ECONOMICS

CFA® Program Curriculum
2016 • LEVEL I • VOLUME 2

Please visit our website at
www.WileyGlobalFinance.com.

FSC
www.fsc.org
MIX
Paper from
responsible sources
FSC® C005928

CONTENTS

Economics

◙ indicates an optional segment

◙ indicates an optional segment

◙ indicates an optional segment

How to Use the CFA Program Curriculum

Congratulations on your decision to enter the Chartered Financial Analyst (CFA®) Program. This exciting and rewarding program of study reflects your desire to become a serious investment professional. You are embarking on a program noted for its high ethical standards and the breadth of knowledge, skills, and abilities it develops. Your commitment to the CFA Program should be educationally and professionally rewarding.

The credential you seek is respected around the world as a mark of accomplishment and dedication. Each level of the program represents a distinct achievement in professional development. Successful completion of the program is rewarded with membership in a prestigious global community of investment professionals. CFA charterholders are dedicated to life-long learning and maintaining currency with the ever-changing dynamics of a challenging profession. The CFA Program represents the first step toward a career-long commitment to professional education.

The CFA examination measures your mastery of the core skills required to succeed as an investment professional. These core skills are the basis for the Candidate Body of Knowledge (CBOK™). The CBOK consists of four components:

- A broad outline that lists the major topic areas covered in the CFA Program (www.cfainstitute.org/cbok);
- Topic area weights that indicate the relative exam weightings of the top-level topic areas (www.cfainstitute.org/level_I);
- Learning outcome statements (LOS) that advise candidates about the specific knowledge, skills, and abilities they should acquire from readings covering a topic area (LOS are provided in candidate study sessions and at the beginning of each reading); and
- The CFA Program curriculum, which contains the readings and end-of-reading questions, that candidates receive upon exam registration.

Therefore, the key to your success on the CFA examinations is studying and understanding the CBOK. The following sections provide background on the CBOK, the organization of the curriculum, and tips for developing an effective study program.

CURRICULUM DEVELOPMENT PROCESS

The CFA Program is grounded in the practice of the investment profession. Beginning with the Global Body of Investment Knowledge (GBIK), CFA Institute performs a continuous practice analysis with investment professionals around the world to determine the knowledge, skills, and abilities (competencies) that are relevant to the profession. Regional expert panels and targeted surveys are conducted annually to verify and reinforce the continuous feedback from the GBIK collaborative website. The practice analysis process ultimately defines the CBOK. The CBOK reflects the competencies that are generally accepted and applied by investment professionals. These competencies are used in practice in a generalist context and are expected to be demonstrated by a recently qualified CFA charterholder.

The Education Advisory Committee, consisting of practicing charterholders, in conjunction with CFA Institute staff, designs the CFA Program curriculum in order to deliver the CBOK to candidates. The examinations, also written by charterholders, are designed to allow you to demonstrate your mastery of the CBOK as set forth in the CFA Program curriculum. As you structure your personal study program, you should emphasize mastery of the CBOK and the practical application of that knowledge. For more information on the practice analysis, CBOK, and development of the CFA Program curriculum, please visit www.cfainstitute.org.

ORGANIZATION OF THE CURRICULUM

The Level I CFA Program curriculum is organized into 10 topic areas. Each topic area begins with a brief statement of the material and the depth of knowledge expected.

Each topic area is then divided into one or more study sessions. These study sessions—18 sessions in the Level I curriculum—should form the basic structure of your reading and preparation.

Each study session includes a statement of its structure and objective and is further divided into specific reading assignments. An outline illustrating the organization of these 18 study sessions can be found at the front of each volume of the curriculum.

The readings and end-of-reading questions are the basis for all examination questions and are selected or developed specifically to teach the knowledge, skills, and abilities reflected in the CBOK. These readings are drawn from content commissioned by CFA Institute, textbook chapters, professional journal articles, research analyst reports, and cases. All readings include problems and solutions to help you understand and master the topic areas.

Reading-specific Learning Outcome Statements (LOS) are listed at the beginning of each reading. These LOS indicate what you should be able to accomplish after studying the reading. The LOS, the reading, and the end-of-reading questions are dependent on each other, with the reading and questions providing context for understanding the scope of the LOS.

You should use the LOS to guide and focus your study because each examination question is based on the assigned readings and one or more LOS. The readings provide context for the LOS and enable you to apply a principle or concept in a variety of scenarios. The candidate is responsible for the entirety of the required material in a study session, which includes the assigned readings as well as the end-of-reading questions and problems.

We encourage you to review the information about the LOS on our website (www.cfainstitute.org/programs/cfaprogram/courseofstudy/Pages/study_sessions.aspx), including the descriptions of LOS "command words" (www.cfainstitute.org/programs/Documents/cfa_and_cipm_los_command_words.pdf).

FEATURES OF THE CURRICULUM

Required vs. Optional Segments   You should read all of an assigned reading. In some cases, though, we have reprinted an entire chapter or article and marked certain parts of the reading as "optional." The CFA examination is based only on the required segments, and the optional segments are included only when it is determined that they might help you to better understand the required segments (by seeing the required material in its full context). When an optional segment begins, you will see an icon and a dashed vertical bar in the outside margin that will continue until the optional segment ends, accompanied by another icon. *Unless the material is specifically marked as optional, you should assume it is required.* You should rely on the required segments and the reading-specific LOS in preparing for the examination.

END OPTIONAL
SEGMENT

End-of-Reading Problems/Solutions   *All problems in the readings as well as their solutions (which are provided directly following the problems) are part of the curriculum and are required material for the exam.* When appropriate, we have included problems within and after the readings to demonstrate practical application and reinforce your understanding of the concepts presented. The problems are designed to help you learn these concepts and may serve as a basis for exam questions. Many of these questions are adapted from past CFA examinations.

Glossary and Index   For your convenience, we have printed a comprehensive glossary in each volume. Throughout the curriculum, a **bolded** word in a reading denotes a term defined in the glossary. The curriculum eBook is searchable, but we also publish an index that can be found on the CFA Institute website with the Level I study sessions.

Source Material   The authorship, publisher, and copyright owners are given for each reading for your reference. We recommend that you use the CFA Institute curriculum rather than the original source materials because the curriculum may include only selected pages from outside readings, updated sections within the readings, and problems and solutions tailored to the CFA Program.

LOS Self-Check   We have inserted checkboxes next to each LOS that you can use to track your progress in mastering the concepts in each reading.

DESIGNING YOUR PERSONAL STUDY PROGRAM

Create a Schedule   An orderly, systematic approach to exam preparation is critical. You should dedicate a consistent block of time every week to reading and studying. Complete all reading assignments and the associated problems and solutions in each study session. Review the LOS both before and after you study each reading to ensure that you have mastered the applicable content and can demonstrate the knowledge, skill, or ability described by the LOS and the assigned reading. Use the LOS self-check to track your progress and highlight areas of weakness for later review.

As you prepare for your exam, we will e-mail you important exam updates, testing policies, and study tips. Be sure to read these carefully. Curriculum errata are periodically updated and posted on the study session page at www.cfainstitute.org. You can also sign up for an RSS feed to alert you to the latest errata update.

Successful candidates report an average of more than 300 hours preparing for each exam. Your preparation time will vary based on your prior education and experience. For each level of the curriculum, there are 18 study sessions. So, a good plan is to devote 15–20 hours per week for 18 weeks to studying the material. Use the final four to six weeks before the exam to review what you have learned and practice with topic and mock exams. This recommendation, however, may underestimate the hours needed for appropriate examination preparation depending on your individual circumstances, relevant experience, and academic background. You will undoubtedly adjust your study time to conform to your own strengths and weaknesses and to your educational and professional background.

You will probably spend more time on some study sessions than on others, but on average you should plan on devoting 15–20 hours per study session. You should allow ample time for both in-depth study of all topic areas and additional concentration on those topic areas for which you feel the least prepared.

An interactive study planner is available in the candidate resources area of our website to help you plan your study time. The interactive study planner recommends completion dates for each topic of the curriculum. Dates are determined based on study time available, exam topic weights, and curriculum weights. As you progress through the curriculum, the interactive study planner dynamically adjusts your study plan when you are running off schedule to help you stay on track for completion prior to the examination.

CFA Institute Topic Exams   The CFA Institute topic exams are intended to assess your mastery of individual topic areas as you progress through your studies. After each test, you will receive immediate feedback noting the correct responses and indicating the relevant assigned reading so you can identify areas of weakness for further study. For more information on the topic tests, please visit www.cfainstitute.org.

CFA Institute Mock Exams   The three-hour mock exams simulate the morning and afternoon sessions of the actual CFA examination, and are intended to be taken after you complete your study of the full curriculum so you can test your understanding of the curriculum and your readiness for the exam. You will receive feedback at the end of the mock exam, noting the correct responses and indicating the relevant assigned readings so you can assess areas of weakness for further study during your review period. We recommend that you take mock exams during the final stages of your preparation for the actual CFA examination. For more information on the mock examinations, please visit www.cfainstitute.org.

Preparatory Providers   After you enroll in the CFA Program, you may receive numerous solicitations for preparatory courses and review materials. When considering a prep course, make sure the provider is in compliance with the CFA Institute Prep Provider Guidelines Program (www.cfainstitute.org/utility/examprep/Pages/index.aspx). Just remember, there are no shortcuts to success on the CFA examinations; reading and studying the CFA curriculum is the key to success on the examination. The CFA examinations reference only the CFA Institute assigned curriculum—no preparatory course or review course materials are consulted or referenced.

SUMMARY

Every question on the CFA examination is based on the content contained in the required readings and on one or more LOS. Frequently, an examination question is based on a specific example highlighted within a reading or on a specific end-of-reading question and/or problem and its solution. To make effective use of the CFA Program curriculum, please remember these key points:

1   All pages of the curriculum are required reading for the examination except for occasional sections marked as optional. You may read optional pages as background, but you will not be tested on them.

2   All questions, problems, and their solutions—found at the end of readings—are part of the curriculum and are required study material for the examination.

3   You should make appropriate use of the topic and mock examinations and other resources available at www.cfainstitute.org.

4 Use the interactive study planner to create a schedule and commit sufficient study time to cover the 18 study sessions, review the materials, and take topic and mock examinations.

5 Some of the concepts in the study sessions may be superseded by updated rulings and/or pronouncements issued after a reading was published. Candidates are expected to be familiar with the overall analytical framework contained in the assigned readings. Candidates are not responsible for changes that occur after the material was written.

FEEDBACK

At CFA Institute, we are committed to delivering a comprehensive and rigorous curriculum for the development of competent, ethically grounded investment professionals. We rely on candidate and member feedback as we work to incorporate content, design, and packaging improvements. You can be assured that we will continue to listen to your suggestions. Please send any comments or feedback to info@cfainstitute.org. Ongoing improvements in the curriculum will help you prepare for success on the upcoming examinations and for a lifetime of learning as a serious investment professional.

Economics

TOPIC LEVEL LEARNING OUTCOME

The candidate should be able to demonstrate a thorough knowledge of microeconomic and macroeconomic principles.

4

Economics

Microeconomic Analysis

This study session focuses on the microeconomic principles used to describe the marketplace behavior of consumers and firms. The first reading explains the concepts and tools of demand and supply analysis—the study of how buyers and sellers interact to determine transaction prices and quantities. The second reading covers the theory of the consumer, which addresses the demand for goods and services by individuals who make decisions to maximize the satisfaction they receive from present and future consumption. The third reading deals with the theory of the firm, focusing on the supply of goods and services by profit-maximizing firms. That reading provides the basis for understanding the cost side of firms' profit equation. The final reading completes the picture by addressing revenue and explains the types of markets in which firms sell output. Overall, the study session provides the economic tools for understanding how product and resource markets function and the competitive characteristics of different industries.

READING ASSIGNMENTS

READING

13

Demand and Supply Analysis: Introduction

by Richard V. Eastin, PhD, and Gary L. Arbogast, CFA

Richard V. Eastin, PhD, is at the University of Southern California (USA). Gary L. Arbogast, CFA (USA).

LEARNING OUTCOMES

Mastery	The candidate should be able to:
☐	a. distinguish among types of markets;
☐	b. explain the principles of demand and supply;
☐	c. describe causes of shifts in and movements along demand and supply curves;
☐	d. describe the process of aggregating demand and supply curves;
☐	e. describe the concept of equilibrium (partial and general), and mechanisms by which markets achieve equilibrium;
☐	f. distinguish between stable and unstable equilibria, including price bubbles, and identify instances of such equilibria;
☐	g. calculate and interpret individual and aggregate demand, and inverse demand and supply functions, and interpret individual and aggregate demand and supply curves;
☐	h. calculate and interpret the amount of excess demand or excess supply associated with a non-equilibrium price;
☐	i. describe types of auctions and calculate the winning price(s) of an auction;
☐	j. calculate and interpret consumer surplus, producer surplus, and total surplus;
☐	k. describe how government regulation and intervention affect demand and supply;
☐	l. forecast the effect of the introduction and the removal of a market interference (e.g., a price floor or ceiling) on price and quantity;
☐	m. calculate and interpret price, income, and cross-price elasticities of demand and describe factors that affect each measure.

1   INTRODUCTION

In a general sense, **economics** is the study of production, distribution, and consumption and can be divided into two broad areas of study: macroeconomics and microeconomics. **Macroeconomics** deals with aggregate economic quantities, such as national output and national income. Macroeconomics has its roots in **microeconomics**, which deals with markets and decision making of individual economic units, including consumers and businesses. Microeconomics is a logical starting point for the study of economics.

This reading focuses on a fundamental subject in microeconomics: demand and supply analysis. **Demand and supply analysis** is the study of how buyers and sellers interact to determine transaction prices and quantities. As we will see, prices simultaneously reflect both the value to the buyer of the next (or marginal) unit and the cost to the seller of that unit. In private enterprise market economies, which are the chief concern of investment analysts, demand and supply analysis encompasses the most basic set of microeconomic tools.

Traditionally, microeconomics classifies private economic units into two groups: consumers (or households) and firms. These two groups give rise, respectively, to the theory of the consumer and theory of the firm as two branches of study. The **theory of the consumer** deals with **consumption** (the demand for goods and services) by utility-maximizing individuals (i.e., individuals who make decisions that maximize the satisfaction received from present and future consumption). The **theory of the firm** deals with the supply of goods and services by profit-maximizing firms. The theory of the consumer and the theory of the firm are important because they help us understand the foundations of demand and supply. Subsequent readings will focus on the theory of the consumer and the theory of the firm.

Investment analysts, particularly equity and credit analysts, must regularly analyze products and services, their costs, prices, possible substitutes, and complements, to reach conclusions about a company's profitability and business risk (risk relating to operating profits). Furthermore, unless the analyst has a sound understanding of the demand and supply model of markets, he or she cannot hope to forecast how external events—such as a shift in consumer tastes or changes in taxes and subsidies or other intervention in markets—will influence a firm's revenue, earnings, and cash flows.

Having grasped the tools and concepts presented in this reading, the reader should also be able to understand many important economic relations and facts and be able to answer questions, such as:

- Why do consumers usually buy more when the price falls? Is it irrational to violate this "law of demand"?

- What are appropriate measures of how sensitive the quantity demanded or supplied is to changes in price, income, and prices of other goods? What affects those sensitivities?

- If a firm lowers its price, will its total revenue also fall? Are there conditions under which revenue might rise as price falls and what are those? Why?

- What is an appropriate measure of the total value consumers or producers receive from the opportunity to buy and sell goods and services in a free market? How might government intervention reduce that value, and what is an appropriate measure of that loss?

- What tools are available that help us frame the trade-offs that consumers and investors face as they must give up one opportunity to pursue another?

- Is it reasonable to expect markets to converge to an equilibrium price? What are the conditions that would make that equilibrium stable or unstable in response to external shocks?
- How do different types of auctions affect price discovery?

This reading is organized as follows. Section 2 explains how economists classify markets. Section 3 covers the basic principles and concepts of demand and supply analysis of markets. Section 4 introduces measures of sensitivity of demand to changes in prices and income. A summary and practice problems conclude the reading.

TYPES OF MARKETS

2

Analysts must understand the demand and supply model of markets because all firms buy and sell in markets. Investment analysts need at least a basic understanding of those markets and the demand and supply model that provides a framework for analyzing them.

Markets are broadly classified as factor markets or goods markets. **Factor markets** are markets for the purchase and sale of factors of production. In capitalist private enterprise economies, households own the factors of production (the land, labor, physical capital, and materials used in production). **Goods markets** are markets for the output of production. From an economics perspective, firms, which ultimately are owned by individuals either singly or in some corporate form, are organizations that buy the services of those factors. Firms then transform those services into intermediate or final goods and services. (**Intermediate goods and services** are those purchased for use as inputs to produce other goods and services, whereas final goods and services are in the final form purchased by households.) These two types of interaction between the household sector and the firm sector—those related to goods and those related to services—take place in factor markets and goods markets, respectively.

In the factor market for labor, households are sellers and firms are buyers. In goods markets: firms are sellers and both households and firms are buyers. For example, firms are buyers of capital goods (such as equipment) and intermediate goods, while households are buyers of a variety of durable and non-durable goods. Generally, market interactions are *voluntary*. Firms offer their products for sale when they believe the payment they will receive exceeds their cost of production. Households are willing to purchase goods and services when the value they expect to receive from them exceeds the payment necessary to acquire them. Whenever the perceived value of a good exceeds the expected cost to produce it, a potential trade can take place. This fact may seem obvious, but it is fundamental to our understanding of markets. If a buyer values something more than a seller, not only is there an opportunity for an exchange, but that exchange will make *both* parties better off.

In one type of factor market, called **labor markets**, households offer to sell their labor services when the payment they expect to receive exceeds the value of the leisure time they must forgo. In contrast, firms hire workers when they judge that the value of the productivity of workers is greater than the cost of employing them. A major source of household income and a major cost to firms is compensation paid in exchange for labor services.

Additionally, households typically choose to spend less on consumption than they earn from their labor. This behavior is called **saving**, through which households can accumulate financial capital, the returns on which can produce other sources of household income, such as interest, dividends, and capital gains. Households may choose to lend their accumulated savings (in exchange for interest) or invest it in ownership claims in firms (in hopes of receiving dividends and capital gains). Households make these savings choices when their anticipated future returns are judged to be more valuable today than the present consumption that households must sacrifice when they save.

Indeed, a major purpose of financial institutions and markets is to enable the transfer of these savings into capital investments. Firms use **capital markets** (markets for long-term financial capital—that is, markets for long-term claims on firms' assets and cash flows) to sell debt (in bond markets) or equity (in equity markets) in order to raise funds to invest in productive assets, such as plant and equipment. They make these investment choices when they judge that their investments will increase the value of the firm by more than the cost of acquiring those funds from households. Firms also use such financial intermediaries as banks and insurance companies to raise capital, typically debt funding that ultimately comes from the savings of households, which are usually net accumulators of financial capital.

Microeconomics, although primarily focused on goods and factor markets, can contribute to the understanding of all types of markets (e.g., markets for financial securities).

EXAMPLE 1

Types of Markets

1 Which of the following markets is *least* accurately described as a factor market? The market for:

   A land.

   B assembly line workers.

   C capital market securities.

2 Which of the following markets is *most* accurately defined as a goods market? The market for:

   A companies.

   B unskilled labor.

   C legal and lobbying services.

Solution to 1:

C is correct.

Solution to 2:

C is correct.

---

3   BASIC PRINCIPLES AND CONCEPTS

In this reading, we will explore a model of household behavior that yields the consumer demand curve. **Demand**, in economics, is the willingness and ability of consumers to purchase a given amount of a good or service at a given price. **Supply** is the willingness of sellers to offer a given quantity of a good or service for a given price. Later, study on the theory of the firm will yield the supply curve.

The demand and supply model is useful in explaining how price and quantity traded are determined and how external influences affect the values of those variables. Buyers' behavior is captured in the demand function and its graphical equivalent, the demand curve. This curve shows both the highest price buyers are willing to pay for each quantity, and the highest quantity buyers are willing and able to purchase at each price. Sellers' behavior is captured in the supply function and its graphical equivalent, the supply curve. This curve shows simultaneously the lowest price sellers are willing to accept for each quantity and the highest quantity sellers are willing to offer at each price.

If, at a given quantity, the highest price that buyers are willing to pay is equal to the lowest price that sellers are willing to accept, we say the market has reached its equilibrium quantity. Alternatively, when the quantity that buyers are willing and able to purchase at a given price is just equal to the quantity that sellers are willing to offer at that same price, we say the market has discovered the equilibrium price. So equilibrium price and quantity are achieved simultaneously, and as long as neither the supply curve nor the demand curve shifts, there is no tendency for either price or quantity to vary from their equilibrium values.

3.1 The Demand Function and the Demand Curve

We first analyze demand. The quantity consumers are willing to buy clearly depends on a number of different factors called variables. Perhaps the most important of those variables is the item's own price. In general, economists believe that as the price of a good rises, buyers will choose to buy less of it, and as its price falls, they buy more. This is such a ubiquitous observation that it has come to be called the **law of demand**, although we shall see that it need not hold in all circumstances.

Although a good's own price is important in determining consumers' willingness to purchase it, other variables also have influence on that decision, such as consumers' incomes, their tastes and preferences, the prices of other goods that serve as substitutes or complements, and so on. Economists attempt to capture all of these influences in a relationship called the **demand function**. (In general, a function is a relationship that assigns a unique value to a dependent variable for any given set of values of a group of independent variables.) We represent such a demand function in Equation 1:

$$Q_x^d = f\left(P_x, I, P_y, \ldots\right) \qquad\qquad \textbf{(1)}$$

where Q_x^d represents the quantity demanded of some good X (such as per household demand for gasoline in gallons per week), P_x is the price per unit of good X (such as $ per gallon), I is consumers' income (as in $1,000s per household annually), and P_y is the price of another good, Y. (There can be many other goods, not just one, and they can be complements or substitutes.) Equation 1 may be read, "Quantity demanded of good X depends on (is a function of) the price of good X, consumers' income, the price of good Y, and so on."

Often, economists use simple linear equations to approximate real-world demand and supply functions in relevant ranges. A hypothetical example of a specific demand function could be the following linear equation for a small town's per-household gasoline consumption per week, where P_y might be the average price of an automobile in $1,000s:

$$Q_x^d = 8.4 - 0.4P_x + 0.06I - 0.01P_y \qquad\qquad \textbf{(2)}$$

The signs of the coefficients on gasoline price (negative) and consumer's income (positive) are intuitive, reflecting, respectively, an inverse and a positive relationship between those variables and quantity of gasoline consumed. The negative sign on average automobile price may indicate that if automobiles go up in price, fewer will be purchased and driven; hence less gasoline will be consumed. As will be discussed later, such a relationship would indicate that gasoline and automobiles have a negative cross-price elasticity of demand and are thus complements.

To continue our example, suppose that the price of gasoline (P_x) is \$3 per gallon, per household income (I) is \$50,000, and the price of the average automobile (P_y) is \$20,000. Then this function would predict that the per-household weekly demand for gasoline would be 10 gallons: $8.4 - 0.4(3) + 0.06(50) - 0.01(20) = 8.4 - 1.2 + 3 - 0.2 = 10$, recalling that income and automobile prices are measured in thousands. Note that the sign on the own-price variable is negative, thus, as the price of gasoline rises, per household weekly consumption would decrease by 0.4 gallons for every dollar increase in gas price. **Own-price** is used by economists to underscore that the reference is to the price of a good itself and not the price of some other good.

In our example, there are three independent variables in the demand function, and one dependent variable. If any one of the independent variables changes, so does the value of quantity demanded. It is often desirable to concentrate on the relationship between the dependent variable and just one of the independent variables at a time, which allows us to represent the relationship between those two variables in a two-dimensional graph (at specific levels of the variables held constant). To accomplish this goal, we can simply hold the other two independent variables constant at their respective levels and rewrite the equation. In economic writing, this "holding constant" of the values of all variables except those being discussed is traditionally referred to by the Latin phrase *ceteris paribus* (literally, "all other things being equal" in the sense of "unchanged"). In this reading, we will use the phrase "holding all other things constant" as a readily understood equivalent for *ceteris paribus*.

Suppose, for example, that we want to concentrate on the relationship between the quantity demanded of the good and its own-price, P_x. Then we would hold constant the values of income and the price of good Y. In our example, those values are 50 and 20, respectively. So, by inserting the respective values, we would rewrite Equation 2 as

$$Q_x^d = 8.4 - 0.4P_x + 0.06(50) - 0.01(20) = 11.2 - 0.4P_x \qquad \textbf{(3)}$$

Notice that income and the price of automobiles are not ignored; they are simply held constant, and they are "collected" in the new constant term, 11.2. Notice also that we can rearrange Equation 3, solving for P_x in terms of Q_x. This operation is called "inverting the demand function," and gives us Equation 4. (You should be able to perform this algebraic exercise to verify the result.)

$$P_x = 28 - 2.5Q_x \qquad \textbf{(4)}$$

Equation 4, which gives the per-gallon price of gasoline as a function of gasoline consumed per week, is referred to as the **inverse demand function**. We need to restrict Q_x in Equation 4 to be less than or equal to 11.2 so price is not negative. Henceforward we assume that the reader can work out similar needed qualifications to the valid application of equations. The graph of the inverse demand function is called the **demand curve**, and is shown in Exhibit 1.[1]

---

1 Following usual practice, here and in other exhibits we will show linear demand curves intersecting the quantity axis at a price of zero, which shows the intercept of the associated demand equation. Real-world demand functions may be non-linear in some or all parts of their domain. Thus, linear demand functions in practical cases are viewed as approximations to the true demand function that are useful for a relevant range of values. The relevant range would typically not include a price of zero, and the prediction for demand at a price of zero should not be viewed as usable.

Exhibit 1   Household Demand Curve for Gasoline

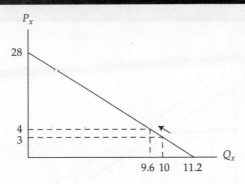

This demand curve is drawn with price on the vertical axis and quantity on the horizontal axis. Depending on how we interpret it, the demand curve shows either the highest quantity a household would buy at a given price or the highest price it would be willing to pay for a given quantity. In our example, at a price of $3 per gallon households would each be willing to buy 10 gallons per week. Alternatively, the highest price they would be willing to pay for 10 gallons per week is $3 per gallon. Both interpretations are valid, and we will be thinking in terms of both as we proceed. If the price were to rise by $1, households would reduce the quantity they each bought by 0.4 units to 9.6 gallons. We say that the slope of the demand curve is 1/−0.4, or −2.5. Slope is always measured as "rise over run," or the change in the vertical variable divided by the change in the horizontal variable. In this case, the slope of the demand curve is $\Delta P / \Delta Q$, where "Δ" stands for "the change in." The change in price was $1, and it is associated with a change in quantity of negative 0.4

3.2 Changes in Demand vs. Movements along the Demand Curve

As we just saw, when own-price changes, quantity demanded changes. This change is called a movement along the demand curve or a change in quantity demanded, and it comes only from a change in own price.

Recall that to draw the demand curve, though, we had to hold everything *except* quantity and own-price constant. What would happen if income were to change by some amount? Suppose that household income rose by $10,000 per year to a value of 60. Then the value of Equation 3 would change to

$$Q_x^d = 8.4 - 0.4P_x + 0.06(60) - 0.01(20) = 11.8 - 0.4P_x \qquad \text{(5)}$$

and Equation 4 would become the new inverse demand function:

$$P_x = 29.5 - 2.5Q_x \qquad \text{(6)}$$

Notice that the slope has remained constant, but the intercepts have both increased, resulting in an outward shift in the demand curve, as shown in Exhibit 2.

Exhibit 2   Household Demand Curve for Gasoline before and after Change in Income

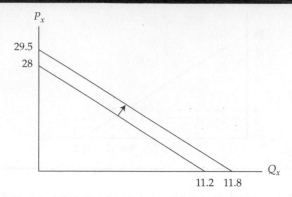

In general, the only thing that can cause a movement along the demand curve is a change in a good's own-price. A change in the value of any *other* variable will shift the entire demand curve. The former is referred to as a *change in quantity demanded*, and the latter is referred to as a *change in demand.*

More importantly, the shift in demand was both a *vertical* shift upward and a *horizontal* shift to the right. That is to say, for any given quantity, the household is now willing to pay a higher price; and at any given price, the household is now willing to buy a greater quantity. Both interpretations of the shift in demand are valid.

EXAMPLE 2

Representing Consumer Buying Behavior with a Demand Function and Demand Curve

An individual consumer's monthly demand for downloadable e-books is given by the equation

$$Q_{eb}^d = 2 - 0.4P_{eb} + 0.0005I + 0.15P_{hb}$$

where Q_{eb}^d equals the number of e-books demanded each month, P_{eb} equals the price of e-books, I equals the household monthly income, and P_{hb} equals the price of hardbound books, per unit. Notice that the sign on the price of hardbound books is positive, indicating that when hardbound books increase in price, more e-books are purchased; thus, according to this equation, the two types of books are substitutes. Assume that the price of e-books is €10.68, household income is €2,300, and the price of hardbound books is €21.40.

1 Determine the number of e-books demanded by this household each month.

2 Given the values for I and P_{hb}, determine the inverse demand function.

3 Determine the slope of the demand curve for e-books.

4 Calculate the vertical intercept (price-axis intercept) of the demand curve if income increases to €3000 per month.

Solution to 1:

Insert given values into the demand function and calculate quantity:

$$Q_{eb}^d = 2 - 0.4(10.68) + 0.0005(2,300) + 0.15(21.40) = 2.088$$

Hence, the household will demand e-books at the rate of 2.088 books per month. Note that this rate is a flow, so there is no contradiction in there being a non-integer quantity. In this case, the outcome means that the consumer buys 23 e-books per 11 months.

Solution to 2:

We want to find the price–quantity relationship holding all other things constant, so first, insert values for I and P_{hb} into the demand function and collect the constant terms:

$$Q_{eb}^d = 2 - 0.4P_{eb} + 0.0005(2,300) + 0.15(21.40) = 6.36 - 0.4P_{eb}$$

Now solve for P_{eb} in terms of Q_{eb}: $P_{eb} = 15.90 - 2.5Q_{eb}$

Solution to 3:

Note from the inverse demand function above that when Q_{eb} rises by one unit, P_{eb} falls by 2.5 euros. So the slope of the demand curve is –2.5, which is the coefficient on Q_{eb} in the inverse demand function. Note it is *not* the coefficient on P_{eb} in the demand function, which is –0.4. It is the inverse of that coefficient.

Solution to 4:

In the demand function, change the value of I to 3,000 from 2,300 and collect constant terms:

$$Q_{eb}^d = 2 - 0.4P_{eb} + 0.0005(3,000) + 0.15(21.40) = 6.71 - 0.4P_{eb}$$

Now solve for P_{eb}: $P_{eb} = 16.78 - 2.5Q_{eb}$. The vertical intercept is 16.78. (Note that this increase in income has shifted the demand curve outward and upward but has not affected its slope, which is still –2.5.)

3.3 The Supply Function and the Supply Curve

The willingness and ability to sell a good or service is called supply. In general, producers are willing to sell their product for a price as long as that price is at least as high as the cost to produce an additional unit of the product. It follows that the willingness to supply, called the **supply function**, depends on the price at which the good can be sold as well as the cost of production for an additional unit of the good. The greater the difference between those two values, the greater is the willingness of producers to supply the good.

In another reading, we will explore the cost of production in greater detail. At this point, we need to understand only the basics of cost. At its simplest level, production of a good consists of transforming inputs, or factors of production (such as land, labor, capital, and materials) into finished goods and services. Economists refer to the "rules" that govern this transformation as the **technology of production**. Because producers have to purchase inputs in factor markets, the cost of production depends on both the technology and the price of those factors. Clearly, willingness to supply is dependent on not only the price of a producer's output, but also additionally on the prices (i.e., costs) of the inputs necessary to produce it. For simplicity, we can assume that the only input in a production process is labor that must be purchased in the labor market. The price of an hour of labor is the wage rate, or W. Hence, we can say that (for any given level of technology) the willingness to supply a good depends on the price of that good and the wage rate. This concept is captured in the following equation, which represents an individual seller's supply function:

$$Q_x^s = f(P_x, W, \ldots) \tag{7}$$

where Q_x^s is the quantity supplied of some good X, such as gasoline, P_x is the price per unit of good X, and W is the wage rate of labor in, say, dollars per hour. It would be read, "The quantity supplied of good X depends on (is a function of) the price of X (its "own" price), the wage rate paid to labor, etc."

Just as with the demand function, we can consider a simple hypothetical example of a seller's supply function. As mentioned earlier, economists often will simplify their analysis by using linear functions, although that is not to say that all demand and supply functions are necessarily linear. One hypothetical example of an individual seller's supply function for gasoline is given in Equation 8:

$$Q_x^s = -175 + 250P_x - 5W \tag{8}$$

Notice that this supply function says that for every increase in price of $1, this seller would be willing to supply an additional 250 units of the good. Additionally, for every $1 increase in wage rate that it must pay its laborers, this seller would experience an increase in marginal cost and would be willing to supply five fewer units of the good.

We might be interested in the relationship between only two of these variables, price and quantity supplied. Just as we did in the case of the demand function, we use the assumption of *ceteris paribus* and hold everything except own-price and quantity constant. In our example, we accomplish this by setting W to some value, say, $15. The result is Equation 9:

$$Q_x^s = -175 + 250P_x - 5(15) = -250 + 250P_x \tag{9}$$

in which only the two variables Q_x^s and P_x appear. Once again, we can solve this equation for P_x in terms of Q_x^s, which yields the *inverse supply function* in Equation 10:

$$P_x = 1 + 0.004Q_x \tag{10}$$

The graph of the inverse supply function is called the **supply curve**, and it shows simultaneously the highest quantity willingly supplied at each price and the lowest price willingly accepted for each quantity. For example, if the price of gasoline were $3 per gallon, Equation 9 implies that this seller would be willing to sell 500 gallons per week. Alternatively, the lowest price she would accept and still be willing to sell 500 gallons per week would be $3. Exhibit 3 represents our hypothetical example of an individual seller's supply curve of gasoline.

Exhibit 3   Individual Seller's Supply Curve for Gasoline

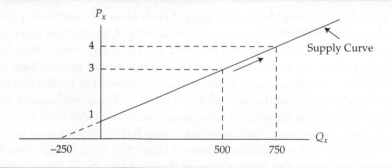

What does our supply function tell us will happen if the retail price of gasoline rises by $1? We insert the new higher price of $4 into Equation 8 and find that quantity supplied would rise to 750 gallons per week. The increase in price has enticed the seller to supply a greater quantity of gasoline per week than at the lower price.

3.4 Changes in Supply vs. Movements along the Supply Curve

As we saw earlier, a change in the (own) price of a product causes a change in the quantity of that good willingly supplied. A rise in price typically results in a greater quantity supplied, and a lower price results in a lower quantity supplied. Hence, the supply curve has a positive slope, in contrast to the negative slope of a demand curve. This positive relationship is often referred to as the **law of supply**.

What happens when a variable other than own-price takes on different values? We could answer this question in our example by assuming a different value for wage rate, say, $20 instead of $15. Recalling Equation 9, we would simply put in the higher wage rate and solve, yielding Equation 11.

$$Q_x^S = -175 + 250P_x - 5(20) = -275 + 250P_x \qquad \text{(11)}$$

This equation, too, can be solved for P_x, yielding the inverse supply function:

$$P_x = 1.1 + 0.004Q_x \qquad \text{(12)}$$

Notice that the constant term has changed, but the slope has remained the same. The result is a shift in the entire supply curve, as illustrated in Exhibit 4:

Exhibit 4   Individual Seller's Supply Curve for Gasoline before and after Increase in Wage Rate

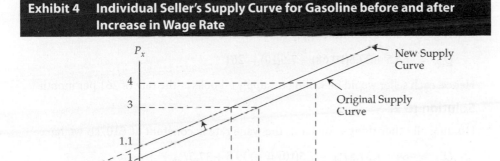

Notice that the supply curve has shifted both vertically upward and horizontally leftward as a result of the rise in the wage rate paid to labor. This change is referred to as a **change in supply**, as contrasted with a **change in quantity supplied** that would result only from a change in this product's own price. Now, at a price of 3, a lower quantity will be supplied: 475 instead of 500. Alternatively, in order to entice this seller to offer the same 500 gallons per week, the price would now have to be 3.1, up from 3 before the change. This increase in lowest acceptable price reflects the now higher marginal cost of production resulting from the increased input price the firm now must pay for labor.

To summarize, a change in the price of a good itself will result in a movement along the supply curve and a change in quantity supplied. A change in any variable other than own-price will cause a shift in the supply curve, called a change in supply. This distinction is identical to the case of demand curves.

Representing Seller Behavior with a Supply Function and Supply Curve

An individual seller's monthly supply of downloadable e-books is given by the equation

$$Q^s_{eb} = -64.5 + 37.5P_{eb} - 7.5W$$

where Q^s_{eb} is number of e-books supplied each month, P_{eb} is price of e-books in euros, and W is the hourly wage rate in euros paid by e-book sellers to workers. Assume that the price of e-books is €10.68 and the hourly wage is €10.

1 Determine the number of e-books supplied each month.

2 Determine the inverse supply function for an individual seller.

3 Determine the slope of the supply curve for e-books.

4 Determine the new vertical intercept of the individual e-book supply curve if the hourly wage were to rise to €15 from €10.

Solution to 1:

Insert given values into the supply function and calculate the number of e-books:

$$Q^s_{eb} = -64.5 + 37.5(10.68) - 7.5(10) = 261$$

Hence, each seller would be willing to supply e-books at the rate of 261 per month.

Solution to 2:

Holding all other things constant, the wage rate is constant at €10, so we have

$$Q^s_{eb} = -64.5 + 37.5P_{eb} - 7.5(10) = -139.5 + 37.5P_{eb}$$

We now solve this for P_{eb}:

$$P_{eb} = 3.72 + 0.0267Q_{eb}$$

Solution to 3:

Note that when Q_{eb} rises by one unit, P_{eb} rises by 0.0267 euros, so the slope of the supply curve is 0.0267, which is the coefficient on Q_{eb} in the inverse supply function. Note that it is *not* 37.5.

Solution to 4:

In the supply function, increase the value of W to €15 from €10:

$$Q^s_{eb} = -64.5 + 37.5P_{eb} - 7.5(15) = -177 + 37.5P_{eb}$$

and invert by solving for P_{eb}:

$$P_{eb} = 4.72 + 0.0267Q_{eb}$$

The vertical intercept is now 4.72. Thus, an increase in the wage rate shifts the supply curve upward and to the left. This change is known as a decrease in supply because at each price the seller would be willing now to supply fewer e-books than before the increase in labor cost.

3.5 Aggregating the Demand and Supply Functions

We have explored the basic concept of demand and supply at the individual household and the individual supplier level. However, markets consist of collections of demanders and suppliers, so we need to understand the process of combining these individual agents' behavior to arrive at market demand and supply functions.

The process could not be more straightforward: simply add all the buyers together and add all the sellers together. Suppose there are 1,000 identical gasoline buyers in our hypothetical example, and they represent the total market. At, say, a price of $3 per gallon, we find that one household would be willing to purchase 10 gallons per week (when income and price of automobiles are held constant at $50,000 and $20,000, respectively). So, 1,000 identical buyers would be willing to purchase 10,000 gallons collectively. It follows that to aggregate 1,000 buyers' demand functions, simply multiply each buyer's quantity demanded by 1,000:

$$Q_x^d = 1{,}000\big(8.4 - 0.4P_x + 0.06I - 0.01P_y\big) = 8{,}400 - 400P_x + 60I - 10P_y \quad \textbf{(13)}$$

where Q_x^d represents the market quantity demanded. Note that if we hold I and P_y at their same respective values of 50 and 20 as before, we can "collapse" the constant terms and write the following Equation 14:

$$Q_x^d = 11{,}200 - 400P_x \quad \textbf{(14)}$$

Equation 14 is just Equation 3 (an individual household's demand function) multiplied by 1,000 households (Q_x^d represents thousands of gallons per week). Again, we can solve for P_x to obtain the market inverse demand function:

$$P_x = 28 - 0.0025Q_x \quad \textbf{(15)}$$

The market demand curve is simply the graph of the market inverse demand function, as shown in Exhibit 5.

Exhibit 5   Aggregate Weekly Market Demand for Gasoline as the Quantity Summation of all Households' Demand Curves

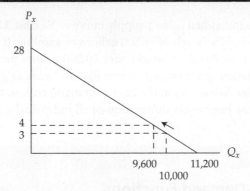

It is important to note that the aggregation process sums all individual buyers' *quantities*, not the *prices* they are willing to pay—that is, we multiplied the demand function, *not* the inverse demand function, by the number of households. Accordingly, the market demand curve has the exact same price intercept as each individual household's demand curve. If, at a price of $28, a single household would choose to buy zero, then it follows that 1,000 identical households would choose, in aggregate, to buy zero as well. On the other hand, if each household chooses to buy 10 at a price of $3, then 1,000 identical households would choose to buy 10,000, as shown in Exhibit 5. Hence, we say that all individual demand curves *horizontally* (quantities), not *vertically* (prices), are added to arrive at the market demand curve.

Now that we understand the aggregation of demanders, the aggregation of suppliers is simple: We do exactly the same thing. Suppose, for example, that there are 20 identical sellers with the supply function given by Equation 8. To arrive at the market supply function, we simply multiply by 20 to obtain:

$$Q_x^s = 20(-175 + 250P_x - 5W) = -3,500 + 5,000P_x - 100W \tag{16}$$

And, if we once again assume W equals \$15, we can "collapse" the constant terms, yielding

$$Q_x^s = 20\left[-175 + 250P_x - 5(15)\right] = -5,000 + 5,000P_x \tag{17}$$

which can be inverted to yield the market inverse supply function:

$$P_x = 1 + 0.0002Q_x \tag{18}$$

Graphing the market inverse supply function yields the market supply curve in Exhibit 6:

Exhibit 6   Aggregate Market Supply as the Quantity Summation of Individual Sellers' Supply Curves

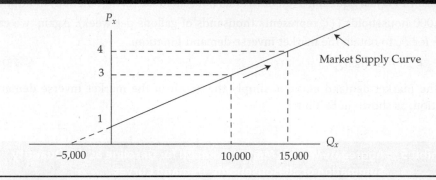

We saw from the individual seller's supply curve in Exhibit 3 that at a price of \$3, an individual seller would willingly offer 500 gallons of gasoline. It follows, as shown in Exhibit 6, that a group of 20 sellers would offer 10,000 gallons per week. Accordingly, at each price, the market quantity supplied is just 20 times as great as the quantity supplied by each seller. We see, as in the case of demand curves, that the market supply curve is simply the horizontal summation of all individual sellers' supply curves.

EXAMPLE 4

Aggregating Demand Functions

An individual consumer's monthly demand for downloadable e-books is given by the equation

$$Q_{eb}^d = 2 - 0.4P_{eb} + 0.0005I + 0.15P_{hb}$$

where Q_{eb}^d equals the number of e-books demanded each month, P_{eb} is the price of e-books in euros, I equals the household monthly income, and P_{hb} equals the price of hardbound books, per unit. Assume that household income is €2,300, and the price of hardbound books is €21.40. The market consists of 1,000 identical consumers with this demand function.

1 Determine the market aggregate demand function.

2 Determine the inverse market demand function.

3 Determine the slope of the market demand curve.

Solution to 1:

Aggregating over the total number of consumers means summing up their demand functions (in the quantity direction). In this case, there are 1,000 consumers with identical individual demand functions, so multiply the entire function by 1,000:

$$Q_{eb} = 1,000(2 - 0.4P_{eb} + 0.0005I + 0.15P_{hb})$$
$$= 2,000 - 400P_{eb} + 0.5I + 150P_{hb}$$

Solution to 2:

Holding I constant at a value of €2,300 and P_{hb} constant at a value of €21.40, we find

$$Q_{eb} = 2,000 - 400P_{eb} + 0.5(2300) + 150(21.40) = 6,360 - 400P_{eb}$$

Now solve for $P_{eb} = 15.90 - 0.0025Q_{eb}$

Solution to 3:

The slope of the market demand curve is the coefficient on Q_{eb} in the inverse demand function, which is −0.0025.

EXAMPLE 5

Aggregating Supply Functions

An individual seller's monthly supply of downloadable e-books is given by the equation

$$Q_{eb}^s = -64.5 + 37.5P_{eb} - 7.5W$$

where Q_{eb}^s is number of e-books supplied, P_{eb} is the price of e-books in euros, and W is the wage rate in euros paid by e-book sellers to laborers. Assume that the price of e-books is €10.68 and wage is €10. The supply side of the market consists of a total of eight identical sellers in this competitive market.

1 Determine the market aggregate supply function.

2 Determine the inverse market supply function.

3 Determine the slope of the aggregate market supply curve.

Solution to 1:

Aggregating supply functions means summing up the quantity supplied by all sellers. In this case, there are eight identical sellers, so multiply the individual seller's supply function by eight:

$$Q_{eb}^s = 8\left(-64.5 + 37.5P_{eb} - 7.5W\right) = -516 + 300P_{eb} - 60W$$

Solution to 2:

Holding W constant at a value of €10, insert that value into the aggregate supply function and then solve for P_{eb} to find the inverse supply function:

$$Q_{eb} = -1,116 + 300P_{eb}$$

Inverting, $P_{eb} = 3.72 + 0.0033Q_{eb}$

Solution to 3:

The slope of the supply curve is the coefficient on Q_{eb} in the inverse supply function, which is 0.0033.

3.6 Market Equilibrium

An important concept in the market model is **market equilibrium**, defined as the condition in which the quantity willingly offered for sale by sellers at a given price is just equal to the quantity willingly demanded by buyers at that same price. When that condition is met, we say that the market has discovered its equilibrium price. An alternative and equivalent condition of equilibrium occurs at that quantity at which the highest price a buyer is willing to pay is just equal to the lowest price a seller is willing to accept for that same quantity.

As we have discovered in the earlier sections, the demand curve shows (for given values of income, other prices, etc.) an infinite number of combinations of prices and quantities that satisfy the demand function. Similarly, the supply curve shows (for given values of input prices, etc.) an infinite number of combinations of prices and quantities that satisfy the supply function. Equilibrium occurs at the unique combination of price and quantity that simultaneously satisfies *both* the market demand function and the market supply function. Graphically, it is the intersection of the demand and supply curves as shown in Exhibit 7.

Exhibit 7	Market Equilibrium Price and Quantity as the Intersection of Demand and Supply

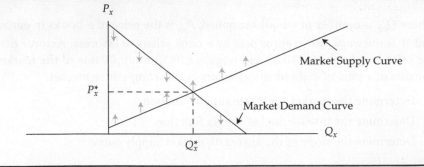

In Exhibit 7, the shaded arrows indicate, respectively, that buyers will be willing to pay any price at or below the demand curve (indicated by ↓), and sellers are willing to accept any price at or above the supply curve (indicated by ↑). Notice that for quantities less than Q_x^*, the highest price buyers are willing to pay exceeds the lowest price sellers are willing to accept, as indicated by the shaded arrows. But for all quantities above Q_x^*, the lowest price willingly accepted by sellers is greater than the highest price willingly offered by buyers. Clearly, trades will not be made beyond Q_x^*.

Algebraically, we can find equilibrium price by setting the demand function equal to the supply function and solving for price. Recall that in our hypothetical example of a local gasoline market, the demand function was given by $Q_x^d = f(P_x, I, P_y)$, and the supply function was given by $Q_x^s = f(P_x, W)$. Those expressions are called **behavioral equations** because they model the behavior of, respectively, buyers and sellers. Variables *other* than own price and quantity are determined outside of the demand and supply model of this particular market. Because of that, they are called **exogenous variables**. Price and quantity, however, are determined within the model for this particular market and are called **endogenous variables**. In our simple example, there are three exogenous variables (I, P_y, and W) and three endogenous variables: P_x, Q_x^d, and Q_x^s. Hence, we have a system of two equations and three unknowns. We need another equation to solve this system. That equation is called the **equilibrium condition**, and it is simply $Q_x^d = Q_x^s$.

Continuing with our hypothetical examples, we could assume that income equals $50 (thousand, per year), the price of automobiles equals $20 (thousand, per automobile), and the hourly wage equals $15. In this case, our equilibrium condition can be represented by setting Equation 14 equal to Equation 17:

$$11,200 - 400P_x = -5,000 + 5,000P_x \qquad (19)$$

and solving for equilibrium, $P_x = 3$.

Equivalently, we could have equated the inverse demand function to the inverse supply function (Equations 15 and 18, respectively)

$$28 - 0.0025Q_x = 1 + 0.0002Q_x \qquad (20)$$

and solved for equilibrium, $Q_x = 10,000$. That is to say, for the given values of I and W, the unique combination of price and quantity of gasoline that results in equilibrium is (3, 10,000).

Note that our system of equations requires explicit values for the exogenous variables to find a unique equilibrium combination of price and quantity. Conceptually, the values of the exogenous variables are being determined in other markets, such as the markets for labor, automobiles, and so on, whereas the price and quantity of gasoline are being determined in the gasoline market. When we concentrate on one market, taking values of exogenous variables as given, we are engaging in what is called **partial equilibrium analysis**. In many cases, we can gain sufficient insight into a market of interest without addressing feedback effects to and from all the other markets that are tangentially involved with this one. At other times, however, we need explicitly to take account of all the feedback mechanisms that are going on in all markets simultaneously. When we do that, we are engaging in what is called **general equilibrium analysis**. For example, in our hypothetical model of the local gasoline market, we recognize that the price of automobiles, a complementary product, has an impact on the demand for gasoline. If the price of automobiles were to rise, people would tend to buy fewer automobiles and probably buy less gasoline. Additionally, though, the price of gasoline probably has an impact on the demand for automobiles that, in turn, can feed back to the gasoline market. Because we are positing a very local gasoline market, it is probably safe to ignore all the feedback effects, but if we are modeling the national markets for gasoline and automobiles, a general equilibrium model might be warranted.

EXAMPLE 6

Finding Equilibrium by Equating Demand and Supply

In the local market for e-books, the aggregate demand is given by the equation

$$Q_{eb}^d = 2{,}000 - 400P_{eb} + 0.5I + 150P_{hb}$$

and the aggregate supply is given by the equation

$$Q_{eb}^s = -516 + 300P_{eb} - 60W$$

where Q_{eb} is quantity of e-books, P_{eb} is the price of an e-book, I is household income, W is wage rate paid to e-book laborers, and P_{hb} is the price of a hard-bound book. Assume I is €2,300, W is €10, and P_{hb} is €21.40. Determine the equilibrium price and quantity of e-books in this local market.

Solution:

Market equilibrium occurs when quantity demanded is equal to quantity supplied, so set $Q_{eb}^d = Q_{eb}^s$ after inserting the given values for the exogenous variables:

$$2{,}000 - 400P_{eb} + 0.5(2{,}300) + 150(21.4) = -516 + 300P_{eb} - 60(10)$$
$$6{,}360 - 400P_{eb} = -1{,}116 + 300P_{eb},$$

which implies that P_{eb} = €10.68, and Q_{eb} = 2,088.

3.7 The Market Mechanism: Iterating toward Equilibrium—or Not

It is one thing to define equilibrium as we have done, but we should also understand the mechanism for reaching equilibrium. That mechanism is what takes place when the market is *not* in equilibrium. Consider our hypothetical example. We found that the equilibrium price was 3, but what would happen if, by some chance, price was actually equal to 4? To find out, we need to see how much buyers would demand at that price and how much sellers would offer to sell by inserting 4 into the demand function and into the supply function.

In the case of quantity demanded, we find that

$$Q_x^d = 11{,}200 - 400(4) = 9{,}600 \tag{21}$$

and in the case of quantity supplied,

$$Q_x^s = -5{,}000 + 5{,}000(4) = 15{,}000 \tag{22}$$

Clearly, the quantity supplied is greater than the quantity demanded, resulting in a condition called **excess supply**, as illustrated in Exhibit 8. In our example, there are 5,400 more units of this good offered for sale at a price of 4 than are demanded at that price.

Exhibit 8   Excess Supply as a Consequence of Price above Equilibrium Price

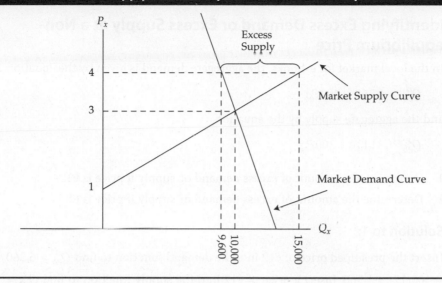

Alternatively, if the market was presented with a price that was too low, say 2, then by inserting the price of 2 into Equations 21 and 22, we find that buyers are willing to purchase 5,400 *more* units than sellers are willing to offer. This result is shown in Exhibit 9.

Exhibit 9   Excess Demand as a Consequence of Price below Equilibrium Price

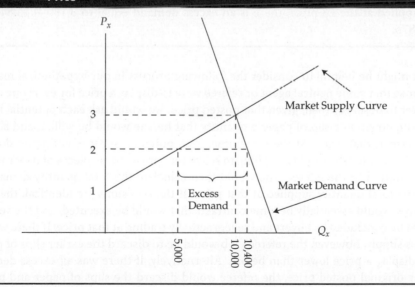

To reach equilibrium, price must adjust until there is neither an excess supply nor an excess demand. That adjustment is called the **market mechanism**, and it is characterized in the following way: In the case of excess supply, price will fall; in the case of excess demand, price will rise; and in the case of neither excess supply nor excess demand, price will not change.

EXAMPLE 7

Identifying Excess Demand or Excess Supply at a Non-equilibrium Price

In the local market for e-books, the aggregate demand is given by the equation

$$Q_{eb}^d = 6{,}360 - 400P_{eb}$$

and the aggregate supply by the equation

$$Q_{eb}^s = -1{,}116 + 300P_{eb}$$

1   Determine the amount of excess demand or supply if price is €12.
2   Determine the amount of excess demand or supply if price is €8.

Solution to 1:

Insert the presumed price of €12 into the demand function to find Q_{eb}^d = 6,360 − 400(12) = 1,560. Insert a price of €12 into the supply function to find Q_{eb}^s = −1,116 + 300(12) = 2,484. Because quantity supplied is greater than quantity demanded at the €12 price, there is an excess supply equal to 2,484 − 1,560 = 924.

Solution to 2:

Insert the presumed price of €8 into the demand function to find Q_{eb}^d = 6,360 − 400(8) = 3,160. Insert a price of €8 into the supply function to find Q_{eb}^s = −1,116 + 300(8) = 1,284. Because quantity demanded is greater than quantity supplied at the €8 price, there is an excess demand equal to 3,160 − 1,284 = 1,876.

It might be helpful to consider the following process in our hypothetical market. Suppose that some neutral agent or referee were to display a price for everyone in the market to observe. Then, given that posted price, we would ask each potential buyer to write down on a slip of paper a quantity that he/she would be willing and able to purchase at that price. At the same time, each potential seller would write down a quantity that he/she would be willing to sell at that price. Those pieces of paper would be submitted to the referee who would then calculate the total quantity demanded and the total quantity supplied at that price. If the two sums are identical, the slips of paper would essentially become contracts that would be executed, and the session would be concluded by buyers and sellers actually trading at that price. If there was an excess supply, however, the referee's job would be to discard the earlier slips of paper and display a price lower than before. Alternatively, if there was an excess demand at the original posted price, the referee would discard the slips of paper and post a higher price. This process would continue until the market reached an equilibrium price at which the quantity willingly offered for sale would just equal the quantity willingly purchased. In this way, the market could tend to move toward equilibrium.[2]

It is not really necessary for a market to have such a referee for it to operate *as if* it had one. Experimental economists have simulated markets in which subjects (usually college students) are given an "order" either to purchase or sell some amount of a

---

2 The process described is known among economists as Walrasian tâtonnement, after the French economist Léon Walras (1834–1910). "Tâtonnement" means roughly, "searching," referring to the mechanism for establishing the equilibrium price.

commodity for a price either no higher (in the case of buyers) or no lower (in the case of sellers) than a set dollar limit. Those limits are distributed among market participants and represent a positively sloped supply curve and a negatively sloped demand curve. The goal for buyers is to buy at a price as far below their limit as possible, and for sellers to sell at a price as far above their limit as possible. The subjects are then allowed to interact in a simulated trading pit by calling out willingness to buy or sell. When two participants come to an agreement on a price, that trade is then reported to a recorder who displays the terms of the deal. Traders are then allowed to observe current prices as they continue to search for a buyer or seller. It has consistently been shown in experiments that this mechanism of open outcry buying and selling (historically, one of the oldest mechanisms used in trading securities) soon converges to the theoretical equilibrium price and quantity inherent in the underlying demand and supply curves used to set the respective sellers' and buyers' limit prices.

In our hypothetical example of the gasoline market, the supply curve is positively sloped, and the demand curve is negatively sloped. In that case, the market mechanism would tend to reach an equilibrium whenever price was accidentally "bumped" away from it. We refer to such an equilibrium as being **stable** because whenever price is disturbed away from equilibrium, it tends to converge back to that equilibrium.[3] It is possible, however, for this market mechanism to result in an unstable equilibrium. Suppose that not only the demand curve has a negative slope but also the supply curve has a negatively sloped segment. For example, at some level of wages, a wage increase might cause workers to supply fewer hours of work if satisfaction ("utility") gained from an extra hour of leisure is greater than the satisfaction obtained from an extra hour of work. Then two possibilities could result, as shown in Panels A and B of Exhibit 10.

Exhibit 10   Stability of Equilibria: I

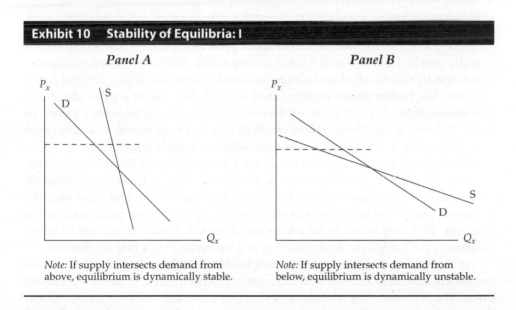

Note: If supply intersects demand from above, equilibrium is dynamically stable.

Note: If supply intersects demand from below, equilibrium is dynamically unstable.

Notice that in Panel A both demand (D) and supply (S) are negatively sloped, but S is steeper and intersects D from above. In this case, if price is above equilibrium, there will be excess supply and the market mechanism will adjust price downward toward equilibrium. In Panel B, D is steeper, which results in S intersecting D from below. In this case, at a price above equilibrium there will be excess demand, and the market mechanism will dictate that price should *rise*, thus leading away from equilibrium.

---

3 In the same sense, equilibrium may sometimes also be referred to as being *dynamically stable*. Similarly, *unstable* or *dynamically unstable* may be used in the sense introduced later.

This equilibrium would be considered **unstable**. If price were accidentally displayed above the equilibrium price, the mechanism would not cause price to converge to that equilibrium, but instead to soar above it because there would be excess demand at that price. In contrast, if price were accidentally displayed below equilibrium, the mechanism would force price even further below equilibrium because there would be excess supply.

If supply were non-linear, there could be multiple equilibria, as shown in Exhibit 11.

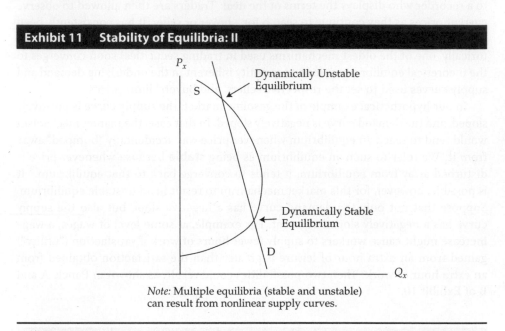

Exhibit 11   Stability of Equilibria: II

Note: Multiple equilibria (stable and unstable) can result from nonlinear supply curves.

Note that there are two combinations of price and quantity that would equate quantity supplied and demanded, hence two equilibria. The lower-priced equilibrium is stable, with a positively sloped supply curve and a negatively sloped demand curve. However, the higher-priced equilibrium is unstable because at a price above that equilibrium price there would be excess demand, thus driving price even higher. At a price below that equilibrium there would be excess supply, thus driving price even lower toward the lower-priced equilibrium, which is a stable equilibrium.

Observation suggests that most markets are characterized by stable equilibria. Prices do not often shoot off to infinity or plunge toward zero. However, occasionally we do observe price bubbles occurring in real estate, securities, and other markets. It appears that prices can behave in ways that are not ultimately sustainable in the long run. They may shoot up for a time but ultimately, if they do not reflect actual valuations, the bubble can burst resulting in a "correction" to a new equilibrium.

As a simple approach to understanding bubbles, consider a case in which buyers and sellers base their expectations of future prices on the rate of change of current prices: if price rises, they take that as a sign that price will rise even further. Under these circumstances, if buyers see an increase in price today, they might actually shift the demand curve to the right, desiring to buy more at each price today because they expect to have to pay more in the future. Alternately, if sellers see an increase in today's price as evidence that price will be even higher in the future, they are reluctant to sell today as they hold out for higher prices tomorrow, and that would shift the supply curve to the left. With a rightward shift in demand and a leftward shift in supply, buyers' and sellers' expectations about price are confirmed and the process begins again. This scenario could result in a bubble that would inflate until someone decides that such high prices can no longer be sustained. The bubble bursts and price plunges.

3.8 Auctions as a Way to Find Equilibrium Price

Sometimes markets really do use auctions to arrive at equilibrium price. Auctions can be categorized into two types depending on whether the value of the item being sold is the same for each bidder or is unique to each bidder. The first case is called **a common value auction** in which there is some actual common value that will ultimately be revealed after the auction is settled. Prior to the auction's settlement, however, bidders must estimate that true value. An example of a common value auction would be bidding on a jar containing many coins. Each bidder could estimate the value; but until someone buys the jar and actually counts the coins, no one knows with certainty the true value. In the second case, called a **private value auction**, each buyer places a subjective value on the item, and in general their values differ. An example might be an auction for a unique piece of art that buyers are hoping to purchase for their own personal enjoyment, not primarily as an investment to be sold later.

Auctions also differ according to the mechanism used to arrive at a price and to determine the ultimate buyer. These mechanisms include the ascending price (or English) auction, the first price sealed bid auction, the second price sealed bid (or Vickery) auction, and the descending price (or Dutch) auction.

Perhaps the most familiar auction mechanism is the **ascending price auction** in which an auctioneer is selling a single item in a face-to-face arena where potential buyers openly reveal their willingness to buy the good at prices that are called out by an auctioneer. The auctioneer begins at a low price and easily elicits nods from buyers. He then raises the price incrementally. In a common value auction, buyers can sometimes learn something about the true value of the item being auctioned from observing other bidders. Ultimately bidders with different maximum amounts they are willing to pay for the item, called **reservation prices**, begin to drop out of the bidding as price rises above their respective reservation prices.[4] Finally, only one bidder is left (who has outbid the bidder with the second highest valuation) and the item is sold to that bidder for his bid price.

Sometimes sellers offer a common value item, such as an oil or timber lease, in a **sealed bid auction**. In this case, bids are elicited from potential buyers, but there is no ability to observe bids by other buyers until the auction has ended. In the **first price sealed bid auction**, the envelopes containing bids are opened simultaneously and the item is sold to the highest bidder for the actual bid price. Consider an oil lease being auctioned by the government. The highest bidder will pay his bid price but does not know with certainty the profitability of the asset on which he is bidding. The profits that are ultimately realized will be learned only after a successful bidder buys and exploits the asset. Bidders each have some expected value they place on the oil lease, and those values can vary among bidders. Typically, some overly optimistic bidders will value the asset higher than its ultimate realizable value, and they might submit bids above that true value. Because the highest bidder wins the auction and must pay his full bid price, he may find that he has fallen prey to the **winner's curse** of having bid more than the ultimate value of the asset. The "winner" in this case will lose money because he has paid more than the value of the asset being auctioned. In recognition of the possibility of being overly optimistic, bidders might bid very conservatively below their expectation of the true value. If all bidders react in this way, the seller might end up with a low sale price.

If the item being auctioned is a private value item, then there is no danger of the winner's curse (no one would bid more than their own true valuation). But bidders try to guess the reservation prices of other bidders, so the most successful winning bidder would bid a price just above the reservation price of the second-highest bidder.

---

4 The term *reservation price* is also used to refer to the minimum price the seller of the auctioned item is willing to accept.

This bid will be below the true reservation price of the highest bidder, resulting in a "bargain" for the highest bidder. To induce each bidder to reveal their true reservation price, sellers can use the **second price sealed bid** mechanism (also known as a Vickery auction). In this mechanism, the bids are submitted in sealed envelopes and opened simultaneously. The winning buyer is the one who submitted the highest bid, but the price she pays is not equal to her own bid. She pays a price equal to the second-highest bid. The optimal strategy for any bidder in such an auction is to bid her actual reservation price, so the second price sealed bid auction induces buyers to reveal their true valuation of the item. It is also true that if the bidding increments are small, the second price sealed bid auction will yield the same ultimate price as the ascending price auction.

Yet another type of auction is called a **descending price auction** or **Dutch auction** in which the auctioneer begins at a very high price—a price so high that no bidder is believed to be willing to pay it.[5] The auctioneer then lowers the called price in increments until there is a willing buyer of the item being sold. If there are many bidders, each with a different reservation price and a unit demand, then each has a perfectly vertical demand curve at one unit and a height equal to his reservation price. For example, suppose the highest reservation price is equal to $100. That person would be willing to buy one unit of the good at a price no higher than $100. Suppose each subsequent bidder also has a unit demand and a reservation price that falls, respectively, in increments of $1. The market demand curve would be a negatively sloped step function; that is, it would look like a stair step, with the width of each step being one unit and the height of each step being $1 lower than the preceding step. For example, at a price equal to $90, 11 people would be willing to buy one unit of the good. If the price were to fall to $89, then the quantity demanded would be 12, and so on.

In the Dutch auction, the auctioneer would begin with a price above $100 and then lower it by increments until the highest reservation price bidder would purchase the unit. Again, the supply curve for this single unit auction would be vertical at one unit, although there might be a seller reserve price that would form the lower bound on the supply curve at that reserve price.

A traditional Dutch auction as just described could be conducted in a single unit or multiple unit format. With a multiple unit format, the price quoted by the auctioneer would be the per-unit price and a winning bidder could take fewer units than all the units for sale. If the winning bidder took fewer than all units for sale, the auctioneer would then lower the price until all units for sale were sold; thus transactions could occur at multiple prices. Modified Dutch auctions (frequently also called simply "Dutch Auctions" in practice) are commonly used in securities markets; the modifications often involve establishing a single price for all purchasers. As implemented in share repurchases, the company stipulates a range of acceptable prices at which the company would be willing to repurchase shares from existing shareholders. The auction process is structured to uncover the minimum price at which the company can buy back the desired number of shares, with the company paying that price to all qualifying bids. For example, if the share price is €25 per share, the company might offer to repurchase 3 million shares in a range of €26 to €28 per share. Each shareholder would then indicate the number of shares and the lowest price at which he or she would be willing to sell. The company would then begin to qualify bids beginning with those shareholders who submitted bids at €26 and continue to qualify bids at higher prices until 3 million shares had been qualified. In our example, that price might be €27. Shareholders who bid between €26 and €27, inclusive, would then be paid €27 per share for their shares.

---

5 The historical use of this auction type for flower auctions in the Netherlands explains the name.

Another Dutch auction variation, also involving a single price and called a **single price auction**, is used in selling US Treasury securities.[6] The single price Treasury bill auction operates as follows: The Treasury announces that it will auction 26-week T-bills with an offering amount of, say, $90 billion with both competitive and non-competitive bidding. Non-competitive bidders state the total face value they are willing to purchase at the ultimate price (yield) that clears the market (i.e., sells all of the securities offered), whatever that turns out to be. Competitive bidders each submit a total face value amount and the price at which they are willing to purchase those bills. The Treasury then ranks those bids in ascending order of yield (i.e., descending order of price) and finds the yield at which the total $90 billion offering amount would be sold. If the offering amount is just equal to the total face value bidders are willing to purchase at that yield, then all the T-bills are sold for that single yield. If there is excess demand at that yield, then bidders would each receive a proportionately smaller total than they offered.

As an example, suppose the following table shows the prices and the offers from competitive bidders for a variety of prices, as well as the total offers from non-competitive bidders, assumed to be $15 billion:

Discount Rate Bid (%)	Bid Price per $100	Competitive Bids ($ billions)	Cumulative Competitive Bids ($ billions)	Non-competitive Bids ($ billions)	Total Cumulative Bids ($ billions)
0.1731	99.91250	10	10	15	25
0.1741	99.91200	15	25	15	40
0.1751	99.91150	20	45	15	60
0.1760	99.91100	12	57	15	72
0.1770	99.91050	10	67	15	82
0.1780	99.91000	5	72	15	87
0.1790	99.90950	10	82	15	97

At yields below 0.1790 percent (prices above 99.90950), there is still excess supply. But at that yield, more bills are demanded than the $90 billion face value of the total offer amount. The clearing yield would be 0.1790 percent (a price of 99.9095 per $100 of face value), and all sales would be made at that single yield. All the non-competitive bidders would have their orders filled at the clearing price, as well as all bidders who bid above that price. The competitive bidders who offered a price of 99.9095 would have 30 percent of their order filled at that price because it would take only 30 percent of the $10 billion ($90 billion − $87 billion offered = $3 billion, or 30 percent of $10 billion) demanded at that price to complete the $90 billion offer amount. That is, by filling 30 percent of the competitive bids at a price of 99.9095, the cumulative competitive bids would sum to $75 billion. This amount plus the $15 billion non-competitive bids adds up to $90 billion.

EXAMPLE 8

Auctioning Treasury Bills with a Single Price Auction

The US Treasury offers to sell $115 billion of 52-week T-bills and requests competitive and non-competitive bids. Non-competitive bids total $10 billion, and competitive bidders in descending order of offer price are as given in the table below:

---

6 Historically, the US Treasury has also used multiple price auctions and in the euro area multiple price auctions are widely used. See http://www.dsta.nl/english/Subjects/Auction_methods for more information.

Discount Rate Bid (%)	Bid Price per $100	Competitive Bids ($ billions)	Cumulative Competitive Bids ($ billions)	Non-competitive Bids ($ billions)	Total Cumulative Bids ($ billions)
0.1575	99.8425	12			
0.1580	99.8420	20			
0.1585	99.8415	36			
0.1590	99.8410	29			
0.1595	99.8405	5			
0.1600	99.8400	15			
0.1605	99.8395	10			

1 Determine the winning price if a single price Dutch auction is used to sell these T-bills.

2 For those bidders at the winning price, what percentage of their order would be filled?

Solution to 1:

Enter the non-competitive quantity of $10 billion into the table. Then find the cumulative competitive bids and the total cumulative bids in the respective columns:

Bid Price per $100	Competitive Bids ($ billions)	Cumulative Competitive Bids ($ billions)	Non-competitive Bids ($ billions)	Total Cumulative Bids ($ billions)
99.8425	12	12	10	22
99.8420	20	32	10	42
99.8415	36	68	10	78
99.8410	29	97	10	107
99.8405	5	102	10	112
99.8400	15	117	10	127
99.8395	10	127	10	137

Note that at a bid price of 99.8400 there would be excess demand of $12 billion (i.e., the difference between $127 billion bid and $115 billion offered), but at the higher price of 99.8405 there would be excess supply. So the winning bid would be at a price of 99.8400.

Solution to 2:

At a price of 99.8400, there would be $15 billion more demanded than at 99.8405 ($127 billion minus $112 billion), and at 99.8405 there would be excess supply equal to $3 billion. So the bidders at the winning bid would have only 3/15, or 20 percent, of their orders filled.

3.9 Consumer Surplus—Value minus Expenditure

To this point, we have discussed the fundamentals of demand and supply curves and explained a simple model of how a market can be expected to arrive at an equilibrium combination of price and quantity. While it is certainly necessary for the analyst to understand the basic working of the market model, it is also crucial to have a sense of why we might care whether the market tends toward equilibrium. This question moves us into the normative, or evaluative, consideration of whether market equilibrium is desirable in any social sense. In other words, is there some reasonable measure we can apply to the outcome of a competitive market that enables us to say whether that outcome is socially desirable? Economists have developed two related concepts called **consumer surplus** and **producer surplus** to address that question. We will begin with consumer surplus, which is a measure of how much net benefit buyers enjoy from the ability to participate in a particular market.

To get an intuitive feel for this concept, consider the last thing you purchased. Maybe it was a cup of coffee, a new pair of shoes, or a new car. Whatever it was, think of how much you actually paid for it. Now contrast that price with the maximum amount you would have been *willing to pay* for it instead of going without it altogether. If those two numbers are different, we say you received some consumer surplus from your purchase. You received a "bargain" because you were willing to pay more than you had to pay.

Earlier we referred to the law of demand, which says that as price falls, consumers are willing to buy more of the good. This observation translates into a negatively sloped demand curve. Alternatively, we could say that the highest price that consumers are willing to pay for an additional unit declines as they consume more and more of it. In this way, we can interpret their *willingness to pay* as a measure of how much they *value* each additional unit of the good. This point is very important: To purchase a unit of some good, consumers must give up something else they value. So the price they are willing to pay for an additional unit of a good is a measure of how much they value that unit, in terms of the other goods they must sacrifice to consume it.

If demand curves are negatively sloped, it must be because the value of each additional unit of the good falls the more of it they consume. We will explore this concept further later, but for now it is enough to recognize that the demand curve can thus be considered a **marginal value curve** because it shows the highest price consumers are willing to pay for each *additional* unit. In effect, the demand curve is the willingness of consumers to pay for each additional unit.

This interpretation of the demand curve allows us to measure the total value of consuming any given quantity of a good: It is the sum of all the marginal values of each unit consumed, up to and including the last unit. Graphically, this measure translates into the area under the consumer's demand curve, up to and including the last unit consumed, as shown in Exhibit 12, in which the consumer is choosing to buy Q_1 units of the good at a price of P_1. The **marginal value** of the Q_1^{th} unit is clearly P_1, because that is the highest price the consumer is willing to pay for that unit. Importantly, however, the marginal value of each unit *up to* the Q_1^{th} is greater than P_1.[7]

Because the consumer would have been willing to pay more for each of those units than she actually paid (P_1), then we can say she received more value than the cost to her of buying them. This concept is referred to as **consumer surplus**, and it is defined as the difference between the value that the consumer places on those units and the amount of money that was required to pay for them. The total value of Q_1 is thus the area of the vertically crosshatched trapezoid in Exhibit 12. The **total expenditure** is only the area of the rectangle with height P_1 and base Q_1. The total consumer surplus received from buying Q_1 units at a level price of P_1 per unit is the *difference* between the area under the demand curve, on the one hand, and the area of the rectangle, $P_1 \times Q_1$, on the other hand. That area is shown as the lightly shaded triangle.

---

7 This assumes that all units of the good are sold at the same price P_1. Because the demand curve is negatively sloped, all units up to the Q_1^{th} have marginal values greater than that price.

Exhibit 12   Consumer Surplus

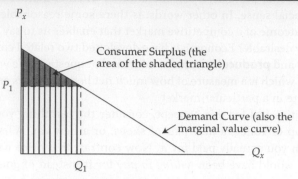

Note: Consumer surplus is the area beneath the demand curve and above the price paid.

EXAMPLE 9

Calculating Consumer Surplus

A market demand function is given by the equation $Q^d = 180 - 2P$. Determine the value of consumer surplus if price is equal to 65.

Solution:

First, insert 65 into the demand function to find the quantity demanded at that price: $Q^d = 180 - 2(65) = 50$. Then, to make drawing the demand curve easier, invert the demand function by solving it for P in terms of Q: $P = 90 - 0.5Q$. Note that the price intercept is 90, and the quantity intercept is 180. Draw the demand curve:

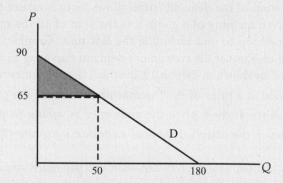

Find the area of the triangle above the price and below the demand curve, up to quantity 50: Area of a triangle is given as $1/2$ Base × Height = $(1/2)(50)(25) = 625$.

3.10 Producer Surplus—Revenue minus Variable Cost

In this section, we discuss a concept analogous to consumer surplus called **producer surplus**. It is the difference between the total revenue sellers receive from selling a given amount of a good, on the one hand, and the total variable cost of producing that amount, on the other hand. **Variable costs** are those costs that change when the level of output changes. Total revenue is simply the total quantity sold multiplied by the price per unit.

The total variable cost (variable cost per unit times units produced) is measured by the area beneath the supply curve, and it is a little more complicated to understand. Recall that the supply curve represents the lowest price that sellers would be willing to accept for each additional unit of a good. In general, that amount is the cost of producing that next unit, called **marginal cost**. Clearly, a seller would never intend to sell a unit of a good for a price *lower* than its marginal cost, because she would lose money on that unit. Alternatively, a producer should be willing to sell that unit for a price that is *higher* than its marginal cost because it would contribute something toward fixed cost and profit, and obviously the higher the price the better for the seller. Hence, we can interpret the marginal cost curve as the lowest price sellers would accept for each quantity, which basically means the marginal cost curve is the supply curve of any competitive seller. The market supply curve is simply the aggregation of all sellers' individual supply curves, as we showed in section 3.5.

Marginal cost curves are likely to have positive slopes. (It is the logical result of the law of diminishing marginal product, which will be discussed in a later reading.) In Exhibit 13, we see such a supply curve. Because its height is the marginal cost of each additional unit, the total variable cost of Q_1 units is measured as the area beneath the supply curve, up to and including that Q_1^{th} unit, or the area of the vertically cross-hatched trapezoid. But each unit is being sold at the same price P_1, so total revenue to sellers is the rectangle whose height is P_1 and base is total quantity Q_1. Because sellers would have been willing to accept the amount of money represented by the trapezoid, but they actually received the larger area of the rectangle, we say they received producer surplus equal to the area of the shaded triangle. So sellers also got a "bargain" because they received a higher price than they would have been willing to accept for each unit.

Exhibit 13   Producer Surplus

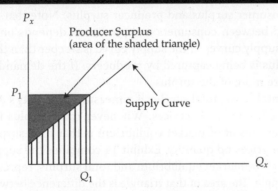

Note: Producer surplus is the area beneath the price and above the supply curve.

EXAMPLE 10

Calculating the Amount of Producer Surplus

A market supply function is given by the equation $Q^s = -15 + P$. Determine the value of producer surplus if price were equal to 65.

Solution:

First, insert 65 into the supply function to find quantity supplied at that price: $Q^s = -15 + (65) = 50$. Then, to make drawing the supply curve easier, invert the supply function by solving for P in terms of Q: $P = 15 + Q$. Note that the price intercept is 15, and the quantity intercept is –15. Draw the supply curve:

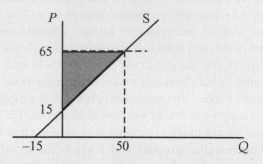

Find the area of the triangle below the price, above the supply curve, up to a quantity of 50: Area = 1/2 Base × Height = (1/2)(50)(50) = 1,250.

3.11 Total Surplus—Total Value minus Total Variable Cost

In the previous sections, we have seen that consumers and producers both receive "a bargain" when they are allowed to engage in a mutually beneficial, voluntary exchange with one another. For every unit up to the equilibrium unit traded, buyers would have been willing to pay more than they actually had to pay. Additionally, for every one of those units, sellers would have been willing to sell it for less than they actually received. The total value to buyers was greater than the total variable cost to sellers. The difference between those two values is called **total surplus**, and it is made up of the sum of consumer surplus and producer surplus. Note that the way the total surplus is divided between consumers and producers depends on the steepness of the demand and supply curves. If the supply curve is steeper than the demand curve, more of the surplus is being captured by producers. If the demand curve is steeper, consumers capture more of the surplus.

In a fundamental sense, total surplus is a measure of society's gain from the voluntary exchange of goods and services. Whenever total surplus increases, society gains. An important result of market equilibrium is that total surplus is maximized at the equilibrium price and quantity. Exhibit 14 combines the supply curve and the demand curve to show market equilibrium and total surplus, represented as the area of the shaded triangle. The area of that triangle is the difference between the trapezoid of total value to society's buyers and the trapezoid of total resource cost to society's sellers. If price measures dollars (or euros) per unit, and quantity measures units per month, then the measure of total surplus is dollars (euros) per month. It is the "bargain" that buyers and sellers together experience when they voluntarily trade the good in a market. If the market ceased to exist, that would be the monetary value of the loss to society.

> **Exhibit 14   Total Surplus as the Area beneath the Demand Curve and above the Supply Curve**

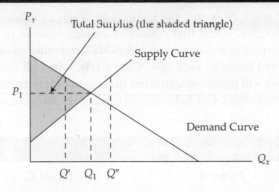

3.12 Markets Maximize Society's Total Surplus

Recall that the market demand curve can be considered the willingness of consumers to pay for each additional unit of a good. Hence, it is society's marginal value curve for that good. Additionally, the market supply curve represents the marginal cost to society to produce each additional unit of that good, assuming no positive or negative externalities. (An **externality** is a case in which production costs or the consumption benefits of a good or service spill over onto those who are not producing or consuming the good or service; a spillover cost (e.g., pollution) is called a **negative externality**, a spillover benefit (e.g., literacy programs) is called a **positive externality**.)

At equilibrium, where demand and supply curves intersect, the highest price that someone is willing to pay is just equal to the lowest price that a seller is willing to accept, which is the marginal cost of that unit of the good. In Exhibit 14, that equilibrium quantity is Q_1. Now, suppose that some influence on the market caused less than Q_1 units to be traded, say only Q' units. Note that the marginal value of the Q'^{th} unit exceeds society's marginal cost to produce it. In a fundamental sense, we could say that society *should* produce and consume it, as well as the next, and the next, all the way up to Q_1. Or suppose that some influence caused more than Q_1 to be produced, say Q'' units. Then what can we say? For all those units beyond Q_1, and up to Q'', society incurred greater cost than the value it received from consuming them. We could say that society *should not* have produced and consumed those additional units. Total surplus was reduced by those additional units because they cost more in the form of resources than the value they provided for society when they were consumed.

There is reason to believe that markets usually trend toward equilibrium and that the condition of equilibrium itself is also optimal in a welfare sense. To delve a little more deeply, consider two consumers, Helen Smith and Tom Warren, who have access to a market for some good, perhaps gasoline or shoes or any other consumption good. We could depict their situations using their individual demand curves juxtaposed on an exhibit of the overall market equilibrium, as in Exhibit 15 where Smith's and Warren's individual demands for a particular good are depicted along with the market demand and supply of that same good. (The horizontal axes are scaled differently because the market quantity is so much greater than either consumer's quantity, but the price axes are identical.)

At the market price of P_x^*, Smith chooses to purchase Q_H, and Warren chooses to purchase Q_T because at that price, the marginal value for each of the two consumers is just equal to the price they have to pay per unit. Now, suppose someone removed one unit of the good from Smith and presented it to Warren. In Panel A of Exhibit 15, the loss of value experienced by Smith is depicted by the dotted trapezoid, and in Panel B of Exhibit 15, the gain in value experienced by Warren is depicted by the crosshatched trapezoid. Note that the increase in Warren's value is necessarily less than the loss in Smith's. Recall that consumer surplus is value minus expenditure. Total consumer surplus is reduced when individuals consume quantities that do not yield equal marginal value to each one. Conversely, when all consumers face the identical price, they will purchase quantities that equate their marginal values across all consumers. Importantly, that behavior maximizes total consumer surplus.

Exhibit 15   How Total Surplus Can Be Reduced by Rearranging Quantity

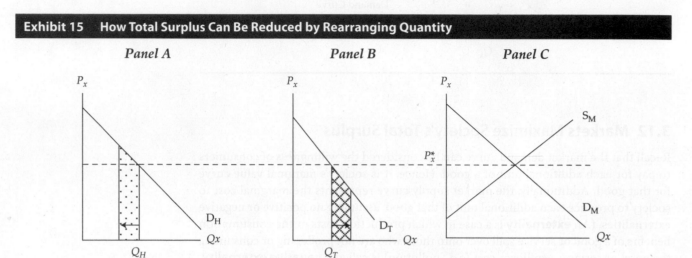

Note: Beginning at a competitive market equilibrium, when one unit is taken from Smith and presented to Warren, total surplus is reduced.

A precisely analogous argument can be made to show that when all producers produce quantities such that their marginal costs are equated across all firms, total producer surplus is maximized. The result of this analysis is that when all consumers face the same market equilibrium price and are allowed to buy all they desire at that price, and when all firms face that same price and are allowed to sell as much as they want at that price, the total of consumer and producer surplus (total surplus) is maximized from that market. This result is the beauty of free markets: They maximize society's net benefit from production and consumption of goods and services.

3.13 Market Interference: The Negative Impact on Total Surplus

Sometimes, lawmakers determine that the market price is "too high" for consumers to pay, so they use their power to impose a ceiling on price below the market equilibrium price. Some examples of ceilings include rent controls (limits on increases in the rent paid for apartments), limits on the prices of medicines, and laws against "price gouging" after a hurricane (i.e., charging opportunistically high prices for goods such as bottled water or plywood). Certainly, price limits benefit anyone who had been paying the old higher price and can still buy all they want at the lower ceiling price. However, the story is more complicated than that. Exhibit 16 shows a market in which a ceiling price, P_c, has been imposed below equilibrium. Let's examine the full impact of such a law.

Exhibit 16   A Price Ceiling

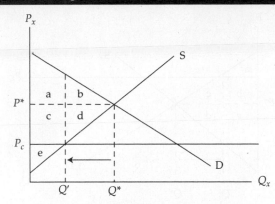

Note: A price ceiling transfers surplus equal to area c from sellers to buyers, but it destroys surplus equal to area b + d, called a deadweight loss.

Prior to imposition of the ceiling price, equilibrium occurs at (P^*, Q^*), and total surplus equals the area given by a + b + c + d + e. It consists of consumer surplus given by a + b, and producer surplus given by c + d + e. When the ceiling is imposed, two things happen: Buyers would like to purchase more at the lower price, but sellers are willing now to sell less. Regardless of how much buyers would like to purchase, though, only Q' would be offered for sale. Clearly, the total quantity that actually gets traded has fallen, and this has some serious consequences. For one thing, any buyer who is still able to buy the Q' quantity has clearly been given a benefit. They used to pay P^* and now pay only P_c per unit. Those buyers gain consumer surplus equal to rectangle c, which used to be part of seller surplus. Rectangle c is surplus that has been transferred from sellers to buyers, but it still exists as part of total surplus. Disturbingly, though, there is a loss of consumer surplus equal to triangle b and a loss of producer surplus equal to triangle d. Those measures of surplus simply no longer exist at the lower quantity. Clearly, surplus cannot be enjoyed on units that are neither produced nor consumed, so that loss of surplus is called a **deadweight loss** because it is surplus that is lost by one or the other group but not transferred to anyone. Thus, after the imposition of a price ceiling at P_c, consumer surplus is given by a + c, producer surplus by e, and the deadweight loss is b + d.[8]

Another example of price interference is a **price floor**, in which lawmakers make it illegal to buy or sell a good or service below a certain price, which is above equilibrium. Again, some sellers who are still able to sell at the now higher floor price benefit from the law, but that's not the whole story. Exhibit 17 shows such a floor price, imposed at P_f above free market equilibrium.

---

8 Technically, the statement assumes that the limited sales are allocated to the consumers with the highest valuations. A detailed explanation, however, is outside the scope of this reading.

Exhibit 17   A Price Floor

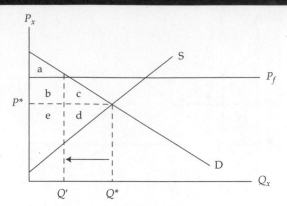

Note: A price floor transfers surplus equal to area b from buyers to sellers, but it destroys surplus equal to area c + d, called a deadweight loss.

At free market equilibrium quantity Q^*, total surplus is equal to a + b + c + d + e, consisting of consumer surplus equal to area a + b + c, and producer surplus equal to area e + d. When the floor is imposed, sellers would like to sell more, but buyers would choose to purchase less. Regardless of how much producers want to sell, however, only Q' will be purchased at the new higher floor price. Those sellers who can still sell at the higher price benefit at the expense of the buyers: There is a transfer of surplus from buyers to sellers equal to rectangle b. Regrettably, however, that's not all. Buyers also lose consumer surplus equal to triangle c, and sellers lose producer surplus equal to triangle d.[9] Once again, no one can benefit from units that are neither produced nor consumed, so there is a deadweight loss equal to triangle c plus triangle d. As a result of the floor, the buyer's surplus is reduced to triangle a.

A good example of a price floor is the imposition of a legal minimum wage in the United States, the United Kingdom, and many other countries. Although controversy remains among some economists on the empirical effects of the minimum wage, most economists continue to believe that a minimum wage can reduce employment. Although some workers will benefit, because they continue to work at the higher wage, others will be harmed because they will no longer be working at the increased wage rate.

EXAMPLE 11

Calculating the Amount of Deadweight Loss from a Price Floor

A market has demand function given by the equation $Q^d = 180 - 2P$, and supply function given by the equation $Q^s = -15 + P$. Calculate the amount of deadweight loss that would result from a price floor imposed at a level of 72.

Solution:

First, solve for equilibrium price of 65 and quantity 50. Then, invert the demand function to find $P = 90 - 0.5Q$, and the supply function to find $P = 15 + Q$. Use these functions to draw the demand and supply curves:

---

9 Technically, this statement assumes that sales are made by the lowest cost producers. A discussion of the point is outside the scope of this reading.

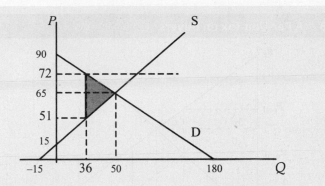

Insert the floor price of 72 into the demand function to find that only 36 would be demanded at that price. Insert 36 into the supply function to find the price of 51 that corresponds to a quantity of 36. Because the price floor would reduce quantity from its equilibrium value of 50 to the new value of 36, the deadweight loss would occur because those 14 units are not now being produced and consumed under the price floor. So deadweight loss equals the area of the shaded triangle: 1/2 Base × Height = (1/2)(72 − 51)(50 − 36) = 147.

Still other policies can interfere with the ability of prices to allocate society's resources. Governments do have legitimate functions to perform in society, and they need to have revenue to finance them. So they often raise revenue by imposing taxes on various goods or activities. One such policy is a per-unit tax, such as an excise tax. By law, this tax could be imposed either on buyers or on sellers, but we shall see that it really doesn't matter at all who legally must pay the tax, the result is the same: more deadweight loss. Exhibit 18 depicts such a tax imposed in this case on buyers. Here, the law simply says that whenever a buyer purchases a unit of some good, he or she must pay a tax of some amount t per unit. Recall that the demand curve is the highest price willingly paid for each quantity. Because buyers probably do not really care who receives the money, government or the seller, their gross willingness to pay is still the same. Because they must pay t dollars to the government, however, their net demand curve would shift vertically downward by t per unit. Exhibit 18 shows the result of such a shift.

Exhibit 18   A Per-Unit Tax on Buyers

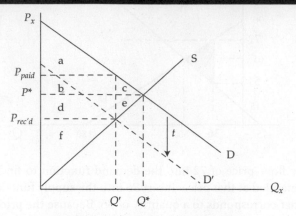

Note: A tax on buyers shifts the demand curve downward by t, imposing a burden on both buyers and sellers, shifting some of the surplus to government but leaving a deadweight loss equal to c plus e.

Originally, the pre-tax equilibrium is where D and S intersect at (P^*, Q^*). Consumer surplus is given by triangle a plus rectangle b plus triangle c, and producer surplus consists of triangle f plus rectangle d plus triangle e. When the tax is imposed, the demand curve shifts vertically downward by the tax per unit, t. This shift results in a new equilibrium at the intersection of S and D'. That new equilibrium price is received by sellers ($P_{rec'd}$). However, buyers now must pay an additional t per unit to government, resulting in a total price paid (P_{paid}) that is higher than before. Sellers receive a lower price and buyers pay a higher price than pretax, so both suffer a burden as a result of this tax, even though it was legally imposed only on buyers. Buyers now have consumer surplus that has been reduced by rectangle b plus triangle c; thus, post-tax consumer surplus is $(a + b + c) - (b + c) = a$. Sellers now have producer surplus that has been reduced by rectangle d plus triangle e; thus post-tax producer surplus is $(f + d + e) - (d + e) = f$. Government receives tax revenue of t per unit multiplied by Q' units. Its total revenue is rectangle b plus rectangle d. Note that the total loss to buyers and sellers $(b + c + d + e)$ is greater than the revenue transferred to government $(b + d)$, so that the tax resulted in a deadweight loss equal to triangle c plus triangle e as $(b + c + d + e) - (b + d) = c + e$.

How would things change if the tax had legally been imposed on sellers instead of buyers? To see the answer, note that the supply curve is the lowest price willingly accepted by sellers, which is their marginal cost. If they now must pay an additional t dollars per unit to government, their lowest acceptable price for each unit is now higher. We show this by shifting the supply curve vertically upward by t dollars per unit, as shown in Exhibit 19.

Exhibit 19 A Per-Unit Tax on Sellers

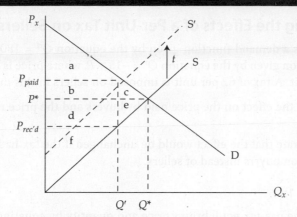

Note: A tax on sellers shifts the supply curve upward by t. Everything is exactly the same as in the case of imposing the tax on buyers.

The new equilibrium occurs at the intersection of S' and D, resulting in the new equilibrium price paid by buyers, P_{paid}. Sellers are paid this price but must remit t dollars per unit to the government, resulting in an after-tax price received ($P_{rec'd}$) that is lower than before the tax. In terms of overall result, absolutely nothing is different from the case in which buyers had the legal responsibility to pay the tax. Tax revenue to the government is the same, buyers' and sellers' reduction in surplus is identical to the previous case, and the deadweight loss is the same as well.

Notice that the share of the total burden of the tax need not be equal for buyers and sellers. In our example, sellers experienced a greater burden than buyers did, regardless of who had the legal responsibility to pay the tax. The relative burden from a tax falls disproportionately on the group (buyers or sellers) that has the steeper curve. In our example, the demand curve is flatter than the supply curve (just slightly so), so buyers bore proportionately less of the burden. Just the reverse would be true if the demand curve had been steeper than the supply curve.

All of the policies we have examined involve government interfering with free markets. Other examples include imposing tariffs on imported goods, setting quotas on imports, or banning the trade of goods. Additionally, governments often impose regulations on the production or consumption of goods to limit or correct the negative effects on third parties that cannot be captured in free market prices. Even the most ardent of free market enthusiasts recognize the justification of some government intervention in the case of public goods, such as for national defense, or where prices do not reflect true marginal social value or cost, as in externalities such as pollution. Social considerations can trump pure economic efficiency, as in the case of child labor laws or human trafficking. What does come from the analysis of markets, however, is the recognition that when social marginal benefits are truly reflected in market demand curves and social marginal costs are truly reflected in supply curves, total surplus is maximized when markets are allowed to operate freely. Moreover, when society does choose to impose legal restrictions, market analysis of the kind we have just examined provides society with a means of at least assessing the deadweight losses that such policies extract from total surplus. In that way, policy makers can perform logical, rigorous cost benefit assessments of their proposed policies to inform their decisions.

EXAMPLE 12

Calculating the Effects of a Per-Unit Tax on Sellers

A market has a demand function given by the equation $Q^d = 180 - 2P$, and a supply function given by the equation $Q^s = -15 + P$, where price is measured in euros per unit. A tax of €2 per unit is imposed on sellers in this market.

1 Calculate the effect on the price paid by buyers and the price received by sellers.

2 Demonstrate that the effect would be unchanged if the tax had been imposed on buyers instead of sellers.

Solution to 1:

Determine the pre-tax equilibrium price and quantity by equating supply and demand: $180 - 2P = -15 + P$. Therefore $P^* = $ €65 before tax. If the tax is imposed on sellers, the supply curve will shift upward by €2. So, to begin, we need to invert the supply function and the demand function: $P = 15 + Q^s$ and $P = 90 - 0.5Q^d$. Now, impose the tax on sellers by increasing the value of P by €2 at each quantity. This step simply means increasing the price intercept by €2. Because sellers must pay €2 tax per unit, the lowest price they are willing to accept for each quantity rises by that amount: $P' = 17 + Q^s$, where "P prime" indicates the new function after imposition of the tax. Because the tax was not imposed on buyers, the inverse demand function remains as it was. Solve for the new equilibrium price and quantity: $90 - 0.5Q = 17 + Q$, so new after-tax $Q = 48.667$. By inserting that quantity into the new inverse demand function, we find that $P_{paid} = $ €65.667. This amount is paid by buyers to sellers, but because sellers are responsible for paying the €2 tax, they receive only €65.667 − €2 = €63.667, after tax. So we find that the tax on sellers has increased the price to buyers by €0.667 while reducing the price received by sellers by €1.33. Out of the €2 tax, buyers bear one-third of the burden and sellers bear two-thirds of the burden. This result is because the demand curve is half as steep as the supply curve. The group with the steepest, less elastic, curve bears the greater burden of a tax, regardless of on whom the legal incidence of the tax is imposed.

Solution to 2:

Instead of adding €2 to the price intercept of supply curve, we now subtract €2 from the price intercept of the demand curve. This step is because buyers' willingness to pay sellers has been reduced by the €2 they must pay in tax per unit. Buyers really don't care who receives their money, they are interested only in the greatest amount they are willing to pay for each quantity. So the new inverse demand function is: $P'' = 88 - 0.5Q$. Using this new inverse demand, we now solve for equilibrium: $88 - 0.5Q = 15 + Q$. (Because buyers must pay the tax, we leave the old supply curve unchanged.) The new equilibrium quantity is therefore $Q = 48.667$, which is exactly as it was when sellers had the obligation to pay the tax. Inserting that number into the old supply function gives us the new equilibrium price of €63.667, which is what buyers must pay sellers. Recall, however, that now buyers must pay €2 in tax per unit, so the price buyers pay after tax is €63.667 + €2 = €65.667. So nothing changes when we impose the statutory obligation on buyers instead of sellers. They still share the ultimate burden of the tax in exactly the same proportion as when sellers had to send the €2 to the taxing authority.

We have seen that government interferences, such as price ceilings, price floors, and taxes, result in imbalances between demand and supply. In general, anything else that intervenes in the process of buyers and sellers finding the equilibrium price can cause imbalances as well. In the simple model of demand and supply, it is assumed that buyers and sellers can interact without cost. Often, however, there can be costs associated with finding a buyer's or a seller's counterpart. There could be a buyer who is willing to pay a price higher than some seller's lowest acceptable price, but if the two cannot find one another, there will be no transaction, resulting in a deadweight loss. The costs of matching buyers with sellers are generally referred to as **search costs**, and they arise because of frictions inherent in the matching process. When these costs are significant, an opportunity may arise for a third party to provide a valuable service by reducing those costs. This role is played by brokers. Brokers do not actually become owners of a good or service that is being bought, but they serve the role of locating buyers for sellers or sellers for buyers. (Dealers, however, actually take possession of the item in anticipation of selling it to a future buyer.) To the extent that brokers serve to reduce search costs, they provide value in the transaction, and for that value they are able to charge a brokerage fee. Although the brokerage fee could certainly be viewed as a transactions cost, it is really a price charged for the service of reducing search costs. In effect, any impediment in the dissemination of information about buyers' and sellers' willingness to exchange goods can cause an imbalance in demand and supply. So anything that improves that information flow can add value. In that sense, advertising can add value to the extent that it informs potential buyers of the availability of goods and services.

DEMAND ELASTICITIES

4

The general model of demand and supply can be highly useful in understanding directional changes in prices and quantities that result from shifts in one or the other curve. At a deeper quantitative level, though, we often need to measure just *how* sensitive quantity demanded or supplied is to changes in the independent variables that affect them. Here is where the concept of *elasticity of demand and supply* plays a crucial role in microeconomics. We will examine several elasticities of demand, but the crucial element is that fundamentally all elasticities are calculated the same way: they are ratios of percentage changes. Let us begin with the sensitivity of quantity demanded to changes in the own-price.

4.1 Own-Price Elasticity of Demand

Recall that when we introduced the concept of a demand function with Equation 1 earlier, we were simply theorizing that quantity demanded of some good, such as gasoline, is dependent on several other variables, one of which is the price of gasoline itself. We referred to the law of demand that simply states the inverse relationship between the quantity demanded and the price. Although that observation is useful, we might want to dig a little deeper and ask, Just how sensitive is quantity demanded to changes in the price of gasoline? Is it highly sensitive, so that a very small rise in price is associated with an enormous fall in quantity, or is the sensitivity only minimal? It might be helpful if we had a convenient measure of this sensitivity.

In Equation 3, we introduced a hypothetical household demand function for gasoline, assuming that the household's income and the price of another good (automobiles) were held constant. It supposedly described the purchasing behavior of a household regarding its demand for gasoline. That function was given by the simple linear expression $Q_x^d = 11.2 - 0.4P_x$. If we were to ask how sensitive quantity is to changes in price in that expression, one plausible answer would be simply to recognize that, according to that demand function, whenever price changes by one unit, quantity changes by 0.4 units in the opposite direction. That is to say, if price were to rise by $1, quantity would fall by 0.4 gallons per week, so the coefficient on the price variable (−0.4) could be the measure of sensitivity we are seeking.

There is a fundamental drawback, however, associated with that measure. Notice that the −0.4 is measured in gallons of gasoline per dollar of price. It is crucially dependent on the *units* in which we measured Q and P. If we had measured the price of gasoline in cents per gallon, instead of dollars per gallon, then the exact same household behavior would be described by the alternative equation $Q_x^d = 11.2 - 0.004P_x$. So, although we could choose the coefficient on price as our measure of sensitivity, we would always need to recall the units in which Q and P were measured when we wanted to describe the sensitivity of gasoline demand. That could be cumbersome.

Because of this drawback, economists prefer to use a gauge of sensitivity that does not depend on units of measure. That metric is called **elasticity**, and it is defined as the ratio of *percentage changes*. It is a general measure of how sensitive one variable is to any other variable. For example, if some variable y depends on some other variable x in the following function: $y = f(x)$, then the elasticity of y with respect to x is defined to be the percentage change in y divided by the percentage change in x, or $\%\Delta y/\%\Delta x$. In the case of **own-price elasticity of demand**, that measure is[10]

$$E_{p_x}^d = \frac{\%\Delta Q_x^d}{\%\Delta P_x} \qquad (23)$$

Notice that this measure is independent of the units in which quantity and price are measured. If, for example, when price rises by 10 percent, quantity demanded falls by 8 percent, then elasticity of demand is simply −0.8. It does not matter whether we are measuring quantity in gallons per week or liters per day, and it does not matter whether we measure price in dollars per gallon or euros per liter; 10 percent is 10 percent, and 8 percent is 8 percent. So the ratio of the first to the second is still −0.8.

We can expand Equation 23 algebraically by noting that the percentage change in any variable x is simply the change in x (denoted "Δx") divided by the level of x. So, we can rewrite Equation 23, using a couple of simple steps, as

$$E_{p_x}^d = \frac{\%\Delta Q_x^d}{\%\Delta P_x} = \frac{\frac{\Delta Q_x^d}{Q_x^d}}{\frac{\Delta P_x}{P_x}} = \left(\frac{\Delta Q_x^d}{\Delta P_x}\right)\left(\frac{P_x}{Q_x^d}\right) \qquad (24)$$

To get a better idea of price elasticity, it might be helpful to use our hypothetical market demand function: $Q_x^d = 11,200 - 400P_x$. For linear demand functions, the first term in the last line of Equation 24 is simply the slope coefficient on P_x in the demand function, or −400. (Technically, this term is the first derivative of Q_x^d with respect to P_x, dQ_x^d/dP_x, which is the slope coefficient for a linear demand function.) So, the elasticity of demand in this case is −400 multiplied by the ratio of price to quantity. Clearly in this case, we need to choose a price at which to calculate the elasticity coefficient. Let's choose the original equilibrium price of $3. Now, we need to find the quantity associated with that particular price by inserting 3 into the demand function and finding $Q = 10,000$. The result of our calculation is that at a price of 3, the elasticity of our market demand function is −400 (3/10,000) = −0.12. How do we

---

10 The reader will also encounter the Greek letter epsilon (ε) being used in the notation for elasticities.

interpret that value? It means, simply, that when price equals 3, a 1 percent rise in price would result in a fall in quantity demanded of only 0.12 percent. (You should try calculating price elasticity when price is equal to, say, $4. Do you find that elasticity equals −0.167?)

In our particular example, when price is $3 per gallon, demand is not very sensitive to changes in price, because a 1 percent rise in price would reduce quantity demanded by only 0.12 percent. Actually, that is not too different from empirical estimates of the actual demand elasticity for gasoline in the United States. When demand is not very sensitive to price, we say demand is **inelastic**. To be precise, when the *magnitude* (ignoring algebraic sign) of the own-price elasticity coefficient has a value less than one, demand is defined to be inelastic. When that magnitude is greater than one, demand is defined to be **elastic**. And when the elasticity coefficient is equal to negative one, demand is said to be **unit elastic**, or **unitary elastic**. Note that if the law of demand holds, own-price elasticity of demand will always be negative, because a rise in price will be associated with a fall in quantity demanded, but it can be either elastic or inelastic. In our hypothetical example, suppose the price of gasoline was very high, say $15 per gallon. In this case, the elasticity coefficient would be −1.154. Therefore, because the magnitude of the elasticity coefficient is greater than one, we would say that demand is elastic at that price.[11]

By examining Equation 24, we should be able to see that for a linear demand curve the elasticity depends on where we calculate it. Note that the first term, $\Delta Q/\Delta P$, will remain constant along the entire demand curve because it is simply the inverse of the slope of the demand curve. But the second term, P/Q, clearly changes depending on where we look. At very low prices, P/Q is very small, so demand is inelastic. But at very high prices, Q is low and P is high, so the ratio P/Q is very high, and demand is elastic. Exhibit 20 illustrates a characteristic of all negatively sloped linear demand curves. Above the midpoint of the curve, demand is elastic; below the midpoint, demand is inelastic; and at the midpoint, demand is unit elastic.

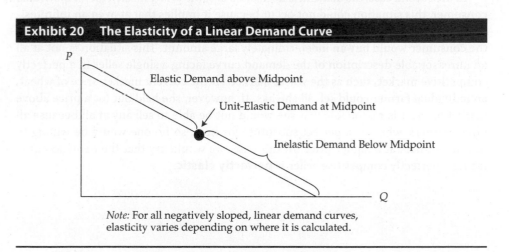

Exhibit 20   The Elasticity of a Linear Demand Curve

P

Elastic Demand above Midpoint

Unit-Elastic Demand at Midpoint

Inelastic Demand Below Midpoint

Q

Note: For all negatively sloped, linear demand curves, elasticity varies depending on where it is calculated.

Sometimes, we might not have the entire demand function or demand curve, but we might have just two observations on price and quantity. In this case, we do not know the slope of the demand curve at a given point because we really cannot say that it is even a linear function. For example, suppose we know that when price is 5,

---

11 For evidence on price elasticities of demand for gasoline, see Molly Espey, "Explaining the Variation in Elasticity Estimates of Gasoline Demand in the United States: A Meta-analysis," *Energy Journal*, vol. 17, no. 3(1996): 49–60. The robust estimates were about −0.26 for short-run elasticity (less than 1 year) and −0.58 for more than a year.

quantity demanded is 9,200, and when price is 6, quantity demanded is 8,800, but we do not know anything more about the demand function. Under these circumstances, economists use something called **arc elasticity**. Arc elasticity of demand is still defined as the percentage change in quantity demanded divided by the percentage change in price. However, because the choice of base for calculating percentage changes has an effect on the calculation, economists have chosen to use the *average* quantity and the *average* price as the base for calculating the percentage changes. (Suppose, for example, that you are making a wage of €10 when your boss says, "I'll increase your wage by 10 percent." You are then earning €11. But later that day, if your boss then reduces your wage by 10 percent, you are then earning €9.90. So, by receiving first a 10 percent raise and then a 10 percent cut in wage, you are worse off. The reason for this is that we typically use the original value as the base, or denominator, for calculating percentages.) In our example, then, the arc elasticity of demand would be:

$$E = \frac{\dfrac{\Delta Q}{Q\ avg}}{\dfrac{\Delta P}{P\ avg}} = \frac{\dfrac{-400}{9{,}000}}{\dfrac{1}{5.5}} = -0.244$$

There are two special cases in which linear demand curves have the same elasticity at all points: vertical demand curves and horizontal demand curves. Consider a vertical demand curve, as in Exhibit 21 Panel A, and a horizontal demand curve, as in Panel B. In the first case, the quantity demanded is the same, regardless of price. Certainly, there could be no demand curve that is perfectly vertical at *all* possible prices, but over some range of prices it is not unreasonable that the same quantity would be purchased at a slightly higher price or a slightly lower price. Perhaps an individual's demand for, say, mustard might obey this description. Obviously, in that price range, quantity demanded is not at all sensitive to price and we would say that demand is **perfectly inelastic** in that range.

In the second case, the demand is horizontal at some price. Clearly, for an individual consumer, this situation could not occur because it implies that at even an infinitesimally higher price the consumer would buy nothing, whereas at that particular price, the consumer would buy an indeterminately large amount. This situation is not at all an unreasonable description of the demand curve facing a single seller in a perfectly competitive market, such as the wheat market. At the current market price of wheat, an individual farmer could sell all she has. If, however, she held out for a price above market price, it is reasonable that she would not be able to sell any at all because all other farmers' wheat is a perfect substitute for hers, so no one would be willing to buy any of hers at a higher price. In this case, we would say that the demand curve facing a perfectly competitive seller is **perfectly elastic**.

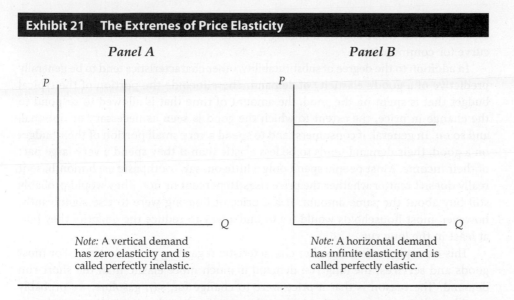

Exhibit 21   The Extremes of Price Elasticity

Panel A

Panel B

Note: A vertical demand has zero elasticity and is called perfectly inelastic.

Note: A horizontal demand has infinite elasticity and is called perfectly elastic.

Own-price elasticity of demand is our measure of how sensitive the quantity demanded is to changes in the price of a good or service, but what characteristics of a good or its market might be informative in determining whether demand is highly elastic or not? Perhaps the most important characteristic is whether there are close substitutes for the good in question. If there are close substitutes for the good, then if its price rises even slightly, a consumer would tend to purchase much less of this good and switch to the substitute, which is now relatively less costly. If there simply are no substitutes, however, then it is likely that the demand is much less elastic. To understand this more fully, consider a consumer's demand for some broadly defined product such as bread. There really are no close substitutes for the category bread, which includes all types from French bread to pita bread to tortillas and so on. So, if the price of all bread were to rise, perhaps a consumer would purchase a little less of it each week, but probably not a significantly smaller amount. Now, however, consider that the consumer's demand for a particular baker's specialty bread instead of the category "bread" as a whole. Surely, there are close substitutes for Baker Bob's Whole Wheat Bread with Sesame Seeds than for bread in general. We would expect, then, that the demand for Baker Bob's special loaf is much more elastic than for the entire category of bread. This fact is why the demand faced by an individual wheat farmer is much more elastic than the entire market demand for wheat; there are much closer substitutes for *her* wheat than for wheat *in general*.

In finance, there exists the question of whether the demand for common stock is perfectly elastic. That is, are there perfect substitutes for a firm's common shares? If so, then the demand curve for its shares should be perfectly horizontal. If not, then one would expect a negatively sloped demand for shares. If demand is horizontal, then an increase in demand (owing to some influence other than positive new information regarding the firm's outlook) would not increase the share price. In contrast, a purely "mechanical" increase in demand would be expected to increase the price if the demand were negatively sloped. One study looked at evidence from 31 stocks whose weights on the Toronto Stock Exchange 300 Index were changed, owing purely to fully anticipated technical reasons that apparently had no relationship to new information about those firms.[12] That is, the demand for those shares shifted rightward.

---

12 Aditya Kaul, Vikas Mehrotra, and Randall Morck, "Demand Curves for Stocks Do Slope Down: New Evidence from an Index Weights Adjustment," *Journal of Finance*, vol. 55(2 April 2000): 893–912.

The authors found that there was a statistically significant 2.3 percent excess return associated with those shares, a finding consistent with a negatively sloped demand curve for common stock.

In addition to the degree of substitutability, other characteristics tend to be generally predictive of a good's elasticity of demand. These include the portion of the typical budget that is spent on the good, the amount of time that is allowed to respond to the change in price, the extent to which the good is seen as necessary or optional, and so on. In general, if consumers tend to spend a very small portion of their budget on a good, their demand tends to be less elastic than if they spend a very large part of their income. Most people spend only a little on, say, toothpaste each month, so it really doesn't matter whether the price rises 10 percent or not. They would probably still buy about the same amount. If the price of housing were to rise significantly, however, most households would try to find a way to reduce the quantity they buy, at least in the long run.

This example leads to another characteristic regarding price elasticity. For most goods and services, the long-run demand is much more elastic than the short-run demand. The reason is that if price were to change for, say, gasoline, we probably would not be able to respond quickly with a significant reduction in the quantity we consume. In the short run, we tend to be locked into modes of transportation, housing and employment location, and so on. The longer the adjustment time, however, the greater the degree to which a household could adjust to the change in price. Hence, for most goods, long-run elasticity of demand is greater than short-run elasticity. Durable goods, however, tend to behave in the opposite way. If the price of washing machines were to fall, people might react quickly because they have an old machine that they know will need to be replaced fairly soon anyway. So when price falls, they might decide to go ahead and make the purchase. If the price of washing machines were to stay low forever, however, it is unlikely that a typical consumer would buy all that many more machines over a lifetime.

Certainly, whether the good or service is seen to be non-discretionary or discretionary would help determine its sensitivity to a price change. Faced with the same percentage increase in prices, consumers are much more likely to give up their Friday night restaurant meal than they are to cut back significantly on staples in their pantry. The more a good is seen as being necessary, the less elastic its demand is likely to be.

In summary, own-price elasticity of demand is likely to be greater (i.e., more sensitive) for items that have many close substitutes, occupy a large portion of the total budget, are seen to be optional instead of necessary, and have longer adjustment times. Obviously, not all of these characteristics operate in the same direction for all goods, so elasticity is likely to be a complex result of these and other characteristics. In the end, the actual elasticity of demand for a particular good turns out to be an empirical fact that can be learned only from careful observation and often, sophisticated statistical analysis.

4.2 Own-Price Elasticity of Demand: Impact on Total Expenditure

Because of the law of demand, an increase in price is associated with a decrease in the number of units demanded of some good or service. But what can we say about the *total expenditure* on that good? That is, what happens to price times quantity when price falls? Recall that elasticity is defined as the ratio of the percentage change in quantity demanded to the percentage change in price. So if demand is elastic, a decrease in price is associated with a larger percentage rise in quantity demanded. For example, if elasticity were equal to negative two, then the percentage change in quantity demanded would be twice as large as the percentage change in price. It follows that a 10 percent fall in price would bring about a rise in quantity of greater magnitude, in this case 20 percent. True, each unit of the good has a lower price, but a sufficiently greater number of units are purchased so that total expenditure (price times quantity) would rise as price falls when demand is elastic.

If demand is inelastic, however, a 10 percent fall in price brings about a rise in quantity less than 10 percent in magnitude. Consequently, when demand is inelastic, a fall in price brings about a fall in total expenditure. If elasticity were equal to negative one, (unitary elasticity) the percentage decrease in price is just offset by an equal and opposite percentage increase in quantity demanded, so total expenditure does not change at all.

In summary, when demand is elastic, price and total expenditure move in *opposite* directions. When demand is inelastic, price and total expenditure move in the *same* direction. When demand is unitary elastic, changes in price are associated with *no change* in total expenditure. This relationship is easy to identify in the case of a linear demand curve. Recall from Exhibit 20 that above the midpoint, demand is elastic; and below the midpoint, demand is inelastic. In the upper section of Exhibit 22, total expenditure ($P \times Q$) is measured as the area of a rectangle whose base is Q and height is P. Notice that as price falls, the inscribed rectangles at first grow in size but then become their largest at the midpoint of the demand curve. Thereafter, as price continues to fall, total expenditure falls toward zero. In the lower section of Exhibit 22, total expenditure is shown for each quantity purchased. Note that it reaches a maximum at the quantity that defines the midpoint, or unit-elastic, point on the demand curve.

Exhibit 22   Elasticity and Total Expenditure

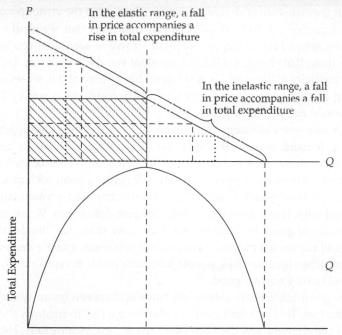

Note: Figure depicts the relationship among changes in price, changes in quantity, and changes in total expenditure. Maximum total expenditure occurs at the unit-elastic point on a linear demand curve (the cross-hatched rectangle).

It should be noted that the relationships just described hold for any demand curve, so it does not matter whether we are dealing with the demand curve of an individual consumer, the demand curve of the market, or the demand curve facing any given seller. For a market, the total expenditure by buyers becomes the total revenue to sellers in that market. It follows, then, that if market demand is elastic, a fall in price will result in an increase in total revenue to sellers as a whole, and if demand is inelastic, a fall in price will result in a decrease in total revenue to sellers. Clearly, if the demand faced by any given seller were inelastic at the current price, that seller could increase revenue by increasing its price. Moreover, because demand is negatively sloped, the increase in price would decrease total units sold, which would almost certainly decrease total cost. So no one-product seller would ever knowingly choose to set price in the inelastic range of its demand.

4.3 Income Elasticity of Demand: Normal and Inferior Goods

In general, elasticity is simply a measure of how sensitive one variable is to change in the value of another variable. Quantity demanded of a good is a function not only of its own price, but also consumer income. If income changes, the quantity demanded can respond, so the analyst needs to understand the income sensitivity as well as price sensitivity.

Income elasticity of demand is defined as the percentage change in quantity demanded divided by the percentage change in income (I), holding all other things constant, and can be represented as in Equation 25.

$$E_I^d = \frac{\%\Delta Q_x^d}{\%\Delta I} = \frac{\frac{\Delta Q_x^d}{Q_x^d}}{\frac{\Delta I}{I}} = \left(\frac{\Delta Q_x^d}{\Delta I}\right)\left(\frac{I}{Q_x^d}\right) \qquad (25)$$

Note that the structure of this expression is identical to the structure of own-price elasticity in Equation 24. Indeed, all elasticity measures that we shall examine will have the same general structure, so essentially if you've seen one, you've seen them all. The only thing that changes is the independent variable of interest. For example, if the income elasticity of demand for some good has a value of 0.8, we would interpret that to mean that whenever income rises by one percent, the quantity demanded at each price would rise by 0.8 percent.

Although own-price elasticity of demand will almost always be negative because of the law of demand, *income* elasticity can be negative, positive, or zero. Positive income elasticity simply means that as income rises, quantity demanded also rises, as is characteristic of most consumption goods. We define a good with positive income elasticity as a **normal good**. It is perhaps unfortunate that economists often take perfectly good English words and give them different definitions. When an economist speaks of a normal good, he is saying nothing other than that the demand for that particular good rises when income increases and falls when income decreases. Hence, if we find that when income rises, people buy more meals at restaurants, then dining out is defined to be a normal good.

For some goods, there is an *inverse* relationship between quantity demanded and consumer income. That is, when people experience a rise in income, they buy absolutely less of some goods, and they buy more when their income falls. Hence, income elasticity of demand for those goods is negative. By definition, goods with *negative* income elasticity are called **inferior goods**. Again, the word inferior means nothing other than that the income elasticity of demand for that good is observed to be negative. It does not necessarily indicate anything at all about the quality of that good. Typical examples of inferior goods might be rice, potatoes, or less expensive cuts of meat. One study found that income elasticity of demand for beer is slightly negative, whereas income elasticity of demand for wine is significantly positive. An economist would therefore say that beer is inferior whereas wine is normal. Ultimately, whether a good is called inferior or normal is simply a matter of empirical statistical analysis. And a good could be normal for one income group and inferior for another income group. (A BMW 3-series automobile might very well be normal for a moderate-income group but inferior for a high-income group of consumers. As their respective income levels rose, the moderate group might purchase more BMWs whereas the upper-income group might buy fewer 3-series as they traded up to a 5- or 7-series.) Clearly, for some goods and some ranges of income, consumer income might not have an impact on purchase decision at all. Hence for those goods, income elasticity of demand is zero.

Thinking back to our discussion of the demand curve, recall that we invoked the assumption of "holding all other things constant" when we plotted the relationship between price and quantity demanded. One of the variables we held constant was consumer income. If income were to change, obviously the whole curve would shift one way or the other. For normal goods, a rise in income would shift the entire demand curve upward and to the right, resulting in an *increase in demand*. If the good were inferior, however, a rise in income would result in a downward and leftward shift in the entire demand curve.

4.4 Cross-price Elasticity of Demand: Substitutes and Complements

It should be clear by now that any variable on the right-hand side of the demand function can serve as the basis for its own elasticity. Recall that the price of another good might very well have an impact on the demand for a good or service, so we should be able to define an elasticity with respect to the *other* price, as well. That elasticity is called the **cross-price elasticity of demand** and takes on the same structure as own-price elasticity and income elasticity of demand, as represented in Equation 26.

$$E^d_{P_y} = \frac{\%\Delta Q^d_x}{\%\Delta P_y} = \frac{\frac{\Delta Q^d_x}{Q^d_x}}{\frac{\Delta P_y}{P_y}} = \left(\frac{\Delta Q^d_x}{\Delta P_y}\right)\left(\frac{P_y}{Q^d_x}\right) \tag{26}$$

Note how similar in structure this equation is to own-price elasticity. The only difference is that the subscript on P is now y, indicating the price of some other good, Y, instead of the own-price, X. This cross-price elasticity of demand measures how sensitive the demand for good X is to changes in the price of some other good, Y, holding all other things constant. For some pairs of goods, X and Y, when the price of Y rises, more of good X is demanded. That is, the cross-price elasticity of demand is positive. Those goods are defined to be **substitutes.** Substitutes are defined empirically. If the cross-price elasticity of two goods is positive, they are substitutes, irrespective of whether someone would consider them "similar."

This concept is intuitive if you think about two goods that are seen to be close substitutes, perhaps like two brands of beer. When the price of one of your favorite brands of beer rises, what would you do? You would probably buy less of that brand and more of a cheaper brand, so the cross-price elasticity of demand would be positive.

Alternatively, two goods whose cross-price elasticity of demand is negative are defined to be **complements**. Typically, these goods would tend to be consumed together as a pair, such as gasoline and automobiles or houses and furniture. When automobile prices fall, we might expect the quantity of autos demanded to rise, and thus we might expect to see a rise in the demand for gasoline. Ultimately, though, whether two goods are substitutes or complements is an empirical question answered solely by observation and statistical analysis. If, when the price of one good rises the demand for the other good also rises, they are substitutes. If the demand for that other good falls, they are complements. And the result might not immediately resonate with our intuition. For example, grocery stores often put something like coffee on sale in the hope that customers will come in for coffee and end up doing their weekly shopping there as well. In that case, coffee and, say, cabbage could very well empirically turn out to be complements even though we do not normally think of consuming coffee and cabbage together as a pair (i.e., that the price of coffee has a relation to the sales of cabbage).

For substitute goods, an increase in the price of one good would shift the demand curve for the other good upward and to the right. For complements, however, the impact is in the other direction: When the price of one good rises, the quantity demanded of the other good shifts downward and to the left.

4.5 Calculating Demand Elasticities from Demand Functions

Although the concept of different elasticities of demand is helpful in sorting out the qualitative and directional effects among variables, the analyst will also benefit from having an empirically estimated demand function from which to calculate the magnitudes as well. There is no substitute for actual observation and statistical (regression) analysis to yield insights into the quantitative behavior of a market. (Empirical analysis, however, is outside the scope of this reading.) To see how an analyst would use such an equation, let us return to our hypothetical market demand function for gasoline in Equation 13 duplicated here:

$$Q_x^d = 8,400 - 400P_x + 60I - 10P_y \qquad\qquad\text{(27)}$$

As we found when we calculated own-price elasticity of demand earlier, we need to identify "where to look" by choosing actual values for the independent variables, P_x, I, and P_y. We choose \$3 for P_x, \$50 (thousands) for I, and \$20 (thousands) for P_y. By inserting these values into the "estimated" demand function (Equation 27), we find that quantity demanded is 10,000 gallons of gasoline per week. We now have everything we need to calculate own-price, income, and cross-price elasticities of demand for our market. Those respective elasticities are expressed in Equations 28, 29, and 30. Each of those expressions has a term denoting the change in quantity divided by the change in each respective variable: $\Delta Q_x/\Delta P_x$, $\Delta Q_x/\Delta I$, and $\Delta Q_x/\Delta P_y$. In each case, those respective terms are given by the coefficients on the variables of interest. Once we recognize this fact, the rest is accomplished simply by inserting values into the elasticity formulas.

$$E_{p_x}^d = \left(\frac{\Delta Q_x^d}{\Delta P_x}\right)\left(\frac{P_x}{Q_x^d}\right) = \left[-400\right]\left[\frac{3}{10,000}\right] = -0.12 \qquad\qquad\text{(28)}$$

$$E_I^d = \left(\frac{\Delta Q_x^d}{\Delta I}\right)\left(\frac{I}{Q_x^d}\right) = \left[60\right]\left[\frac{50}{10,000}\right] = 0.30 \qquad\qquad\text{(29)}$$

$$E_{p_y}^d = \left(\frac{\Delta Q_x^d}{\Delta P_y}\right)\left(\frac{P_y}{Q_x^d}\right) = \left[-10\right]\left[\frac{20}{10,000}\right] = -0.02 \qquad\qquad\text{(30)}$$

In our example, at a price of \$3, the own-price elasticity of demand is −0.12, meaning that a 1 percent increase in the price of gasoline would bring about a decrease in quantity demanded of only 0.12 percent. Because the absolute value of the own-price elasticity is less than one, we characterize demand as being *inelastic* at that price, so an increase in price would result in an increase in total expenditure on gasoline by consumers in that market. Additionally, the income elasticity of demand is 0.30, meaning that a 1 percent increase in income would bring about an increase of 0.30 percent in the quantity demanded of gasoline. Because that elasticity is positive (but small), we would characterize gasoline as a *normal* good: An increase in income would cause consumers to buy more gasoline. Finally, the cross-price elasticity of demand between gasoline and automobiles is –0.02, meaning that if the price of automobiles rose by 1 percent, the demand for gasoline would fall by 0.02 percent. We would therefore characterize gasoline and automobiles as *complements* because the cross-price elasticity is negative. The magnitude is, however, quite small, so we would conclude that the complementary relationship is quite weak.

EXAMPLE 13

Calculating Elasticities from a Given Demand Function

An individual consumer's monthly demand for downloadable e-books is given by the equation $Q_{eb}^d = 2 - 0.4P_{eb} + 0.0005I + 0.15P_{hb}$, where Q_{eb}^d equals the number of e-books demanded each month, I equals the household monthly income, P_{eb} equals the price of e-books, and P_{hb} equals the price of hardbound books. Assume that the price of e-books is €10.68, household income is €2,300, and the price of hardbound books is €21.40.

1 Determine the value of own-price elasticity of demand for e-books.

2 Determine the income elasticity of demand for e-books.

3 Determine the cross-price elasticity of demand for e-books with respect to the price of hardbound books.

Solution to 1:

Recall that own-price elasticity of demand is given by $(\Delta Q_{eb}/\Delta P_{eb})(P_{eb}/Q_{eb})$, and notice from the demand function that $\Delta Q_{eb}/\Delta P_{eb} = -0.4$. Inserting the given variable values into the demand function yields $Q_{eb} = 2.088$. So at a price of €10.68, the own-price elasticity of demand equals $(-0.4)(10.68/2.088) = -2.046$, which is elastic because in absolute value the elasticity coefficient is greater than one.

Solution to 2:

Recall that income elasticity of demand is given by $(\Delta Q_{eb}/\Delta I)(I/Q_{eb})$. Notice from the demand function that $\Delta Q_{eb}/\Delta I = 0.0005$. Inserting in the values for I and Q_{eb} yields income elasticity of $(0.0005)(2,300/2.088) = 0.551$, which is positive, so e-books are a normal good.

Solution to 3:

Recall that cross-price elasticity of demand is given by $(\Delta Q_{eb}/\Delta P_{hb})(P_{hb}/Q_{eb})$, and notice from the demand function that $\Delta Q_{eb}/\Delta P_{hb} = 0.15$. Inserting in the values for P_{hb} and Q_{eb} yields a cross-price elasticity of demand for e-books of $(0.15)(21.40/2.088) = 1.537$, which is positive, implying that e-books and hardbound books are substitutes.

SUMMARY

This reading has surveyed demand and supply analysis. Because markets (goods, factor, and capital) supply the foundation for today's global economy, an understanding of the demand and supply model is essential for any analyst who hopes to grasp the implications of economic developments on investment values. Among the points made are the following:

- The basic model of markets is the demand and supply model. The demand function represents buyers' behavior and can be depicted (in its inverse demand form) as a negatively sloped demand curve. The supply function represents sellers' behavior and can be depicted (in its inverse supply form) as a positively sloped supply curve. The interaction of buyers and sellers in a market results in equilibrium. Equilibrium exists when the highest price willingly paid by buyers is just equal to the lowest price willingly accepted by sellers.

- Goods markets are the interactions of consumers as buyers and firms as sellers of goods and services produced by firms and bought by households. Factor markets are the interactions of firms as buyers and households as sellers of land, labor, capital, and entrepreneurial risk-taking ability. Capital markets are used by firms to sell debt or equity to raise long-term capital to finance the production of goods and services.

- Demand and supply curves are drawn on the assumption that everything *except* the price of the good itself is held constant (an assumption known as *ceteris paribus* or "holding all other things constant"). When something other than price changes, the demand curve or the supply curve will shift relative to the other curve. This shift is referred to as a change in demand or supply, as opposed to quantity demanded or quantity supplied. A new equilibrium generally will be obtained at a different price and a different quantity than before. The market mechanism is the ability of prices to adjust to eliminate any excess demand or supply resulting from a shift in one or the other curve.

- If, at a given price, the quantity demanded exceeds the quantity supplied, there is excess demand and price will rise. If, at a given price, the quantity supplied exceeds the quantity demanded, there is excess supply and price will fall.

- Sometimes auctions are used to seek equilibrium prices. Common value auctions sell items that have the same value to all bidders, but bidders can only estimate that value before the auction is completed. Overly optimistic bidders overestimate the true value and end up paying a price greater than that value. This result is known as the winner's curse. Private value auctions sell items that (generally) have a unique subjective value for each bidder. Ascending price auctions use an auctioneer to call out ever increasing prices until the last, highest bidder ultimately pays his/her bid price and buys the item. Descending price, or Dutch, auctions begin at a very high price and then reduce that price until one bidder is willing to buy at that price. Second price sealed bid auctions are sometimes used to induce bidders to reveal their true reservation prices in private value auctions. Treasury notes and some other financial instruments are sold using a form of Dutch auction (called a single price auction) in which competitive and non-competitive bids are arrayed in descending price (increasing yield) order. The winning bidders all pay the same price, but marginal bidders might not be able to fill their entire order at the market clearing price.

- Markets that work freely can optimize society's welfare, as measured by consumer surplus and producer surplus. Consumer surplus is the difference between the total value to buyers and the total expenditure necessary to purchase a given amount. Producer surplus is the difference between the total revenue received by sellers from selling a given amount and the total variable cost of production of that amount. When equilibrium price is reached, total surplus is maximized.

- Sometimes, government policies interfere with the free working of markets. Examples include price ceilings, price floors, and specific taxes. Whenever the imposition of such a policy alters the free market equilibrium quantity (the quantity that maximizes total surplus), there is a redistribution of surplus between buyers and sellers; but there is also a reduction of total surplus, called deadweight loss. Other influences can result in an imbalance between demand and supply. Search costs are impediments in the ability of willing buyers and willing sellers to meet in a transaction. Brokers can add value if they reduce search costs and match buyers and sellers. In general, anything that improves information about the willingness of buyers and sellers to engage will reduce search costs and add value.

- Economists use a quantitative measure of sensitivity called elasticity. In general, elasticity is the ratio of the percentage change in the dependent variable to the percentage change in the independent variable of interest. Important specific elasticities include own-price elasticity of demand, income elasticity of demand, and cross-price elasticity of demand.

- Based on algebraic sign and magnitude of the various elasticities, goods can be classified into groups. If own-price elasticity of demand is less than one in absolute value, demand is called "inelastic"; it is called "elastic" if own-price elasticity of demand is greater than one in absolute value. Goods with positive income elasticity of demand are called normal goods, and those with negative income elasticity of demand are called inferior goods. Two goods with negative cross-price elasticity of demand—a drop in the price of one good causes an increase in demand for the other good—are called complements. Goods with positive cross-price elasticity of demand—a drop in the price of one good causes a decrease in demand for the other—are called substitutes.

- The relationship among own-price elasticity of demand, changes in price, and changes in total expenditure is as follows: If demand is elastic, a reduction in price results in an increase in total expenditure; if demand is inelastic, a reduction in price results in a decrease in total expenditure; if demand is unitary elastic, a change in price leaves total expenditure unchanged.

PRACTICE PROBLEMS

1   Which of the following markets is *most* accurately characterized as a goods market? The market for:

    A   coats.

    B   sales clerks.

    C   cotton farmland.

2   The observation "as a price of a good falls, buyers buy more of it" is *best* known as:

    A   consumer surplus.

    B   the law of demand.

    C   the market mechanism.

3   Two-dimensional demand and supply curves are drawn under which of the following assumptions?

    A   Own price is held constant.

    B   All variables but quantity are held constant.

    C   All variables but own price and quantity are held constant.

4   The slope of a supply curve is *most* often:

    A   zero.

    B   positive.

    C   negative.

5   Assume the following equation

$$Q_x^s = -4 + \frac{1}{2}P_x - 2W$$

    where Q_x^s is the quantity of good X supplied, P_x is the price of good X, and W is the wage rate paid to laborers. If the wage rate is 11, the vertical intercept on a graph depicting the supply curve is *closest* to:

    A   −26.

    B   −4.

    C   52.

6   Movement along the demand curve for good X occurs due to a change in:

    A   income.

    B   the price of good X.

    C   the price of a substitute for good X.

The following information relates to Questions 7–10

A producer's supply function is given by the equation

$$Q_S^s = -55 + 26P_s - 1.3W$$

where Q_S^s is the quantity of steel supplied by the market, P_s is the per unit price of steel, and W is the per unit price of labor.

7 If the price of labor rises, what happens to the steel producer's supply curve? The supply curve:

   A shifts to the left.

   B shifts to the right.

   C remains unchanged.

8 If the unit price of labor is 10, which equation is *closest* to the expression for the inverse supply function?

   A $P_s = 2.6 + 0.04Q_S^s$.

   B $Q_S^s = 42 + 26P_s$.

   C $Q_S^s = -68 + 26P_s$.

9 If the unit price of labor is 10, the slope of the supply curve is *closest* to:

   A −1.30.

   B 0.04.

   C 26.00.

10 Assume the supply side of the market consists of exactly five identical sellers. If the unit price of labor is 20, which equation is *closest* to the expression for the market inverse supply function?

   A $P_s = 2.6 + 0.008Q_S^s$.

   B $P_s = 3.1 + 0.008Q_S^s$.

   C $P_s = 3.1 + 0.04Q_S^s$.

---

11 Which of the following statements about market equilibrium is *most* accurate?

   A The difference between quantity demanded and quantity supplied is zero.

   B The demand curve is negatively sloped and the supply curve is positively sloped.

   C For any given pair of market demand and supply curves, only one equilibrium point can exist.

12 Which of the following statements *best* characterizes the market mechanism for attaining equilibrium?

   A Excess supply causes prices to fall.

   B Excess demand causes prices to fall.

   C The demand and supply curves shift to reach equilibrium.

13 An auction in which the auctioneer starts at a high price and then lowers the price in increments until there is a willing buyer is *best* called a:

A Dutch auction.

B Vickery auction.

C private-value auction.

14 Which statement is *most likely* to be true in a single-price US Treasury bill auction?

A Only some non-competitive bids would be filled.

B Bidders at the highest winning yield may only get a portion of their order filled.

C All bidders at a yield higher than the winning bid would get their entire order filled.

15 The winner's curse in common value auctions is *best* described as the winning bidder paying:

A more than the value of the asset.

B a price not equal to one's own bid.

C more than intended prior to bidding.

16 A wireless phone manufacturer introduced a next-generation phone that received a high level of positive publicity. Despite running several high-speed production assembly lines, the manufacturer is still falling short in meeting demand for the phone nine months after introduction. Which of the following statements is the *most* plausible explanation for the demand/supply imbalance?

A The phone price is low relative to the equilibrium price.

B Competitors introduced next-generation phones at a similar price.

C Consumer incomes grew faster than the manufacturer anticipated.

17 A per-unit tax on items sold that is paid by the seller will *most likely* result in the:

A supply curve shifting vertically upward.

B demand curve shifting vertically upward.

C demand curve shifting vertically downward.

18 Which of the following statements *most* accurately and completely describes a deadweight loss?

A A transfer of surplus from one party to another.

B A reduction in either the buyer's or seller's surplus.

C A reduction in total surplus resulting from market interference.

19 If an excise tax is paid by the buyer instead of the seller, which of the following statements is *most likely* to be true? The price (including tax):

A paid will be higher than if the seller had paid the tax.

B received will be lower than if the seller had paid the tax.

C received will be the same as if the seller had paid the tax.

20 A quota on an imported good below the market-clearing quantity will *most likely* lead to which of the following effects?

A The supply curve shifts upward.

B The demand curve shifts upward.

C Some of the buyer's surplus transfers to the seller.

21 Assume a market demand function is given by the equation

$$Q^d = 50 - 0.75P$$

where Q^d is the quantity demanded and P is the price. If P equals 10, the value of the consumer surplus is *closest* to:

A 67.

B 1,205.

C 1,667.

22 Which of the following *best* describes producer surplus?

A Revenue minus variable costs.

B Revenue minus variable plus fixed costs.

C The area above the supply curve and beneath the demand curve and to the left of the equilibrium point.

23 Assume a market supply function is given by the equation

$$Q_s = -7 + 0.6P$$

where Q_s is the quantity supplied and P is the price. If P equals 15, the value of the producer surplus is *closest* to:

A 3.3.

B 41.0.

C 67.5.

The following information relates to Questions 24–26

The market demand function for four-year private universities is given by the equation

$$Q^d_{pr} = 84 - 3.1P_{pr} + 0.8I + 0.9P_{pu}$$

where Q^d_{pr} is the number of applicants to private universities per year in thousands, P_{pr} is the average price of private universities (in thousands of USD), I is the household monthly income (in thousands of USD), and P_{pu} is the average price of public (government-supported) universities (in thousands of USD). Assume that P_{pr} is equal to 38, I is equal to 100, and P_{pu} is equal to 18.

24 The price elasticity of demand for private universities is *closest* to:

A −3.1.

B −1.9.

C 0.6.

25 The income elasticity of demand for private universities is *closest* to:

A 0.5.

B 0.8.

C 1.3.

26 The cross-price elasticity of demand for private universities with respect to the price of public universities is *closest* to:

A 0.3.

B 3.1.

C 3.9.

---

27 If the cross-price elasticity between two goods is negative, the two goods are classified as:

A normal.

B substitutes.

C complements.

SOLUTIONS

1 A is correct. Coats are finished goods, the result of the output of production.

2 B is correct.

3 C is correct. In order to draw demand and supply curves, own price and own quantity must be allowed to vary. However, all other variables are held constant to focus on the relation of own price with quantity.

4 B is correct. Producers generally will supply a greater quantity of a good at higher prices for the good.

5 C is correct. Because the supply curve is the graph of the inverse supply function, solve for the inverse supply function given the wage rate of 11:

$$Q_x^s = -4 + \frac{1}{2}P_x - 2(11)$$

$$= -26 + \frac{1}{2}P_x$$

$$Q_x^s + 26 = \frac{1}{2}P_x$$

$$P_x = 52 + 2Q_x^s$$

The vertical intercept is 52.

6 B is correct. The demand curve shows quantity demanded as a function of own price only.

7 A is correct. The supply curve (which is the graph of the inverse supply function) shifts to the left. The producer is only willing to sell any given quantity at a higher price due to the increase in costs.

8 A is correct. The inverse supply function is *closest to* $P_S = 2.6 + 0.04Q_S^s$.

$$\text{Start with the supply equation:} \quad Q_S^s = -55 + 26P_S - 1.3W$$
$$\text{Insert } W = 10: \qquad = -55 + 26P_S - 1.3(10)$$
$$= -68 + 26P_S$$
$$\text{Solve for } P_S: \quad P_S = 2.6 + 0.04Q_S^s \text{ (the inverse supply function)}$$

9 B is correct. The slope coefficient of Q_S^s in the inverse supply function, which gives the supply curve, is 0.04.

10 B is correct. Start with the equation $Q_S^s = -55 + 26P_S - 1.3W$. Insert the unit price of labor at 20 and, to aggregate for five suppliers, multiply the individual producer's supply function by 5:

$$Q_S^s = 5(-55 + 26P_S - 1.3(20))$$

$$Q_S^s = -275 + 130P_S - 130$$

$$Q_S^s = -405 + 130P_S$$

Invert the equation to get the market inverse supply function: $P_S = 3.1 + 0.008Q_S^s$.

11 A is correct. At market equilibrium the quantity demanded just equals quantity supplied, and thus, the difference between the two is zero.

12 A is correct. Excess supply at a given price implies that there is not enough demand at that price. So the price must fall until it reaches the point at which the demand and supply curves intersect.

13 A is correct. The basic Dutch auction is a descending-price auction.

14 B is correct. Non-competitive bids and bidders at lower yields will get their orders filled first. Securities may then not be available to fill demand entirely at the highest winning yield.

15 A is correct. The winning bidder in such auctions may be overly optimistic about the underlying value of the item won.

16 A is correct. The situation described is one of excess demand because, in order for markets to clear at the given level of quantity supplied, the company would need to raise prices.

17 A is correct. The lowest acceptable price to the supplier at any given quantity must now increase because part of the price is paid as a per-unit tax. Thus, the supply curve shifts upward.

18 C is correct. A deadweight loss is the surplus lost by both the producer and the consumer and not transferred to anyone.

19 C is correct. The trade price should be the same whether the tax is imposed on the buyer or on the seller.

20 C is correct. A quota will cause excess demand, raising the price of the good and moving it up and to the left along the demand curve. This should shift some of the buyer's surplus to the seller.

21 B is correct. We find consumer surplus as the area of the triangle formed by the y (price) axis, the inverse demand curve, and a line segment from the y axis to the inverse demand function at $P = 10$.

Put the price into the demand equation: $Q^d = 50 - 0.75(10)$

$Q^d = 42.5$ (this is the base of the triangle)

Invert the demand function by solving for P: $-0.75P = Q^d - 50$

$P = -1.33Q^d + 66.67$

Note the price intercept is 66.67. The height of the triangle is $66.67 - 10 = 56.67$. The consumer surplus is the area of the triangle above the price of 10 and below the demand curve, with base equal to the quantity of 42.5: 1/2 Base × Height = $(1/2)(42.5)(66.7 - 10) = 1,205$.

22 A is correct. Producer surplus is the difference between the total revenue that sellers receive from selling a given amount of a good and the total variable cost of producing that amount.

23 A is correct. With a linear supply curve, producer surplus is equal to the area of a triangle with base equal to the market clearing price minus the price intercept, height equal to the market clearing quantity, and bounded by the supply curve as the hypotenuse. Given a (market clearing) price of 15, quantity is 2:

$Q_s = -7 + 0.6(15) = 2$

Next find the inverse supply function:

$P = (1/0.6)7 + (1/0.6)Q_s$

$P = 11.67 + 1.67Q_s$

Note that the price intercept is 11.7 and the quantity intercept is −7.0. Thus, producer surplus is 1/2 Base × Height = $(1/2)(2)(15 - 11.7) = 3.3$.

24 B is correct. From the demand function:

$$\Delta Q_{pr}^d / \Delta P_{pr} = -3.1 \text{ (the coefficient in front of own price)}$$

Solve for Q_{pr}^d:
$$Q_{pr}^d = 84 - 3.1 P_{pr} + 0.8I + 0.9 P_{pu}$$
$$= 84 - 3.1(38) + 0.8(100) + 0.9(18)$$
$$= 62.4$$

At $P_{pr} = 38$, price elasticity of demand $= \left(\Delta Q_{pr}^d / \Delta P_{pr} \right) \left(P_{pr} / Q_{pr}^d \right)$
$$= (-3.1)(38/62.4)$$
$$= -1.9$$

25 C is correct. From the demand function:

$$\Delta Q_{pr}^d / \Delta I = 0.8 \text{ (coefficient in front of the income variable)}$$

Solve for Q_{pr}^d:
$$Q_{pr}^d = 84 - 3.1 P_{pr} + 0.8I + 0.9 P_{pu}$$
$$= 84 - 3.1(38) + 0.8(100) + 0.9(18)$$
$$= 62.4$$

At $I = 100$, the income elasticity of demand $= \left(\Delta Q_{pr}^d / \Delta I \right) \left(I / Q_{pr}^d \right)$
$$= (0.8)(100/62.4)$$
$$= 1.3$$

26 A is correct. From the demand function:

$$\Delta Q_{pr}^d / \Delta P_{pu} = 0.9 \text{ (the coefficient in front of } P_{pu})$$

Solve for Q_{pr}^d:
$$Q_{pr}^d = 84 - 3.1 P_{pr} + 0.8I + 0.9 P_{pu}$$
$$= 84 - 3.1(38) + 0.8(100) + 0.9(18)$$
$$= 62.4$$

At $P = 38$, and $P_{pu} = 18$, the cross-price elasticity of demand $= \left(\Delta Q_{pr}^d / \Delta P_{pu} \right) \left(P_{pu} / Q_{pr}^d \right)$
$$= (0.9)(18/62.4)$$
$$= 0.3$$

27 C is correct. With complements, consumption goes up or down together. With a negative cross-price elasticity, as the price of one good goes up, the demand for both falls.

READING

14

Demand and Supply Analysis: Consumer Demand

by Richard V. Eastin, PhD, and Gary L. Arbogast, CFA

Richard V. Eastin, PhD, is at the University of Southern California (USA). Gary L. Arbogast, CFA (USA).

LEARNING OUTCOMES

Mastery	The candidate should be able to:
☐	a. describe consumer choice theory and utility theory;
☐	b. describe the use of indifference curves, opportunity sets, and budget constraints in decision making;
☐	c. calculate and interpret a budget constraint;
☐	d. determine a consumer's equilibrium bundle of goods based on utility analysis;
☐	e. compare substitution and income effects;
☐	f. distinguish between normal goods and inferior goods and explain Giffen goods and Veblen goods in this context.

INTRODUCTION

1

By now it should be clear that economists are model builders. In the previous reading, we examined one of their most fundamental models, the model of demand and supply. And as we have seen, models begin with simplifying assumptions and then find the implications that can then be compared to real-world observations as a test of the model's usefulness. In the model of demand and supply, we *assumed* the existence of a demand curve and a supply curve, as well as their respective negative and positive slopes. That simple model yielded some very powerful implications about how markets work, but we can delve even more deeply to explore the underpinnings of demand and supply. In this reading, we examine the theory of the consumer as a way of understanding where consumer demand curves originate. In a subsequent reading, the origins of the supply curve are sought in presenting the theory of the firm.

This reading is organized as follows: Section 2 describes consumer choice theory in more detail. Section 3 introduces utility theory, a building block of consumer choice theory that provides a quantitative model for a consumer's preferences and tastes. Section 4 surveys budget constraints and opportunity sets. Section 5 covers the determination of the consumer's bundle of goods and how that may change in response to changes in income and prices. Section 6 examines substitution and income effects for different types of goods. A summary and practice problems conclude the reading.

2   CONSUMER THEORY: FROM PREFERENCES TO DEMAND FUNCTIONS

The introduction to demand and supply analysis in the previous reading basically assumed that the demand function exists, and focused on understanding its various characteristics and manifestations. In this reading, we address the foundations of demand and supply analysis and seek to understand the sources of consumer demand through the theory of the consumer, also known as consumer choice theory. **Consumer choice theory** can be defined as the branch of microeconomics that relates consumer demand curves to consumer preferences. Consumer choice theory begins with a fundamental model of how consumer preferences and tastes might be represented. It explores consumers' willingness to trade off between two goods (or two baskets of goods), both of which the consumer finds beneficial. Consumer choice theory then recognizes that to consume a set of goods and services, consumers must purchase them at given market prices and with a limited income. In effect, consumer choice theory first models what the consumer would like to consume, and then it examines what the consumer can consume with limited income. Finally, by superimposing what the consumer would *like* to do onto what the consumer *can* do, we arrive at a model of what the consumer *would* do under various circumstances. Then by changing prices and income, the model develops consumer demand as a logical extension of consumer choice theory.

Although consumer choice theory attempts to model consumers' preferences or tastes, it does not have much to say about *why* consumers have the tastes and preferences they have. It still makes assumptions, but does so at a more fundamental level. Instead of assuming the existence of a demand curve, it derives a demand curve as an implication of assumptions about preferences. Note that economists are not attempting to predict the behavior of any single consumer in any given circumstance. Instead, they are attempting to build a consistent model of aggregate market behavior in the form of a market demand curve.

Once we model the consumer's preferences, we then recognize that consumption is governed not only by preferences but also by the consumer's **budget constraint** (the ability to purchase various combinations of goods and services, given his or her income). Putting preference theory together with the budget constraint gives us the demand curve we are seeking. In the following sections, we explore these topics in turn.

UTILITY THEORY: MODELING PREFERENCES AND TASTES

3

At the foundation of consumer behavior theory is the assumption that the consumer knows his or her own tastes and preferences and tends to take rational actions that result in a more preferred consumption "bundle" over a less preferred bundle. To build a consistent model of consumer choice, we need to begin with a few assumptions about preferences.

3.1 Axioms of the Theory of Consumer Choice

First, let us be clear about the consumption opportunities over which the consumer is assumed to have preferences. We define a **consumption bundle** or **consumption basket** as a specific combination of the goods and services that the consumer would like to consume. We could almost literally conceive of a basket containing a given amount of, say, shoes, pizza, medical care, theater tickets, piano lessons, and all the other things that a consumer might enjoy consuming. Each of those goods and services can be represented in a given basket by a non-negative quantity, respectively, of all the possible goods and services. Any given basket could have zero of one or more of those goods. A distinctly different consumption bundle would contain all of the same goods but in different quantities, again allowing for the possibility of a zero quantity of one or more of the goods. For example, bundle A might have the same amount of all but one of the goods and services as bundle B but a different amount of that one. Bundles A and B would be considered two distinct bundles.

Given this understanding of consumption bundles, the first assumption we make about a given consumer's preferences is simply that she is able to make a comparison between any two possible bundles. That is, given bundles A and B, she must be able to say either that she prefers A to B, or she prefers B to A, or she is *indifferent* between the two. This is the assumption of **complete preferences** (also known as the axiom of completeness), and although it does not appear to be a particularly strong assumption, it is not trivial either. It rules out the possibility that she could just say, "I recognize that the two bundles are different, but in fact they are *so* different that I simply cannot compare them at all." A loving father might very well say that about his two children. In effect, the father neither prefers one to the other nor is, in any meaningful sense, indifferent between the two. The assumption of complete preferences cannot accommodate such a response.

Second, we assume that when comparing any three distinct bundles, A, B, and C, if A is preferred to B, and simultaneously B is preferred to C, then it must be true that A is preferred to C. This assumption is referred to as the assumption of **transitive preferences**, and it is assumed to hold for indifference as well as for strict preference. This is a somewhat stronger assumption because it is essentially an assumption of rationality. We would say that if a consumer prefers a skiing holiday to a diving holiday and a diving holiday to a backpacking holiday and at the same time prefers a backpacking holiday to a skiing holiday, then he is acting irrationally. Transitivity rules out this kind of inconsistency. If you have studied psychology, however, you will no doubt have seen experiments that show subjects violating this assumption, especially in cases of many complex options being offered to them.

When we state these axioms, we are not saying that we believe them actually to be true in every instance, but we assume them for the sake of building a model. A model is a simplification of the real world phenomena we are trying to understand. Necessarily, axioms must be at some level inaccurate and incomplete representations of the phenomena we are trying to model. If that were not the case, the "model" would not be a simplification; it would be a reflection of the complex system we are attempting to model and thus would not help our understanding very much.

Finally, we usually assume that in at least one of the goods, the consumer could never have so much that she would refuse any more, even if it were free. This assumption is sometimes referred to as the "more is better" assumption or the assumption of **non-satiation**. Clearly, for some things, more *is* worse, such as air pollution or trash. In those cases, the *good* is then the *removal* of that *bad*, so we can usually reframe our model to accommodate the non-satiation assumption. In particular, when we later discuss the concept of risk for an investor, we will recognize that for many, more risk is worse than less risk, all else being equal. In that analysis, we shall model the willingness of the investor to trade off between increased investment returns and increased certainty, which is the absence of risk.

EXAMPLE 1

Axioms Concerning Preferences

Helen Smith enjoys, among other things, eating sausages. She also enjoys reading Marcel Proust. Smith is confronted with two baskets: Basket A, which contains several other goods and a package of sausages, and B, which contains identical quantities of the other goods as Basket A, but instead of the sausages, it contains a book by Proust. When asked which basket she prefers, she replies, "I like them both, but sausages and a book by Proust are *so* different that I simply cannot compare the two baskets." Determine whether Smith is obeying all the axioms of preference theory.

Solution:

Smith is violating the assumption of complete preferences. This assumption states that a consumer must be able to compare any two baskets of goods, either preferring one to the other or being indifferent between the two. If she complies with this assumption, she must be able to compare these two baskets of goods.

3.2 Representing the Preference of a Consumer: The Utility Function

Armed with the assumptions of completeness, transitivity, and non-satiation, we ask whether there might be a way for a given consumer to represent his own preferences in a consistent manner. Let us consider presenting him with all possible bundles of all the possible goods and services he could consider. Now suppose we give him paper and pencil and ask him to assign a number to each of the bundles. (The assumption of completeness ensures that he, in fact, could do that.) All he must do is write a number on a paper and lay it on each of the bundles. The only restrictions are these: Comparing any two bundles, if he prefers one to the other, he must assign a higher number to the bundle he prefers. And if he is indifferent between them, he must assign the same number to both. Other than that, he is free to begin with any number he wants for the first bundle he considers. In this way, he is simply ordering the bundles according to his preferences over them.

Of course, each of these possible bundles has a specific quantity of each of the goods and services. So, we have two sets of numbers. One set consists of the pieces of paper he has laid on the bundles. The other is the set of numerical quantities of the goods that are contained in each of the respective bundles. Under "reasonable assumptions" (the definition of which is not necessary for us to delve into at this level), it is possible to come up with a rule that translates the quantities of goods in each basket into the number that our consumer has assigned to each basket. That "assignment rule" is called the **utility function** of that particular consumer. The single task of that utility function is to translate each basket of goods and services into a number that rank orders the baskets according to our particular consumer's preferences. The number itself is referred to as the utility of that basket and is measured in **utils**, which are just quantities of happiness, or well-being, or whatever comes to mind such that more of it is better than less of it.

In general, we can represent the utility function as

$$U = f\left(Q_{x_1}, Q_{x_2}, ..., Q_{x_n}\right)$$ (1)

where the Qs are the quantities of each of the respective goods and services in the bundles. In the case of two goods—say, ounces of wine (W) and slices of bread (B)—a utility function might be simply

$$U = f(W,B) = WB$$ (2)

or the product of the number of ounces of wine and the number of slices of bread. The utility of a bundle containing 4 ounces of wine along with 2 slices of bread would equal 8 utils, and it would rank lower than a bundle containing 3 ounces of wine along with 3 slices of bread, which would yield 9 utils.

The important point to note is that the utility function is just a ranking of bundles of goods. If someone were to replace all those pieces of paper with new numbers that maintained the same ranking, then the new set of numbers would be just as useful a utility function as the first in describing our consumer's preferences. This characteristic of utility functions is called an *ordinal*, as contrasted to a *cardinal*, ranking. Ordinal rankings are weaker measures than cardinal rankings because they do not allow the calculation and ranking of the *differences* between bundles.

3.3 Indifference Curves: The Graphical Portrayal of the Utility Function

It will be convenient for us to represent our consumer's preferences graphically, not just mathematically. To that end, we introduce the concept of an **indifference curve**, which represents all the combinations of two goods such that the consumer is entirely indifferent among them. This is how we construct such a curve: Consider bundles that contain only two goods so that we can use a two-dimensional graph to represent them—as in Exhibit 1, where a particular bundle containing W_a ounces of wine along with B_a slices of bread is represented as a single point, a. The assumption of non-satiation (more is always better) ensures that all bundles lying directly above, directly to the right of, or both above and to the right (more wine and more bread) of point a must be preferred to bundle a. That set of bundles is called the "preferred-to-bundle-a" set. Correspondingly, all the bundles that lie directly below, to the left of, and both below and to the left of bundle a must yield less utility and therefore would be called the "dominated-by-bundle-a" set.

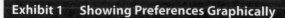

Exhibit 1   Showing Preferences Graphically

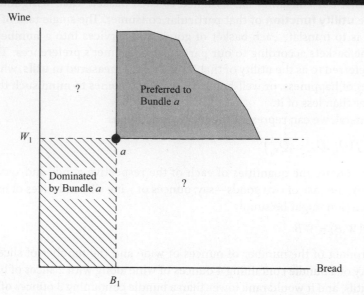

Note: A given bundle of two goods is represented as a single point, *a*, in the two-dimensional graph. Non-satiation allows us to rank-order many, but not all, other bundles, relative to *a*, leaving some questions unanswered.

To determine our consumer's preferences, suppose we present a choice between bundle *a* and some bundle *a'*, which contains more bread but less wine than *a*. Non-satiation is not helpful to us in this case, so we need to ask the consumer which he prefers. If he strictly prefers *a'*, then we would remove a little bread and ask again. If he strictly prefers *a*, then we would add a little bread, and so on. Finally, after a series of adjustments, we could find just the right combination of bread and wine such that the new bundle *a'* would be equally satisfying to our consumer as bundle *a*. That is to say, our consumer would be indifferent between consuming bundle *a* or bundle *a'*. We would then choose a bundle, say *a''*, that contains more wine and less bread than bundle *a*, and we would again adjust the goods such that the consumer is once again indifferent between bundle *a* and bundle *a''*. By continuing to choose bundles and make adjustments, it would be possible to identify all possible bundles such that the consumer is just indifferent among each of them and bundle *a*. Such a set of points is represented in Exhibit 2, where the indifference curve through point *a* represents that set of bundles. Notice that the "preferred-to-bundle-*a*" set has expanded to include all bundles that lie in the region above and to the right of the indifference curve. Correspondingly, the "dominated-by-bundle-*a*" set has expanded to include all bundles that lie in the region below and to the left of the indifference curve.

Exhibit 2   An Indifference Curve

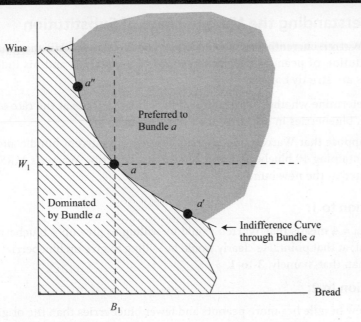

Note: An indifference curve shows all combinations of two goods such that the consumer is indifferent between them.

The indifference curve represents our consumer's unique preferences over the two goods wine and bread. Its negative slope simply represents that both wine and bread are seen as "good" to this consumer; in order to maintain indifference, a decrease in the quantity of wine must be compensated for by an increase in the quantity of bread. Its curvature tells us something about the strength of his willingness to trade off one good for the other. The indifference curve in Exhibit 2 is characteristically drawn to be *convex* when viewed from the origin. This indicates that the willingness to give up wine to obtain a little more bread diminishes the more bread and the less wine the bundle contains.

We capture this willingness to give up one good to obtain a little more of the other in the phrase **marginal rate of substitution** of bread for wine, MRS_{BW}. The MRS_{BW} is the rate at which the consumer is willing to give up wine to obtain a small increment of bread, holding utility constant (i.e., movement along an indifference curve). Notice that the convexity implies that at a bundle like a'', which contains rather a lot of wine and not much bread, the consumer would be willing to give up a considerable amount of wine in exchange for just a little more bread. (The slope of the indifference curve is quite steep at that point.) However, at a point like a', which contains considerably more bread but less wine than a'', the consumer is not ready to sacrifice nearly as much wine to obtain a little more bread. This suggests that the value being placed on bread, in terms of the amount of wine the consumer is willing to give up for bread, diminishes the more bread and less wine he has. It follows that the MRS_{BW} is the negative of the slope of the tangent to the indifference curve at any given bundle. If, at some point, the slope of the indifference curve had value -2.5, it means that, starting at that particular bundle, our consumer would be willing to sacrifice wine to obtain bread at the rate of 2.5 ounces of wine per slice of bread. Because of the convexity assumption—that MRS_{BW} must diminish as he moves toward more bread and less wine—the MRS_{BW} is continuously changing as he moves along his indifference curve.

EXAMPLE 2

Understanding the Marginal Rate of Substitution

Tom Warren currently has 50 blueberries and 20 peanuts. His marginal rate of substitution of peanuts for blueberries, MRS_{pb} equals 4, and his indifference curves are strictly convex.

1 Determine whether Warren would be willing to trade at the rate of 3 of his blueberries in exchange for 1 more peanut.

2 Suppose that Warren is indifferent between his current bundle and one containing 40 blueberries and 25 peanuts. Describe Warren's MRS_{pb} evaluated at the new bundle.

Solution to 1:

MRS_{pb} = 4 means that Warren would be willing to give up 4 blueberries for 1 peanut, at that point. He clearly would be willing to give up blueberries at a rate less than that, namely, 3-to-1.

Solution to 2:

The new bundle has more peanuts and fewer blueberries than the original one, and Warren is indifferent between the two, meaning that both bundles lie on the same indifference curve, where blueberries are plotted on the vertical axis and peanuts on the horizontal axis. Because his indifference curves are strictly convex and the new bundle lies below and to the right of his old bundle, his MRS_{pb} must be less than 4. That is to say, his indifference curve at the new point must be less steep than at the original bundle.

3.4 Indifference Curve Maps

There was nothing special about our initial choice of bundle a as a starting point for the indifference curve. We could have begun with a bundle containing more of both goods. In that case, we could have gone through the same process of trial and error, and we would have ended up with another indifference curve, this one passing through the new point and lying above and to the right of the first one. Indeed, we could construct any number of indifference curves in the same manner simply by starting at a different initial bundle. The result is an entire family of indifference curves, called an **indifference curve map**, and it represents our consumer's entire utility function. The word *map* is appropriate because the entire set of indifference curves comprises a contour map of this consumer's utility function. Each contour, or indifference curve, is a set of points in which each point shares a common level of utility with the others. Moving upward and to the right from one indifference curve to the next represents an increase in utility, and moving down and to the left represents a decrease. The map could look like that in Exhibit 3.

Exhibit 3 An Indifference Curve Map

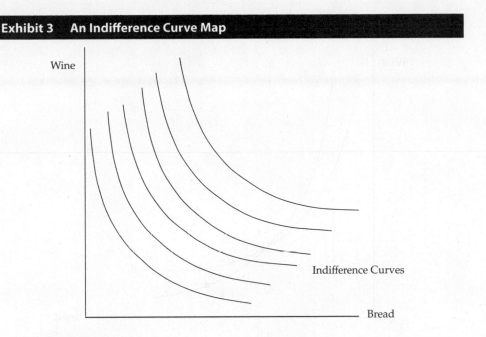

Wine

Indifference Curves

Bread

Note: The indifference curve map represents the consumer's utility function. Any curve above and to the right represents a higher level of utility.

Because of the completeness assumption, there will be one indifference curve passing through every point in the set. Because of the transitivity assumption, no two indifference curves for a given consumer can ever cross. Exhibit 4 shows why. If bundle *a* and bundle *b* lie on the same indifference curve, the consumer must be indifferent between the two. If *a* and *c* lie on the same indifference curve, she must be indifferent between these two bundles as well. But because bundle *c* contains more of both wine and bread than bundle *b*, she must prefer *c* to *b*, which violates transitivity of preferences. So we see that indifference curves will generally be strictly convex and negatively sloped, and they cannot cross. These are the only restrictions we place on indifference curve maps.

Exhibit 4   Why One Person's Indifference Curves Cannot Cross

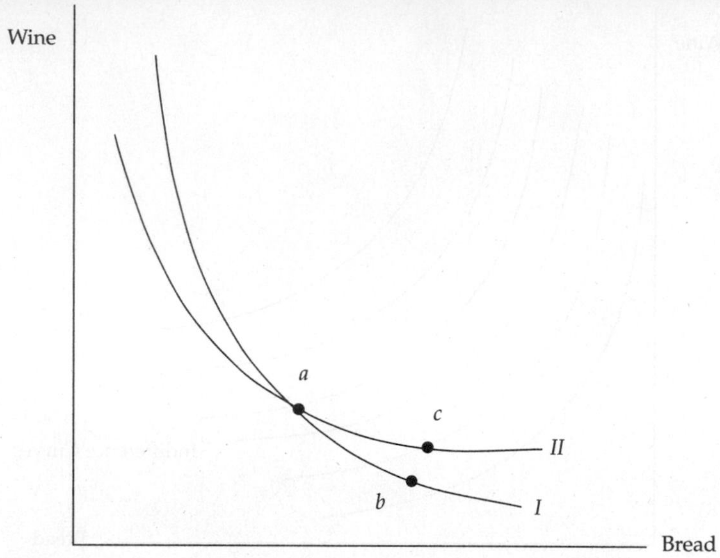

Note: Two indifference curves for a given individual cannot cross because the transitivity assumption would be violated.

3.5 Gains from Voluntary Exchange: Creating Wealth through Trade

There is no requirement that all consumers have the same preferences. Take the case of Helen Smith and Tom Warren. The indifference curves for Smith will likely be different from Warren's. And although *for any given individual* two indifference curves cannot cross, there is no reason why two indifference curves for two different consumers cannot intersect. Consider Exhibit 5, in which we observe an indifference curve for Smith and one for Warren. Suppose they are initially endowed with identical bundles, represented by *a*. They each have exactly identical quantities of bread and wine. Note, however, that because their indifference curves intersect at that point, their slopes are different. Warren's indifference curve is steeper at point *a* than is Smith's. This means that Warren's MRS_{BW} is greater than Smith's MRS_{BW}. That is to say, Warren is willing, at that point, to give up more wine for an additional slice of bread than Smith is. That also means that Smith is willing to give up more bread for an additional ounce of wine than Warren is. Therefore, we observe that Warren has a relatively stronger preference for bread compared to Smith, and Smith has a relatively stronger preference for wine than Warren.

Exhibit 5   Two Consumers with Different Preferences

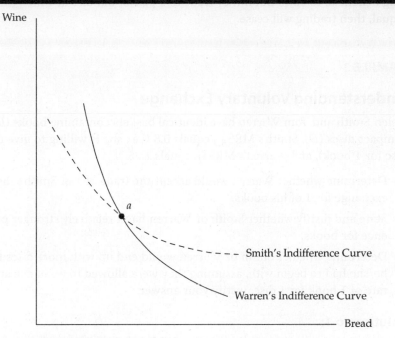

Note: When two consumers have different preferences, they will have different marginal rates of substitution when evaluated at identical bundles. Here, Warren has a relatively strong preference for bread because he is willing to give up more wine for another slice of bread than is Smith.

Suppose that the slope of Warren's indifference curve at point *a* is equal to −2, and the slope of Smith's indifference curve at point *a* is equal to −½. Warren is willing to give up 2 ounces of wine for 1 slice of bread, and Smith is willing to give up only ½ ounce of wine for 1 slice of bread. But that means she would be willing to give up 2 slices of bread for 1 ounce of wine. What would happen if Warren and Smith are allowed to exchange bread for wine? Suppose they are allowed to exchange at the ratio of one ounce of wine for one slice of bread. Would they both agree to an exchange at that ratio? Yes. Warren would be willing to give up two ounces of wine for a slice of bread, so he would certainly be willing to give up only one ounce of wine for one slice of bread. Correspondingly, Smith would be willing to give up two slices of bread for one ounce of wine, so she would certainly be willing to give up only one slice of bread for one ounce of wine. If they actually made such a trade at the one-to-one ratio, then Smith would end up with more wine and less bread than she started with, and Warren would end up with more bread and less wine than he started with.

We could say that Warren is better off by the value to him of one ounce of wine because he was *willing* to give up two ounces but only *had to* give up one ounce for his slice of bread. What about Smith? She is better off by the value to her of one slice of bread because she was *willing* to give up two slices of bread for her one additional ounce of wine but only *had to* give up one slice. Both Smith and Warren are better off after they trade. There is no more bread or wine than when they began, but there is greater *wealth* because both are better off than before they traded with each other. Both Smith and Warren ended on higher indifference curves than when they began.

As Smith gives up slices of bread for more ounces of wine, her MRS_{BW} increases; her indifference curve becomes steeper. Simultaneously, as Warren gives up ounces of wine for more slices of bread, his MRS_{BW} decreases; his indifference curve becomes less steep. Eventually, if they continue to trade, their MRSs will reach equality and there will be no further gains to be achieved from additional exchange. Initially, it was the differences in their willingness to trade one good for the other that made trading beneficial to both. But if they trade to a pair of bundles at which their MRSs are equal, then trading will cease.

EXAMPLE 3

Understanding Voluntary Exchange

Helen Smith and Tom Warren have identical baskets containing books (B) and compact discs (D). Smith's MRS_{BD} equals 0.8 (i.e., she is willing to give up 0.8 disc for 1 book), and Warren's MRS_{BD} equals 1.25.

1   Determine whether Warren would accept the trade of 1 of Smith's discs in exchange for 1 of his books.

2   State and justify whether Smith or Warren has a relatively stronger preference for books.

3   Determine whether Smith or Warren would end up with more discs than he/she had to begin with, assuming they were allowed to exchange at the rate of 1 book for 1 disc. Justify your answer.

Solution to 1:

Warren's MRS_{BD} equals 1.25, meaning that he is willing to give up 1.25 discs for 1 more book. Another way to say this is that Warren requires at least 1.25 discs to compensate him for giving up 1 book. Because Smith only offers one disc, Warren will not accept the offer. (Of course, Smith would not voluntarily give up one disc for one of Warren's books. Her MRS_{BD} is only 0.8, meaning that she would be willing to give up, at most, 0.8 disc for a book; so she would not have offered one disc for a book anyway.)

Solution to 2:

Because Warren is willing to give up 1.25 discs for a book and Smith is willing to give up only 0.8 disc for a book, Warren has a relatively stronger preference for books.

Solution to 3:

Smith would have more discs than she originally had. Because Smith has a relatively stronger preference for discs and Warren has a relatively stronger preference for books, Smith would trade books for discs and so would end up with more discs.

---

4   THE OPPORTUNITY SET: CONSUMPTION, PRODUCTION, AND INVESTMENT CHOICE

Above, we have examined the trade-offs that economic actors (e.g., consumers, companies, investors) are *willing* to make. In this section, we recognize that circumstances almost always impose constraints on the trade-offs that these actors *are able* to make. In other words, we need to explore how to model the constraints on behavior that are imposed by the fact that we live in a world of scarcity: There is simply not enough of everything to satisfy the needs and desires of everyone at a given time. Consumers must generally purchase goods and services with their limited incomes and at given market prices. Companies, too, must divide their limited input resources in order to produce different products. Investors are not able to choose *both* high returns *and* low risk simultaneously. Choices must be made, and here we examine how to represent the set of choices from which to choose.

4.1 The Budget Constraint

Previously, we examined what would happen if Warren and Smith were each given an endowment of bread and wine and were allowed to exchange at some pre-determined ratio. Although that circumstance is possible, a more realistic situation would be if Warren or Smith had a given income with which to purchase bread and wine at fixed market prices. Let Warren's income be given by I, the price he must pay for a slice of bread be P_B, and the price he must pay for an ounce of wine be P_W. Warren has freedom to spend his income any way he chooses, so long as the expenditure on bread plus the expenditure on wine does not exceed his income per time period. We can represent this **income constraint** (or **budget constraint**) with the following expression:

$$P_B Q_B + P_W Q_W \leq I \qquad (3)$$

This expression simply constrains Warren to spend, in total, no more than his income. At this stage of our analysis, we are assuming a one-period model. In effect, then, Warren has no reason *not* to spend all of his income. The weak inequality becomes a strict equality, as shown in Equation 4, because there would be no reason for Warren to save any of his income if there is "no tomorrow."

$$P_B Q_B + P_W Q_W = I \qquad (4)$$

From this equation, we see that if Warren were to spend all of his income only on bread, he could buy I/P_B slices of bread. Or if he were to confine his expenditure to wine alone, he could buy I/P_W ounces of wine. Alternatively, he could spread his income across bread and wine expenditures any way he chooses. Graphically, then, his budget constraint would appear as in Exhibit 6:

Exhibit 6 The Budget Constraint

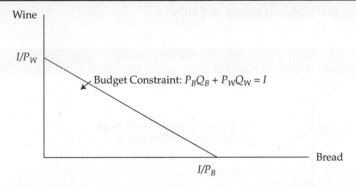

Note: The budget constraint shows all the combinations of bread and wine that the consumer could purchase with a fixed amount of income, I, paying prices P_B and P_W, respectively.

A simple algebraic manipulation of Equation 4 yields the budget constraint in the form of an intercept and slope:

$$Q_W = \frac{I}{P_W} - \frac{P_B}{P_W} Q_B \qquad (5)$$

Notice that the slope of the budget constraint is equal to $-P_B/P_W$, and it shows the amount of wine that Warren would have to give up if he were to purchase another slice of bread. If the price of bread were to rise, the budget constraint would become steeper, pivoting through the vertical intercept. Alternatively, if the price of wine were to rise, the budget constraint would become less steep, pivoting downward through the horizontal intercept. If income were to rise, the entire budget constraint would shift outward, parallel to the original constraint, as shown in Exhibit 7:

Exhibit 7   Changing Prices and Income

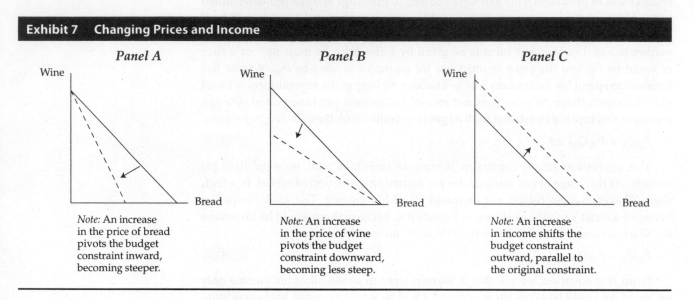

Panel A

Note: An increase in the price of bread pivots the budget constraint inward, becoming steeper.

Panel B

Note: An increase in the price of wine pivots the budget constraint downward, becoming less steep.

Panel C

Note: An increase in income shifts the budget constraint outward, parallel to the original constraint.

As a specific example of a budget constraint, suppose Smith has $60 to spend on bread and wine per month, the price of a slice of bread is $0.50, and the price of an ounce of wine is $0.75. If she spent all of her income on bread, she could buy 120 slices of bread. Or she could buy up to 80 ounces of wine if she chose to buy no bread. Obviously, she can spend half her income on each good, in which case she could buy 60 slices of bread and 40 ounces of wine. The entire set of bundles that Smith could buy with her $60 budget is shown in Exhibit 8:

Exhibit 8   A Specific Example of a Budget Constraint

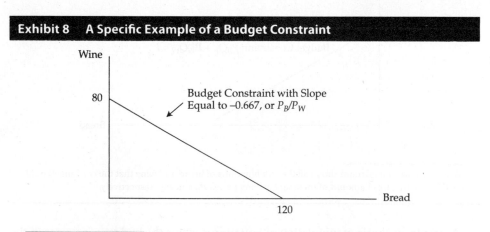

Budget Constraint with Slope Equal to –0.667, or P_B/P_W

Note: This exhibit shows Smith's budget constraint if she has an income of $60 and must pay $0.50 per slice of bread and $0.75 per ounce of wine.

EXAMPLE 4

The Budget Constraint

Nigel's Pub has a total budget of £128 per week to spend on cod and lamb. The price of cod is £16 per kilogram, and the price of lamb is £10 per kilogram.

1 Calculate Nigel's budget constraint.

2 Construct a diagram of Nigel's budget constraint.

3 Determine the slope of Nigel's budget constraint.

Solution to 1:

The budget constraint is simply that the sum of the expenditure on cod plus the expenditure on lamb be equal to his budget: $128 = 16 Q_C + 10 Q_L$. Rearranging, it can also be written in intercept slope form: $Q_C = 128/P_C - (P_L/P_C) Q_L = 8 - 0.625 Q_L$.

Solution to 2:

We can choose to measure either commodity on the vertical axis, so we arbitrarily choose cod. Note that if Nigel spends his entire budget on cod, he could buy 8kg. On the other hand, if he chooses to spend the entire budget on lamb, he could buy 12.8kg. Of course, he could spread his £128 between the two goods in any proportions he chooses, so the budget constraint is drawn as follows:

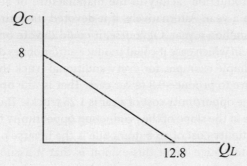

Solution to 3:

With quantity of cod measured on the vertical axis, the slope is equal to $-(P_L/P_C) = -10/16 = -0.625$. (*Note*: If we had chosen to measure quantity of lamb on the vertical axis, the slope would be inverted: $-(P_C/P_L) = -1.6$.)

4.2 The Production Opportunity Set

Companies face constraints on their production opportunities, just as consumers face limits on the bundles of goods that they can consume. Consider a company that produces two products using the same production capacity. For example, an automobile company might use the same factory to produce either automobiles or light trucks. If so, then the company is constrained by the limited capacity to produce vehicles. If it produces more trucks, it must reduce its production of automobiles; likewise, if it produces more automobiles, it must produce fewer trucks. The company's **production opportunity frontier** shows the maximum number of units of one good it can produce, for any given number of the other good that it chooses to manufacture. Such a frontier for the vehicle company might look something like that in Exhibit 9.

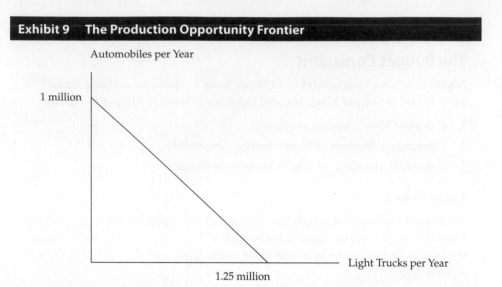

Exhibit 9   The Production Opportunity Frontier

Note: The production opportunity frontier for a vehicle manufacturer shows the maximum number of autos for any given level of truck production. In this example, the opportunity cost of a truck is 0.8 autos.

There are two important things to notice about this example. First, if the company devoted its entire production facility to the manufacture of automobiles, it could produce 1 million in a year. Alternatively, if it devoted its entire plant to trucks, it could produce 1.25 million a year. Of course, it could devote only part of the year's production to trucks, in which case it could produce automobiles during the remainder of the year. In this simple example, for every additional truck the company chooses to make, it would have to produce 0.8 fewer cars. That is, the **opportunity cost** of a truck is 0.8 cars, or the opportunity cost of a car is 1.25 trucks. The opportunity cost of trucks is the negative of the slope of the production opportunity frontier: 1/1.25. And of course, the opportunity cost of an automobile is the inverse of that ratio, or 1.25.

The other thing to notice about this exhibit is that it assumes the opportunity cost of a truck is independent of how many trucks (and cars) the company produces. The production opportunity frontier is linear with a constant slope. Perhaps a more realistic example would be to increase marginal opportunity cost. As more and more trucks are produced, fewer inputs that are particularly well suited to producing truck inputs could be transferred to assist in their manufacture, causing the cost of trucks (in terms of cars) to rise as more trucks are produced. In this event, the production opportunity frontier would become steeper as the company moved its production point away from cars and toward more trucks, resulting in a frontier that would be concave as viewed from the origin.

4.3 The Investment Opportunity Set

The investment opportunity set is examined in detail in readings on investments, but it is appropriate to examine it briefly here because we are learning about constraints on behavior. Consider possible investments in which one option might be to invest in an essentially risk-free asset, such as a US Treasury bill. There is virtually no possibility that the US government would default on a 90-day obligation to pay back an investor's purchase price, plus interest. Alternatively, an investor could put her money into a broadly diversified index of common shares. This investment will necessarily be more risky because of the fact that share prices fluctuate. If investors inherently find risk distasteful, then they will be reluctant to invest in a risky asset unless they expect to receive, on average, a higher rate of return. Hence, it is reasonable to expect that a broadly diversified index of common shares will have an expected return that exceeds that of the risk-free asset, or else no one would hold that portfolio.

Our hypothetical investor could choose to put some of her funds in the risk-free asset and the rest in the common shares index. For each additional dollar invested in the common shares index, she can expect to receive a higher return, though not with certainty; so, she is exposing herself to more risk in the pursuit of a higher return. We can structure her investment opportunities as a frontier that shows the highest expected return consistent with any given level of risk, as shown in Exhibit 10. The investor's choice of a portfolio on the frontier will depend on her level of risk aversion.

Exhibit 10   The Investment Opportunity Frontier

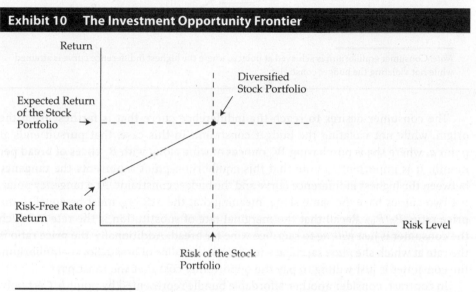

Note: The investment opportunity frontier shows that as the investor chooses to invest a greater proportion of assets in the market portfolio, she can expect a higher return but also higher risk.

CONSUMER EQUILIBRIUM: MAXIMIZING UTILITY SUBJECT TO THE BUDGET CONSTRAINT

5

It would be wonderful if we could all consume as much of everything as we wanted, but unfortunately, most of us are constrained by income and prices. We now superimpose the budget constraint onto the preference map to model the actual choice of our consumer. This is a constrained (by the resources available to pay for consumption) optimization problem that every consumer must solve: Choose the bundle of goods and services that gets us as high on our ranking as possible, while not exceeding our budget.

5.1 Determining the Consumer's Equilibrium Bundle of Goods

In general, the consumer's constrained optimization problem consists of maximizing utility, subject to the budget constraint. If, for simplicity, we assume there are only two goods, wine and bread, then the problem appears graphically as in Exhibit 11.

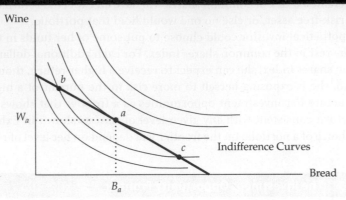

Exhibit 11   Consumer Equilibrium

Note: Consumer equilibrium is achieved at point *a*, where the highest indifference curve is attained while not violating the budget constraint.

The consumer desires to reach the indifference curve that is farthest from the origin, while not violating the budget constraint. In this case, that pursuit ends at point *a*, where she is purchasing W_a ounces of wine along with B_a slices of bread per month. It is important to note that this equilibrium point represents the tangency between the highest indifference curve and the budget constraint. At a tangency point, the two curves have the same slope, meaning that the MRS_{BW} must be equal to the price ratio, P_B/P_W. Recall that the marginal rate of substitution is the rate at which the consumer is just *willing* to sacrifice wine for bread. Additionally, the price ratio is the rate at which she *must* sacrifice wine for another slice of bread. So, at equilibrium, the consumer is just willing to pay the opportunity cost that she must pay.

In contrast, consider another affordable bundle represented by point *b*. Certainly, the consumer is able to purchase that bundle because it lies on her budget constraint. However, the MRS_{BW} at that point is greater than the price ratio, meaning that she is *willing* to give up wine to obtain bread at a rate greater than she *must*. Hence, she will be better off moving downward along the budget constraint until she reaches the tangent point at *a*. In effect, she is willing to pay a higher price than she must for each additional unit of bread until she reaches B_a. For all of the units that she consumes up to B_a, we could say that the consumer is receiving consumer surplus, a concept we visited above when discussing the demand curve. Importantly, she would not purchase slices of bread beyond B_a at these prices because at a point like *c*, the marginal rate of substitution is less than the price ratio—meaning that the price for that additional unit is above her willingness to pay. Even though she could afford bundle *c*, it would not be the best use of her income.

EXAMPLE 5

Consumer Equilibrium

Currently, a consumer is buying both sorbet and gelato each week. His MRS_{GS} [marginal rate of substitution of gelato (*G*) for sorbet (*S*)] equals 0.75. The price of gelato is €1 per scoop, and the price of sorbet is €1.25 per scoop.

1   Determine whether the consumer is currently optimizing his budget over these two desserts. Justify your answer.

2   Explain whether the consumer should buy more sorbet or more gelato, given that he is not currently optimizing his budget.

Solution to 1:

In this example, the condition for consumer equilibrium is $MRS_{GS} = P_G/P_S$. Because $P_G/P_S = 0.8$ and $MRS_{GS} = 0.75$, the consumer is clearly not allocating his budget in a way that maximizes his utility, subject to his budget constraint.

Solution to 2:

The MRS_{GS} is the rate at which the consumer is willing to give up sorbet to gain a small additional amount of gelato, which is 0.75 scoops of sorbet to gain one scoop of gelato. The price ratio, P_G/P_S (0.8), is the rate at which he *must* give up sorbet to gain an additional small amount of gelato. In this case, the consumer would be better off spending a little less on gelato and a little more on sorbet.

5.2 Consumer Response to Changes in Income: Normal and Inferior Goods

The consumer's behavior is constrained by his income and the prices he must pay for the goods he consumes. Consequently, if one or more of those parameters changes, the consumer is likely to change his consumption behavior. We first consider an increase in income. Recall from Exhibit 7, Panel C, that an increase in income simply shifts the budget constraint outward from the origin, parallel to itself. Exhibit 12 indicates such a shift and shows how the consumer would respond, in this case, by buying more of both bread and wine.

Exhibit 12	The Effect of an Increase in Income on a Normal Good

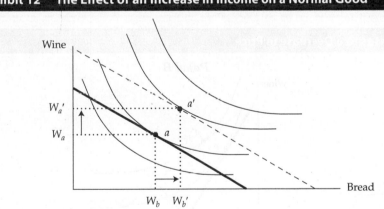

Note: The effect of an increase in income when both goods are normal is to increase the consumption of both.

As we discovered, there is no restriction that the purchase of every good must respond to an increase in income with an increase in quantity. There, we defined *normal goods* as those with a positive response to an increase in income and *inferior goods* as those with a negative response to an increase in income. Suppose that bread is an inferior good for a particular consumer, whereas wine is a normal good. Exhibit 13 shows this consumer's purchase behavior when income increases. As income rises, the consumer purchases less bread but more wine.

Exhibit 13   The Effect of an Increase in Income on an Inferior Good

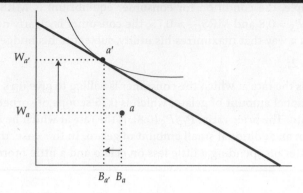

Note: The effect of an increase in income on the purchase of bread, an inferior good in this example, reduces the consumption of that good.

5.3 How the Consumer Responds to Changes in Price

We now hold income and the price of one good (wine) constant but decrease the price of the other good (bread). Recall that a decrease in the price of bread pivots the budget constraint outward along the horizontal axis but leaves the vertical intercept unchanged—as in Exhibit 14, where we examine two responses to the decrease in the price of bread.

Exhibit 14   Elastic and Inelastic Responses to a Decrease in Price

Panel A

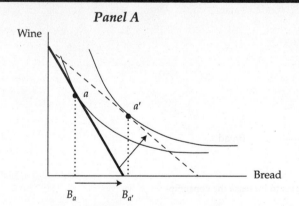

Panel B

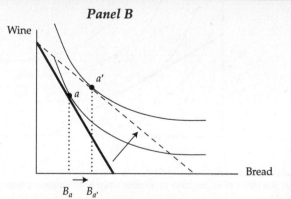

Note: When the price of bread falls, this consumer moves from bundle *a* to bundle *a'*, showing an elastic response.

Note: When the price of bread falls, this consumer moves from bundle *a* to bundle *a'*, showing an inelastic response.

In both cases, when the price of bread falls, the consumer buys more bread. But in the first case, he is quite responsive to the price change, responding with an elastic demand for bread. In the second case, the consumer is still responsive but much less so than the first consumer; this consumer's response to the price change is inelastic.

REVISITING THE CONSUMER'S DEMAND FUNCTION

6

We have now come to the reason why we wanted to explore consumer theory in the first place: We want to have a sound theoretical foundation for our use of consumer demand curves. Although we could merely assume that a consumer has a demand curve, we derive a richer understanding of that curve if we start with a more fundamental recognition of the consumer's preferences and her response to changes in the parameters that constrain her behavior in the marketplace.

6.1 Consumer's Demand Curve from Preferences and Budget Constraints

Recall that to draw a consumer's demand curve, we appealed to the assumption of "holding all other things constant" and held preferences, income, and the prices of all but one good constant. Graphically, we show such an exercise by representing a given utility function with a set of indifference curves, and then we superimpose a set of budget constraints, each one representing a different price of one of the goods. Exhibit 15 shows the result of this exercise. Notice that we are "stacking" two exhibits vertically to show both the indifference curves and budget constraints and the demand curve below them. In the upper exhibit, we have rotated the budget constraint rightward, indicating successively lower prices of bread, P_B^1, P_B^2, P_B^3, P_B^4, while holding income constant at I.

Exhibit 15   Deriving a Demand Curve

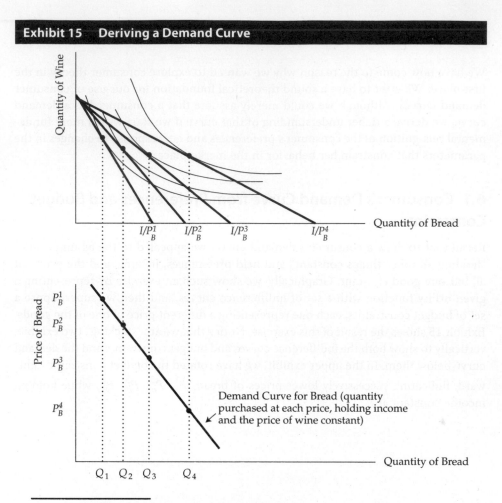

Note: A demand curve for bread is derived from the indifference curve map and a set of budget constraints representing different prices of bread.

This pair of diagrams deserves careful inspection. Notice first that the vertical axes are not the same. In the upper diagram, we represent the quantity of the *other* good, wine, whose price is being held constant, along with income. Hence, the budget constraints all have the same vertical intercept. But the price of bread is falling as we observe ever less steep budget constraints with horizontal intercepts moving rightward. Confronted with each respective budget constraint, the consumer finds the tangent point as indicated. This point corresponds to the respective quantities of bread, Q_1, Q_2, Q_3, and Q_4. Note also that the horizontal axes of the two diagrams are identical. They measure the quantity of bread purchased. Importantly, the vertical axis in the lower diagram measures the price of bread. As the price of bread falls, this consumer chooses to buy ever greater quantities, as indicated. The price–quantity combinations that result trace out this consumer's demand curve for bread in the lower diagram. For each tangent point in the upper diagram, there is a corresponding point in the lower diagram, tracing out the demand curve for bread.

6.2 Substitution and Income Effects for a Normal Good

The law of demand says that when price falls, quantity demanded rises; however, it doesn't say why. We can answer that question by delving a little more deeply into consumer theory. When there is a decline in the price of a good that the consumer has been buying, two things happen. The good now becomes *relatively* less costly as compared to other goods. That is, it becomes more of a bargain than other things the consumer could purchase; thus, more of this good gets substituted for other goods in the consumer's market basket. Additionally, though, with the decline in that price, the consumer's **real income** rises. We're not saying that the size of the consumer's paycheck changes; we're saying that the amount of goods that can be purchased with the same amount of money has increased. If this good is a normal good, then increases in income lead to increased purchases of this good. So the consumer tends to buy more when price falls for both reasons: the substitution effect and the income effect of a change in the price of a good.

A close look at indifference curves and budget constraints can demonstrate how these effects can be separated. Consider Exhibit 16, where we analyze Warren's response to a decrease in the price of bread. When the price of bread falls, as indicated by the pivoting in budget constraints from BC_1 to BC_2, Warren buys more bread, increasing his quantity from Q_a to Q_c. That is the net effect of both the substitution effect and the income effect. We can see the partial impact of each of these effects by engaging in a mental exercise. Part of Warren's response is because of his increase in real income. We can remove that effect by subtracting some income from him, while leaving the new lower price in place. The dashed budget constraint shows the reduction in income that would be just sufficient to move Warren back to his original indifference curve. Notice that we are moving BC_2 inward, parallel to itself until it becomes just tangent to Warren's original indifference curve at point b. The price decrease was a good thing for Warren. An offsetting bad thing would be an income reduction. If the income reduction is just sufficient to leave Warren as well off but no better off than before the price change, then we have effectively removed the real income effect of the decrease in price. What's left of his response must be due to the pure substitution effect alone. So, we say that the substitution effect is shown by the move from point a to point b. If his income reduction were then restored, the resulting movement from point b to point c must be the pure income effect.

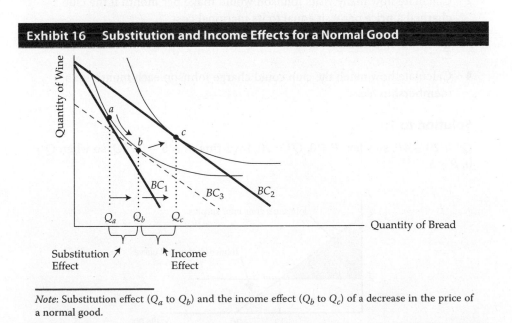

Exhibit 16   Substitution and Income Effects for a Normal Good

Note: Substitution effect (Q_a to Q_b) and the income effect (Q_b to Q_c) of a decrease in the price of a normal good.

An important thing to notice is that the pure substitution effect must always be in the direction of purchasing more when the price falls and purchasing less when the price rises. This is because of the diminishing marginal rate of substitution, or the convexity of the indifference curve. Look again at Exhibit 16. Note that the substitution effect is the result of changing from budget constraint 1 to budget constraint 3—or moving the budget constraint along the original indifference curve, while maintaining tangency. Note that in the process, the budget constraint becomes less steep, just as the marginal rate of substitution decreases. Warren is no better off than before the changes, but his behavior has changed: He now buys more bread and less wine than before the offsetting changes in income and price. This reason for negatively sloped demand curves never changes.

Sellers can sometimes use income and substitution effects to their advantage. Think of something you often buy, perhaps lunch at your favorite café. How much would you be willing to pay for a "lunch club membership card" that would allow you to purchase lunches at, say, half price? If the café could extract from you the maximum amount each month that you would be willing to pay for the half-price option, then it would successfully have removed the income effect from you in the form of a monthly fixed fee. Notice that Exhibit 16 implies that you would end up buying more lunches each month than before you purchased the discount card, even though you would be no better or worse off than before. This is a way that sellers are sometimes able to extract consumer surplus by means of creative pricing schemes. It's a common practice among big box retailers, sports clubs, and other users of what is called "two-part tariff pricing."

EXAMPLE 6

Two-Part Tariff Pricing

Nicole Johnson's monthly demand for visits to her health club is given by the following equation: $Q^d = 20 - 4P$, where Q^d is visits per month and P is euros per visit. The health club's marginal cost is fixed at €2 per visit.

1   Determine Johnson's demand curve for health club visits per month.

2   Calculate how many visits Johnson would make per month if the club charged a price per visit equal to its marginal cost.

3   Calculate Johnson's consumer surplus at the price determined in Question 2.

4   Calculate how much the club could charge Johnson each month for a membership fee.

Solution to 1:

$Q^d = 20 - 4P$, so when $P = 0$, $Q^d = 20$. Inverting, $P = 5 - 0.25Q$, so when $Q = 0$, $P = 5$.

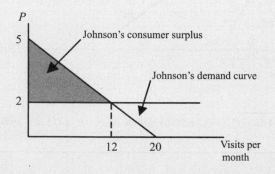

Solution to 2:

$Q^d = 20 - 4(2) = 12$. Johnson would make 12 visits per month at a price of €2 per visit.

Solution to 3:

Johnson's consumer surplus can be measured as the area under her demand curve and above the price she pays, for a total of 12 visits: $CS = (\frac{1}{2})(12)(3) = 18$. Johnson would enjoy €18 per month consumer surplus.

Solution to 4:

The club could extract all of Johnson's consumer surplus by charging her a monthly membership fee of €18 plus a per-visit price of €2. This is called a two-part tariff because it assesses one price per unit of the item purchased plus a per-month fee (sometimes called an "entry fee") equal to the buyer's consumer surplus evaluated at the per-unit price.

6.3 Income and Substitution Effects for an Inferior Good

We know that for some consumers and some goods, an increase in income leads to a decrease in the quantity purchased at each price. These goods are called *inferior* goods, and they have negative income elasticity of demand. When price falls, these goods still exhibit substitution and income effects, but they are in opposite directions. Consider Exhibit 17, in which we see a fairly standard set of indifference curves and budget constraints. But in this case, bread is an inferior good.

Exhibit 17   Income and Substitution Effects for an Inferior Good

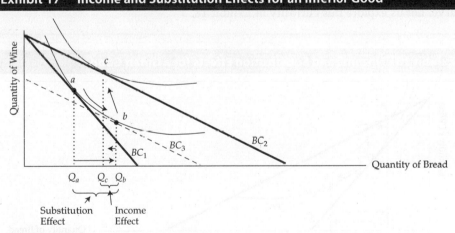

Note: The income effect of a price decrease for an inferior good is opposite to the substitution effect, tending to mitigate the change in quantity.

Notice that when the bread's price falls, as indicated by the shift from budget constraint 1 (BC_1) to budget constraint 2 (BC_2), the consumer buys more bread, just as we would expect. That is, the consumer's demand curve is still negatively sloped. When we apply the income adjustment to isolate substitution effect from income effect, we shift the budget constraint back to constraint 3, reducing income sufficiently to place the consumer back on the original indifference curve. As before, the substitution effect is shown as a movement along the original indifference curve from point *a* to point *b*. The income effect is, as before, a movement from one indifference curve to the other, as shown by the movement from point *b* to point *c*. In this case, however, the income effect partially offsets the substitution effect, causing demand to be less elastic than if the two effects reinforced each other.

We see that for inferior goods, the income effect and the substitution effect are in opposite directions: The decrease in price causes the consumer to buy more, but the income effect tends to mitigate that effect. It's still true that a decrease in the price of bread represents an increase in real income. But in the case of an inferior good, the increased income causes the consumer to want to buy less of the good, not more. As long as the income effect has a lower magnitude than the substitution effect, the consumer still ends up buying more at the lower price. However, she buys a little less than she would if the good were normal. It is possible, though highly unlikely, for the income effect to have greater magnitude than the substitution effect. We examine that case next.

In the case of savings, the same type of effects can apply. For example, say interest rates rise. Individuals may save more because the reward (price) for saving has risen, and individuals substitute future consumption for present consumption. However, higher interest rates also imply that less saving is required to attain a given future amount of money. If the latter effect (the income effect) dominates, then it is possible to observe higher interest rates resulting in less savings.

6.4 Negative Income Effect Larger than Substitution Effect: Giffen Goods

In theory, it is possible for the income effect to be so strong and so negative as to overpower the substitution effect. If that were to occur, then a decrease in price could result in a *decrease* in quantity demanded and a *positively sloped* individual demand curve. Let us explore this curiosity in Exhibit 18.

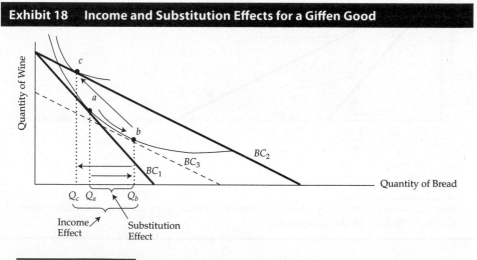

Exhibit 18   Income and Substitution Effects for a Giffen Good

Note: Income and substitution effects of a fall in price for a Giffen good: When price declines, the consumer chooses to buy less of the good.

Once again, we decrease the price of bread as indicated by the pivoting of the budget constraint form BC_1 to BC_2, and then we move the budget constraint parallel to itself leftward until it just touches the original indifference curve at point *b* to remove the income effect. What is left is the substitution effect. As always, the substitution effect causes the consumer to substitute more bread for less wine in the basket, as indicated by the movement along the indifference curve from point *a* to point *b*. But notice the odd result when we "give back" the income and move from BC_3 to BC_2. The income effect for this inferior good (from point *b* to point *c*) is once again opposite in direction to the substitution effect, as is true for all inferior goods. But in this curious case, its magnitude overwhelms the substitution effect: Point *c* lies *to the left* of point *a*. The consumer actually buys less of the good when its price falls, resulting in a positively sloped demand curve. If we reversed the analysis and increased the price of bread, this consumer would buy more bread when its price rose. Those inferior goods whose income effect is negative and greater in magnitude than the substitution effect are known as **Giffen goods**. Importantly, all Giffen goods must be inferior, but not all inferior goods are Giffen goods.

This curious result is originally attributed to Robert Giffen, who suspected that Irish peasants might have responded this way to increased prices of staples during the Irish potato famine in the nineteenth century. He reasoned that staples, such as potatoes, comprised a very large portion of the peasants' total budget. Additionally, potatoes could be a very inferior good, which simply means that when incomes fell, the peasants bought a lot more potatoes; and when incomes rose, they bought a lot fewer. Now because potatoes took up such a large part of total expenditures, any increase in the price of potatoes would result in a very substantial decrease in real income. This combination of strong inferiority coupled with a large amount of the budget spent on potatoes could, in theory, result in the negative income effect not only being opposite in direction to the substitution effect, but in fact overwhelming it.

Although some empirical studies have suggested the existence of Giffen goods, even if they existed they would be extraordinarily rare. Moreover, although they might exist for some small subset of consumers, it is highly unlikely that consumers as a whole would behave this way. So Giffen goods' role in microeconomics is greater than their role in the empirical world. True, they result in a positively sloped demand curve and they do not violate any of the axioms of consumer choice theory. But any company's manager who believes that if she raises the price of her product she will sell *more* of it is very likely to be disappointed.

EXAMPLE 7

Income and Substitution Effects of a Decrease in Price

Consider the following diagram of budget constraints and indifference curves for a consumer choosing to allocate her budget between books and shoes. Determine whether shoes are normal, inferior, or Giffen goods for this consumer.

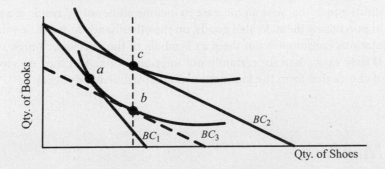

Solution:

When the price of shoes falls, the original budget constraint pivots from BC_1 to BC_2. The original tangent point was at *a* and is now at *c*. We can separate the substitution effect from the income effect by removing enough income to put the consumer back on the old indifference curve at point *b*. This is shown as a shift in the budget constraint from BC_2 to BC_3, a parallel shift. The substitution effect is, therefore, from point *a* to point *b*, along the original indifference curve. The income effect is from point *b* to point *c*, but note that those two points are on the same vertical line. In this case, shoes are on a borderline between normal and inferior. There is zero income effect. (If point *c* had been to the right of point *b*, shoes would be normal. And if *c* had been to the left of point *b*, they would be inferior. Finally, if *c* had been to the left of point *a*, shoes would be a Giffen good.)

6.5 Veblen Goods: Another Possibility for a Positively Sloped Demand Curve

Standard choice theory assumes that the consumer can always make comparisons among all pairs of bundles of goods and identify preferences before knowing anything about the prices of those baskets. Then, as we've seen, the consumer is constrained by income and prices and makes actual choices of which bundles to purchase with limited income. It is important to note that those preferences are assumed to exist even before knowing the prices at which those goods could be purchased. It is possible, however, that an item's price tag *itself* might help determine the consumer's preferences for it. Thorstein Veblen posited just such a circumstance in his concept of **conspicuous consumption**. According to this way of thinking, a consumer might derive utility out of being known by others to consume a so-called *high status* good, such as a luxury automobile or a very expensive piece of jewelry. Importantly, it is the high price itself that partly imparts value to such a good. If that is the case, then a consumer would actually value a good more if it had a higher price. So, it is argued that by increasing the price of a **Veblen good**, the consumer would be *more inclined* to purchase it, not less. In the extreme, it could be argued that the consumer's demand for such a good could be positively sloped, though this need not necessarily follow. In fact, of course, if any seller actually faced a positively sloped demand curve for her product, the rational response would be to increase price because she would sell more at the higher price. Ultimately, at some very high price, demand would necessarily become negatively sloped.

It is important to recognize that, although Veblen goods and Giffen goods share some characteristics, they are in fact quite different. Whether or not they actually exist, Giffen goods are not inconsistent with the fundamental axioms of demand theory. True, they would result in a violation of the law of demand, but that law is not a logical necessity. It is simply recognition that in virtually all observed cases, demand curves are negatively sloped. Giffen goods certainly would not be considered examples of "status goods," because an increase in income alone would result in a reduced interest in purchasing them. Veblen goods, on the other hand, derive their value from the ostentatious consumption of them as symbols of the purchaser's high status in society. If they exist, they are certainly not inferior goods. And they do violate the axioms of choice that form the foundation of accepted demand theory.

SUMMARY

This reading has explored how consumer preferences over baskets of goods and budget constraints translate into the demand curves posited by the demand and supply model of markets. Among the major points made are the following.

▪ Consumer choice theory is the branch of microeconomics that relates consumer demand curves to consumer preferences. Utility theory is a quantitative model of consumer preferences and is based on a set of axioms (assumptions that are assumed to be true). If consumer preferences are complete, transitive, and insatiable, those preferences can be represented by an ordinal utility function and depicted by a set of indifference curves that are generally negatively sloped, convex from below, and do not cross for a given consumer.

■ A consumer's relative strength of preferences can be inferred from his marginal rate of substitution of good X for good Y (MRS_{XY}), which is the rate at which the consumer is willing to sacrifice good Y to obtain an additional small increment of good X. If two consumers have different marginal rates of substitution, they can both benefit from the voluntary exchange of one good for the other.

■ A consumer's attainable consumption options are determined by her income and the prices of the goods she must purchase to consume. The set of options available is bounded by the budget constraint, a negatively sloped linear relationship that shows the highest quantity of one good that can be purchased for any given amount of the other good being bought.

■ Analogous to the consumer's consumption opportunity set are, respectively, the production opportunity set and the investment opportunity set. A company's production opportunity set represents the greatest quantity of one product that a company can produce, for any given amount of the other good it produces. The investment opportunity set represents the highest return an investor can expect, for any given amount of risk undertaken.

■ Consumer equilibrium is obtained when utility is maximized, subject to the budget constraint, generally depicted as a tangency between the highest attainable indifference curve and the fixed budget constraint. At that tangency, the MRS_{XY} is just equal to the two goods' price ratio, P_X/P_Y—or that bundle such that the rate at which the consumer is just willing to sacrifice good Y for good X is equal to the rate at which, based on prices, she must sacrifice good Y for good X.

■ If the consumer's income and the price of all other goods are held constant and the price of good X is varied, the set of consumer equilibria that results will yield that consumer's demand curve for good X. In general, we expect the demand curve to have a negative slope (the law of demand) because of two influences: income and substitution effects of a decrease in price. Normal goods have a negatively sloped demand curve. For normal goods, income and substitution effects reinforce one another. However, for inferior goods, the income effect offsets part or all of the substitution effect. In the case of the Giffen good, the income effect of this very inferior good overwhelms the substitution effect, resulting in a positively sloped demand curve.

■ In accepted microeconomic consumer theory, the consumer is assumed to be able to judge the value of any given bundle of goods without knowing anything about their prices. Then, constrained by income and prices, the consumer is assumed to be able to choose the optimal bundle of goods that is in the set of available options. It is possible to conceive of a situation in which the consumer cannot truly value a good until the price is known. In these Veblen goods, the price is used by the consumer to signal the consumer's status in society. Thus, to some extent, the higher the price of the good, the more value it offers to the consumer. In the extreme case, this could possibly result in a positively sloped demand curve. This result is similar to a Giffen good, but the two goods are fundamentally different.

PRACTICE PROBLEMS

1 A child indicates that she prefers going to the zoo over the park and prefers going to the beach over the zoo. When given the choice between the park and the beach, she chooses the park. Which of the following assumptions of consumer preference theory is she *most likely* violating?

   A Non-satiation.

   B Complete preferences.

   C Transitive preferences.

2 Which of the following ranking systems *best* describes consumer preferences within a utility function?

   A Util.

   B Ordinal.

   C Cardinal.

3 Which of the following statements *best* explains why indifference curves are generally convex as viewed from the origin?

   A The assumption of non-satiation results in convex indifference curves.

   B The marginal rate of substitution of one good for another remains constant along an indifference curve.

   C The marginal utility gained from one additional unit of a good versus another diminishes the more one has of the first good.

4 If a consumer's marginal rate of substitution of good X for good Y (MRS_{XY}) is equal to 2, then the:

   A consumer is willing to give up 2 units of X for 1 unit of Y.

   B slope of a line tangent to the indifference curve at that point is 2.

   C slope of a line tangent to the indifference curve at that point is −2.

5 In the case of two goods, x and y, which of the following statements is *most likely* true? Maximum utility is achieved:

   A along the highest indifference curve below the budget constraint line.

   B at the tangency between the highest attainable indifference curve and the budget constraint line.

   C when the marginal rate of substitution is equal to the ratio of the price of good y to the price of good x.

6 In the case of a normal good with a decrease in own price, which of the following statements is *most likely* true?

   A Both the substitution and income effects lead to an increase in the quantity purchased.

   B The substitution effect leads to an increase in the quantity purchased, while the income effect has no impact.

   C The substitution effect leads to an increase in the quantity purchased, while the income effect leads to a decrease.

7 For a Giffen good, the:

   A demand curve is positively sloped.

   B substitution effect overwhelms the income effect.

    C income and substitution effects are in the same direction.

8 Which of the following statements *best* illustrates the difference between a Giffen good and a Veblen good?

    A The Giffen good alone is an inferior good.

    B The substitution effect for each is in opposite directions.

    C The Veblen good alone has a positively sloped demand curve.

SOLUTIONS

1   C is correct. If the child prefers the zoo over the park and the beach over the zoo, then she should prefer the beach over the park according to the axiom of transitive preferences.

2   B is correct. Utility functions only allow ordinal rankings of consumer preferences.

3   C is correct. The slope of the indifference curve at any point gives the marginal rate of substitution of one good for another. The curve is convex because the marginal value of one good versus another decreases the more one has of the first good.

4   C is correct. The marginal rate of substitution is equal to the negative of the slope of the tangent to the indifference curve at that point, or −2.

5   B is correct. Maximum utility is achieved where the highest attainable indifference curve intersects with just one point (the tangency) on the budget constraint line.

6   A is correct. In the case of normal goods, the income and substitution effects are reinforcing, leading to an increase in the amount purchased after a drop in price.

7   A is correct. The income effect overwhelms the substitution effect such that an increase in the price of the good results in greater demand for the good, resulting in a positively sloped demand curve.

8   A is correct. Veblen goods are not inferior goods, whereas Giffen goods are. An increase in income for consumers of a Veblen good leads to an increase in the quantity purchased at each price. The opposite is true for a Giffen good.

15

Demand and Supply Analysis: The Firm

by Gary L. Arbogast, CFA, and Richard V. Eastin, PhD

Gary L. Arbogast, CFA (USA). Richard V. Eastin, PhD, is at the University of Southern California (USA).

LEARNING OUTCOMES

Mastery	The candidate should be able to:
☐	**a.** calculate, interpret, and compare accounting profit, economic profit, normal profit, and economic rent;
☐	**b.** calculate and interpret and compare total, average, and marginal revenue;
☐	**c.** describe a firm's factors of production;
☐	**d.** calculate and interpret total, average, marginal, fixed, and variable costs;
☐	**e.** determine and describe breakeven and shutdown points of production;
☐	**f.** describe approaches to determining the profit-maximizing level of output;
☐	**g.** describe how economies of scale and diseconomies of scale affect costs;
☐	**h.** distinguish between short-run and long-run profit maximization;
☐	**i.** distinguish among decreasing-cost, constant-cost, and increasing-cost industries and describe the long-run supply of each;
☐	**j.** calculate and interpret total, marginal, and average product of labor;
☐	**k.** describe the phenomenon of diminishing marginal returns and calculate and interpret the profit-maximizing utilization level of an input;
☐	**l.** determine the optimal combination of resources that minimizes cost.

1   INTRODUCTION

In studying decision making by consumers and businesses, microeconomics gives rise to the theory of the consumer and theory of the firm as two branches of study.

The **theory of the consumer** is the study of consumption—the demand for goods and services—by utility-maximizing individuals. The **theory of the firm**, the subject of this reading, is the study of the supply of goods and services by profit-maximizing firms. Conceptually, profit is the difference between revenue and costs. Revenue is a function of selling price and quantity sold, which are determined by the demand and supply behavior in the markets into which the firm sells/provides its goods or services. Costs are a function of the demand and supply interactions in resource markets, such as markets for labor and for physical inputs. The main focus of this reading is the cost side of the profit equation for companies competing in market economies under perfect competition. A subsequent reading will examine the different types of markets into which a firm may sell its output.

The study of the profit-maximizing firm in a single time period is the essential starting point for the analysis of the economics of corporate decision making. Furthermore, with the attention given to earnings by market participants, the insights gained by this study should be practically relevant. Among the questions this reading will address are the following:

- How should profit be defined from the perspective of suppliers of capital to the firm?

- What is meant by factors of production?

- How are total, average, and marginal costs distinguished, and how is each related to the firm's profit?

- What roles do marginal quantities (selling prices and costs) play in optimization?

This reading is organized as follows: Section 2 discusses the types of profit measures, including what they have in common, how they differ, and their uses and definitions. Section 3 covers the revenue and cost inputs of the profit equation and the related topics of breakeven analysis, shutdown point of operation, market entry and exit, cost structures, and scale effects. In addition, the economic outcomes related to a firm's optimal supply behavior over the short run and long run are presented in this section. A summary and practice problems conclude the reading.

2   OBJECTIVES OF THE FIRM

This reading assumes that the objective of the firm is to maximize profit over the period ahead. Such analysis provides both tools (e.g., optimization) and concepts (e.g., productivity) that can be adapted to more-complex cases and also provides a set of results that may offer useful approximations in practice. The price at which a given quantity of a good can be bought or sold is assumed to be known with certainty (i.e., the theory of the firm under conditions of certainty). The main contrast of this type of analysis is to the theory of the firm under conditions of uncertainty, where prices, and therefore profit, are uncertain. Under market uncertainty, a range of possible profit outcomes is associated with the firm's decision to produce a given quantity of goods or services over a specific time period. Such complex theory typically makes simplifying assumptions. When managers of for-profit companies have been surveyed about the objectives of the companies they direct, researchers have often concluded that a) companies frequently have multiple objectives; b) objectives can often be classified as focused on profitability (e.g., maximizing profits, increasing market share) or on controlling risk (e.g., survival, stable earnings growth); and c) managers in different countries may have different emphases.

Finance experts frequently reconcile profitability and risk objectives by stating that the objective of the firm is, or should be, **shareholder wealth maximization** (i.e., to maximize the market value of shareholders' equity). This theory states that firms try, or should try, to increase the wealth of their owners (shareholders) and that market prices balance returns against risk. However, complex corporate objectives may exist in practice. Many analysts view profitability as the single most important measure of business performance. Without profit, the business eventually fails; with profit, the business can survive, compete, and prosper. The question is: What is profit? Economists, accountants, investors, financial analysts, and regulators view profit from different perspectives. The starting point for anyone who is doing profit analysis is to have a solid grasp of how various forms of profit are defined and how to interpret the profit based on these different definitions.

By defining profit in general terms as the difference between total revenue and total costs, profit maximization involves the following expression:

$$\Pi = TR - TC \tag{1}$$

where Π is profit, TR is total revenue, and TC is total costs. TC can be defined as accounting costs or economic costs, depending on the objectives and requirements of the analyst for evaluating profit. The characteristics of the product market, where the firm sells its output or services, and of the resource market, where the firm purchases resources, play an important role in the determination of profit. Key variables that determine TC are the level of output, the firm's efficiency in producing that level of output when utilizing inputs, and resource prices as established by resource markets. TR is a function of output and product price as determined by the firm's product market.

2.1 Types of Profit Measures

The economics discipline has its own concept of profit, which differs substantially from what accountants consider profit. There are thus two basic types of profit—accounting and economic—and analysts need to be able to interpret each correctly and to understand how they are related to each other. In the theory of the firm, however, *profit* without further qualification refers to *economic profit*.

2.1.1 *Accounting Profit*

Accounting profit is generally defined as net income reported on the income statement according to standards established by private and public financial oversight bodies that determine the rules for financial reporting. One widely accepted definition of accounting profit—also known as net profit, net income, or net earnings—states that it equals revenue less all **accounting (or explicit) costs**. Accounting or explicit costs are payments to non-owner parties for services or resources that they supply to the firm. Often referred to as the "bottom line" (the last income figure in the income statement), accounting profit is what is left after paying all accounting costs—whether the expense is a cash outlay or not. When accounting profit is negative, it is called an **accounting loss**. Equation 2 summarizes the concept of accounting profit:

$$\text{Accounting profit} = \text{Total revenue} - \text{Total accounting costs} \tag{2}$$

When defining profit as accounting profit, the TC term in Equation 1 becomes total accounting costs, which include only the explicit costs of doing business. Let us consider two businesses: a start-up company and a publicly traded corporation. Suppose that for the start-up, total revenue in the business's first year is €3,500,000 and total accounting costs are €3,200,000. Accounting profit is €3,500,000 − €3,200,000 = €300,000. The corresponding calculation for the publicly traded corporation, let us suppose, is $50,000,000 − $48,000,000 = $2,000,000. Note that total accounting costs in either case include interest expense—which represents the return required by suppliers of debt capital—because interest expense is an explicit cost.

2.1.2 Economic Profit and Normal Profit

Economic profit (also known as **abnormal profit** or **supernormal profit**) may be defined broadly as accounting profit less the implicit opportunity costs not included in total accounting costs.

$$\text{Economic profit} = \text{Accounting profit} - \text{Total implicit opportunity costs} \quad \textbf{(3a)}$$

We can define a term, **economic cost**, equal to the sum of total accounting costs and implicit opportunity costs. Economic profit is therefore equivalently defined as:

$$\text{Economic profit} = \text{Total revenue} - \text{Total economic costs} \quad \textbf{(3b)}$$

For publicly traded corporations, the focus of investment analysts' work, the cost of equity capital is the largest and most readily identified implicit opportunity cost omitted in calculating total accounting cost. Consequently, economic profit can be defined for publicly traded corporations as accounting profit less the required return on equity capital.

Examples will make these concepts clearer. Consider the start-up company for which we calculated an accounting profit of €300,000 and suppose that the entrepreneurial executive who launched the start-up took a salary reduction of €100,000 per year relative to the job he left. That €100,000 is an opportunity cost of involving him in running the start-up. Besides labor, financial capital is a resource. Suppose that the executive, as sole owner, makes an investment of €1,500,000 to launch the enterprise and that he might otherwise expect to earn €200,000 per year on that amount in a similar risk investment. Total implicit opportunity costs are €100,000 + €200,000 = €300,000 per year and economic profit is zero: €300,000 − €300,000 = €0. For the publicly traded corporation, we consider the cost of equity capital as the only implicit opportunity cost identifiable. Suppose that equity investment is $18,750,000 and shareholders' required rate of return is 8 percent so that the dollar cost of equity capital is $1,500,000. Economic profit for the publicly traded corporation is therefore $2,000,000 (accounting profit) less $1,500,000 (cost of equity capital) or $500,000.

For the start-up company, economic profit was zero. Total economic costs were just covered by revenues and the company was not earning a euro more nor less than the amount that meets the opportunity costs of the resources used in the business. Economists would say the company was earning a normal profit (economic profit of zero). In simple terms, **normal profit** is the level of accounting profit needed to just cover the implicit opportunity costs ignored in accounting costs. For the publicly traded corporation, normal profit was $1,500,000: normal profit can be taken to be the cost of equity capital (in money terms) for such a company or the dollar return required on an equal investment by equity holders in an equivalently risky alternative investment opportunity. The publicly traded corporation actually earned $500,000 in excess of normal profit, which should be reflected in the common shares' market price.

Thus, the following expression links accounting profit to economic profit and normal profit:

$$\text{Accounting profit} = \text{Economic profit} + \text{Normal profit} \quad \textbf{(4)}$$

When accounting profit equals normal profit, economic profit is zero. Further, when accounting profit is greater than normal profit, economic profit is positive; and when accounting profit is less than normal profit, economic profit is negative (the firm has an **economic loss**).

Economic profit for a firm can originate from sources such as:

- competitive advantage;
- exceptional managerial efficiency or skill;
- difficult to copy technology or innovation (e.g., patents, trademarks, and copyrights);
- exclusive access to less-expensive inputs;
- fixed supply of an output, commodity, or resource;
- preferential treatment under governmental policy;
- large increases in demand where supply is unable to respond fully over time;
- exertion of monopoly power (price control) in the market; and
- market barriers to entry that limit competition.

Any of the above factors may lead the firm to have positive net present value investment (NPV) opportunities. Access to positive NPV opportunities and therefore profit in excess of normal profits in the short run may or may not exist in the long run, depending on the potential strength of competition. In highly competitive market situations, firms tend to earn the normal profit level over time because ease of market entry allows for other competing firms to compete away any economic profit over the long run. Economic profit that exists over the long run is usually found where competitive conditions persistently are less than perfect in the market.

2.1.3 *Economic Rent*

The surplus value known as **economic rent** results when a particular resource or good is fixed in supply (with a vertical supply curve) and market price is higher than what is required to bring the resource or good onto the market and sustain its use. Essentially, demand determines the price level and the magnitude of economic rent that is forthcoming from the market. Exhibit 1 illustrates this concept, where P_1 is the price level that yields a normal profit return to the business that supplies the item. When demand increases from Demand$_1$ to Demand$_2$, price rises to P_2, where at this higher price level economic rent is created. The amount of this economic rent is calculated as $(P_2 - P_1) \times Q_1$. The firm has not done anything internally to merit this special reward: It benefits from an increase in demand in conjunction with a supply curve that does not fully adjust with an increase in quantity when price rises.

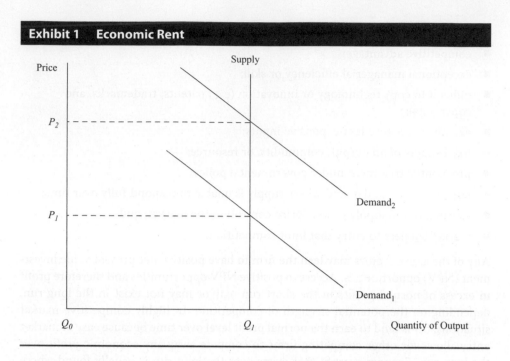

Exhibit 1   Economic Rent

Because of their limited availability in nature, certain resources—such as land and specialty commodities—possess highly **inelastic supply** curves in both the short run and long run (shown in Exhibit 1 as a vertical supply curve). When supply is relatively inelastic, a high degree of market demand can result in pricing that creates economic rent. This economic rent results from the fact that when price increases, the quantity supplied does not change or, at the most, increases only slightly. This is because of the fixation of supply by nature or by such artificial constraints as government policy.

How is the concept of economic rent useful in financial analysis? Commodities or resources that command economic rent have the potential to reward equity investors more than what is required to attract their capital to that activity, resulting in greater shareholders' wealth. Evidence of economic rent attracts additional capital funds to the economic endeavor. This new investment capital increases shareholders' value as investors bid up share prices of existing firms. Any commodity, resource, or good that is fixed or nearly fixed in supply has the potential to yield economic rent. From an analytical perspective, one can obtain industry supply data to calculate the **elasticity of supply**, which measures the sensitivity of quantity supplied to a change in price. If quantity supplied is relatively unresponsive (**inelastic**) to price changes, then a potential condition exists in the market for economic rent. A reliable forecast of changes in demand can indicate the degree of any economic rent that is forthcoming from the market in the future. When one is analyzing fixed or nearly fixed supply markets (e.g., gold), a fundamental comprehension of demand determinants is necessary to make rational financial decisions based on potential economic rent.

EXAMPLE 1

Economic Rent and Investment Decision Making

The following market data show the global demand, global supply, and price on an annual basis for gold over the period 2006–2008. Based on the data, what observation can be made about market demand, supply, and economic rent?

Year	2006	2007	2008	Percent Change 2006–2008
Supply (in metric tons)	3,569	3,475	3,508	−1.7
Demand (in metric tons)	3,423	3,552	3,805	+11.2
Average spot price (in US$)	603.92	695.39	871.65	+44.3

Source: GFMS and World Gold Council.

Solution:

The amount of total gold supplied to the world market over this period has actually declined slightly by 1.7 percent during a period when there was a double-digit increase of 11.2 percent in demand. As a consequence, the spot price has dramatically increased by 44.3 percent. Economic rent has resulted from this market relationship of a relatively fixed supply of gold and a rising demand for it.

2.2 Comparison of Profit Measures

All three types of profit are interconnected because, according to Equation 4, accounting profit is the summation of normal and economic profit. In the short run, the normal profit rate is relatively stable, which makes accounting and economic profit the two variable terms in the profit equation. Over the longer term, all three types of profit are variable, where the normal profit rate can change according to investment returns across firms in the industry.

Normal profit is necessary to stay in business in the long run; positive economic profit is not. A business can survive indefinitely by just making the normal profit return for investors. Failing to earn normal profits over the long run has a debilitating impact on the firm's ability to access capital and to function properly as a business enterprise. Consequently, the market value of equity and shareholders' wealth deteriorates whenever risk to achieving normal profit materializes and the firm fails to reward investors for their risk exposure and for the opportunity cost of their equity capital.

To summarize, the ultimate goal of analyzing the different types of profit is to determine how their relationships to one another influence the firm's market value of equity. Exhibit 2 compares accounting, normal, and economic profits in terms of how a firm's market value of equity is impacted by the relationships among the three types of profit.

Exhibit 2	Relationship of Accounting, Normal, and Economic Profit to Equity Value	
Relationship between Accounting Profit and Normal Profit	**Economic Profit**	**Firm's Market Value of Equity**
Accounting profit > Normal profit	Economic profit > 0 and firm is able to protect economic profit over the long run	Positive effect
Accounting profit = Normal profit	Economic profit = 0	No effect
Accounting profit < Normal profit	Economic profit < 0 implies economic loss	Negative effect

3　ANALYSIS OF REVENUE, COSTS, AND PROFITS

To fully comprehend the dimensions of profit maximization, one must have a detailed understanding of the revenue and cost variables that determine profit.

Revenue and cost flows are calculated in terms of total, average, and marginal. A total is the summation of all individual components. For example, total cost is the summation of all costs that are incurred by the business. Total revenue is the sum of the revenues from all the business's units. In the theory of the firm, averages and marginals are calculated with respect to the quantity produced and sold in a single period (as opposed to averaging a quantity over a number of time periods). For example, average revenue is calculated by dividing total revenue by the number of items sold. To calculate a marginal term, take the change in the total and divide by the change in the quantity number.

Exhibit 3 shows a summary of the terminology and formulas pertaining to profit maximization, where profit is defined as total revenue minus total economic costs. Note that the definition of profit is the economic version, which recognizes that the implicit opportunity costs of equity capital, in addition to explicit accounting costs, are economic costs. The first main category consists of terms pertaining to the revenue side of the profit equation: total revenue, average revenue, and marginal revenue. Cost terms follow with an overview of the different types of costs—total, average, and marginal.

Exhibit 3　Summary of Profit, Revenue, and Cost Terms

Term	Calculation
Profit	
(Economic) profit	Total revenue minus total economic cost; $(TR - TC)$
Revenue	
Total revenue (TR)	Price times quantity $(P \times Q)$, or the sum of individual units sold times their respective prices; $\Sigma(P_i \times Q_i)$
Average revenue (AR)	Total revenue divided by quantity; $(TR \div Q)$
Marginal revenue (MR)	Change in total revenue divided by change in quantity; $(\Delta TR \div \Delta Q)$
Costs	
Total fixed cost (TFC)	Sum of all fixed expenses; here defined to include all opportunity costs
Total variable cost (TVC)	Sum of all variable expenses, or per unit variable cost times quantity; (per unit $VC \times Q$)
Total costs (TC)	Total fixed cost plus total variable cost; $(TFC + TVC)$
Average fixed cost (AFC)	Total fixed cost divided by quantity; $(TFC \div Q)$
Average variable cost (AVC)	Total variable cost divided by quantity; $(TVC \div Q)$
Average total cost (ATC)	Total cost divided by quantity; $(TC \div Q)$ or $(AFC + AVC)$
Marginal cost (MC)	Change in total cost divided by change in quantity; $(\Delta TC \div \Delta Q)$

3.1　Profit Maximization

In free markets—and even in regulated market economies—profit maximization tends to promote economic welfare and a higher standard of living, and creates wealth for investors. Profit motivates businesses to use resources efficiently and to concentrate on activities in which they have a competitive advantage. Most economists believe that profit maximization promotes allocational efficiency—that resources flow into their highest valued uses.

Overall, the functions of profit are as follows:

- Rewards entrepreneurs for risk taking when pursuing business ventures to satisfy consumer demand.

- Allocates resources to their most-efficient use; input factors flow from sectors with economic losses to sectors with economic profit, where profit reflects goods most desired by society.

- Spurs innovation and the development of new technology.

- Stimulates business investment and economic growth.

There are three approaches to calculate the point of profit maximization. First, given that profit is the difference between total revenue and total costs, maximum profit occurs at the output level where this difference is the greatest. Second, maximum profit can also be calculated by comparing revenue and cost for each individual unit of output that is produced and sold. A business increases profit through greater sales as long as per-unit revenue exceeds per-unit cost on the next unit of output sold. Profit maximization takes place at the point where the last individual output unit breaks even. Beyond this point, total profit decreases because the per-unit cost is higher than the per-unit revenue from successive output units. A third approach compares the revenue generated by each resource unit with the cost of that unit. Profit contribution occurs when the revenue from an input unit exceeds its cost. The point of profit maximization is reached when resource units no longer contribute to profit. All three approaches yield the same profit-maximizing quantity of output. (These approaches will be explained in greater detail later.)

Because profit is the difference between revenue and cost, an understanding of profit maximization requires that we examine both of those components. Revenue comes from the demand for the firm's products, and cost comes from the acquisition and utilization of the firm's inputs in the production of those products.

3.1.1 *Total, Average, and Marginal Revenue*

This section briefly examines demand and revenue in preparation for addressing cost. Unless the firm is a pure **monopolist** (i.e., the only seller in its market), there is a difference between market demand and the demand facing an individual firm. A later reading will devote much more time to understanding the various competitive environments (perfect competition, monopolistic competition, oligopoly, and monopoly), known as **market structure**. To keep the analysis simple at this point, we will note that competition could be either perfect or imperfect. In **perfect competition**, the individual firm has virtually no impact on market price, because it is assumed to be a very small seller among a very large number of firms selling essentially identical products. Such a firm is called a **price taker**. In the second case, the firm does have at least some control over the price at which it sells its product because it must lower its price to sell more units. This relationship is shown in Exhibit 5.

Exhibit 4 presents total, average, and marginal revenue data for a firm under the assumption that the firm is price taker at each relevant level of quantity of goods sold. Consequently, the individual seller faces a horizontal demand curve over relevant output ranges at the price level established by the market (see Exhibit 5). The seller can offer any quantity at this set market price without affecting price. In contrast, **imperfect competition** is where an individual firm has enough share of the market (or can control a certain segment of the market) and is therefore able to exert some influence over price. Instead of a large number of competing firms, imperfect competition involves a smaller number of firms in the market relative to perfect competition and in the extreme case only one firm (i.e., monopoly). Under any form of imperfect competition, the individual seller confronts a negatively sloped demand curve, where price and the quantity demanded by consumers are inversely related. In this case, price to the firm declines when a greater quantity is offered to the market; price to the firm increases when a lower quantity is offered to the market. This is shown in Exhibits 6 and 7.

Exhibit 4	Total, Average, and Marginal Revenue under Perfect Competition			
Quantity Sold (Q)	Price (P)	Total Revenue (TR)	Average Revenue (AR)	Marginal Revenue (MR)
0	100	0	—	—
1	100	100	100	100
2	100	200	100	100
3	100	300	100	100
4	100	400	100	100
5	100	500	100	100
6	100	600	100	100
7	100	700	100	100
8	100	800	100	100
9	100	900	100	100
10	100	1,000	100	100

The **quantity** or **quantity demanded** variable is the amount of the product that consumers are willing and able to buy at each price level. The quantity sold can be affected by the business through such activities as sales promotion, advertising, and competitive positioning of the product that would take place under the market model of imperfect competition. Under perfect competition, however, total quantity in the market is influenced strictly by price, while non-price factors are not important. Once consumer preferences are established in the market, price determines the quantity demanded by buyers. Together, price and quantity constitute the firm's demand curve, which becomes the basis for calculating the total, average, and marginal revenue.

In Exhibit 4, **price** is the market price as established by the interactions of the market demand and supply factors. Since the firm is a price taker, price is fixed at 100 at all levels of output.

Total revenue (TR) is tabulated as price times the quantity of units sold. At 1 unit TR is 100 (calculated as 100×1 unit); at 10 units it is 1,000 (calculated as 100×10 units). At zero quantity, obviously, total revenue is always zero. Under perfect competition, for each increment in quantity, total revenue increases by the price level, which is constant to the firm. This relationship is shown in Exhibit 4—where the increase in total revenue from one quantity to the next equals 100, which is equal to the price.

Average revenue (AR) is quantity sold divided into total revenue. The mathematical outcome of this calculation is simply the price that the firm receives in the market for selling a given quantity. For any firm that sells at a uniform price, average revenue will equal price. For example, AR at 3 units is 100 (calculated as $300 \div 3$ units); at 8 units it is also 100 (calculated as $800 \div 8$ units).

Marginal revenue (MR) is the change in total revenue divided by the change in quantity sold; it is simply the additional revenue from selling one more unit. For example, in Exhibit 4, MR at 4 units is 100 [calculated as $(400 - 300) \div (4 - 3)$]; at

9 units it is also 100 [calculated as $(900 - 800) \div (9 - 8)$]. In a competitive market in which price is constant to the individual firm regardless of the amount of output offered, marginal revenue is equal to average revenue, where both are the same as the market price. Reviewing the revenue data in Exhibit 4, price, average revenue, and marginal revenue are all equal to 100. In the case of imperfect competition, MR declines with greater output and is less than AR at any positive quantity level, as will become clear with Exhibit 7.

Exhibit 5 graphically displays the revenue data from Exhibit 4. For an individual firm operating in a market setting of perfect competition, MR equals AR and both are equal to a price that stays the same across all levels of output. Because price is fixed to the individual seller, the firm's demand curve is a horizontal line at the point where the market sets the price. In Exhibit 5, at a price of 100, $P_1 = MR_1 = AR_1 =$ Demand$_1$. Marginal revenue, average revenue, and the firm's price remain constant until market demand and supply factors cause a change in price. For instance, if price increases to 200 because of an increase in market demand, the firm's demand curve shifts from Demand$_1$ to Demand$_2$ with corresponding increases in MR and AR as well. Total revenue increases from TR_1 to TR_2 when price increases from 100 to 200. At a price of 100, total revenue at 10 units is 1,000; however, at a price of 200, total revenue would be 2,000 for 10 units.

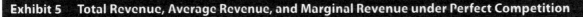

Exhibit 5   Total Revenue, Average Revenue, and Marginal Revenue under Perfect Competition

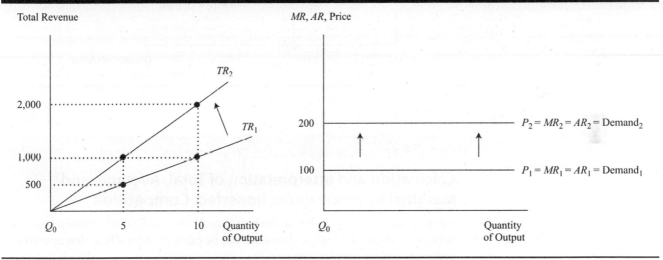

Exhibit 6 graphically illustrates the general shapes and relationships for TR, AR, and MR under imperfect competition. MR is positioned below the price and AR lines. TR peaks when MR equals zero at point Q_1.

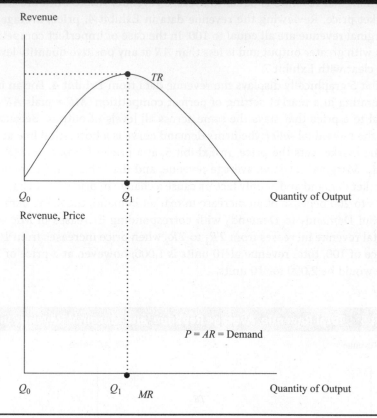

Exhibit 6   Total Revenue, Average Revenue, and Marginal Revenue under Imperfect Competition

---

EXAMPLE 2

Calculation and Interpretation of Total, Average, and Marginal Revenue under Imperfect Competition

Given quantity and price data in the first two columns of Exhibit 7, total revenue, average revenue, and marginal revenue can be calculated for a firm that operates under imperfect competition.

Exhibit 7

Quantity (Q)	Price (P)	Total Revenue (TR)	Average Revenue (AR)	Marginal Revenue (MR)
0	100	0	—	—
1	99	99	99	99
2	98	196	98	97
3	97	291	97	95
4	96	384	96	93
5	95	475	95	91
6	94	564	94	89
7	93	651	93	87
8	92	736	92	85

Exhibit 7   (Continued)

Quantity (Q)	Price (P)	Total Revenue (TR)	Average Revenue (AR)	Marginal Revenue (MR)
9	91	819	91	83
10	90	900	90	81

Describe how total revenue, average revenue, and marginal revenue change as quantity sold increases from 0 to 10 units.

Solution:

Total revenue increases with a greater quantity, but the rate of increase in TR (as measured by marginal revenue) declines as quantity increases. Average revenue and marginal revenue decrease when output increases, with MR falling faster than price and AR. Average revenue is equal to price at each quantity level. Exhibit 8 shows the relationships among the revenue variables presented in Exhibit 7.

Exhibit 8   Total Revenue, Average Revenue, and Marginal Revenue for Exhibit 7 Data

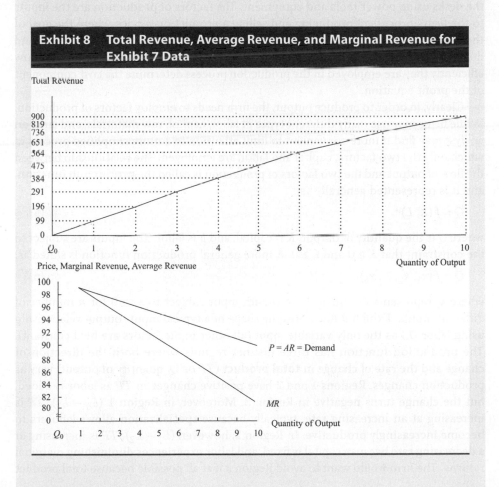

3.1.2 *Factors of Production*

Revenue generation occurs when output is sold in the market. However, costs are incurred before revenue generation takes place as the firm purchases resources, or what are commonly known as the factors of production, in order to produce a product or service that will be offered for sale to consumers. Factors of production, the inputs to the production of goods and services, include:

- *land*, as in the site location of the business;
- *labor*, which consists of the inputs of skilled and unskilled workers as well as the inputs of firms' managers;
- *capital*, which in this context refers to *physical capital*—such tangible goods as equipment, tools, and buildings. Capital goods are distinguished as inputs to production that are themselves produced goods; and
- *materials*, which in this context refers to any goods the business buys as inputs to its production process.[1]

For example, a business that produces solid wood office desks needs to acquire lumber and hardware accessories as raw materials and hire workers to construct and assemble the desks using power tools and equipment. The factors of production are the inputs to the firm's process of producing and selling a product or service where the goal of the firm is to maximize profit by satisfying the demand of consumers. The types and quantities of resources or factors used in production, their respective prices, and how efficiently they are employed in the production process determine the cost component of the profit equation.

Clearly, in order to produce output, the firm needs to employ factors of production. While firms may use many different types of labor, capital, raw materials, and land, an analyst may find it more convenient to limit attention to a more simplified process in which only the two factors, capital and labor, are employed. The relationship between the flow of output and the two factors of production is called the **production function**, and it is represented generally as:

$$Q = f(K, L) \tag{5}$$

where Q is the quantity of output, K is capital, and L is labor. The inputs are subject to the constraint that $K \geq 0$ and $L \geq 0$. A more general production function is stated as:

$$Q = f(x_1, x_2, \dots x_n) \tag{6}$$

where x_i represents the quantity of the ith input subject to $x_i \geq 0$ for n number of different inputs. Exhibit 9 illustrates the shape of a typical input–output relationship using labor (L) as the only variable input (all other input factors are held constant). The production function has three distinct regions where both the direction of change and the rate of change in **total product** (*TP* or Q, quantity of output) vary as production changes. Regions 1 and 2 have positive changes in *TP* as labor is added, but the change turns negative in Region 3. Moreover, in Region 1 ($L_0 - L_1$), *TP* is increasing at an increasing rate, typically because specialization allows laborers to become increasingly productive. In Region 2, however, ($L_1 - L_2$), *TP* is increasing at a decreasing rate because capital is fixed, and labor experiences diminishing marginal returns. The firm would want to avoid Region 3 if at all possible because total product

---

1 Because this factor may include such processed materials as steel and plastic that the firm purchases as inputs to production, the name *materials* was chosen in preference to another, traditional, name for this factor, *raw materials*. Candidates may encounter a number of variations in the classification and terminology for the factors of production.

or quantity would be declining rather than increasing with additional input: There is so little capital per unit of labor that additional laborers would possibly "get in each other's way". Point A is where TP is maximized.

Exhibit 9   A Firm's Production Function

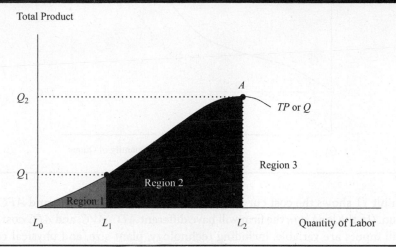

EXAMPLE 3

Factors of Production

A group of business investors are in the process of forming a new enterprise that will manufacture shipping containers to be used in international trade.

1   What decisions about factors of production must the start-up firm make in beginning operations?

2   What objective should guide the firm in its purchase and use of the production factors?

Solution to 1:

The entrepreneurs must decide where to locate the manufacturing facility in terms of an accessible site (land) and building (physical capital), what to use in the construction of the containers (materials), and what labor input to use.

Solution to 2:

Overall, any decision involving the input factors should focus on how that decision affects costs, profitability, and risk—such that shareholders' wealth is maximized.

3.1.3 Total, Average, Marginal, Fixed, and Variable Costs

Exhibit 10 shows the graphical relationships among total costs, total fixed cost, and total variable cost. The curve for total costs is a parallel shift of the total variable cost curve and always lies above the total variable cost curve by the amount of total fixed cost. At zero production, total costs are equal to total fixed cost because total variable cost at this output level is zero.

Exhibit 10   Total Costs, Total Variable Cost, and Total Fixed Cost

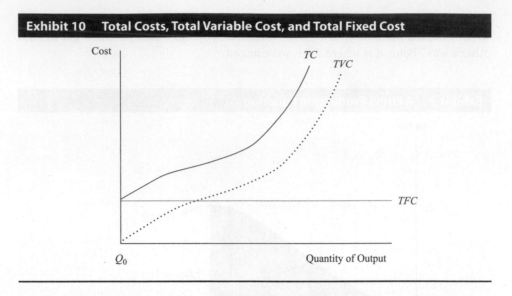

Exhibit 11 shows the cost curve relationships among *ATC*, *AVC*, and *AFC* in the short run. (In the long run, the firm will have different *ATC*, *AVC*, and *AFC* cost curves when all inputs are variable, including technology, plant size, and physical capital.) The difference between *ATC* and *AVC* at any output quantity is the amount of *AFC*. For example, at Q_1 the distance between *ATC* and *AVC* is measured by the value of *A*, which equals the amount of fixed cost as measured by amount *B* at Q_1. Similarly, at Q_2, the distance between *ATC* and *AVC* of *X* equals amount *Y* of *AFC*. The vertical distance between *ATC* and *AVC* is exactly equal to the height of *AFC* at each quantity. Both average total cost and average variable cost take on a bowl-shaped pattern in which each curve initially declines, reaches a minimum-cost output level, and then increases after that point. Point *S*, which corresponds to Q_{AVC}, is the minimum point on the *AVC* (such as 2 units in Exhibit 13). Similarly, point *T*, which corresponds to Q_{ATC}, is the minimum point on *ATC* (such as 3 units in Exhibit 13). As shown in Exhibit 11, when output increases, average fixed cost declines as *AFC* approaches the horizontal quantity axis.

Exhibit 11   Average Total Cost, Average Variable Cost, and Average Fixed Cost

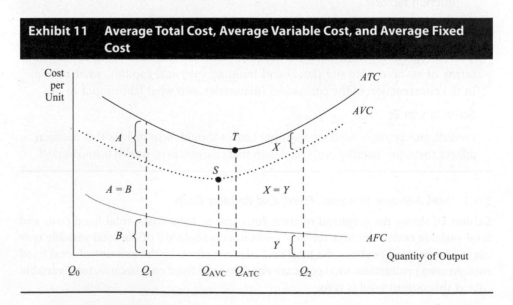

Exhibit 12 displays the cost curve relationships for *ATC*, *AVC*, and *MC* in the short run. The marginal cost curve intersects both the *ATC* and *AVC* at their respective minimum points. This occurs at points *S* and *T*, which correspond to Q_{AVC} and Q_{ATC}, respectively. Mathematically, when marginal cost is less than average variable cost, *AVC* will be decreasing. The opposite occurs when *MC* is greater than *AVC*. For example, in Exhibit 13, *AVC* begins to increase beyond 2 units, where *MC* exceeds *AVC*. The same relationship holds true for *MC* and *ATC*. Referring again to Exhibit 13, *ATC* declines up to 3 units when *MC* is less than *ATC*. After 3 units, *ATC* increases as *MC* exceeds *ATC*. Initially, the marginal cost curve declines, but at some point it begins to increase in reflection of an increasing rate of change in total costs as the firm produces more output. Point *R* (Exhibit 12), which corresponds to Q_{MC}, is the minimum point on the marginal cost curve.

Exhibit 12   Average Total Cost, Average Variable Cost, and Marginal Cost

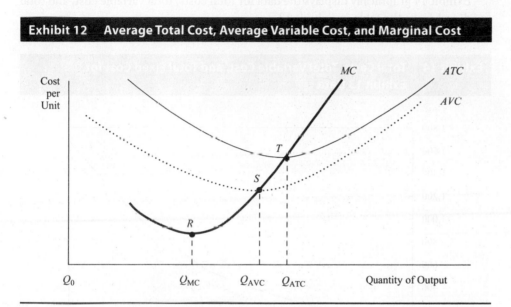

Exhibit 13 shows an example of how total, average, and marginal costs are derived. Total costs are calculated by summing total fixed cost and total variable cost. Marginal cost is derived by taking the change in total costs as the quantity variable changes.

Exhibit 13   Total, Average, Marginal, Fixed, and Variable Costs

Quantity (Q)	Total Fixed Cost[a] (TFC)	Average Fixed Cost (AFC)	Total Variable Cost (TVC)	Average Variable Cost (AVC)	Total Costs (TC)	Average Total Cost (ATC)	Marginal Cost (MC)
0	100	—	0	—	100	—	—
1	100	100.0	50	50.0	150	150.0	50
2	100	50.0	75	37.5	175	87.5	25
3	100	33.3	125	41.7	225	75.0	50
4	100	25.0	210	52.5	310	77.5	85
5	100	20.0	300	60.0	400	80.0	90
6	100	16.7	450	75.0	550	91.7	150
7	100	14.3	650	92.9	750	107.1	200
8	100	12.5	900	112.5	1,000	125.0	250

(continued)

Exhibit 13   (Continued)

Quantity (Q)	Total Fixed Cost[a] (TFC)	Average Fixed Cost (AFC)	Total Variable Cost (TVC)	Average Variable Cost (AVC)	Total Costs (TC)	Average Total Cost (ATC)	Marginal Cost (MC)
9	100	11.1	1,200	133.3	1,300	144.4	300
10	100	10.0	1,550	155.0	1,650	165.0	350

[a] Includes all opportunity costs.

Exhibit 14 graphically displays the data for total costs, total variable cost, and total fixed cost from the table in Exhibit 13.

Exhibit 14   Total Costs, Total Variable Cost, and Total Fixed Cost for Exhibit 13 Data

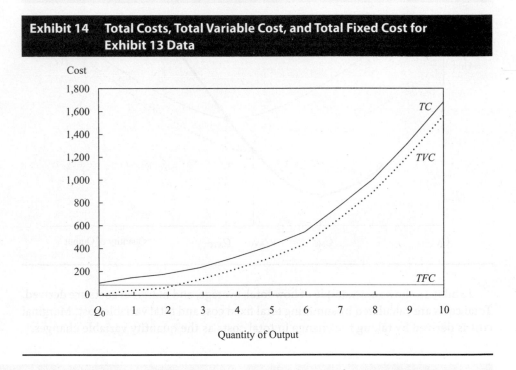

Total costs (*TC*) are the summation of all costs, where costs are classified according to fixed or variable. Total costs increase as the firm expands output and decrease when production is cut. The rate of increase in total costs declines up to a certain output level and, thereafter, accelerates as the firm gets closer to full utilization of capacity. The rate of change in total costs mirrors the rate of change in total variable cost. In Exhibit 13, *TC* at 5 units is 400—of which 300 is variable cost and 100 is fixed cost. At 10 units, total costs are 1,650, which is the sum of 1,550 in variable cost and 100 in fixed cost.

Total fixed cost (*TFC*) is the summation of all expenses that do not change when production varies. It can be a sunk or unavoidable cost that a firm has to cover whether it produces anything or not, or it can be a cost that stays the same over a range of production but can change to another constant level when production moves outside of that range. The latter is referred to as a **quasi-fixed cost**, although it remains categorized as part of *TFC*. Examples of fixed costs are debt service, real estate lease agreements, and rental contracts. Quasi-fixed cost examples would be certain utilities and administrative salaries that could be avoided or be lower when output is zero but would assume higher constant values over different production ranges. Normal profit is considered to be a fixed cost because it is a return required by investors on their equity capital regardless of output level. At zero output, total costs are always equal to the amount of total fixed cost that is incurred at this production point. In Exhibit 13, total fixed cost remains at 100 throughout the entire production range.

Other fixed costs evolve primarily from investments in such fixed assets as real estate, production facilities, and equipment. As a firm grows in size, fixed asset expansion occurs along with a related increase in fixed cost. However, fixed cost cannot be arbitrarily cut when production declines. Regardless of the volume of output, an investment in a given level of fixed assets locks the firm into a certain amount of fixed cost that is used to finance the physical capital base, technology, and other capital assets. When a firm downsizes, the last expense to be cut is usually fixed cost.

Total variable cost (TVC), which is the summation of all variable expenses, has a direct relationship with quantity. When quantity increases, total variable cost increases; total variable cost declines when quantity decreases. At zero production, total variable cost is always zero. Variable cost examples are payments for labor, raw materials, and supplies. As indicated above, total costs mirror total variable cost, with the difference being a constant fixed cost. The change in total variable cost (which defines marginal cost) declines up to a certain output point and then increases as production approaches capacity limits. In Exhibit 13, total variable cost increases with an increase in quantity. However, the change from 1 to 2 units is 25, calculated as $(75 - 50)$; the change from 9 to 10 units is 350, calculated as $(1,550 - 1,200)$.

Another approach to calculating total variable cost is to determine the variable cost per unit of output and multiply this cost figure by the number of production units. Per unit variable cost is the cost of producing each unit exclusive of any fixed cost allocation to production units. One can assign variable cost individually to units or derive an average variable cost per unit.

Whenever a firm initiates a downsizing, retrenchment, or defensive strategy, variable cost is the first to be considered for reduction given its variability with output. However, variable cost is reducible only so far because all firms have to maintain a minimum amount of labor and other variable resources to function effectively.

Exhibit 15 illustrates the relationships among marginal cost, average total cost, average variable cost, and average fixed cost for the data presented in Exhibit 13.

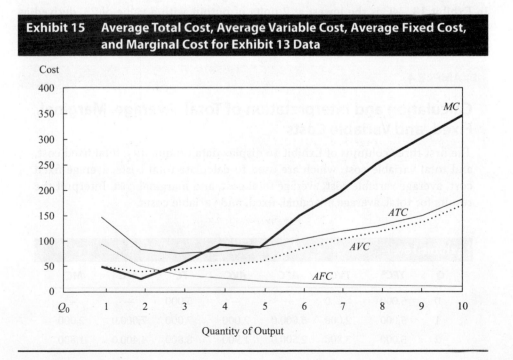

Exhibit 15   Average Total Cost, Average Variable Cost, Average Fixed Cost, and Marginal Cost for Exhibit 13 Data

Dividing total fixed cost by quantity yields **average fixed cost** (*AFC*), which decreases throughout the production span. A declining average fixed cost reflects spreading a constant cost over more and more production units. At high production volumes, *AFC* may be so low that it is a small proportion of average total cost. In Exhibit 13, *AFC* declines from 100 at 1 unit, to 20 at 5 units, and then to 10 at an output level of 10 units.

Average variable cost (*AVC*) is derived by dividing total variable cost by quantity. For example, average variable cost at 5 units is (300 ÷ 5) or 60. Over an initial range of production, average variable cost declines and then reaches a minimum point. Thereafter, cost increases as the firm utilizes more of its production capacity. This higher cost results primarily from production constraints imposed by the fixed assets at higher volume levels. The minimum point on the *AVC* coincides with the lowest average variable cost. However, the minimum point on the *AVC* does not correspond to the least-cost quantity for average total cost. In Exhibit 13, average variable cost is minimized at 2 units, whereas average total cost is the lowest at 3 units.

Average total cost (*ATC*) is calculated by dividing total costs by quantity or by summing average fixed cost and average variable cost. For instance, in Exhibit 13, at 8 units *ATC* is 125 [calculated as (1,000 ÷ 8) or (*AFC* + *AVC* = 12.5 + 112.5)]. Average total cost is often referenced as per-unit cost and is frequently called average cost. The minimum point on the average total cost curve defines the output level that has the least cost. The cost-minimizing behavior of the firm would dictate operating at the minimum point on its *ATC* curve. However, the quantity that maximizes profit (such as Q_3 in Exhibit 17) may not correspond to the ATC-minimum point. The minimum point on the *ATC* curve is consistent with maximizing profit per-unit, but it is not necessarily consistent with maximizing total profit. In Exhibit 13, the least-cost point of production is 3 units; *ATC* is 75, derived as [(225 ÷ 3) or (33.3 + 41.7)]. Any other production level results in a higher *ATC*.

Marginal cost (*MC*) is the change in total cost divided by the change in quantity. Marginal cost also can be calculated by taking the change in total variable cost and dividing by the change in quantity. It represents the cost of producing an additional unit. For example, at 9 units marginal cost is 300, calculated as [(1,300 − 1,000) ÷ (9 − 8)]. Marginal cost follows a J-shaped pattern whereby cost initially declines but turns higher at some point in reflection of rising costs at higher production volumes. In Exhibit 13, *MC* is the lowest at 2 units of output with a value of 25, derived as [(175 − 150) ÷ (2 − 1)].

EXAMPLE 4

Calculation and Interpretation of Total, Average, Marginal, Fixed, and Variable Costs

The first three columns of Exhibit 16 display data on quantity, total fixed cost, and total variable cost, which are used to calculate total costs, average fixed cost, average variable cost, average total cost, and marginal cost. Interpret the results for total, average, marginal, fixed, and variable costs.

Exhibit 16							
Q	*TFC*[a]	*TVC*	*AFC*	*AVC*	*TC*	*ATC*	*MC*
0	5,000	0	—	—	5,000	—	—
1	5,000	2,000	5,000.0	2,000	7,000	7,000.0	2,000
2	5,000	3,800	2,500.0	1,900	8,800	4,400.0	1,800

Exhibit 16   (Continued)

Q	TFCª	TVC	AFC	AVC	TC	ATC	MC
3	5,000	5,400	1,666.7	1,800	10,400	3,466.7	1,600
4	5,000	8,000	1,250.0	2,000	13,000	3,250.0	2,600
5	5,000	11,000	1,000.0	2,200	16,000	3,200.0	3,000
6	5,000	15,000	833.3	2,500	20,000	3,333.3	4,000
7	5,000	21,000	714.3	3,000	26,000	3,714.3	6,000
8	5,000	28,800	625.0	3,600	33,800	4,225.0	7,800
9	5,000	38,700	555.6	4,300	43,700	4,855.6	9,900
10	5,000	51,000	500.0	5,100	56,000	5,600.0	12,300

ª Includes all opportunity costs

Solution:

Total fixed cost remains unchanged at 5,000 throughout the entire production range, while average fixed cost continuously declines from 5,000 at one unit to 500 by 10 units. Both average variable cost and marginal cost initially decline and then reach their lowest level at 3 units, with costs of 1,800 and 1,600, respectively. Beyond 3 units, both average variable cost and marginal cost increase, indicating that the cost of production rises with greater output. The least-cost point for average total cost is 3,200 at 5 units. At zero output, total costs are 5,000, which equal the amount of total fixed cost.

Exhibit 17 displays the firm's supply curve, shutdown point, and breakeven level of operation under perfect competition in the short run. The firm's **short-run supply curve** is the bold section of the marginal cost curve that lies above the minimum point (point A) on the average variable cost curve. If the firm operates below this point (for example between C and A), it shuts down because of its inability to cover variable costs in full. Between points A and B, the firm can operate in the short run because it is meeting variable cost payments even though it is unable to cover all of its fixed costs. In the long run, however, the firm is not able to survive if fixed costs are not completely covered. Any operating point above point B (the minimum point on ATC), such as point D, generates an economic profit.

A firm's **shutdown point** occurs when average revenue is less than average variable cost (any output below $Q_{shutdown}$), which corresponds to point A in Exhibit 17. Shutdown is defined as a situation in which the firm stops production but still confronts the payment of fixed costs in the short run as a business entity. In the short run, a business is capable of operating in a loss situation as long as it covers its variable costs even though it is not earning sufficient revenue to cover all fixed cost obligations. If variable costs cannot be covered in the short run ($P < AVC$), the firm will shut down operations and simply absorb the unavoidable fixed costs. This problem occurs at output Q_1, which corresponds to point C where price is less than average variable cost. However, in the long run, to remain in business, the price must cover all costs. Therefore, in the long run, at any price below the breakeven point, the firm will exit the market, i.e., the firm will no longer participate in the market. Point D, which corresponds to output Q_3, is a position where economic profit occurs because price is greater than ATC.

Exhibit 17   A Firm's Short-Run Supply Curve, Breakeven Point, and Shutdown Point under Perfect Competition

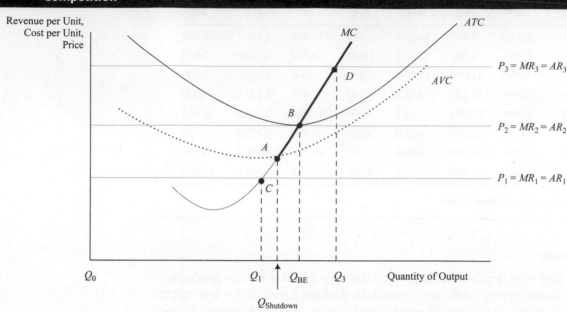

In the case of perfect competition, the **breakeven point** is the quantity where price, average revenue, and marginal revenue equal average total cost. It is also defined as the quantity where total revenue equals total costs. Firms strive to reach initial breakeven as soon as possible to avoid start-up losses for any extended period of time. When businesses are first established, there is an initial period where losses occur at low quantity levels. In Exhibit 17, the breakeven quantity occurs at output Q_{BE}, which corresponds to point B where price is tangent to the minimum point on the ATC. (Keep in mind that normal profit as an implicit cost is included in ATC as a fixed cost.)

Exhibit 18 shows the breakeven point under perfect competition using the total revenue–total cost approach. Actually, there are two breakeven points—lower (point E) and upper (point F). Below point E, the firm is losing money (economic losses), and beyond that point is the region of profitability (shaded area) that extends to the upper breakeven point. Within this profit area, a specific quantity (Q_{max}) maximizes profit as the largest difference between TR and TC. Point F is where the firm leaves the profit region and incurs economic losses again. This second region of economic losses develops when the firm's production begins to reach the limits of physical capacity, resulting in diminished productivity and an acceleration of costs. Obviously, the firm would not produce beyond Q_{max} because it is the optimal production point that maximizes profit.

Exhibit 18   A Firm's Breakeven Points Using Total Revenue and Total Costs under Perfect Competition

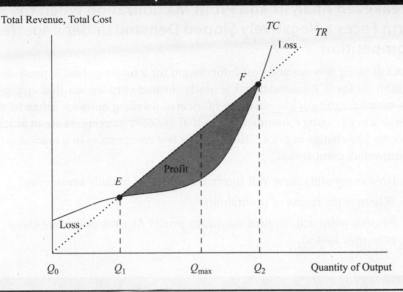

Breakeven points, profit regions, and economic loss ranges are influenced by demand and supply conditions, which change frequently according to the market behavior of consumers and firms. A high initial breakeven point is riskier than a low point because it takes a larger volume and, usually, a longer time to reach. However, at higher output levels it yields more return in compensation for this greater risk.

In the case where TC exceeds TR, as shown in Exhibit 19, the firm will want to minimize the economic loss (as long as $TR > TVC$), which is defined as the smallest difference between TC and TR. This occurs at Q_{min}, where the economic loss is calculated as $(TC_M - TR_N)$ on the vertical axis.

Exhibit 19   Loss Minimization Using Total Revenue and Total Costs

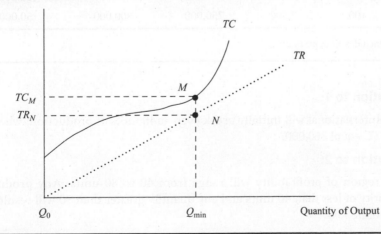

Breakeven Analysis and Profit Maximization When the Firm Faces a Negatively Sloped Demand under Imperfect Competition

The following revenue and cost information for a future period is presented in Exhibit 20 for WR International, a newly formed corporation that engages in the manufacturing of low-cost, pre-fabricated dwelling units for urban housing markets in emerging economies. (Note that quantity increments are in blocks of 10 for a 250 change in price.) The firm has few competitors in a market setting of imperfect competition.

1   How many units must WR International sell to initially break even?

2   Where is the region of profitability?

3   At what point will the firm maximize profit? At what points are there economic losses?

Exhibit 20

Quantity (Q)	Price (P)	Total Revenue (TR)	Total Costs (TC)[a]	Profit
0	10,000	0	100,000	(100,000)
10	9,750	97,500	170,000	(72,500)
20	9,500	190,000	240,000	(50,000)
30	9,250	277,500	300,000	(22,500)
40	9,000	360,000	360,000	0
50	8,750	437,500	420,000	17,500
60	8,500	510,000	480,000	30,000
70	8,250	577,500	550,000	27,500
80	8,000	640,000	640,000	0
90	7,750	697,500	710,000	(12,500)
100	7,500	750,000	800,000	(50,000)

[a] Includes all opportunity costs

Solution to 1:

WR International will initially break even at 40 units of production, where *TR* and *TC* equal 360,000.

Solution to 2:

The region of profitability will range from 40 to 80 units. Any production quantity of less than 40 units and any quantity greater than 80 will result in an economic loss.

Solution to 3:

Maximum profit of 30,000 will occur at 60 units. Lower profit will occur at any output level that is higher or lower than 60 units. From zero quantity to 40 units and for quantities beyond 80 units, economic losses occur.

Given the relationships among total revenue, total variable cost, and total fixed cost, Exhibit 21 summarizes the decisions to operate, shut down production, or exit the market in both the short run and long run. As previously discussed, the firm must cover variable cost before fixed cost. In the short run, if total revenue cannot cover total variable cost, the firm shuts down production to minimize loss, which would equal the amount of fixed cost. If total variable cost exceeds total revenue in the long run, the firm will exit the market as a business entity to avoid the loss associated with fixed cost at zero production. By terminating business operations through market exit, investors escape the erosion in their equity capital from economic losses. When total revenue is enough to cover total variable cost but not all of total fixed cost, the firm can survive in the short run but will be unable to maintain financial solvency in the long run.

Exhibit 21

Revenue–Cost Relationship	Short-Run Decision	Long-Term Decision
$TR \geq TC$	Stay in market	Stay in market
$TR > TVC$ but $TR < TFC + TVC$	Stay in market	Exit market
$TR < TVC$	Shut down production to zero	Exit market

EXAMPLE 6

Shutdown Analysis

For the most recent financial reporting period, a business domiciled in Ecuador (which recognizes the US dollar as an official currency) has revenue of $2 million and total costs of $2.5 million, which are or can be broken down into total fixed cost of $1 million and total variable cost of $1.5 million. The net loss on the firm's income statement is reported as $500,000 (ignoring tax implications). In prior periods, the firm had reported profits on its operations.

1 What decision should the firm make regarding operations over the short term?

2 What decision should the firm make regarding operations over the long term?

3 Assume the same business scenario except that revenue is now $1.3 million, which creates a net loss of $1.2 million. What decision should the firm make regarding operations in this case?

Solution to 1:

In the short run, the firm is able to cover all of its total variable cost but only half of its $1 million in total fixed cost. If the business ceases to operate, its loss is $1 million, the amount of total fixed cost, whereas the net loss by operating is minimized at $500,000. The firm should attempt to operate by negotiating special arrangements with creditors to buy time to return operations back to profitability.

Solution to 2:

If the revenue shortfall is expected to persist over time, the firm should cease operations, liquidate assets, and pay debts to the extent possible. Any residual for shareholders would decrease the longer the firm is allowed to operate unprofitably.

Solution to 3:

The firm would minimize loss at $1 million of total fixed cost by shutting down compared with continuing to do business where the loss is $1.2 million. Shareholders will save $200,000 in equity value by pursuing this option. Unquestionably, the business will have a rather short life expectancy if this loss situation were to continue.

When evaluating profitability, particularly of start-up firms and businesses using turnaround strategies, analysts should consider highlighting breakeven and shutdown points in their financial research. Identifying the unit sales levels where the firm enters or leaves the production range for profitability and where the firm can no longer function as a viable business entity provides invaluable insight to investment decisions.

3.1.4 Output Optimization and Maximization of Profit

Profit maximization occurs when

■ the difference between total revenue (TR) and total costs (TC) is the greatest;

■ marginal revenue (MR) equals marginal cost (MC); and

■ the revenue value of the output from the last unit of input employed equals the cost of employing that input unit (as later developed in Equation 12).

All three approaches derive the same profit-maximizing output level. In the first approach, a firm starts by forecasting unit sales, which becomes the basis for estimates of future revenue and production costs. By comparing predicted total revenue to predicted total costs for different output levels, the firm targets the quantity that yields the greatest profit. When using the marginal revenue–marginal cost approach, the firm compares the change in predicted total revenue (MR) with the change in predicted total costs (MC) by unit of output. If MR exceeds MC, total profit is increased by producing more units because each successive unit adds more to total revenue than it does to total costs. If MC is greater than MR, total profit is decreased when additional units are produced. The point of profit maximization occurs where MR equals MC. The third method compares the estimated cost of each unit of input to that input's contribution with projected total revenue. If the increase in projected total revenue coming from the input unit exceeds its cost, a contribution to total profit is evident. In turn, this justifies further employment of that input. On the other hand, if the increase in projected total revenue does not cover the input unit's cost, total profit is diminished. Profit maximization based on the employment of inputs occurs where the next input unit for each type of resource used no longer makes any contribution to total profit.

Combining revenue and cost data from Exhibits 4 and 13, Exhibit 22 demonstrates the derivation of the optimal output level that maximizes profit for a firm under perfect competition. Profit is calculated as the difference between total revenue and total costs. At zero production, an economic loss of 100 occurs, which is equivalent to total fixed cost. Upon initial production, the firm incurs an economic loss of 50 on the first unit but breaks even by unit 2. The region of profitability ranges from 2 to 6 units. Within this domain, total profit is maximized in the amount of 100 at 5 units of output. No other quantity level yields a higher profit. At this 5-unit level, marginal revenue exceeds marginal cost. But at unit 6, marginal revenue is less than marginal cost, which results in a lower profit because unit 6 costs more to produce than what it generates in revenue. Unit 6 costs 150 to produce but contributes only 100 to total revenue, which yields a 50 loss on that unit. As a result, profit drops from 100 to 50. At unit 7 and beyond, the firm begins to lose money again as it passes the upper breakeven mark and enters a second economic loss zone.

Exhibit 22   Profit Maximization under Perfect Competition

Quantity (Q)	Price (P)	Total Revenue (TR)	Total Costs (TC)[a]	Profit (P)	Marginal Revenue (MR)	Marginal Cost (MC)
0	100	0	100	(100)	—	—
1	100	100	150	(50)	100	50
2	100	200	175	25	100	25
3	100	300	225	75	100	50
4	100	400	310	90	100	85
5	100	500	400	100	100	90
6	100	600	550	50	100	150
7	100	700	750	(50)	100	200
8	100	800	1,000	(200)	100	250
9	100	900	1,300	(400)	100	300
10	100	1,000	1,650	(650)	100	350

[a] Includes all opportunity costs

Exhibits 23 and 24 display the data from Exhibit 22 to illustrate profit maximization under perfect competition using the $(TR - TC)$ and $(MR = MC)$ approaches. Exhibit 24 highlights profit maximization based on comparing how much each unit of output costs to produce (MC) to how much each unit contributes to revenue (MR). Each unit up to and including unit 5 contributes to profit in that each unit's marginal revenue exceeds its marginal cost. Starting at unit 6 and thereafter, the marginal revenue for each unit is less than the marginal cost. This results in a reduction in profit. Profit maximization occurs where MR equals MC. In this case, the optimal decision for the firm using a comparison of MR and MC is to produce 5 units.[2]

---

2 Marginal analysis is a common and valuable optimization tool that is used to determine the point of profit maximization and the optimal employment of resources. It is often said that the firm makes decisions "on the margin."

Exhibit 23   Profit Maximization Using Total Revenue and Total Costs from Exhibit 22

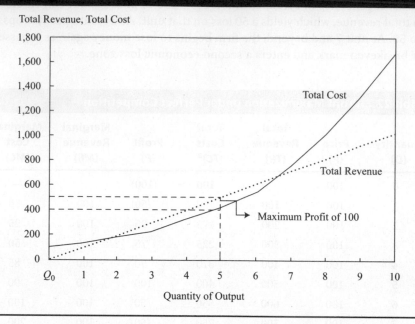

Exhibit 24   Profit Maximization Using Marginal Revenue and Marginal Cost from Exhibit 22

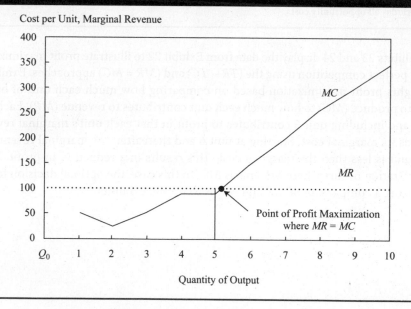

It should be noted that under imperfect competition, the firm faces a negatively sloped demand curve. As the firm offers a greater quantity to the market, price decreases. In contrast, a firm under perfect competition has an insignificant share of the market and is able to sell more without impacting market price. Obviously, the type of market structure in which a firm operates as a seller has an impact on the firm's profit in terms of the price received when output levels vary.

EXAMPLE 7

Profit Maximization and the Breakeven Point under Imperfect Competition

Exhibit 25 shows revenue and cost data for a firm that operates under the market structure of imperfect competition.

1 At what point does the firm break even over its production range in the short run?

2 What is the quantity that maximizes profit given total revenue and total costs?

3 Comparing marginal revenue and marginal cost, determine the quantity that maximizes profit.

Exhibit 25

Q	P	TR	TC[a]	Profit	MR	MC
0	1,000	0	550	(550)	—	—
1	995	995	1,000	(5)	995	450
2	990	1,980	1,500	480	985	500
3	985	2,955	2,100	855	975	600
4	980	3,920	2,800	1,120	965	700
5	975	4,875	3,600	1,275	955	800
6	970	5,820	4,600	1,220	945	1,000
7	965	6,755	5,800	955	935	1,200
8	960	7,680	7,200	480	925	1,400
9	955	8,595	8,800	(205)	915	1,600
10	950	9,500	10,800	(1,300)	905	2,000

[a] Includes all opportunity costs.

Solution to 1:

The breakeven point occurs between unit 1 and unit 2, where profit increases from (5) to 480.

Solution to 2:

At an output level of 5 units, the firm maximizes profit in the amount of 1,275, calculated as the difference between TR of 4,875 and TC of 3,600.

Solution to 3:

Profit maximization occurs at 5 units, where MR of 955 exceeds MC of 800, which yields a profit contribution of 155. However, at 6 units, MR of 945 is less than the MC of 1,000, resulting in a loss of 55 and a reduction in profit from 1,275 to 1,220.

Exhibit 26 summarizes the $(TR - TC)$ and $(MR = MC)$ profit-maximization approaches for firms operating under perfect competition. (Profit maximization using inputs is discussed in Section 3.2.2.)

Exhibit 26	Summary of Profit Maximization and Loss Minimization under Perfect Competition
Revenue–Cost Relationship	**Actions by Firm**
$TR = TC$ and $MR > MC$	Firm is operating at lower breakeven point; increase Q to enter profit territory.
$TR \geq TC$ and $MR = MC$	Firm is at maximum profit level; no change in Q.
$TR < TC$ and $TR \geq TVC$ but $(TR - TVC) < TFC$ (covering TVC but not TFC)	Find level of Q that minimizes loss in the short run; work toward finding a profitable Q in the long run; exit market if losses continue in the long run.
$TR < TVC$ (not covering TVC in full)	Shut down in the short run; exit market in the long run.
$TR = TC$ and $MR < MC$	Firm is operating at upper breakeven point; decrease Q to enter profit territory.

Profit acts as an efficient allocator of equity capital to investment opportunities whereby shareholders' wealth is increased. Equity flows from low-return business investments to high-return business investments as it seeks the greatest return potential on a risk-adjusted basis. Basic economic theory describes how consumer choice voiced through the price mechanism in competitive markets directs resources to their most efficient use according to what consumers need and want. In the end, it is profitability—which evolves from the interactions of demand and supply factors in product and resource markets—that decides where financial capital is employed.

3.1.5 *Economies of Scale and Diseconomies of Scale*

Rational behavior dictates that the firm select an operating size or scale that maximizes profit over any time frame. The time frame for the firm can be separated into the short run and long run based on the ability of the firm to adjust the quantities of the fixed resources it employs. The short run is defined as a time period in which at least one of the factors of production is fixed. The most likely inputs to be held constant in defining the short run are technology, physical capital, and plant size. Usually, a firm cannot change these inputs in a relatively short period of time given the inflexible nature of their use. The long run is defined as a time period in which all factors of production are variable, including technology, physical capital, and plant size. Additionally, in the long run, firms can enter or exit the market based on decisions regarding profitability. The long run is often referred to as the **planning horizon** in which the firm can choose the short-run position or optimal operating size that maximizes profit over time.

The time required for long-run adjustments varies by industry. For example, the long run for a small business using very little in the way of technology and physical capital may be less than a year. On the other hand, for a capital-intensive firm, the long run may be more than a decade. However, given enough time, all production factors are variable, which allows the firm to choose an operating size or plant capacity based on different technologies and physical capital. In this regard, costs and profits will differ between the short run and long run.

The fixed-input constraint in the short run along with input prices establish the firm's **short-run average total cost curve** (SRATC). This defines what the per-unit cost will be for any quantity in the short run. The SRATC and the demand for the firm's product determine short-run profit. The selection of technology, physical capital, and plant size is a key determinant of the short-run cost curve for the firm. As the firm switches to newer technologies and physical capital, a corresponding change in short-run costs occurs. In the long run, a firm has the opportunity for greater profit potential based on the ability to lower its costs ■ through choices of more-efficient technology and physical capital and a wider selection of production capacities.

Exhibit 27 displays the **long-run average total cost curve** (LRATC), which is derived from the short-run average total cost curves that are available to the firm.[3] The business has a choice of five technology-physical capital options and plant capacities over the long run, each with its own short-run cost curve. The LRATC consists of sections of these individual short-run cost curves. For example, from zero production to Q_1 output, $SRATC_1$ yields the lowest per unit cost. Between Q_1 and Q_2, the lowest cost per unit is attainable with $SRATC_2$, which represents a larger production capacity. $SRATC_3$ and $SRATC_4$ would provide for the lowest average cost over time for output levels of $Q_2 - Q_4$ and $Q_4 - Q_5$, respectively. For any output greater than Q_5, $SRATC_5$ becomes the preferred curve for minimizing average total cost. Tangentially connecting all of the least-cost SRATC segments by way of an envelope curve creates the LRATC. (Assuming an unlimited number of possible technologies, plant sizes, and physical capital combinations—and therefore a theoretically unlimited number of SRATC—the LRATC becomes a smooth curve rather than a segmented one as indicated by the bold segments of the five SRATC's in Exhibit 27.) The LRATC shows the lowest cost per unit at which output can be produced over a long period of time when the firm is able to make technology, plant size, and physical capital adjustments. If the same technologies and physical capital are available and adaptable to every firm in the industry, then all firms would have the same LRATC. However, firms could be at different positions on this homogenous LRATC depending on their operating size that is based on output.

Exhibit 27 Long-Run Average Total Cost Curve

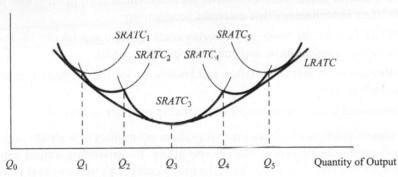

Over the long run, as a business expands output, it can utilize more efficient technology and physical capital and take advantage of other factors to lower the costs of production. This development is referred to as **economies of scale** or **increasing returns to scale** as a firm moves to lower cost structures when it grows in size. Output increases by a larger proportion than the increase in inputs. The opposite effect can result after a certain volume level at which the business faces higher costs as it expands in size. This outcome is called **diseconomies of scale** or **decreasing returns to scale**, where the firm becomes less efficient with size. In this case, output increases by a smaller proportion than the increase in inputs. Diseconomies of scale often result from the firm becoming too large to be managed efficiently even though better technology can be increasing productivity within the business. Both economies and diseconomies

---

3 Some writers use short-run average cost (SRAC) and long-run average cost (LRAC) in the same sense as SRATC and LRATC, respectively.

of scale can occur at the same time; the impact on long-run average total cost depends on which dominates. If economies of scale dominate, LRATC decreases with increases in output; the reverse holds true when diseconomies of scale prevail.

Referring back to Exhibit 27, economies of scale occur from Q_0 (zero production) to output level Q_3, where Q_3 is the cost-minimizing level of output for $SRATC_3$. It is evident throughout this production range that per-unit costs decline as the firm produces more. Over the production range of Q_3 to Q_5, diseconomies of scale are occurring as per-unit costs increase when the firm expands output. Under perfect competition, given the five SRATC selections that are available to the firm throughout the production range $Q_0 - Q_5$, $SRATC_3$ is the optimal technology, plant capacity, and physical capital choice, with Q_3 being the target production size for the firm that would minimize cost over the long term.

Perfect competition forces the firm to operate at the minimum point on the LRATC because market price will be established at this level over the long run. If the firm is not operating at this least-cost point, its long-term viability will be threatened. The minimum point on the LRATC is referred to as the **minimum efficient scale** (MES). The MES is the optimal firm size under perfect competition over the long run where the firm can achieve cost competitiveness.

As the firm grows in size, economies of scale and a lower average total cost can result from the following factors:

- Division of labor and management in a large firm with numerous workers, where each worker can specialize in one task rather than perform many duties, as in the case of a small business (as such, workers in a large firm become more proficient at their jobs).

- Being able to afford more-expensive, yet more-efficient equipment and to adapt the latest in technology that increases productivity.

- Effectively reducing waste and lowering costs through marketable byproducts, less energy consumption, and enhanced quality control.

- Better use of market information and knowledge for more-effective managerial decision making.

- Discounted prices on resources when buying in larger quantities.

A classic example of a business that realizes economies of scale through greater physical capital investment is the electric utility. By expanding output capacity to accommodate a larger customer base, the utility company's per-unit cost will decline. Economies of scale help to explain why electric utilities have naturally evolved from localized entities to regional and multi-region enterprises. Wal-Mart, the world's largest retailer, is an example of a business that uses bulk purchasing power to obtain deep discounts from suppliers to keep costs and prices low. Wal-Mart also utilizes the latest in technology to monitor point-of-sale transactions to have timely market information to respond to changes in customer buying behavior. This leads to economies of scale through lower distribution and inventory costs.

The factors that can lead to diseconomies of scale, inefficiencies, and rising costs when a firm increases in size include:

- So large that it cannot be properly managed.

- Overlap and duplication of business functions and product lines.

- Higher resource prices because of supply constraints when buying inputs in large quantities.

General Motors (GM) is an example of a business that has realized diseconomies of scale by becoming too large. Scale diseconomies have occurred through product overlap and duplication (i.e., similar or identical automobile models), where the fixed cost for these models is not spread over a large volume of output. (Recently, the company has decided to discontinue various low-volume product models that overlapped with other models.) GM has numerous manufacturing plants throughout the world and sells vehicles in over a hundred countries. Given this geographical dispersion in production and sales, the company has had communication and management coordination problems, which have resulted in higher costs. Also, GM has had significantly higher labor costs when compared with its competitors. By being the largest producer in the market, it has been a target of labor unions for higher compensation and benefits packages relative to other firms.

Strategically, when a firm is operating in the economies of scale region, expanding production capacity will increase the firm's competitiveness through lower costs. Firm expansion is often facilitated with a growth or business combination (i.e., merger or acquisition) strategy. On the other hand, when a business is producing in the area of diseconomies of scale, the objective is to downsize to reduce costs and become more competitive. From an investment perspective, a firm operating at the minimum point of the industry LRATC under perfect competition should be valued higher than a firm that is not producing at this least-cost quantity.

The LRATC can take various forms given the development of new technology and growth prospects for an industry over the long term. Exhibit 28 displays examples of different average total cost curves that firms can realize over the long run. Panel A shows that scale economies dissipate rapidly at low output levels. This implies that a firm with a low volume of output can be more cost competitive than a firm that is producing a high output volume. Panel B indicates a lower and lower average cost over time as firm size increases. The larger the business, the more competitive it is and the greater its potential investment value. Finally, Panel C shows the case of **constant returns to scale** (i.e., output increases by the same proportion as the increase in inputs) over the range of production from Q_1 to Q_2, indicating that size does not give a firm a competitive edge over another firm within this range. In other words, a firm that is producing the smaller output Q_1 has the same long-run average total cost as a firm producing the higher output Q_2.

Exhibit 28   Types of Long-Run Average Total Cost Curves

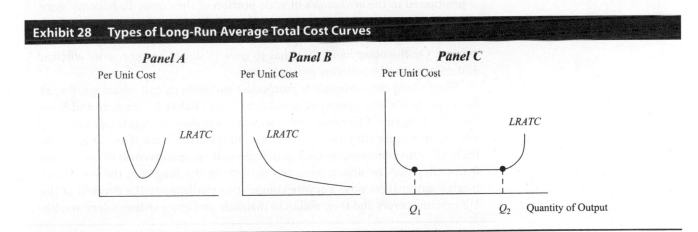

EXAMPLE 8

Long-Run Average Total Cost Curve

Exhibit 29 displays the long-run average total cost curve ($LRATC_{US}$) and the short-run average total cost curves for three hypothetical US-based automobile manufacturers—Starr Vehicles (Starr), Rocket Sports Cars (Rocket), and General Auto (GenAuto). The long-run average total cost curve ($LRATC_{foreign}$)

for foreign-owned automobile companies that compete in the US auto market is also indicated in the graph. (The market structure implicit in the exhibit is imperfect competition.)

To what extent are the cost relationships depicted in Exhibit 29 useful for an economic and financial analysis of the three US-based auto firms?

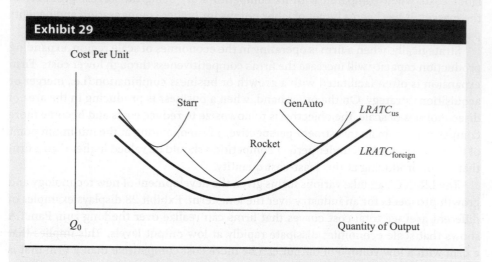

Exhibit 29

Solution:

First, it is observable that the foreign auto companies have a lower LRATC compared with that of the US automobile manufacturers. This competitive position places the US firms at a cost and possible pricing disadvantage in the market with the potential to lose market share to the lower-cost foreign competitors. Second, only Rocket operates at the minimum point of the $LRATC_{US}$, whereas GenAuto is situated in the region of diseconomies of scale and Starr is positioned in the economies of scale portion of the curve. To become more efficient and competitive, GenAuto needs to downsize and restructure, which means moving down the $LRATC_{US}$ curve to a smaller, yet lower-cost production volume. On the other hand, Starr has to grow in size to become more efficient and competitive by lowering per-unit costs.

From a long-term investment prospective and given its cost advantage, Rocket has the potential to create more investment value relative to GenAuto and Starr. Over the long run, if GenAuto and Starr can lower their average total costs, they will become more attractive to investors. On the other hand, if any or all of the three US auto companies cannot match the cost competitiveness of the foreign firms, they may be driven from the market. In the long run, the lower-cost foreign automakers pose a severe competitive challenge to the survival of the US manufacturers and their ability to maintain and grow shareholders' wealth.

3.1.6 *Profit Maximization in the Short Run and Long Run*

No matter the time span, the firm's supply behavior centers on the objective of profit maximization. In the short term, when technology and physical capital are fixed, maximum profit (or minimal loss) is determined where marginal cost equals marginal revenue (points A and B in Exhibit 30). Cases of profit maximization and loss minimization are illustrated in Exhibit 30 for a firm operating under perfect competition in the short run. In Panel A, the firm realizes economic profit because TR is greater than TC and price exceeds SRATC in the production range of Q_1–Q_2. Q_{max} is the output level that maximizes economic profit. Panel B shows the case of loss minimization because TC exceeds TR and SRATC is above the price level. Q_{min} yields the least loss of all possible production quantities. Note that in this case, the short-run loss is still less than fixed cost, so the firm should continue operating in the short run.

Exhibit 30	Profit Maximization and Loss Minimization in the Short Run under Perfect Competition

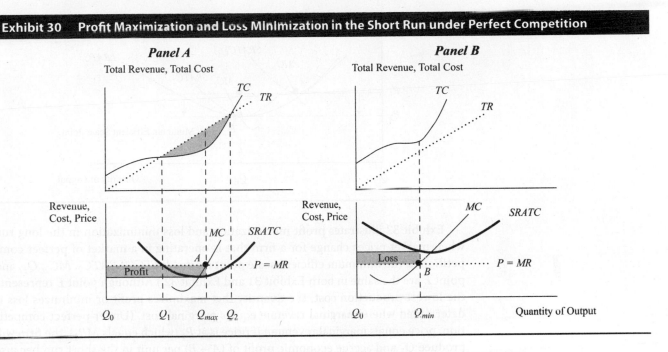

Exhibit 31 illustrates long-run profit maximization under perfect competition given the long-run average total cost curve when economies of scale occur. In the long run under perfect competition, the firm will operate at the minimum efficient scale point on its long-run average total cost curve. This least-cost point is illustrated in Exhibit 31 as point E at output level Q_E. In comparison to the point of minimum efficient scale, any other output quantity results in a higher cost.

In the short run given $SRATC_1$ and P_1, the firm is making only normal profit because price equals average total cost at point A. By realizing economies of scale in the long run, the firm can move down the LRATC to $SRATC_2$ and produce Q_F. If the firm still receives P_1, economic profit is forthcoming at Q_E in the amount of $(B - E)$ per unit. However, economic profit with no barriers to entry under perfect competition leads to more competitors, a greater market supply, and, subsequently, a lower price in the long run. The price to the firm will decline to P_2, and economic profit will disappear with the long-run equilibrium for the firm occurring at point E, the minimum efficient scale. At point E, the firm is making only normal profit because in the long run under perfect competition, economic profit is zero.

Exhibit 31   Long-Run Profit Maximization and Minimum Efficient Scale under Perfect Competition

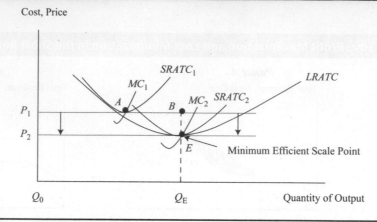

Exhibit 32 illustrates profit maximization and loss minimization in the long run when market prices change for a firm that is operating in a market of perfect competition at the minimum efficient scale point on its LRATC. ($SRATC_2$, MC_2, Q_E, and point E are the same in both Exhibit 31 and Exhibit 32.) Although point E represents the lowest production cost, the quantity that maximizes profit or minimizes loss is determined where marginal revenue equals marginal cost. (Under perfect competition, price equals marginal revenue.) If price is at P_1 (which equals MR_1), the firm will produce Q_1 and accrue economic profit of $(A - B)$ per unit in the short run because price is greater than average total cost. In the long run, economic profit attracts new competitors who drive price down, resulting in zero economic profit. Profitability declines to the level at P_2, where price is tangent to average total cost at point E. If price is at P_3 (which equals MR_3), the firm will produce Q_3 and realize an economic loss of $(C - D)$ per unit in the short run because average total cost is greater than price. In the long run, firms will exit the market; as a result, price rises to P_2, eliminating economic losses. Again, profitability for the firm returns to the normal level at point E, where price matches average total cost. The long-term equilibrium for the firm occurs at point E, which corresponds to Demand$_2$, MR_2, a price of P_2, and an output level of Q_E.

Exhibit 32   Profit Maximization and Loss Minimization in the Long Run under Perfect Competition

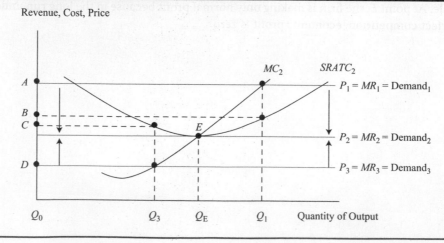

3.1.7 The Long-Run Industry Supply Curve and What It Means for the Firm

The **long-run industry supply curve** shows the relationship between quantities supplied and output prices for an industry when firms are able to enter or exit the industry in response to the level of short-term economic profit (i.e., perfect competition) and when changes in industry output influence resource prices over the long run. Exhibit 33 illustrates three types of long-run supply curves based on increasing costs, decreasing costs, and constant costs to firms competing under perfect competition.

Exhibit 33   Long-Run Supply Curves for the Firm

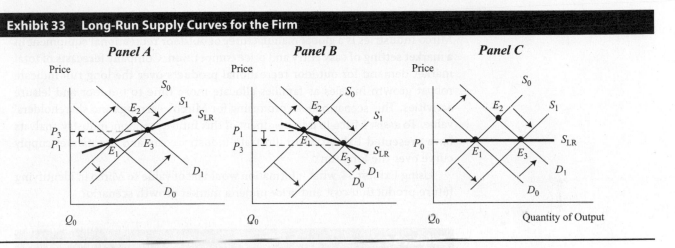

An **increasing-cost industry** exists when prices and costs are higher when industry output is increased in the long run. This is demonstrated in Panel A. Assuming zero economic profit at E_1, when demand increases from D_0 to D_1, price rises and economic profit results at E_2 in the short run. Over the long term in response to this economic profit, new competitors will enter the industry and existing firms will expand output, resulting in an increase in supply from S_0 to S_1 and a long-term equilibrium at E_3. If the increase in demand for resources from this output expansion leads to higher prices for some or all inputs, the industry as a whole will face higher production costs and charge a higher price for output. As indicated by S_{LR} in Panel A, the long-run supply curve for the industry will have a positive slope over the long run. The firm in an increasing-cost industry will experience higher resource costs so market price must rise in order to cover these costs. The petroleum, coal, and natural gas industries are prime examples of increasing-cost industries, where the supply response to long-run demand growth results in higher output prices because of the rising costs of energy production.

Panel B shows the case of a **decreasing-cost industry**, where the supply increase from S_0 to S_1 leads to a lower price for output in the market. Firms are able to charge a lower price because of a reduction in their resource costs. Decreasing costs can evolve from technological advances, producer efficiencies that come from a larger firm size, and economies of scale of resource suppliers (i.e., lower resource prices) that are passed on to resource buyers when industry output expands. The long-run supply curve for the industry will have a negative slope, as displayed by S_{LR} in Panel B. As a result, the firm in a decreasing-cost industry will experience lower resource costs and can then charge a lower price.[4] Possible examples of decreasing-cost industries are semiconductors and personal computers, where the rapid growth in demand over the past decade has led to substantially lower prices.

---

4 The individual firm's supply curve is still upward sloping even though the industry's long-run supply curve is negatively sloped. This means that in the long run, the firm's supply curve shifts to the right when industry costs decrease. This results in a lower price charged by the firm for each quantity.

In some cases, firms in the industry will experience no change in resource costs and output prices over the long run. This type of industry is known as a **constant-cost industry**. This is displayed in Panel C, where the long-run supply curve (S_{LR}) for the industry is a horizontal line indicating a constant price level when the industry increases output.

EXAMPLE 9

A Firm Operating in an Increasing-Cost Industry

Mirco Industries is a global manufacturer of outdoor recreational equipment in a market setting of easy entry and price competition. Company forecasts of total market demand for outdoor recreational products over the long run indicate robust growth in sales as families allocate more time to outdoor and leisure activities. This scenario looks promising for Mirco's earnings and shareholders' value. To assist Mirco in its assessment of this future scenario, industry analysts have presented Exhibit 34 to illustrate industry costs and the market supply curve over the long run.

Using Exhibit 34, what information would be of value to Mirco in identifying future production cost and price under a market growth scenario?

Exhibit 34

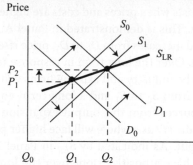

Note: Market demand increases from D_0 to D_1. The market responds with an increase in supply from S_0 to S_1. In the long run, the price of P_2 will be higher than the original price of P_1.

Solution:

As indicated by the upward slope of the long-run industry supply curve, Mirco will experience an increase in production costs over the long run because of higher resource prices when the industry expands production and new firms enter the industry in response to an increase in market demand. To cover the higher production costs, Mirco will ultimately charge the higher market price of P_2 relative to the current price of P_1.

3.2 Productivity

In general terms, **productivity** is defined as the average output per unit of input. Any production factor can be used as the input variable. However, it has been a common practice to use the labor resource as the basis for measuring productivity. In this regard, productivity is based on the number of workers used or the number of work-hours performed. In many cases, labor is easier to quantify relative to the other types of resources used in production. As such, productivity is typically stated as output per worker or output per labor hour.

Why is productivity important? Cost minimization and profit maximization behavior dictate that the firm strives to maximize productivity—that is, produce the most output per unit of input or produce any given level of output with the least amount of inputs. A firm that lags behind the industry in productivity is at a competitive disadvantage and, as a result, is most likely to face decreases in future earnings and shareholders' wealth. An increase in productivity lowers production costs, which leads to greater profitability and investment value. Furthermore, productivity benefits (e.g., increased profitability) can be fully or partially distributed to other stakeholders of the business, such as consumers in the form of lower prices and employees in the form of enhanced compensation. Transferring some or all of the productivity rewards to non-equity holders creates synergies that benefit shareholders over time.

The benefits from increased productivity are as follows:

- Lower business costs, which translate into increased profitability.

- An increase in the market value of equity and shareholders' wealth resulting from an increase in profit.

- An increase in worker rewards, which motivates further productivity increases from labor.

Undoubtedly, increases in productivity reinforce and strengthen the competitive position of the firm over the long run. A fundamental analysis of a company should examine the firm's commitment to productivity enhancements and the degree to which productivity is integrated into the competitive nature of the industry or market. In some cases, productivity is not only an important promoter of growth in firm value over the long term, but it is also the key factor for economic survival. A business that lags the market in terms of productivity often finds itself less competitive, while at the same time confronting profit erosion and deterioration in shareholders' wealth. Whenever productivity is a consideration in the equity valuation of the firm, the first step for the analyst is to define measures of productivity. Typical productivity measures for the firm are based on the concepts of total product, average product, and marginal product of labor.

3.2.1 *Total, Average, and Marginal Product of Labor*

When measuring a firm's operating efficiency, it is easier and more practical to use a single resource factor as the input variable rather than a bundle of the different resources that the firm uses in producing units of output. As discussed in the previous section, labor is typically the input that is the most identifiable and calculable for measuring productivity. However, any input that is not difficult to quantify can be used. An example will illustrate the practicality of using a single factor input, such as labor, to evaluate the firm's output performance. A business that manually assembles widgets has 50 workers, one production facility, and an assortment of equipment and hand tools. The firm would like to assess its productivity when it utilizes these three types of input factors to produce widgets. In this case, the most appropriate method is to use labor as the input factor for determining productivity because the firm uses a variety of physical capital and only one plant building.

To illustrate the concepts of total product, average product, and marginal product, labor is used as the input variable. Exhibit 35 provides a summary of definitions and tabulations for these three concepts.

Exhibit 35	Definitions and Calculations for Total, Marginal, and Average Product of Labor
Term	**Calculation**
Total product	Sum of the output from all inputs during a time period; usually illustrated as the total output (TP or Q) using labor (L)
Average product	Total product divided by the quantity of a given input; measured as total product divided by the number of workers used at that output level; ($TP \div L$) or ($Q \div L$)
Marginal product	The amount of additional output resulting from using one more unit of input assuming other inputs are fixed; measured by taking the difference in total product and dividing by the change in the quantity of labor; ($\Delta TP \div \Delta L$) or ($\Delta Q \div \Delta L$)

Measured on the basis of the labor input, **total product** (TP or Q) is defined as the aggregate sum of production for the firm during a time period. As a measure of productivity, total product provides superficial information as to how effective and efficient the firm is in terms of producing output. For instance, three firms—Company A, Company B, and Company C—that comprise the entire industry have total output levels of 100,000 units, 180,000 units, and 200,000 units, respectively. Obviously, Company C dominates the market with a 41.7 percent share, followed by Company B's 37.5 percent share and Company A's 20.8 percent portion of the market. This information says little about how efficient each firm is in generating its total output level. Total product only provides an insight into the firm's production volume relative to the industry; it does not show how efficient the firm is in producing its output.

Average product (AP) measures the productivity of inputs on average and is calculated by dividing total product by the total number of units for a given input that is used to generate that output. Average product is usually measured on the basis of the labor input. It is a representative or overall measure of labor's productivity: Some workers are more productive than average, and others are less productive than average.

Given the aforementioned production levels for the three firms, Company A employs 100 workers, and Company B and Company C utilize 200 and 250 workers, respectively. Calculating average product of labor for each of the three firms yields the following productivity results: Company A→1,000 units of output per worker, Company B→900 units per worker, and Company C→800 units per worker. It is apparent that Company A is the most efficient firm, although it has the lowest share of the total market. Company C has the largest portion of the total market, but it is the least efficient of the three. Given that Company A can maintain its productivity advantage over the long run, it will be positioned to generate the greatest return on investment through lower costs and higher profit outcomes relative to the other firms in the market.

Marginal product (MP), also known as marginal return, measures the productivity of each unit of input and is calculated by taking the difference in total product from adding another unit of input (assuming other resource quantities are held constant). Typically, it is measured in terms of labor's performance; thereby, it is a gauge of productivity of the individual additional worker rather than an average across all workers.

Exhibit 36 provides a numerical illustration for total, average, and marginal products of labor.

Exhibit 36	Total, Average, and Marginal Product of Labor		
Labor (L)	Total Product (TP_L)	Average Product (AP_L)	Marginal Product (MP_L)
0	0	—	—
1	100	100	100
2	210	105	110
3	300	100	90
4	360	90	60
5	400	80	40
6	420	70	20
7	350	50	(70)

Total product increases as the firm adds labor until worker 7, where at that point total production declines by 70 units. Obviously, the firm does not want to employ any worker that has negative productivity. In this case, no more than six workers are considered for employment with the firm.

At an employment level of five workers, AP and MP are 80 units (400 ÷ 5) and 40 units [(400 − 360) ÷ (5 − 4)], respectively. The productivity of the fifth worker is 40 units, while the average productivity for all five workers is 80 units, twice that of worker 5.

A firm has a choice of using total product, average product, marginal product, or some combination of the three to measure productivity. Total product does not provide an in-depth view of a firm's state of efficiency. It is simply an indication of a firm's output volume and potential market share. Therefore, average product and marginal product are better gauges of a firm's productivity because both can reveal competitive advantage through production efficiency. However, individual worker productivity is not easily measurable when workers perform tasks collectively. In this case, average product is the preferred measure of productivity performance.

3.2.2 Marginal Returns and Productivity

Referring to the marginal product column in Exhibit 36, worker 2 has a higher output of 110 units compared with worker 1 who produces 100 units; there is an increase in return when employees are added to the production process. This economic phenomenon is known as **increasing marginal returns**, where the marginal product of a resource increases as additional units of that input are employed. However, successive workers beyond number 2 have lower and lower marginal product to the point where the last worker has a negative return. This observation is called the **law of diminishing returns**. Diminishing returns can lead to a negative marginal product as evidenced with worker 7. There is no question that a firm does not want to employ a worker or input that has a negative impact on total output.

Initially, a firm can experience increasing returns from adding labor to the production process because of the concepts of specialization and division of labor. At first, by having too few workers relative to total physical capital, the understaffing situation requires employees to multi-task and share duties. As more workers are added, employees can specialize, become more adept at their individual functions, and realize an increase in marginal productivity. But after a certain output level, the law of diminishing returns becomes evident.

Assuming all workers are of equal quality and motivation, the decline in marginal product is related to the short run, where at least one resource (typically plant size, physical capital, and/or technology) is fixed. When more and more workers are added to a fixed plant size-technology-physical capital base, the marginal return of the labor factor eventually decreases because the fixed input restricts the output potential of additional workers. One way of understanding the law of diminishing returns is to void the principle and assume that the concept of increasing returns lasts indefinitely. As more workers are added, or when any input is increased, the marginal output continuously increases. At some point, the world's food supply could be grown on one hectare of land or all new automobiles could be manufactured in one factory. Physically, the law of increasing returns is not possible in perpetuity, even though it can clearly be evident in the early stages of production.

Another element resulting in diminishing returns is the quality of labor itself. In the previous discussion, it was assumed all workers were of equal ability. However, that assumption may not be entirely valid when the firm's supply of labor has varying degrees of human capital. In that case, the business would want to employ the most productive workers first; then, as the firm's labor demand increased, less-productive workers would be hired. When the firm does not have access to an adequate supply of homogenous human capital, or for that matter any resource, diminishing marginal product occurs at some point.

EXAMPLE 10

Calculation and Interpretation of Total, Average, and Marginal Product

Average product and marginal product can be calculated on the basis of the production relationship between the number of machines and total product, as indicated in the first two columns of Exhibit 37.

1   Interpret the results for total, average, and marginal product.

2   Indicate where increasing marginal returns change to diminishing marginal returns.

Exhibit 37

Machines (K)	Total Product (TP_K)	Average Product (AP_K)	Marginal Product (MP_K)
0	0	—	—
1	1,000	1,000	1,000
2	2,500	1,250	1,500
3	4,500	1,500	2,000
4	6,400	1,600	1,900
5	7,400	1,480	1,000
6	7,500	1,250	100
7	7,000	1,000	(500)

Solution to 1:

Total product increases to six machines, where it tops out at 7,500. Because total product declines from machine 6 to machine 7, the marginal product for machine 7 is negative 500 units. Average product peaks at 1,600 units with four machines.

Solution to 2:

Increasing returns are evident up to machine 3, where marginal product equals 2,000 units of output. Beyond machine 3, decreasing returns develop because MP_K declines when more machines are added to the production process.

The data provided in Exhibit 38 show productivity changes for various US industries over the period 2000–2007. The coal mining and newspaper sectors have several years of negative changes in productivity, which do not reinforce prospects for long-term growth in profitability. Declines in productivity raise production costs and reduce profit. For the most part, the other industries have solid productivity increases from year to year, even though in some cases the change is volatile. On a trend basis, productivity increases appear to have peaked in the period 2002–2004 and then edged downward during the latter part of the period. Declining productivity makes a firm or industry less competitive over time; however, any adverse impact on profitability stemming from lower or negative productivity may be offset by rising demand for the product.

Exhibit 38	Productivity Changes for Selected Sectors, 2000–2007								
Sector	NAICS[1]	2000	2001	2002	2003	2004	2005	2006	2007
Coal mining	212,100	4.9%	−1.3%	−2.3%	1.5%	0.0%	−4.9%	−7.5%	1.2%
Newspaper publishers	511,110	5.5	−4.3	−0.6	5.1	−5.6	2.4	4.0	−1.8
Auto	336,100	−10.6	0.3	14.5	12.0	1.1	4.6	10.2	4.8
Commercial banking	522,110	3.9	−2.3	4.3	4.5	5.5	1.3	2.9	0.9
Merchandise stores	452,000	5.9	3.8	3.5	6.0	2.8	3.2	3.3	0.5
Air transportation	481,000	1.9	−5.3	9.9	10.2	12.7	7.6	5.1	1.8

[1]North American Industry Classification System.
Note: Productivity is defined by the US Bureau of Labor Statistics as output per worker-hour.
Source: US Bureau of Labor Statistics, "Productivity and Costs by Industry: Annual Rates of Change."

Productivity is a key element in the determination of costs and profit to the firm, especially over the long term. Although productivity can fluctuate widely in the short run (as indicated in Exhibit 38) for a variety of reasons, secular patterns in output per unit of labor denote more meaningful relationships among productivity, costs, profits, and the competitive status of the firm with respect to the industry. To summarize, the analyst should study the productivity levels of the firm over the long run and do an evaluation of how the firm's efficiency compares with the industry standard. A firm that lags the industry in productivity may find itself at a competitive disadvantage with the end result of profit erosion and negative implications for shareholders' wealth. Once evident, productivity issues cause the firm's market value of equity to be discounted.

As previously discussed, a major determinant of the cost component of the profit equation is the degree of efficiency in which the firm uses resources in producing output as defined by the firm's production function. Given the relationship between output and inputs, marginal product (MP) and average product (AP) form the basis for marginal cost (MC) and average variable cost (AVC). Actually, MC and AVC are respective mirror images of MP and AP. Exhibit 39 illustrates this relationship in the short run by showing three areas of interest.

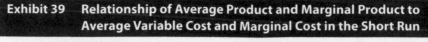

Exhibit 39   Relationship of Average Product and Marginal Product to Average Variable Cost and Marginal Cost in the Short Run

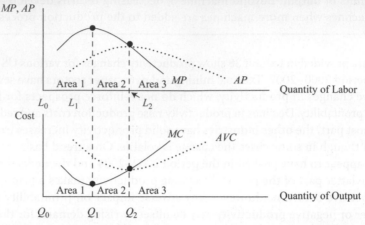

Area 1 shows an increasing MP from L_0 to L_1. The increases in MP result in declining marginal costs from Q_0 to Q_1. As MP or productivity peaks at L_1, MC is minimized at Q_1. Diminishing marginal returns take over in Areas 2 and 3, where a decreasing marginal product results in higher marginal costs. Not only does MP impact MC, but the shape of the AVC also is based on the pattern of AP. At L_2, AP is maximized, while its corresponding output level of Q_2 is consistent with the minimum position on the AVC curve. Note that when MP is greater than AP, AP is increasing; when MP is less than AP, AP is declining. A similar relationship holds true for MC and AVC. When MC is less than AVC, AVC is decreasing; the opposite occurs when MC is greater than AVC. In Area 3, AP is declining, which creates an upturn in the AVC curve.

Technology, quality of human and physical capital, and managerial ability are key factors in determining the production function relationship between output and inputs. The firm's production function establishes what productivity is in terms of TP, MP, and AP. In turn, productivity significantly influences total, marginal, and average costs to the firm, and costs directly impact profit. Obviously, what happens at the production level in terms of productivity impacts the cost level and profitability.

Because revenue, costs, and profit are measured in monetary terms, the productivity of the different input factors requires comparison on a similar basis. In this regard, the firm wants to maximize output per monetary unit of input cost. This goal is denoted by the following expression:

$$MP_{input} / P_{input} \tag{7}$$

where MP_{input} is the marginal product of the input factor and P_{input} is the price of that factor (i.e., resource cost).

When using a combination of resources, a least-cost optimization formula is constructed as follows:

$$\frac{MP_1}{\text{Price of input 1}} = \ldots = \frac{MP_n}{\text{Price of input } n} \tag{8}$$

where the firm utilizes n different resources. Using a two-factor production function consisting of labor and physical capital, Equation 9 best illustrates this rule of least cost:

$$\frac{MP_L}{P_L} = \frac{MP_K}{P_K} \tag{9}$$

where MP_L and MP_K are the marginal products of labor and physical capital, respectively. P_L is the price of labor or the wage rate, and P_K is the price of physical capital. For example, if MP_L/P_L equals two and MP_K/P_K is four, physical capital yields twice the output per monetary unit of input cost versus labor. It is obvious that the firm will want to use physical capital over labor in producing additional output because it provides more productivity on an equivalent cost basis. However, as more physical capital is employed, the firm's MP of capital declines because the law of diminishing returns impacts production. Physical capital is added until its ratio of MP per monetary unit of input cost matches that of labor: $MP_K/P_K = MP_L/P_L = 2.$[5] At this point, both inputs are added when expanding output until their ratios differ. When their ratios diverge, the input with the higher ratio will be employed over the other lower ratio input when the firm increases production.

EXAMPLE 11

Determining the Optimal Input Combination

Canadian Global Electronic Corp. (CGEC) uses three types of labor—unskilled, semi-skilled, and skilled—in the production of electronic components. The firm's production technology allows for the substitution of one type of labor for another. Also, the firm buys labor in a perfectly competitive resource market in which the price of labor stays the same regardless of the number of workers hired. In the following table, the marginal productivity and compensation in Canadian dollars for each type of labor is displayed.

What labor type should the firm hire when expanding output?

Type of Labor	Marginal Product (MP_{input}) per Day	Compensation (P_{input}) per Day (\$)	$\dfrac{MP_{input}}{P_{input}}$
Unskilled (U)	200 units (MP_U)	100 (P_U)	2 units per \$
Semi-skilled (SS)	500 units (MP_{SS})	125 (P_{SS})	4 units per \$
Skilled (S)	1,000 units (MP_S)	200 (P_S)	5 units per \$

Solution:

The firm minimizes cost and enhances profitability by adding skilled labor over the other two types because it has the highest ratio of MP to input price. As the marginal product of skilled labor declines with additional workers, MP_S/P_S decreases. When it declines to the same value as semi-skilled labor, both skilled and semi-skilled workers are added because their productivity per Canadian dollar of input cost is identical. Again, a diminishing marginal product decreases both ratios. When all three labor inputs have the same MP_{input}/P_{input}, the firm will add all three labor types at the same time when expanding output.

---

5 This assumes that MP_L is independent of physical capital K. However, as more K is used, MP_L could actually increase because labor will become more productive when using more physical capital. In this case, $MP_K/P_K = MP_L/P_L$ at some point between 2 and 4.

Equations 7, 8, and 9 derive the physical output per monetary unit of input cost. However, to determine the profit-maximizing utilization level of an input, the firm must measure the revenue value of the input's *MP* and then compare this figure with the cost of the input. The following equations represent this relationship:

Marginal product × Product price = Price of the input   **(10)**

Marginal revenue product = Price of the input   **(11)**

Marginal revenue product (*MRP*) is calculated as the *MP* of an input unit times the price of the product. This term measures the value of the input to the firm in terms of what the input contributes to *TR*. It is also defined as the change in *TR* divided by the change in the quantity of the resource employed. If an input's *MRP* exceeds its cost, a contribution to profit is evident. For example, when the *MP* of the last unit of labor employed is 100 and the product price is 2.00, the *MRP* for that unit of labor (MRP_L) is 200. When the input price of labor is 125, the surplus value or contribution to profit is 75. In contrast, if *MRP* is less than the input's price, a loss would be incurred from employing that input unit. If the *MP* of the next unit of labor is 50 with a product price of 2.00, MRP_L will now be 100. With the same labor cost of 125, the firm would incur a loss of 25 when employing this input unit. Profit maximization occurs when the *MRP* equates to the price or cost of the input for each type of resource that is used in the production process.

In the case of multiple factor usage, the following equation holds true for *n* inputs:

$$\frac{MRP_1}{\text{Price of input 1}} = \cdots = \frac{MRP_n}{\text{Price of input } n} = 1$$ **(12)**

When profit is maximized, *MRP* equals the input price for each type of resource used and all MRP_{input}/P_{input} are equal to one.

EXAMPLE 12

Profit Maximization Using the Marginal Revenue Product and Resource Cost Approach

Using the data from the previous case of Canadian Global Electronic Corp., the table below shows the *MRP* per labor type when product price in Canadian dollars is $0.50. *MRP* per day is calculated as the *MP* per type of labor from Example 11 multiplied by the product price.

Which type of labor contributes the most to profitability?

Type of Labor	Marginal Revenue Product (MRP_{input}) per Day ($)	Compensation (P_{input}) per Day ($)	$\dfrac{MRP_{input}}{P_{input}}$
Unskilled (*U*)	100 (MRP_U)	100 (P_U)	1.0
Semi-skilled (*SS*)	250 (MRP_{SS})	125 (P_{SS})	2.0
Skilled (*S*)	500 (MRP_S)	200 (P_S)	2.5

Solution:

Calculating the MRP_{input}/P_{input} values for the different labor categories yields ratio numbers of 1.0, 2.0, and 2.5 for unskilled, semi-skilled, and skilled labor, respectively. The firm adds skilled labor first because it is the most profitable to employ, as indicated by MRP_S/P_S being the highest ratio of the three labor inputs. The contribution to profit by employing the next skilled worker is $300, calculated as ($500 − $200). However, with the employment of additional skilled workers, MRP_S declines because of diminishing returns that are associated with the MP component. At the point where the skilled labor ratio drops below 2.0—for example, to 1.5—semi-skilled labor becomes feasible to hire because its MRP exceeds its compensation by more than that of skilled labor.[6] Again, the diminishing returns effect decreases MRP when additional semi-skilled workers are hired. In the case of unskilled labor, MRP_U equals the cost of labor; hence, no further contribution to profit accrues from adding this type of labor. In fact, adding another unskilled worker would probably reduce total profit because the next worker's compensation is likely to exceed MRP as a result of a declining MP. The input level that maximizes profit is where $MRP_U/P_U = MRP_{SS}/P_{SS} = MRP_S/P_S = 1$.

SUMMARY

When assessing financial performance, a micro exploration of a firm's profitability reveals more information to the analyst relative to the typical macro examination of overall earnings. Crucial issues evolve when the firm fails to reward investors properly for their equity commitment and when the firm's operating status is non-optimal in regard to resource employment, cost minimization, and profit maximization.

Among the points made in this reading are the following:

- The two major concepts of profits are accounting profit and economic profit. Economic profit equals accounting profit minus implicit opportunity costs not included in accounting costs. Profit in the theory of the firm refers to economic profit.

- Normal profit is an economic profit of zero. A firm earning a normal profit is earning just enough to cover the explicit and implicit costs of resources used in running the firm, including, most importantly for publicly traded corporations, debt and equity capital.

- Economic profit is a residual value in excess of normal profit and results from access to positive NPV investment opportunities.

- The factors of production are the inputs to the production of goods and services and include land, labor, capital, and materials.

- Profit maximization occurs at the following points:
  - Where the difference between total revenue and total costs is the greatest.
  - Where marginal revenue equals marginal cost.
  - Where marginal revenue product equals the resource cost for each type of input.

- When total costs exceed total revenue, loss minimization occurs where the difference between total costs and total revenue is the least.

- In the long run, all inputs to the firm are variable, which expands profit potential and the number of cost structures available to the firm.

---

6 The next semi-skilled worker contributes $125 (derived as $250 − $125) per day to profit, while the next skilled worker's contribution, based on a ratio of 1.5, is $100 ($MRP_S$ of $300 minus compensation of $200 per day).

- Under perfect competition, long-run profit maximization occurs at the minimum point of the firm's long-run average total cost curve.

- In an economic loss situation, a firm can operate in the short run if total revenue covers variable cost but is inadequate to cover fixed cost; however, in the long run, the firm will exit the market if fixed costs are not covered in full.

- In an economic loss situation, a firm shuts down in the short run if total revenue does not cover variable cost in full and eventually exits the market if the shortfall is not reversed.

- Economies of scale lead to lower average total cost; diseconomies of scale lead to higher average total cost.

- A firm's production function defines the relationship between total product and inputs.

- Average product and marginal product, which are derived from total product, are key measures of a firm's productivity.

- Increases in productivity reduce business costs and enhance profitability.

- An industry supply curve that is positively sloped in the long run will increase production costs to the firm. An industry supply curve that is negatively sloped in the long run will decrease production costs to the firm.

- In the short run, assuming constant resource prices, increasing marginal returns reduce the marginal costs of production and decreasing marginal returns increase the marginal costs of production.

PRACTICE PROBLEMS

1 Normal profit is *best* described as:

   A zero economic profit.

   B total revenue minus all explicit costs.

   C the sum of accounting profit plus economic profit.

2 A firm supplying a commodity product in the marketplace is *most likely* to receive economic rent if:

   A demand increases for the commodity and supply is elastic.

   B demand increases for the commodity and supply is inelastic.

   C supply increases for the commodity and demand is inelastic.

3 Entrepreneurs are *most likely* to receive payment or compensation in the form of:

   A rent.

   B profit.

   C wages.

4 The marketing director for a Swiss specialty equipment manufacturer estimates the firm can sell 200 units and earn total revenue of CHF500,000. However, if 250 units are sold, revenue will total CHF600,000. The marginal revenue per unit associated with marketing 250 units instead of 200 units is *closest* to:

   A CHF 2,000.

   B CHF 2,400.

   C CHF 2,500.

5 An agricultural firm operating in a perfectly competitive market supplies wheat to manufacturers of consumer food products and animal feeds. If the firm were able to expand its production and unit sales by 10% the *most likely* result would be:

   A a 10% increase in total revenue.

   B a 10% increase in average revenue.

   C an increase in total revenue of less than 10%.

6 An operator of a ski resort is considering offering price reductions on weekday ski passes. At the normal price of €50 per day, 300 customers are expected to buy passes each weekday. At a discounted price of €40 per day 450 customers are expected to buy passes each weekday. The marginal revenue per customer earned from offering the discounted price is *closest* to:

   A €20.

   B €40.

   C €50.

7 The marginal revenue per unit sold for a firm doing business under conditions of perfect competition will *most likely* be:

   A equal to average revenue.

   B less than average revenue.

   C greater than average revenue.

The following information relates to Questions 8–10

A firm's director of operations gathers the following information about the firm's cost structure at different levels of output:

Exhibit 1		
Quantity (Q)	Total Fixed Cost (TFC)	Total Variable Cost (TVC)
0	200	0
1	200	100
2	200	150
3	200	200
4	200	240
5	200	320

8 Refer to the data in Exhibit 1. When quantity produced is equal to 4 units, the average fixed cost (AFC) is *closest* to:

A 50.

B 60.

C 110.

9 Refer to the data in Exhibit 1. When the firm increases production from 4 to 5 units, the marginal cost (MC) is *closest* to:

A 40.

B 64.

C 80.

10 Refer to the data in Exhibit 1. The level of unit production resulting in the lowest average total cost (ATC) is *closest* to:

A 3.

B 4.

C 5.

11 The short-term breakeven point of production for a firm operating under perfect competition will *most likely* occur when:

A price is equal to average total cost.

B marginal revenue is equal to marginal cost.

C marginal revenue is equal to average variable costs.

12 The short-term shutdown point of production for a firm operating under perfect competition will *most likely* occur when:

A price is equal to average total cost.

B marginal revenue is equal to marginal cost.

C marginal revenue is less than average variable costs.

13 When total revenue is greater than total variable costs but less than total costs, in the short term a firm will *most likely*:

A exit the market.

B stay in the market.

C shut down production.

14 A profit maximum is *least likely* to occur when:

A average total cost is minimized.

B marginal revenue equals marginal cost.

C the difference between total revenue and total cost is maximized.

15 A firm that increases its quantity produced without any change in per-unit cost is experiencing:

A economies of scale.

B diseconomies of scale.

C constant returns to scale.

16 A firm is operating beyond minimum efficient scale in a perfectly competitive industry. To maintain long-term viability the *most likely* course of action for the firm is to:

A operate at the current level of production.

B increase its level of production to gain economies of scale.

C decrease its level of production to the minimum point on the long-run average total cost curve.

17 Under conditions of perfect competition, in the long run firms will *most likely* earn:

A normal profits.

B positive economic profits.

C negative economic profits.

18 A firm engages in the development and extraction of oil and gas, the supply of which is price inelastic. The *most likely* equilibrium response in the long run to an increase in the demand for petroleum is that oil prices:

A increase, and extraction costs per barrel fall.

B increase, and extraction costs per barrel rise.

C remain constant, and extraction costs per barrel remain constant.

19 A firm develops and markets consumer electronic devices in a perfectly competitive, decreasing-cost industry. The firm's products have grown in popularity. The *most likely* equilibrium response in the long run to rising demand for such devices is for selling prices to:

A fall and per-unit production costs to decrease.

B rise and per-unit production costs to decrease.

C remain constant and per-unit production costs to remain constant.

The following information relates to Questions 20–21

The manager of a small manufacturing firm gathers the following information about the firm's labor utilization and production:

Exhibit 2	
Labor (L)	**Total Product (TP)**
0	0
1	150
2	320
3	510
4	660
5	800

20 Refer to the data in Exhibit 2. The number of workers resulting in the highest level of average product of labor is *closest* to:

A 3.

B 4.

C 5.

21 Refer to the data in Exhibit 2. The marginal product of labor demonstrates increasing returns for the firm if the number of workers is *closest* to but not more than:

A 2.

B 3.

C 4.

22 A firm experiencing an increase in the marginal product of labor employed would *most likely*:

A allow an increased number of workers to specialize and become more adept at their individual functions.

B find that an increase in workers cannot be efficiently matched by other inputs that are fixed such as property, plant, and equipment.

C find that the supply of skilled workers is limited, and additional workers lack essential skills and aptitudes possessed by the current workforce.

23 For a manufacturing company to achieve the most efficient combination of labor and capital, and therefore minimize total costs for a desired level of output, it will *most likely* attempt to equalize the:

A average product of labor to the average product of capital.

B marginal product per unit of labor to the marginal product per unit of capital.

C marginal product obtained per dollar spent on labor to the marginal product per dollar spent on capital.

24 A firm will expand production by 200 units and must hire at least one additional worker. The marginal product per day for one additional unskilled worker is 100 units. The marginal product per day for one additional skilled worker is 200 units. Wages per day are $200 for an unskilled worker and $450 for a skilled worker. The firm will *most likely* minimize costs at the higher level of production by hiring:

A one additional skilled worker.

    B two additional unskilled workers.

    C either a skilled worker or two unskilled workers.

25 A Mexican firm employs unskilled, semi-skilled, and skilled labor in a cost-minimizing mix at its manufacturing plant. The marginal product of unskilled labor is considerably lower than semi-skilled and skilled labor, but the equilibrium wage for unskilled labor is only 300 pesos per day. The government passes a law that mandates a minimum wage of 400 pesos per day. Equilibrium wages for semi-skilled and skilled labor exceed this minimum wage and therefore are not affected by the new law. The firm will *most likely* respond to the imposition of the minimum wage law by:

    A employing more unskilled workers at its plant.

    B employing fewer unskilled workers at its plant.

    C keeping the mix of unskilled, semi-skilled, and skilled workers the same.

The following information relates to Questions 26–27

A firm produces handcrafted wooden chairs, employing both skilled craftsmen and automated equipment in its plant. The selling price of a chair is €100. A craftsman earns €900 per week and can produce ten chairs per week. Automated equipment leased for €800 per week can produce ten chairs per week.

26 The marginal revenue product (per week) of hiring an additional craftsman is *closest* to:

    A €100.

    B €900.

    C €1,000.

27 The firm would like to increase weekly output by 50 chairs. The firm would *most likely* enhance profits by:

    A hiring additional craftsmen.

    B leasing additional automated equipment.

    C leasing additional automated equipment and hiring additional craftsmen in equal proportion.

SOLUTIONS

1   A is correct. Normal profit is the level of accounting profit such that implicit opportunity costs are just covered; thus, it is equal to a level of accounting profit such that economic profit is zero.

2   B is correct. Economic rent results when a commodity is fixed in supply (highly inelastic) and the market price is higher than what is required to bring the commodity to market. An increase in demand in this circumstance would result in a rising price and increased potential for economic rent.

3   B is correct. Profit is the return to entrepreneurship for its contribution to the economic process.

4   A is correct. Marginal revenue per unit is defined as the change in total revenue divided by the change in quantity sold. $MR = \Delta TR \div \Delta Q$. In this case, change in total revenue equals CHF100,000, and change in total units sold equals 50. CHF100,000 ÷ 50 = CHF2,000.

5   A is correct. In a perfectly competitive market, an increase in supply by a single firm will not affect price. Therefore, an increase in units sold by the firm will be matched proportionately by an increase in revenue.

6   A is correct. Marginal revenue per unit is defined as the change in total revenues divided by the change in quantity sold. $MR = \Delta TR \div \Delta Q$. In this case, change in total revenue per day equals €3,000 [(450 x €40) − (300 x €50)], and change in units sold equals 150 (450 − 300). €3,000 ÷ 150 = €20.

7   A is correct. Under perfect competition, a firm is a price taker at any quantity supplied to the market, and $AR = MR = $ Price.

8   A is correct. Average fixed cost is equal to total fixed cost divided by quantity produced: AFC = TFC/Q = 200/4 = 50.

9   C is correct. Marginal cost is equal to the change in total cost divided by the change in quantity produced. $MC = \Delta TC/\Delta Q$ = 80/1 = 80.

10 C is correct. Average total cost is equal to total cost divided by quantity produced. At 5 units produced the average total cost is 104. $ATC = TC/Q$ = 520/5 = 104.

11 A is correct. Under perfect competition, price equals marginal revenue. A firm breaks even when marginal revenue equals average total cost.

12 C is correct. The firm should shut down production when marginal revenue is less than average variable cost.

13 B is correct. When total revenue is enough to cover variable costs but not total fixed costs in full, the firm can survive in the short run but would be unable to maintain financial solvency in the long run.

14 A is correct. The quantity at which average total cost is minimized does not necessarily correspond to a profit maximum.

15 C is correct. Output increases in the same proportion as input increases occur at constant returns to scale.

16 C is correct. The firm operating at greater than long-run efficient scale is subject to diseconomies of scale. It should plan to decrease its level of production.

17 A is correct. Competition should drive prices down to long-run marginal cost, resulting in only normal profits being earned.

18 B is correct. The development and extraction of scarce oil and gas is an increasing-cost industry. A positive shift in demand will cause firms to increase supply, but at higher costs. The higher costs associated with increasing supply will cause prices to rise.

19 A is correct. A positive shift in demand will cause firms to increase supply, but at decreasing costs. The decreasing cost per unit will be passed on to consumers and cause prices to fall in the long run.

20 A is correct. Three workers produce the highest average product equal to 170. $AP = 510/3 = 170$.

21 B is correct. Marginal product is equal to the change in total product divided by the change in labor. The increase in MP from 2 to 3 workers is 190: $MP = \Delta TP/\Delta L = (510 - 320)/(3 - 2) = 190/1 = 190$.

22 A is correct. Adding new workers in numbers sufficient for them to specialize in their roles and functions should increase marginal product of labor.

23 C is correct. Costs are minimized when substitution of labor for capital (or the reverse) does not result in any cost savings, which is the case when the marginal product per dollar spent is equalized across inputs.

24 B is correct. An expansion in production by 200 units can be achieved by two unskilled workers at a total cost of $400, or $2 per unit produced. $400/200 = $2 per unit produced.

25 B is correct. The firm employs labor of various types in a cost-minimizing combination. Profit is maximized when marginal revenue product is equalized across each type of labor input. If the wage rate of unskilled workers increases, the marginal product produced per dollar spent to employ unskilled labor will decline. The original employment mix is no longer optimal, so the firm will respond by shifting away from unskilled workers to workers whose wages are unaffected by the minimum wage law.

26 C is correct. The marginal revenue product is the marginal product of an additional craftsman (10 chairs) times the price per chair (€100). $10 \times €100 = €1,000$.

27 B is correct. The marginal revenue product for additional power tools is €1,000, which exceeds the €800 cost of the tools by €200. $(10 \times €100 = €1,000) - €800 = €200$.

READING

16

The Firm and Market Structures

by Richard G. Fritz, PhD, and Michele Gambera, PhD, CFA

Richard G. Fritz, PhD, is at Georgia Institute of Technology (USA). Michele Gambera, PhD, CFA, is at UBS Global Asset Management (USA).

LEARNING OUTCOMES

Mastery	The candidate should be able to:
☐	a. describe characteristics of perfect competition, monopolistic competition, oligopoly, and pure monopoly;
☐	b. explain relationships between price, marginal revenue, marginal cost, economic profit, and the elasticity of demand under each market structure;
☐	c. describe a firm's supply function under each market structure;
☐	d. describe and determine the optimal price and output for firms under each market structure;
☐	e. explain factors affecting long-run equilibrium under each market structure;
☐	f. describe pricing strategy under each market structure;
☐	g. describe the use and limitations of concentration measures in identifying market structure;
☐	h. identify the type of market structure within which a firm operates.

INTRODUCTION

1

The purpose of this reading is to build an understanding of the importance of market structure. As different market structures result in different sets of choices facing a firm's decision makers, an understanding of market structure is a powerful tool in analyzing issues such as a firm's pricing of its products and, more broadly, its potential to increase profitability. In the long run, a firm's profitability will be determined by the forces associated with the market structure within which it operates. In a highly competitive market, long-run profits will be driven down by the forces of competition. In less competitive markets, large profits are possible even in the long run; in the short run, any outcome is possible. Therefore, understanding the forces behind the market structure will aid the financial analyst in determining firms' short- and long-term prospects.

Section 2 introduces the analysis of market structures. The section addresses questions such as: What determines the degree of competition associated with each market structure? Given the degree of competition associated with each market structure, what decisions are left to the management team developing corporate strategy? How does a chosen pricing and output strategy evolve into specific decisions that affect the profitability of the firm? The answers to these questions are related to the forces of the market structure within which the firm operates.

Sections 3, 4, 5, and 6 analyze demand, supply, optimal price and output, and factors affecting long-run equilibrium for perfect competition, monopolistic competition, oligopoly, and pure monopoly, respectively.

Section 7 reviews techniques for identifying the various forms of market structure. For example, there are accepted measures of market concentration that are used by regulators of financial institutions to judge whether or not a planned merger or acquisition will harm the competitive nature of regional banking markets. Financial analysts should be able to identify the type of market structure a firm is operating within. Each different structure implies a different long-run sustainability of profits. A summary and practice problems conclude the reading.

2 ANALYSIS OF MARKET STRUCTURES

Traditionally, economists classify a market into one of four structures: perfect competition, monopolistic competition, oligopoly, and monopoly. Section 2.1 explains that four-way classification in more detail. Section 2.2 completes the introduction by providing and explaining the major points to evaluate in determining the structure to which a market belongs.

2.1 Economists' Four Types of Structure

Economists define a market as a group of buyers and sellers that are aware of each other and are able to agree on a price for the exchange of goods and services. While the internet has extended a number of markets worldwide, certain markets are limited by geographic boundaries. For example, the internet search engine Google operates in a worldwide market. In contrast, the market for premixed cement is limited to the area within which a truck can deliver the mushy mix from the plant to a construction site before the compound becomes useless. Thomas L. Friedman's international best seller *The World Is Flat*[1] challenges the concept of the geographic limitations of the market. If the service being provided by the seller can be digitized, its market expands worldwide. For example, a technician can scan your injury in a clinic in Switzerland. That radiographic image can be digitized and sent to a radiologist in India to be read. As a customer (i.e., patient), you may never know that part of the medical service provided to you was the result of a worldwide market.

Some markets are highly concentrated, with the majority of total sales coming from a small number of firms. For example, in the market for small consumer batteries, three firms controlled 87 percent of the US market (Duracell 43 percent, Energizer 33 percent, and Rayovac 11 percent) as of 2005. Other markets are very fragmented, such as automobile repairs, where small independent shops often dominate and large

---

1 Friedman (2006).

chains may or may not exist. New products can lead to market concentration: It is estimated that the Apple iPod had a world market share of over 70 percent among MP3 players in 2009.

THE IMPORTANCE OF MARKET STRUCTURE

Consider the evolution of television broadcasting. As the market environment for television broadcasting evolved, the market structure changed, resulting in a new set of challenges and choices. In the early days, there was only one choice: the "free" analog channels that were broadcast over the airwaves. In most countries, there was only one channel, owned and run by the government. In the United States, some of the more populated markets were able to receive more channels because local channels were set up to cover a market with more potential viewers. By the 1970s, new technologies made it possible to broadcast by way of cable connectivity and the choices offered to consumers began to expand rapidly. Cable television challenged the "free" broadcast channels by offering more choice and a better-quality picture. The innovation was expensive for consumers and profitable for the cable companies. By the 1990s, a new alternative began to challenge the existing broadcast and cable systems: satellite television. Satellite providers offered a further expanded set of choices, albeit at a higher price than the free broadcast and cable alternatives. In the early 2000s, satellite television providers lowered their pricing to compete directly with the cable providers. Today, cable program providers, satellite television providers, and terrestrial digital broadcasters that offer premium and pay-per-view channels compete for customers who are increasingly finding content on the internet.

This is a simple illustration of the importance of market structure. As the market for television broadcasting became increasingly competitive, managers had to make decisions regarding product packaging, pricing, advertising, and marketing in order to survive in the changing environment.

Market structure can be broken down into four distinct categories: perfect competition, monopolistic competition, oligopoly, and monopoly.

We start with the most competitive environment, **perfect competition**. Unlike some economic concepts, perfect competition is not merely an ideal based on assumptions. Perfect competition is a reality—for example, in several commodities markets, where sellers and buyers have a strictly homogeneous product and no single producer is large enough to influence market prices. Perfect competition's characteristics are well recognized and its long-run outcome unavoidable. Profits under the conditions of perfect competition are driven to the required rate of return paid by the entrepreneur to borrow capital from investors (so-called normal profit or rental cost of capital). This does not mean that all perfectly competitive industries are doomed to extinction by a lack of profits. On the contrary, millions of businesses that do very well are living under the pressures of perfect competition.

Monopolistic competition is also highly competitive; however, it is considered a form of imperfect competition. Two economists, Edward H. Chamberlin (US) and Joan Robinson (UK), identified this hybrid market and came up with the term because there are strong elements of competition in this market structure and also some monopoly-like conditions. The competitive characteristic is a notably large number of firms, while the monopoly aspect is the result of product differentiation. That is, if the seller can convince consumers that its product is uniquely different from other, similar products, then the seller can exercise some degree of pricing power over the market. A good example is the brand loyalty associated with soft drinks such as Coca-Cola. Many of Coca-Cola's customers believe that their beverages are truly different from and better than all other soft drinks. The same is true for fashion creations and cosmetics.

The **oligopoly** market structure is based on a relatively small number of firms supplying the market. The small number of firms in the market means that each firm must consider what retaliatory strategies the other firms will pursue when prices and production levels change. Consider the pricing behavior of commercial airline companies. Pricing strategies and route scheduling are based on the expected reaction of the other carriers in similar markets. For any given route—say, from Paris, France, to Chennai, India—only a few carriers are in competition. If one of the carriers changes its pricing package, others will likely retaliate. Understanding the market structure of oligopoly markets can help in identifying a logical pattern of strategic price changes for the competing firms.

Finally, the least competitive market structure is **monopoly**. In pure monopoly markets, there are no other good substitutes for the given product or service. There is a single seller, which, if allowed to operate without constraint, exercises considerable power over pricing and output decisions. In most market-based economies around the globe, pure monopolies are regulated by a governmental authority. The most common example of a regulated monopoly is the local electrical power provider. In most cases, the monopoly power provider is allowed to earn a normal return on its investment and prices are set by the regulatory authority to allow that return.

2.2 Factors That Determine Market Structure

Five factors determine market structure:

1 The number and relative size of firms supplying the product;

2 The degree of product differentiation;

3 The power of the seller over pricing decisions;

4 The relative strength of the barriers to market entry and exit; and

5 The degree of non-price competition.

The number and relative size of firms in a market influence market structure. If there are many firms, the degree of competition increases. With fewer firms supplying a good or service, consumers are limited in their market choices. One extreme case is the monopoly market structure, with only one firm supplying a unique good or service. Another extreme is perfect competition, with many firms supplying a similar product. Finally, an example of relative size is the automobile industry, in which a small number of large international producers (e.g., Ford and Toyota) are the leaders in the global market, and a number of small companies either have market power because they are niche players (e.g., Ferrari) or have little market power because of their narrow range of models or limited geographical presence (e.g., Škoda).

In the case of monopolistic competition, there are many firms providing products to the market, as with perfect competition. However, one firm's product is differentiated in some way that makes it appear better than similar products from other firms. If a firm is successful in differentiating its product, the differentiation will provide pricing leverage. The more dissimilar the product appears, the more the market will resemble the monopoly market structure. A firm can differentiate its product through aggressive advertising campaigns; frequent styling changes; the linking of its product with other, complementary products; or a host of other methods.

When the market dictates the price based on aggregate supply and demand conditions, the individual firm has no control over pricing. The typical hog farmer in Nebraska and the milk producer in Bavaria are **price takers**. That is, they must accept whatever price the market dictates. This is the case under the market structure of perfect competition. In the case of monopolistic competition, the success of product differentiation determines the degree with which the firm can influence price. In the case of oligopoly, there are so few firms in the market that price control becomes possible. However, the small number of firms in an oligopoly market invites complex pricing strategies. Collusion, price leadership by dominant firms, and other pricing strategies can result.

The degree to which one market structure can evolve into another and the difference between potential short-run outcomes and long-run equilibrium conditions depend on the strength of the barriers to entry and the possibility that firms fail to recoup their original costs or lose money for an extended period of time and are therefore forced to exit the market. Barriers to entry can result from very large capital investment requirements, as in the case of petroleum refining. Barriers may also result from patents, as in the case of some electronic products and drug formulas. Another entry consideration is the possibility of high exit costs. For example, plants that are specific to a special line of products, such as aluminum smelting plants, are non-redeployable, and exit costs would be high without a liquid market for the firm's assets. High exit costs deter entry and are therefore also considered barriers to entry. In the case of farming, the barriers to entry are low. Production of corn, soybeans, wheat, tomatoes, and other produce is an easy process to replicate; therefore, those are highly competitive markets.

Non-price competition dominates those market structures where product differentiation is critical. Therefore, monopolistic competition relies on competitive strategies that may not include pricing changes. An example of non-price competition is product differentiation through marketing. In other circumstances, non-price competition may occur because the few firms in the market feel dependent on each other. Each firm fears retaliatory price changes that would reduce total revenue for all of the firms in the market. Because oligopoly industries have so few firms, each firm feels dependent on the pricing strategies of the others. Therefore, non-price competition becomes a dominant strategy.

Exhibit 1   Characteristics of Market Structure

Market Structure	Number of Sellers	Degree of Product Differentiation	Barriers to Entry	Pricing Power of Firm	Non-price Competition
Perfect competition	Many	Homogeneous/ Standardized	Very Low	None	None
Monopolistic competition	Many	Differentiated	Low	Some	Advertising and Product Differentiation
Oligopoly	Few	Homogeneous/ Standardized	High	Some or Considerable	Advertising and Product Differentiation
Monopoly	One	Unique Product	Very High	Considerable	Advertising

From the perspective of the owners of the firm, the most desirable market structure is that with the most control over price, because this control can lead to large profits. Monopoly and oligopoly markets offer the greatest potential control over price; monopolistic competition offers less control. Firms operating under perfectly competitive market conditions have no control over price. From the consumers' perspective, the most desirable market structure is that with the greatest degree of competition, because prices are generally lower. Thus, consumers would prefer as many goods and services as possible to be offered in competitive markets.

As often happens in economics, there is a trade-off. While perfect competition gives the largest quantity of a good at the lowest price, other market forms may spur more innovation. Specifically, there may be high costs in researching a new product, and firms will incur such costs only if they expect to earn an attractive return on their research investment. This is the case often made for medical innovations, for example—the cost of clinical trials and experiments to create new medicines would bankrupt perfectly competitive firms but may be acceptable in an oligopoly market structure. Therefore, consumers can benefit from less-than-perfectly-competitive markets.

PORTER'S FIVE FORCES AND MARKET STRUCTURE

A financial analyst aiming to establish market conditions and consequent profitability of incumbent firms should start with the questions framed by Exhibit 1: How many sellers are there? Is the product differentiated? and so on. Moreover, in the case of monopolies and quasi monopolies, the analyst should evaluate the legislative and regulatory framework: Can the company set prices freely, or are there governmental controls? Finally, the analyst should consider the threat of competition from potential entrants.

This analysis is often summarized by students of corporate strategy as "Porter's five forces," named after Harvard Business School professor Michael E. Porter. His book, *Competitive Strategy*, presented a systematic analysis of the practice of market strategy. Porter (2008) identified the five forces as:

- Threat of entry;
- Power of suppliers;
- Power of buyers (customers);
- Threat of substitutes; and
- Rivalry among existing competitors.

It is easy to note the parallels between four of these five forces and the columns in Exhibit 1. The only "orphan" is the power of suppliers, which is not at the core of the theoretical economic analysis of competition, but which has substantial weight in the practical analysis of competition and profitability.

Some stock analysts (e.g., Dorsey 2004) use the term "economic moat" to suggest that there are factors protecting the profitability of a firm that are similar to the moats (ditches full of water) that used to protect some medieval castles. A deep moat means that there is little or no threat of entry by invaders, i.e. competitors. It also means that customers are locked in because of high switching costs.

3 PERFECT COMPETITION

Perfect competition is characterized by the five conditions presented in Exhibit 1, above:

1 There are a large number of potential buyers and sellers.
2 The products offered by the sellers are virtually identical.
3 There are few or easily surmountable barriers to entry and exit.
4 Sellers have no market-pricing power.
5 Non-price competition is absent.

While few markets achieve the distinction of being perfectly competitive, it is useful to establish the outcome associated with this market structure as a benchmark against which other market structures can be compared. The most typical example of perfect competition is found in certain aspects of the agriculture industry, such as the large number of farmers growing corn for animal feed. Corn is a primary source of food for pork, beef, and poultry production. A bushel of corn from Farmer Brown is virtually identical to a bushel of corn from Farmer Lopez. If a hog farmer needs corn to feed his hogs, it does not matter whether the corn comes from Farmer Brown or Farmer Lopez. Furthermore, the aggregate corn market is well defined, with active futures and spot markets. Information about the corn market is easy and inexpensive to access, and there is no way to differentiate the product, such as by advertising. Agribusiness is capital intensive, but where arable land is relatively abundant and water is available, the barriers to entry (e.g., capital and expertise) for corn production are relatively low.

3.1 Demand Analysis in Perfectly Competitive Markets

The price of a homogeneous product sold in a competitive market is determined by the demand and supply in that market. Economists usually represent demand and supply in a market through demand and supply curves in a two-axis plane, where quantity and price are shown on the x-axis and y-axis, respectively. Economists believe that demand functions have negative slopes, as shown in Exhibit 2. That is, at high prices, less is demanded. For normal goods and services, as the price declines, the quantity demanded increases. This concept is based on two effects: the income effect and the substitution effect. The income effect results from the increased purchasing power the consumer has when prices fall. With lower prices, the consumer can afford to purchase more of the product. The substitution effect comes from the increasing attractiveness of the lower-priced product. If soybean prices are unchanged and corn prices decrease, hog farmers will substitute corn for soybeans as feed for their animals.

Exhibit 2   Market Demand in Perfect Competition

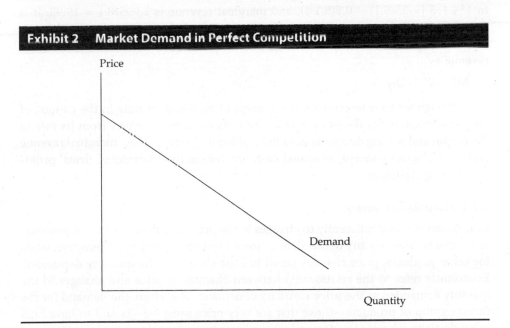

Assume the demand for this product can be specified as

$$Q_D = 50 - 2P$$

where Q_D is the quantity of demand and P is the product's price. This demand function can be rearranged in terms of price:

$$P = 25 - 0.5Q_D$$

In this form, total revenue (TR) is equal to price times quantity, or $P \times Q_D$. Thus,

$$TR = PQ_D = 25Q_D - 0.5Q_D^2$$

Average revenue (AR) can be found by dividing TR by Q_D. Therefore,

$$AR = TR/Q_D = \left(25Q_D - 0.5Q_D^2\right)\Big/Q_D = 25 - 0.5Q_D$$

Note that the AR function is identical to the market demand function. The assumption here is that the relationship between price and quantity demanded is linear. Clearly, that may not be the case in the real market. Another simplifying assumption made is that the price of the product is the only determinant of demand. Again, that is not likely in the real market. For example, economic theory suggests that consumer income is another important factor in determining demand. The prices of related goods and services, such as substitutes and complements, are also considered factors affecting demand for a particular product.

Marginal revenue (MR) is the change in total revenue per extra increment sold when the quantity sold changes by a small increment, ΔQ_D. Substituting $(Q_D + \Delta Q_D)$ into the total revenue (TR) equation, marginal revenue can be expressed as:

$$MR = \frac{\Delta TR}{\Delta Q_D} = \frac{\left[25(Q_D + \Delta Q_D) - 0.5\left(Q_D^2 + 2Q_D\Delta Q_D + \Delta Q_D^2\right)\right] - \left[25Q_D - 0.5Q_D^2\right]}{\Delta Q_D}$$

$$= \frac{25\Delta Q_D - Q_D\Delta Q_D - 0.5\Delta Q_D^2}{\Delta Q_D} = 25 - Q_D - 0.5\Delta Q_D$$

For example, suppose $Q_D = 5$ and $\Delta Q_D = 1$, then total revenue increases from 112.50 $[= 25(5) - 0.5\ (5^2)]$ to 132 $[= 25(6) - 0.5(6^2)]$, and marginal revenue is 19.5 = (132 − 112.5)/1. Note that marginal revenue is equal to $(25 - Q_D - 0.5\Delta Q_D)$. Now suppose that ΔQ_D is much smaller, for example $\Delta Q_D = 0.1$. In this case, total revenue increases to 114.495 $[= 25(5.1) - 0.5(5.1^2)]$, and marginal revenue is 1.995/0.1 = 19.95. It is straightforward to confirm that as ΔQ_D gets smaller marginal revenue gets closer to $20 = 25 - Q_D$. So, for very small changes in the quantity sold we can write marginal revenue as[2]

$$MR = 25 - Q_D$$

Although we have introduced the concept of marginal revenue in the context of the demand curve for the market as a whole, its usefulness derives from its role in the output and pricing decisions of individual firms. As we will see, marginal revenue and an analogous concept, marginal cost, are critical in determining firms' profit-maximizing strategies.

3.1.1 Elasticity of Demand

Consumers respond differently to changes in the price of different kinds of products and services. The quantity demanded for some products is very price sensitive, while for other products, price changes result in little change in the quantity demanded. Economists refer to the relationship between changes in price and changes in the quantity demanded as the price elasticity of demand. Therefore, the demand for the former group of products—those that are very price sensitive—is said to have high price elasticity, whereas the demand for the latter group is said to have low price elasticity. Understanding the sensitivity of demand changes to changes in price is critical to understanding market structures.

Price elasticity of demand measures the percentage change in the quantity demanded given a percentage change in the price of a given product. Because the relationship of demand to price is negative, the price elasticity of demand would be negative. *Many economists, however, present the price elasticity as an absolute value,*

---

2 Readers who are familiar with calculus will recognize this as the derivative of total revenue with respect to the quantity sold.

so that price elasticity has a positive sign. We will follow that convention. Higher price elasticity indicates that consumers are very responsive to changes in price. Lower values for price elasticity imply that consumers are not very responsive to price changes. Price elasticity can be measured with the following relationship:

$$\varepsilon_P = -(\% \text{ change in } Q_D) \div (\% \text{ change in } P)$$

where ε_P is price elasticity of demand, Q_D is the quantity demanded, and P is the product's price.

Price elasticity of demand falls into three categories. When demand is very responsive to price change, it is identified as *elastic*. When demand is not responsive to price change, it is identified as *inelastic*. When the percentage change in quantity demanded is exactly the same as the percentage change in price, the demand is called *unitary elastic*.

$\varepsilon_P > 1$ Demand is elastic

$\varepsilon_P = 1$ Demand is unitary elastic

$\varepsilon_P < 1$ Demand is inelastic

Price elasticity of demand depends on several factors. *Price elasticity will be higher if there are many close substitutes for the product.* If a product has many good alternatives, consumers will be more sensitive to price changes. For example, carbonated beverages ("soft drinks") have many close substitutes. It takes strong brand loyalty to keep customer demand high in the soft drink market when one brand's price is strategically lowered; the price elasticity of demand for Coca-Cola has been estimated to be 3.8. For products with numerous close substitutes, demand is highly elastic. For products with few close substitutes, demand is lower in price elasticity and would be considered price inelastic. The demand for first-class airline tickets is often seen as inelastic because only very wealthy people are expected to buy them; the demand for economy-class tickets is elastic because the typical consumer for this product is more budget-conscious. Consumers do not consider economy-class airline tickets a close substitute for first-class accommodations, particularly on long flights.

The airline ticket example introduces another determinant of price elasticity of demand. *The greater the share of the consumer's budget spent on the item, the higher the price elasticity of demand.* Expensive items, such as durable goods (e.g., refrigerators and televisions), tend to have higher elasticity measures, while less expensive items, such as potatoes and salt, have lower elasticity values. Consumers will not change their normal salt consumption if the price of salt decreases by 10 percent. Instead, they will buy their next package of salt when they run out, with very little regard to the price change.

The airline ticket also makes a good example for the final factor determining price elasticity. *Price elasticity of demand also depends on the length of time within which the demand schedule is being considered.* Holiday airline travel is highly price elastic. Consumers shop vigorously for vacation flights because they have time to plan their holiday. Business airline travelers typically have less flexibility in determining their schedules. If your business requires a face-to-face meeting with a client, then the price of the ticket is somewhat irrelevant. If gasoline prices increase, there is very little you can do in the short run but pay the higher price. However, evidence of commuter choices indicates that many use alternative transportation methods after the gasoline price spikes. In the long run, higher gasoline prices will lead consumers to change their modes of transportation, trading in less efficient vehicles for automobiles with higher gas mileage or public transit options where available.

There are two extreme cases of price elasticity of demand. One extreme is the **horizontal demand schedule**. This term implies that at a given price, the response in the quantity demanded is infinite. *This is the demand schedule faced by a perfectly competitive firm, because it is a price taker,* as in the case of a corn farmer. If the corn farmer tried to charge a higher price than the market price, nobody would buy her product. On the other hand, the farmer has no incentive to sell at a lower price because she can sell all she can produce at the market price. In a perfectly competitive market the quantity supplied by an individual firm has a negligible effect on the market price. In the case of *perfect price elasticity*, the measure is $\varepsilon_P = \infty$.

The other extreme is the **vertical demand schedule**. The vertical demand schedule implies that some fixed quantity is demanded, regardless of price. An example of such demand is the diabetic consumer with the need for a certain amount of insulin. If the price of insulin goes up, the patient will not consume less of it. The amount desired is set by the patient's medical condition. The measure for *perfect price inelasticity* is $\varepsilon_P = 0$.

The nature of the elasticity calculation and consumer behavior in the marketplace imply that for virtually any product (excluding cases of perfect elasticity and perfect inelasticity), demand is more elastic at higher prices and less elastic (more inelastic) at lower prices. For example, at current low prices, the demand for table salt is very inelastic. However, if table salt increased in price to hundreds of dollars per ounce, consumers would become more responsive to its price changes. Exhibit 3 reports several empirical estimates of price elasticity of demand.

Exhibit 3	Empirical Price Elasticities[3]
Commodity (Good/Service)	Price Elasticity of Market Demand
Alcoholic beverages consumed at home	
Beer	0.84
Wine	0.55
Liquor	0.50
Coffee	
Regular	0.16
Instant	0.36
Credit charges on bank cards	2.44
Furniture	3.04
Glassware/china	1.20
International air transportation United States/Europe	1.20
Shoes	0.73
Soybean meal	1.65
Tomatoes	2.22

3.1.2 *Other Factors Affecting Demand*

There are two other important forces that influence shifts in consumer demand. One influential factor is consumer income and the other is the price of a related product. For normal goods, as consumer income increases, the demand increases. The degree to which consumers respond to higher incomes by increasing their demand for goods and services is referred to as income elasticity of demand. **Income elasticity of demand**

---

3 Various sources, as noted in McGuigan, Moyer, and Harris (2008), p. 95. These are the elasticities with respect to the product's own price; by convention, they are shown here as positive numbers.

measures the responsiveness of demand to changes in income. The calculation is similar to that of price elasticity, with the percentage change in income replacing the percentage change in price. Note the new calculation below:

$$\varepsilon_Y = (\% \text{ change in } Q_D) \div (\% \text{ change in } Y)$$

where ε_Y is income elasticity of demand, Q_D is the quantity demanded, and Y is consumer income. For normal goods, the measure ε_Y will be a positive value. That is, as consumers' income rises, more of the product is demanded. For products that are considered luxury items, the measure of income elasticity will be greater than one. There are other goods and services that are considered inferior products. For inferior products, as consumer income rises, less of the product is demanded. Inferior products will have negative values for income elasticity. For example, a person on a small income may watch television shows, but if this person had more income, she would prefer going to live concerts and theater performances; in this example, television shows would be the inferior good.

As a technical issue, the difference between price elasticity of demand and income elasticity of demand is that the demand adjustment for price elasticity represents a movement *along the demand schedule* because the demand schedule represents combinations of price and quantity. The demand adjustment for income elasticity represents a *shift in the demand curve* because with a higher income one can afford to purchase more of the good at any price. For a normal good, an increase in income would shift the demand schedule out to the right, away from the origin of the graph, and a decrease in income would shift the demand curve to the left, toward the origin.

The final factor influencing demand for a product is the change in price of a related product, such as a strong substitute or a complementary product. If a close competitor in the beverage market lowers its price, consumers will substitute that product for your product. Thus, your product's demand curve will shift to the left, toward the origin of the graph. **Cross-price elasticity of demand** is the responsiveness of the demand for product A that is associated with the change in price of product B:

$$\varepsilon_X = (\% \text{ change in } Q_{DA}) \div (\% \text{ change in } P_B)$$

where ε_X is cross-price elasticity of demand, Q_{DA} is the quantity demanded of product A, and P_B is the price of product B.

When the cross-price elasticity of demand between two products is *positive*, the two products are considered to be **substitutes**. For example, you may expect to have positive cross-price elasticity between honey and sugar. If the measure of cross-price elasticity is *negative*, the two products are referred to as **complements** of each other. For example, if the price of DVDs goes up, you would expect consumers to buy fewer DVD players. In this case, the cross-price elasticity of demand would have a negative value.

Reviewing cross-price elasticity values provides a simple test for the degree of competition in the market. The more numerous and the closer the substitutes for a product, the lower the pricing power of firms selling in that market; the fewer the substitutes for a product, the greater the pricing power. One interesting application was a US Supreme Court case involving the production and sale of cellophane by DuPont.[4] The court noted that the relevant product market for DuPont's cellophane was the broader flexible packaging materials market. The Supreme Court found the cross-price elasticity of demand between cellophane and other flexible packaging materials to be sufficiently high and exonerated DuPont from a charge of monopolizing the market.

Because price elasticity of demand relates changes in price to changes in the quantity demanded, there must be a logical relationship between marginal revenue and price elasticity. Recall that marginal revenue equals the change in total revenue

---

4 *US v. DuPont*, 351 US 377 (1956), as noted in McGuigan, Moyer, and Harris (2008).

given a change in output or sales. An increase in total revenue results from a decrease in price that results in an increase in sales. In order for the increase in the quantity demanded to be sufficient to offset the decline in price, the percentage change in quantity demanded must be greater than the percentage decrease in price. The relationship between TR and price elasticity is as follows:

$\varepsilon_P > 1$ Demand is elastic $\qquad\qquad\qquad\qquad$ $\uparrow P \rightarrow$ TR $\downarrow$ and $\downarrow P \rightarrow$ TR $\uparrow$

$\varepsilon_P = 1$ Demand is unitary elastic $\qquad\qquad$ $\updownarrow P \rightarrow$ no change in TR

$0 < \varepsilon_P < 1$ Demand is inelastic $\qquad\qquad$ $\uparrow P \rightarrow$ TR $\uparrow$ and $\downarrow P \rightarrow$ TR $\downarrow$

Total revenue is maximized when marginal revenue is zero. The logic is that as long as marginal revenue is positive (i.e., each additional unit sold contributes to additional total revenue), total revenue will continue to increase. Only when marginal revenue becomes negative will total revenue begin to decline. Therefore, the percentage decrease in price is greater than the percentage increase in quantity demanded. The relationship between MR and price elasticity can be expressed as

$$MR = P[1 - (1/\varepsilon_P)]$$

An understanding of price elasticity of demand is an important strategic tool. It would be very useful to know in advance what would happen to your firm's total revenue if you increased the product's price. If you are operating in the inelastic portion of the demand curve, increasing the price of the product will increase total revenue. On the other hand, if you are operating in the elastic portion of the product's demand curve, increasing the price will decrease total revenue.

Decision makers can also use the relationship between marginal revenue and price elasticity of demand in other ways. For example, suppose you are a farmer considering planting soybeans or some other feed crop, such as corn. From Exhibit 3, we know that soybean meal's price elasticity of demand has been estimated to be 1.65. We also know that the current (August 2010) soybean meal price is \$330.14 per metric ton. Therefore, by solving the equation above, we find that the expected marginal revenue per metric ton of soybean meal is \$130.05. Soybeans may prove to be a profitable crop for the farmer. However, just a few years earlier, in August of 2006, the price of a metric ton of soybean meal was \$175.91. Given the crop's price elasticity of demand, the estimated marginal revenue per metric ton was then \$69.30. The lower price translates into lower marginal revenue and might induce the farmer to plant a more profitable feed crop instead.

How do business decision makers decide what level of output to bring to the market? To answer that question, the firm must understand its cost of resources, its production relations, and its supply function. Once the supply function is well defined and understood, it is combined with the demand analysis to determine the profit-maximizing levels of output.

3.1.3 *Consumer Surplus: Value Minus Expenditure*

To this point, we have discussed the fundamentals of supply and demand curves and explained a simple model of how a market can be expected to arrive at an equilibrium combination of price and quantity. While it is certainly necessary for the analyst to understand the basic workings of the market model, it is also crucial to have a sense of why we might care about the nature of the equilibrium. In this section we review the concept of **consumer surplus,** which is helpful in understanding and evaluating business pricing strategies. Consumer surplus is defined as the difference between the value that a consumer places on the units purchased and the amount of money that was required to pay for them. It is a measure of the value gained by the buyer from the transaction.

To get an intuitive feel for the concept of consumer surplus, consider the last thing you purchased. Whatever it was, think of how much you actually paid for it. Now contrast that price with the maximum amount you *would have been willing to pay* rather than go without the item altogether. If those two numbers are different, we say you received some consumer surplus from your purchase. You got a "bargain" because you would have been willing to pay more than you had to pay.

Earlier, we referred to the law of demand, which says that as price falls, consumers are willing to buy more of the good. This observation translates into a negatively sloped demand curve. Alternatively, we could say that the highest price that consumers are willing to pay for an additional unit declines as they consume more and more of a good. In this way, we can interpret their *willingness to pay* as a measure of how much they *value* each additional unit of the good. This is a very important point: In order to purchase a unit of some good, consumers must give up something else they value. So the price they are willing to pay for an additional unit of a good is a measure of how much they value that unit, in terms of the other goods they must sacrifice to consume it.

If demand curves are negatively sloped, it must be because the value of each additional unit of the good falls as more of the good is consumed. We shall explore this concept further below, but for now, it is enough to recognize that the demand curve can therefore be considered a **marginal value curve**, because it shows the highest price consumers would be willing to pay for each additional unit. In effect, the demand curve is the willingness of consumers to pay for each additional unit.

This interpretation of the demand curve allows us to measure the total value of consuming any given quantity of a good. It is the sum of all the marginal values of each unit consumed, up to and including the last unit. Graphically, this measure translates into the area under the consumer's demand curve, up to and including the last unit consumed, as shown in Exhibit 4, where the consumer is choosing to buy Q_1 units of the good at a price of P_1. The marginal value of the Q_1^{th} unit is clearly P_1, because that is the highest price the consumer is willing to pay for that unit. Importantly, however, the marginal value of each unit *up to* the Q_1^{th} is greater than P_1.

Exhibit 4   Consumer Surplus

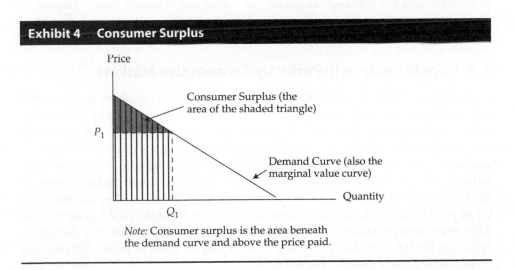

Note: Consumer surplus is the area beneath the demand curve and above the price paid.

Because the consumer would have been willing to pay more for each of those units than she actually paid (P_1), we can say she received more value than the cost to her of buying them. This extra value is the buyer's consumer surplus. The *total value* of quantity Q_1 to the buyer is the area of the vertically crosshatched trapezoid in Exhibit 4. The *total expenditure* is only the area of the rectangle with height P_1 and base Q_1 (bottom section). The total consumer surplus received from buying Q_1 units at a level price of P_1 per unit is the difference between the area under the demand curve and the area of the rectangle $P_1 \times Q_1$. The resulting area is shown as the lightly shaded triangle (upper section).

EXAMPLE 1

Consumer Surplus

A market demand function is given by the equation $Q_D = 180 - 2P$. Find the value of consumer surplus if price is equal to 65.

Solution:

First, input 65 into the demand function to find the quantity demanded at that price: $Q_D = 180 - 2(65) = 50$. Then, to make drawing the demand curve easier, invert the demand function by solving for P in terms of Q_D: $P = 90 - 0.5Q_D$. Note that the price intercept is 90 and the quantity intercept is 180. Draw the demand curve:

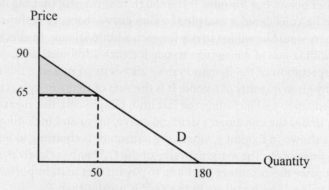

Find the area of the triangle above the price of 65 and below the demand curve, up to quantity 50: Area = ½ (Base)(Height) = ½ (50)(25) = 625.

3.2 Supply Analysis in Perfectly Competitive Markets

Consider two corn farmers, Mr. Brown and Ms. Lopez. They both have land available to them to grow corn and can sell at one price, say 3 currency units per kilogram. They will try to produce as much corn as is profitable at that price. If the price is driven up to 5 currency units per kilogram by new consumers entering the market—say, ethanol producers—Mr. Brown and Ms. Lopez will try to produce more corn. To increase their output levels, they may have to use less productive land, increase irrigation, use more fertilizer, or all three. Their production costs will likely increase. They will both still try to produce as much corn as possible in order to profit at the new, higher price of 5 currency units per kilogram. Exhibit 5 illustrates this example. Note that the supply functions for the individual firms have positive slopes. Thus, as prices increase, the firms supply greater quantities of the product.

Exhibit 5   Firm and Market Supply in Perfect Competition

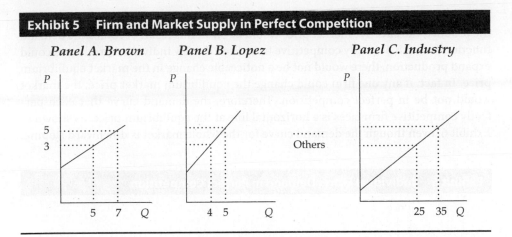

Notice that the market supply curve is the sum of the supply curves of the individual firms—Brown, Lopez, and others—that make up the market. Assume that the supply function for the market can be expressed as a linear relationship, as follows:

$$Q_S = 10 + 5P, \text{ or } P = -2 + 0.2Q_S,$$

where Q_S is the quantity supplied and P is the price of the product.

Before we analyze the optimal supply level for the firm, we need to point out that economic costs and profits differ from accounting costs and profits in a significant way. **Economic costs** include all the remuneration needed to keep the productive resource in its current employment or to acquire the resource for productive use.

In order to evaluate the remuneration needed to keep the resource in its current use and attract new resources for productive use, economists refer to the resource's **opportunity cost**. Opportunity cost is measured by determining the resource's next best opportunity. If a corn farmer could be employed in an alternative position in the labor market with an income of 50,000, then the opportunity cost of the farmer's labor is 50,000. Similarly, the farmer's land and capital could be leased to another farmer or sold and reinvested in another type of business. The return foregone by not doing so is an opportunity cost. In economic terms, total cost includes the full normal market return on all the resources utilized in the business. **Economic profit** is the difference between TR and total cost (TC). Economic profit differs from accounting profit because accounting profit does not include opportunity cost. Accounting profit includes only explicit payments to outside providers of resources (e.g. workers, vendors, lenders) and depreciation based on the historic cost of physical capital.

3.3 Optimal Price and Output in Perfectly Competitive Markets

Carrying forward our examples from Sections 3.1 and 3.2, we can now combine the market supply and demand functions to solve for the equilibrium price and quantity, where Q^* represents the equilibrium level of both supply and demand.

$$P = 25 - 0.5Q_D = -2 + 0.2Q_S = P$$
$$25 - 0.5Q_D = -2 + 0.2Q_S$$
$$27 = 0.7Q^*$$
$$Q^* = 38.57$$

According to the market demand curve, the equilibrium price is

$$P = 25 - 0.5Q^* = 25 - 0.5(38.57) = 25 - 19.29 = 5.71.$$

With many firms in the market and total output in the market of almost 39 units of the product, the effective market price would be 5.71. This result becomes the demand function for each perfectly competitive firm. Even if a few individual producers could expand production, there would not be a noticeable change in the market equilibrium price. In fact, if any one firm could change the equilibrium market price, the market would not be in perfect competition. Therefore, the demand curve that each perfectly competitive firm faces is a horizontal line at the equilibrium price, as shown in Exhibit 6, even though the demand curve for the whole market is downward sloping.

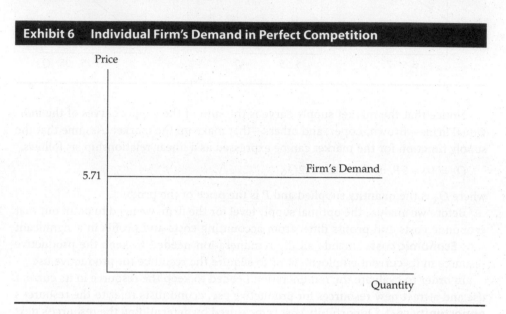

Exhibit 6   Individual Firm's Demand in Perfect Competition

EXAMPLE 2

Demand Curves in Perfect Competition

Is it possible that the demand schedule faced by Firm A is horizontal while the demand schedule faced by the market as a whole is downward sloping?

A No, because Firm A can change its output based on demand changes.

B No, because a horizontal demand curve means that elasticity is infinite.

C Yes, because consumers can go to another firm if Firm A charges a higher price, and Firm A can sell all it produces at the market price.

Solution:

C is correct. Firm A cannot charge a higher price and has no incentive to sell at a price below the market price.

To analyze the firm's revenue position, recall that average revenue is equivalent to the firm's demand function. Therefore, the horizontal line that represents the firm's demand curve is the firm's AR schedule.

Marginal revenue is the incremental increase in total revenue associated with each additional unit sold. For every extra unit the firm sells, it receives 5.71. Thus, the firm's MR schedule is also the horizontal line at 5.71. TR is calculated by multiplying AR by the quantity of products sold. Total revenue is the area under the AR line at the point where the firm produces the output. In the case of perfect competition, the following conditions hold for the individual firm:

Price = Average revenue = Marginal revenue

The next step is to develop the firm's cost functions. The firm knows that it can sell the entire product it produces at the market's equilibrium price. How much should it produce? That decision is determined by analysis of the firm's costs and revenues. A corn farmer uses three primary resources: land, labor, and capital. In economics, capital is any man-made aid to production. For the corn farmer, his or her capital includes the irrigation system, tractors, harvesters, trucks, grain bins, fertilizer, and so forth. The labor includes the farmer, perhaps members of the farmer's family, and hired labor. In the initial stages of production, only the farmer and the farmer's family are cultivating the land, with a significant investment in capital. They have a tractor, fertilizer, irrigation equipment, grain bins, seed, and a harvester. The investment in land and capital is relatively high compared with the labor input. In this production phase, the average cost of producing a bushel of corn is high. As they begin to expand by adding labor to the collection of expensive land and capital, the average cost of producing corn begins to decline—for example, because one tractor can be used more intensively to plow a larger amount of land. When the combination of land, labor, and capital approaches an efficient range, the average cost of producing a bushel of corn declines.

Given a certain level of technology, there is a limit to the increase in productivity. Eventually something begins to cause declining marginal productivity. That is, each additional unit of input produces a progressively smaller increase in output. This force is called the **law of diminishing returns**. This "law" helps define the shape of the firm's cost functions. Average cost and marginal cost will be U-shaped. Over the initial stages of output, average and marginal costs will decline. At some level of output, the law of diminishing returns will overtake the efficiencies in production and average and marginal costs will increase.

Average cost (AC) is Total cost (TC) divided by Output (Q). Therefore,

AC = TC/Q

Note that we have defined average cost (AC) in terms of total costs. Many authors refer to this as "average total cost" to distinguish it from a related concept, "average variable cost," which omits fixed costs. In the reminder of this reading, *average cost should be understood to mean average total cost.*

Marginal cost (MC) is the change in TC associated with an incremental change in output:

MC = ΔTC/ΔQ

By definition, fixed costs do not vary with output, so marginal cost reflects only changes in variable costs.[5] MC declines initially because processes can be made more efficient and specialization makes workers more proficient at their tasks. However, at some higher level of output, MC begins to increase (e.g., must pay workers a higher wage to have them work overtime and, in agriculture, less fertile land must be brought into production). MC and AC will be equal at the level of output where AC is minimized. This is a mathematical necessity and intuitive. If you employ the least expensive labor in the initial phase of production, average and marginal cost will decline. Eventually, additional labor will be more costly. For example, if the labor market is at or near full employment, in order to attract additional workers, you must pay higher wages than

---

5 Readers who are familiar with calculus will recognize that MC is simply the derivative of total cost with respect to quantity produced.

they are currently earning elsewhere. Thus, the additional (marginal) labor is more costly, and the higher cost increases the overall average as soon as MC exceeds AC. Exhibit 7 illustrates the relationship between AC and MC.

Exhibit 7   Individual Firm's Short-Run Cost Schedules

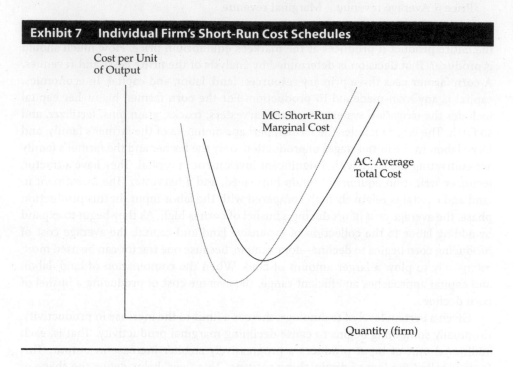

Now combine the revenue and cost functions from Exhibits 6 and 7. In short-run equilibrium, the perfectly competitive firm can earn an economic profit (or an economic loss). In this example, the equilibrium price, 5.71, is higher than the minimum AC. The firm will always maximize profit at an output level where MR = MC. Recall that in perfect competition, the horizontal demand curve is the marginal revenue and average revenue schedules. By setting output at point A in Exhibit 8, where MR = MC, the firm will maximize profits. Total revenue is equal to $P \times Q$—in this case, 5.71 times Q_C. Total cost is equal to Q_C times the average cost of producing Q_C, at point B in Exhibit 8. The difference between the two areas is economic profit.

Exhibit 8   Perfectly Competitive Firm's Short-Run Equilibrium

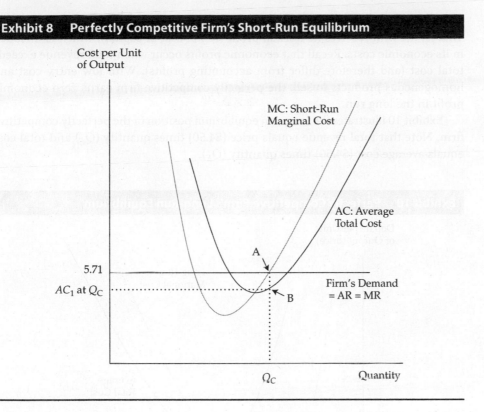

3.4 Factors Affecting Long-Run Equilibrium in Perfectly Competitive Markets

In the long run, economic profit will attract other entrepreneurs to the market, resulting in the production of more output. The aggregate supply will increase, shifting the industry supply (S_1) curve to the right, away from the origin of the graph. For a given demand curve, this increase in supply at each price level will lower the equilibrium price, as shown in Exhibit 9.

Exhibit 9   Perfectly Competitive Market with Increased Supply

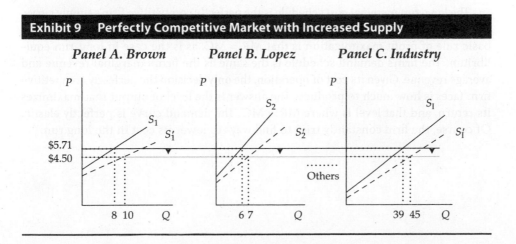

In the long run, the perfectly competitive firm will operate at the point where marginal cost equals the minimum of average cost, because at that point, entry is no longer profitable: In equilibrium, price equals not only marginal cost (firm equilibrium) but also minimum average cost, so that total revenues equal total costs. This result implies that the perfectly competitive firm operates with zero economic profit. That is, the firm receives its normal profit (rental cost of capital), which is included in its economic costs. Recall that economic profits occur when total revenue exceeds total cost (and therefore differ from accounting profits). With low entry cost and homogeneous products to sell, the perfectly competitive firm earns zero economic profit in the long run.

Exhibit 10 illustrates the long-run equilibrium position of the perfectly competitive firm. Note that total revenue equals price ($4.50) times quantity ($Q_E$) and total cost equals average cost ($4.50) times quantity ($Q_E$).

Exhibit 10   Perfectly Competitive Firm's Long-Run Equilibrium

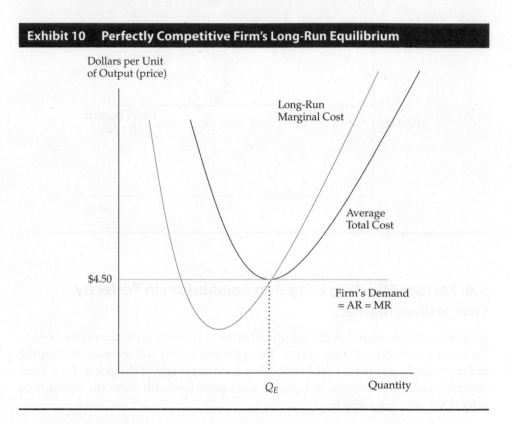

The long-run marginal cost schedule is the perfectly competitive firm's supply curve. The firm's demand curve is dictated by the aggregate market's equilibrium price. The basic rule of profit maximization is that MR = MC, as is the case in long-run equilibrium. The firm's demand schedule is the same as the firm's marginal revenue and average revenue. Given its cost of operation, the only decision the perfectly competitive firm faces is how much to produce. The answer is the level of output that maximizes its return, and that level is where MR = MC. The demand curve is perfectly elastic. Of course, the firm constantly tries to find ways to lower its cost in the long run.

SCHUMPETER ON INNOVATION AND PERFECT COMPETITION

The Austrian-American economist Joseph A. Schumpeter[6] pointed out that technical change in economics can happen in two main ways:

1 Innovation of process: a new, more efficient way to produce an existing good or service.

2 Innovation of product: a new product altogether or an innovation upon an existing product.

Innovation of process is related to production methods. For example, instead of mixing cement by hand, since the invention of the electric engine it has been possible to use electric mixers. A more recent innovation has been to use the internet to provide technical support to personal computer users: A technician can remotely log on to the customer's PC and fix problems instead of providing instructions over the phone. The result is likely the same, but the process is more efficient.

Innovation of product is related to the product itself. MP3 players, smart phones, robot surgery, and GPS vehicle monitoring have existed only for a few years. They are new products and services. While portable music players existed before the MP3 player, no similar service existed before GPS monitoring of personal vehicles and freight trucks was invented.

How does the reality of continuous innovation of product and process, which is a characteristic of modern economies, fit into the ideal model of perfect competition, where the product is made by a huge number of tiny, anonymous suppliers? This seems a contradiction because the tiny suppliers cannot all be able to invent new products—and indeed, the markets for portable music players and smart phones do not look like perfect competition.

Schumpeter suggested that perfect competition is more of a long run type of market. In the short run, a company develops a new process or product and is the only one to take advantage of the innovation. This company likely will have high profits and will outpace any competitors. A second stage is what Schumpeter called the swarming (as when a group of bees leaves a hive to follow a queen): In this case, some entrepreneurs notice the innovation and follow the innovator through imitation. Some of them will fail, while others will succeed and possibly be more successful than the initial innovator. The third stage occurs when the new technology is no longer new because everyone has imitated it. At this point, no economic profits are realized, because the new process or product is no longer a competitive advantage, in the sense that everyone has it—which is when perfect competition prevails and we have long-run equilibrium until a new innovation of process or product is introduced.

MONOPOLISTIC COMPETITION

4

Early in the 20th century, economists began to realize that most markets did not operate under the conditions of perfect competition.[7] Many market structures exhibited characteristics of strong competitive forces; however, other distinct non-competitive factors played important roles in the market. As the name implies, monopolistic competition is a hybrid market. *The most distinctive factor in monopolistic competition is product differentiation.* Recall the characteristics from Exhibit 1:

1 There are a large number of potential buyers and sellers.

---

6 See part 2 of Schumpeter (1942) for the famous "creative destruction" process.
7 Chamberlin (1933).

2 The products offered by each seller are close substitutes for the products offered by other firms, and each firm tries to make its product look different.

3 Entry into and exit from the market are possible with fairly low costs.

4 Firms have some pricing power.

5 Suppliers differentiate their products through advertising and other non-price strategies.

While the market is made up of many firms that compose the product group, each producer attempts to distinguish its product from that of the others. Product differentiation is accomplished in a variety of ways. For example, consider the wide variety of communication devices available today. Decades ago, when each communication market was controlled by a regulated single seller (the telephone company), all telephones were alike. In the deregulated market of today, the variety of physical styles and colors is extensive. All versions accomplish many of the same tasks.

The communication device manufacturers and providers differentiate their products with different colors, styles, networks, bundled applications, conditional contracts, functionality, and more. Advertising is usually the avenue pursued to convince consumers there is a difference between the goods in the product group. Successful advertising and trademark branding result in customer loyalty. A good example is the brand loyalty associated with Harley-Davidson motorcycles. Harley-Davidson's customers believe that their motorcycles are truly different from and better than all other motorcycles. The same kind of brand loyalty exists for many fashion creations and cosmetics.

The extent to which the producer is successful in product differentiation determines pricing power in the market. Very successful differentiation results in a market structure that resembles the single-seller market (monopoly). However, because there are relatively low entry and exit costs, competition will, in the long run, drive prices and revenues down toward an equilibrium similar to perfect competition. Thus, the hybrid market displays characteristics found in both perfectly competitive and monopoly markets.

4.1 Demand Analysis in Monopolistically Competitive Markets

Because each good sold in the product group is somewhat different from the others, the demand curve for each firm in the monopolistic competition market structure is downward sloping to the right. Price and the quantity demanded are negatively related. Lowering the price will increase the quantity demanded, and raising the price will decrease the quantity demanded. There will be ranges of prices within which demand is elastic and (lower) prices at which demand is inelastic. Exhibit 11 illustrates the demand, marginal revenue, and cost structures facing a monopolistically competitive firm in the short run.

Exhibit 11   Short-Run Equilibrium in Monopolistic Competition

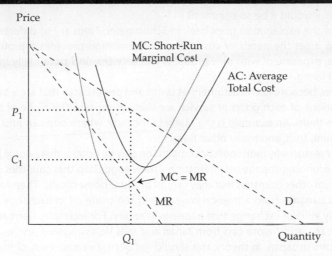

In the short run, the profit-maximizing choice is the level of output where MR = MC. Because the product is somewhat different from that of the competitors, the firm can charge the price determined by the demand curve. Therefore, in Exhibit 11, Q_1 is the ideal level of output and P_1 is the price consumers are willing to pay to acquire that quantity. Total revenue is the area of the rectangle $P_1 \times Q_1$.

4.2 Supply Analysis in Monopolistically Competitive Markets

In perfect competition, the firm's supply schedule is represented by the marginal cost schedule. In monopolistic competition, there is no well-defined supply function. The information used to determine the appropriate level of output is based on the intersection of MC and MR. However, the price that will be charged is based on the market demand schedule. The firm's supply curve should measure the quantity the firm is willing to supply at various prices. That information is not represented by either marginal cost or average cost.

4.3 Optimal Price and Output in Monopolistically Competitive Markets

As seen in Section 4.1, in the short run, the profit-maximizing choice is the level of output where MR = MC and total revenue is the area of the rectangle $P_1 \times Q_1$ in Exhibit 11.

The average cost of producing Q_1 units of the product is C_1, and the total cost is the area of the rectangle $C_1 \times Q_1$. The difference between TR and TC is economic profit. The profit relationship is described as

$$\pi = TR - TC$$

where π is total profit, TR is total revenue, and TC is total cost.

THE BENEFITS OF IMPERFECT COMPETITION

Is monopolistic competition indeed imperfect—that is, is it a bad thing? At first, one would say that it is an inefficient market structure because prices are higher and the quantity supplied is less than in perfect competition. At the same time, in the real world, we see more markets characterized by monopolistic competition than markets meeting the strict conditions of perfect competition. If monopolistic competition were that inefficient, one wonders, why would it be so common?

A part of the explanation goes back to Schumpeter. Firms try to differentiate their products to meet the needs of customers. Differentiation provides a profit incentive to innovate, experiment with new products and services, and potentially improve the standard of living.

Moreover, because each customer has tastes and preferences that are a bit different, slight variations of each good or service are likely to capture the niche of the market that prefers them. An example is the market for candy, where one can find chocolate, liquorice, mint, fruit, and many other flavors.

A further reason why monopolistic competition may be good is that people like variety. Traditional economic theories of international trade suggested that countries should buy products from other countries that they cannot produce domestically. Therefore, Norway should buy bananas from a tropical country and sell crude oil in exchange. But this is not the only kind of exchange that happens in reality: For example, Germany imports Honda, Subaru, and Toyota cars from Japan and sells Volkswagen, Porsche, Mercedes, and BMW cars to Japan. In theory, this should not occur because each of the countries produces good cars domestically and does not need to import them. The truth, however (see, for example, Krugman 1989), is that consumers in both countries enjoy variety. Some Japanese drivers prefer to be at the steering wheel of a BMW; others like Hondas, and the same happens in Germany. Variety and product differentiation, therefore, are not necessarily bad things.

4.4 Factors Affecting Long-Run Equilibrium in Monopolistically Competitive Markets

Because TC includes all costs associated with production, including opportunity cost, economic profit is a signal to the market, and that signal will attract more competition. Just as with the perfectly competitive market structure, with relatively low entry costs, more firms will enter the market and lure some customers away from the firm making an economic profit. The loss of customers to new entrant firms will drive down the demand for all firms producing similar products. In the long run for the monopolistically competitive firm, economic profit will fall to zero. Exhibit 12 illustrates the condition of long-run equilibrium for monopolistic competition.

Exhibit 12   Long-Run Equilibrium in Monopolistic Competition

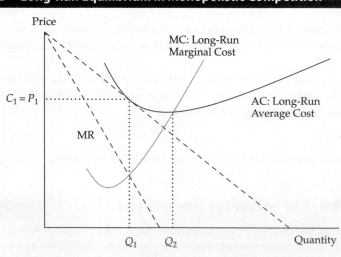

In long-run equilibrium, output is still optimal at the level where MR = MC, which is Q_1 in Exhibit 12. Again, the price consumers are willing to pay for any amount of the product is determined from the demand curve. That price is P_1 for the quantity Q_1 in Exhibit 12, and total revenue is the area of the rectangle $P_1 \times Q_1$. Notice that unlike long-run equilibrium in perfect competition, in the market of monopolistic competition, the equilibrium position is at a higher level of average cost than the level of output that minimizes average cost. Average cost does not reach its minimum until output level Q_2 is achieved. Total cost in this long-run equilibrium position is the area of the rectangle $C_1 \times Q_1$. Economic profit is total revenue minus total cost. In Exhibit 12, economic profit is zero because total revenue equals total cost: $P_1 \times Q_1 = C_1 \times Q_1$.

In the hybrid market of monopolistic competition, zero economic profit in long-run equilibrium resembles perfect competition. However, the long-run level of output, Q_1, is less than Q_2, which corresponds to the minimum average cost of production and would be the long run level of output in a perfectly competitive market. In addition, the economic cost in monopolistic competition includes some cost associated with product differentiation, such as advertising. In perfect competition, there are no costs associated with advertising or marketing because all products are homogeneous. Prices are lower, but consumers may have little variety.

OLIGOPOLY

5

An oligopoly market structure is characterized by only a few firms doing business in a relevant market. The products must all be similar and, to a great extent, be substitutes for one another. In some oligopoly markets, the goods or services may be differentiated by marketing and strong brand recognition, as in the markets for breakfast cereals and for bottled or canned beverages. Other examples of oligopoly markets are made up of homogeneous products with little or no attempt at product differentiation, such as petroleum and cement. *The most distinctive characteristic of oligopoly markets is the small number of firms that dominate the market. There are so few firms in the relevant market that their pricing decisions are interdependent.* That is, each firm's pricing decision is based on the expected retaliation by the other firms. Recall from Exhibit 1 the characteristics of oligopoly markets:

1   There are a small number of potential sellers.

2   The products offered by each seller are close substitutes for the products offered by other firms and may be differentiated by brand or homogeneous and unbranded.

3   Entry into the market is difficult, with fairly high costs and significant barriers to competition.

4   Firms typically have substantial pricing power.

5   Products are often highly differentiated through marketing, features, and other non-price strategies.

Because there are so few firms, each firm can have some degree of pricing power, which can result in substantial profits. Another by-product of the oligopoly market structure is the attractiveness of price collusion. Even without price collusion, a dominant firm may easily become the price maker in the market. Oligopoly markets without collusion typically have the most sophisticated pricing strategies. Examples of non-colluding oligopolies include the US tobacco market and the Thai beer market.

In 2004, four firms controlled 99 percent of the US tobacco industry.[8] Brands owned by Singha Co. and by ThaiBev controlled over 90 percent of the Thai beer market in 2009. (This situation is expected to change soon, as the Association of Southeast Asian Nations trade agreement will open the doors to competition from other ASEAN producers.) Perhaps the most well-known oligopoly market with collusion is the OPEC cartel, which seeks to control prices in the petroleum market by fostering agreements among oil-producing countries.

5.1 Demand Analysis and Pricing Strategies in Oligopoly Markets

Oligopoly markets' demand curves depend on the degree of pricing interdependence. In a market where collusion is present, the aggregate market demand curve is divided up by the individual production participants. Under non-colluding market conditions, each firm faces an individual demand curve. Furthermore, non-colluding oligopoly market demand characteristics depend on the pricing strategies adopted by the participating firms. There are three basic pricing strategies: pricing interdependence, the Cournot assumption, and the Nash equilibrium.

The first pricing strategy is to assume pricing interdependence among the firms in the oligopoly. A good example of this situation is any market where there are "price wars," such as the commercial airline industry. For example, flying out of the Atlanta, Georgia, hub, Delta Air Lines and AirTran Airways jointly serve several cities. AirTran is a low-cost carrier and typically offers lower fares to destinations out of Atlanta. Delta tends to match the lower fares for those cities also served by AirTran when the departure and arrival times are similar to its own. However, when Delta offers service to the same cities at different time slots, Delta's ticket prices are higher.

The most common pricing strategy assumption in these price war markets is that competitors will match a price reduction and ignore a price increase. The logic is that by lowering its price to match a competitor's price reduction, the firm will not experience a reduction in customer demand. Conversely, by not matching the price increase, the firm stands to attract customers away from the firm that raised its prices. The oligopolist's demand relationship must represent the potential increase in market share when rivals' price increases are not matched and no significant change in market share when rivals' price decreases are matched.

Given a prevailing price, the price elasticity of demand will be much greater if the price is increased and less if the price is decreased. The firm's customers are more responsive to price increases because its rivals have lower prices. Alternatively, the firm's customers are less responsive to price decreases because its rivals will match its price change.

This implies that the oligopolistic firm faces two different demand structures, one associated with price increases and another relating to price reductions. Each demand function will have its own marginal revenue structure as well. Consider the demand and marginal revenue functions in Exhibit 13(A). The functions $D_P\uparrow$ and $MR_P\uparrow$ represent the demand and marginal revenue schedules associated with higher prices, while the functions $D_P\downarrow$ and $MR_P\downarrow$ represent the lower prices' demand and marginal revenue schedules. The two demand schedules intersect at the prevailing price (i.e., the price where price increase and price decrease are both equal to zero).

---

8 These examples are based on "Industry Surveys," Net Advantage Database, Standard & Poor's; and Market Share Reports, Gale Research, annual issues, as noted in McGuigan, Moyer, and Harris (2008).

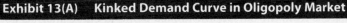

Exhibit 13(A)   Kinked Demand Curve in Oligopoly Market

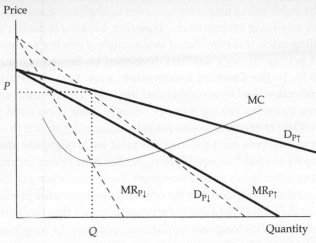

This oligopolistic pricing strategy results in a kinked demand curve, with the two segments representing the different competitor reactions to price changes. The kink in the demand curve also yields a discontinuous marginal revenue structure, with one part associated with the price increase segment of demand and the other relating to the price decrease segment. Therefore, the firm's overall demand equals the relevant portion of $D_{P\uparrow}$ and the relevant portion of $D_{P\downarrow}$. Exhibit 13(B) represents the firm's new demand and marginal revenue schedules. The firm's demand schedule in Exhibit 13(B) is segment $D_{P\uparrow}$ and $D_{P\downarrow}$, where overall demand $D = D_{P\uparrow} + D_{P\downarrow}$.

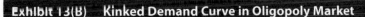

Exhibit 13(B)   Kinked Demand Curve in Oligopoly Market

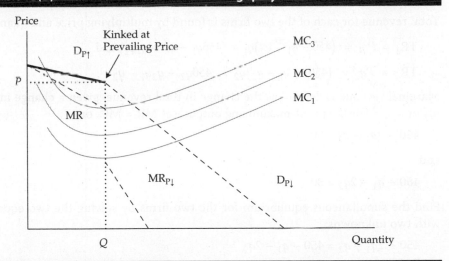

Notice in Exhibit 13(B) that a wide variety of cost structures are consistent with the prevailing price. If the firm has relatively low marginal costs, MC_1, the profit-maximizing pricing rule established earlier, MR = MC, still holds for the oligopoly firm. Marginal cost can rise to MC_2 and MC_3 before the firm's profitability is challenged. If the marginal cost curve MC_2 passes through the gap in marginal revenue, the most profitable price and output combination remains unchanged at the prevailing price and original level of output.

Criticism of the kinked demand curve analysis focuses on its inability to determine what the prevailing price is from the outset. The kinked demand curve analysis does help explain why stable prices have been observed in oligopoly markets and is therefore a useful tool for analyzing such markets. However, because it cannot determine the original prevailing price, it is considered an incomplete pricing analysis.

The second pricing strategy was first developed by French economist Augustin Cournot in 1838. In the **Cournot assumption**, each firm determines its profit-maximizing production level by assuming that the other firms' output will not change. This assumption simplifies pricing strategy because there is no need to guess what the other firm will do to retaliate. It also provides a useful approach to analyzing real-world behavior in oligopoly markets. Take the most basic oligopoly market situation, a two-firm duopoly market.[9] In equilibrium, neither firm has an incentive to change output, given the other firm's production level. Each firm attempts to maximize its own profits under the assumption that the other firm will continue producing the same level of output in the future. The Cournot strategy assumes that this pattern continues until each firm reaches its long-run equilibrium position. In long-run equilibrium, output and price are stable: There is no change in price or output that will increase profits for either firm.

Consider this example of a duopoly market. Assume that the aggregate market demand has been estimated to be

$$Q_D = 450 - P$$

The supply function is represented by constant marginal cost MC = 30.

The Cournot strategy's solution can be found by setting $Q_D = q_1 + q_2$, where q_1 and q_2 represent the output levels of the two firms. Each firm seeks to maximize profit, and each firm believes the other firm will not change output as it changes its own output (Cournot's assumption). The firm will maximize profit where MR = MC. Rearranging the aggregate demand function in terms of price, we get:

$$P = 450 - Q_D = 450 - q_1 - q_2, \text{ and MC} = 30$$

Total revenue for each of the two firms is found by multiplying price and quantity:

$$TR_1 = Pq_1 = (450 - q_1 - q_2)q_1 = 450q_1 - q_1^2 - q_1q_2, \text{ and}$$

$$TR_2 = Pq_2 = (450 - q_1 - q_2)q_2 = 450q_2 - q_2q_1 - q_2^2$$

Marginal revenue is defined as the change in total revenue, given a change in sales (q_1 or q_2).[10] For the profit-maximizing output, set MR = MC, or

$$450 - 2q_1 - q_2 = 30$$

and

$$450 - q_1 - 2q_2 = 30$$

Find the simultaneous equilibrium for the two firms by solving the two equations with two unknowns:

$$450 - 2q_1 - q_2 = 450 - q_1 - 2q_2$$

---

9 The smallest possible oligopoly market is a duopoly, which is made up of only two sellers.

10 The marginal revenue formulas can be obtained using the technique introduced in section 3.1. For the market demand function, total revenue is $P \times Q = 450Q - Q^2$ and our technique yields MR = $\Delta TR/\Delta Q$ = $450 - 2Q$. For the individual firms in the Cournot duopoly, $MR_1 = \Delta TR_1/\Delta q_1 = 450 - 2q_1 - q_2$, and $MR_2 = \Delta TR_2/\Delta q_2 = 450 - q_1 - 2q_2$. Each of these marginal revenue formulas is, of course, the derivative of the relevant total revenue formula with respect to the relevant quantity.

Because $q_2 = q_1$ under Cournot's assumption, insert this solution into the demand function and solve as

$$450 - 2q_1 - q_1 = 450 - 3q_1 = 30$$

Therefore, $q_1 = 140$, $q_2 = 140$, and $Q = 280$.
The price is $P = 450 - 280 = 170$.

In the Cournot strategic pricing solution, the market equilibrium price will be 170 and the aggregate output will be 280 units. This result, known as the Cournot equilibrium, differs from the perfectly competitive market equilibrium because the perfectly competitive price will be lower and the perfectly competitive output will be higher. In general, non-competitive markets have higher prices and lower levels of output in equilibrium when compared with perfect competition. In competition, the equilibrium is reached where price equals marginal cost.

$$P_C = MR_C = MC, \text{ so } 450 - Q = 30$$

where P_C is the competitive firm's equilibrium price.

$$Q = 420, \text{ and } P_C = 30.$$

Exhibit 14 describes the oligopoly, competitive, and monopoly market equilibrium positions, where P_M is the monopoly optimum price, P_C is the competitive price, and $P_{Cournot}$ is the oligopoly price under the Cournot assumption.

Exhibit 14   Cournot Equilibrium in Duopoly Market

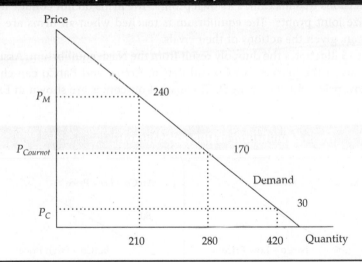

In the later discussion regarding monopoly market structure, equilibrium will be established where MR = MC. That solution is also shown in Exhibit 14. The monopoly firm's demand schedule is the aggregate market demand schedule. Therefore, the solution is

$$MR = MC$$

From Footnote 10, MR = 450 − 2Q; therefore,

$$450 - 2Q = 30 \quad \text{and} \quad Q = 210$$

From the aggregate demand function, solve for price:

$$P_M = 450 - 210 = 240$$

Note that the Cournot solution falls between the competitive equilibrium and the monopoly solution.

It can be shown that as the number of firms increases from two to three, from three to four, and so on, the output and price equilibrium positions move toward the competitive equilibrium solution. This result has historically been the theoretical basis for the antitrust policies established in the United States.

The third pricing strategy is attributed to one of the 1994 Nobel Prize winners, John Nash, who first developed the general concepts. In the previous analysis, the concept of market equilibrium occurs when firms are achieving their optimum remuneration under the circumstances they face. In this optimum environment, the firm has no motive to change price or output level. Existing firms are earning a normal return (zero economic profit), leaving no motive for entry to or exit from the market. All firms in the market are producing at the output level where price equals the average cost of production.

In **game theory** (the set of tools that decision makers use to consider responses by rival decision makers), the **Nash equilibrium** is present when two or more participants in a non-cooperative game have no incentive to deviate from their respective equilibrium strategies after they have considered and anticipated their opponent's rational choices or strategies. In the context of oligopoly markets, the Nash equilibrium is an equilibrium defined by the characteristic that none of the oligopolists can increase its profits by unilaterally changing its pricing strategy. The assumption is made that each participating firm does the best it can, given the reactions of its rivals. Each firm anticipates that the other firms will react to any change made by competitors by doing the best they can under the altered circumstances. The firms in the oligopoly market have interdependent actions. The actions are non-cooperative, with each firm making decisions that maximize its own profits. The firms do not collude in an effort to maximize joint profits. The equilibrium is reached when all firms are doing the best they can, given the actions of their rivals.

Exhibit 15 illustrates the duopoly result from the Nash equilibrium. Assume there are two firms in the market, ArcCo and BatCo. ArcCo and BatCo can charge high prices or low prices for the product. The market outcomes are shown in Exhibit 15.

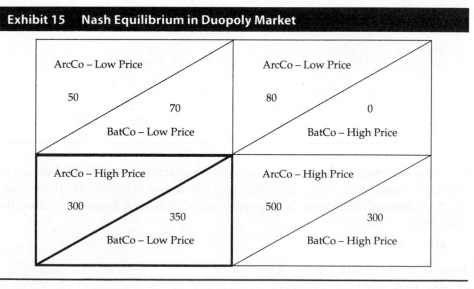

Exhibit 15   Nash Equilibrium in Duopoly Market

For example, the top left solution indicates that when both ArcCo and BatCo offer the product at low prices, ArcCo earns a profit of 50 and BatCo earns 70. The top right solution shows that if ArcCo offers the product at a low price, BatCo earns zero profits. The solution with the maximum joint profits is the lower right equilibrium, where both firms charge high prices for the product. Joint profits are 800 in this solution.

However, the Nash equilibrium requires that each firm behaves in its own best interest. BatCo can improve its position by offering the product at low prices when ArcCo is charging high prices. In the lower left solution, BatCo maximizes its profits at 350. While ArcCo can earn 500 in its best solution, it can do so only if BatCo also agrees to charge high prices. This option is clearly not in BatCo's best interest because it can increase its return from 300 to 350 by charging lower prices.

This scenario brings up the possibility of collusion. If ArcCo agrees to share at least 51 of its 500 when both companies are charging high prices, BatCo should also be willing to charge high prices. While, in general, such collusion is unlawful in most countries, it remains a tempting alternative. Clearly, conditions in oligopolistic industries encourage collusion, with a small number of competitors and interdependent pricing behavior. Collusion is motivated by several factors: increased profits, reduced cash flow uncertainty, and improved opportunities to construct barriers to entry.

When collusive agreements are made openly and formally, the firms involved are called a **cartel**. In some cases, collusion is successful; other times, the forces of competition overpower collusive behavior. There are six major factors that affect the chances of successful collusion.[11]

1 *The number and size distribution of sellers.* Successful collusion is more likely if the number of firms is small or if one firm is dominant. Collusion becomes more difficult as the number of firms increases or if the few firms have similar market shares. When the firms have similar market shares, the competitive forces tend to overshadow the benefits of collusion.

2 *The similarity of the products.* When the products are homogeneous, collusion is more successful. The more differentiated the products, the less likely it is that collusion will succeed.

3 *Cost structure.* The more similar the firms' cost structures, the more likely it is that collusion will succeed.

4 *Order size and frequency.* Successful collusion is more likely when orders are frequent, received on a regular basis, and relatively small. Frequent small orders, received regularly, diminish the opportunities and rewards for cheating on the collusive agreement.

5 *The strength and severity of retaliation.* Oligopolists will be less likely to break the collusive agreement if the threat of retaliation by the other firms in the market is severe.

6 *The degree of external competition.* The main reason to enter into the formal collusion is to increase overall profitability of the market, and rising profits attract competition. For example, the average extraction cost of a barrel of crude oil from the Persian Gulf is $3, while the average cost from the Alaskan fields is $30. It is more likely that crude oil producers in the Persian Gulf will successfully collude because of the similarity in their cost structures. If OPEC had held crude oil prices down below $30 per barrel, there would not have been a viable economic argument to explore oil fields in Alaska. Extracting petroleum from Canadian tar sands becomes economically attractive only at prices above $50 per barrel. OPEC's successful cartel raised crude oil prices to the point where outside sources became economically possible and in doing so increased the competition the cartel faces.

There are other possible oligopoly strategies that are associated with decision making based on game theory. The Cournot equilibrium and the Nash equilibrium are examples of specific strategic games. A strategic game is any interdependent behavioral

---

11 McGuigan, Moyer, and Harris (2008).

choice employed by individuals or groups that share a common goal (e.g., military units, sports teams, or business decision makers). Another prominent decision-making strategy in oligopolistic markets is the first-mover advantage in the **Stackelberg model**, named after the economist who first conceptualized the strategy.[12] The important difference between the Cournot model and the Stackelberg model is that Cournot assumes that in a duopoly market, decision making is simultaneous, while Stackelberg assumes that decisions are made sequentially. In the Stackelberg model, the leader firm chooses its output first and then the follower firm chooses after observing the leader's output. It can be shown that the leader firm has a distinct advantage, being a first mover.[13] In the Stackelberg game, the leader can aggressively overproduce to force the follower to scale back its production or even punish or eliminate the weaker opponent. This approach is sometimes referred to as a "top dog" strategy.[14] The leader earns more than in Cournot's simultaneous game, while the follower earns less. Many other strategic games are possible in oligopoly markets. The important conclusion is that the optimal strategy of the firm depends on what its adversary does. The price and marginal revenue the firm receives for its product depend on both its decisions and its adversary's decisions.

5.2 Supply Analysis in Oligopoly Markets

As in monopolistic competition, the oligopolist does not have a well-defined supply function. That is, there is no way to determine the oligopolist's optimal levels of output and price independent of demand conditions and competitor's strategies. However, the oligopolist still has a cost function that determines the optimal level of supply. Therefore, the profit-maximizing rule established earlier is still valid: The level of output that maximizes profit is where MR = MC. The price to charge is determined by what price consumers are willing to pay for that quantity of the product. Therefore, the equilibrium price comes from the demand curve, while the output level comes from the relationship between marginal revenue and marginal cost.

Consider an oligopoly market in which one of the firms is dominant and thus able to be the price leader. Dominant firms generally have 40 percent or greater market share. When one firm dominates an oligopoly market, it does so because it has greater capacity, has a lower cost structure, was first to market, or has greater customer loyalty than other firms in the market.

Assuming there is no collusion, the dominant firm becomes the price maker, and therefore its actions are similar to monopoly behavior in its segment of the market. The other firms in the market follow the pricing patterns of the dominant firm. Why wouldn't the price followers attempt to gain market share by undercutting the dominant firm's price? The most common explanation is that the dominant firm's supremacy often stems from a lower cost of production. Usually, the price followers would rather charge a price that is even higher than the dominant firm's price choice. If they attempt to undercut the dominant firm, the followers risk a price war with a lower-cost producer that can threaten their survival. Some believe that one explanation for the price leadership position of the dominant firm is simply convenience. Only one firm has to make the pricing decisions, and the others can simply follow its lead.

---

12 Von Stackelberg (1952). See also Kelly (2003), pp. 115–120, for a comparison between the Cournot and Stackelberg equilibriums.
13 Nicholson and Snyder (2008), p. 543.
14 Fudenberg and Tirole (1984), pp. 361–368.

Exhibit 16 establishes the dominant firm's pricing decision. The dominant firm's demand schedule, D_L, is a substantial share of the total market demand, D_T. The low-cost position of the dominant firm is represented by its marginal cost, MC_L. The sum of the marginal costs of the price followers is established as ΣMC_F and represents a higher cost of production than that of the price leader.

Exhibit 16   Dominant Oligopolist's Price Leadership

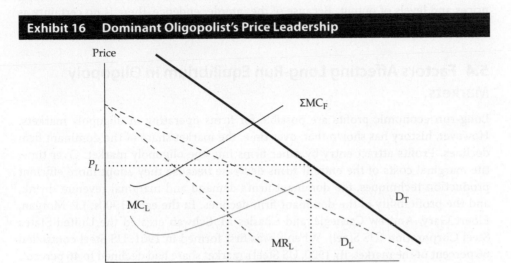

There is an important reason why the total demand curve and the leader demand curve are not parallel in Exhibit 16: Remember that the leader is the low-cost producer. Therefore, as price decreases, fewer of the smaller suppliers will be able to profitably remain in the market, and several will exit because they do not want to sell below cost. Therefore, the leader will have a larger market share as P decreases, which implies that Q_L increases at a low price, exactly as shown by a steeper D_T in the diagram.

The price leader identifies its profit-maximizing output where $MR_L = MC_L$, at output Q_L. This is the quantity it wants to supply; however, the price it will charge is determined by its segment of the total demand function, D_L. At price P_L, the dominant firm will supply quantity Q_L of total demand, D_T. The price followers will supply the difference to the market, $(Q_T - Q_L) = Q_F$. Therefore, neither the dominant firm nor the follower firms have a single functional relationship that determines the quantity supplied at various prices.

5.3 Optimal Price and Output in Oligopoly Markets

From the discussion above, it is clear that there is no single optimum price and output analysis that fits all oligopoly market situations. The interdependence among the few firms that make up the oligopoly market provides a complex set of pricing alternatives, depending on the circumstances in each market. In the case of the kinked demand curve, the optimum price is the prevailing price at the kink in the demand function. However, as previously noted, the kinked demand curve analysis does not provide insight into what established the prevailing price in the first place.

Perhaps the case of the dominant firm, with the other firms following the price leader, is the most obvious. In that case, the optimal price is determined at the output level where MR = MC. The profit-maximizing price is then determined by the output position of the segment of the demand function faced by the dominant firm. The price followers have little incentive to change the leader's price. In the case of the Cournot assumption, each firm assumes that the other firms will not alter their output following the dominant firm's selection of its price and output level.

Therefore, again, the optimum price is determined by the output level where MR = MC. In the case of the Nash equilibrium, each firm will react to the circumstances it faces, maximizing its own profit. These adjustments continue until there are stable prices and levels of output. Because of the interdependence, there is no certainty as to the individual firm's price and output level.

5.4 Factors Affecting Long-Run Equilibrium in Oligopoly Markets

Long-run economic profits are possible for firms operating in oligopoly markets. However, history has shown that, over time, the market share of the dominant firm declines. Profits attract entry by other firms into the oligopoly market. Over time, the marginal costs of the entrant firms decrease because they adopt more efficient production techniques, the dominant firm's demand and marginal revenue shrink, and the profitability of the dominant firm declines. In the early 1900s, J.P. Morgan, Elbert Gary, Andrew Carnegie, and Charles M. Schwab created the United States Steel Corporation (US Steel). When it was first formed in 1901, US Steel controlled 66 percent of the market. By 1920, US Steel's market share had declined to 46 percent, and by 1925 its market share was 42 percent.

In the long run, optimal pricing strategy must include the reactions of rival firms. History has proven that pricing wars should be avoided because any gains in market share are temporary. Decreasing prices to drive competitors away lowers total revenue to all participants in the oligopoly market. Innovation may be a way—though sometimes an uneconomical one—to maintain market leadership.

OLIGOPOLIES: APPEARANCE VERSUS BEHAVIOR

When is an oligopoly not an oligopoly? There are two extreme cases of this situation. A normal oligopoly has a few firms producing a differentiated good, and this differentiation gives them pricing power.

At one end of the spectrum, we have the oligopoly with a credible threat of entry. In practice, if the oligopolists are producing a good or service that can be easily replicated, has limited economies of scale, and is not protected by brand recognition or patents, they will not be able to charge high prices. The easier it is for a new supplier to enter the market, the lower the margins. In practice, this oligopoly will behave very much like a perfectly competitive market.

At the opposite end of the spectrum, we have the case of the cartel. Here, the oligopolists collude and act as if they were a single firm. In practice, a very effective cartel enacts a cooperative strategy. As shown in Section 5.1, instead of going to a Nash equilibrium, the cartel participants go to the more lucrative (for them) cooperative equilibrium.

A cartel may be explicit (that is, based on a contract) or implicit (based on signals). An example of signals in a duopoly would be that one of the firms reduces its prices and the other does not. Because the firm not cutting prices refuses to start a price war, the firm that cut prices may interpret this signal as a "suggestion" to raise prices to a higher level than before, so that profits may increase for both.

MONOPOLY

6

Monopoly market structure is at the opposite end of the spectrum from perfect competition. For various reasons, there are significant barriers to entry such that a single firm produces a highly specialized product and faces no threat of competition. There are no good substitutes for the product in the relevant market, and the market demand function is the same as the individual firm's demand schedule. *The distinguishing characteristics of monopoly are that a single firm represents the market and significant barriers to entry exist.* Exhibit 1 identified the characteristics of monopoly markets:

1 There is a single seller of a highly differentiated product.

2 The product offered by the seller has no close substitute.

3 Entry into the market is very difficult, with high costs and significant barriers to competition.

4 The firm has considerable pricing power.

5 The product is differentiated through non-price strategies such as advertising.

Monopoly markets are unusual. With a single seller dominating the market, power over price decisions is significant. For a single seller to achieve this power, there must be factors that allow the monopoly to exist. One obvious source of monopoly power would be a patent or copyright that prevents other firms from entering the market. Patent and copyright laws exist to reward intellectual capital and investment in research and development. In so doing, they provide significant barriers to entry.

Another possible source of market power is control over critical resources used for production. One example is De Beers Consolidated Mines Limited. De Beers owned or controlled all diamond mining operations in South Africa and established pricing agreements with other important diamond producers. In doing so, De Beers was able to control the prices for cut diamonds for decades. Technically, De Beers was a near-monopoly dominant firm rather than a pure monopoly, although its pricing procedure for cut diamonds resembled monopoly behavior.

Perhaps the most common form of monopolistic market power occurs as the result of government-controlled authorization. In most urban areas, a single source of water and sewer services is offered. In some cases, these services are offered by a government-controlled entity. In other cases, private companies provide the services under government regulation. Such "natural" monopolies require a large initial investment that benefits from economies of scale; therefore, government may authorize a single seller to provide a certain service because having multiple sellers would be too costly. For example, electricity in most markets is provided by a single seller. Economies of scale result when significant capital investment benefits from declining long-run average costs. In the case of electricity, a large gas-fueled power plant producing electricity for a large area is substantially more efficient than having a small diesel generator for every building. That is, the average cost of generating and delivering a kilowatt of electricity will be substantially lower with the single power station, but the initial fixed cost of building the power station and the lines delivering electricity to each home, factory, and office will be very high.

In the case of natural monopolies, limiting the market to a single seller is considered beneficial to society. One water and sewer system is deemed better for the community than dozens of competitors because building multiple infrastructures for running water and sewer service would be particularly expensive and complicated. One electrical power grid supplying electricity for a community can make large capital investments in generating plants and lower the long-run average cost, while multiple power grids would lead to a potentially dangerous maze of wires. Clearly, not all monopolies are in a position to make significant economic profits. Regulators, such as public utility commissions in the United States, attempt to determine what a normal return for the monopoly owners' investment should be, and they set prices accordingly. Nevertheless, monopolists attempt to maximize profits.

Not all monopolies originate from "natural" barriers. For some monopolists, barriers to entry do not derive from increasing returns to scale. We mentioned that marketing and brand loyalty are sources of product differentiation in monopolistic competition. In some highly successful cases, strong brand loyalty can become a formidable barrier to entry. For example, if the Swiss watchmaker Rolex is unusually successful in establishing brand loyalty, so that its customers think there is no close substitute for its product, then the company will have monopoly-like pricing power over its market.

The final potential source of market power is the increasing returns associated with network effects. Network effects result from synergies related to increasing market penetration. By achieving a critical level of adoption, Microsoft was able to extend its market power through the network effect—for example, because most computer users know how to use Microsoft Word. Therefore, for firms, Word is cheaper to adopt than other programs because almost every new hire will be proficient in using the software and will need no further training. At some level of market share, a network-based product or service (think of Facebook or eBay) reaches a point where each additional share point increases the probability that another user will adopt.[15] These network effects increase the value to other potential adopters. In Microsoft's case, the network effects crowded out other potential competitors, including Netscape's internet browser, that might have led to applications bypassing Windows. Eventually, Microsoft's operating system's market share reached 92 percent of the global market. Similar situations occur in financial markets: If a publicly listed share or a derivative contract is more frequently traded on a certain exchange, market participants wishing to sell or buy the security will go to the more liquid exchange because they expect to find a better price and faster execution there.

6.1 Demand Analysis in Monopoly Markets

The monopolist's demand schedule is the aggregate demand for the product in the relevant market. Because of the income effect and the substitution effect, demand is negatively related to price, as usual. The slope of the demand curve is negative and therefore downward sloping. The general form of the demand relationship is

$$Q_D = a - bP \quad \text{or, rewritten,} \quad P = a/b - (1/b)Q_D$$

Therefore, total revenue $= \text{TR} = P \times Q = (a/b)Q_D - (1/b)Q_D^2$

Marginal revenue is the change in revenue given a change in the quantity demanded. Because an increase in quantity requires a lower price, the marginal revenue schedule is steeper than the demand schedule. If the demand schedule is linear, then the marginal revenue curve is twice as steep as the demand schedule.[16]

$$\text{MR} = \Delta \text{TR}/\Delta Q = (a/b) - (2/b)\,Q_D$$

The demand and marginal revenue relationship is expressed in Exhibit 17.

---

15 When a network-based device reaches a 30 percent share, the next 50 percentage points are cheaper to promote, according to McGuigan, Moyer, and Harris (2008).
16 Marginal revenue can be found using the technique shown in section 3.1 or, for readers who are familiar with calculus, by taking the derivative of the total revenue function: $\text{MR} = \Delta \text{TR}/\Delta Q = (a/b) - (2/b)Q_D$.

Exhibit 17   Monopolist's Demand and Marginal Revenue

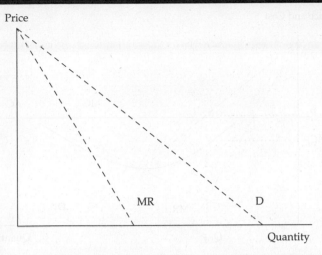

Suppose a company operating on a remote island is the single seller of natural gas. Demand for its product can be expressed as

$Q_D = 400 - 0.5P$, which can be rearranged as
$P = 800 - 2Q_D$

Total revenue is $P \times Q = TR = 800Q_D - 2Q_D^2$, and marginal revenue is MR = 800 $- 4Q_D$.[17]

In Exhibit 17, the demand curve's intercept is 800 and the slope is –2. The marginal revenue curve in Exhibit 17 has an intercept of 800 and a slope of –4.

Average revenue is TR/Q_D; therefore, $AR = 800 - 2Q_D$, which is the same as the demand function. In the monopoly market model, average revenue is the same as the market demand schedule.

6.2 Supply Analysis in Monopoly Markets

A monopolist's supply analysis is based on the firm's cost structure. As in the market structures of monopolistic competition and oligopoly, the monopolist does not have a well-defined supply function that determines the optimal output level and the price to charge. The optimal output is the profit-maximizing output level. The profit-maximizing level of output occurs where marginal revenue equals marginal cost, MR = MC.

Assume the natural gas company has determined that its total cost can be expressed as

$TC = 20,000 + 50Q + 3Q^2$

Marginal cost is $\Delta TC/\Delta Q = MC = 50 + 6Q$.[18]

Supply and demand can be combined to determine the profit-maximizing level of output. Exhibit 18 combines the monopolist's demand and cost functions.

---

17 $MR = \Delta TR/\Delta Q = 800 - 4Q$; see footnote 16.
18 The marginal cost equation can be found in this case by applying the technique used to find the marginal revenue equation in section 3.1, or by taking the derivative of the total cost function.

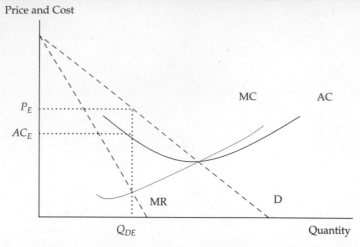

Exhibit 18   Monopolist's Demand, Marginal Revenue, and Cost Structures

In Exhibit 18, the demand and marginal revenue functions are clearly defined by the aggregate market. However, the monopolist does not have a supply curve. The quantity that maximizes profit is determined by the intersection of MC and MR, Q_{DE}.

The price consumers are willing to pay for this level of output is P_E, as determined by the demand curve, P_E.

The profit-maximizing level of output is MR = MC: $800 - 4Q_D = 50 + 6Q_D$; therefore, $Q_D = 75$ when profit is maximized.

Total profit equals total revenue minus total cost:

$$\pi = 800Q - 2Q_D^2 - \left(20,000 + 50Q_D + 3Q_D^2\right) = -20,000 + 750Q_D - 5Q_D^2$$

Profit is represented by the difference between the area of the rectangle $Q_{DE} \times P_E$, representing total revenue, and the area of the rectangle $Q_{DE} \times AC_E$, representing total cost.

MONOPOLISTS AND THEIR INCENTIVES

In theoretical models, which usually take product quality and technology as given, monopolists can choose to vary either price or quantity. In real life, they also have the ability to vary their product.

A monopolist can choose to limit quality if producing a higher-quality product is costly and higher quality does not increase profits accordingly. For example, the quality of domestically produced cars in most developed countries improved dramatically once foreign imports became more available. Before the opening of borders to foreign imports, the single incumbent that dominated the market (for example, Fiat in Italy) or the small group of incumbents acting as a collusive oligopoly (such as the Detroit "Big Three" in the United States) were the effective monopolists of their domestic automobile markets. Rust corrosion, limited reliability, and poor gas mileage were common.[19]

Similarly, regulated utilities may have limited incentives to innovate. Several studies, including Gomez-Ibanez (2003), have found that state-owned and other monopoly telephone utilities tended to provide very poor service before competition was introduced. Poor service may not be limited to poor connection quality but may also include extensive delays in adding new users and limited introduction of new services, such as caller ID or automatic answering services.

---

19 For more on this topic, see Banker, Khosla, and Sinha (1998).

Intuitively, a monopolist will not spend resources on quality control, research and development, or even customer relations unless there is a threat of entry of a new competitor or unless there is a clear link between such expenses and a profit increase. In contrast, in competitive markets, including oligopoly, innovation and quality are often ways to differentiate the product and increase profits.

6.3 Optimal Price and Output in Monopoly Markets

Continuing the natural gas example from above, the total profit function can be solved using the quadratic formula.[20] Another method to solve the profit function is to evaluate $\Delta\pi/\Delta Q_D$ and set it equal to zero. This identifies the point at which profit is unaffected by changes in output.[21] Of course, this will give the same result as we found by equating marginal revenue with marginal cost. The monopoly will maximize profits when $Q^* = 75$ units of output and the price is set from the demand curve at 650.

$P^* = 800 - 2(75) = 650$ per unit

To find total maximum profits, substitute these values into the profit function above:

$$\pi = -20{,}000 + 750Q_D - 5Q_D^2 = -20{,}000 + 750(75) - 5\left(75^2\right) = 8{,}125$$

Note that the price and output combination that maximizes profit occurs in the elastic portion of the demand curve in Exhibit 18. This must be so because marginal revenue and marginal cost will always intersect where marginal revenue is positive. This fact implies that quantity demanded responds more than proportionately to prices changes, i.e. demand is elastic, at the point at which MC = MR. As noted earlier, the relationship between marginal revenue and price elasticity, E_P, is:

$\text{MR} = P[1 - 1/E_P]$

In monopoly, MR = MC; therefore,

$P[1 - 1/E_P] = \text{MC}$

The firm can use this relationship to determine the profit-maximizing price if the firm knows its cost structure and the price elasticity of demand, E_P. For example, assume the firm knows that its marginal cost is constant at 75 and recent market analysis indicates that price elasticity is estimated to be 1.5. The optimal price is solved as

$P[1 - 1/1.5] = 75$ and

$P = 225$

Exhibit 18 indicated that the monopolist wants to produce at Q_E and charge the price of P_E. Suppose this is a natural monopoly that is operating as a government franchise under regulation. Natural monopolies are usually found where production is based on significant economies of scale and declining cost structure in the market. Examples include electric power generation, natural gas distribution, and the water and sewer industries. These are often called public utilities. Exhibit 19 illustrates such a market in long-run equilibrium.

---

20 The quadratic formula, where $aQ^2 + bQ + c = 0$, is $Q = \left\{-b \pm \sqrt{\left(b^2 - 4ac\right)}\right\}/2a$.

21 Maximum profit occurs where $\Delta\pi/\Delta Q_D = 0 = 750 - 10Q_D$. Therefore, profits are maximized at $Q_D = 75$.

Exhibit 19   Natural Monopoly in a Regulated Pricing Environment

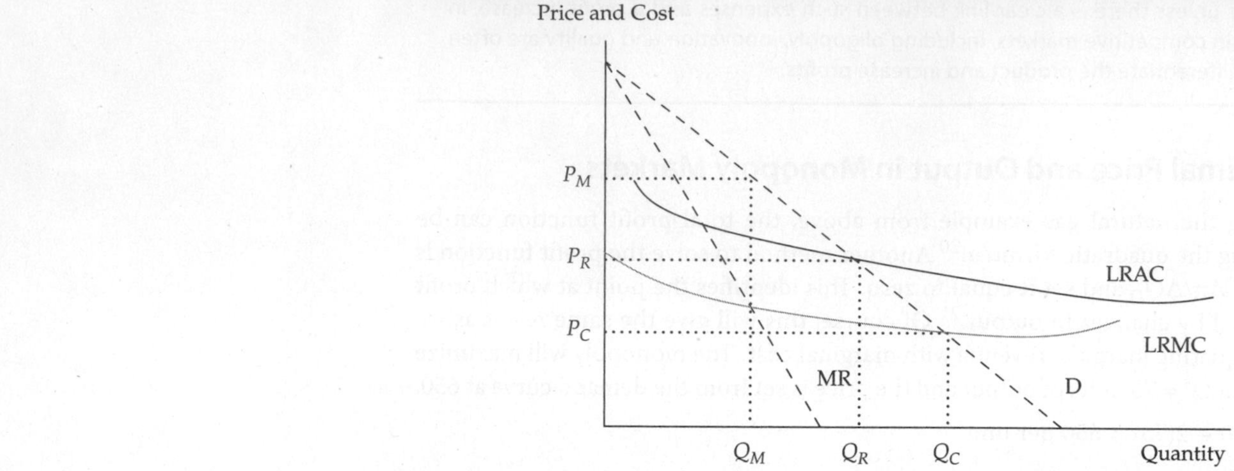

In Exhibit 19, three possible pricing and output solutions are presented. The first is what the monopolist would do without regulation: The monopolist would seek to maximize profits by producing Q_M units of the product, where long-run marginal cost equals marginal revenue, LRMC = MR. To maximize profits, the monopolist would raise the price to the level the demand curve will accept, P_M.

In perfect competition, the price and output equilibrium occurs where price is equal to the marginal cost of producing the incremental unit of the product. In a competitive market, the quantity produced would be higher, Q_C, and the price lower, P_C. For this regulated monopoly, the competitive solution would be unfair because at output Q_C, the price P_C would not cover the average cost of production. One possibility is to subsidize the difference between the long-run average cost, LRAC, and the competitive price, P_C, for each unit sold.

Another solution is for the regulator to set the price at the point where long-run average cost equals average revenue. Recall that the demand curve represents the average revenue the firm receives at each output level. The government regulator will attempt to determine the monopolistic firm's long-run average cost and set the output and price so that the firm receives a fair return on the owners' invested capital. The regulatory solution is output level Q_R, with the price set at P_R. Therefore, the regulatory solution is found between the unregulated monopoly equilibrium and the competitive equilibrium.

6.4 Price Discrimination and Consumer Surplus

Monopolists can be more or less effective in taking advantage of their market structure. At one extreme, we have a monopolist that charges prices and supplies quantities that are the same as they would be in perfect competition; this scenario may be a result of regulation or threat of entry (if the monopolist charged more, another company could come in and price the former monopolist out of the market). At the opposite extreme, hated by all consumers and economists, is the monopolist that extracts the entire consumer surplus. This scenario is called **first-degree price discrimination**, where a monopolist is able to charge each customer the highest price the customer is willing to pay. This is called price discrimination because the monopolist charges a different price to each client. How can this be? For example, if the monopolist knows the exact demand schedule of the customer, then the monopolist is able to capture the entire consumer surplus. In practice, the monopolist is able to measure how often the product is used and charges the customer the highest price the consumer is willing to pay for that unit of good. Another possibility is that public price disclosure is non-existent, so that no customer knows what the other customers are paying. Interestingly, not every consumer is worse off in this case, because some consumers may be charged a price that is below that of perfect competition, as long as the marginal revenue exceeds the marginal cost.

In **second-degree price discrimination** the monopolist offers a menu of quantity-based pricing options designed to induce customers to self-select based on how highly they value the product. Such mechanisms include volume discounts, volume surcharges, coupons, product bundling, and restrictions on use. In practice, producers can use not just the quantity but also the quality (e.g., "professional grade") to charge more to customers that value the product highly.

Third-degree price discrimination happens when customers are segregated by demographic or other traits. For example, some econometric software is licensed this way: A student version can handle only small datasets and is sold for a low price; a professional version can handle very large datasets and is sold at a much higher price because corporations need to compute the estimates for their business and are therefore willing to pay more for a license. Another example is that airlines know that passengers who want to fly somewhere and come back the same day are most likely business people; therefore, one-day roundtrip tickets are generally more expensive than tickets with a return flight at a later date or over a weekend.

Price discrimination has many practical applications when the seller has pricing power. The best way to understand how this concept works is to think of consumer surplus: As seen in this reading, a consumer may be willing to pay more for the first unit of a good, but to buy a second unit she will want to pay a lower price, thus getting a better deal on the first unit. In practice, sellers can sometimes use income and substitution effects to their advantage. Think of something you often buy, perhaps lunch at your favorite café. How much would you be willing to pay for a "lunch club membership card" that would allow you to purchase lunches at, say, half price? If the café could extract from you the maximum amount each month that you would be willing to pay for the half-price option, then it would successfully have removed the income effect from you in the form of a monthly fixed fee. Notice that a downward-sloping demand curve implies that you would end up buying more lunches each month than before you purchased the discount card, even though you would be no better or worse off than before. This is a way that sellers are sometimes able to extract consumer surplus by means of creative pricing schemes. It's a common practice among big-box retailers, sports clubs, and other users of what is called "two-part tariff pricing," as in the example below.

EXAMPLE 3

Price Discrimination

Nicole's monthly demand for visits to her health club is given by the following equation: $Q_D = 20 - 4P$, where Q_D is visits per month and P is euros per visit. The health club's marginal cost is fixed at €2 per visit.

1   Draw Nicole's demand curve for health club visits per month.

2   If the club charged a price per visit equal to its marginal cost, how many visits would Nicole make per month?

3   How much consumer surplus would Nicole enjoy at that price?

4   How much could the club charge Nicole each month for a membership fee?

Solution to 1:

$Q_D = 20 - 4P$, so when $P = 0$, $Q_D = 20$. Inverting, $P = 5 - 0.25Q_D$, so when $Q = 0$, $P = 5$.

Solution to 2:

$Q_D = 20 - 4(2) = 12$. Nicole would make 12 visits per month at a price of €2 per visit.

Solution to 3:

Nicole's consumer surplus can be measured as the area under her demand curve and above the price she pays for a total of 12 visits, or $(0.5)(12)(3) = 18$. Nicole would enjoy a consumer surplus of €18 per month.

Solution to 4:

The club could extract all of Nicole's consumer surplus by charging her a monthly membership fee of €18 plus a per-visit price of €2. This pricing method is called a two-part tariff because it assesses one price per unit of the item purchased plus a per-month fee (sometimes called an "entry fee") equal to the buyer's consumer surplus evaluated at the per-unit price.

6.5 Factors Affecting Long-Run Equilibrium in Monopoly Markets

The unregulated monopoly market structure can produce economic profits in the long run. In the long run, all factors of production are variable, while in the short run, some factors of production are fixed. Generally, the short-run factor that is fixed is the capital investment, such as the factory, machinery, production technology, available arable land, and so forth. The long-run solution allows for all inputs, including technology, to change. In order to maintain a monopoly market position in the long run, the firm must be protected by substantial and ongoing barriers to entry. If the monopoly position is the result of a patent, then new patents must be continuously added to prevent the entry of other firms into the market.

For regulated monopolies, such as natural monopolies, there are a variety of long-run solutions. One solution is to set the price equal to marginal cost, $P = MC$. However, that price will not likely be high enough to cover the average cost of production, as Exhibit 19 illustrated. The answer is to provide a subsidy sufficient to compensate the firm. The national rail system in the United States, Amtrak, is an example of a regulated monopoly operating with a government subsidy.

National ownership of the monopoly is another solution. Nationalization of the natural monopoly has been a popular solution in Europe and other parts of the world. The United States has generally avoided this potential solution. One problem with this arrangement is that once a price is established, consumers are unwilling to accept price increases, even as factor costs increase. Politically, raising prices on products from government-owned enterprises is highly unpopular.

Establishing a governmental entity that regulates an authorized monopoly is another popular solution. Exhibit 19 illustrated the appropriate decision rule. The regulator sets price equal to long-run average cost, $P_R = LRAC$. This solution assures that investors will receive a normal return for the risk they are taking in the market. Given that no other competitors are allowed, the risk is lower than in a highly competitive market environment. The challenge facing the regulator is determining the authentic risk-related return and the monopolist's realistic long-run average cost.

The final solution is to franchise the monopolistic firm through a bidding war. Again, the public goal is to select the winning firm based on price equaling long-run average cost. Retail outlets at rail stations and airports and concession outlets at stadiums are examples of government franchises. The long-run success of the monopoly franchise depends on its ability to meet the goal of pricing its products at the level of its long-run average cost.

EXAMPLE 4

Monopolies and Efficiency

Are monopolies *always* inefficient?

A   No, because if they charge more than average cost they are nationalized.

B   Yes, because they charge all consumers more than perfectly competitive markets would.

C   No, because economies of scale and regulation (or threat of entry) may give a better outcome for buyers than perfect competition.

Solution:

C is correct. Economies of scale and regulation may make monopolies more efficient than perfect competition.

IDENTIFICATION OF MARKET STRUCTURE

7

Monopoly markets and other situations where companies have pricing power can be inefficient because producers constrain output to cause an increase in prices. Therefore, there will be less of the good being consumed and it will be sold at a higher price, which is generally inefficient for the market as a whole. This is why competition law regulates the degree of market competition in several industries of different countries.

Market power in the real world is not always as clear as it is in textbook examples. Governments and regulators often have the difficult task of measuring market power and establishing whether a firm has a dominant position that may resemble a monopoly. For example, in the 1990s, US regulators prosecuted agricultural corporation Archer Daniels Midland (ADM) for conspiring with Japanese competitors to fix the price of lysine, an amino acid used as an animal feed additive. The antitrust action resulted in a settlement that involved over US$100 million in fines paid by the cartel members. Another example occurred in the 1970s, when US antitrust authorities broke up the local telephone monopoly, leaving AT&T the long-distance business (and opening that business to competitors), and required AT&T to divest itself of the local telephone companies it owned. This antitrust decision brought competition, innovation, and lower prices to the US telephone market.

European regulators (specifically, the European Commission) have affected the mergers and monopoly positions of European corporations (as in the case of the companies Roche, Rhone-Poulenc, and BASF, which were at the center of a vitamin price-fixing case) as well as non-European companies (such as Intel) that do business in Europe. Moreover, the merger between the US company General Electric and the European company Honeywell was denied by the European Commission on grounds of excessive market concentration.

Quantifying excessive market concentration is difficult. Sometimes, regulators need to measure whether something that has not yet occurred might generate excessive market power. For example, a merger between two companies might allow the combined company to be a monopolist or quasi monopolist in a certain market.

A financial analyst hearing news about a possible merger should always consider the impact of competition law (sometimes called antitrust law)—that is, whether a proposed merger may be blocked by regulators in the interest of preserving a competitive market.

7.1 Econometric Approaches

How should one measure market power? The theoretical answer is to estimate the elasticity of demand and supply in a market. If demand is very elastic, the market must be very close to perfect competition. If demand is rigid (inelastic), companies *may* have market power. This is the approach taken in the cellophane case mentioned in Section 3.1.2.

From the econometric point of view, this estimation requires some attention. The problem is that observed price and quantity are the equilibrium values of price and quantity and do not represent the value of either supply or demand. Technically, this is called the problem of endogeneity, in the sense that the equilibrium price and quantity are jointly determined by the interaction of demand and supply. Therefore, to have an appropriate estimation of demand and supply, we will need to use a model with two equations, namely, an equation of demanded quantity (as a function of price, income of the buyers, and other variables) and an equation of supplied quantity (as a function of price, production costs, and other variables). The estimated parameters will then allow us to compute elasticity.

Regression analysis is useful in computing elasticity but requires a large number of observations. Therefore, one may use a time-series approach and, for example, look at 20 years of quarterly sales data for a market. However, the market structure may have changed radically over those 20 years, and the estimated elasticity may not apply to the current situation. Moreover, the supply curve may change as a result of a merger among large competitors, and the estimation based on past data may not be informative regarding the future state of the market post merger.

An alternative approach is a cross-sectional regression analysis. Instead of looking at total sales and average prices in a market over time (the time-series approach mentioned above), we can look at sales from different companies in the market during the same year, or even at single transactions from many buyers and companies. Clearly, this approach requires substantial data-gathering effort, and therefore, this estimation method can be complicated. Moreover, different specifications of the explanatory variables (for example, using total GDP rather than median household income or per-capita GDP to represent income) may sometimes lead to dramatically different estimates.

7.2 Simpler Measures

Trying to avoid the above drawbacks, analysts often use simpler measures to estimate elasticity. The simplest measure is the concentration ratio, which is the sum of the market shares of the largest N firms. To compute this ratio, one would, for example, add the sales values of the largest 10 firms and divide this figure by total market sales. This number is always between zero (perfect competition) and 100 percent (monopoly).

The main advantage of the concentration ratio is that it is simple to compute, as shown above. The disadvantage is that it does not directly quantify market power. In other words, is a high concentration ratio a clear signal of monopoly power? The analysis of entry in Section 2 explains clearly that this is not the case: A company may be the only incumbent in a market, but if the barriers to entry are low, the simple presence of a *potential* entrant may be sufficient to convince the incumbent to behave like a firm in perfect competition. For example, a sugar wholesaler may be the only one in a country, but the knowledge that other large wholesalers in the food industry might easily add imported sugar to their range of products should convince the sugar wholesaler to price its product as if it were in perfect competition.

Another disadvantage of the concentration ratio is that it tends to be unaffected by mergers among the top market incumbents. For example, if the largest and second-largest incumbents merge, the pricing power of the combined entity is likely to be larger than that of the two pre-existing companies. But the concentration ratio may not change much.

CALCULATING THE CONCENTRATION RATIO

Suppose there are eight producers of a certain good in a market. The largest producer has 35 percent of the market, the second largest has 25 percent, the third has 20 percent, the fourth has 10 percent, and the remaining four have 2.5 percent each. If we computed the concentration ratio of the top three producers, it would be 35 + 25 + 20 = 80 percent, while the concentration ratio of the top four producers would be 35 + 25 + 20 + 10 = 90 percent.

If the two largest companies merged, the new concentration ratio for the top three producers would be 60 (the sum of the market shares of the merged companies) + 20 + 10 = 90 percent, and the concentration ratio for the four top producers would be 92.5 percent. Therefore, this merger affects the concentration ratio very mildly, even though it creates a substantial entity that controls 60 percent of the market.

For example, the effect of consolidation in the US retail gasoline market has resulted in increasing degrees of concentration. In 1992, the top four companies in the US retail gasoline market shared 33 percent of the market. By 2001, the top four companies controlled 78 percent of the market (Exxon Mobil 24 percent, Shell 20 percent, BP/Amoco/Arco 18 percent, and Chevron/Texaco 16 percent).

To avoid the known issues with concentration ratios, economists O.C. Herfindahl and A.O. Hirschman suggested an index where the market shares of the top N companies are first squared and then added. If one firm controls the whole market (a monopoly), the Herfindahl-Hirschman index (HHI) equals 1. If there are M firms in the industry with equal market shares, then the HHI equals $(1/M)$. This provides a useful gauge for interpreting an HHI. For example, an HHI of 0.20 would be analogous to having the market shared equally by 5 firms.

The HHI for the top three companies in the example in the box above would be $0.35^2 + 0.25^2 + 0.20^2 = 0.225$ before the merger, while after the merger, it would be $0.60^2 + 0.20^2 + 0.10^2 = 0.410$, which is substantially higher than the initial 0.225. This is why the HHI is widely used by competition regulators. However, just like the concentration ratio, the HHI does not take the possibility of entry into account, nor does it consider the elasticity of demand. As a consequence, the HHI has limited use for a financial analyst trying to estimate the potential profitability of a company or group of companies.

EXAMPLE 5

The Herfindahl-Hirschman Index

Suppose a market has 10 suppliers, each of them with 10 percent of the market. What are the concentration ratio and the HHI of the top four firms?

A Concentration ratio 4 percent and HHI 40

B Concentration ratio 40 percent and HHI 0.4

C Concentration ratio 40 percent and HHI 0.04

Solution:

C is correct. The concentration ratio for the top four firms is 10 + 10 + 10 + 10 = 40 percent, and the HHI is $0.10^2 \times 4 = 0.01 \times 4 = 0.04$.

SUMMARY

In this reading, we have surveyed how economists classify market structures. We have analyzed the distinctions between the different structures that are important for understanding demand and supply relations, optimal price and output, and the factors affecting long-run profitability. We also provided guidelines for identifying market structure in practice. Among our conclusions are the following:

- Economic market structures can be grouped into four categories: perfect competition, monopolistic competition, oligopoly, and monopoly.

- The categories differ because of the following characteristics: The number of producers is many in perfect and monopolistic competition, few in oligopoly, and one in monopoly. The degree of product differentiation, the pricing power of the producer, the barriers to entry of new producers, and the level of non-price competition (e.g., advertising) are all low in perfect competition, moderate in monopolistic competition, high in oligopoly, and generally highest in monopoly.

- A financial analyst must understand the characteristics of market structures in order to better forecast a firm's future profit stream.

- The optimal marginal revenue equals marginal cost. However, only in perfect competition does the marginal revenue equal price. In the remaining structures, price generally exceeds marginal revenue because a firm can sell more units only by reducing the per unit price.

- The quantity sold is highest in perfect competition. The price in perfect competition is usually lowest, but this depends on factors such as demand elasticity and increasing returns to scale (which may reduce the producer's marginal cost). Monopolists, oligopolists, and producers in monopolistic competition attempt to differentiate their products so that they can charge higher prices.

- Typically, monopolists sell a smaller quantity at a higher price. Investors may benefit from being shareholders of monopolistic firms that have large margins and substantial positive cash flows.

- Competitive firms do not earn economic profit. There will be a market compensation for the rental of capital and of management services, but the lack of pricing power implies that there will be no extra margins.

- While in the short run firms in any market structure can have economic profits, the more competitive a market is and the lower the barriers to entry, the faster the extra profits will fade. In the long run, new entrants shrink margins and push the least efficient firms out of the market.

- Oligopoly is characterized by the importance of strategic behavior. Firms can change the price, quantity, quality, and advertisement of the product to gain an advantage over their competitors. Several types of equilibrium (e.g., Nash, Cournot, kinked demand curve) may occur that affect the likelihood of each of the incumbents (and potential entrants in the long run) having economic profits. Price wars may be started to force weaker competitors to abandon the market.

- Measuring market power is complicated. Ideally, econometric estimates of the elasticity of demand and supply should be computed. However, because of the lack of reliable data and the fact that elasticity changes over time (so that past data may not apply to the current situation), regulators and economists often use simpler measures. The concentration ratio is simple, but the HHI, with little more computation required, often produces a better figure for decision making.

REFERENCES

Banker, R.D., I. Khosla, and K.K. Sinha. 1998. "Quality and Competition." *Management Science*, vol. 44, no. 9:1179–1192.

Chamberlin, Edward H. 1933. *The Theory of Monopolistic Competition*. Cambridge, MA: Harvard University Press.

Dorsey, Pat. 2004. *The Five Rules for Successful Stock Investing: Morningstar's Guide to Building Wealth and Winning in the Market*. Hoboken, NJ: John Wiley & Sons.

Friedman, Thomas L. 2006. *The World Is Flat: A Brief History of the Twenty-first Century*. New York: Farrar, Straus and Giroux.

Fudenberg, Drew, and Jean Tirole. 1984. "The Fat Cat Effect, the Puppy Dog Ploy and the Lean and Hungry Look." *American Economic Review*, vol. 74, no. 2:361–366.

Gomez-Ibanez, Jose A. 2003. *Regulating Infrastructure: Monopoly, Contracts, and Discretion*. Cambridge, MA: Harvard University Press.

Kelly, Anthony. 2003. *Decision Making Using Game Theory: An Introduction for Managers*. Cambridge, UK: Cambridge University Press.

Krugman, Paul R. 1989. "Industrial Organization and International Trade." In *Handbook of Industrial Organization*, vol. 2. Edited by Richard Schmalensee and Robert Willig. Amsterdam: Elsevier B.V.

McCloskey, D. 1982. *The Applied Theory of Price*. 2nd ed. New York: Macmillan.

McGuigan, James R., R. Charles Moyer, and Frederick H. Harris. 2008. *Managerial Economics: Applications, Strategy and Tactics*. 11th ed. Mason, OH: Thomson South-Western.

Porter, Michael E. 2008. "The Five Competitive Forces that Shape Strategy." *Harvard Business Review*, vol. 86, no. 1:78–93.

Nicholson, Walter, and Christopher M. Snyder. 2008. *Microeconomic Theory: Basic Principles and Extensions*. 10th ed. Mason, OH: Thomson South-Western.

Schumpeter, Joseph A. 1942. *Capitalism, Socialism and Democracy*. New York: HarperCollins.

von Stackelberg, Heinrich. 1952. *The Theory of the Market Economy*. New York: Oxford University Press.

PRACTICE PROBLEMS

1 A market structure characterized by many sellers with each having some pricing power and product differentiation is *best* described as:

   A oligopoly.

   B perfect competition.

   C monopolistic competition.

2 A market structure with relatively few sellers of a homogeneous or standardized product is *best* described as:

   A oligopoly.

   B monopoly.

   C perfect competition.

3 Market competitors are *least likely* to use advertising as a tool of differentiation in an industry structure identified as:

   A monopoly.

   B perfect competition.

   C monopolistic competition.

4 Upsilon Natural Gas, Inc. is a monopoly enjoying very high barriers to entry. Its marginal cost is $40 and its average cost is $70. A recent market study has determined the price elasticity of demand is 1.5. The company will *most likely* set its price at:

   A $40.

   B $70.

   C $120.

5 The demand schedule in a perfectly competitive market is given by $P = 93 - 1.5Q$ (for $Q \leq 62$) and the long-run cost structure of each company is:

Total cost:	$256 + 2Q + 4Q^2$
Average cost:	$256/Q + 2 + 4Q$
Marginal cost:	$2 + 8Q$

   New companies will enter the market at any price greater than:

   A 8.

   B 66.

   C 81.

6 Companies *most likely* have a well-defined supply function when the market structure is:

   A oligopoly.

   B perfect competition.

   C monopolistic competition.

7 Aquarius, Inc. is the dominant company and the price leader in its market. One of the other companies in the market attempts to gain market share by undercutting the price set by Aquarius. The market share of Aquarius will *most likely*:

   A increase.

   B decrease.

   C stay the same.

8 SigmaSoft and ThetaTech are the dominant makers of computer system software. The market has two components: a large mass-market component in which demand is price sensitive, and a smaller performance-oriented component in which demand is much less price sensitive. SigmaSoft's product is considered to be technically superior. Each company can choose one of two strategies:

- *Open architecture (Open):* Mass market focus allowing other software venders to develop products for its platform.

- *Proprietary (Prop):* Allow only its own software applications to run on its platform.

Depending upon the strategy each company selects, their profits would be:

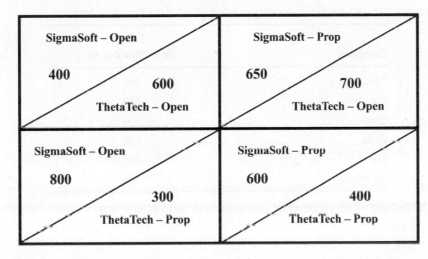

The Nash equilibrium for these companies is:

   A proprietary for SigmaSoft and proprietary for ThetaTech.

   B open architecture for SigmaSoft and proprietary for ThetaTech.

   C proprietary for SigmaSoft and open architecture for ThetaTech.

9 A company doing business in a monopolistically competitive market will *most likely* maximize profits when its output quantity is set such that:

   A average cost is minimized.

   B marginal revenue equals average cost.

   C marginal revenue equals marginal cost.

10 Oligopolistic pricing strategy *most likely* results in a demand curve that is:

   A kinked.

   B vertical.

   C horizontal.

11 Collusion is *less likely* in a market when:

   A the product is homogeneous.

   B companies have similar market shares.

   C the cost structures of companies are similar.

12 If companies earn economic profits in a perfectly competitive market, over the long run the supply curve will *most likely*:

   A shift to the left.

   B shift to the right.

C remain unchanged.

13 Over time, the market share of the dominant company in an oligopolistic market will *most likely*:

A increase.

B decrease.

C remain the same.

14 A government entity that regulates an authorized monopoly will *most likely* base regulated prices on:

A marginal cost.

B long run average cost.

C first degree price discrimination.

15 An analyst gathers the following market share data for an industry:

Company	Sales (in millions of €)
ABC	300
Brown	250
Coral	200
Delta	150
Erie	100
All others	50

The industry's four-company concentration ratio is *closest* to:

A 71%.

B 86%.

C 95%.

16 An analyst gathered the following market share data for an industry comprised of five companies:

Company	Market Share (%)
Zeta	35
Yusef	25
Xenon	20
Waters	10
Vlastos	10

The industry's three-firm Herfindahl-Hirschmann Index is *closest* to:

A 0.185.

B 0.225.

C 0.235.

17 One disadvantage of the Herfindahl-Hirschmann Index is that the index:

A is difficult to compute.

B fails to reflect low barriers to entry.

C fails to reflect the effect of mergers in the industry.

18 In an industry comprised of three companies, which are small-scale manufacturers of an easily replicable product unprotected by brand recognition or patents, the *most* representative model of company behavior is:

> **A**   oligopoly.
>
> **B**   perfect competition.
>
> **C**   monopolistic competition.

19   Deep River Manufacturing is one of many companies in an industry that make a food product. Deep River units are identical up to the point they are labeled. Deep River produces its labeled brand, which sells for $2.20 per unit, and "house brands" for seven different grocery chains which sell for $2.00 per unit. Each grocery chain sells both the Deep River brand and its house brand. The *best* characterization of Deep River's market is:

> **A**   oligopoly.
>
> **B**   perfect competition.
>
> **C**   monopolistic competition.

SOLUTIONS

1 C is correct. Monopolistic competition is characterized by many sellers, differentiated products, and some pricing power.

2 A is correct. Few sellers of a homogeneous or standardized product characterizes an oligopoly.

3 B is correct. The product produced in a perfectly competitive market cannot be differentiated by advertising or any other means.

4 C is correct. Profits are maximized when MR = MC. For a monopoly, MR = $P[1 - 1/E_p]$. Setting this equal to MC and solving for P:

$$\$40 = P[1 - (1/1.5)] = P \times 0.333$$
$$P = \$120$$

5 B is correct. The long-run competitive equilibrium occurs where MC = AC = P for each company. Equating MC and AC implies $2 + 8Q = 256/Q + 2 + 4Q$.

Solving for Q gives $Q = 8$. Equating MC with price gives $P = 2 + 8Q = 66$. Any price above 66 yields an economic profit because P = MC > AC, so new companies will enter the market.

6 B is correct. A company in a perfectly competitive market must accept whatever price the market dictates. The marginal cost schedule of a company in a perfectly competitive market determines its supply function.

7 A is correct. As prices decrease, smaller companies will leave the market rather than sell below cost. The market share of Aquarius, the price leader, will increase.

8 C is correct. In the Nash model, each company considers the other's reaction in selecting its strategy. In equilibrium, neither company has an incentive to change its strategy. ThetaTech is better off with open architecture regardless of what SigmaSoft decides. Given this choice, SigmaSoft is better off with a proprietary platform. Neither company will change its decision unilaterally.

9 C is correct. The profit maximizing choice is the level of output where marginal revenue equals marginal cost.

10 A is correct. The oligopolist faces two different demand structures, one for price increases and another for price decreases. Competitors will lower prices to match a price reduction, but will not match a price increase. The result is a kinked demand curve.

11 B is correct. When companies have similar market shares, competitive forces tend to outweigh the benefits of collusion.

12 B is correct. The economic profit will attract new entrants to the market and encourage existing companies to expand capacity.

13 B is correct. The dominant company's market share tends to decrease as profits attract entry by other companies.

14 B is correct. This allows the investors to receive a normal return for the risk they are taking in the market.

15 B is correct. The top four companies in the industry comprise 86 percent of industry sales: (300 + 250 + 200 + 150)/(300 + 250 + 200 + 150 + 100 + 50) = 900/1050 = 86%.

16 B is correct. The three-firm Herfindahl-Hirschmann Index is $0.35^2 + 0.25^2 + 0.20^2 = 0.225$.

17 B is correct. The Herfindahl-Hirschmann Index does not reflect low barriers to entry that may restrict the market power of companies currently in the market.

18 B is correct. The credible threat of entry holds down prices and multiple incumbents are offering undifferentiated products.

19 C is correct. There are many competitors in the market, but some product differentiation exists, as the price differential between Deep River's brand and the house brands indicates.

5

Economics

Macroeconomic Analysis

This study session covers fundamental macroeconomic concepts. The first reading provides the building blocks of aggregate output and income measurement, aggregate demand and supply analysis, and the analysis of the factors affecting economic growth. The second reading explains fluctuations in economic activity, known as business cycles, which have important effects on businesses and investment markets. The third reading discusses monetary and fiscal policy and how they are used by central banks and governments to mitigate the severity of economic fluctuations and to achieve other policy goals.

READING ASSIGNMENTS

Reading 17	Aggregate Output, Prices, and Economic Growth by Paul R. Kutasovic, PhD, CFA, and Richard G. Fritz, PhD
Reading 18	Understanding Business Cycles by Michele Gambera, PhD, CFA, Milton Ezrati, and Bolong Cao, PhD, CFA
Reading 19	Monetary and Fiscal Policy by Andrew Clare, PhD, and Stephen Thomas, PhD

READING

17

Aggregate Output, Prices, and Economic Growth

by Paul R. Kutasovic, PhD, CFA, and Richard G. Fritz, PhD

Paul R. Kutasovic, PhD, CFA, is at New York Institute of Technology (USA). Richard G. Fritz, PhD, is at Georgia Institute of Technology (USA).

LEARNING OUTCOMES

Mastery	The candidate should be able to:
☐	a. calculate and explain gross domestic product (GDP) using expenditure and income approaches;
☐	b. compare the sum-of-value-added and value-of-final-output methods of calculating GDP;
☐	c. compare nominal and real GDP and calculate and interpret the GDP deflator;
☐	d. compare GDP, national income, personal income, and personal disposable income;
☐	e. explain the fundamental relationship among saving, investment, the fiscal balance, and the trade balance;
☐	f. explain the IS and LM curves and how they combine to generate the aggregate demand curve;
☐	g. explain the aggregate supply curve in the short run and long run;
☐	h. explain causes of movements along and shifts in aggregate demand and supply curves;
☐	i. describe how fluctuations in aggregate demand and aggregate supply cause short-run changes in the economy and the business cycle;
☐	j. distinguish between the following types of macroeconomic equilibria: long-run full employment, short-run recessionary gap, short-run inflationary gap, and short-run stagflation;
☐	k. explain how a short-run macroeconomic equilibrium may occur at a level above or below full employment;
☐	l. analyze the effect of combined changes in aggregate supply and demand on the economy;

(continued)

1   INTRODUCTION

In the field of economics, *microeconomics* is the study of the economic activity and behavior of individual economic units, such as a household, a company, or a market for a particular good or service, and *macroeconomics* is the study of the aggregate activities of households, companies, and markets. Macroeconomics focuses on national aggregates, such as total *investment*, the amount spent by all businesses on plant and equipment; total *consumption*, the amount spent by all households on goods and services; the rate of change in the general level of prices; and the overall level of interest rates.

Macroeconomic analysis examines a nation's aggregate output and income, its competitive and comparative advantages, the productivity of its labor force, its price level and inflation rate, and the actions of its national government and central bank. The objective of macroeconomic analysis is to address such fundamental questions as:

- What is an economy's aggregate output, and how is aggregate income measured?
- What factors determine the level of aggregate output/income for an economy?
- What are the levels of aggregate demand and aggregate supply of goods and services within the country?
- Is the level of output increasing or decreasing, and at what rate?
- Is the general price level stable, rising, or falling?
- Is unemployment rising or falling?
- Are households spending or saving more?
- Are workers able to produce more output for a given level of inputs?
- Are businesses investing in and expanding their productive capacity?
- Are exports (imports) rising or falling?

From an investment perspective, investors must be able to evaluate a country's current economic environment and to forecast its future economic environment in order to identify asset classes and securities that will benefit from economic trends occurring within that country. Macroeconomic variables—such as the level of inflation, unemployment, consumption, government spending, and investment—affect the overall level of activity within a country. They also have different impacts on the growth and profitability of industries within a country, the companies within those industries, and the returns of the securities issued by those companies.

This reading is organized as follows: Section 2 describes gross domestic product and related measures of domestic output and income. Section 3 discusses short-run and long-run aggregate demand and supply curves, the causes of shifts and movements along those curves, and factors that affect equilibrium levels of output, prices, and interest rates. Section 4 discusses sources, sustainability, and measures of economic growth. A summary and practice problems complete the reading.

AGGREGATE OUTPUT AND INCOME

2

The **aggregate output** of an economy is the value of all the goods and services produced in a specified period of time. The **aggregate income** of an economy is the value of all the payments earned by the suppliers of factors used in the production of goods and services. Because the value of the output produced must accrue to the factors of production, aggregate output and aggregate income within an economy must be equal.

There are four broad forms of payments (i.e., income): compensation of employees, rent, interest, and profits. Compensation of employees includes wages and benefits (primarily employer contributions to private pension plans and health insurance) that individuals receive in exchange for providing labor. **Rent** is payment for the use of property. **Interest** is payment for lending funds. **Profit** is the return that owners of a company receive for the use of their capital and the assumption of financial risk when making their investments. Although businesses are the direct owners of much of the property and physical capital in the economy, by virtue of owning the businesses, households are the ultimate owners of these assets and hence the ultimate recipients of the profits. In reality, of course, a portion of profits are usually retained within businesses to help finance maintenance and expansion of capacity. Similarly, because the government is viewed as operating on a non-profit basis, any revenue it receives from ownership of companies and/or property may be viewed as being passed back to households in the form of lower taxes. Therefore, for simplicity, it is standard in macroeconomics to attribute all income to the household sector unless the analysis depends on a more precise accounting.

Aggregate *expenditure*, the total amount spent on the goods and services produced in the (domestic) economy during the period, must also be equal to aggregate output and aggregate income. However, some of this expenditure may come from foreigners in the form of net exports.[1] Thus, aggregate output, aggregate income, and aggregate expenditure all refer to different ways of decomposing the same quantity.

Exhibit 1 illustrates the flow of inputs, output, income, and expenditures in a very simple economy. Households supply the factors of production (labor and capital) to businesses in exchange for wages and profit (aggregate income) totaling £100. These flows are shown by the top two arrows. Companies use the inputs to produce goods and services (aggregate output) which they sell to households (aggregate expenditure) for £100. The output and expenditure flows are shown by the bottom two arrows. Aggregate output, income, and expenditure are all equal to £100.

In this simplified example, households spend all of their income on domestically produced goods and services. They do not buy foreign goods, save for the future, or pay taxes. Similarly, businesses do not sell to foreigners or the government and do not invest to increase their productive capacity. These important components of the economy will be added in Section 2.2. But first we need to discuss how output and income are measured.

---

1 Note that "aggregate expenditure" as defined here does *not* equal the amount spent by *domestic* residents on goods and services because it includes exports (purchases of domestic products by foreigners) and excludes imports (purchases of foreign products by domestic residents). Thus, spending by domestic residents does not necessarily equal domestic income/output. Indeed, within any given period, it usually does not. This will be explained in more detail in Section 2.2.3.

Exhibit 1	Output, Income, and Expenditure in a Simple Economy: The Circular Flow

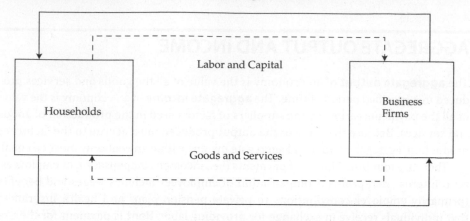

Income £100 (= Wages + Profits)

Labor and Capital

Households   Business Firms

Goods and Services

Consumption Expenditure £100

2.1 Gross Domestic Product

Gross domestic product (GDP) measures

- the market value of all final goods and services produced within the economy in a given period of time (output definition) or, equivalently,

- the aggregate income earned by all households, all companies, and the government within the economy in a given period of time (income definition).

Intuitively, GDP measures the flow of output and income in the economy.[2] GDP represents the broadest measure of the value of economic activity occurring within a country during a given period of time.

Therefore, GDP can be determined in two different manners. In the income approach, GDP is calculated as the total amount earned by households and companies in the economy. In the expenditure approach, GDP is calculated as the total amount spent on the goods and services produced within the economy during a given period. For the economy as a whole, total income must equal total expenditures, so the two approaches yield the same result.

Many developed countries use a standardized methodology for measuring GDP. This methodology is described in the official handbook of the Organisation for Economic Co-Operation and Development (Paris: OECD Publishing). The OECD reports the national accounts for many developed nations. In the United States, the National Income and Product Accounts (also called NIPA, or national accounts, for short) is the official US government accounting of all the income and expenditure flows in the US economy. The national accounts are the responsibility of the US Department of

---

2 Some textbooks and countries measure flows of income and output by using gross national product (GNP) rather than GDP. The difference is subtle but can be important in some contexts. GDP includes production within national borders regardless of whether the factors of production (labor, capital, and property) are owned domestically or by foreigners. In contrast, GNP measures output produced by domestically owned factors of production regardless of whether the production occurs domestically or overseas.

Commerce and are published in its *Survey of Current Business*. In Canada, similar data are available from Statistics Canada, whereas in China, the National Bureau of Statistics of China provides GDP data.

To ensure that GDP is measured consistently over time and across countries, the following three broad criteria are used:

- All goods and services included in the calculation of GDP *must be produced during the measurement period*. Therefore, items produced in previous periods—such as houses, cars, machinery, or equipment—are excluded. In addition, transfer payments from the government sector to individuals, such as unemployment compensation or welfare benefits, are excluded. Capital gains that accrue to individuals when their assets appreciate in value are also excluded.

- The only goods and services included in the calculation of GDP are those whose value *can be determined by being sold in the market*. This enables the price of goods or services to be objectively determined. For example, a liter of extra virgin olive oil is more valuable than a liter of spring water because the market price of extra virgin olive oil is higher than the market price of spring water. The value of labor used in activities that are not sold on the market, such as commuting, gardening, etc., is also excluded from GDP. By-products of production processes are also excluded if they have no explicit market value, such as air pollution, water pollution, and acid rain.

- Only the market value of final goods and services is included in GDP. Final goods and services are those that are not resold. *Intermediate goods* are goods that are resold or used to produce another good.[3] The value of intermediate goods is excluded from GDP because additional value is added during the production process, and all the value added during the entire production process is reflected in the final sale price of the finished good. An alternative approach to measuring GDP is summing all the value added during the production and distribution processes. The most direct approach, however, is to sum the market value of all the final goods and services produced within the economy in a given time period.

Two distinct, but closely related, measurement methods can be used to calculate GDP based on expenditures: value of final output and sum of value added. These two methods are illustrated in Exhibit 2. In this example, a farmer sells wheat to a miller. The miller grinds the wheat into flour and sells it to a baker who makes bread and sells it to a retailer. Finally, the bread is sold to retail customers. The wheat and flour are both intermediate goods in this example because they are used as inputs to produce another good. Thus, they are not counted (directly) in GDP. For the purposes of GDP, the value of the final product is €1.00, which includes the value added by the bread retailer as a distributor of the bread. If, in contrast, the baker sold directly to the public, the value counted in GDP would be the price at which the baker sold the bread, €0.78. The left column of the exhibit shows the total revenue received at each stage of the process, whereas the right column shows the value added at each stage. Note that the market value of the final product (€1.00) is equal to the sum of the value added at each of the stages. Thus, the contribution to GDP can be measured as either the final sale price or the sum of the value added at each stage.

---

3 "Final goods" should not be confused with so-called final sales, and "intermediate goods" should not be confused with inventories. GDP includes both final sales to customers and increases in companies' inventories. If sales exceed current production, then GDP is less than final sales by the amount of goods sold out of inventory.

Exhibit 2   Value of Final Product Equals Income Created

	Receipts at Each Stage (€)	Value Added (= Income Created) at Each Stage (€)	
Receipts of farmer from miller	0.15	0.15	Value added by farmer
Receipts of miller from baker	0.46	0.31	Value added by miller
Receipts of baker from retailer	0.78	0.32	Value added by baker
Receipts of retailer from final customer	1.00	0.22	Value added by retailer
	1.00	1.00	
	Value of final output	Total value added = Total income created	

EXAMPLE 1

Contribution of Automobile Production to GDP

Exhibit 3 provides simplified information on the cost of producing an automobile in the United States at various stages of the production process. The example assumes the automobile is produced and sold domestically and assumes no imported material is used. Calculate the contribution of automobile production to GDP using the value-added method, and show that it is equivalent to the expenditure method. What impact would the use of imported steel or plastics have on GDP?

Exhibit 3   Cost of Producing Automobiles

Stage of Production	Sales Value ($)
1 Production of basic materials	
Steel	1,000
Plastics	3,000
Semiconductors	1,000
2 Assembly of automobile (manufacturer price)	15,000
3 Wholesale price for automobile dealer	16,000
4 Retail price	18,000

Solution:

GDP includes only the value of final goods and ignores intermediate goods in order to avoid double counting. Thus, the final sale price of $18,000 and not the total sales value of $54,000 (summing sales at all the levels of production) would be included in GDP. Alternatively, we can avoid double counting by calculating and summing the value added at each stage. At each stage of production, the difference between what a company pays for its inputs and what it receives for the product is its contribution to GDP. The value added for each stage of production is computed as follows:

Stage of Production	Sales Value ($)	Value Added ($)	
1 Production of basic materials			
Steel	1,000	1,000	
Plastics	3,000	3,000	
Semiconductors	1,000	1,000	
Total Inputs		5,000	(sum of 3 inputs)
2 Assembly of car (manufacturer price)	15,000	10,000	= (15,000 − 5,000)
3 Wholesale price for car dealer	16,000	1,000	= (16,000 − 15,000)
4 Retail price	18,000	2,000	= (18,000 − 16,000)
Total expenditures	18,000		
Total value added		18,000	

Thus, the sum of the value added by each stage of production is equal to $18,000, which is equal to the final selling price of the automobile. If some of the inputs (steel, plastics, or semiconductors) are imported, the value added would be reduced by the amount paid for the imports.

2.1.1 Goods and Services Included at Imputed Values

As a general rule, only the value of goods and services whose *value can be determined by being sold in the market* are included in the measurement of GDP. Owner-occupied housing and government services, however, are two examples of services that are not sold in the marketplace but are still included in the measurement of GDP.

When a household (individual) rents a place to live, he or she is buying housing services. The household pays the owner of the property rent in exchange for shelter. The income that a property owner receives is included in the calculation of GDP. However, when a household purchases a home, it is implicitly paying itself in exchange for the shelter. As a result, the government must estimate (impute) a value for this owner-occupied rent, which is then added to GDP.

The value of government services provided by police officers, firemen, judges, and other government officials is a key factor that affects the level of economic activity. However, valuing these services is difficult because they are not sold in a market like other services; individual customers cannot decide how much to consume or how much they are willing to pay. Therefore, these services are simply included in GDP at their cost (e.g., wages paid) with no value added attributed to the production process.

For simplicity and global comparability, the number of goods and services with imputed values that are included in the measurement of GDP are limited. In general, non-market activity is excluded from GDP. Thus, activities performed for one's own benefit, such as cooking, cleaning, and home repair, are excluded. Activities in the so-called underground economy are also excluded. The underground economy reflects economic activity that people hide from the government either because it is illegal or because they are attempting to evade taxation. Undocumented laborers who are paid "off the books" are one example. The illegal drug trade is another. Similarly, barter transactions, such as neighbors exchanging services with each other (for example, helping your neighbor repair her fence in exchange for her plowing your garden), are excluded from GDP.

Exhibit 4 shows the estimated size of the underground economy in various countries as a percentage of nominal GDP. The estimates range from 8 percent in the United States to 60 percent in Peru. Based on these estimates, the US national income accounts fail to account for roughly 7.4 percent (= 8/108) of economic activity, whereas in Peru, the national accounts miss roughly 37.5 percent (= 60/160) of the economy. For most of the countries shown, the national accounts miss 12–20 percent of the economy.

Exhibit 4	Underground Economy as a Percentage of Nominal GDP (2006)
Country	**Underground Economy as a Percentage of Nominal GDP (%)**
Peru	60.0
Mexico	32.1
South Korea	27.5
Costa Rica	26.8
Greece	26.0
India	24.4
Italy	23.1
Spain	20.2
Sweden	16.3
Germany	15.4
Canada	14.1
China	14.0
France	13.2
Japan	8.9
United States	8.0

Source: Friedrich Schneider and Andreas Buehm, Linz University, 2009.

It should be clear from these estimates of the underground economy that the reliability of official GDP data varies considerably across countries. Failure to capture a significant portion of activity is one problem. Poor data collection practices and unreliable statistical methods within the official accounts are also potential problems.

2.1.2 *Nominal and Real GDP*

In order to evaluate an economy's health, it is often useful to remove the effect of changes in the general price level on GDP because higher (lower) income driven solely by changes in the price level is not indicative of a higher (lower) level of economic activity. To accomplish this, economists use **real GDP**, which indicates what would have been the total expenditures on the output of goods and services if prices were unchanged. **Per capita real GDP** (real GDP divided by the size of the population) has often been used as a measure of the average standard of living in a country.

Suppose we are interested in measuring the GDP of an economy. For the sake of simplicity, suppose that the economy consists of a single automobile maker and that in 2009, 300,000 vehicles are produced with an average market price of €18,750. GDP in 2009 would be €5,625,000,000. Economists define the value of goods and services measured at current prices as **nominal GDP**. Suppose that in 2010, 300,000 vehicles are again produced but that the average market price for a vehicle increases by 7 percent to €20,062.50. GDP in 2010 would be €6,018,750,000. Even though no more cars were produced in 2010 than in 2009, it appears that the economy grew by (€6,018,750,000/€5,625,000,000) − 1 = 7% between 2009 and 2010, although it actually did not grow at all.

Nominal and real GDP can be expressed as

Nominal $GDP_t = P_t \times Q_t$

where

P_t = Prices in year t
Q_t = Quantity produced in year t

Real $GDP_t = P_B \times Q_t$

where

P_B = Prices in the base year

Taking the base year to be 2009 and putting in the 2009 and 2010 numbers gives:

Nominal GDP_{2009} = (€18,750 × 300,000) = €5,625,000,000

Real GDP_{2009} = (€18,750 × 300,000) = €5,625,000,000

Nominal GDP_{2010} = (€20,062.50 × 300,000) = €6,018,750,000

Real GDP_{2010} = (€18,750 × 300,000) = €5,625,000,000

In this example, real GDP did not change between 2009 and 2010 because the total output remained the same: 300,000 vehicles. The difference between nominal GDP in 2010 and real GDP in 2010 was the 7 percent inflation rate.

Now suppose that the auto manufacturer produced 3 percent more vehicles in 2010 than in 2009 (i.e., production in 2010 was 309,000 vehicles). Real GDP would increase by 3 percent from 2009 to 2010. With a 7 percent increase in prices, nominal GDP for 2010 would now be

Nominal GDP_{2010} = (1.03 × 300,000) × (1.07 × €18,750)
= (309,000 × €20,062.50)
= €6,199,312,500

The **implicit price deflator for GDP**, or simply the **GDP deflator**, is defined as

$$\text{GDP deflator} = \frac{\text{Value of current year output at current year prices}}{\text{Value of current year output at base year prices}} \times 100$$

Thus, in the example the GDP deflator for 2010 is [(309,000 × €20,062.50)/ (309,000 × €18,750)](100) = (1.07)(100) = 107. The GDP deflator broadly measures the aggregate changes in prices across the overall economy, and hence changes in the deflator provide a useful gauge of inflation within the economy.

Real GDP is equal to nominal GDP divided by the GDP deflator scaled by 100:

Real GDP = [Nominal GDP/(GDP deflator/100)]

This relation gives the GDP deflator its name. That is, the measure of GDP in terms of current prices, nominal GDP, is adjusted for inflation by dividing it by the deflator. The expression also shows that the GDP deflator is the ratio of nominal GDP to real GDP scaled by 100:

GDP deflator = (Nominal GDP/Real GDP) × 100

Thus, real GDP for 2010 would be

Real GDP_{2010} = [Nominal GDP/(GDP deflator/100)]
= [€6,199,312,500/(107/100)]
= €5,793,750,000

Note that €5,793,750,000 represents 3 percent real growth over 2009 GDP and 3 percent higher real GDP for 2010 than under the assumption of no growth in unit car sales in 2010.

What would be the increase in *nominal* GDP for 2010 compared with 2009 with the 3 percent greater automobile production and 7 percent inflation?

(Nominal GDP$_{2010}$/Nominal GDP$_{2009}$) − 1

= (€6,199,312,500/€5,625,000,000) − 1

= 0.102

So, nominal GDP would increase by 10.2 percent, which equals [(1.07 × 1.03) − 1] or approximately 7% + 3% = 10%. Which number is more informative about growth in economic activity, 3 percent real growth or 10.2 percent nominal growth? The real growth rate is more informative because it exactly captures increases in output. Nominal growth, by blending price changes with output changes, is less directly informative about output changes. In summary, real economic growth is measured by the percentage change in real GDP. When measuring real economic activity or when comparing one nation's economy to another, real GDP and real GDP growth should be used because they more closely reflect the quantity of output available for consumption and investment.

EXAMPLE 2

Calculating the GDP Deflator

John Lambert is an equity analyst with Equitytrust, a Canadian investment management firm that primarily invests in Canadian stocks and bonds. The investment policy committee for the firm is concerned about the possibility of inflation. The implicit GDP deflator is an important measure of the overall price level in the economy, and changes in the deflator provide an important gauge of inflation within the economy. GDP data have been released by Statistics Canada and are shown in Exhibit 5. Lambert is asked by the committee to use the GDP data to calculate the implicit GDP price deflator from 2005 to 2009 and the inflation rate for 2009.

Exhibit 5   Real and Nominal GDP for Canada

	Seasonally adjusted at annual rates (SAAR)				
	2005	2006	2007	2008	2009
GDP at market prices (million C$)	1,373,845	1,450,405	1,529,589	1,599,608	1,527,258
Real GDP (million 2002 C$)	1,247,807	1,283,033	1,311,260	1,318,054	1,285,604

Solution:

The implicit GDP price deflator measures inflation across all sectors of the economy, including the consumer, business, government, exports, and imports. It is calculated as the ratio of nominal to real GDP and reported as an index number with the base year deflator equal to 100. The implicit GDP price deflator for the Canadian economy for 2009 is calculated as (1,527,258/1,285,604) × 100 = 118.8. The results for the other years are shown in the following table:

	2005	2006	2007	2008	2009
GDP at market prices (million C$)	1,373,845	1,450,405	1,529,589	1,599,608	1,527,258
Real GDP (million 2002 C$)	1,247,807	1,283,033	1,311,260	1,318,054	1,285,604
Implicit GDP price deflator	110.1	113.0	116.6	121.4	118.8

The inflation rate is calculated as a percentage change in the index. For 2009, the annual inflation rate is equal to $[(118.8/121.4) - 1]$ or -2.1 percent. This shows that Canada actually experienced deflation in 2009 even though prices are still above their level in 2007.

2.2 The Components of GDP

Having defined GDP and discussed how it is measured, we can now consider the major components of GDP, the flows among the four major sectors of the economy—the household sector, the business sector, the government sector, and the foreign or external sector (comprising transactions with the "rest of the world")—and the markets through which they interact. An expression for GDP, based on the expenditure approach, is

$$GDP = C + I + G + (X - M) \qquad \text{(1)}$$

where

C = Consumer spending on final goods and services

I = Gross private domestic investment, which includes business investment in capital goods (e.g., plant and equipment) and changes in inventory (**inventory investment**)

G = Government spending on final goods and services

X = Exports

M = Imports

Exhibit 6 shows the flow of expenditures, income, and financing among the four sectors of the economy and the three principal markets. In the exhibit, solid arrows point in the direction of expenditure on final goods and services. For simplicity, corresponding flows of output are not shown separately. The flow of factors of production is also shown with a solid arrow. Financial flows, including income and net taxes, are shown with dashed arrows pointing to the recipient of funds.

Exhibit 6   Output, Income, and Expenditure Flows

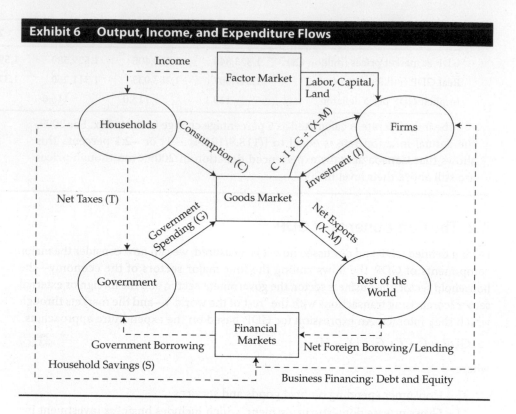

2.2.1 *The Household and Business Sectors*

The very top portion of Exhibit 6 shows the services of labor, land, and capital flowing through the *factor market* to business firms and the flow of income back from firms to households. Households spend part of their income on consumption (*C*) and save (*S*) part of their income for future consumption. Current consumption expenditure flows through the *goods market* to the business sector. Household saving flows into the *financial markets* where it provides funding for businesses that need to borrow or raise equity capital. Firms borrow or raise equity primarily to finance investment (*I*) in inventory, property, plant, and equipment. Investment (*I*) is shown flowing from firms through the goods market and back to firms because the business sector both demands and produces the goods needed to build productive capacity (*capital goods*).

In most developed economies, like Italy and the United States, expenditures on capital goods represent a significant portion of GDP. Investments (expenditures) on capital goods accounted for approximately 21.1 percent of Italy's GDP in 2007, while in the United States investments accounted for approximately 18.4 percent of GDP. In some developing countries, notably China (40.0 percent) and India (33.8 percent), investment spending accounts for a substantially larger share of the economy.[4] As we will examine in greater detail later, investment spending is an important determinant of an economy's long-term growth rate. At the same time, investment spending is the most volatile component of the economy, and changes in capital spending, especially spending on inventories, are one of the main factors causing short-run economic fluctuations.

---

4 See Exhibit 27 later in this reading for investment details for other countries. OECD.Stat Extracts: Country Statistical Profiles 2009 (stats.oecd.org) and *Economic Report of the President* (Washington, DC: US Government Printing Office, 2010): Table B-12, page 345.

2.2.2 The Government Sector

The government sector collects taxes from households and businesses. For simplicity, only the taxes collected from the household sector are shown in Exhibit 6. In turn, the government sector purchases goods and services (G) from the business sector. For example, the government sector hires construction companies to build roads, schools, and other infrastructure goods. Government expenditure (G) also reflects spending on the military, police and fire protection, the postal service, and other government services. Provision of these services makes the government a major source of employment in most countries. To keep Exhibit 6 simple, however, government employment and the corresponding income are not explicitly shown.

Governments also make transfer payments to households. In general, these are designed to address social objectives such as maintaining minimum living standards, providing health care, and assisting the unemployed with retraining and temporary support. In Exhibit 6, transfer payments are subtracted from taxes and reflected in net taxes (T).

Transfer payments are not included in government expenditures on goods and services (G) because they represent a monetary transfer by the government of tax revenue back to individuals with no corresponding receipt of goods or services. The household spending facilitated by the transfer payments is, of course, included in consumption (C) and, hence, GDP. It is worth noting that transfers do not always take the form of direct payments to beneficiaries. Instead, the government may pay for or even directly provide goods or services to individuals. For example, universal health care programs often work in this way.

If, as is usually the case, government expenditure (G) exceeds net taxes (T), then the government has a *fiscal deficit* and must borrow in the financial markets. Thus, the government may compete with businesses in the financial markets for the funds generated by household saving. The only other potential source of funds in an economy is capital flows from the rest of the world. These will be discussed in the next section.

In 2007, the ratio of general government spending (which includes central government as well as state, provincial, and local government) to GDP in Italy was 44.8 percent while in the United States it was 31.2 percent. In countries where the government provides more services, such as universal health care in Italy, the government's contribution to GDP is greater. France's government sector represents 46.3 percent of GDP. In other countries, the public sector makes up a smaller share. For example, in Costa Rica, which has no standing army or navy, government spending is 16.1 percent of GDP. Exhibit 7 shows data on tax revenues, general government spending, and transfer payments as a share of nominal GDP.

Exhibit 7	**General Government Spending and Taxes as a Percentage of GDP (2007)**			
		General Government Spending as a Percentage of GDP		
Country	**General Government Tax Revenues as a Percentage of GDP**	**Total**	**Goods and Services and Debt Service**	**Transfer Payments**
Canada	33.3%	31.9%	17.1%	14.8%
Mexico	20.5	22.6	Not available	Not available
United States	28.3	31.2	19.5	11.7
Japan	28.1	30.5	14.9	15.6
South Korea	28.7	24.0	15.7	8.3
France	43.6	46.3	20.2	26.1

(continued)

Exhibit 7　(Continued)

Country	General Government Tax Revenues as a Percentage of GDP	General Government Spending as a Percentage of GDP		
		Total	**Goods and Services and Debt Service**	**Transfer Payments**
Germany	36.2	36.0	13.7	22.3
Greece	31.3	36.7	19.8	16.9
Italy	43.3	44.8	21.5	23.3
Spain	37.2	35.3	16.6	18.7
Sweden	48.2	44.5	17.7	26.8
Costa Rica	14.0	16.1	Not available	Not available

Sources: OECD Stat Extracts: Country Statistical Profiles 2009 (stats.oecd.org) and *Revenue Statistics 1965–2008: 2009 Edition* (OECD).

2.2.3 *The External Sector*

Trade and capital flows involving the rest of the world are shown in the bottom right quadrant of Exhibit 6. Net exports ($X - M$) reflects the difference between the value of goods and services sold to foreigners—exports (X)—and the portion of domestic consumption (C), investment (I), and government expenditure (G) that represents purchases of goods and services from the rest of the world—imports (M).

A **balance of trade deficit** means that the domestic economy is spending more on foreign goods and services than foreign economies are spending on domestic goods and services. It also means that the country is spending more than it produces because domestic saving is not sufficient to finance domestic investment plus the government's fiscal balance. A trade deficit must be funded by borrowing from the rest of the world through the financial markets. The rest of the world is able to provide this financing because, by definition, it must be running a corresponding trade surplus and spending less than it produces.

It bears emphasizing that trade and capital flows between an economy and the rest of the world must balance. One area's deficit is another's surplus, and vice versa. This is an accounting identity that must hold. In effect, having allowed a country to run a trade deficit, foreigners must, in aggregate, finance it. However, the financing terms may or may not be attractive.

Exhibit 8 reports trade balances for the United States with selected countries. Note that Canada was the largest trading partner, both in terms of exports and imports, in 2008. China was a close second in selling goods to US markets, but China is not an important consumer of US goods. Hence, the US trade deficit with China was the largest by far. Overall, in 2008 the US balance of trade deficit was $231,115 million.

Exhibit 8　US International Trade in Goods—Selected Countries, 2008 (millions of US dollars)

	Exports	Imports	Balance
Total, all countries	1,276,994	2,117,245	−840,251
Europe	321,151	440,802	−119,651
Euro area	198,538	277,728	−79,190
France	28,603	44,036	−15,433
Germany	54,209	97,597	−43,388

Exhibit 8   (Continued)

	Exports	Imports	Balance
Italy	15,330	36,140	−20,810
Canada	261,872	342,920	−81,048
Mexico	151,147	219,808	−68,661
China	69,552	337,963	−268,411
India	17,623	25,739	−8,116
Japan	64,457	139,587	−75,130

Source: Economic Report of the President (Washington, DC: US Government Printing Office, 2010): Table B-105, page 451.

2.3 GDP, National Income, Personal Income, and Personal Disposable Income

This section examines the calculation of GDP and other income measures in detail by means of an analysis of data from Statistics Canada.

Exhibit 9 provides data on the level of Canadian GDP and its components measured at market prices (nominal GDP), leaving certain quantities to be determined.

Exhibit 9   GDP Release for the Canadian Economy
(millions of C$ at market prices, seasonally adjusted at annual rates)

	2005	2006	2007	2008	2009
Expenditure based:					
Consumer spending	758,966	801,742	851,603	890,351	898,728
Government spending	259,857	277,608	293,608	314,329	333,942
Government gross fixed investment	37,067	41,151	45,321	50,955	59,078
Business gross fixed investment	255,596	283,382	301,885	313,574	269,394
Exports	519,435	524,075	534,718	563,948	438,553
Deduct: Imports	468,270	487,674	505,055	539,012	464,722
Change in inventories*	10,614	9,362	8,266	5,472	−8,180
Statistical discrepancy	580	759	−757	−9	465
GDP at Market Prices	**1,373,845**	**1,450,405**	**1,529,589**	**1,599,608**	*TBD*
Income based:					
Wages, salaries, and supplementary labor income	695,093	743,392	784,885	818,613	819,066
Corporate profits before tax**	185,855	194,024	203,392	210,756	149,438
Government business enterprise profits before taxes	15,293	14,805	15,493	16,355	12,975
Interest income	61,421	66,404	71,589	83,998	63,947
Unincorporated business net income, including rent	85,234	86,750	90,411	94,559	99,879
Taxes less subsidies on factors of production	61,982	64,536	67,900	71,094	70,604
Taxes less subsidies on products	93,302	96,052	98,816	94,840	93,030

(continued)

Exhibit 9   (Continued)

	2005	2006	2007	2008	2009
National Income	1,198,180	1,265,963	1,332,486	1,390,215	*TBD*
Statistical discrepancy	−581	−759	757	10	−466
Capital consumption allowance	176,246	185,201	196,346	209,383	218,785
GDP at Market Prices	1,373,845	1,450,405	1,529,589	1,599,608	*TBD*
Undistributed corporate profits	91,926	96,793	90,829	110,431	56,969
Corporate income taxes	51,631	47,504	54,867	53,176	34,319
Transfer payments: government to consumer	136,247	145,754	154,609	163,979	174,390
Personal Income	1,035,586	1,106,832	1,174,683	1,224,653	*TBD*
Personal Disposable Income	794,269	853,190	901,634	949,484	965,628
Interest paid to business	14,029	16,978	19,063	19,558	18,115
Consumer transfers to foreigners	4,395	4,483	5,533	5,117	4,737
Personal saving	16,878	29,987	25,435	34,458	*TBD*

* Includes change in government inventory.
** Includes inventory valuation adjustment.
Source: Statistics Canada.

The exhibit shows the two approaches to measuring GDP: 1) expenditures on final output measured as the sum of sales to the final users and 2) the sum of the factor incomes generated in the production of final output. In theory, the two approaches should provide the same estimate of GDP. As shown in the exhibit, however, in practice they differ because of the use of different data sources. The difference is accounted for by a *statistical discrepancy*. Market analysts more closely follow the expenditure approach because the expenditure data are more timely and reliable than data for the income components.[5]

Using the expenditure approach, Statistics Canada measures Canadian GDP as follows:

GDP = Consumer spending on goods and services

+ Business gross fixed investment

+ Change in inventories

+ Government spending on goods and services

+ Government gross fixed investment

+ Exports − Imports

+ Statistical discrepancy

---

5 As shown in Exhibit 9, Statistics Canada divides the total statistical discrepancy roughly equally (with opposite signs) between the income- and expenditure-based measures of GDP. In the US national accounts, the statistical discrepancy appears only in the income-based breakdown of GDP because the expenditures data are believed to be more accurate than the income data.

Note that the Canadian national income accounts classify a portion of government expenditures as gross fixed investment. Not all countries make this distinction. The United States, for example, does not. Also note that the change in business inventories must be included in expenditures. Otherwise, goods produced but not yet sold would be left out of GDP.

The income-based approach calculates GDP as the sum of factor incomes and essentially measures the cost of producing final output. However, two of the costs entering into the gross value of output are not really earned by a factor of production. These items, depreciation and indirect taxes, are discussed below. GDP is estimated in the income approach as follows:[6]

GDP = National income + Capital consumption allowance + Statistical discrepancy

where **national income** is the income received by all factors of production used in the generation of final output:

National income = Compensation of employees

+ Corporate and government enterprise profits before taxes

+ Interest income

+ Unincorporated business net income (proprietor's income)

+ Rent

+ Indirect business taxes less subsidies

Compensation of employees includes wages and supplements to wages, which are primarily payments for pensions and health insurance. Corporate profits before taxes include three items: 1) dividends paid to households, 2) undistributed corporate profits (retained earnings) that remain in the business sector, and 3) corporate taxes paid to government. Interest income is the interest paid by businesses to households, government, and foreigners to compensate them for the loan of a financial asset. Unincorporated net income, including rent, is the earnings that flow to unincorporated proprietors and farm operators for running their own business. "Indirect business taxes less subsidies" reflects taxes and subsidies included in the final price of the good or service. It is the (net) portion of national income that is directly paid to the government. In the Canadian accounts, these are measured in two ways: 1) "taxes less subsidies on products," which includes sales taxes, fuel taxes, and import duties, and 2) "taxes less subsidies on factors of production," which is mainly property taxes and payroll taxes.

The **capital consumption allowance** (CCA) is a measure of the wear and tear (depreciation) of the capital stock that occurs in the production of goods and services. This measure acknowledges the fact that some income/output must be allocated to replacement of the existing capital stock as it wears out. Loosely speaking, one may think of Profit + CCA as the total amount earned by capital, with the CCA being the amount that must be earned and reinvested just to maintain the existing productivity of the capital.

Along with the GDP report, Statistics Canada and other government statistical agencies provide information on personal income and saving. **Personal income** is a broad measure of household income and measures the ability of consumers to make purchases. As such, it is one of the key determinants of consumption spending. Personal

---

6 Construction of the national income accounts varies across countries. In the United States, for example, national income is defined to include income received by US-owned factors of production even if the income is generated outside the United States. To compute US GDP, the national income data must be adjusted for net foreign factor income. No adjustment is required in the Canadian data since the data are measured on a geographic basis equivalent to GDP.

income includes all income received by households, whether earned or unearned. It differs from national income in that some of the income earned by the factors of production (indirect business taxes, corporate income taxes, retained earnings) is not received by households and instead goes to the government or business sectors. Similarly, households receive some income from governments (transfer payments, such as social insurance payments, unemployment compensation, and disability payments) that is not earned. Thus, the following adjustments are made to national income in order to derive personal income:

Personal income = National income

- Indirect business taxes

- Corporate income taxes

- Undistributed corporate profits

+ Transfer payments

Personal disposable income (PDI) is equal to personal income less personal taxes. It measures the amount of after-tax income that households have to spend on goods and services or to save. Thus, it is the most relevant, and most closely watched, measure of income for household spending and saving decisions.

Finally, household saving is equal to PDI less three items: consumption expenditures, interest paid by consumers to business, and personal transfer payments to foreigners. The corresponding measure of saving for the business sector equals undistributed corporate profits plus the capital consumption allowance.

EXAMPLE 3

Canadian GDP Release and Other Measures of Production and Income

The investment policy committee at Equitytrust asks John Lambert to review the Canadian GDP data shown in Exhibit 9 and data from the Department of Finance Canada that show that the combined federal–provincial government deficit for 2009 was 84,249 (million C$), with the federal deficit at 55,590 (million C$).

1 Calculate 2009 GDP using the expenditure approach, and indicate how the expenditures are represented in Exhibit 6.

2 Calculate 2009 GDP using the income approach.

3 Calculate personal income for 2009.

4 Using the Canadian data for 2009, calculate the level of household saving (S), the saving rate, and net taxes (T) paid by the household sector. Given that the combined government budget deficit was 84,249 (million C$) in 2009, calculate tax revenues for the Canadian economy.

5 Calculate the impact of foreign trade on the Canadian economy in 2009 and Canada's net foreign borrowing/lending in 2009.

6 Calculate the net amount of borrowing/lending by the business sector in 2009.

Solutions:

(All numbers in millions)

Solution to 1:

In the expenditure approach, nominal GDP is calculated as the sum of spending by the major sectors in the economy:

GDP = Consumer spending on goods and services + Business gross fixed investment + Government spending on goods and services + Government gross fixed investment + Exports − Imports + Change in inventories + Statistical discrepancy

Substituting the numbers from Exhibit 9,

GDP = 898,728 + 269,394 + 333,942 + 59,078 + 438,553

= − 464,722 − 8,180 + 465

= C\$1,527,258

In Exhibit 6, these expenditures are represented by the arrows pointing to the goods market and by the arrow pointing back to firms labeled as $C + I + G + (X − M)$.

Solution to 2:

On the income side, nominal GDP is equal to national income plus the capital consumption allowance plus a statistical discrepancy. National income is defined as the sum of income received by the factors of production and is given by

National income = Compensation of employees + Corporate and government enterprise profits before taxes + Interest income + Unincorporated business net income (proprietor's income) + Rent + Inventory valuation adjustment + Indirect business taxes - Subsidies

Substituting in the numbers from Exhibit 9, we get C\$1,308,939, where indirect business taxes are equal to 70,604 + 93,030 = C\$163,634. Using this result,

GDP = 1,308,939 + 218,785 − 466 = C\$1,527,258

Solution to 3:

Personal income is calculated as

Personal income = National income − Indirect business taxes − Corporate income taxes − Undistributed corporate profits + Transfer payments

Substituting in the numbers from Exhibit 9,

Personal income = 1,308,939 − (70,604 + 93,030) − 34,319 − 56,969 + 174,390

= C\$1,228,407

Solution to 4:

Household saving is equal to personal disposable income less three items: consumption expenditures, interest paid by consumers to business, and personal transfer payments to foreigners. Consumption (C) is given in Exhibit 9 as C\$898,728. Substituting the numbers, saving (S) = 965,628 − 898,728 − 18,115 − 4,737 = C\$44,048.

The Canadian saving rate for 2009 = (44,048/965,628) = 4.6%

Net taxes paid by the household sector consists of two components: 1) taxes paid by households to the government minus 2) government transfer payments to households. From Exhibit 9, government transfer payments to households for 2009 were C\$174,390. The tax outlay for households in 2009 is the difference between personal income and personal disposable income. Therefore, tax payments by households to government equal

1,228,407 − 965,628 = C\$262,779

Thus, net taxes going to government (T) from the household sector is C$88,389. However, personal taxes do not cover all sources of receipts for government. Government receipts also come from such sources as corporate income taxes, indirect taxes on businesses and consumers, and contributions for social insurance. The total tax receipts for all levels of government can be estimated from the deficit information. From Exhibit 9, government spending for 2009 totaled (333,942 + 59,078) = C$393,020. Therefore, total tax revenue from all sources is equal to 393,020 minus 84,249 or C$308,771.

Solution to 5:

The international sector had a large impact on the Canadian economy in 2009. Exports declined sharply—by 22.2 percent—going from C$563,948 in 2008 to C$438,553 in 2009. Imports declined from C$539,012 in 2008 to C$464,722 in 2009, a 13.8 percent decrease. As a result, the Canadian economy moved from a trade surplus of C$24,936 in 2008 to a deficit of C$26,169 in 2009. This huge swing in the trade balance had a very significant negative impact on the Canadian economy and subtracted from GDP growth.

Canada funded the large trade deficit in 2009 by borrowing C$26,169 from the rest of the world through the financial markets. As discussed in Section 2.2.3, trade and capital flows between an economy and the rest of the world must balance. A trade deficit must be funded by a capital inflow.

Solution to 6:

Borrowing by the business sector depends on the level of saving in the sector (i.e., internally generated funds) and the level of business investment in both fixed assets and inventories (i.e., the amount that must be financed). For 2009, gross saving in the business sector is equal to undistributed corporate profits (56,969) plus the capital consumption allowance (218,785). Thus, business saving is C$275,754. Because this number exceeds business fixed and inventory investment of C$261,214 (269,394 − 8,180), the business sector was a net lender of funds totaling C$14,540.

---

3   AGGREGATE DEMAND, AGGREGATE SUPPLY, AND EQUILIBRIUM

In this section, we will build a model of aggregate demand and aggregate supply and use it to discuss how aggregate output and the level of prices are determined in the economy. **Aggregate demand** (AD) represents the quantity of goods and services that households, businesses, government, and foreign customers want to buy at any given level of prices. **Aggregate supply** (AS) represents the quantity of goods and services producers are willing to supply at any given level of prices. It also reflects the amount of labor and capital that households are willing to offer into the marketplace at given real wage rates and cost of capital.

3.1 Aggregate Demand

As we will see, the aggregate demand curve looks like the ordinary demand curves that we encounter in microeconomics: quantity demanded increases as the price level declines. But our intuitive understanding of that relationship—lower price allows us to buy more of a good *with a given level of income*—does not apply here because income is not fixed. Instead, aggregate income/expenditure is to be determined within the model along with the price level. Thus, we will need to explain the relationship between price and quantity demanded somewhat differently.

The aggregate demand curve represents the combinations of aggregate income and the price level at which two conditions are satisfied. First, aggregate expenditure equals aggregate income. As indicated in our discussion of GDP accounting, this must always be true after the fact. The new aspect here is the requirement that *planned* expenditure equal *actual* (or realized) income. To understand the distinction, consider business inventories. If businesses end up with more inventory than they planned, then the difference represents unplanned (or unintended) business investment and actual output in the economy exceeded *planned* expenditure by that amount. Second, the available real money supply is willingly held by households and businesses.

The first condition—equality of planned expenditures and actual income/output—gives rise to what is called the *IS curve*. The second condition—equilibrium in the money market—is embodied in what is called the *LM curve*. When we put them together, we get the aggregate demand curve.

3.1.1 *Balancing Aggregate Income and Expenditure: The IS Curve*

Total expenditure on domestically produced output comes from four sources: household consumption (C), investments (I), government spending (G), and net exports ($X - M$). This can be expressed as

$$\text{Expenditure} = C + I + G + (X - M)$$

Personal disposable income is equal to GDP (Y) plus transfer payments (F) minus retained earnings and depreciation (= business saving, S_B) minus direct and indirect taxes (R). Households allocate disposable income between consumption of goods and services (C) and household saving (S_H). Therefore,

$$Y + F - S_B - R = C + S_H$$

Rearranging this equation, we get

$$Y = C + S + T$$

where $T = (R - F)$ denotes net taxes and $S = (S_B + S_H)$ denotes total private sector saving.

Because total expenditures must be identical to aggregate income (Y), we have the following relationship:

$$C + S + T = C + I + G + (X - M)$$

By rearranging this equation, we get the following fundamental relationship among domestic saving, investment, the fiscal balance, and the trade balance:

$$S = I + (G - T) + (X - M) \qquad \textbf{(2)}$$

This equation shows that domestic private saving is used or absorbed in one of three ways: investment spending (I), financing government deficits ($G - T$), and building up financial claims against overseas economies [positive trade balance, ($X - M$) > 0]. If there is a trade deficit [($X - M$) < 0], then domestic private saving is being supplemented by inflows of foreign saving and overseas economies are building up financial claims against the domestic economy.

By rearranging the identity, we can examine the implications of government deficits and surpluses:

$$G - T = (S - I) - (X - M)$$

A fiscal deficit [($G - T$) > 0] implies that the private sector must save more than it invests [($S - I$) > 0] or the country must run a trade deficit [($X - M$) < 0] with corresponding inflow of foreign saving, or both.

EXAMPLE 4

Foreign Capital Inflows Help Finance Government Deficits

The budgetary situation changed dramatically in Canada during 2009. As noted in Example 3, the Department of Finance Canada reported that in 2009 the combined federal–provincial government had a deficit of 82,249 (million C$). Thus, the government sector operated at a deficit that needed to be financed. How was this deficit financed?

Solution:

Using the formula $G - T = (S - I) - (X - M)$ shows that a budget deficit is financed through either higher domestic saving (S), lower business investment (I), or borrowing from foreigners ($X - M$). Private saving is given by

Private saving = Household saving + Undistributed corporate profits

+ Capital consumption allowance

Household saving for 2009 is given in the solution to part 4 of Example 3. Using that figure and the 2009 values for undistributed corporate profits and capital consumption allowance from Exhibit 9, we get

Private saving = 44,048 + 56,969 + 218,785 = C$319,802

Comparing this number to the level of private investment in 2009 shows that private sector saving exceeded investment spending by C$58,588 [319,802 − (269,394 − 8,180)]. Thus, domestic private saving financed over 71 percent of the deficit (58,588/82,249).

To finance the rest of the government deficit, foreign imports (M) would have to exceed exports (X) by C$23,661. From Exhibit 9, the actual trade deficit (amount of foreign borrowing) was C$26,169, slightly greater than the amount required. This difference is largely due to the statistical discrepancy caused by different data sources being used for expenditure-based and income-based estimates of GDP.

Equation 2 is the key relationship that must hold in order for aggregate income and aggregate expenditure to be equal. Up to this point, we have treated it as simply an accounting identity. We now need to think of it as the outcome of explicit decisions on the part of households, businesses, government, and foreigners. When we do so, we are faced with the question of what underlies these decisions and how the requisite balance is established.

Economists have found that the dominant determinant of consumption spending is disposable income ($Y - S_B - T$). This can be expressed formally by indicating that consumption is a function $C(\cdot)$ of disposable income,

$$C = C(Y - S_B - T)$$

or, dropping the technically correct but practically insignificant adjustment for retained earnings and depreciation (S_B), a function of GDP minus net taxes,

$$C = C(Y - T)$$

When households receive an additional unit of income, some proportion of this additional income is spent and the remainder is saved. The **marginal propensity to consume** (MPC) represents the proportion of an additional unit of disposable income that is consumed or spent. Because the amount that is not spent is saved, the **marginal propensity to save** (MPS) is MPS = 1 − MPC.

According to the consumption function, either an increase in real income or a decrease in taxes will increase aggregate consumption. Somewhat more sophisticated models of consumption recognize that consumption depends not only on current disposable income but also on wealth. Except for the very rich, individuals tend to spend a higher fraction of their current income as their wealth increases because with higher current wealth, there is less need to save to provide for future consumption.

Exhibit 10 shows household consumption expenditures as a percentage of GDP for selected countries.

Exhibit 10	Household Final Consumption Expenditures as a Percentage of GDP, 2007[7]
United States	70.1
Mexico	65.4
Italy	58.7
France	56.7
Germany	56.6
Canada	56.5
Japan	56.3

These figures reflect the *average propensity to consume* (APC)—that is, the ratio C/Y—rather than a measure of how the next unit of income would be divided between spending and saving, the MPC. However, they are reasonable proxies for the MPC in each country. Comparing Germany's 56.6 percent APC with Mexico's 65.4 percent, the implication is that the Mexican economy is more sensitive to changes in disposable household income than the German economy. All other things being equal, macroeconomic policies that increase disposable household income, such as lowering government taxes, would have a larger impact on the economies of Mexico (65.4 percent) and the United States (70.1 percent) than similar policies would have in Germany (56.6 percent) or France (56.7 percent).

Companies are the primary source of investment spending (I). They make investment decisions in order to expand their stock of physical capital, such as building new factories or adding new equipment to existing facilities. A definition of physical capital is *any manmade aid to production*. Companies also buy investment goods, such as manufacturing plants and equipment to replace existing facilities and equipment that wear out. Total investment, including replacement of worn-out capital, is called *gross investment*, as opposed to *net investment*, which reflects only the addition of new capacity. GDP includes gross investment; hence the name *gross* domestic product. Total investment spending in such developed countries as Italy, Germany, the United Kingdom, and the United States ranged between 18 and 22 percent of GDP in 2007.[8]

Investment decisions depend primarily on two factors: the level of interest rates and aggregate output/income. The level of interest rates reflects the cost of financing investment. The level of aggregate output serves as a proxy for the expected profitability of new investments. When an economy is underutilizing its resources, interest rates are typically very low and yet investment spending often remains dormant because the expected return on new investments is also low. Conversely, when output is high

---

7 OECD.Stat Extracts: Country Statistical Profiles 2009 (stats.oecd.org).
8 OECD.Stat Extracts: Country Statistical Profiles 2009 (stats.oecd.org) and *Economic Report of the President*, (Washington, DC: US Government Printing Office, 2010): Table B-2, page 330. See Exhibit 27 in this reading for investment details on other countries.

and companies have little spare capacity, the expected return on new investments is high. Thus, investment decisions may be modeled as a decreasing function $I(\cdot,\cdot)$ of the **real interest rate** (nominal interest rate minus the expected rate of inflation) and an increasing function of the level of aggregate output. Formally,

$$I = I(r, Y)$$

where I is investment spending, r is the real interest rate, and Y is, as usual, aggregate income. This investment function leaves out some important drivers of investment decisions, such as the availability of new and better technology. Nonetheless, it reflects the two most important considerations: the cost of funding (represented by the real interest rate) and the expected profitability of the new capital (proxied by the level of aggregate output).

Many government spending decisions are insensitive to the current level of economic activity, the level of interest rates, the currency exchange rate, and other economic factors. Thus, economists often treat the level of government spending on goods and services (G) as an *exogenous* policy variable determined outside the macroeconomic model. In essence, this means that the adjustments required to maintain the balance among aggregate spending, income, and output must occur primarily within the private sector.

Tax policy may also be viewed as an exogenous policy tool. However, the actual amount of net taxes (T) collected is closely tied to the level of economic activity. Most countries impose income taxes or value-added taxes (VAT) or both that increase with the level of income or expenditure. Similarly, at least some transfer payments to the household sector are usually based on economic need and are hence inversely related to aggregate income. Each of these factors makes net taxes (T) rise and fall with aggregate income, Y. The government's fiscal balance can be represented as

$$G - T = \bar{G} - t(Y)$$

where $\bar{G}$ is the exogenous level of government expenditure and $t(Y)$ indicates that net taxes are an (increasing) function of aggregate income, Y. The fiscal balance decreases (smaller deficit or larger surplus) as aggregate income (Y) increases and increases as income declines. This effect is called an *automatic stabilizer* because it tends to mitigate changes in aggregate output.

Net exports ($X - M$) are primarily a function of income in the domestic country and in the rest of the world and the relative prices of domestic and foreign goods and services. As domestic income rises, some of the additional demand that is induced will be for imported goods. Thus, net exports will decline. An increase in income in the rest of the world will lead to an increase in demand for the domestic country's products and hence an increase net exports. A decrease in the relative price of domestically produced goods and services, perhaps because of a depreciation of the currency, will shift demand toward these products and hence increase net exports.

We are now in a position to describe how aggregate expenditure and income are brought into balance. Slightly rearranging Equation 2, equality of expenditure and income implies

$$S - I = (G - T) + (X - M)$$

Based on the discussion above, we know that both the government's fiscal balance and the trade balance decrease as income rises because of net taxes and imports, respectively. Hence, the right-hand side of this equation declines with income. This is shown by the downward-sloping line in Exhibit 11. Assuming the direct effect of higher income on saving is larger than the impact on investment, the left-hand side of the equation increases as income rises. This is shown by the solid upward-sloping line in Exhibit 11. Note that this line is drawn for a given level of the real interest rate, r_0. The intersection of these curves shows the level of income at which expenditure and income balance. At higher levels of income, the saving–investment differential $(S - I)$ exceeds the combined fiscal and trade balances, implying "excess saving" or insufficient expenditure. At lower levels of income, the saving–investment differential is smaller than the combined fiscal and trade balances, implying planned expenditure exceeds output (= income).

Exhibit 11   Balancing Aggregate Income and Expenditure

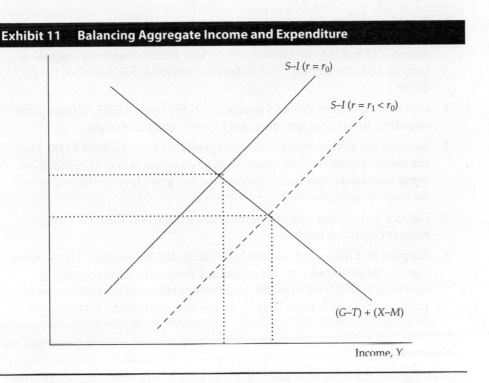

The dashed, upward-sloping line in the exhibit reflects a lower real interest rate, $r_1 < r_0$. This line lies to the right of the solid line because for any value of the saving–investment differential $(S - I)$, the higher level of investment induced by a lower real interest rate requires a higher level of income to induce higher saving. With a lower real interest rate, the curves intersect at a higher level of income. Thus, we see that *equilibrating income and expenditure entails an inverse relationship between income and the real interest rate*. Economists refer to this relationship as the *IS curve* because investment (I) and saving (S) are the primary components that adjust to maintain the balance between aggregate expenditure and income. The IS curve is illustrated in Exhibit 12 in the next section.

EXAMPLE 5

The IS Curve

The following equations are given for a hypothetical economy:

$$
\begin{aligned}
C &= 2{,}000 + 0.7(Y - T) & \text{Consumption function} \\
I &= 400 + 0.2Y - 30r & \text{Investment function} \\
G &= 1{,}500 & \text{Government spending} \\
(X - M) &= 1{,}000 - 0.1Y & \text{Net export function} \\
T &= -200 + 0.3Y & \text{Tax function}
\end{aligned}
$$

1   Based on these equations, determine the combinations of aggregate income (Y) and the real interest rate (r) that are consistent with equating income and expenditure. That is, find the equation that describes the IS curve.

2   Given a real interest rate of 4 percent, find the level of GDP, consumption spending, investment spending, net exports, and tax receipts.

3   Suppose the government increased expenditure from 1,500 to 2,000. Find the new IS curve. Does the increase in government spending result in an equal increase in equilibrium income for any given level of the real interest rate? Why or why not?

4   Given a real interest rate of 4 percent, determine how the increased government spending is funded.

5   Suppose that the output/income level calculated in Question 2 is the most that can be produced with the economy's resources. If the economy is operating at that level when the government increases expenditure from 1,500 to 2,000, what must happen to maintain the balance between expenditure and income?

Solution to 1:

Starting with the basic GDP identity $Y = C + I + G + (X - M)$ and substituting for each expenditure component using the equations above gives

$$Y = 2{,}000 + 0.7(Y - T) + 400 + 0.2Y - 30r + 1{,}500 + 1{,}000 - 0.1Y$$

Substituting in the tax equation and solving for Y, we get

$$
\begin{aligned}
Y &= 2{,}000 + 0.7(Y + 200 - 0.3Y) + 400 + 0.2Y - 30r + 1{,}500 + 1{,}000 - 0.1Y \\
&= 5{,}040 + 0.59Y - 30r \\
Y &= 12{,}292.7 - 73.2r
\end{aligned}
$$

The final equation is the IS curve. It summarizes combinations of income and the real interest rate at which income and expenditure are equal. Equivalently, it reflects equilibrium in the goods market.

Solution to 2:

If the real interest rate is 4 percent, then GDP and the components of GDP are

$$
\begin{aligned}
Y &= 12{,}292.7 - 73.2(4) = 11{,}999.9 \\
T &= -200 + 0.3(11{,}999.9) = 3{,}399.9 \\
C &= 2{,}000 + 0.7(11{,}999.9 - 3{,}399.9) = 8{,}020 \\
I &= 400 + 0.2(11{,}999.9) - 30(4) = 2{,}680.0 \\
(X - M) &= 1{,}000 - 0.10(11{,}999.9) = -200.0
\end{aligned}
$$

Solution to 3:

Following the steps above but with $G = 2{,}000$, the IS curve is

$$Y = 13{,}512.2 - 73.2r$$

At any given level of the interest rate, aggregate income increases by 1,219.5 = (13,512.2 − 12,292.7). This is 2.44 (= 1,219.5/500) times the increase in government spending. The increase in government spending has a "multiplier" effect on equilibrium income because as income rises, both consumption and investment spending also rise, leading to an even greater increase in income, which leads to even more spending, etc. However, some of the increased private spending goes for imports, and higher income also induces higher taxes and saving. The condition for equality of income and expenditure can be written as

$$G = (S - I) + T + (M - X)$$

So the increase in government spending must be balanced by some combination of 1) an increase in saving relative to investment, 2) an increase in taxes, and 3) a rise in imports relative to exports. Given the interest rate, each of these will be induced by an increase in aggregate income. Because saving (S) equals $Y - C - T$,

$$\Delta S = \Delta Y - \Delta C - \Delta T = \Delta Y - \left[0.7(\Delta Y - \Delta T)\right] - \Delta T$$
$$= \Delta Y(1 - 0.7) + \Delta T(0.7 - 1)$$
$$= 0.3\Delta Y - 0.3\Delta T = 0.3\Delta Y - 0.3(0.3)\Delta Y$$
$$= 0.3(1 - 0.3)\Delta Y = 0.21\Delta Y$$

Using this result along with the investment, tax, and trade balance functions gives

$$\Delta G = (0.21 - 0.2)\Delta Y + 0.3\Delta Y + 0.1\Delta Y = 0.41\Delta Y$$

So, $\Delta Y = (1 / 0.41)\Delta G = 2.44\Delta G$.

Note that an extra unit of income increases saving by 0.21 but also increases investment spending by 0.20. So, in this hypothetical economy, the saving–investment differential ($S - I$) is very insensitive to the level of aggregate income. All else the same, this implies that relatively large changes in income are required to restore the expenditure/income balance whenever there is a change in spending behavior.

Solution to 4:

Using the results above,

$$\text{Change in fiscal balance} = \Delta G - \Delta T = \Delta G\left[1 - 0.3(2.44)\right]$$
$$= 0.268(500) = 134$$
$$\text{Change in trade balance} = \Delta(X - M) = 2.44\Delta G(-0.1)$$
$$= -0.244(500) = -122$$
$$\text{Change in } (S - I) = \Delta(S - I) = 2.44\Delta G(0.21 - 0.20)$$
$$= 0.0244(5) = 12$$

So, the increase in government spending (500) is ultimately financed by a large increase in taxes (500 − 134 = 366), a very small increase in private sector excess saving (12), and an increase in capital flows from abroad (122).

Solution to 5:

If the economy is operating at maximum output, then an increase in government expenditure must "crowd out" an equal amount of private expenditure in order to keep total expenditure equal to output/income. In this simple model, this implies that the real interest rate must rise enough that investment spending falls by the amount of the increase in government spending. Using the new IS curve equation from Question 3 and the original level of income from Question 2, we need the interest rate such that

$$Y = 13{,}512.2 - 73.2r = 11{,}999.9 => r = 20.66\%$$

So the real interest rate would soar from 4 percent to 20.66 percent to choke off investment spending.

3.1.2 Equilibrium in the Money Market: The LM Curve

The IS curve tells us what level of income is consistent with a given level of the real interest rate but does not address the appropriate level of interest rates, nor does it depend on the price level. In order to determine the interest rate and introduce a connection between output and the price level, we must consider supply and demand in the financial markets. To keep the model as simple as possible, we will deal explicitly with demand and supply for only one financial asset: money. All other assets (e.g., stocks and bonds) are implicitly treated as a composite alternative to holding money. In some of the subsequent discussion, however, we will note differential impacts on equity and fixed-income securities.

The *quantity theory of money* equation provides a straightforward connection among the nominal money supply (M), the price level (P), and real income/expenditure (Y):

$$MV = PY$$

In this equation, V is the *velocity of money*, the average rate at which money circulates through the economy to facilitate expenditure. This equation essentially defines V. The equation begins to have economic content only when we make assumptions about how velocity is related to such economic variables as the interest rate. In the simplest case, if velocity is assumed to be constant, then the quantity theory of money equation implies that the money supply determines the nominal value of output (PY). Therefore, an increase in the money supply will increase the nominal value of output. However, this equation alone cannot tell us how that increase would be split between price and quantity.

The quantity theory equation can be rewritten in terms of the supply and demand for real money balances:

$$M/P = (M/P)_D = kY$$

where $k = 1/V$ reflects how much money people want to hold for every currency unit of real income. The demand for real money balances is typically assumed to depend inversely on the interest rate because a higher interest rate encourages investors to shift their assets out of money (bank deposits) into higher-yielding securities. Although the quantity theory of money suggests that the demand for real money balances is proportional to real income, this need not be the case. The important point is that money demand increases with income. Thus, demand for real money balances is an increasing function $M(\cdot,\cdot)$ of real income and a decreasing function of the interest rate. Equilibrium in the money market requires

$$M/P = M(r,Y)$$

Holding the real money supply (M/P) constant, this equation implies a positive relationship between real income (Y) and the real interest rate (r). Given the real money supply, an increase in real income must be accompanied by an increase in the interest rate in order to keep the demand for real money balances equal to the supply. This relationship, which economists refer to as the *LM curve*, is shown by the upward-sloping curve in Exhibit 12.

Exhibit 12   The IS and LM Curves

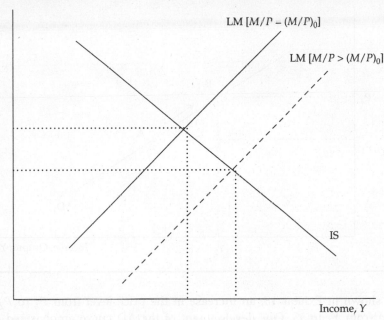

Real Interest Rate, r

LM $[M/P - (M/P)_0]$

LM $[M/P > (M/P)_0]$

IS

Income, Y

The intersection of the IS and LM curves determines the combination of real income and the real interest rate that is consistent with both the equality of income and (planned) expenditure (the IS curve) and equilibrium in the money market (the LM curve). In Exhibit 12, the dashed LM curve reflects a higher real money supply than the solid LM curve. With a higher real money supply, the intersection of the IS and LM curves occurs at a higher level of real income and a lower level of the real interest rate.

3.1.3 *The Aggregate Demand Curve*

If the nominal money supply (M) is held constant, then a higher or lower real money supply (M/P) arises because of changes in the lower price. If the price level declines, the real money supply increases and, as shown in Exhibit 12, real income increases while the real interest rate declines. Conversely, an increase in the price level leads to a decline in real income and an increase in the real interest rate. This inverse relationship between the price level and real income is illustrated in Exhibit 13. This is the **aggregate demand curve** (AD curve).

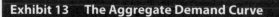

Exhibit 13   The Aggregate Demand Curve

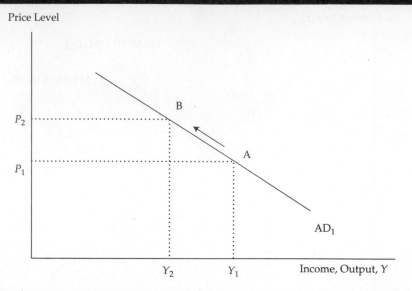

As shown in Exhibit 13, an increase in the price level from P_1 to P_2 reduces income from Y_1 to Y_2. Our development of the AD curve emphasized only one channel through which prices affect the quantity of output demanded (i.e., planned real expenditure)—the interest rate. There are, however, other mechanisms. Higher prices erode the purchasing power of retirees and others whose income is fixed in nominal terms. Similarly, higher prices reduce the real value of nominal assets (e.g., stocks and bonds) and may reduce consumption relative to current income as people seek to rebuild the real purchasing power of their wealth. Higher domestic prices also make domestically produced goods more expensive relative to imports (assuming a constant currency exchange rate). In each case, lower prices have the opposite effect, increasing aggregate expenditure and income.

It should be clear that many interesting and important aspects of the economy are subsumed into the AD curve: saving, investment, trade and capital flows, interest rates, asset prices, fiscal and monetary policy, and more. All of these disappear behind a deceptively simple relationship between price and output/income.

Before moving on to consider aggregate supply, let's look more closely at the interaction of interest rates and income implicit in movements along the AD curve. For simplicity, we assume there are no changes in the fiscal or trade balances so that maintaining the balance between aggregate expenditure and aggregate income requires that changes in investment spending equal changes in private saving. As the price level increases, the real money supply (M/P) declines. To induce a corresponding decline in money demand, the interest rate must rise so that other assets are more attractive and income must fall to reduce the transactional need for money balances. The higher interest rate induces companies to reduce investment spending. The decline in income reduces household saving. *The slope of the AD curve depends on the relative sensitivities of investment, saving, and money demand to income and the interest rate.* The AD curve will be flatter if

- investment expenditure is highly sensitive to the interest rate;
- saving is insensitive to income;
- money demand is insensitive to interest rates; and
- money demand is insensitive to income.

The first two conditions directly imply that income will have to move more to induce a large enough change in saving to match the change in investment spending. All else equal, each of the last two conditions implies that a larger change in the interest rate is required to bring money demand in line with money supply. This, in turn, implies a larger change in investment spending and a correspondingly larger change in saving and income.

EXAMPLE 6

Aggregate Demand

The money demand and supply equations for our hypothetical economy are

$$M_d/P = -300 + 0.5Y - 30r \quad \text{(real money demand)}$$
$$M/P = 5,200/P \quad \text{(real money supply)}$$

1 Find the equation for the LM curve.

2 Using the IS curve from Question 1 of Example 5, find the equation of the AD curve.

3 Find the levels of GDP and the interest rate if $P = 1$.

4 What will happen to GDP and the interest rate if the price level rises to 1.1 or falls to 0.9?

5 Suppose investment spending were more sensitive to the interest rate so that the IS becomes ($Y = 12,292.7 - 150r$). What happens to the slope of the AD curve? What does this imply about the effectiveness of monetary policy?

Solution to 1:

Setting the real money supply equal to real money demand and rearranging, we get the LM equation:

$$Y = 600 + 2(M/P) + 60r$$

Or with $M = 5,200$,

$$Y = 600 + 10,400/P + 60r \text{ (LM equation)}$$

Solution to 2:

From Question 1 of Example 5, the IS equation is $Y = 12,292.7 - 73.2\,r$. We now have two equations and two unknowns. The easiest way to solve this problem is to multiply the LM curve by 1.22 (= 73.2/60.0) and then add the equations:

$$1.22Y = 732 + 2.44(M/P) + 73.2r \quad \text{(LM equation)}$$
$$Y = 12,292.7 - 73.2r \quad \text{(IS equation)}$$

Adding the two equations and solving for Y,

$$Y = 5,867.0 + 1.099(M/P) \quad \text{(AD curve)}$$
$$= 5,867.0 + 5,715.3/P \quad \text{(with } M = 5,200)$$

Solution to 3:

If $P = 1$, the AD curve gives GDP as $Y = 5,867.0 + 5,715.3 = 11,582.3$. From the money demand and supply equation, the equilibrium interest rate is

$$5,200/1 = -300 + 0.5(11,582.3) - 30r => r = 9.7\%$$

Solution to 4:

If the price level increases to 1.1, GDP declines to $Y = 5,867.0 + 5,715.3/1.1 = 11,062.7$. If the price level falls to 0.9, GDP increases to $Y = 5,867.0 + 5,715.3/0.9 = 12,217.3$. To find the interest rate in each case, we plug these values for Y into the IS curve.

$$\text{If } P = 1.1: \ Y = 11,062.7 = 12,292.7 - 73.2\,r => r = 16.8\%$$
$$\text{If } P = 0.9: \ Y = 12,217.3 = 12,292.7 - 73.2\,r => r = 1.0\%$$

Thus, we have the following relationship among the price level, GDP, and the interest rate:

Price Level	GDP	Interest Rate
0.9	12,217.3	1.0
1.0	11,582.3	9.7
1.1	11,062.7	16.8

The inverse relationship between GDP and the price level is the AD curve. The inverse relationship between GDP and the interest rate reflects the IS curve.

Solution to 5:

If the interest rate parameter in the IS curve is 150 instead of 73.2, we can multiply the LM equation by 2.5 (= 150/60) instead of 1.22 (= 73.2/60) to get the system of equations:

$$2.5Y = 1,500 + 5(M/P) + 150r \quad \text{(LM equation)}$$
$$Y = 12,292.7 - 150r \quad \text{(IS equation)}$$

Adding these equations and solving for Y gives

$$Y = 3,940.77 + 1.429(M/P) \quad \text{(new AD curve)}$$
$$= 3,940.77 + 7,428.6/P \quad \text{(with } M = 5,200)$$

Comparing the new AD curve to the original AD curve indicates that output (Y) is now more sensitive to the price level. That is, the AD curve is flatter. Monetary policy is now more effective because, at any given price level, an increase in M has a greater impact on Y. This can be understood as follows: As the real money supply increases, the interest rate must fall and/or expenditure must increase in order to induce households to hold the increased money supply. With investment spending now more sensitive to the interest rate, income will have to rise by more in order to increase saving by a corresponding amount.

3.2 Aggregate Supply

Aggregate demand only tells us the relationship between the price level and the amount of output demanded at those prices. To understand what price and output level will prevail in the economy, we need to add aggregate supply, the amount of output producers are willing to provide at various prices. The **aggregate supply curve** (AS curve) represents the level of domestic output that companies will produce at each price level. Unlike the demand side, we must distinguish between the short- and long-run AS curves, which differ with respect to how wages and other input prices respond to changes in final output prices. "Long run" and "short run" are relative terms and are necessarily imprecise with respect to calendar time. The "long run" is long enough that wages, prices, and expectations can adjust but not long enough that physical capital is a variable input. Capital and the available technology to use that capital remain fixed. This condition implies a period of at least a few years and perhaps a decade. The truly long run in which even the capital stock is variable may be thought of as covering multiple decades. Consideration of the very long run is postponed to our discussion of economic growth in Section 4.

In the very short run, perhaps a few months or quarters, companies will increase or decrease output to some degree without changing price. This is shown in Exhibit 14 by the horizontal line labeled VSRAS. If demand is somewhat stronger than expected, companies earn higher profit by increasing output as long as they can cover their variable costs. So they will run their plant and equipment more intensively, demand more effort from their salaried employees, and increase the hours of employees who are paid on the basis of hours worked. If demand is somewhat weaker than projected, companies can run their plants less intensively, cut labor hours, and utilize staff to perform maintenance and carry out efficiency-enhancing projects that are often postponed during busier periods.

Exhibit 14   Aggregate Supply Curve

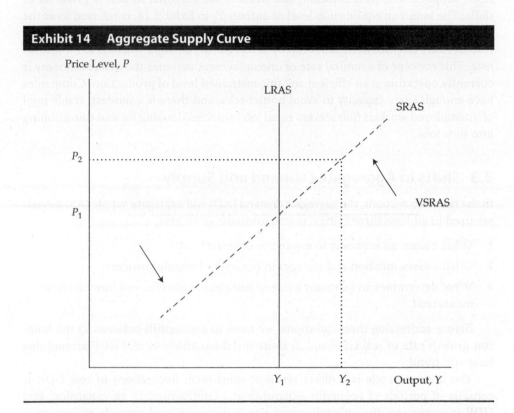

Over somewhat longer periods, the AS curve is upward sloping because more costs become variable. This is represented by the short-run aggregate supply (SRAS) curve in Exhibit 14. In most businesses, wages are adjusted once a year, but for companies with union contracts, several years may pass before the contracts expire. The prices for raw materials and other inputs may also be established under long-term contracts. Hence, wages and other input costs are relatively inflexible in the short run and do not fully adjust to changes in output prices. As the price level rises, most companies enjoy higher profit margins and hence expand production. In Exhibit 14, when prices move from P_1 to P_2, the quantity of aggregate output supplied increases from Y_1 to Y_2. Conversely, a reduction in the price level squeezes profit margins and causes companies to reduce production.

Over time, however, wages and other input prices tend to "catch up" with the prices of final goods and services. In other words, wages and prices that are inflexible or slow to adjust in the short run adjust to changes in the price level over the long run. Thus, over the long run, when the aggregate price level changes, wages and other input prices change proportionately so that the higher aggregate price level has no impact on aggregate supply. This is illustrated by the vertical long-run aggregate supply (LRAS) curve in Exhibit 14. As prices move from P_1 to P_2, the quantity of output supplied remains at Q_1 in the long run. The only change that occurs is that prices shift to a higher level (from P_1 to P_2).

The position of the LRAS curve is determined by the potential output of the economy. The amount of output produced depends on the fixed amount of capital and labor and the available technology. This classical model of aggregate supply can be expressed as

$$Y = F\left(\overline{K},\overline{L}\right) = \overline{Y}$$

where $\overline{K}$ is the fixed amount of capital and $\overline{L}$ is the available labor supply. The stock of capital is assumed to incorporate the existing technological base.[9] The available labor supply is also held constant, and workers are assumed to have a given set of skills. The long-run equilibrium level of output, Y_1 in Exhibit 14, is referred to as the *full employment*, or *natural*, level of output. At this level of output, the economy's resources are deemed to be fully employed and (labor) *unemployment is at its natural rate*. This concept of a natural rate of unemployment assumes the macroeconomy is currently operating at an efficient and unconstrained level of production. Companies have enough spare capacity to avoid bottlenecks, and there is a modest, stable pool of unemployed workers (job seekers equal job vacancies) looking for and transitioning into new jobs.

3.3 Shifts in Aggregate Demand and Supply

In the next two sections, the aggregate demand (AD) and aggregate supply (AS) models are used to address three critical macroeconomic questions:

1   What causes an economy to expand or contract?

2   What causes inflation and changes in the level of unemployment?

3   What determines an economy's rate of sustainable growth, and how can it be measured?

Before addressing these questions, we need to distinguish between 1) the long-run growth rate of real GDP and 2) short-run fluctuations in real GDP around this long-run trend.

The business cycle is a direct result of short-term fluctuations of real GDP. It consists of periods of economic expansion and contraction. In an expansion, real GDP is increasing, the unemployment rate is declining, and capacity utilization is rising. In a contraction, real GDP is decreasing, the unemployment rate is rising, and capacity utilization is declining. Shifts in the AD and AS curves determine the short-run changes in the economy associated with the business cycle. In addition, the AD–AS model provides a framework for estimating the sustainable growth rate of an economy, which is addressed in Section 4.

From an asset allocation perspective, it is important to determine the current phase of the business cycle as well as how fast the economy is growing relative to its sustainable growth rate. The expected rate of return on equities and fixed-income securities, for example, depends on estimates of the growth rate of GDP and inflation. For equities, GDP growth is the primary determinant of aggregate corporate profits. For fixed-income securities, the expected rate of inflation determines the spread

---

9 Note that investment, *I*, reflects replacement of worn-out capital plus the change in capital, ΔK. Over short periods of time, net investment is assumed to have a negligible effect on aggregate supply. The cumulative effect of investment on economic growth is discussed in Section 4.

between real and nominal rates of return. In order to use the AD and AS model to analyze the economy and to make investment decisions, we need to first understand what factors cause the curves to shift.

3.3.1 *Shifts in Aggregate Demand*

In addition to price, factors that influence the level of spending by households, companies, governments, and foreigners (i.e., the aggregate level of expenditures) will cause the AD curve to shift. A shift to the right represents an increase in aggregate demand at any price level. Exhibit 15 shows this as a shift from AD_1 to AD_2. A shift to the left represents a decrease in aggregate demand at any price level. This is indicated by a move from AD_1 to AD_3. Key factors that directly or indirectly influence the level of aggregate expenditures and cause the aggregate demand curve to shift include changes in

- household wealth;
- consumer and business expectations;
- capacity utilization;
- monetary policy;
- the exchange rate;
- growth in global economy; and
- fiscal policy (government spending and taxes).

Exhibit 15   Shifts in the Aggregate Demand Curve

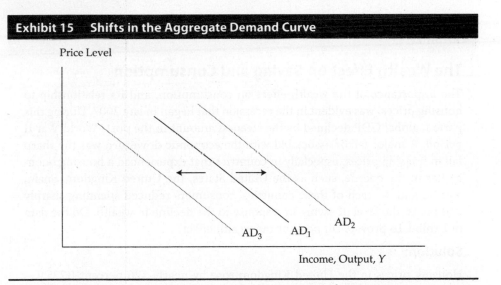

Household Wealth   Household wealth includes the value of both financial assets (e.g., cash, savings accounts, investment securities, and pensions) and real assets (e.g., real estate). The primary reason households save a portion of their current income is to accumulate wealth for consumption in the future. The proportion of disposable income that households save depends partly on the value of the financial and real assets that they have already accumulated. If these assets increase in value, households will tend to save less and spend a greater proportion of their income because they will still be able to meet their wealth accumulation goals. As a result, an increase in household wealth increases consumer spending and shifts the aggregate demand curve to the right. In contrast, a decline in wealth will reduce consumer spending and shift the AD curve to the left. This is often referred to as the **wealth effect** and is one explanation for how changes in equity prices affect economic activity. Higher equity prices increase household wealth, which increases consumer spending and reduces the amount saved out of current income. Economic studies estimate that an increase or decrease in wealth in developed countries increases or decreases annual consumer spending by 3–7 percent of the change in wealth.[10] A smaller but still statistically significant wealth effect has been found in a number of emerging markets (developing countries).[11]

Exhibit 16   Housing Prices and the Saving Rate in the United Kingdom

Year	Housing Prices (first quarter of each year) (Index 2000 Q1 = 100)	Saving Rate (%)
2000	100	4.7
2002	122.7	5.8
2004	180.5	3.7
2006	206.3	2.9
2007	225.9	2.1
2008	220.5	1.2
2009	192.7	7.0

Source: Office of National Statistics, United Kingdom.

EXAMPLE 7

The Wealth Effect on Saving and Consumption

The importance of the wealth effect on consumption, and its relationship to housing prices, was evident in the recession that began in late 2007. During this period, global GDP declined by the steepest amount in the post–World War II period. A major factor associated with the economic downturn was the sharp fall in housing prices, especially in countries that experienced a housing boom earlier in the decade, such as the United States, the United Kingdom, Spain, and Ireland. In each of these countries, consumers reduced spending sharply and raised the level of saving in response to the decline in wealth. Do the data in Exhibit 16 provide support for the wealth effect?

Solution:

Housing prices in the United Kingdom rose by nearly 126 percent [(225.9 − 100)/100] between 2000 and 2007. As predicted, the saving rate declined (with a lag), going from an average of 5.3 percent of income in 2000 and 2002 to 1.2 percent in 2008. Then, as housing prices fell by 14.7 percent between 2007 and 2009, the saving rate rose dramatically from 1.2 percent in 2008 to 7 percent in 2009. Of course, the decline in housing prices was not the only factor contributing to the increase in the saving rate. Stock prices also declined in this period, further reducing wealth in the United Kingdom, and the recession raised uncertainty over future jobs and income.

---

10 See, for example, Case, Quigley, and Shiller (2005).
11 See Funke (2004).

Consumer and Business Expectations   Psychology has an important impact on consumer and business spending. When consumers are confident about their future income and the stability/safety of their jobs, they tend to spend a higher portion of their disposable income. This shifts the AD curve to the right. Consumer spending declines and the AD curve shifts to the left when consumers become less confident. Similarly, when businesses are optimistic about their future growth and profitability, they spend (invest) more on capital projects, which also shifts the AD curve to the right.

Capacity Utilization   Capacity utilization is a measure of how fully an economy's production capacity is being used. Companies with excess capacity have little incentive to invest in new property, plant, and equipment. In contrast, when companies are operating at or near full capacity, they will need to increase investment spending in order to expand production. Data from the OECD and the US Federal Reserve indicate that when aggregate capacity utilization reaches 82 to 85 percent, production blockages arise, prompting companies to increase their level of investment spending. This shifts the AD curve to the right.

Fiscal Policy   **Fiscal policy** is the use of taxes and government spending to affect the level of aggregate expenditures.[12] An increase in government spending, one of the direct components of AD, shifts the AD curve to the right, whereas a decrease in government spending shifts the AD curve to the left. Taxes affect GDP indirectly through their effect on consumer spending and business investment. Lower taxes will increase the proportion of personal income and corporate pre-tax profits that consumers and businesses have available to spend and will shift the AD curve to the right. In contrast, higher taxes will shift the AD curve to the left.

Monetary Policy   *Money* is generally defined as currency in circulation plus deposits at commercial banks. **Monetary policy** refers to action taken by a nation's central bank to affect aggregate output and prices through changes in bank reserves, reserve requirements, or its target interest rate.

Most countries have fractional reserve banking systems in which each bank must hold reserves (vault cash plus deposits at the central bank) at least equal to the required reserve ratio times its customer deposits. Banks with excess reserves can lend them to banks that need reserves to meet their reserve requirements. The central bank can increase the money supply by 1) buying securities from banks, 2) lowering the required reserve ratio, and/or 3) reducing its target for the interest rate at which banks borrow and lend reserves among themselves. In each case, the opposite action would decrease the money supply.

When the central bank buys securities from banks in an open-market operation, it pays for them with a corresponding increase in bank reserves. This increases the amount of deposits banks can accept from their customers—that is, the money supply. Similarly, cutting the required reserve ratio increases the level of deposits (i.e., money) consistent with a given level of reserves in the system. If the central bank chooses to target an interbank lending rate, as the Federal Reserve targets the federal funds rate in the United States, then it must add or drain reserves via open-market operations to maintain the target interest rate. If it raises (lowers) its target interest rate, it will have to drain (add) reserves in order to make reserves more (less) expensive in the interbank market. Thus, open-market operations and interest rate targeting are very closely related. The main distinction is whether the central bank chooses to target a

---

12 Government spending and taxes may be adjusted for other purposes too. In macroeconomics, however, the term "fiscal policy" is usually reserved for actions intended to affect the overall level of expenditure.

level of reserves and let the market determine the interest rate or chooses to target the interest rate and let the market (banks) determine the level of reserves they desire to hold at that rate.

An increase in the money supply shifts the AD curve to the right so that each price level corresponds to a higher level of income and expenditure.[13] There are various channels through which the additional expenditures may be induced. For example, the interest rate reduction required to induce investors to hold the additional money balances will encourage companies to investment more and households to borrow to purchase durable goods, such as cars. In addition, banks may facilitate greater expenditure by raising credit limits and loosening credit standards. Conversely, a reduction in the money supply shifts the AD curve to the left.

Exhibit 17 illustrates the short-run and long-run effect of expansionary monetary policy. Suppose the central bank expands the money supply in an attempt to stimulate demand when the economy is already in long-run equilibrium. The expansionary policy will shift the AD curve to the right, from AD_1 to AD_2. In the very short run, output will expand from Y_1 to Y_2 without an increase in the price level. After operating at higher-than-normal production rates for a few months or quarters, companies will begin to push for price increases and input prices will begin to rise as well. The aggregate supply curve will steepen, and prices will increase to P_3 while output declines to Y_3. As input prices become more flexible, the AS curve will steepen until, in the long run, it is vertical and output has returned to the long-run natural level, Y_1, with prices rising to P_4. Thus, expanding the money supply increases output in the short run, but in the long run it affects only the price level.

Exhibit 17   Short-Run and Long-Run Effect of Monetary Expansion

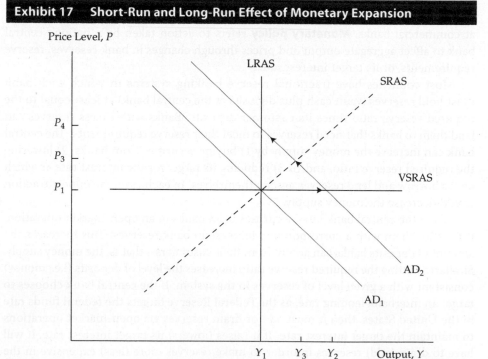

---

13 An unusual but important special case known as a *liquidity trap* occurs if a) banks are willing to hold virtually unlimited excess reserves rather than expand their balance sheets by taking deposits and making loans and/or b) demand for money balances by households and companies is insensitive to the level of income. In a liquidity trap, monetary policy will be ineffective and the AD curve will not shift despite the central bank's efforts. Some have argued that this was a reasonable description of the US situation in 2010.

Exchange Rate   An exchange rate is the price of one currency relative to another. Changes in the exchange rate affect the price of exports and imports and thus aggregate demand. For example, a lower euro relative to other currencies makes European exports cheaper in world markets and foreign products sold in Europe (European imports) more expensive. Therefore, a lower euro should cause European exports to increase and imports to decline, causing the AD curve to shift to the right. Conversely, a stronger euro reduces exports and raises imports, and the AD curve shifts to the left.

Growth in the Global Economy   International trade is what links countries together and creates a global economy. Faster economic growth in foreign markets encourages foreigners to buy more products from domestic producers and increases exports. For example, rapid GDP growth in China has increased Chinese demand for foreign products. Japan has benefited from this rapid growth because it has exported more products to China. In terms of the AD and AS model, the AD curve for Japan has shifted to the right because of increased demand for Japanese products in China, resulting in higher exports. A decline in the growth rate of China's economy would have a negative effect on the Japanese economy because exports would be lower. This would cause the Japanese AD curve to shift to the left.

What happens to interest rates when the AD curve shifts? In the case of an increase in the money supply, the interest rate declines at each price level because the increase in income (Y) increases saving and rates must decline to induce a corresponding increase in investment spending (I). In each of the other cases considered above, a rightward shift in the AD curve will increase the interest rate at each price level. With the real money supply held constant, the interest rate must rise as income increases. The increase in the interest rate reduces the demand for money at each level of expenditure/income and, therefore, allows expenditure/income to increase without an increase in the money supply. In terms of the quantity theory of money equation, this corresponds to a higher velocity of money, V.

The main factors that shift the AD curve are summarized in Exhibit 18. In each case, the impact of the factor is considered in isolation. In practice, however, various factors may be at work simultaneously and there may be interaction among them. This is especially true with regard to expectational factors—consumer and business confidence—which are likely to be influenced by other developments.

Exhibit 18 Impact of Factors Shifting Aggregate Demand		
An Increase in the Following Factors:	**Shifts the AD Curve:**	**Reason:**
Stock prices	Rightward: Increase in AD	Higher consumption
Housing prices	Rightward: Increase in AD	Higher consumption
Consumer confidence	Rightward: Increase in AD	Higher consumption
Business confidence	Rightward: Increase in AD	Higher investment
Capacity utilization	Rightward: Increase in AD	Higher investment
Government spending	Rightward: Increase in AD	Government spending a component of AD
Taxes	Leftward: Decrease in AD	Lower consumption and investment
Bank reserves	Rightward: Increase in AD	Lower interest rate, higher investment and possibly higher consumption
Exchange rate (foreign currency per unit domestic currency)	Leftward: Decrease in AD	Lower exports and higher imports
Global growth	Rightward: Increase in AD	Higher exports

EXAMPLE 8

Shifts in Aggregate Demand

Francois Ubert is a portfolio manager with EuroWorld, a French investment management firm. Ubert is considering increasing his clients' portfolio exposure to Brazilian equities. Before doing so, he asks you to prepare a report on the following recent economic events in Brazil and to summarize the impact of each event on the Brazilian economy and on Brazilian equity and fixed-income securities.

1 The Brazilian central bank reduced bank reserves, resulting in a lower money supply.

2 The capacity utilization rate in Brazil is currently estimated to be 86.4 percent, a 2.7 percent increase from the previous year.

3 Corporate profits reported by Brazilian companies increased by 30 percent over last year's levels, and corporations have revised their forecasts of future profitability upward.

4 The government recently announced that it plans to start construction on a number of hydroelectric projects to reduce Brazil's reliance on imported oil.

5 Forecasts by private sector economists project that the European economy will enter a recession in the next year.

Solution to 1:

This monetary policy action is designed to reduce consumption and business investment spending. The reduction in real money balances will increase interest rates and discourage lending within the banking system. Higher interest rates and tighter credit will reduce both investment and consumption expenditures and shift the AD curve to the left. The prices of fixed-income securities will fall because of the rise in interest rates. The reduction in aggregate output should lower corporate profits, and it is likely that equity prices will also fall.

Solution to 2:

Capacity utilization is a key factor determining the level of investment spending. A current utilization rate of over 86 percent and an increase from the previous year indicate a growing lack of spare capacity in the Brazilian economy. As a result, businesses will probably increase their level of capital spending. This will increase AD and shift the AD curve to the right. Higher economic activity (income/output) will cause upward pressure on interest rates and may have a negative impact on fixed-income securities. Higher income/output should increase corporate profits and is likely to have a positive impact on equity securities.

Solution to 3:

Expected corporate profits are an important determinant of the level of investment spending. The large increase in expected profits will raise the level of investment spending and increase aggregate demand. This will shift the AD curve to the right. The increase in corporate profits and the resulting increase in economic output should have a positive impact on equities. The increase in output will put upward pressure on interest rates and downward pressure on the prices of fixed-income securities.

Solution to 4:

Fiscal policy uses government spending to influence the level and growth rate of economic activity. The announcement indicates an increase in government spending, which is a direct component of AD. Therefore, higher spending on the projects will increase AD and shift the AD curve to the right. The increase in output and expenditure should be positive for equities. But it will be negative for existing fixed-income investments because higher interest rates will be required to induce investors to buy and hold the government debt issued to fund the new projects.

Solution to 5:

A recession in Europe will decrease the demand for Brazilian exports by European households and businesses and shift the AD curve to the left. The resulting decline in income and downward pressure on prices will be positive for fixed-income securities but negative for equities.

3.3.2 Shifts in Short-Run Aggregate Supply

Factors that change the cost of production or expected profit margins will cause the SRAS curve to shift. These factors include changes in

- nominal wages;
- input prices, including the price of natural resources;
- expectations about future output prices and the overall price level;
- business taxes and subsidies; and
- the exchange rate.

In addition, factors that shift the long-run AS curve (see Section 3.3.3) will also shift the SRAS curve by a corresponding amount because the SRAS and LRAS reflect the same underlying resources and technology. As the economy's resources and technology change, the full employment (or natural) level of output changes, and both the LRAS and SRAS shift accordingly.

Change in Nominal Wages Changes in nominal wages shift the short-run AS curve because wages are often the largest component of a company's costs. An increase in nominal wages raises production costs, resulting in a decrease in AS and a leftward shift in the SRAS curve. Lower wages shift the AS curve to the right. It is important to note that changes in nominal wages have no impact on the LRAS curve.

A better way to measure the impact of labor costs on the AS curve is to measure the change in unit labor cost. We define the change in unit labor cost as

% Change in unit labor cost = % Change in nominal wages

    − % Change in productivity

EXAMPLE 9

Unit Labor Cost and Short-Run Aggregate Supply

Suppose Finnish workers are paid €20 an hour and are able to produce 100 cell phones in an hour. The labor cost per cell phone is €0.20 (€20 divided by 100 units). If the wages per hour for Finnish workers rise by 10 percent from €20 to €22 and they are able to raise their productivity by 10 percent, what is the impact on unit labor cost and the short-run aggregate supply curve?

Solution:

The workers can now produce 110 cell phones per hour, and unit labor cost will not change (22/110 = 0.20). In this case, the SRAS curve will remain in its original position. If wages had increased by 20 percent instead of 10 percent, then unit labor cost would have increased and the SRAS would shift to the left. Conversely, if the wage increase were only 5 percent, then unit labor cost would have decreased and the SRAS would shift to the right.

Change in Input Prices   The price of raw materials is an important component of cost for many businesses. Lower input prices reduce the cost of production, which, in turn, makes companies willing to produce more at any output price. This is reflected in a rightward shift of the SRAS curve. Conversely, higher input prices increase production costs, which, in turn, causes companies to reduce production at any output price. This shifts the SRAS curve to the left. During the 1970s, high oil prices caused the SRAS curve in most countries to shift to the left. In contrast, in the mid-1980s, declining oil prices lowered the cost of production and shifted the SRAS curve in most countries to the right. Oil prices currently have a smaller impact on the global economy than in the 1970s and 1980s because most countries have reduced their reliance on oil and improved their energy efficiency so that they now use less energy per unit of GDP.

Change in Expectations about Future Prices   The impact of expected future prices on current output decisions is not as straightforward as it might seem. First, each company is primarily concerned about the price of its own output rather than the general price level. The latter may be more reflective of its costs. If it expects its own output price to rise (fall) relative to the general price level, then it may increase (decrease) production in response to the perceived change in its profit margin. As more and more companies become optimistic (pessimistic) about their ability to raise the relative price of their product, the SRAS will shift to the right (left). In the aggregate, of course, companies can neither raise nor lower their prices relative to the general price level. Hence, shifts in the SRAS driven by such price expectations are likely to be modest and temporary. Second, considering future prices introduces a temporal aspect into decision making. If the future price level is expected to be higher, companies may decide to produce more today in order to expand inventory available for future sale. But they will only do so if the cost of carrying inventory (financing, storage, and spoilage) is less than they expect to save on production costs by producing more today and less in the future. Conversely, they may cut current production and sell out of existing inventory if they expect future prices (and costs) to be lower.

The upshot is that expectations of higher (lower) future prices are likely to shift the SRAS curve to the right (left), but the impact may be modest and/or temporary.

Change in Business Taxes and Subsidies   Higher business taxes increase production costs per unit and shift the short-run AS curve to the left. Business subsidies are a payment from the government to the producer. Subsidies for businesses lower their production costs and shift the SRAS curve to the right.

Change in the Exchange Rate   Many countries import raw materials, including energy and intermediate goods. As a result, changes in the exchange rate can affect the cost of production and, therefore, aggregate supply. A higher Yen relative to the Euro will lower the cost of raw materials and intermediate goods imported to Japan from Europe. This, in turn, will lower the production costs of Japanese producers and shift the AS curve in Japan to the right. A lower Yen will have the opposite effect.

3.3.3 *Shifts in Long-Run Aggregate Supply*

As discussed above, the position of the LRAS curve is determined by the potential output of the economy. **Potential GDP** measures the productive capacity of the economy and is the level of real GDP that can be produced at full employment. Potential GDP is not a static concept but can increase each year at a steady rate as the economy's resource capacity grows. Therefore, any factor increasing the resource base of an economy causes the LRAS curve to shift as shown in Exhibit 19.

Exhibit 19   Shift in Long-Run Aggregate Supply (LRAS) Curve

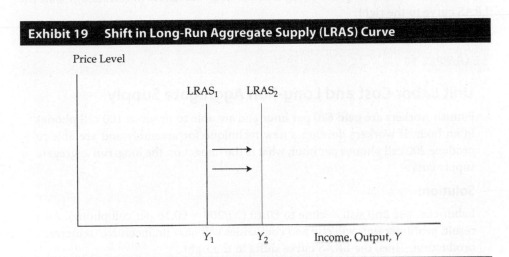

These factors include changes in

- supply of labor and quality of labor forces (human capital);
- supply of natural resources;
- supply of physical capital; and
- productivity and technology.

Supply of Labor   The larger the supply of labor, the more output the economy can produce. The labor supply depends on growth in the population, the labor force participation rate (the percentage of the population working or looking for work), and net immigration. The determinants of the labor supply are discussed in more detail in Section 4. Increases in the labor supply shift the LRAS curve to the right. Decreases shift the curve to the left.

Supply of Natural Resources   Natural resources are essential inputs to the production process and include everything from available land to oil to water. Increased availability of natural resources shifts the LRAS curve to the right.

Supply of Physical Capital   Investment in new property, plant, equipment, and software is an essential ingredient for growth. An increase in the stock of physical capital will increase the capacity of the economy to produce goods and services. Simply put, if workers are provided with more and better equipment to use, they should be able to produce more output than they could with the older equipment. Thus, strong growth in business investment, which increases the supply of physical capital, shifts the LRAS curve to the right.

Supply of Human Capital   Another way to raise the productive capacity of a country is to increase human capital—the quality of the labor force—through training, skills development, and education. Improvement in the quality of the labor force shifts the LRAS curve to the right.

Labor Productivity and Technology   Another important factor affecting the productive capacity of an economy is how efficient labor is in transforming inputs into final goods and services. **Productivity** measures the efficiency of labor and is the amount of output produced by workers in a given period of time—for example, output per hour worked. An increase in productivity decreases labor cost, improves profitability, and results in higher output. Two of the main drivers of labor productivity—physical capital per worker and the quality of the workforce—have been discussed above. The third key determinant of productivity is technology. Advances in technology shift the LRAS curve to the right.

EXAMPLE 10

Unit Labor Cost and Long-Run Aggregate Supply

Finnish workers are paid €20 per hour and are able to produce 100 cell phones in an hour. If workers develop a new technique for assembly and are able to produce 200 cell phones per hour, what is the impact on the long-run aggregate supply curve?

Solution:

Labor cost per unit will decline to €0.10 (20/200 = €0.10 per cell phone). As a result, profit per unit will rise and companies will have an incentive to increase production. Thus, the LRAS curve shifts to the right.

The factors shifting the AS curve are summarized in Exhibit 20. Rightward shifts in the SRAS or LRAS curves are defined as an increase in supply. Leftward shifts in the SRAS or LRAS curves represent a decrease in supply.

Exhibit 20	Impact of Factors Shifting Aggregate Supply		
An Increase in	**Shifts SRAS**	**Shifts LRAS**	**Reason**
Supply of labor	Rightward	Rightward	Increases resource base
Supply of natural resources	Rightward	Rightward	Increases resource base
Supply of human capital	Rightward	Rightward	Increases resource base
Supply of physical capital	Rightward	Rightward	Increases resource base
Productivity and technology	Rightward	Rightward	Improves efficiency of inputs
Nominal wages	Leftward	No impact	Increases labor cost
Input prices (e.g., energy)	Leftward	No impact	Increases cost of production
Expectation of future prices	Rightward	No impact	Anticipation of higher costs and/or perception of improved pricing power
Business taxes	Leftward	No impact	Increases cost of production
Subsidy	Rightward	No impact	Lowers cost of production
Exchange rate	Rightward	No impact	Lowers cost of production

As with our summary of factors that shift the AD curve, Exhibit 20 considers each of the factors affecting aggregate supply in isolation. In practice, various factors will be at work simultaneously, and there may be interaction among them. This is especially important with respect to interaction between factors listed as affecting only SRAS and those that also impact LRAS.

For example, consider an increase in the cost of natural resource inputs (e.g., energy). This shifts the SRAS curve to the left, but according to Exhibit 20, it has no effect on LRAS. This presumes that there has not been a permanent change in the relative prices of the factors of production. If there has been a permanent change, companies will be forced to conserve on the now more expensive input and will not be able to produce as efficiently. The LRAS curve would, therefore, shift to the left, just as it would if the available supply of natural resources had declined relative to the supply of other inputs. Indeed, that is the most likely cause of a permanent change in relative input prices.

EXAMPLE 11

Shifts in Aggregate Supply

John Donovan is a portfolio manager for a global mutual fund. Currently, his fund has 10 percent of its assets invested in Chinese equities. He is considering increasing the fund's allocation to the Chinese equity market. His decision will be based on an analysis of the following economic developments and their impact on the Chinese economy and equity market. What is the impact on SRAS and LRAS from the following factors?

1 Global oil prices, currently near their longer-run trend at $75 a barrel, have increased from $35 a barrel over the last three years because of strong demand from China and India.

2 The number of students studying engineering has dramatically increased at Chinese universities over the last decade.

3 Wages for China's workers are rising, leading some multinational companies to consider shifting their investments to Vietnam or India.

4 Recent data show that business investment as a share of GDP is over 40 percent in China.

5 The People's Bank of China is likely to permit the yuan to appreciate by 10 percent over the next year.

Solution to 1:

Higher energy prices cause a decrease in short-run AS and shift the SRAS curve to the left. Because oil prices are back to their longer-run trend, the leftward shift in SRAS essentially reverses a previous shift that occurred when oil prices fell to $35, and it is likely that there will be no impact on the LRAS curve. Lower output and profit are likely to have a negative effect on Chinese equity prices.

Solution to 2:

More students studying engineering indicates an improvement in the quality of the labor force—an increase in human capital. As a result, AS increases and the AS curve shifts to the right. Both short-run and long-run curves are affected. Higher output and profits may be expected to have a positive effect on Chinese equity prices.

Solution to 3:

The increase in wages increases labor costs for businesses, causes short-run aggregate supply to decline, and shifts the SRAS curve to the left. Lower output and profit should have a negative effect on Chinese equity prices.

Solution to 4:

The high level of business investment indicates that the capital stock in China is growing at a fast rate. This means that workers have more capital to use, which increases their productivity. Thus, AS increases and the AS curve shifts to the right. Both short-run AS and long-run AS are affected. Higher output should have a positive effect on Chinese equity prices.

Solution to 5:

The probable appreciation of the yuan means that the cost of imported raw materials, such as iron ore, coal, and oil, will be lower for Chinese companies. As a result, short-run AS increases and the SRAS curve shifts to the right. The LRAS curve may also shift to the right if the appreciation of the yuan is permanent and global commodity prices do not fully adjust. Higher output and profit should have a positive effect on Chinese equity prices.[14]

The implications of the above factors for equity investment in China are ambiguous. If the long-run effects dominate, however, then the net impact should be positive. The positive factors—the high level of investment and the growing pool of engineering students—have a lasting impact on output and profit. The negative factors—higher wages and oil prices—should be temporary because wages will realign with the price level and the increase in oil prices appears to offset a previous temporary decline. The reduction in raw material prices due to the stronger currency is positive for output, profit, and equities in the short run and perhaps in the long run as well.

3.4 Equilibrium GDP and Prices

Now that we have discussed the components of the AD and AS model, we can combine them to determine the real level of GDP and the price level. Equilibrium occurs where the AD and AS curves intersect. At this point, the quantity of aggregate output demanded (or the level of aggregate expenditures) is equal to the quantity of aggregate output supplied. In Exhibit 21, equilibrium price and GDP occur at P_1 and Y_1. If the price level is above P_1, then the quantity of output supplied exceeds the amount demanded. This situation would result in unsold inventories and would require a reduction in production and in prices. If the price level is below P_1, then the quantity of aggregate output demanded exceeds the quantity of aggregate output supplied. This situation would result in a shortage of goods that would put upward pressure on prices.

It is important to understand that short-run macroeconomic equilibrium may occur at a level above or below full employment. We consider four possible types of macroeconomic equilibrium:

1 Long-run full employment

2 Short-run recessionary gap

3 Short-run inflationary gap

4 Short-run stagflation

---

14 The alert reader may have noted that the stronger yuan will also reduce export demand and shift the AD curve to the left. The combined impact of the AD and AS shifts on output, profit, and equity prices is ambiguous.

From an investment perspective, the performance of asset classes and financial markets will differ in each of the above cases as the economy makes the adjustment toward the macroeconomic equilibrium. We look at these differences later in the reading.

3.4.1 Long-Run Equilibrium

Exhibit 21 shows the long-run full employment equilibrium for an economy. In this case, equilibrium occurs where the AD curve intersects the SRAS curve at a point on the LRAS curve. Because equilibrium occurs at a point on the LRAS curve, the economy is at potential real GDP. Both labor and capital are fully employed, and everyone who wants a job has one. *In the long run, equilibrium GDP is equal to potential GDP.*

Exhibit 21   Long-Run Macroeconomic Equilibrium

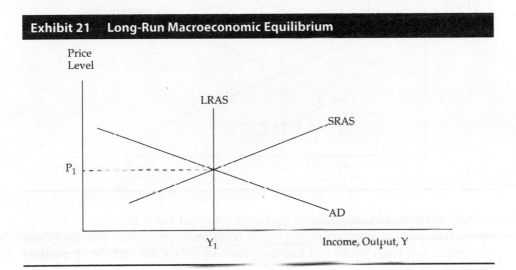

In practice, the level of potential GDP is difficult to measure with precision. Because of fluctuations arising from shifts in the AD and SRAS curves, the economy rarely operates at potential GDP. Thus, potential GDP is not observable from the data on actual GDP. In addition, potential GDP is determined by factors that are themselves difficult to measure (see Section 4.2). Thus, "bottom-up" estimates of the *level* of potential output are also quite imprecise. However, as will be discussed in Section 4, economists have confidence that the long-run *growth rate* of potential GDP can be estimated well enough to provide meaningful guidance for analysts and policymakers. Hence, in the short run, economists generally focus on factors that cause actual GDP to grow faster or slower than their estimate of the long-run growth rate of potential output. In addition, they focus on measures that indicate, albeit imprecisely, the extent to which the economy is operating above or below its productive capacity, such as unemployment and capacity utilization.

3.4.2 Recessionary Gap

Cyclical fluctuations in real GDP and prices are caused by shifts in both the AD and SRAS curves. A decline in AD or a leftward shift in the AD curve results in lower GDP and lower prices. Such declines in AD lead to economic contractions, and if such declines drive demand below the economy's potential GDP, the economy goes into a recession. In Exhibit 22, when aggregate demand falls, the equilibrium shifts from Point A to Point B. Real GDP contracts from Y_1 to Y_2, and the aggregate price level falls from P_1 to P_2. Because of the decline in demand, companies reduce their workforce and the unemployment rate rises. The economy is in recession,[15] and the recessionary gap is measured as the difference between Y_2 and Y_1 or the amount by which equilibrium output is below potential GDP. Thus, a recessionary gap occurs when the AD curve intersects the short-run AS curve at a short-run equilibrium level of GDP below potential GDP. *Most importantly, in contrast to full employment, equilibrium GDP is below potential GDP.*

Exhibit 22   Recessionary Gap

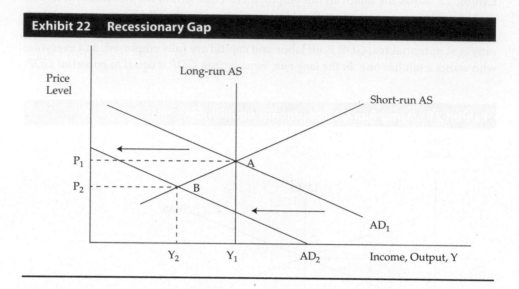

Any of the factors discussed in Section 3.3.1 could cause the shift in the AD curve. Tightening of monetary policy, higher taxes, more pessimistic consumers and businesses, and lower equity and housing prices all reduce AD and are all possible causes of a recession.

The question is, How does the economy return to full employment? There is considerable debate among economists about the answer to this question. Some economists argue that an automatic, self-correcting mechanism will push the economy back to its potential, without the need for government action. The idea is that because of the decline in prices and higher unemployment, workers will be willing to accept lower nominal wages. Workers will do this because each currency unit of wages now buys more goods and services because of their lower price. As a result, lower wages and input prices will cause the SRAS curve to shift to the right (see Exhibit 20) and push the economy back to full employment and potential GDP.

The problem is that this price mechanism can take several years to work. As an alternative, government can use the tools of fiscal and monetary policy to shift the AD curve to the right (from Point B to Point A in Exhibit 22) and move the economy back to full employment. On the fiscal side, policymakers can reduce taxes or increase government spending. On the monetary side, the central bank can lower interest rates or increase the money supply. The problem, however, is that variable lags in the effectiveness of these policy measures imply that policy adjustments may end up reinforcing rather than counteracting underlying shifts in the economy.

Investment Implications of a Decrease in AD   Aggregate demand and aggregate supply are theoretical measures that are very hard to measure directly. Most governments, however, publish statistics that provide an indication of the direction that aggregate

---

15 A **recession** is defined as a period during which real GDP decreases (i.e., "negative growth") for at least two successive quarters or a period of significant decline in total output, income, employment, and sales usually lasting from six months to a year.

demand and supply are moving over time. For example, statistics on consumer sentiment, factory orders for durable and nondurable goods, the value of unfilled orders, the number of new housing starts, the number of hours worked, and changes in inventories provide an indication of the direction of aggregate demand. If these statistics suggest that a recession is caused by a decline in AD, the following conditions are likely to occur:

- Corporate profits will decline.
- Commodity prices will decline.
- Interest rates will decline.
- Demand for credit will decline.

This suggests the following investment strategy:

- Reduce investments in **cyclical companies**[16] because their earnings are likely to decline the most in an economic slowdown.
- Reduce investments in commodities and/or commodity-oriented companies because the decline in commodity prices will slow revenue growth and reduce profit margins.
- Increase investments in **defensive companies**[17] because they are likely to experience only modest earnings declines in an economic slowdown.
- Increase investments in investment-grade or government-issued fixed-income securities. The prices of these securities should increase as interest rates decline.
- Increase investments in long-maturity fixed-income securities because their prices will be more responsive to the decline in interest rates than the prices of shorter-maturity securities.
- Reduce investments in speculative equity securities and in fixed-income securities with low credit quality ratings.

As with most investment strategies, this strategy will be most successful if it is implemented before other market participants recognize the opportunities and asset prices adjust.

EXAMPLE 12

Using AD and AS: The Recession of 2007–2009

Many Asian economies were more adversely affected than the United States by the global recession that began in late 2007. In the first quarter of 2009, real GDP fell at an annualized rate of 16 percent in Japan, 11 percent in Singapore, and 9 percent in Taiwan, compared with a 6 percent annualized decline in the United States. Using the data on exports as a share of GDP shown in Exhibit 23, explain how the following economic factors contributed to the recession in the Asian economies:

1　Collapse of house prices and home construction in the United States.

---

16 Cyclical companies are companies with sales and profits that regularly expand and contract with the business cycle or state of economy (for example, automobile and chemical companies).

17 Defensive companies are companies with sales and profits that have little sensitivity to the business cycle or state of the economy (for example, food and pharmaceutical companies).

2   Oil prices rising from around $30 a barrel in 2004 to nearly $150 a barrel
     in 2008. (*Note*: Most of the markets in eastern Asia, such as Hong Kong,
     Japan, South Korea, and Taiwan, rely on imports for almost all of their
     oil and energy needs. In contrast, the United States has a large domestic
     energy industry and imports about one-half of its oil.)

3   The dramatic reduction in credit availability following the collapse or near
     collapse of major financial institutions in 2008.

Exhibit 23	Exports as a Share of GDP, 2007	
Market	Exports as a Percentage of GDP	Percentage of Exports Going to United States
Singapore	186	11.2
Hong Kong	166	11.5
Taiwan	62	11.6
South Korea	53	10.9
Germany	47	7.1
China	37	26.4
Mexico	28	80.2
Kenya	27	8.2
Japan	17	20.1
India	14	17.0
United States	12	—
Ethiopia	11	6.7

Sources: World Bank: World Development Indicators and OECD Stat Extracts.

Solution to 1:

The collapse in housing prices caused housing construction spending, a component of business investment, to decline in the United States. The decline in
housing prices also caused a sharp fall in household wealth. As a result, consumption spending in the United States declined because of the wealth effect.
The decline in both consumption and housing construction shifted the AD
curve for the United States to the left, resulting in a US recession. The link to
the Asian economies was through global trade because exports represent such
a large share of the Asian countries' GDP. In 2007, exports as a share of GDP
(Exhibit 23) were 186 percent in Singapore, 62 percent in Taiwan, 53 percent in
South Korea, and 37 percent in China. In turn, each of these markets exports a
significant amount of goods and services to the United States; e.g., over 26 percent
of Chinese exports were going to the United States. Thus, the recession in the
United States and especially the decline in US consumption spending caused a
sharp fall in exports among these countries. This lowered their AD and caused
the AD curve to shift to the left, resulting in a recessionary gap in these countries.

Solution to 2:

The rise in oil prices increased input cost and shifted the short-run AS curve
to the left. Because the eastern Asian economies are heavily dependent on
imported oil, their economies were more adversely affected than the economy
of the United States.

Solution to 3:

The decline in housing prices caused financial institutions in the United States to suffer large losses on housing-related loans and securities. Several large lenders collapsed, and the US Treasury and the Federal Reserve had to intervene to prevent a wave of bankruptcies among large financial institutions. As a result of the crisis, it became difficult for households and businesses to obtain credit to finance their spending. This caused AD to fall and increased the severity of the recession in the United States, resulting in a significant decline in US imports and thus exports from the Asian countries. In addition, the financial crisis made it more difficult to get trade finance, further reducing exports from Asia.

In summary, global investors need to be aware of the growing linkages among countries and the extent that one country's economic growth depends on demand from within as well as from outside of that country. Data on exports as a percentage of a country's GDP provide an indication of this dependence. Although Japan is often viewed as an export-driven economy, Exhibit 23 shows that exports are only 17 percent of its GDP. Similarly, the economy of India depends largely on domestic spending for growth because exports account for only 14 percent of GDP.

3.4.3 *Inflationary Gap*

Increases in AD lead to economic expansions as real GDP and employment increase. If the expansion drives the economy beyond its production capacity, however, **inflation**[18] will occur. As summarized in Exhibit 18, higher government spending, lower taxes, a more optimistic outlook among consumers and businesses, a weaker domestic currency, rising equity and housing prices, and an increase in the money supply would each stimulate aggregate demand and shift the AD curve to the right. If aggregate supply does not increase to match the increase in AD, a rise in the overall level of prices will result.

In Exhibit 24, an increase in AD will shift the equilibrium level of GDP from Point A to Point B. Real output increases from Y_1 to Y_2, and the aggregate price level rises from P_1 to P_2. As a result of the increase in aggregate demand, companies increase their production and hire more workers. The unemployment rate declines. Once an economy reaches its potential GDP, however, companies must pay higher wages and other input prices to further increase production. The economy now faces an inflationary gap, measured by the difference between Y_2 and Y_1 in Exhibit 24. *An inflationary gap occurs when the economy's short-run level of equilibrium GDP is above potential GDP, resulting in upward pressure on prices.*

---

18 The inflation rate is defined as the increase in the general price level from one period to the next.

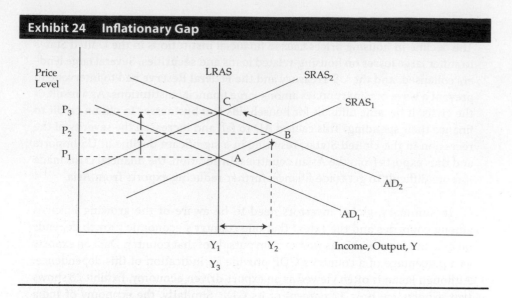

Exhibit 24   Inflationary Gap

GDP cannot remain at Y_2 for long because the economy is over-utilizing its resources—i.e., extra shifts of workers are hired and plant and equipment are operating at their maximum capacity. Eventually, workers become tired and plant and equipment wear out. The increase in the general price level and input prices will set in motion the process of returning the economy back to potential GDP. Higher wages and input prices shift the SRAS supply curve to the left (from $SRAS_1$ to $SRAS_2$), moving the economy to Point C in Exhibit 24. Again, this self-correcting mechanism may work slowly.

A nation's government and/or its central bank can attempt to use the tools of fiscal and monetary policy to control inflation by shifting the AD curve to the left (AD_2 to AD_1 in Exhibit 24) so that the return to full employment occurs without the price increase. From a fiscal perspective, policymakers can raise taxes or cut government spending. From a monetary perspective, the central bank can reduce bank reserves, resulting in a decrease in the growth of the money supply and higher interest rates.

Investment Implications of an Increase in AD Resulting in an Inflationary Gap   If economic statistics (consumer sentiment, factory orders for durable and nondurable goods, etc.) suggest that there is an expansion caused by an increase in AD, the following conditions are likely to occur:

- Corporate profits will rise.
- Commodity prices will increase.
- Interest rates will rise.
- Inflationary pressures will build.

This suggests the following investment strategy:

- Increase investment in cyclical companies because they are expected to have the largest increase in earnings.
- Reduce investments in defensive companies because they are expected to have only a modest increase in earnings.
- Increase investments in commodities and commodity-oriented equities because they will benefit from higher production and output.
- Reduce investments in fixed-income securities, especially longer-maturity securities, because they will decline in price as interest rates rise. Raise exposure to speculative fixed-income securities (junk bonds) because default risks decrease in an economic expansion.

3.4.4 Stagflation: Both High Inflation and High Unemployment

Structural fluctuations in real GDP are caused by fluctuations in SRAS. Declines in aggregate supply bring about **stagflation**—high unemployment and increased inflation. Increases in aggregate supply conversely give rise to high economic growth and low inflation.

Exhibit 25 shows the case of a decline in aggregate supply, perhaps caused by an unexpected increase in basic material and oil prices. The equilibrium level of GDP shifts from Point A to B. The economy experiences a recession as GDP falls from Y_1 to Y_2, but the price level, instead of falling, rises from P_1 to P_2. Over time, the reduction in output and employment should put downward pressure on wages and input prices and shift the SRAS curve back to the right, re-establishing full employment equilibrium at Point A. However, this mechanism may be painfully slow. Policymakers may use fiscal and monetary policy to shift the AD curve to the right, as previously discussed, but at the cost of a permanently higher price level at Point C.

Exhibit 25   Stagflation

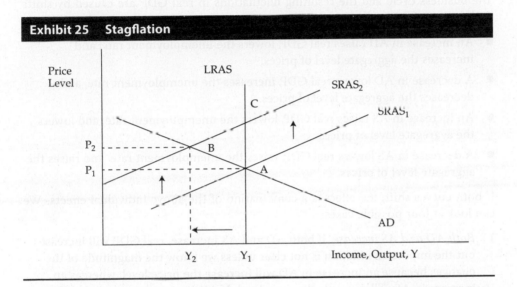

The global economy experienced stagflation in the mid-1970s and early 1980s. Both unemployment and inflation soared. The problem was caused by a sharp decline in aggregate supply fueled by higher input prices, especially the price of oil. In 1973, the price of oil quadrupled. A steep global recession began in late 1973 and lasted through early 1975. The recession was unusual because prices rose rather than declined as would be expected in a typical demand-caused downturn. In 1979–1980, the price of oil doubled. Higher energy prices shifted the SRAS curve to the left, as shown in Exhibit 25, leading to a global recession in 1980–1982. In the United States, the contraction in output was reinforced by the Federal Reserve's decision to tighten monetary policy to fight the supply-induced inflation.

Investment Implications of Shift in AS   Labor and raw material costs, including energy prices, determine the direction of shifts in short-run aggregate supply: Higher costs for labor, raw materials, and energy lead to a decrease in aggregate supply, resulting in lower economic growth and higher prices. Conversely, lower labor costs, raw material prices, and energy prices lead to an increase in aggregate supply, resulting in higher economic growth and a lower aggregate price level. Productivity is also an important factor. Higher rates of productivity growth shift the AS to the right, resulting in higher output and lower unit input prices. Lower rates of productivity growth do the opposite and shift the AS curve to the left.

From an investment perspective, a decline in AS (leftward shift of the SRAS curve) suggests

- reducing investment in fixed income because rising output prices (i.e., inflation) put upward pressure on nominal interest rates;

- reducing investment in most equity securities because profit margins are squeezed and output declines; and

- increasing investment in commodities or commodity-based companies because prices and profits are likely to rise.

On the other hand, an increase in AS (rightward shift of the SRAS curve) due to higher productivity growth or lower labor, raw material, and energy costs is favorable for most asset classes other than commodities.

3.4.5 Conclusions on AD and AS

The business cycle and the resulting fluctuations in real GDP are caused by shifts in the AD and AS curves. The impact of these shifts can be summarized as follows:

- An increase in AD raises real GDP, lowers the unemployment rate, and increases the aggregate level of prices.

- A decrease in AD lowers real GDP, increases the unemployment rate, and decreases the aggregate level of prices.

- An increase in AS raises real GDP, lowers the unemployment rate, and lowers the aggregate level of prices.

- A decrease in AS lowers real GDP, raises the unemployment rate, and raises the aggregate level of prices.

If both curves shift, the effect is a combination of the above individual effects. We can look at four possible cases:

1 *Both AD and AS increase.* If both AD and AS increase, real GDP will increase but the impact on inflation is not clear unless we know the magnitude of the changes because an increase in AD will increase the price level, whereas an increase in AS will decrease the price level. If AD increases more than AS, the price level will increase. If AS increases more than AD, however, the price level will decline.

2 *Both AD and AS decrease.* If both AD and AS decrease, real GDP and employment will decline, but the impact on the price level is not clear unless we know the magnitude of the changes because a decrease in AD decreases the price level, whereas a decrease in AS increases the price level. If AD decreases more than AS, the price level will fall. If AS decreases more than AD, the price level will rise.

3 *AD increases and AS decreases.* If AD increases and AS declines, the price level will rise, but the effect on real GDP is not clear unless we know the magnitude of the changes because an increase in AD increases real GDP, whereas a decrease in AS decreases real GDP. If AD increases more than AS declines, GDP will rise. If AS decreases more than AD increases, real GDP will fall.

4 *AD decreases and AS increases.* If AD decreases and AS increases, the price level will decline but the impact on real GDP is not clear unless we know the magnitudes of the changes because a decrease in AD decreases real GDP, whereas an increase in AS increases real GDP. If AD decreases more than AS increases, real GDP will fall. If AS increases more than AD declines, real GDP will rise.

Exhibit 26 summarizes these four cases.

		Effect on	Effect on Aggregate
Change in AS	**Change in AD**	**Real GDP**	**Price Level**
Increase	Increase	Increase	Indeterminate
Decrease	Decrease	Decrease	Indeterminate
Increase	Decrease	Indeterminate	Decrease
Decrease	Increase	Indeterminate	Increase

Exhibit 26   Effect of Combined Changes in AS and AD

Whether the growth of the economy is demand- or supply-driven has an impact on asset prices. Demand-driven expansions are normally associated with rising interest rates and inflation, whereas contractions are associated with lower inflation and interest rates. Supply-driven expansions are associated with lower inflation and interest rates, whereas supply-driven contractions are associated with rising inflation and interest rates.

EXAMPLE 13

Investment Strategy Based on AD and AS Curves

An analyst is evaluating the possibility of investing in China, Italy, Mexico, or Brazil. What are the equity and fixed-income investment opportunities in these countries based on the following events?

1   The Chinese government announced a spending plan of $1.2 trillion or 13 percent of GDP. In addition, the central bank of China eased monetary policy, resulting in a surge of lending.

2   The Italian government announced a decline in labor productivity, and it expects this trend to continue into the future.

3   In response to rising inflationary pressure, the Mexican central bank tightened monetary policy, and the government announced tax increases and spending cuts to balance the budget.

4   A major discovery of oil off the coast of Brazil lowered oil prices, while the Brazilian government announced a major increase in spending on public infrastructure to stimulate the economy.

Solution to 1:

Stimulative fiscal and monetary policies should result in a demand-driven expansion. Investors should reduce investments in fixed-income securities and defensive companies and invest in cyclical companies and commodities. As a result, the prospects for growth-oriented equity investments look favorable in China.

Solution to 2:

A decline in labor productivity will result in a decline in AS; i.e., the AS curve will shift to the left. This is typically a poor investment environment. Investors should reduce investments in both fixed-income and equity securities and invest in commodities. Entry into Italian stocks and bonds does not look attractive.

Solution to 3:

The policy measures put in place by the Mexican government and central bank will cause a drop in AD and likely result in a recession. Investors should increase their investments in fixed-income securities because interest rates will most likely decline as the recession deepens. This is a poor environment for equity securities.

Solution to 4:

This is a situation where both the AD and AS curves will shift. The increase in spending on public infrastructure will shift the AD curve to the right, resulting in higher aggregate expenditures and prices. Lower oil prices will shift the AS curve to the right, resulting in higher GDP but lower prices. Thus, GDP will clearly increase, but the impact on prices and inflation is indeterminate. As a result, investors should increase their investment in equity securities; however, the impact on fixed-income securities is unclear.

EXAMPLE 14

Using AD and AS to Explain Japan's Economic Problem

Japan has experienced sluggish growth in real GDP for nearly two decades following the bursting of an asset and investment bubble in the late 1980s. At the same time, Japan has experienced deflation (declining prices) over this period. The reasons for this protracted period of stagnation continue to be debated among economists. Failure to recognize a change in the Japanese growth rate has hurt many investors, especially those taking a long-term perspective. From their peak in 1989, Japanese equity prices, as measured by the Nikkei index, fell by over 60 percent before bottoming out in mid-1992. Since that time, the market has been essentially flat despite considerable volatility.

The performance of the Japanese economy can be explained using the AD and AS model. The protracted slowdown of growth in Japan beginning in the early 1990s can be linked to the effect of the collapse of the equity and commercial real estate markets in the late 1980s and to excessive investment in capital goods (new factories and equipment) in the 1980s. These problems were compounded by persistent weakness in the banking sector, a profound lack of confidence among businesses and consumers, and negative demographics with slow growth in the working age population.

The sum of these developments caused a decline in both the AD and AS curves. Aggregate demand declined, causing the AD curve to shift to the left for the following reasons:

■ The wealth effect due to the decline in equity and real estate prices sharply reduced consumption spending. Asset prices have yet to recover from the fall.

■ Excessive investment in capital goods caused a sharp decline in business investment.

■ Lack of confidence among businesses and consumers.

■ Problems in the banking sector made monetary policy ineffective because banks were unable to lend, which negatively affected both consumer and business spending.

AS declined for the following reasons:

- Marked slowing in private investment spending reduced the capital stock. This also reduced potential GDP.

- Slow population growth limited the growth in the labor supply. This also reduced potential GDP.

- Higher energy prices slowed growth because of Japan's heavy dependence on imported energy.

As would be expected, the declines in both AD and AS resulted in slow GDP growth. The fact that prices fell indicates that the AD curve shifted more than the AS curve.

ECONOMIC GROWTH AND SUSTAINABILITY

4

We now shift focus from the short-run cyclical movement of the economy to its long-term growth rate. Economic growth is calculated as the annual percentage change in real GDP or the annual change in real per capita GDP:

- Growth in real GDP measures how rapidly the total economy is expanding.
- Per capita GDP, defined as real GDP divided by population, determines the standard of living in each country and the ability of the average person to buy goods and services.

Economic growth is important because rapid growth in per capita real GDP can transform a poor nation into a wealthy one. Even small differences in the growth rate of per capita GDP, if sustained over time, have a large impact on an economy's standard of living. One should think of the growth rate of GDP as the equivalent of a rate of return on a portfolio. Small differences in return compounded over many years make a big difference. Nevertheless, there is a limit to how fast an economy can grow. Faster growth is not always better for an economy because there are costs associated with excess growth, such as higher inflation, potential environmental damage, and the lower consumption and higher savings needed to finance the growth.

This raises the issue of sustainable growth, which requires an understanding of the concept of potential GDP. Recall that potential GDP measures the productive capacity of the economy and is the level of real GDP that an economy could produce if capital and labor are fully employed. In order to grow over time, an economy must add to its productive capacity. Thus, the **sustainable rate of economic growth** is measured by the rate of increase in the economy's productive capacity or potential GDP. It is important to note that economists cannot directly measure potential output. Instead, they estimate it using a variety of techniques discussed later in this reading.

For global investors, estimating the sustainable rate of economic growth for an economy is important for both asset allocation and security selection decisions. Investors need to understand how the rate of economic growth differs among countries and whether these growth rates are sustainable. When examining the GDP data, global investors need to address a number of questions, including the following:

1 What are the underlying determinants or sources of growth for the country?

2 Are these sources of growth likely to remain stable or change over time?

3 How can we measure and forecast sustainable growth for different countries?

4.1 The Production Function and Potential GDP

The neoclassical or Solow growth model is the framework used to determine the underlying sources of growth for an economy. The model shows that the economy's productive capacity and potential GDP increase for two reasons:

1 accumulation of such inputs as capital, labor, and raw materials used in production, and

2 discovery and application of new technologies that make the inputs in the production process more productive—that is, able to produce more goods and services for the same amount of input.

The model is based on a **production function** that provides the quantitative link between the level of output that the economy can produce and the inputs used in the production process, given the state of technology. A two-factor production function with labor and capital as the inputs is expressed mathematically as

$$Y = AF(L, K)$$

where Y denotes the level of aggregate output in the economy, L is the quantity of labor or number of workers in the economy, K is the capital stock or the equipment and structures used to produce goods and services, and A represents technological knowledge or **total factor productivity** (TFP). TFP is a scale factor that reflects the portion of growth that is not accounted for by the capital and labor inputs. The main factor influencing TFP is technological change. Like potential GDP, TFP is not directly observed in the economy and must be estimated.

The production function shows that output in the economy depends on inputs and the level of technology. The economy's capacity to produce goods grows when these inputs increase and/or technology advances. The more technologically advanced an economy is, the more output it is able to produce from a given amount of inputs.

Two assumptions about the production function provide a link to microeconomics. First, we assume that the production function has constant returns to scale. This means that if all the inputs in the production process are increased by the same percentage, then output will rise by that percentage. Thus, doubling all inputs would double output. Second, we assume that the production function exhibits **diminishing marginal productivity** with respect to any individual input. This property plays an important role in assessing the contribution of labor and capital to economic growth. Marginal productivity looks at the extra output that is produced from a one-unit increase in an input if the other inputs are unchanged. It applies to any input as long as the other inputs are held constant. For example, if we have a factory of a fixed size and we add more workers to the factory, the marginal productivity of labor measures how much additional output each additional worker will produce.

Diminishing marginal productivity means that at some point the extra output obtained from each additional unit of the input will decline. In the above example, if we hire more workers at the existing factory (fixed capital input in this case), output will rise by a smaller and smaller amount with each additional worker. Traditionally, economists focused on the labor input and how the productivity of labor would decline given a fixed amount of land. The traditional growth theory, where labor is the only (variable) input, was developed by Thomas Malthus in his 1798 publication, *Essay on the Principle of Population*. Malthus argued that as the population and labor force grew, the additional output produced by an additional worker would decline essentially to zero and there would be no long-term economic growth. This gloomy forecast caused others to label economics the "dismal science."

The dire prediction implied by declining marginal productivity of labor never materialized, and economists changed the focus of the analysis away from labor to capital. In this case, if we add more and more capital to a fixed number of workers, the amount of additional output contributed by each additional amount of capital will fall. Thus, if capital grows faster than labor, capital will become less productive, resulting in slower and slower growth. Diminishing marginal productivity of capital has two major implications for potential GDP:

1 Long-term sustainable growth cannot rely solely on **capital deepening investment** that increases the stock of capital relative to labor. More generally, increasing the supply of some input(s) relative to other inputs will lead to diminishing returns and cannot be the basis for sustainable growth.

2 Given the relative scarcity and hence high productivity of capital in developing countries, the growth rates of developing countries should exceed those of developed countries. As a result, there should be a **convergence** of incomes between developed and developing countries over time.

Because of diminishing returns to capital, the only way to sustain growth in potential GDP per capita is through technological change or growth in total factor productivity. This results in an upward shift in the production function: The economy produces more goods and services using the same level of labor and capital inputs. In terms of the formal production function shown above, this is reflected by an increase in the technology parameter, A.

Using the production function, Robert Solow developed a model that explained the contribution of labor, capital, and technology (total factor productivity) to economic growth. The growth accounting equation shows that the rate of growth of potential output equals growth in technology plus the weighted average growth rate of labor and capital.

$$\text{Growth in potential GDP} = \text{Growth in technology} + W_L(\text{Growth in labor})$$
$$+ W_C(\text{Growth in capital})$$

where W_L and W_C are the relative shares of capital and labor in national income. The capital share is the sum of corporate profits, net interest income, net rental income, and depreciation divided by GDP. The labor share is employee compensation divided by GDP. For the United States, W_L and W_C are roughly 0.7 and 0.3, respectively.

The growth accounting equation highlights a key point: The contribution of labor and capital to long-term growth depends on their respective shares of national income. For the United States, because labor's share is higher, an increase in the growth rate of labor will have a significantly larger impact (roughly double) on potential GDP growth than will an equivalent increase in the growth rate of capital.

The growth accounting equation can be further modified to explain growth in per capita GDP. Because it measures the standard of living and purchasing power of the average person in an economy, per capita GDP is more relevant than the absolute level of GDP in comparing economic performance among countries. Transforming the growth accounting equation into per capita terms results in the following equation:

$$\text{Growth in per capita potential GDP} = \text{Growth in technology}$$
$$+ W_C(\text{Growth in capital-to-labor ratio})$$

The capital-to-labor ratio measures the amount of capital available per worker and is weighted by the share of capital in national income. Because capital's share in national income in the US economy is 0.3, a 1 percent increase in the amount of capital available for each worker increases per capita output by only 0.3 percent. The equation shows that improvements in technology are more important than capital in raising an economy's standard of living.

4.2 Sources of Economic Growth

The growth accounting equation focuses on the main determinants of growth—capital, labor and technology—and omits a number of other sources of growth to simplify the analysis. For many countries, however, natural resource and human capital inputs play an important role in explaining economic growth. Therefore, there are five important sources of growth for an economy:

■ Labor supply;

■ Human capital;

■ Physical capital;

■ Technology; and

■ Natural resources.

These sources of growth determine the capacity of the economy to supply goods and services.

Labor Supply   Growth in the number of people available for work (quantity of work-force) is an important source of economic growth and partially accounts for the superior growth performance, among the advanced economies, of the US economy versus the European and Japanese economies. Most developing countries, such as China, India, and Mexico, have a large potential labor supply. We can measure the potential size of the labor input as the total number of hours available for work, which is given by

Total hours worked = Labor force × Average hours worked per worker

The **labor force** is defined as the portion of the working age population (over the age of 16) that is employed or available for work but not working (unemployed). The contribution of labor to overall output is also affected by changes in the average hours worked per worker. Average hours worked is highly sensitive to the business cycle. However, the long-term trend has been toward a shorter workweek in the advanced countries. This development is the result of legislation, collective bargaining agreements, and the growth of part-time and temporary work.

Human Capital   In addition to the quantity of labor, the quality of the labor force is important. Human capital is the accumulated knowledge and skill that workers acquire from education, training, and life experience. It measures the quality of the workforce. In general, better-educated and skilled workers will be more productive and more adaptable to changes in technology.

An economy's human capital is increased through investment in education and on-the-job training. Like physical capital, investment in education is costly. Studies show that there is a significant return on education. That is, people with more education earn higher wages. Moreover, education may also have a spillover or externality impact: Increasing the educational level of one person not only raises the output of that person but also the output of those around him or her. The spillover effect operates through the link between education and advances in technology. Education not only improves the quality of the labor force but also encourages growth through innovation. Investment in health is also a major contributor to human capital, especially in developing countries.

Physical Capital Stock   The physical **capital stock** (accumulated amount of buildings, machinery, and equipment used to produce goods and services) increases from year to year as long as net investment (gross investment less depreciation of capital) is positive. Thus, countries with a higher rate of investment should have a growing physical capital stock and a higher rate of GDP growth. Exhibit 27 shows the level of business investment as a share of GDP. The exhibit shows significant variation across countries, with the investment share in the United States being low in comparison to other developed countries.

As is evident in Exhibit 27, the correlation between economic growth and investment is high. Countries that devote a large share of GDP to investment, such as China, India, and South Korea, have high growth rates. The fastest-growing countries in Europe over the last decade, Ireland and Spain, have the highest investment-to-GDP ratios. Countries that devote a smaller share of GDP to investment, such as Brazil and Mexico, have slower growth rates. The data show why the Chinese economy has expanded at such a rapid rate, achieving an annual GDP growth rate of over 10 percent over the last two decades. Investment spending in China on new factories, equipment, and infrastructure as a percentage of GDP is the highest in the world. In recent years, China devoted over 40 percent of its GDP to investment spending.

Exhibit 27	Business Investment as a Percentage of GDP				
Developed economies	1994	2000	2005	2007	Average Annual Real GDP Growth, 1991–2009 (%)
United States	17.2	19.9	19.2	18.4	2.2
Japan	28.5	25.2	23.3	23.2	1.1
Germany	22.6	21.5	17.4	18.7	1.4
France	18.4	19.5	20.0	21.5	1.5
Italy	18.5	20.3	20.7	21.1	1.0
United Kingdom	16.1	17.1	16.9	17.8	2.2
Canada	18.8	19.2	21.3	22.6	2.1
Ireland	16.1	23.1	26.6	26.3	5.1
Spain	20.7	25.8	29.4	31.0	2.6
Australia	23.9	22.0	27.0	27.7	3.2
South Korea	36.4	31.1	29.3	28.8	4.9
New Zealand	20.9	20.4	24.1	22.9	2.7

Developing countries	1994	2000	2005	2007	Average Annual Real GDP Growth, 1991–2009 (%)
Brazil	18.5	16.8	15.9	17.5	2.8
China	34.5	34.3	41.0	40.0	10.2
India	NA	22.9	30.4	33.8	6.4
Indonesia	24.8	19.9	23.6	24.9	4.6
Mexico	19.4	21.4	20.1	20.8	2.4
Turkey	22.9	20.4	21.0	21.5	3.4

Source: OECD StatLink.

Technology The most important factor affecting economic growth is technology, especially in developed countries such as the United States. **Technology** refers to the process a company uses to transform inputs into outputs. Technological advances are discoveries that make it possible to produce more or higher-quality goods and services with the same resources or inputs. At the same time, technological progress results in the creation of new goods and services. Finally, technological progress improves how efficiently businesses are organized and managed.

Technological advances are very important because they allow an economy to overcome the limits imposed by diminishing marginal returns. Thus, an economy will face limits to growth if it relies exclusively on expanding the inputs or factors of production.

Because most technological change is embodied in new machinery, equipment, and software, physical capital must be replaced, and perhaps expanded, in order to take advantage of changes in technology. One of the key drivers of growth in developed countries over the last decade has been the information technology (IT) sector. Growth in the IT sector has been driven by technological innovation that has caused the price of key technologies, such as semiconductors, to fall dramatically. The steep declines in prices have encouraged investment in IT at the expense of other assets. The sector has grown very fast and has made a significant contribution to economic growth, employment, and exports.

Countries can innovate through expenditures, both public and private, on research and development (R&D). Thus, expenditures on R&D and the number of patents issued, although not directly measuring innovation, provide some useful insight into innovative performance. Countries can also acquire new technology through imitation or copying the technology developed elsewhere. The embodiment of technology in capital goods can also enable relatively poor countries to jump ahead of the technology leaders.

Total factor productivity (TFP) is the component of productivity that proxies technological progress and organizational innovation. TFP is the amount by which output would rise because of improvements in the production process. It is calculated as a residual, the difference between the growth rate of potential output and the weighted average growth rate of capital and labor. Specifically,

TFP growth = Growth in potential GDP

$$- \left[W_L \left(\text{Growth in labor} \right) + W_C \left(\text{Growth in capital} \right) \right]$$

Natural Resources   Raw materials are an essential input to growth and include everything from available land to oil to water. Historically, consumption of raw materials has increased as economies have grown. There are two categories of natural resources:

1 **Renewable resources** are those that can be replenished, such as a forest. For example, if a tree is cut, a seedling can be planted and a new forest harvested in the future.

2 **Non-renewable resources** are finite resources that are depleted once they are consumed. Oil and coal are examples.

Natural resources account for some of the differences in growth among countries. Today, such countries as Brazil and Australia, as well as those in the Middle East, have relatively high per capita incomes because of their resource base. Countries in the Middle East have large pools of oil. Brazil has an abundance of land suitable for large-scale agricultural production, making it a major exporter of coffee, soybeans, and beef.

Even though natural resources are important, they are not necessary for a country to achieve a high level of income provided it can acquire the requisite inputs through trade. Countries in eastern Asia, such as Japan and South Korea, have experienced rapid economic growth but own few natural resources.

China's Economic Growth

Chinese economic growth, as measured by real GDP, has averaged about 10 percent since the late 1970s. On the demand side, high rates of business investment spending (over 40 percent of GDP as shown in Exhibit 27) and export growth have fueled growth. On the supply side, there have been three major sources of growth over the last few decades:

1 rapid capital accumulation due to the high rate of investment,

2 adoption of more advanced technology from developed countries, and

3 a large increase in the non-farm labor force as people have moved from the interior rural areas to the urban areas on the coast.

China has not needed to rely on innovating new technology because it has pursued an export-oriented strategy based on imitation and replication of foreign products. Domestic natural resources have also not been an important driver of growth; China is a net importer of natural resources.

China faces three problems going forward that are likely to slow its growth rate. First, it is quite likely that its workforce will begin to shrink within the next decade. As a result of its long-standing one-child policy, overall population growth is very low (0.6 percent per year), and the number of people over 65 is the fastest-growing segment of the population. Thus, it is likely that the workforce will shrink over time. The impact may, however, be mitigated by the ongoing shift of workers from rural to urban areas of the country. In addition, China is investing heavily in education to improve the quality of the workforce.

The second potential problem arises from reliance on very high levels of investment spending. The high rate of investment has raised concerns about excess capacity in many industries and low rates of return on new investments in general. Because of diminishing returns to capital, further increases in capital per worker (capital deepening investment) will generate progressively smaller increases in real GDP per worker. In essence, China may be beyond the point where exceptional real growth can be sustained by simply adopting existing technology and deploying more of it.

The third potential problem looms on the demand side. The Chinese household sector has an extremely high propensity to save—so high that despite the very high level of investment spending, China runs a substantial current account surplus. If investment spending declines as a share of GDP, China will be left with a serious deficiency of aggregate demand unless household consumption and/or government expenditure expand to fill the void.

In summary, China faces significant growth challenges. Decades of a policy designed to limit population growth may shift labor force growth into reverse just when the potency of rapid capital accumulation wanes. Meanwhile, even if very high levels of investment spending will not sustain historical levels of aggregate *supply* growth, any significant reduction in investment spending could be devastating to aggregate *demand* without a corresponding acceleration in household consumption.

4.3 Measures of Sustainable Growth

Measuring how fast an economy can grow is an important exercise. Economists project potential GDP into the future to forecast the sustainable growth path for the economy. An economy's potential GDP is an unobserved concept that is approximated using a number of alternative methods. It is important to note that estimates of the economy's potential growth can change as new data become available. Being able to understand such a change is critical for financial analysts because equity returns are highly dependent on the sustainable rate of economic growth.

We discussed in the previous section that the growth rate of potential GDP depends on the rate of technological progress as well as the growth rate of

- the labor force;
- physical and human capital; and
- natural resources.

How can we summarize all of these forces driving economic growth and develop a method to measure/estimate the growth rate of potential GDP? One way is to use the growth accounting equation discussed in Section 4.1.

$$\text{Growth in potential GDP} = \text{Growth in technology} + W_L(\text{Growth in labor})$$
$$+ W_C(\text{Growth in capital})$$

The problem with this approach is that there are no observed data on potential GDP or on total factor productivity and both must be estimated. In addition, data on the capital stock and the labor and capital shares of national income are not available for many countries, especially the developing countries.

As an alternative, we can focus on the productivity of the labor force, where we generally have more reliable data. **Labor productivity** is defined as the quantity of goods and services (real GDP) that a worker can produce in one hour of work. Our standard of living improves if we produce more goods and services for each hour of work. Labor productivity is calculated as real GDP for a given year divided by the total number of hours worked in that year, counting all workers. We use total hours, rather than the number of workers, to adjust for the fact that not everyone works the same number of hours.

$$\text{Labor productivity} = \text{Real GDP/Aggregate hours}$$

Therefore, we need to understand the forces that make labor more productive. Productivity is determined by the factors that we examined in the preceding section: education and skill of workers (human capital), investments in physical capital, and improvements in technology. An increase in any of these factors will increase the productivity of the labor force. The factors determining labor productivity can be derived from the production functions under the assumption of constant returns to scale, where a doubling of inputs causes output to double as well. Dividing the production function by $1/L$, we get the following:

$$Y/L = AF(1, K/L)$$

where Y/L is output per worker, which is a measure of labor productivity. The equation states that labor productivity depends on physical capital per worker (K/L) and technology (A). Recall that "A" can also be interpreted as total factor productivity. As this equation indicates, labor productivity and total factor productivity are related but distinct concepts. TFP is a scale factor that does not depend on the mix of inputs. Changes in TFP are measured as a residual, capturing growth that cannot be attributed to specific inputs. On the other hand, as shown in this equation, labor productivity— output per worker—depends on both the general level of productivity (reflected in TFP) and the mix of inputs. Increases in either TFP or the capital-to-labor ratio boost labor productivity. Because both output and labor input can be observed, labor productivity can be measured directly.

Labor productivity is a key concept for measuring the health and prosperity of an economy and its sustainable rate of growth. An analyst examining the growth prospects for an economy needs to focus on the labor productivity data for that country.

Labor productivity largely explains the differences in the living standards and the long-term sustainable growth rates among countries. The distinction between the level and growth rate of productivity is important to understand. Exhibit 28 provides such a comparison for selected countries.

Exhibit 28	Labor Productivity: Level vs. Growth Rate in Select Countries	
	Level of Labor Productivity (2008 GDP per hour worked)	Labor Productivity Average Annual Growth Rate, 2001–2008
United States	$55.3	2.0%
Ireland	54.7	2.4
France	53.2	1.3
Germany	50.5	1.5
Sweden	45.9	2.0
United Kingdom	44.9	2.1
Canada	43.2	0.9
Spain	42.5	0.9
Italy	41.1	0.0
Japan	38.3	1.9
Greece	32.1	2.2
South Korea	25.3	4.7
Turkey	23.8	NA
Mexico	18.6	0.5

Source: OECD Stat Extracts.

Level of Labor Productivity The higher the level of labor productivity, the more goods and services the economy can produce with the same number of workers. The level of labor productivity depends on the accumulated stock of human and physical capital and is much higher in the developed countries. For example, China has a population of over 1.3 billion people, compared with slightly over 300 million people in the United States. Because of its much larger population, China has significantly more workers than the United States. The US economy as measured by real GDP is much larger, however, because US workers are much more productive than Chinese workers. As shown in Exhibit 28, the United States has the highest level of productivity in the world, producing over $55 of GDP per hour worked. Similarly, workers in France, Germany, and Ireland have high levels of productivity. In comparison, Mexican workers produce only $18.6 worth of GDP per hour worked. Thus, US workers are nearly three times more productive than Mexican workers.

Growth Rate of Labor Productivity The growth rate of labor productivity is the percentage increase in productivity over a year. It is among the economic statistics that economists and financial analysts watch most closely. In contrast to the level of productivity, the growth rate of productivity is typically higher in the developing countries where human and physical capital is scarce but growing rapidly.

If productivity growth is rapid, it means the same number of workers can produce more and more goods and services. In this case, companies can afford to pay higher wages and still make a profit. Thus, high rates of productivity growth will translate into rising profits and higher stock prices.

In contrast, persistently low productivity growth suggests the economy is in bad shape. Without productivity gains, businesses have to either cut wages or boost prices in order to increase profit margins. Low rates of productivity growth should be associated with slow growth in profits and flat or declining stock prices.

EXAMPLE 16

Prospects for Equity Returns in Mexico

John Todd, CFA, manages a global mutual fund with nearly 30 percent of its assets invested in Europe. Because of the low population growth rate, he is concerned about the long-term outlook for the European economies. With potentially slower economic growth in Europe, the environment for equities may be less attractive. Therefore, he is considering reallocating some of the assets from Europe to Mexico. Based on the data in Exhibits 27 and 28, do you think that investment opportunities are favorable in Mexico? According to the OECD, the Mexican population increased by 0.8 percent in 2008, compared with a 0.3 percent increase in the European Union (27 countries).

Solution:

Other than the higher population growth rate, the potential sources of growth for Mexico are not favorable. The level of business investment (Exhibit 27) in Mexico is quite low, especially in comparison to China, and even below that of many of the advanced economies in Europe, such as Spain and Italy. The level of labor productivity in Mexico is well below that in most European countries. This is not surprising given that the amount of capital per worker in Mexico is much lower than that in Europe. What is surprising and of concern is the rate of labor productivity growth in Mexico. Labor productivity in Mexico is growing at a 0.5 percent annual rate, well below that of Germany, France, and the United Kingdom. This means that the rightward shift in the AS curve is greater for the European countries than for Mexico, despite the more favorable demographic trend in Mexico. In addition, it implies that there is more potential for expanding profit margins in Europe than in Mexico. Thus, the analysis of potential growth does not suggest a favorable outlook for equity returns in Mexico. In the absence of more favorable considerations—e.g., compelling equity valuations—John Todd should decide not to reallocate assets from Europe to Mexico.

Measuring Sustainable Growth   Labor productivity data can be used to estimate the rate of sustainable growth of the economy. A useful way to describe potential GDP is as a combination of aggregate hours worked and the productivity of those workers:

Potential GDP = Aggregate hours worked × Labor productivity

Transforming the above equation into growth rates, we get the following:

Potential growth rate = Long-term growth rate of labor force

+ Long-term labor productivity growth rate

Thus, potential growth is a combination of the long-term growth rate of the labor force and the long-term growth rate of labor productivity. Therefore, if the labor force is growing at 1 percent per year and productivity per worker is rising at 2 percent per year, then potential GDP (adjusted for inflation) is rising at 3 percent per year.

EXAMPLE 17

Estimating the Rate of Growth in Potential GDP

Exhibit 29 provides data on sources of growth for Canada, Germany, Japan, and the United States. Estimate the growth rates of the labor force, labor productivity, and potential GDP for each country by averaging the growth rates for these variables for the last two decades.

Exhibit 29	Sources of Growth: Average Annual Growth Rate			
	1971–1980	**1981–1990**	**1991–2000**	**2001–2008**
Canada				
Labor force	2.1%	1.8%	1.1%	1.5%
Productivity	1.8	1.0	1.8	0.9
GDP	4.0	2.8	2.9	2.4
Germany				
Labor force	−0.9%	0.0%	−0.4%	−0.4%
Productivity	3.7	2.3	2.5	1.5
GDP	2.9	2.3	2.1	1.0
Japan				
Labor force	0.3%	0.5%	−0.9%	−0.7%
Productivity	4.2	3.4	2.2	2.1
GDP	4.5	3.9	1.2	1.4
United States				
Labor force	1.6%	1.8%	1.5%	0.3%
Productivity	1.6	1.4	1.8	2.0
GDP	3.2	3.2	3.3	2.2

Solution:

Potential GDP is calculated as the sum of the trend growth rate in the labor force and the trend growth rate in labor productivity. The growth in the labor force can differ from the population growth rate because of changes in the labor force participation rate and changes in hours worked per person. Estimating based on the average for the last two decades gives

	Projected Growth in Labor Force	**Projected Growth in Labor Productivity**	**Projected Growth in Potential GDP**
Canada	1.3%	1.3%	2.6%
Germany	−0.4	2.0	1.6
Japan	−0.8	2.1	1.3
United States	0.9	1.9	2.8

The most striking result is the difference in labor force growth in Germany and Japan in contrast to that in the United States and Canada. Most of the difference between the growth rates in potential GDP among these countries can be explained by the demographic factor. The results suggest that Japan's sluggish growth over the last two decades is likely to continue. The weak productivity growth in Canada is of concern and is indicative of a low rate of innovation among Canadian companies.

EXAMPLE 18

Prospects for Fixed-Income Investments

As a fixed-income analyst for a large Canadian bank, you have just received the latest GDP forecast from the OECD for Canada, Germany, Japan, and the United States. The forecast is given below:

Exhibit 30 OECD GDP Forecast	
	Projected Average Annual GDP Growth (2010–2012)
Canada	4.0%
Germany	1.5
Japan	0.5
United States	3.8

To evaluate the future prospects for fixed-income investments, analysts must estimate the future rate of inflation and assess the possibility of changes in monetary policy by the central bank. An important indicator for both of these factors is the degree of slack in the economy. One way to measure the degree of slack in the economy is to compare the growth rates of actual GDP and potential GDP.

Based on the estimates of potential GDP from the previous example and the information in Exhibit 30, evaluate the prospects for fixed-income investments in each of the countries.

Solution:

In comparing the OECD forecast for GDP growth with the estimated growth rate in potential GDP, there are two cases to consider:

1 If actual GDP is growing at a faster rate than potential GDP, it signals growing inflationary pressures and an increased likelihood that the central bank will raise interest rates.

2 If actual GDP is growing at a slower rate than potential GDP, it signals growing resource slack, less inflationary pressures, and an increased likelihood that the central bank will reduce rates or leave them unchanged.

Exhibit 31 provides a comparison of actual and potential GDP for the above countries.

Exhibit 31	Actual vs. Potential GDP	
	Projected Average Annual GDP Growth (2010–2012)	**Potential GDP Growth**
Canada	4.0%	2.6%
Germany	1.5	1.6
Japan	0.5	1.3
United States	3.8	2.8

The data suggest that inflationary pressure will grow in the United States and Canada and that both the Federal Reserve and the Bank of Canada will eventually raise interest rates. Thus, the environment for bond investing is not favorable in the United States and Canada, because bond prices are likely to decline.

With Germany growing at its potential rate of GDP growth, the rate of inflation should neither rise nor fall. Monetary policy is set by the European Central Bank (ECB), but data on the German economy play a big role in the ECB's decision. Based on the above data, no change in ECB policy is likely. For bond investors, little change in bond prices is likely in Germany, so investors need to focus on the interest (coupon) income received from the bond.

Finally, growing resource slack in Japan will put downward pressure on inflation and may force the Bank of Japan to keep rates low. Bond prices should rise in this environment.

SUMMARY

This reading introduces important macroeconomic concepts and principles for macroeconomic forecasting and related investment decision making. Macroeconomics examines the economy as a whole by focusing on a country's aggregate output of final goods and services, total income, aggregate expenditures, and the general price level. The first step in macroeconomic analysis is to measure the size of an economy. Gross domestic product enables us to assign a monetary value to an economy's level of output or aggregate expenditures. The interaction of aggregate demand and aggregate supply determines the level of GDP as well as the general price level. The business cycle reflects shifts in aggregate demand and short-run aggregate supply. The long-term sustainable growth rate of the economy depends on growth in the supply and quality of inputs (labor, capital, and natural resources) and advances in technology. From an investment perspective, macroeconomic analysis and forecasting are important because business profits, asset valuations, interest rates, and inflation rates depend on the business cycle in the short to intermediate term and on the drivers of sustainable economic growth in the long term. In addition, it is important to understand fiscal and monetary policies' economic impact on and implications for inflation, household consumption and saving, capital investment, and exports.

- GDP is the market value of all final goods and services produced within a country in a given time period.
- GDP can be valued by looking at either the total amount spent on goods and services produced in the economy or the income generated in producing those goods and services.

- GDP counts only final purchases of newly produced goods and services during the current time period. Transfer payments and capital gains are excluded from GDP.

- With the exception of owner-occupied housing and government services, which are estimated at imputed values, GDP includes only goods and services that are valued by being sold in the market.

- Intermediate goods are excluded from GDP in order to avoid double counting.

- GDP can be measured either from the value of final output or by summing the value added at each stage of the production and distribution process. The sum of the value added by each stage is equal to the final selling price of the good.

- Nominal GDP is the value of production using the prices of the current year. Real GDP measures production using the constant prices of a base year. The GDP deflator equals the ratio of nominal GDP to real GDP.

- Households earn income in exchange for providing—directly or indirectly through ownership of businesses—the factors of production (labor, capital, natural resources including land). From this income, they consume, save, and pay net taxes.

- Businesses produce most of the economy's output/income and invest to maintain and expand productive capacity. Companies retain some earnings but pay out most of their revenue as income to the household sector and as taxes to the government.

- The government sector collects taxes from households and businesses and purchases goods and services from the private business sector.

- Foreign trade consists of exports and imports. The difference between the two is net exports. If net exports are positive (negative), then the country spends less (more) than it earns. Net exports are balanced by accumulation of either claims on the rest of the world (net exports > 0) or obligations to the rest of the world (net exports < 0).

- Capital markets provide a link between saving and investment in the economy.

- From the expenditure side, GDP includes personal consumption (C), gross private domestic investment (I), government spending (G), and net exports ($X - M$).

- The major categories of expenditure are often broken down into subcategories. Gross private domestic investment includes both investment in fixed assets (plant and equipment) and the change in inventories. In some countries, government investment spending is separated from other government spending.

- National income is the income received by all factors of production used in the generation of final output. It equals GDP minus the capital consumption allowance (depreciation) and a statistical discrepancy.

- Personal income reflects pre-tax income received by households. It equals national income plus transfers minus undistributed corporate profits, corporate income taxes, and indirect business taxes.

- Personal disposable income equals personal income minus personal taxes.

- Private saving must equal investment plus the fiscal and trade deficits. That is, $S = I + (G - T) + (X - M)$.

- Consumption spending is a function of disposable income. The marginal propensity to consume represents the fraction of an additional unit of disposable income that is spent.

- Investment spending depends on the average interest rate and the level of aggregate income. Government purchases and tax policy are often considered to be exogenous variables determined outside the macroeconomic model. Actual taxes collected depend on income and are, therefore, endogenous—that is, determined within the model.

- The IS curve reflects combinations of GDP and the real interest rate such that aggregate income/output equals planned expenditures. The LM curve reflects combinations of GDP and the interest rate such that demand and supply of real money balances are equal.

- Combining the IS and LM relationships yields the aggregate demand curve.

- Aggregate demand and aggregate supply determine the level of real GDP and the price level.

- The aggregate demand curve is the relationship between real output (GDP) demanded and the price level, holding underlying factors constant. Movements along the aggregate demand curve reflect the impact of price on demand.

- The aggregate demand curve is downward sloping because a rise in the price level reduces wealth, raises real interest rates, and raises the price of domestically produced goods versus foreign goods. The aggregate demand curve is drawn assuming a constant money supply.

- The aggregate demand curve will shift if there is a change in a factor, other than price, that affects aggregate demand. These factors include household wealth, consumer and business expectations, capacity utilization, monetary policy, fiscal policy, exchange rates, and foreign GDP.

- The aggregate supply curve is the relationship between the quantity of real GDP supplied and the price level, keeping all other factors constant. Movements along the supply curve reflect the impact of price on supply.

- The short-run aggregate supply curve is upward sloping because higher prices result in higher profits and induce businesses to produce more and laborers to work more. In the short run, some prices are sticky, implying that some prices do not adjust to changes in demand.

- In the long run, all prices are assumed to be flexible. The long-run aggregate supply curve is vertical because input costs adjust to changes in output prices, leaving the optimal level of output unchanged. The position of the curve is determined by the economy's level of potential GDP.

- The level of potential output, also called the full employment or natural level of output, is unobservable and difficult to measure precisely. This concept represents an efficient and unconstrained level of production at which companies have enough spare capacity to avoid bottlenecks and there is a balance between the pool of unemployed workers and the pool of job openings.

- The long-run aggregate supply curve will shift because of changes in labor supply, supply of physical and human capital, and productivity/technology.

- The short-run supply curve will shift because of changes in potential GDP, nominal wages, input prices, expectations about future prices, business taxes and subsidies, and the exchange rate.

- The business cycle and short-term fluctuations in GDP are caused by shifts in aggregate demand and aggregate supply.

- When the level of GDP in the economy is below potential GDP, such a recessionary situation exerts downward pressure on the aggregate price level.

- When the level of GDP is above potential GDP, such an overheated situation puts upward pressure on the aggregate price level.

- Stagflation, a combination of high inflation and weak economic growth, is caused by a decline in short-run aggregate supply.

- The sustainable rate of economic growth is measured by the rate of increase in the economy's productive capacity or potential GDP.

- Growth in real GDP measures how rapidly the total economy is expanding. Per capita GDP, defined as real GDP divided by population, reflects the standard of living in a country. Real GDP growth rates and levels of per capita GDP vary widely among countries.

- The sources of economic growth include the supply of labor, the supply of physical and human capital, raw materials, and technological knowledge.

- Output can be described in terms of a production function. For example, $Y = AF(L, K)$ where L is the quantity of labor, K is the capital stock, and A represents technological knowledge or total factor productivity. The function $F(\cdot)$ is assumed to exhibit constant returns to scale but diminishing marginal productivity for each input individually.

- Total factor productivity is a scale factor that reflects the portion of output growth that is not accounted for by changes in the capital and labor inputs. TFP is mainly a reflection of technological change.

- Based on a two-factor production function, Potential GDP growth = Growth in TFP + W_L (Growth in labor) + W_C (Growth in capital), where W_L and W_C (= 1 − W_L) are the shares of labor and capital in GDP.

- Diminishing marginal productivity implies that
  - Increasing the supply of some input(s) relative to other inputs will lead to diminishing returns and cannot be the basis for sustainable growth. In particular, long-term sustainable growth cannot rely solely on capital deepening, that is, increasing the stock of capital relative to labor.
  - Given the relative scarcity and hence high productivity of capital in developing countries, the growth rate of developing countries should exceed that of developed countries.

- The labor supply is determined by population growth, the labor force participation rate, and net immigration. The capital stock in a country increases with investment. Correlation between long-run economic growth and the rate of investment is high.

- In addition to labor, capital, and technology, human capital—essentially, the quality of the labor force—and natural resources are important determinants of output and growth.

- Technological advances are discoveries that make it possible to produce more and/or higher-quality goods and services with the same resources or inputs. Technology is the main factor affecting economic growth in developed countries.

- The sustainable rate of growth in an economy is determined by the growth rate of the labor supply plus the growth rate of labor productivity.

REFERENCES

Case, K., J. Quigley, and R. Shiller. 2005. "Comparing Wealth Effects: The Stock Market versus the Housing Market." *Advances in Macroeconomics*, vol. 5, no. 1.

Funke, N. 2004. "Is There a Stock Market Wealth Effect in Emerging Markets?" *International Monetary Fund* (March).

PRACTICE PROBLEMS

1   Which of the following statements is the *most* appropriate description of gross domestic product (GDP)?

    A   The total income earned by all households, firms, and the government whose value can be verified.

    B   The total amount spent on all final goods and services produced within the economy over a given time period.

    C   The total market value of resalable and final goods and services produced within the economy over a given time period.

2   The component *least likely* to be included in a measurement of gross domestic product (GDP) is:

    A   the value of owner occupied rent.

    B   the annual salary of a local police officer.

    C   environmental damage caused by production.

3   Which of the following conditions is *least likely* to increase a country's GDP?

    A   An increase in net exports.

    B   Increased investment in capital goods.

    C   Increased government transfer payments.

4   Which of the following would be included in Canadian GDP for a given year? The market value of:

    A   wine grown in Canada by US citizens.

    B   electronics made in Japan and sold in Canada.

    C   movies produced outside Canada by Canadian film makers.

5   Suppose a painting is produced and sold in 2010 for £5,000. The expenses involved in producing the painting amounted to £2,000. According to the sum-of-value-added method of calculating GDP, the value added by the final step of creating the painting was:

    A   £2,000.

    B   £3,000.

    C   £5,000.

6   A GDP deflator less than 1 indicates that an economy has experienced:

    A   inflation.

    B   deflation.

    C   stagflation.

7   The *most* accurate description of nominal GDP is:

    A   a measure of total expenditures at current prices.

    B   the value of goods and services at constant prices.

    C   a measure to compare one nation's economy to another.

8   From the beginning to the ending years of a decade, the annual value of final goods and services for country X increased from €100 billion to €300 billion. Over that time period, the GDP deflator increased from 111 to 200. Over the decade, real GDP for country X increased by approximately:

    A   50%.

B 67%.

C 200%.

9 If the GDP deflator values for 2008 and 2010 were 190 and 212.8, respectively, which of the following *best* describes the annual growth rate of the overall price level?

A 5.8%.

B 6%.

C 12%.

10 The numerator of the GDP price deflator reflects:

A the value of base year output at current prices.

B the value of current year output at current prices.

C the value of current year output at base year prices.

11 Consider the following data for 2010 for a hypothetical country:

Account name	Amount ($ trillions)
Consumption	15.0
Capital consumption allowance	1.5
Government spending	3.8
Imports	1.7
Gross private domestic investment	4.0
Exports	1.5

Based only on the data given, the gross domestic product and national income are respectively *closest* to:

A 21.1 and 20.6.

B 22.6 and 21.1.

C 22.8 and 20.8.

12 In calculating personal income for a given year, which of the following would *not* be subtracted from national income?

A Indirect business taxes.

B Undistributed corporate profits.

C Unincorporated business net income.

13 Equality between aggregate expenditure and aggregate output implies that the government's fiscal deficit must equal:

A Private saving – Investment – Net exports.

B Private saving – Investment + Net exports.

C Investment – Private saving + Net exports.

14 Because of a sharp decline in real estate values, the household sector has increased the fraction of disposable income that it saves. If output and investment spending remain unchanged, which of the following is *most likely*?

A A decrease in the government deficit.

B A decrease in net exports and increased capital inflow.

C An increase in net exports and increased capital outflow.

15 Which curve represents combinations of income and the real interest rate at which planned expenditure equals income?

A The IS curve.

B   The LM curve.

C   The aggregate demand curve.

16   An increase in government spending would shift the:

   A   IS curve and the LM curve.

   B   IS curve and the aggregate demand curve.

   C   LM curve and the aggregate demand curve.

17   An increase in the nominal money supply would shift the:

   A   IS curve and the LM curve.

   B   IS curve and the aggregate demand curve.

   C   LM curve and the aggregate demand curve.

18   An increase in the price level would shift the:

   A   IS curve.

   B   LM curve.

   C   aggregate demand curve.

19   As the price level declines along the aggregate demand curve, the interest rate is *most likely* to:

   A   decline.

   B   increase.

   C   remain unchanged.

20   The full employment, or natural, level of output is *best* described as:

   A   the maximum level obtainable with existing resources.

   B   the level at which all available workers have jobs consistent with their skills.

   C   a level with a modest, stable pool of unemployed workers transitioning to new jobs.

21   Which of the following *best* describes the aggregate supply curve in the short-run (e.g., 1 to 2 years)? The short run aggregate supply curve is:

   A   flat because output is more flexible than prices in the short run.

   B   vertical because wages and other input prices fully adjust to the price level.

   C   upward sloping because input prices do not fully adjust to the price level in the short run.

22   If wages were automatically adjusted for changes in the price level, the short-run aggregate supply curve would *most likely* be:

   A   flatter.

   B   steeper.

   C   unchanged.

23   The *least likely* cause of a decrease in aggregate demand is:

   A   higher taxes.

   B   a weak domestic currency.

   C   a fall in capacity utilization.

24   Which of the following is *most likely* to cause the long-run aggregate supply curve to shift to the left?

   A   Higher nominal wages.

   B   A decline in productivity.

   C   A increase in corporate taxes.

25   Increased household wealth will *most likely* cause an increase in:

    A household saving.

    B investment expenditures.

    C consumption expenditures.

26 The *most likely* outcome when both aggregate supply and aggregate demand increase is:

    A a rise in inflation.

    B higher employment.

    C an increase in nominal GDP.

27 Which of the following is *least likely* to be caused by a shift in aggregate demand?

    A Stagflation.

    B A recessionary gap.

    C An inflationary gap.

28 Following a sharp increase in the price of energy, the overall price level is *most likely* to rise in the short run:

    A and remain elevated indefinitely unless the central bank tightens.

    B but be unchanged in the long run unless the money supply is increased.

    C and continue to rise until all prices have increased by the same proportion.

29 Among developed economies, which of the following sources of economic growth is *most likely* to explain superior growth performance?

    A Technology.

    B Capital stock.

    C Labor supply.

30 Which of the following can be measured directly?

    A Potential GDP.

    B Labor productivity.

    C Total factor productivity.

31 The sustainable growth rate is *best* estimated as:

    A the weighted average of capital and labor growth rates.

    B growth in the labor force plus growth of labor productivity.

    C growth in total factor productivity plus growth in the capital-to-labor ratio.

32 In the neoclassical or Solow growth model, an increase in total factor productivity reflects an increase in:

    A returns to scale.

    B output for given inputs.

    C the sustainable growth rate.

The following information relates to Questions 33–34

An economic forecasting firm has estimated the following equation from historical data based on the neoclassical growth model:

Potential output growth = 1.5 + 0.72 × Growth of labor + 0.28 × Growth of capital

33 The intercept (1.5) in this equation is *best* interpreted as:

A   the long-run sustainable growth rate.

B   the growth rate of total factor productivity.

C   above trend historical growth that is unlikely to be sustained.

34 The coefficient on the growth rate of labor (0.72) in this equation is *best* interpreted as:

A   the labor force participation rate.

B   the marginal productivity of labor.

C   the share of income earned by labor.

---

35 Convergence of incomes over time between emerging market countries and developed countries is *most likely* due to:

A   total factor productivity.

B   diminishing marginal productivity of capital.

C   the exhaustion of non-renewable resources.

SOLUTIONS

1 B is correct. GDP is the total amount spent on all final goods and services produced within the economy over a specific period of time.

2 C is correct. By-products of production processes that have no explicit market value are not included in GDP.

3 C is correct. Government transfer payments, such as unemployment compensation or welfare benefits, are excluded from GDP.

4 A is correct. Canadian GDP is the total market value of all final goods and services produced in a given time period within Canada. The wine was produced in Canada and counts towards Canadian GDP.

5 B is correct. This is the value added by the artist: £5,000 – £2,000 = £3,000.

6 B is correct. The GDP Deflator = Nominal GDP/Real GDP. To get a ratio less than 1, real GDP exceeds nominal GDP, which indicates that prices have decreased and, accordingly, deflation has occurred.

7 A is correct. Nominal GDP is defined as the value of goods and services measured at current prices. Expenditure is used synonymously with the value of goods and services since aggregate expenditures must equal aggregate output of an economy.

8 B is correct. Real GDP in the first year was €100 billion/1.11 = €90 and in the last year it was €300 billion/2.00 = €150. Thus, (€150 – €90)/€90 = 0.67 or 67%.

9 A is correct: $(212.8/190)^{1/2} - 1 = 0.0583$ or 5.8%.

10 B is correct.

$$\text{GDP deflator} = \frac{\text{Value of current year output at current year prices}}{\text{Value of current year output at base year prices}} \times 100$$

11 B is correct. GDP = Consumption + Gross private domestic investment + Government Spending + Exports – Imports = 15 + 4 + 3.8 + 1.5 – 1.7 = 22.6. National income = GDP – CCA = 22.6 – 1.5 = 21.1

12 C is correct. Unincorporated business net income is also known as proprietor's income and is included in personal income.

13 A is correct. The fundamental relationship among saving, investment, the fiscal balance, and the trade balance is $S = I + (G - T) + (X - M)$. This form of the relationship shows that private saving must fund investment expenditures, the government fiscal balance, and net exports (= net capital outflows). Rearranging gives $G - T = (S - I) - (X - M)$. The government's fiscal deficit $(G - T)$ must be equal to the private sector's saving/investment balance $(S - I)$ minus net exports.

14 C is correct. The fundamental relationship among saving, investment, the fiscal balance, and the trade balance is $S = I + (G - T) + (X - M)$. Given the levels of output and investment spending, an increase in saving (reduction in consumption) must be offset by either an increase in the fiscal deficit or an increase in net exports. Increasing the fiscal deficit is not one of the choices, so an increase in net exports and corresponding increase in net capital outflows (increased lending to foreigners and/or increased purchases of assets from foreigners) is the correct response.

15 A is correct. The IS curve represents combinations of income and the real interest rate at which planned expenditure equals income.

16 B is correct. The IS curve represents combinations of income and the real interest rate at which planned expenditure equals income. Equivalently, it represents combinations such that

$$S(Y) = I(r) + (G - T) + (X - M)$$

where $S(Y)$ indicates that planned saving is a (increasing) function of income and $I(r)$ indicates that planned investment is a (decreasing) function of the real interest rate. To maintain this relationship, an increase in government spending (G) requires an increase in saving at any given level of the interest rate (r). This implies an increase in income (Y) at each interest rate level—a rightward shift of the IS curve. Unless the LM curve is vertical, the IS and LM curves will intersect at a higher level of aggregate expenditure/income. Since the LM curve embodies a constant price level, this implies an increase in aggregate expenditure at each price level—a rightward shift of the Aggregate Demand curve.

17 C is correct. The LM curve represents combinations of income and the interest rate at which the demand for real money balances equals the supply. For a given price level, an increase in the nominal money supply is also an increase in the real money supply. To increase the demand for real money balances, either the interest must decline or income must increase. Therefore, at each level of the interest rate, income (= expenditure) must increase—a rightward shift of the LM curve. Since the IS curve is downward sloping (higher income requires a lower interest rate), a rightward shift in the LM curve means that the IS and LM curves will intersect at a higher level of aggregate expenditure/income. This implies a higher level of aggregate expenditure at each price level—a rightward shift of the Aggregate Demand curve.

18 B is correct. The LM curve represents combinations of income and the interest rate at which the demand for real money balances equals the supply. For a given nominal money supply, an increase in the price level implies a decrease in the real money supply. To decrease the demand for real money balances, either the interest must increase or income must decrease. Therefore, at each level of the interest rate, income (= expenditure) must decrease—a leftward shift of the LM curve.

19 A is correct. A decrease in the price level increases the real money supply and shifts the LM curve to the right. Since the IS curve is downward sloping, the IS and LM curves will intersect at a higher level of income and a lower interest rate.

20 C is correct. At the full employment, or natural, level of output the economy is operating at an efficient and unconstrained level of production. Companies have enough spare capacity to avoid bottlenecks, and there is a modest, stable pool of unemployed workers (job seekers equal job vacancies) looking for and transitioning into new jobs.

21 C is correct. Due to long-term contracts and other rigidities, wages and other input costs do not fully adjust to changes in the price level in the short-run. Given input prices, firms respond to output price changes by expanding or contracting output to maximize profit. Hence, the SRAS is upward sloping.

22 B is correct. The slope of the short-run aggregate supply curve reflects the extent to which wages and other input costs adjust to the overall price level. Automatic adjustment of wages would mitigate the impact of price changes on profitability. Hence, firms would not adjust output as much in response to changing output prices—the SRAS curve would be steeper.

23 B is correct. A weak domestic currency will result in an increase in aggregate demand at each price level—a rightward shift in the AD curve. A weaker currency will cause a country's exports to be cheaper in global markets. Conversely, imports will be more expensive for domestic buyers. Hence, the net exports component of aggregate demand will increase.

24 B is correct. Productivity measures the efficiency of labor and is the amount of output produced by workers in a given period of time. A decline in productivity implies decreased efficiency. A decline in productivity increases labor costs, decreases profitability and results in lower output at each output price level—a leftward shift in both the short-run and long-run aggregate supply curves.

25 C is correct. The wealth effect explains the impact of increases or decreases in household wealth on economic activity. Household wealth includes financial and real assets. As asset values increase, consumers save less and spend more out of current income since they will still be able to meet their wealth accumulation goals. Therefore, an increase in household wealth results in a rightward shift in the aggregate demand curve.

26 B is correct. Higher aggregate demand (AD) and higher aggregate supply (AS) raise real GDP and lower unemployment, meaning employment levels increase.

27 A is correct. Stagflation occurs when output is declining and prices are rising. This is most likely due to a decline in aggregate supply—a leftward shift of the SRAS curve. Depending on the source of the shift, the LRAS may shift too.

28 B is correct. An increase in energy prices will shift the short-run aggregate supply curve (SRAS) to the left, reducing output and increasing prices. If there is no change in the aggregate demand curve, in particular if the central bank does not expand the money supply, slack in the economy will put downward pressure on in input prices, shifting the SRAS back to its original position. In the long run, the price level will be unchanged.

29 A is correct. Technology is the most important factor affecting economic growth for developed countries. Technological advances are very important because they allow an economy to overcome the limits imposed by diminishing marginal returns.

30 B is correct. Labor productivity can be directly measured as output/hour.

31 B is correct. Output growth is equal to the growth rate of the labor force plus the growth rate of labor productivity, i.e. output per worker. Unlike total factor productivity, output per worker is observable, so this is the most practical way to approach estimation of sustainable growth.

32 B is correct. Total factor productivity (TFP) is a scale factor primarily reflecting technology. An increase in TFP means that output increases for any level of factor inputs.

33 B is correct. The estimated equation is the standard Solow growth accounting equation. The intercept is the growth rate of total factor productivity.

34 C is correct. In the standard Solow growth accounting equation, the coefficient on each factor's growth rate is its share of income.

35 B is correct. Diminishing marginal productivity of capital means that as a country accumulates more capital per worker the incremental boost to output declines. Thus, all else the same, economies grow more slowly as they become more capital intensive. Given the relative scarcity and hence high marginal productivity of capital in developing countries, they tend to grow more rapidly than developed countries. This leads to convergence in income levels over time.

Understanding Business Cycles

by Michele Gambera, PhD, CFA, Milton Ezrati, and Bolong Cao, PhD, CFA

Michele Gambera, PhD, CFA, is at UBS Global Asset Management (USA). Milton Ezrati (USA). Bolong Cao, PhD, CFA, is at Ohio University (USA).

LEARNING OUTCOMES

Mastery	The candidate should be able to:
☐	a. describe the business cycle and its phases;
☐	b. describe how resource use, housing sector activity, and external trade sector activity vary as an economy moves through the business cycle;
☐	c. describe theories of the business cycle;
☐	d. describe types of unemployment and measures of unemployment;
☐	e. explain inflation, hyperinflation, disinflation, and deflation;
☐	f. explain the construction of indices used to measure inflation;
☐	g. compare inflation measures, including their uses and limitations;
☐	h. distinguish between cost-push and demand-pull inflation;
☐	i. describe economic indicators, including their uses and limitations;

INTRODUCTION

1

Agricultural societies experience good harvest years and bad ones. Weather is a main factor influencing whether the crops will be abundant or scarce, but of course there are also other factors, including plant and animal diseases. Ancient writings include stories of alternating good and bad production years. Modern diversified economies are less influenced by weather and diseases.

Whereas the reading on national income accounting and growth focuses on long-term economic growth and the factors that help foster it, this reading addresses short-term movements in economic activity. Some of the factors causing such short-term movements are the same as those causing economic growth, such as changes in population, technology, and capital. However, other factors, such as money and inflation, are more specific to short-term fluctuations.

This reading is organized as follows. Section 2 describes the business cycle and its phases, explaining the behaviors of businesses and households that typically characterize phases and transitions between phases. Section 3 provides an introduction to business cycle theory, in particular how different economic schools of thought interpret the business cycle and their recommendations with respect to it. Section 4 introduces basic concepts concerning unemployment and inflation, two important economic policy concerns that are sensitive to the business cycle. Section 5 discusses variables that fluctuate in predictable time relationships with the economy, focusing on variables whose movements have value in predicting the future course of the economy. A summary and practice problems conclude the reading.

2 OVERVIEW OF THE BUSINESS CYCLE

Burns and Mitchell (1946) define the business cycle as follows:

> Business cycles are a type of fluctuation found in the aggregate economic activity of nations that organize their work mainly in business enterprises: a cycle consists of expansions occurring at about the same time in many economic activities, followed by similarly general recessions, contractions, and revivals which merge into the expansion phase of the next cycle; this sequence of events is recurrent but not periodic; in duration, business cycles vary from more than one year to 10 or 12 years.

This long definition is rich with important insights. First, business cycles are typical of economies that rely mainly on business enterprises—therefore, not agrarian societies or centrally planned economies. Second, a cycle has an expected sequence of phases representing alternation between expansion and contraction. Third, such phases occur at about the same time throughout the economy—that is, not just in agriculture or not just in tourism but in almost all sectors. Fourth, cycles are recurrent (i.e., they happen again and again over time) but not periodic (i.e., they do not all have the exact same intensity and/or duration). Finally, cycles typically last between 1 and 12 years.

Although Burns and Mitchell's definition may appear obvious in part, it indeed remains helpful even more than 60 years after it was written. Many investors like to think that there are simple regularities that occur at exactly the same time, every year or cycle: For example, shares always rally in January and big crashes occur in October. Of course, things are quite more complex. The truth, as Burns and Mitchell remind us, is that history never repeats itself exactly, but it certainly has similarities that can be taken into account when analyzing the present and forecasting the future.

2.1 Phases of the Business Cycle

A business cycle consists of four phases: trough, expansion, peak, contraction. The period of **expansion** occurs after the **trough** (lowest point) of a business cycle and before its **peak** (highest point), and **contraction** is the period after the peak and before the trough.[1] During the expansion phase, aggregate economic activity is increasing (*aggregate* is used because some individual economic sectors may not be growing). The contraction—often called a **recession**, but may be called a **depression** when

---

1 For more information, see www.nber.org/cycles/recessions.html.

exceptionally severe—is a period in which aggregate economic activity is declining (although some individual sectors may be growing). Business cycles are usually viewed as fluctuations around the trend growth of an economy, so such points as peaks and troughs are relative to the individual cycle.

Panel A of Exhibit 1 shows a stylized representation of the business cycle and Panel B provides a description of some important characteristics of each phase. The description distinguishes between early and late stages of the expansion phase, which are close to cycle turning points. Panel B also describes how several important economic variables evolve through the course of a business cycle.

Exhibit 1   Panel A: Schematic of Business Cycle Phases

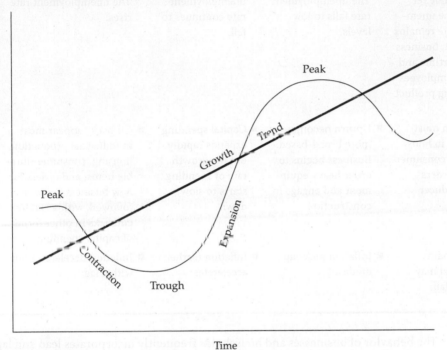

Level of National Economic Activity

Peak

Trend

Growth

Expansion

Peak

Contraction

Trough

Time

Exhibit 1	Panel B: Characteristics			
	Early Expansion (Recovery)	**Late Expansion**	**Peak**	**Contraction (Recession)**
Economic Activity	▪ Gross domestic product (GDP), industrial production, and other measures of economic activity turn from decline to expansion.	▪ Activity measures show an accelerating rate of growth.	▪ Activity measures show decelerating rate of growth.	▪ Activity measures show outright declines.
Employment	▪ Layoffs slow (and net employment turns positive), but new hiring does not yet occur and the unemployment rate remains high. At first, business turns to overtime and temporary employees to meet rising product demands.	▪ Business begins full time rehiring as overtime hours rise. The unemployment rate falls to low levels.	▪ Business slows its rate of hiring; however, the unemployment rate continues to fall.	▪ Business first cuts hours and freezes hiring, followed by outright layoffs. The unemployment rate rises.
Consumer and Business Spending	▪ Upturn often most pronounced in housing, durable consumer items, and orders for light producer equipment.	▪ Upturn becomes more broad-based. Business begins to order heavy equipment and engage in construction.	▪ Capital spending expands rapidly, but the growth rate of spending starts to slow down.	▪ Cutbacks appear most in industrial production, housing, consumer durable items, and orders for new business equipment, followed, with a lag, by cutbacks in other forms of capital spending.
Inflation	▪ Inflation remains moderate and may continue to fall.	▪ Inflation picks up modestly.	▪ Inflation further accelerates.	▪ Inflation decelerates but with a lag.

The behavior of businesses and households frequently incorporates lead and lags, relative to what are established as turning points in a business cycle. For example, unemployment may not start decreasing immediately after the expansion phase starts because companies may want to fully use their existing workforce and wait to hire new employees until they are sure that the economy is indeed getting better. However, gradually all economic variables are going to revert toward their normal range of values (e.g., GDP growth will be a positive number). If any countercyclical economic policies were adopted during the recession, they would be gradually phased out; for example, if the central bank reduced interest rates to fight the recession, they should start increasing rates toward their historical norms. Central banks are the monetary authority in most modern economies.

During a recession, investors place relatively high values on such safer assets as government securities and shares of companies with steady (or growing) positive cash flows, such as utilities and producers of staple goods. Such preferences reflect the fact that the marginal value of a safe income stream increases in periods when employment is insecure or declining. When asset markets expect the end of a recession and the beginning of an expansion phase, they will re-price risky assets upward. When an expansion is in sight, the markets will start incorporating higher profit expectations into the prices of corporate bonds and stocks, particularly those of such cyclical companies as producers of discretionary goods, for example automobiles. Typically, equity markets will hit the trough about three to six months before the economy and well before the economic indicators turn up. Indeed, the equity stock market is classified as a leading indicator of the economy.

When an economy's expansion is well established, a later part of an expansion called a **boom** often follows. The boom is still an expansionary phase, which is characterized by economic growth "testing the limits" of the economy. For example, companies expand so much that they will have difficulty finding qualified workers, and therefore will start bidding wars to hire competitor's employees. The accompanying rise in labor costs causes a reduction of profits. Another example is that companies start believing that the economy will continue expanding for the foreseeable future, and therefore decide to borrow money to expand their production capacity. Clearly, these two examples represent situations that cannot go on forever; salaries and invested capital cannot grow exponentially without affecting profit margins. At this point, the government and/or its central bank often steps in to attempt to correct excesses. Consider the following situation. The central bank is concerned that excessive salary growth may lead to inflation. For example, companies will try to pass on higher production costs to their customers or excessive borrowing may cause investors to have cash flow problems. At the height of the boom phase, the economy is said to be overheating (just like the engine of a car that has been pushed to an excessive level).

During the boom, the riskiest assets will often have substantial price increases. Safe assets, such as government bonds that were more highly prized during the recession, may have lower prices and thus higher yields. In addition, investors may fear higher inflation, which also contributes to higher nominal yields.

The end of the expansion, or boom, is characterized by the peak of the business cycle, which is also the beginning of the contraction (also known as downturn). Here, either because of restrictive economic policies established to tame an overheated economy or because of other shocks, such as energy prices or a credit crisis, the economy stumbles and starts slowing down. Unemployment will increase and GDP growth will decrease during this part of the business cycle.

EXAMPLE 1

When Do Recessions Begin and End?

A simple and commonly referred to rule is: A recession has started when a country or region experiences two consecutive quarters of negative real GDP growth. Real GDP growth is a measure of the "real" or "inflation-adjusted" growth of the overall economy. This rule can be misleading because it does not indicate a recession if real GDP growth is negative in one quarter, slightly positive the next quarter, and again negative in the next quarter. Many analysts question this result. This issue is why, in some countries, there are statistical and economic committees that apply the principles stated by Burns and Mitchell to several macroeconomic variables (and not just real GDP growth) as a basis to identify business cycle peaks and troughs. The National Bureau of Economic Research (NBER) is the well-known organization that dates business cycles in the United States. Interestingly, the economists and statisticians on NBER's Business Cycle Dating Committee analyze numerous time series of data focusing on employment, industrial production, and sales. Because the data are available with a delay (preliminary data releases can be revised even one year after the period they refer to), it also means that the Committee's determinations may take place well after the business cycle turning points have occurred. As we will see later in the reading, there are practical indicators that may help economists understand in advance if a cyclical turning point is about to happen.

1 Which of the following rules is *most* commonly used to determine when recessions start? Recessions start when:

A the central bank runs out of foreign reserves.

B real GDP has two consecutive quarters of negative growth.

C economic activity experiences a material decline in two business sectors.

2 Suppose you are interested in forecasting earnings growth for a company active in a country where no official business cycle dating committee (such as the NBER) exists. Which variables would you consider to estimate peaks and troughs of that country's business cycles, in addition to any existing index of leading indicators?

A Inflation, the central bank's discount rate, and unemployment.

B The DJIA, equity market average book value, and monetary base.

C Unemployment, GDP growth, industrial production, and inflation.

Solution to 1:

B is correct. GDP is the measure for the whole economy, whereas foreign reserves or a limited number of sectors may not have material impact on the whole economy.

Solution to 2:

C is correct. The discount rate, the monetary base, and stock market indices are not direct measures of economic activities. The first two are determined by monetary policy, which react to economic activities, whereas the stock market indices tend to be forward looking.

The types of assets that tend to outperform during the contraction phase vary with the events that trigger the crisis. For example, in the case of a bank crisis, investors may panic and try to sell risky assets at any price, hoping to buy safer assets. In the case of a slowdown as a result of restrictive economic policies within the country, investors may try to buy shares of exporting companies.

Investors, who are often optimists in the expansion phase, tend to be overly pessimistic at the bottom of the recession. During recent economic history in many countries, such as the United States, economic contractions have been shorter than expansions.

Many economic variables and sectors of the economy have distinctive cyclical patterns. Knowledge of these patterns can offer insight into likely cyclical directions overall or can be particularly applicable to an investment strategy that requires more specific rather than general cyclical insights for investment success. The following sections provide overviews of how the use of resources (the factors of production) typically evolves through the business cycle and how the sectors of real estate and external trade characteristically behave.

2.2 Resource Use through the Business Cycle

This section provides a broad overview of how the use of resources needed to produce goods and services typically evolves during a business cycle.

There are significant links between fluctuations in inventory, employment, and investment in physical capital with economic fluctuations. When a downturn starts, for example because of a monetary or fiscal tightening, aggregate demand (AD) decreases, shifting the AD curve left; as a result, inventories start to accumulate. Exhibit 2 displays this shift from AD_1 to AD_2 along with the long-run aggregate supply (LRAS) and short-run aggregate supply (SRAS) curves. This shift occurs because demand decreases and companies end up with an excess of inputs and intermediate products ready for production, as well as final products ready for sale. As a consequence, companies may slow down production, thus idling workers (e.g., no more overtime) and physical capital (e.g., the equipment is used at less than full capacity), which further decreases aggregate demand and shifts the AD curve even further to the left (in Exhibit 2, AD_2 shifts to AD_3). In total, the equilibrium has moved to lower prices (from $Price_a$ to $Price_b$) and lower GDP (from GDP_a to GDP_b).

Exhibit 2   Policy-Triggered Recession

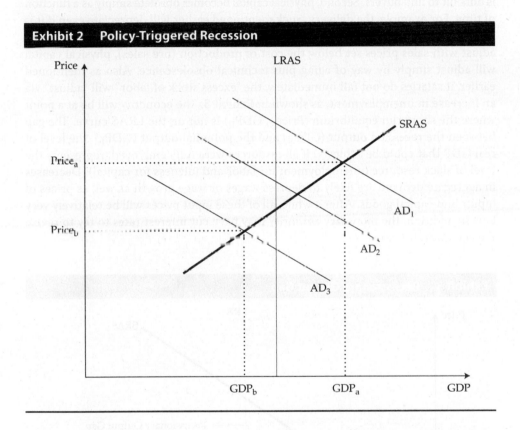

Companies do not start firing workers right away. First of all, if it is just a temporary slowdown for the economy, these workers may be needed again soon, so it is better to retain their jobs. In particular, selecting and training new workers is costly and it is efficient to keep workers on payroll, even if they are not fully utilized, while waiting out a short period of slow business. Second, some economists suggest that there is an implicit bond of loyalty between a company and its workers, and thus workers will be more productive if they know that the company is not disposing of them at the first sign of economic trouble.

Even though companies may not fire workers right away, they will likely reduce production and stop ordering new inventories and new production equipment. For example, if business slows down, there is no need to order an additional delivery truck—the existing trucks will be sufficient because there are fewer deliveries to make. If a large enough number of companies act similarly, the slow patch in business will be exacerbated. By the same token, if workers start worrying that lean years are coming, they may start saving more so they have more reserves. These actions will also reduce AD and further slow down the economy.

If the downturn becomes more severe, companies will start switching into recession mode—that is, they will cut all non-essential costs. This step often means terminating consultants, workers beyond the strict minimum, any standing supply orders, advertising campaigns, and so on. Capacity utilization will be low, and few companies will invest in new equipment and structures. In addition, because of the gloomy economic framework, banks will be wary of lending because bankruptcy risks will increase. Companies will try to liquidate their inventories of unsold products. As a result, the AD curve has a dramatic shift left toward an even lower GDP, and the economy enters what seems to be a downward spiral.

In an economic downturn, companies will probably not sell physical capital. First, it is difficult to find buyers. Second, physical capital becomes obsolete simply as a function of time. For example, the delivery truck mentioned earlier will depreciate even if it is being used at less than full capacity. Therefore, although the stock of inventories can adjust with sales prices set below the cost of production (fire sales), physical capital will adjust simply by way of aging plus technical obsolescence. Also as mentioned earlier, if salaries do not fall immediately, the "excess stock of labor" will "adjust" via an increase in unemployment, as shown in Exhibit 3. The economy will be at a point where the short-run equilibrium (Price$_R$, GDP$_R$) is not on the LRAS curve. The gap between the recession output (GDP$_R$) and the potential output (GDP$_P$), the level of real GDP that could be achieved if all resources were fully employed, represents the level of slack resource (unemployment for labor and idleness for capital). Decreases in aggregate demand are likely to depress wages or wage growth as well as prices of inputs and capital goods. After a while, all of these input prices will be relatively very low. In addition, the monetary authority may have cut interest rates to try to revive the economy.

Exhibit 3   Recessionary Output Gap

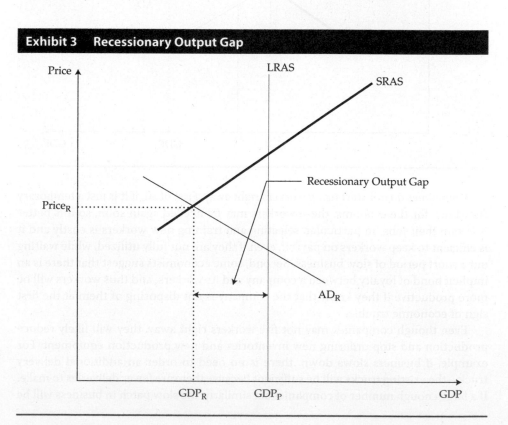

As the price or inflation rate starts to fall, consumers and companies begin to purchase more—that is, aggregate quantity demanded of output begins to rise. (The short-run equilibrium moves downward along the AD curve.) A consequence of these economic influences is that some companies will increase production because of inventories being low. Also, because interest rates have been cut lower, some companies and households will determine that building a more efficient warehouse or renovating a home has become relatively cheap, and therefore, will decide to start investing in structures, housing, and durable goods (equipment for companies, appliances for households). This stage is the turning point of the business cycle, when aggregate demand gradually starts to increase (the aggregate demand curve shifts right).

When the economic revival begins, companies will not immediately start the costly process of selecting and hiring new workers. They will wait for the expansion to give clear signs of life. However, if enough new investment triggers an increase in aggregate demand, companies will start replenishing their inventories. Low inventories mean that even if companies buy a little bit of inventory, there will be a short-term boom in demand for inputs and intermediate products, which will further support aggregate demand. This stage is often called inventory rebuilding or restocking in the financial press and may be followed by further capital expenditure (the one truck is now not sufficient for all deliveries). Demand for all factors of production increases.

As aggregate demand continues to grow, the boom phase of the cycle begins. Two different results of a boom phase could occur. First, the economy may experience shortages, and the demand for factors of production may exceed supply. Another possibility is that the excess demand comes from an overly optimistic buildup in production capacity, which means that supply of capital will greatly exceed demand a few months down the road (think of the excessive amount of fiber optic investments during the 1990s technology boom or the residential overbuilding in many countries during the 2000s housing bubble). These are possible triggers for the next recession.

2.2.1 Fluctuation in Capital Spending

This section describes how capital spending typically fluctuates with the business cycle. Because business profits and cash flows are extremely sensitive to the pace of economic activity, spending on new equipment and commercial structures is sensitive. Shifts in capital spending tend to affect the overall economic cycle in three stages or phases.

First, the downturn in spending on equipment usually occurs abruptly as final demand starts to fall off. Businesses, seeing a decline in sales and expecting a drop in profits and free cash flow, will halt new ordering and cancel existing orders if possible because they have no reason to expand production capacity in such a situation. The initial cuts occur in orders for technology and light equipment because there are short lead times from order to delivery and cutbacks simply require managers to decide against any additional orders. Because it sometimes takes longer to cancel or even halt construction activity or the installation of larger, more complex pieces of equipment, cutbacks in these areas unfold with a longer lag. Typically, the initial cutbacks at this phase exaggerate the economy's downward thrust. Then later, as the general cyclical downturn matures, cutbacks in spending on structures and heavy equipment add to the negative cyclical momentum.

In the second phase, when the economy begins its initial recovery, sales are still at such low levels that a business hardly utilizes all its existing capacity and has little need to expand it. But although capacity utilization remains low, orders begin to pick up tentatively for two reasons. First, the economic improvement creates growth in earnings and free cash flow that give businesses the financial wherewithal to increase spending. Second, the upturn in sales convinces managers to reinstate the more radical cancellations made in the uncertainty of the initial cyclical weakness, typically in equipment with a high rate of obsolescence, such as software, systems, and technological hardware. The shock of profit declines during a recession also instills a more general desire to make purchases that enhance efficiency more than those that expand capacity. As in the downturn, movements in new orders provide the first signal of recovery.

The third phase develops much later in the cyclical upturn, after a long period of output growth begins to strain the economy's overall productive capacity. Orders and sales at this phase of the cycle focus on capacity expansion and involve a higher proportion of heavy and complex equipment, warehouses, and factories. As the economic growth picks up speed, the capacity utilization starts to rise, a trend that cannot substitute for capital spending. In fact, spending on new capacity usually begins long before capacity would seem to need additions. This seeming disconnect occurs because economies are always changing their needs. Much that counts as capacity in the statistics becomes less relevant even though the underlying assets remain fully serviceable. The composition of the economy's capacity may not be optimal for the current economic structure, necessitating spending for new capital. A company, for instance, that needs more transportation equipment cannot substitute with a surplus of forklifts, although they are counted in overall capacity. Similarly, a company that needs warehouse space in the suburbs of Mumbai gains little relief from the surplus warehouse space in Goa. This last phase in the cyclical spending cycle may then occur surprisingly soon after capacity utilization picks up. Orders, of course, give the usual early indication of this phase.

The most watched indicator of the future direction of capital spending is orders for capital equipment because they precede moves in actual shipments.

EXAMPLE 2

Capital Spending

1 The most likely reason that US analysts often follow new orders for capital goods excluding defense and aircraft is because:

   A the military is part of the public sector.

   B aircraft and military orders are often the same so there is double counting.

   C armed forces and airlines tend to place infrequent and large (i.e., lumpy) orders, which create a false signal for the index.

2 Orders for equipment decline before construction orders in a recession because:

   A businesses are uncertain about cyclical directions.

   B they are easier to cancel than large construction contracts.

   C business values light equipment less than structures and heavy machinery.

Solution to 1:

C is correct. Business cycle indicators need to represent the activities in the whole economy and thus should not be influenced by some particular sectors that may have uncorrelated fluctuations.

> ### Solution to 2:
>
> B is correct. Because it usually takes much longer time to plan and complete large construction projects than for equipment orders, construction projects may be less influenced by business cycles.
>
> ---
>
> *Note*: New orders statistics include orders that will be delivered over several years. For example, it is common for airlines to order 40 airplanes to be delivered over five years. Therefore, analysts use "core" orders that exclude defense and aircrafts for a better understanding of the economy's trend.

2.2.2 *Fluctuation in Inventory Levels*

Inventory accumulation and decumulation by businesses can also occur with such rapidity (i.e., rapidly and with large movements) that they have a much greater effect on economic growth than justified by their relatively small aggregate size. The key indicator in this area is the inventory–sales ratio that measures the outstanding stock of available inventories to the level of sales. The interaction of this gauge with the cycle develops in three distinct stages.

First, toward the top of the economic cycle, as sales fall or slow, it usually takes businesses a while to cut back on new production. Inventories, as a consequence, accumulate involuntarily, which combined with a fall in sales prompts a sudden rise in inventory–sales ratios. Because these inventories count positively in the accounting for the whole economy, this rise falsely blunts signs of economic weakness, and so practitioners look for figures that abstract from inventory swings that are commonly called "final sales." To adjust and sell off these unwanted inventories, a business has to cut production below even reduced sales levels. That action causes subsequent indicators in the overall economy to look weaker than they otherwise might have been. Although final sales offer a reality check, the production cutbacks involved in the inventory decumulations lead to order cancellations and layoffs that can subsequently cut final sales further and deepen cyclical corrections.

Second, with businesses producing at rates below the sales volumes necessary to dispose of unwanted inventories, inventory–sales ratios begin to fall back toward normal. When these indicators return to acceptable levels and businesses no longer have any need to further reduce inventories, they will raise production levels even without any sales growth just to cease the decline in inventory levels. This step results in a seemingly improved economic situation, even if sales remain depressed. Again, final sales provide a reality check on the underlying economic situation. As a business reaches this phase in the cycle, the seemingly minor increase in production levels can actually mark the beginning of the cyclical turn because the relief of finally adjusting inventories can slow or stop the rate of staff layoffs and do the same for the business's other demands for inputs.

The third stage occurs as sales generally begin their cyclical upturn. In a manner analogous to but the opposite of the initial cyclical downturn, a business may initially fail to keep production on pace with sales, which causes it to lose inventory to the initial sales increase. The subsequent fall in inventory–sales ratios, when it occurs in the face of rising sales, quickly prompts a surge in production not only to catch up with sales but also to replenish depleted inventories. However, sometimes during short or severe recessions, when businesses have not had time to adjust or reduce inventories to acceptable levels, only the initial sales increase is necessary to adjust inventories, thereby making increased production unnecessary and extending the lag to the cyclical pickup in production. But whether the production upturn occurs with a short or a long lag, it typically marks the turn in hiring patterns and for a time can markedly exaggerate the cyclical strength.

EXAMPLE 3

Inventory Fluctuation

1   Though a small part of the overall economy, inventories can reflect growth significantly because they:
    A   reflect general business sentiment.
    B   tend to move forcefully up or down.
    C   determine the availability of goods for sale.

2   Inventories tend to rise when:
    A   inventory–sales ratios are low.
    B   inventory–sales ratios are high.
    C   economic activity begins to rebound.

3   Inventories will often fall early in a recovery because:
    A   businesses need profit.
    B   sales outstrip production.
    C   businesses ramp up production because of increased economic activity.

Solution to 1:

B is correct. As stated in the reading, inventory level fluctuates dramatically over the business cycle.

Solution to 2:

A is correct. When the economy starts to recover, sales of inventories can outpace production, which results in low inventory–sales ratios. Companies then need to accumulate more inventories to restore the ratio to normal level.

Solution to 3:

B is correct. The companies are slow to increase production in early recovery phase because they first want to confirm the recession is over. Increasing output also takes time after the downsizing during the recession.

2.2.3 *Consumer Behavior*

As the largest single sector of almost every developed economy (70 percent of the US economy), patterns of household consumption determine overall economic direction more than any other sector. Patterns of consumption are critical to practitioners who, for any number of diverse reasons, have a particular interest in the sector. For example, marketers or equity analysts covering consumer product companies would have a high interest in the sector.

The two primary measures of household consumption are retail sales and, where available, a broad-based indicator of consumer spending that also includes purchases outside purely retail establishments, such as utilities, household services, and so on. Often these are presented in nominal terms and deflated to indicate directions of real or unit purchases and growth. Some indicators can make much finer distinctions, such as tracking spending, both real and nominal, of the more specific groups of consumer products. The three major divisions are: 1) durable goods, such as autos, appliances, and furniture; 2) nondurable goods, such as food, medicine, cosmetics, and clothing; and 3) services, such as medical treatment, entertainment, communications, and hairdressers. Because durable purchases usually replace items with longer useful lives, households in hard times can postpone such purchases more readily than spending on either services or nondurable goods. Comparing trends in durable purchases to those in the other categories can give practitioners a notion of the economy's progress through the cycle, with weakness in durables spending an early indication of general economic weakness, and the catch-up in such spending a harbinger of a more general cyclical recovery.

Beyond direct observations of consumer spending and its mix, practitioners can also gauge future directions by analyzing consumer confidence or sentiment to ascertain how aggressive consumers may be in their spending. Usually, such information is in the form of surveys intended to provide practitioners with a general guide to trends. But in practice, they frequently do not reflect actual consumer behavior because survey respondents answer what they imagine are the preferences of the typical consumer, indicating behavior contrary to their own.

Growth in income provides a more solid indication of consumption prospects, and household income figures are widely available in most countries. Especially relevant is after-tax income or what is frequently called "disposable" income. Some analysts chart consumer spending less from an examination of gross or even after-tax income than from a concept termed "permanent income." Permanent income abstracts away from temporary income unsustainable losses or gains and tries to capture the income flow on which households believe they can rely. Spending on durables tends to rise and fall with the gains and losses whatever their cause, but the basic level of consumption reflects this notion of permanent income.

Even after making such distinctions, consumer spending frequently diverges from income, no matter how it is measured. An analysis of the savings rate can assist practitioners in this regard. Calculated in different ways in different countries and sometimes in different ways within the same country, cross-border comparisons of saving rates are difficult. But because all aim in one way or another to measure the percent of income households set aside from spending, variations in saving rates can capture consumers' willingness to reduce spending out of current income. The savings rate also reflects future income uncertainties perceived by consumers (precautionary savings). Therefore, it indicates consumers' ability to spend despite possible lower income in the future. Thus a rise in the savings rate, usually measured as a percent of income, could indicate a certain caution among households and signal economic weakening. Certainly that was the case in Europe and the United States during the global financial crisis that led into the 2008–2009 recession. At the same time, the greater the stock of savings in the household sector and the wider the gap between ongoing income and spending, the greater the capability among households to pick up their spending, even ahead of income. So, although unusually high savings may at first say something negative about the cyclical outlook, they point longer-term to the potential for recovery.

EXAMPLE 4

Consumer Behavior

1 Durable goods have the most pronounced cyclical behavior because:
   A they have a longer useful life.
   B their purchase cannot be delayed.
   C they are needed more than nondurable goods or services.

2 Permanent income provides a better guide to:
   A savings rates.

B spending on services.

C spending on durable goods.

Solution to 1:

A is correct. Durable goods are usually big ticket items, the life span of which can be extended with repairs and without incurring the high replacement costs. So consumers tend to delay replacement when economic outlook is not favorable.

Solution to 2:

B is correct. Households adjust consumption based on perceived permanent income level rather than temporary earning fluctuations. Savings rate and durable goods consumption are more related to the short-term uncertainties caused by recessions.

2.3 Housing Sector Behavior

Although generally a much smaller part of the overall economy than consumer spending, housing can move up and down so rapidly that it can count more in overall economic movements than the sector's relatively small size might suggest. Almost every major economy offers statistics on new and existing home sales, residential construction activity, and sometimes, importantly, the inventory of unsold homes on the market. Statistics are also potentially available for the average or median price of homes, sometimes recorded by type of housing unit and sometimes as the price per square foot or square meter. Whatever the specific statistics, the relationships in this area typically follow fairly regular cyclical patterns.

Because many home buyers finance their purchase with a mortgage, the sector is especially sensitive to interest rates. Home buying and consequently construction activity expand in response to lower mortgage rates and contract in response to higher mortgage rates.

Beyond such interest rate effects, housing also follows its own internal cycle. When housing prices are low relative to average incomes, and especially when mortgage rates are also low, the cost of owning a house falls and demand for housing increases. Often indicators of the cost of owning a house are available to compare household incomes with the cost of supporting an average house, both its price and the expense of a typical mortgage. Commonly, housing prices and mortgage rates rise disproportionately as expansionary cycles mature, bringing on an increase in relative housing costs, even as household incomes rise. The resulting slowdown of house sales can lead to a cyclical downturn first in buying and then, as the inventory of unsold houses builds, in actual construction activity.

These links, clear as they are, are far from mechanical. If housing prices have risen rapidly in the recent past, for instance, many people will buy to gain exposure to the expected price gains, even as the purchase in other respects becomes harder to rationalize. Such behavior can extend the cycle upward and may result in a more severe correction. This result occurs because "late buying" activity invites overbuilding. The large inventory of unsold homes eventually puts downward pressure on real estate prices, catching late buyers, who have stretched their resources. This pattern occurred in many countries during the 2008–2009 global financial crisis.

Behind such cyclical considerations, housing, more than most economic sectors, responds to demographics, in particular the pace of family or household formation in an economy. Not every economy has data on family formation, but almost all offer information on the growth of particular age groups or cohorts in their respective populations. A focus on those cohorts, typically 25- to 40-year-olds, when household formation commonly occurs, usually can substitute for direct measures of net family formation. Adjusted for older people who are vacating existing homes, such calculations serve as an indicator of underlying, longer-term, secular housing demand. Although such measures have little to do with business cycles, they do offer a gauge, along with affordability, of how quickly the housing market can correct excess and return to growth. In China, for instance, where the government recently estimated a need for about 400 million more urban housing units over the next 25 years, housing demand will more quickly reverse cyclical weakness than in such economies as Italy or Japan where net new family formation is relatively slight.

EXAMPLE 5

Housing Sector Behavior

1 Housing is more sensitive than other sectors of the economy to:

A interest rates.

B permanent income.

C government spending.

2 Apart from questions of affordability, house buying also reflects:

A the rate of family formation.

B speculation on housing prices.

C both the rate of family formation and speculation on housing prices.

Solution to 1:

A is correct. Because real estate purchases are usually financed with mortgage loans, interest rate changes directly influence the monthly payment amounts.

Solution to 2:

C is correct. Family formation constitutes the actual need for housing, whereas speculation on housing prices reflects the fact that real estate has investment value.

2.4 External Trade Sector Behavior

The external trade sector varies tremendously in size and importance from one economy to another. In such places as Singapore and Hong Kong, for instance, where almost all inputs are imported and the bulk of their economies' output finds its way to the export market, trade (counting exports and imports together) easily exceeds their GDP. In other places, such as the United States with its huge continental economy, external trade assumes a much smaller part of GDP, although in recent decades the relative size of international trade has grown in almost every country in the world. Because the external trade sector can be very important for some countries, the business cycles of the large open economies in the world can be transmitted to them through international trade.

Typically, imports rise, all else equal, with the pace of domestic GDP growth, as needs and wants or generally rising demand also increase purchases of goods and services from abroad. Thus, imports respond to the domestic cycle. Exports are less a reflection of the domestic cycle than of cycles in the rest of the world. If these external cycles are strong, all else equal, exports will grow even if the domestic economy should experience a decline in growth. To understand the impact of exports, financial analysts need to understand the strength of the major trading partners of the economy under consideration. The net effect of trade offsets cyclical weakness, and depending on the importance of exports to the economy, could erase it altogether. Most practitioners look at the net difference between exports and imports (they use the balance of payments, which calculates trade's contribution to the economy as exports less imports). For these reasons, such differences can mean the pattern of external trade balances is entirely different from the rest of the domestic economic cycle.

Currency also has an independent effect that can move trade in directions strikingly different from the domestic economic cycle. When a nation's currency appreciates, foreign goods seem cheaper than domestic goods to the domestic population, prompting, all else equal, a relative rise in imports. At the same time, such currency appreciation makes that nation's exports more expensive on global markets, impairing their prospects. Of course, currency depreciation has the opposite effects. Although currency moves are sometimes violent, they only have a significant effect on trade and the balance of payments when they cumulate in a single direction for some time. Moves from one month or quarter to the next, however great, have a minimal effect until they persist. Thus cumulative currency movements that take place over a period of years will have an impact on trade flows that will persist even if the currency subsequently moves in a contrary direction for a temporary period.

Financial analysts need to consider a wide range of variables, both in the domestic economy and abroad, to assess relative GDP growth rates and then superimpose on those rates currency considerations to ascertain whether they reinforce other cyclical forces or counteract them. Generally, GDP growth differentials in global economic growth rates between countries have the most immediate and straightforward effect because domestic changes raise or reduce imports and foreign economic activity changes raise or reduce exports. Currency moves have a more complex and, despite the drama of short-term currency moves, a more gradual effect.

EXAMPLE 6

External Trade

1 Imports generally respond to:

   A the level of exports.

   B domestic industrial policy.

   C the pace of domestic GDP growth.

2 Exports generally respond to the:

   A level of unionization.

   B pace of global growth.

   C pace of domestic GDP growth.

Solution to 1:

C is correct. As a part of aggregate demand, imports reflect the domestic needs for foreign goods, which vary together with domestic economic growth.

Solution to 2:

B is correct. Exports reflect the foreign demands on domestic output, which depend on the conditions of global economy.

THEORIES OF THE BUSINESS CYCLE

3

Business cycles have been recognized since the early days of economic theory, and considerable effort has gone into identifying different cycles and explaining them. Until the 1930s, however, the general view was that they were a natural feature of the economy and the pain of recessions is temporary. But the depth and severity of the 1930s downturn (known as the Great Depression) created a crisis in economic theory.

After the Great Depression (which began in 1929), the debate between various economic schools of thought (Neoclassical, Austrian, and Keynesian) spurred important innovations in the way the business cycle was described and explained. Similarly, after the dramatic recessions triggered by the oil shocks of 1973 and 1979, the old paradigm was taken apart and new developments in economics and quantitative methods led to an improved understanding of short-term economic dynamics. In this section, we will review and summarize some of the main theories.

3.1 Neoclassical and Austrian Schools

Neoclassical analysis relied on the concept of general equilibrium—that is, all markets will reach equilibrium because of the "invisible hand, or free market," and the price will be found for every good at which supply equals demand. All resources are used efficiently based on the principle of marginal cost equaling marginal revenue, and no involuntary unemployment of labor or capital takes place. In practice, because the neoclassical school provides that the invisible hand will reallocate capital and labor so that they will be used to produce whatever consumers want, it does not allow for "fluctuations found in the aggregate economic activity." If a shock of any origin shifts either the aggregate demand or aggregate supply curve, the economy will quickly readjust and reach its equilibrium via lower interest rates and lower wages.

Neoclassical economists rely on **Say's law**: All that is produced will be sold because supply creates its own demand. French economist J.B. Say pointed out that if something is produced, the capital and labor used for that production will have to be compensated. This compensation of the factors (interest for capital and wages for labor) creates purchasing power in the sense that the workers receive a paycheck and thus can buy goods and services they need. Widespread declines in demand would be strictly temporary.

In the neoclassical school, a massive crisis, such as the Great Depression of the 1930s with widespread unemployment of more than 20 percent throughout the industrialized world, is impossible. Yet, it happened. The crisis started in the United States and successively affected many other countries.

The 1929 crisis helped introduce a breakthrough in economic theory because the crisis touched many sectors at the same time and in a dramatic fashion. Because the neoclassical theory denied the possibility of a prolonged depression, it could not be used to explain how to fight such a depression. The main adjustment mechanism proposed by the neoclassical school—cuts in wages—was difficult to achieve and, as we shall see, was questioned by the Keynesian school.

The Austrian school, including F. von Hayek and L. von Mises, shared some views of the neoclassical school, but focused more on two topics that were largely unimportant in the neoclassical framework: money and government. Money was not necessary in the neoclassical model, because the exchange of goods and services could occur in the form of barter and still reach general equilibrium. Money was seen just as a way to simplify exchange. Similarly, the role of government in the neoclassical model was quite limited because the economy could take care of itself and little else was needed of the government besides upholding the law and securing the borders.

Von Hayek argued that fluctuations are caused by governments that try to increase GDP and employment (thus perhaps increasing voters' consensus) by adopting expansionary monetary policies. Governments lower the market interest rate below its natural value (aggregate demand shifts right) and thus lead companies to overinvest (an inflationary gap). Once companies realize that they have accumulated too much equipment and too many structures, they will suddenly stop investing, which depresses aggregate demand (aggregate demand shifts left dramatically) and causes a crisis throughout the economy. To reach the new equilibrium, all prices including wages must decrease.

As a result of manipulating interest rates the economy exhibits fluctuations that would not have happened otherwise. Therefore, Austrian economists advocate limited government intervention in the economy, lest the government causes a boom-and-bust cycle. The best thing to do in the recession phase is to allow the necessary market adjustment to take place as quickly as possible.

The Austrian school has a theory of what causes the business cycle: It is misguided government intervention. The Neoclassical school does not have a theory of the business cycle, and the closest it gets to it is Schumpeter's creative destruction theory, which shows cycles within industries as a result of technological progress but no economy-wide fluctuations.[2] Schumpeter formulated a theory of innovations, which explained cycles limited to individual industries: When an inventor comes up with a new product (e.g., the digital music player in recent decades) or a new, better way to produce an existing good or service (e.g., radio frequency identification tracking of inventories), then the entrepreneur that introduces the new discovery will likely have bigger profits and may drive the existing producers out of business. Therefore, innovations can generate crises that affect only the industry affected by the new invention. Neoclassical economics recognizes that business cycles exist but treats them as temporary disequilibria.

3.2 Keynesian and Monetarist Schools

The Keynesian and Monetarist schools of economic thought have been among the most influential. Their prescriptions concerning the business cycle are discussed in the following sections.

3.2.1 *Keynesian School*

As previously mentioned, if a recession occurs, the Neoclassical and Austrian schools argue in general that no government intervention is needed. Unemployment and excess supply of goods will be solved by allowing market prices to decrease (including wages) until all markets clear: Supply equals demand and factors of production are fully employed.

British economist John Maynard Keynes[3] disagreed with both Neoclassical and Austrian views. He observed that a generalized price and wage reduction (solely brought about through market forces), necessary to bring markets back to equilibrium during a recession, would be hard to attain. For example, workers may not want to see their nominal compensation decrease because nobody likes a pay cut.

But Keynes thought that even if workers agreed to accept lower salaries, this situation might exacerbate the crisis by reducing aggregate demand rather than solving it because lower salary expectations would shift aggregate demand left. For example,

---

2 Joseph Alois Schumpeter was born in Austria and studied with members of the Austrian school, such as Menger and Hayek, but he was more Neoclassical than Austrian in the economic sense. He taught in the United States for many years.

3 John Maynard Keynes' name is often mentioned in full, with first and middle name, to avoid confusion with his father, John Neville Keynes, who was also an economist.

if wages fell, workers would need to cut back on their spending. This response would cause a further contraction in the demand for all sorts of goods and services, starting from the more expensive items, such as durable goods, and move in a "domino effect" through the economy (the downward spiral of the AD curve continuously shifting left, as mentioned earlier).

Further, Keynes believed there could be circumstances in which lower interest rates would not reignite growth because business confidence or "animal spirit" was too low. As a consequence, Keynes advocated government intervention in the form of fiscal policy. While he accepted the possibility that markets would reach the equilibrium envisioned by Neoclassical and Austrian economists over the long run, he famously quipped that "in the long run, we are all dead;" that is, the human suffering is excessive while waiting for all shocks to be absorbed and for the economy to return to equilibrium.

When crises occur, the government should intervene to keep capital and labor employed by deliberately running a larger fiscal deficit. This intervention would limit the damages of major recessions. Although this concept continues to be a highly politically charged debate, many economists agree that government expenditure can limit the negative effect of major economic crises in the short term. The practical criticisms that are often expressed about Keynesian fiscal policy are:

1   Fiscal deficits mean higher government debt that needs to be serviced and repaid eventually. There is a danger that government finances could move out of control.

2   Keynesian cyclical policies are focused on the short term. In the long run, the economy may come back and the presence of the expansionary policy may cause it to "overheat"—that is, to have unsustainably fast economic growth, which causes inflation and other problems. This result is because of the typical lags involved in expansionary policy taking effect on the economy.

3   Fiscal policy takes time to implement. Quite often, by the time stimulatory fiscal policy kicks in, the economy is already recovering. (Monetary policy determines the available quantities of money and loans in an economy.)

Keynes' writings did not advocate a continuous presence of the government in the economy, nor did he suggest using economic policy to "fine tune" the business cycle. He only advocated decisive action in case of a serious economic crisis, such as the Great Depression.

EXAMPLE 7

The Perspective of Hyman Minsky

A different view of business cycles came from Hyman Minsky. His view had something in common with the Austrian school and something in common with Keynes. Minsky believed that excesses in financial markets exacerbate economic fluctuations. For example, a rapid growth of credit, often given to risky ventures in the late expansion phase of the cycle, will be followed by a "credit crunch" during the down-swing phase. Minsky traced excesses to a type of complacency in which people underestimate the risk of events that have not occurred in a while. Therefore, if the economy has been in a long expansion, people may think that the market works very well and that the expansion will last forever—that is, extrapolating past experiences. In this sense, Minsky could be seen as a precursor of behavioral finance, which is the branch of finance that studies how cognition biases, such as overconfidence and short memory, induce investors to be overconfident and make suboptimal choices.

The term **Minsky moment** has been coined for a point in business cycle when, after individuals become overextended in borrowing to finance speculative investments, people start realizing that something is likely to go wrong and a panic ensues leading to asset sell-offs. The subprime crisis that affected many industrialized countries starting in 2008 has been represented as a "Minsky moment"[4] because it came after years in which risk premiums (e.g., the differentials, or spreads, between very risky bonds and very safe bonds) were at historically low levels. Typically, low risk premiums suggest that no adverse events are expected—in other words, investors believe that because the economy and the markets have been enjoying a protracted expansion, there is no reason to worry about the future. As a consequence, many market observers suggest that business cycles are being tamed. This kind of view of the world leads people to underestimate risk, for example, by not doing the appropriate diligent research before granting a loan or before purchasing a security—in a word, complacency.

The "Minsky moment" has been compared with a cartoon in which a cartoon character walks over a cliff without realizing that it is doing so. When he looks down and sees that he is walking on thin air, he panics and falls to the bottom of the canyon—just like the world economy in 2008.

A warning in 2005 by Alan Greenspan, then chairman of the US Federal Reserve,[5] was not taken seriously by market participants. Greenspan said that historically, extended periods of low risk premiums always ended badly. This warning was to a large extent in line with Minsky's view: People tend to extrapolate the recent past, and if little volatility has occurred recently, they may think that low volatility will persist indefinitely.

Some market analysts, after the crisis, pointed out that not even Greenspan knew how accurate his remark would turn out to be. As explained by Reinhardt and Rogoff (2009) and Siegel (2010), when rates were very low, investors tried to get extra yield by investing in complex and potentially more risky assets, such as securitized subprime mortgages and collateralized debt obligations whose credit-worthiness was much lower than expected.

As soon as the economy started having difficulties, the value of many risky securities dropped dramatically, placing investors globally into a state of panic and causing a dramatic fall in aggregate demand. The crisis is another example of why thinking that a new era has started and the things learned from analyzing the past no longer apply is generally a very costly mistake.

3.2.2 Monetarist School

The Monetarist school, generally identified with Milton Friedman, objected to Keynesian intervention for four main reasons:

1 The Keynesian model does not recognize the supreme importance of the money supply. If the money supply grows too fast, there will be an unsustainable boom, and if it grows too slowly, there will be a recession. Friedman focused mainly on broad measures of money, such as M^2.

---

4 Paul McCulley (for example, see McCulley 2010) originated this expression.
5 Alan Greenspan, Chairman of the US Federal Reserve at the time, remarked in 2005: "Thus, this vast increase in the market value of asset claims is in part the indirect result of investors accepting lower compensation for risk. Such an increase in market value is too often viewed by market participants as structural and permanent. To some extent, those higher values may be reflecting the increased flexibility and resilience of our economy. But what they perceive as newly abundant liquidity can readily disappear. Any onset of increased investor caution elevates risk premiums and, as a consequence, lowers asset values and promotes the liquidation of the debt that supported higher asset prices. This is the reason that history has not dealt kindly with the aftermath of protracted periods of low risk premiums."

2 The Keynesian model lacks a complete representation of utility-maximizing agents and is thus not logically sound.

3 Keynes' short-term view failed to consider the long-term costs of government intervention (e.g., growing government debt and high cost of interest on this debt).

4 The timing of governments' economic policy responses was uncertain, and the stimulative effects of a fiscal expansion may take effect after the crisis was over, and thus cause more harm than good.[6]

Therefore, Monetarists advocate a focus on maintaining steady growth of the money supply, and otherwise a very limited role for government in the economy. Fiscal and monetary policy should be clear and consistent over time, so all economic agents can forecast government actions. In this way, the uncertainty of economic fluctuations would not be increased by any uncertainty about the timing and magnitude of economic policies and their lagged effects.

According to the Monetarist school, business cycles may occur both because of exogenous shocks and because of government intervention. It is better to let aggregate demand and supply find their own equilibrium than to risk causing further economic fluctuations. However, a key part of monetarist thought is that the money supply needs to continue to grow at a moderate rate. If it falls, as occurred in the 1930s, the economic downturn could be severe, whereas if money grows too fast, inflation will follow.

3.3 The New Classical School

Starting in the 1970s, economists such as Robert Lucas started questioning the foundations of the models used to explain business cycles. Among other things, Lucas agreed with Friedman (1968) and pointed out that the models should try to represent the actions of economic agents with a utility function and a budget constraint, just like the models used in microeconomics. This approach has come to be known as **new classical macroeconomics**—an approach to macroeconomics that seeks the macroeconomic conclusions of individuals maximizing utility on the basis of rational expectations and companies maximizing profits. The assumption is made that all agents are roughly alike, and thus solving the problem of one agent is the same as solving that of millions of similar agents (or the per capita income and consumption of the average agent).

The New Classical models are dynamic in the sense of describing fluctuations over many periods and present general equilibrium in the sense of determining all prices rather than one price. The models by Edward C. Prescott and Finn E. Kydland, who are among the pioneers of this approach, have an economic agent that has to face external shocks (e.g., as a result of changes in technology, tastes, or world prices) and thus optimizes its choices to reach the highest utility. If all agents act in similar fashion, the markets will gradually adjust toward equilibrium.

3.3.1 *Models without Money: Real Business Cycle Theory*

New Classical economists comment that some policy recommendations made in the past were rather illogical: for example, if everybody knows that in a recession the government will give out low rate loans to corporations that want to invest in new equipment and structures, why would any reasonable company invest outside

---

6 Markets may react differently to changes in interest rates and other tools of monetary policy. There is a long chain of events from the time when interest rates are cut, to when banks change the rates they charge clients, to when a company sees that rates are lower and thus decides to invest in new equipment, to when the equipment is finally purchased. Therefore, by the time these events all happen, the economy may be in expansion and the new investment may lead the economy to overheating.

recessions unless absolutely required to? Obviously, if most companies thought that, they would stop investing, thus causing a recession that otherwise would not have occurred. Essentially, the government's anti-cyclical policy could cause a recession.

Because, just like the neoclassical models, the initial New Classical models did not include money, they were called real business cycle models (often abbreviated as RBC). Cycles have real causes, such as the aforementioned changes in technology, whereas monetary variables, such as inflation, are assumed to have no effect on GDP and unemployment.[7]

RBC models of the business cycle conclude that expansions and contractions represent efficient operation of the economy in response to external real shocks. Because the level of economic activity at any time is consistent with maximizing expected utility, the policy recommendation of RBC theory is for government *not* to intervene in the economy with discretionary fiscal and monetary policy.

Critics of RBC models often focus on the labor market. Because RBC models rely on efficient markets, it follows that unemployment can only be short term: apart from frictional unemployment,[8] if markets are efficient, a person who does not have a job can only be a person who does not want to work. If a person is unemployed, in the context of efficient markets, he just needs to lower his wage rate until he finds an employer who hires him. This assumption is logical because if markets are perfectly flexible, all markets must find equilibrium and full employment.

Therefore, as suggested particularly by the earliest RBC models, a person is unemployed because he or she is asking for wages that are too high, or in other words, this person's utility function is maximized by having more leisure (e.g., free time to visit museums, watch games on TV, and enjoy time with friends) and less consumption (which could be increased by giving up some leisure and finding a job). However, the observation that during a recession many people are eagerly searching for jobs and are unable to find employment despite dropping their asking wages substantially suggests that this theory is unrealistic.

Although many find this explanation unconvincing, RBC theorists argue that, undeniably, markets would clear if people were rational and avoided unrealistic expectations of earnings or simply enjoyed their leisure accompanied by optimally meager consumption.

An interesting feature of RBC models is that they give aggregate supply a more prominent role than many other theories. For example, supply has a limited importance in the Keynesian theory, probably because Keynes was more concerned with the Great Depression, which was largely a crisis of aggregate demand. RBC models show that supply shocks, such as advances in technology or changes in the relative prices of inputs, cause the aggregate supply (AS) to shift left. A new technology can change potential GDP, for example, thus moving long-run AS to the right. Adjustment will be needed because not all companies can adopt the new technology at once, and therefore short-run AS will not jump to the new equilibrium immediately. Similarly, an increase of energy prices shifts short-run AS to the left (higher prices and lower GDP). In the long run companies and households can learn to use less of the expensive energy inputs (substitution effect), and therefore long-run AS will shift right (higher GDP) if the economy learns to produce more goods with less energy.

---

7 See Plosser (1989) and Romer (2005, chapter 4) for an introduction to RBC models. Basically, RBC models assume that economic agents are fully rational and that markets function with no imperfection or friction. As a consequence, any changes in monetary aggregates or other monetary policies will promptly cause changes in price levels and other variables without affecting real GDP or employment.

8 Frictional unemployment indicates the people who in economic statistics appear to be unemployed, but in reality are moving between jobs. Because there is always someone who has just left his or her job and is about to start a new one, or someone who just entered the job market and has already found a job but has not started yet, we know that a small part of the statistically unemployed are people between jobs.

3.3.2 *Models with Money*

Inflation is often seen as a cause of business cycles, because when monetary policy ends up being too expansionary, the economy grows at an unsustainable pace—creating an inflationary gap. The result is that, for example, suppliers cannot keep up with demand. In this environment, prices will tend to grow faster than normal—that is, inflation.

As a consequence, the central bank will often intervene to limit inflation by "tightening" monetary policy, which generally means increasing interest rates, so that the cost of borrowing will be higher and demand for goods and services will slow down (a leftward shift in aggregate demand caused by the higher cost of money). This response will decrease equilibrium GDP and can result in a recession.

Given that inflation appears to trigger policy responses from central banks, it is an important part of modern business cycles. Therefore, it can be helpful to use models that include money to explain economic growth. As mentioned earlier, RBC models assume that transactions could occur with barter, and thus do not explicitly include money. More recent dynamic general equilibrium models (for example, Christiano, Eichenbaum, and Evans 2005) include money and inflation.

Monetary policy can be incorporated into dynamic general equilibrium models with money. In one type of model, the economy receives shocks from changes in technology and consumer preferences (like in the RBC case), but can also receive shocks from monetary policy, which sometimes can tame the business cycle and at other times may exacerbate it.

Another group of dynamic general equilibrium models are the **Neo-Keynesians** or **New Keynesians**.[9] Like the New Classical school, the Neo-Keynesian school attempts to place macroeconomics on sound microeconomic foundations. In contrast to the New Classical school the Neo-Keynesian school assumes slow-to-adjust ("sticky") prices and wages. The Neo-Keynesian models show that markets do not reach equilibrium immediately and seamlessly, but even small imperfections may cause markets to be in disequilibrium for a long time. As a consequence, government intervention as advocated in the 1930s by Keynes may be useful to eliminate unemployment and bring markets toward equilibrium.

The typical example of these imperfections, which also appeared in Keynes' work, is that workers do not want their wages to decrease to help the market reach a new equilibrium (i.e., wages are often downwardly sticky).[10] Another possibility that some economists suggested in the 1980s is called the "menu costs" explanation: It is costly for companies to continuously adjust prices to make markets clear, just like it would be costly for a restaurant to print new menus daily with updated prices.[11] Another explanation is that every time an economic shock hits a company, the company will need some time to reorganize its production.

EXAMPLE 8

Real Business Cycle Models

1 The main difference between New Classical (RBC) and Neo-Keynesian models is that the New Classical models:

A are monetarist.

---

9 For an introduction to Neo-Keynesian models, see Romer (2005, chapter 5) and Mankiw (1989).

10 As mentioned earlier, Keynes thought that even if workers agreed to accept lower wages, this might exacerbate the crisis rather than solving it because lower wage expectations would shift AD left.

11 Clearly, both this example and the "menu costs" name were initially envisioned before personal computers and laser printers became affordable and widely used. Still, one can imagine the cost for a store owner to replace the price tags on every item in the store on a daily basis, and also how this would confuse shoppers.

B use utility-maximizing agents, whereas Neo-Keynesian does not.

C assume that prices adjust quickly to changes in supply and demand, whereas Neo-Keynesians assume that prices adjust slowly.

2 Basic RBC models focus on the choices of a typical individual, who can choose between consuming more (thus giving up leisure) and enjoying leisure more (thus giving up consumption). What causes persistent unemployment in this model?

A Contractionary monetary policy causes a shock to real variables.

B The economy returns to equilibrium promptly, thus persistent unemployment does not exist.

C The utility function: If the individual prefers leisure much more than consumption, she will forego consumption and instead choose unemployment to enjoy more leisure when the market salary is low.

Solution to 1:

C is correct. A key feature of Keynesian macroeconomics is the stickiness of prices. In contrast, Classical views assume flexible price adjustments that ensure market clearing. Modern theories always assume rational economic representative agents in the economy as the "micro" foundation of macroeconomics. Thus they are the "New" models.

Solution to 2:

C is correct. Shocks in the standard New Classical model can only have a temporary effect, thus A is not the right answer. Unemployment can still exist when the labor market is cleared, so a rational explanation is provided in C.

In recent years, a consensus concerning business cycles has gradually started building in macroeconomics. It is too early to say that economists agree on all causes of and remedies for business fluctuations, but at least an analytical framework has emerged, which encompasses both New Classical and Neo-Keynesian approaches. Woodford (2009), among others, shows that new research seems to be leading to a unified approach.

The debate about business cycles often receives a politically partisan treatment in the press because some people are generally against government intervention in the economy (for example, because it may lead to large deficits) and others are in favor (for example, because it may alleviate the effects of a large economic shock). It is important to base investment decisions on analysis and not on politics; the financial analyst must try as much as possible to set personal biases aside.

However, there is little doubt that central banks are very actively trying to manage the business cycle by raising interest rates when the economy becomes too hot and inflation accelerates and cutting rates when the economy is weak. In the 2008–2009 downturn, when official interest rates approached zero, this policy was extended to include "quantitative easing" to try to lower interest rates further out on the yield curve to stimulate the economy.

EXAMPLE 9

Analyzing Government Expenditure

Simple criteria for the financial analyst wondering if a government's expenditure is excessive (i.e., unsustainably high and/or of an inappropriate composition) include the following:[12]

1   Does the government always have a deficit no matter the cyclical phase, or does it have surpluses during economic booms?

2   Does the government have a deficit because of a defined series of necessary investments that will improve the productivity of the country, or is it spending most of its money in salaries for patronage employees and on infrastructure of questionable uses?

3   Is the growth rate of debt (government budget deficit as a percentage of GDP) higher than GDP growth? If so, the debt level will not likely be sustainable.

When government expenditures are excessive, inflation often follows. After that, a recession may occur because the central bank takes necessary measures to slow down an overheated economy. That is, if government purchases increase aggregate demand too much, thus causing inflation (expansionary fiscal policy), the central bank will intervene to stop prices from increasing too quickly (tightening or contractionary monetary policy).

UNEMPLOYMENT AND INFLATION

4

Many governments state economic policy objectives related to limiting the rate at which citizens are unemployed and containing price inflation (i.e., preserving the purchasing power of a domestic currency). The relationships of these variables to the business cycle are discussed in the following sections. In general, unemployment is at its highest just as the recovery starts and is at its lowest at the peak of the economy.

4.1 Unemployment

A typical cause of business cycle downturns is a tight labor market—that is, one with low unemployment. An overheated economy leads to inflation when unemployment is very low. Workers ask for higher wages because they expect prices of goods and services to keep going up, and at the same time they have market power against employers because are few available workers to be hired. This upward pressure on wages coupled with the impact of wage escalator clauses (automatic increases in wages as the consumer price index grows) triggers a price-wage inflationary spiral. This issue was a particular problem in industrialized countries in the 1960s and 1970s and remains an issue today.

A key aspect in this process is inflation expectations. Because inflation expectations are high, the request for higher wages is stronger, which induces employers to increase prices in advance to keep their profit margins stable. This avalanche process grows with time. Central banks act, sometimes drastically, to slow down the economy and reset inflationary expectations throughout the economy at a low level, so that

---

12 For a more formal and data-rich approach, see Reinhardt and Rogoff (2009).

if everyone expects low inflation, the inflationary spiral itself will stop. An effect of these policies is a deep recession. Therefore, whenever a financial analyst sees signs of a price-wage spiral in the making, a reasonable response would be to consider the effect of both high inflation and sharp tightening of monetary policy.

This example shows that measures of labor market conditions are important in assessing whether an economy is at risk of cyclical downturn.

The following are the definitions of a few terms that are used to summarize the state of the labor market:

- **Employed**: number of people with a job. This figure normally does not include people working in the informal sector (e.g., unlicensed cab drivers, illegal workers, etc.).

- **Labor force**: number of people who either have a job or are actively looking for a job. This number excludes retirees, children, stay-at-home parents, full-time students, and other categories of people who are neither employed nor actively seeking employment.

- **Unemployed**: people who are actively seeking employment but are currently without a job. Some special subcategories include:

  - **Long-term unemployed**: people who have been out of work for a long time (more than 3–4 months in many countries) but are still looking for a job.

  - **Frictionally unemployed**: people who are not working at the time of filling out the statistical survey because they just left one job and are about to start another job. That is, the frictionally unemployed have a job waiting for them and are not 100 percent unemployed—it is just that they have not started the new job yet.

- **Unemployment rate**: ratio of unemployed to labor force.

- **Activity ratio** (or Participation ratio): ratio of labor force to total population of working age (i.e., those between 16 and 64 years of age).

- **Underemployed**: person who has a job but has the qualifications to work a significantly higher-paying job. For example, a lawyer who is out of work and takes a job in a bookstore could call herself underemployed. This lawyer would count as employed for the computation of the unemployment rate (she does have a job, even if it may not be her highest paying job). Although the unemployment rate statistic is criticized for not taking the issue of underemployment into account, it may be difficult to classify whether a person is truly underemployed—for example, the lawyer may find legal work too stressful and prefers working at the bookstore. However, data for part-time working is sometimes a good proxy.

- **Discouraged worker**: person who has stopped looking for a job. Perhaps because of a weak economy, the discouraged worker has given up seeking employment. Discouraged workers are statistically outside the labor force (similar to children and retirees), which means they are not counted in the official unemployment rate. During bad recessions, the unemployment rate may actually decrease because many discouraged workers stop seeking work, such as stay-at-home mothers who ideally would prefer to work. It is important to observe the participation rate together with the unemployment rate to understand if unemployment is decreasing because of an improved economy or because of an increase in discouraged workers. Discouraged workers and underemployed people may be considered examples of "hidden unemployment."

- **Voluntarily unemployed**: person voluntarily outside the labor force, such as a jobless worker refusing an available vacancy for which the wage is lower than their threshold or those who retired early.

4.1.1 *The Unemployment Rate*

The unemployment rate is certainly the most quoted measure of unemployment; it attempts to measure those people who have no work but would work if they could find it, generally stated as a percent of the overall workforce. In the United States, the indicator emerges from a monthly survey of households by the US Bureau of Labor Statistics, which asks how many household members have jobs and how many of working age do not but are seeking work. Other statistical bureaus rely on other sources for the calculation, using claims for unemployment assistance, for instance, or their equivalent. Some measure the workforce simply as those of working age, regardless of whether they are ready or willing to work. These differences can make precise international comparisons problematic. One solution is to use the International Labour Organization (ILO) statistics that try to estimate on a consistent basis. As indicated earlier, some statistical agencies add perspective with other measures; for example, what proportion of those who have ceased work are discouraged, underemployed, or have opted out of the workforce for other reasons or are working part-time.

Although these various unemployment measures provide insight to the state of the economy, they are inaccurate in pointing to cyclical directions on at least two counts, both of which make unemployment a lagging economic indicator of the business cycle.

In the first place, the unemployment rate tends to point to a past economic condition—that is, it lags the cycle—because the labor force expands and declines in response to the economic environment. Compounding the inaccuracy, when times get hard, discouraged workers cease searching for work, reducing the number typically counted as unemployed and making the jobs market look stronger than it really is. Conversely, when the jobs market picks up, these people return to the search, and because they seldom find work immediately, they at least initially raise the calculation of those unemployed, giving the false impression of the lack of recovery in the jobs market, when, in fact, it is the improvement that brought these people back into the workforce in the first place. Sometimes this cyclical flow of new jobs seekers is so great that the unemployment rate actually rises even as the economic recovery gains momentum. Those agencies that measure the workforce in terms of the working-age population avoid this bias, because this demographic (working-age population) remains more or less constant regardless of the state of the labor market. But this approach introduces biases of its own, such as counting as unemployed people who have severe disabilities and could never seek work.

The second reason the unemployment indicator tends to lag the cycle comes from the typical reluctance of businesses to lay off people. The reluctance may stem from a desire to retain good workers for the long run, or just reflect constraints written into labor contracts that make layoffs expensive. The reluctance makes the various measures of unemployment rise more slowly as the economy slides into recession than they otherwise might. Then as the recovery develops, a business waits to hire until it has fully employed the workers it has kept on the payroll during the recession; this delay causes decreases in the unemployment rate to lag in the cyclical recovery, sometimes for a long time.

4.1.2 *Overall Payroll Employment and Productivity Indicators*

To get a better picture of the employment cycle, practitioners often rely on more straightforward measures of payroll growth. By measuring the size of payrolls, practitioners sidestep such issues as the ebb and flow of discouraged workers and can more directly point to cyclical directions. These statistics, however, do have biases of their own. It is hard, for instance, to count employment in smaller businesses, which, especially in many developed economies, are the main drivers of employment growth. Still, there is a clear indication of economic trouble when payrolls shrink and a clear indication of recovery when they rise.

The application of other variables can also assist in understanding the employment situation and its use in determining cyclical directions. Two of the most straightforward are measures of hours worked, especially overtime, and the use of temporary workers. A business does not want to make mistakes with full-time staff, either hiring or firing. Thus, at the first signs of economic weakness, managers cut back hours, especially overtime. Such movements can simply reflect minor month-to-month production shifts, but if followed by cutbacks in part-time and temporary staff, the picture gives a strong signal of economic weakness, especially if confirmed by other independent indicators. Similarly, on the cyclical upswing, a business turns first to increases in overtime and hours. If a business then increases temporary staffing, it gives a good signal of economic recovery long before any movement in rehiring fulltime staff again, especially if confirmed by independent cyclical indicators.

Productivity measures also offer insight into this cyclical process. Because productivity is usually measured by dividing output by hours worked, a business's tendency to keep workers on the payroll even as output falls usually prompts a reduction in measured productivity. If measures are available promptly enough, this sign of cyclical weakness might precede even the change in hours. This drop in productivity precedes any change in full-time payrolls. Productivity also responds promptly when business conditions improve and the business first begins to utilize its underemployed workers, which occurs earlier than any upturn in full-time payrolls.

On a more fundamental level, productivity can also pick up in response to technological breakthroughs or improved training techniques. As already mentioned, such changes affect potential GDP. If strong enough, they can negatively affect employment trends, keeping them slower than they would be otherwise by relieving the need for additional staff to increase production. But these influences usually unfold over decades and mean little to cyclical considerations, which, at most, unfold over years. What is more, there are few statistical indicators to gauge the onset of technological change, restraining analysts to the use of anecdotal evidence or occasional longitudinal studies.

EXAMPLE 10

Analyzing Unemployment

1 Comparisons of unemployment among countries:

   A   are impossible.

   B   show which countries are more prosperous.

   C   must take into account different unemployment measurement methods.

2 Unemployment frequently lags the cycle because:

   A   it takes time to compile the employment data.

   B   businesses are reluctant to dismiss and hire workers.

   C   workers must give notice to employers before quitting jobs.

3 Productivity offers perspective on the business cycle by:

   A   showing the need for new employees.

   B   assessing the skill set of existing employees.

   C   measuring the intensity of work flow for existing employees.

Solution to 1:

C is correct. Different countries use different statistical scope and ratio definitions and these differences have to be reconciled before meaningful conclusions can be made from cross-country comparisons.

Solution to 2:

B is correct. Besides labor hoarding by employers because of the costs related to hiring and firing, the variations of labor force over business cycles also contribute to this feature of the unemployment rate.

Solution to 3:

C is correct. Because employers would like to keep the workforce relatively stable, productivity falls as output declines in a downturn because it is measured as the ratio of output over hours worked. Similarly productivity rises as output recovers.

4.2 Inflation

The overall price level changes at varying rates during different phases of a business cycle. Thus, when studying business cycles, it is important to understand the statistics related to this phenomenon. In general, the inflation rate is pro-cyclical (that is it goes up and down *with* the cycle), but with a lag of a year or more.

Inflation refers to a sustained rise in the overall level of prices in an economy. Economists use various price indices to measure the overall price level, also called the aggregate price level. The **inflation rate** is the percentage change in a price index—that is, the speed of overall price level movements. Investors follow the inflation rate closely, not only because it can help to infer the state of the economy but also because an unexpected change may result in a change in monetary policy, which can in turn have a large and immediate impact on asset prices. In developing countries, very high inflation rates can lead to social unrest or even shifts of political power, which constitutes political risk for investments in those economies.

Central banks, the monetary authority in most modern economies, monitor the domestic inflation rates closely when conducting monetary policy, which in turn determines the available quantities of money and loans in an economy. A high inflation rate combined with fast economic growth and low unemployment usually indicates the economy is overheating, which may trigger some policy movements to cool it down. However, if a high inflation rate is combined with a high level of unemployment and a slowdown of the economy—an economic state known as **stagflation** (for stagnation plus inflation)—the economy will typically be left to correct itself because no short-term economic policy is thought to be effective.

4.2.1 Deflation, Hyperinflation, and Disinflation

There are various terms related to the levels and changes of the inflation rate.

- **Deflation**: A sustained decrease in aggregate price level, which corresponds to a negative inflation rate—that is, an inflation rate of less than 0 percent.

- **Hyperinflation**: An extremely fast increase in aggregate price level, which corresponds to an extremely high inflation rate—for example, 500 to 1000 percent per year.

- **Disinflation**: A decline in the inflation rate, such as from around 15 to 20 percent to 5 or 6 percent. Disinflation is very different from deflation because even after a period of disinflation, the inflation rate remains positive and the aggregate price level keeps rising (although at a slower speed).

Inflation means that the same amount of money can purchase less real goods or services in the future. So, the value of money or the purchasing power of money decreases in an inflationary environment. When deflation occurs, the value of money actually increases. Because most debt contracts are written in fixed monetary amounts, the liability of a borrower also rises in real terms during deflation. As the price level falls, the revenue of a typical company also falls during a recession. Facing increasing real debt, a company that is short of cash usually cuts its spending, investment, and workforce sharply. Less spending and high unemployment then further exacerbate the economic contraction. To avoid getting too close to deflation, the consensus on the preferred inflation rate is around 2 percent per year for developed economies. Deflation occurred in the United States during the Great Depression and briefly during the recession of 2008–2009 following the global financial crisis. Since the late 1990s, Japan has experienced several episodes of deflation.

Hyperinflation usually occurs when large scale government spending is not backed by real tax revenue and the monetary authority accommodates government spending with unlimited money supply. Hyperinflation is often triggered by the shortage of supply created during or after a war, economic regime transition, or prolonged economic distress of an economy caused by political instability. During hyperinflation, people are eager to change their cash into real goods because prices are rising very fast. As a result, money changes hands at extremely high frequency. The government also has to print more money to support its increased spending. As more cash chases a limited supply of goods and services, the rate of price increases accelerates. After World War I, a famous case of hyperinflation occurred in Germany from 1923 to 1924. During the peak of this episode, prices doubled every 3.7 days. After World War II, Hungary experienced a severe hyperinflation during which prices doubled every 15.6 hours at its peak in 1946. In 1993, the inflation rate in Ukraine peaked at 10,155 percent per year. In January 1994, the *monthly* inflation rate peaked at 313 million percent in Yugoslavia. The most recent hyperinflation in Zimbabwe reached a peak of *monthly* inflation at 79.6 billion percent in the middle of November 2008. Because the basic cause for hyperinflation is too much money in circulation, regaining control of the money supply is the key to ending hyperinflation.

Exhibit 4 shows recent episodes of disinflation in selected countries around the world. The first episode happened during the early 1980s. Because of the two oil crises in the 1970s, many countries around the world were experiencing high levels of inflation. In Exhibit 4, the annual inflation rates in most counties around 1980 ranged between 10 and 20 percent. Even though this level is still far from hyperinflation, it generated social pressure against inflationary monetary policy. At the cost of a severe recession early in the 1980s, these countries brought inflation rates down to around 5 percent on average by 1985. In the first years of the 1990s, inflationary experience varied widely in world markets as some countries entered recessions, such as the United States and the United Kingdom, and others boomed. However, from the beginning to the end of the decade, there was a broad-based decline in inflation rates; in some countries annual inflation rates were below 2 percent by the end of the decade. In many countries, the decline in inflation was attributed to high productivity growth rates.

Exhibit 4	Two Episodes of Disinflation around the World Annual Inflation Rates								
	First Episode					Second Episode			
Year	1979	1980	1983	1984	1985	1990	1991	1998	1999
Country									
Australia	9.1	10.2	10.1	3.9	6.7	7.3	3.2	0.9	1.5
Canada	9.1	10.1	5.9	4.3	4.0	4.8	5.6	1.0	1.7

| Exhibit 4 | (Continued) | | | | | | | | |

| | First Episode | | | | | Second Episode | | | |
Year	1979	1980	1983	1984	1985	1990	1991	1998	1999
Finland	7.5	11.6	8.4	7.1	5.2	6.1	4.3	1.4	1.2
France	10.6	13.6	9.5	7.7	5.8	3.2	3.2	0.6	0.5
Germany	4.0	5.4	3.3	2.4	2.1	2.7	4.0	1.0	0.6
Italy	14.8	21.1	14.6	10.8	9.2	6.5	6.3	2.0	1.7
Japan	3.7	7.8	1.9	2.3	2.0	3.1	3.3	0.7	−0.3
Korea	18.3	28.7	3.4	2.3	2.5	8.6	9.3	7.5	0.8
Spain	15.7	15.6	12.2	11.3	8.8	6.7	5.9	1.8	2.3
Sweden	7.2	13.7	8.9	8.0	7.4	10.4	9.4	−0.3	0.5
United Kingdom	13.4	18.0	4.6	5.0	6.1	7.0	7.5	1.6	1.3
United States	11.3	13.5	3.2	4.3	3.5	5.4	4.2	1.6	2.2
Average	10.4	14.1	7.2	5.8	5.3	6.0	5.5	1.6	1.2
G–7 Countries	9.6	12.5	4.6	4.6	3.9	4.8	4.4	1.3	1.4

Source: The Organisation for Economic Co-Operation and Development (OECD).

4.2.2 *Measuring Inflation: The Construction of Price Indices*

Because the inflation rate is measured as the percentage change of a price index, it is important to understand how a price index is constructed so that the inflation rate derived from that index can be accurately interpreted. A **price index** represents the average prices of a basket of goods and services, and various methods can be used to average the different prices. Exhibit 5 shows a simple example of the change of a consumption basket over time.

| Exhibit 5 | Consumption Basket and Prices over Two Months | | | |

Time	January 2010		February 2010	
Goods	Quantity	Price	Quantity	Price
Rice	50 kg	¥3/kg	70 kg	¥4/kg
Gasoline	70 liters	¥4.4/liter	60 liters	¥4.5/liter

For January 2010, the total value of the consumption basket is:

Value of rice + Value of gasoline = $(50 \times 3) + (70 \times 4.4) = ¥458$

A price index uses the relative weight of a good in a basket to weight the price in the index. Therefore, the same consumption basket in February 2010 is worth:

Value of rice + Value of gasoline = $(50 \times 4) + (70 \times 4.5) = ¥515$

The price index in the base period is usually set to 100. So if the price index in January 2010 is 100, then the price index in February 2010 is:

$$\text{Price index in February 2010} = \frac{515}{458} \times 100 = ¥112.45$$

$$\text{The inflation rate} = \frac{112.45}{100} - 1 = 0.1245 = 12.45\%$$

A price index created by holding the composition of the consumption basket constant is called a **Laspeyres index**. Most price indices around the world are Laspeyres indices because the survey data on the consumption basket is only available with a lag. In many countries, the basket is updated every five years. Because most price indices are created to measure the cost of living, simply using a fixed basket of goods and services has three serious biases:

▪ The substitution bias: As the price of one good or service rises, people may substitute it with other goods or services that have a lower price. This substitution will result in an upward bias in the measured inflation rate based on a Laspeyres index.

▪ The quality bias: As the quality of the same product improves over time, it satisfies people's needs and wants better. One such example is the quality of cars. Over the years, the prices of cars have been rising but the safety and reliability of cars have also been enhanced. If not adjusted for quality, the measured inflation rate will experience another upward bias.

▪ New product bias: New products are frequently introduced and a fixed basket of goods and services will not include them. In general, this situation again creates an upward bias in the inflation rate.

It is relatively easy to resolve the quality bias and new product bias. Many countries adjust for the quality of the products in a basket, a practice called hedonic pricing. New products can be introduced into the basket over time. The substitution bias can be somewhat resolved by using chained price index formula. One such example is the **Fisher index**, which is the geometric mean of the Laspeyres index and the **Paasche index**. The latter is an index formula using the current composition of the basket. Using the consumption basket for February 2010 in Exhibit 5, the value of the Paasche index is

$$\text{Paasche Index}_{02/2010} = I_P = \frac{(70 \times 4) + (60 \times 4.5)}{(70 \times 3) + (60 \times 4.4)} \times 100$$

$$= \frac{550}{474} \times 100 = 116.03$$

The value of the Fisher index is

$$\text{Fisher Index}_{02/2010} = \sqrt{I_P \times I_L} = \sqrt{116.03 \times 112.45} = 114.23$$

where I_L is the Laspeyres index.

4.2.3 Price Indices and Their Usage

Most countries use their own consumer price index (CPI) to track inflation in the domestic economy. Exhibit 6 shows the different weights for various categories of goods and services in the consumer price indices of different countries.

Exhibit 6	The Consumption Basket of Different Consumer Price Indices					
Country	Japan	China	India	Germany	United States	United States
Name of Index	CPI	CPI	CPI(UNME)	HICP	PCE	CPI-U
Year[a]	2005	2005	1984/85	2008	2009	2007/08
Category (%):						
Food and Beverage	25.9	34	47.1	16.7	7.8	14.8
Housing and Utility	27.2	13	21.9	23.1	18.8	37.4

					United	
Country	Japan	China	India	Germany	States	United States
Furniture	3.4	6	2.0	6.1	2.5	4.6
Apparel	4.6	9	7.0	5.3	3.2	3.7
Medical Care	4.5	10	2.5	4.4	16.2	6.5
Transportation and Communication	13.9	10	5.2	17.6	9.1	20.1
Education and Recreation	14.6	14	6.8	13.3	7.0[b]	9.5
Others	5.9	4	7.5	13.5	35.4	3.5

[a] The base year of the weights where it is appropriate.
[b] Recreation only.
Source: Government websites and authors' calculation.

As shown in Exhibit 6, in different countries the consumer price indices have different names and different weights on various categories of goods and services. For example, food weights are higher in the CPI for China and India, but less for the developed countries. The scope of the index is also different among countries. For China, Japan, and Germany, the surveys used to collect data for CPI cover both urban and rural areas. The CPI for the United States covers only urban areas using a household survey, which is why it is called the CPI-U. On the other hand, the **personal consumption expenditures** (PCE) price index covers all personal consumption in the United States using business surveys. The **producer price index** (PPI) is another important inflation measure. The PPI reflects the price changes experienced by domestic producers in a country. Because price increases may eventually pass through to consumers, the PPI can influence the future CPI. The items in the PPI include fuels, farm products (such as grains and meat), machinery and equipment, chemical products (such as drugs and paints), transportation equipment, metals, pulp and paper, and so on. These products are usually further grouped by stage-of-processing categories: crude materials, intermediate materials, and finished goods. Similar to the CPI, scope and weights vary among countries. The differences in the weights can be much more dramatic for the PPI than for the CPI because different countries may specialize in different industries. In some countries, the PPI is called the **wholesale price index** (WPI).

As an important inflation indicator, many economic activities are indexed to a certain price index. For example, the United States' **Treasury Inflation-Protected Securities** (TIPS) adjusts the bond's principal according to the US CPI-U index. The terms of labor contracts and commercial real estate leases may adjust periodically according to the CPI. Recurring payments in business contracts can be linked to the PPI or its sub-indices for a particular category of products.

Central banks usually use a consumer price index to monitor inflation. For example, the European Central Bank (the ECB), the central bank for the European Union (EU) focuses on the harmonised index of consumer prices (HICP). Each member country in the EU first reports their own individual HICP and then Eurostat, the statistical office for the EU, aggregates the country level HICPs with country weights. There are exceptions, however. The Reserve Bank of India follows the inflation in India using WPI. Because food items only represent about 27 percent in the India WPI (much lower than the 70 percent in the India rural CPI), the rural CPIs can rise faster than the WPI when there is high food price inflation. Besides the weight differences, the wholesale prices in the WPI also understate market prices because they do not take into account retail margins (markups). The choice of inflation indicator may also change over time. The central bank of the United States, known as the Federal Reserve Board (the Fed) once focused on the CPI-U produced by the Bureau of Labor Statistics under the US Department of Labor. Because the CPI-U is a Laspeyres index and it has the previously discussed upward biases, the Fed switched in 2000 to the PCE index, a Fisher index produced by the Bureau of Economic Analysis under the US Department of Commerce. The PCE index also has the advantage that it covers the complete range of consumer spending rather than just a basket.

EXAMPLE 11

Headline and Core Inflation

Headline inflation refers to the inflation rate calculated based on the price index that includes all goods and services in an economy. **Core inflation** usually refers to the inflation rate calculated based on a price index of goods and services except food and energy. Policymakers often choose to focus on the core inflation rate when reading the trend in the economy and making economic policies. The reason is that policymakers are trying to avoid overreaction to short-term fluctuations in food and energy prices that may not have a significant impact on future headline inflation.

The ultimate goal for policymakers is to control headline inflation, which reflects the actual cost of living. The fluctuations in the prices of food and energy are often the result of short-term changes in supply and demand. These changes in the prices of energy, particularly oil, are internationally determined and not necessarily reflective of the domestic business cycle. These imbalances may not persist, or even if some changes are permanent, the economy may be able to absorb them over time. These possibilities make headline inflation a noisy predictor. The core inflation rate may be a better signal of the trend in domestically driven inflation. To the extent that some trends in the headline inflation rate are permanent, policymakers need to pay attention to these as well.

Besides tracking inflation, financial analysts also use the price index to deflate GDP (i.e., to eliminate the price effect in nominal GDP data so as to identify trends in real economic growth). Many countries publish a particular price index, called the GDP deflator, for that purpose. Sub-indices are also commonly available and may prove more valuable to an analyst with an interest in a particular industry or company.

EXAMPLE 12

Sub-Indices and Relative Prices

As mentioned previously, a sub-index refers to the price index for a particular category of goods or services. **Relative price** is the price of a specific good or service in comparison with those of other goods and services. Good examples for relative prices include the prices for food and energy. The movements in a sub-index or a relative price may be difficult to detect in the headline inflation rate. Because macroeconomic policy decision-makers rely heavily on the headline inflation rate, they may not be aware of price movements at the sub-index level. These prices movements, however, can be very useful for analyzing the prospects of an industry or a company. For example, if the producer price index for the machinery used by an industry rises quickly, the allowable capital depreciation permitted by the existing tax code may not generate sufficient tax benefits for the companies in that industry to meet future replacement expenses. The future profitability of the industry may decline for this reason. The decline in prices for flat screen televisions provides an example of relative price movements. The price drop for these TVs may help to lower inflation pressure but can hurt manufacturers' profits.

EXAMPLE 13

Inflation

1   Which one of the following economic phenomena related to inflation cannot be determined by using observations of the inflation rate alone?

A   Deflation.

B   Stagflation.

C   Hyperinflation.

2   If a price index is calculated based on a fixed basket of goods, in an inflationary environment the inflation rate calculated based on this index over time will:

A   overstate the actual cost of living.

B   understate the actual cost of living.

C   track the actual cost of living quite closely.

Solution to 1:

B is correct. A high inflation rate alone does not indicate stagflation, which happens if high unemployment occurs together with high inflation.

Solution to 2:

A is correct. The upward biases, such as the substitution bias or quality bias, will overstate the actual cost of living.

4.2.4 Explaining Inflation

Economists describe two types of inflation: **cost-push**, in which rising costs, usually wages, compel businesses to raise prices generally; and **demand-pull**, in which increasing demand raise prices generally, which then are reflected in a business's costs as workers demand wage hikes to catch up with the rising cost of living. Whatever the sequence by which prices and costs rise in an economy, the fundamental cause is the same: excessive demands—either for raw materials, finished goods, or labor—that outstrip the economy's ability to respond. The initial signs appear in the areas with the greatest constraints: the labor market, the commodity market, or in some area of final output. Even before examining particular cost and price measures, practitioners, when considering inflation, look to indicators that might reveal when the economy faces such constraints.

4.2.4.1 Cost-Push Inflation   In the area of cost-push, or wage-push, inflation, analysts can look for signs in commodity prices because commodities are an input to production. But because wages are the single biggest cost to businesses, they focus most particularly on the labor market. Because the object is to gauge demand relative to capacity, the unemployment rate is key, as well as measures of the number of workers available to meet the economy's expanding needs. Obviously, the higher the unemployment rate, the lower the likelihood that shortages will develop in labor markets, whereas the lower the unemployment rate, the greater likelihood that shortages will drive up wages. Because the unemployment rate generally only counts people who are looking for work, some practitioners argue that it fails to account for the economy's full labor potential, and they state that a tight labor market will bring people out in search of work and ease any potential wage strains. To account for this issue and to modify the unemployment rate indicator, these practitioners also look at the participation rate of people in the workforce, arguing that it gives a fuller and more accurate picture of potential than the unemployment rate.

Analysis in this area recognizes that not all labor is alike. Structural factors related to training deficiencies, cultural patterns in all or some of the population, inefficiencies in the labor market, and the like can mean that the economy will effectively face labor shortages long before the unemployment rate reaches very low figures. This effective unemployment rate, below which pressure emerges in labor markets, is frequently referred to as the **non-accelerating inflation rate of unemployment** (NAIRU) or, drawing on the work of the Nobel Prize winner Milton Friedman, the **natural rate of unemployment** (NARU). Of course, these rates vary from one economy to another and over time in a single economy. It is this rate rather than full employment that determines when an economy will experience bottlenecks in the labor market and wage-push inflationary pressures.

Take, for example, the technology sector. It has grown so rapidly in some economies that training in the workforce cannot keep up with demand. This sector can, as a consequence, face shortages of trained workers and attendant wage pressures even though the economy as a whole seems to have considerable slack in the overall labor market. Until training (supply) catches up with demand, that economy may carry a high NARU and NAIRU, yet experience wage and inflation pressure at rates of unemployment that in other places and circumstances might suggest ample slack in the labor market and much less wage-push pressure.

Of course, such assessments of wage-push inflation also find indicators in direct observations of the wage trends that, when they accelerate, might force businesses to raise prices (initiating the wage-price spiral mentioned earlier in this reading). Statistical agencies provide a wide array of wage-cost indicators, such as hourly wage gauges, weekly earnings, and overall labor costs, including the outlays for benefits. Some of these indicators include the effects of special overtime pay or bonuses, others do not. And although these measures give an idea of the cost to businesses and hence the kind of wage-push inflationary pressure, a complete picture only emerges when practitioners examine such trends alongside productivity measures.

Productivity, or output per hour, is an essential part of this inflation analysis because the output available from each worker determines the number of units over which businesses can spread the cost of worker compensation. The greater each worker's output is per hour, the lower price businesses need to charge for each unit of output to cover hourly labor costs. And by extension, the faster output per hour grows, the faster labor compensation can expand without putting undue pressure on businesses' costs per unit of output. The equation for this **unit labor cost** (ULC) indicator, as it is called, is as follows:

$$ULC = W/O$$

where:

ULC = unit labor costs
O = output per hour per worker
W = total labor compensation per hour per worker

Many factors can affect labor productivity across time and between economies. The cyclical swings have already been described, as have the effects of technology and training. The pace of development also tends to increase worker productivity because the more sophisticated equipment, systems, and technologies workers have at their disposal, the higher their output per hour. Whatever causes the productivity growth, if it fails to keep up with worker compensation, unit costs to a business rise and, as a business tries to protect its profit margins, prices generally come under increasing upward pressure. Generally this situation occurs because heavy demand for labor relative to available labor resources has pushed up compensation faster than productivity. Practitioners look for this relationship in this mix of indicators to identify cost- or wage-push inflationary pressure.

EXAMPLE 14

Unemployment Too High

Which of the following is true about NARU and NAIRU?

A They only work in monetarist models.

B They may change over time given changes in technology and economic structure.

C They do not account for bottlenecks in the labor market.

Solution:

B is correct. The NARU and NAIRU may change over time. A is incorrect. NARU and NAIRU are the unemployment rates at which the inflation rate will not rise because of a shortage of labor. This concept does not tie to a particular school of macroeconomic models. C is incorrect because those rates determine when an economy will experience bottlenecks in the labor market.

4.2.4.2 Demand-Pull Inflation The search for indicators from the demand-pull side of the inflation question brings financial analysts back to the relationship between actual and potential real GDP and industrial capacity utilization. In a manner entirely analogous to the unemployment rate in the labor market, the higher the rate of capacity utilization or the closer actual GDP is to potential, the more likely an economy will suffer shortages, bottlenecks, a general inability to satisfy demand, and hence, price increases—initially in commodities but ultimately more generally. And, of course, the more an economy operates below its potential or the lower the rate of capacity utilization, the less such supply pressure will exist and the greater likelihood of a slowdown in inflation, or outright deflation. In addition to these macro indicators, practitioners will also look for signs of inflationary pressure in commodity prices, in part because they are a cost to business, but more as a general sign of excess demand. For an individual economy, such observations could be misleading, however, because commodities trade in a global market and accordingly reflect global economic conditions more than those in an individual economy.

From an entirely different perspective, Monetarists contend that inflation is fundamentally a monetary phenomenon. A surplus of money, they argue, will inflate the money price of everything in the economy. Stated in terms of straightforward supply and demand relationships, a surplus of money would bring down its value just as a surplus in any market would bring down the price of the product in excess. Because the price of money is stated in terms of the products it can buy, its declining value would have an expression in higher prices generally, that is, in inflation. This Monetarist argument, as it is called, finds a more simple expression in the old saying that inflation results when too much money chases too few goods. Although it seems distant from other explanations of inflation, in practice, it is not that distinct. The excess of money creates the inflation by increasing liquidity, which ultimately causes a rapid rise in demand. In this sense, the Monetarist argument is a special case under the more general heading of demand-pull concepts of inflation. The practical distinction between the monetarist and other approaches is in identifying the initial cause of the demand excess.

Financial analysts can track this effect by examining various money supply indicators, usually provided by the central bank. To detect an inflationary potential or the opposite, they note accelerations or decelerations in money growth from past trends. Obviously, accelerations, in the absence of a special explanation, signal the potential for inflationary pressure. In applying this approach, practitioners also compare money growth with the growth of the nominal economy, represented by nominal GDP. If money growth outpaces the growth of the nominal economy, there is an inflationary potential, especially if money growth has also accelerated from its trend. There is a disinflationary or deflationary potential if money growth trails the economy's rate of expansion, especially if it has also decelerated from its trend.

EXAMPLE 15

Velocity of Money (I)

Some practitioners view the likelihood of inflationary pressure from the vantage point of the ratio of nominal GDP to money supply, commonly called the "velocity of money." If this ratio remains stable around a constant or a historical trend, they see reason to look for relative price stability. If velocity falls, it could suggest a surplus of money that might have inflationary potential, but much depends on why it has declined. If velocity has fallen because a cyclical correction has brought down the GDP numerator relative to the money denominator, then practitioners view prospects as more likely to lead to a cyclical upswing to reestablish the former relationship than inflationary pressure. If velocity has fallen, however, because of an increase in the money denominator, then inflationary pressure becomes more likely. If velocity rises, financial analysts might be concerned about a shortage of money in the economy and disinflation or deflation.

The 2008–2009 global recession and financial crisis offers an extreme example of these velocity ambiguities. As the global economy slipped into recession, which held back the GDP numerator in velocity measures, central banks, most notably the Federal Reserve in the United States, tried to help financial institutions cope by injecting huge amounts of money into their respective financial systems, raising the velocity denominator. Velocity measures plummeted accordingly. The expectation is that subsequent GDP growth as economies and financial markets heal will bring velocity back to a more normal level and trend. That said, the fear is that the monetary surge will, over the very long run, lead to inflation. For policy makers, this situation has created a very difficult policy choice. On the one side, they need to sustain the supply of money to help their respective economies cope with the after effects of the financial crisis. On the other side, they need ultimately to withdraw any monetary excess to preclude potential inflationary pressures.

4.2.5 *Inflation Expectations*

Beyond demand-pull, monetary, and cost-push inflation considerations, practitioners also need to account for the effect of inflation expectations. Once inflation becomes embedded in an economy, businesses, workers, consumers, and economic actors of every kind begin to expect it and build those expectations into their actions. This reaction, in turn, creates an inflationary momentum of its own in a manner much like the wage-price spiral mentioned earlier in the reading. Such expectations give inflation something of a self-sustaining character and cause it to persist in an economy even after its initial cause has disappeared. High inflation rates persisted in the 1970s and early 1980s in Europe and the United States on the basis of expectations even after these economies had sunk into recession. The resulting slow or negative economic growth combined with high unemployment and rising inflation was termed "stagflation."

Measuring inflation expectations is not easy. Some practitioners gauge expectations by relying on past inflation trends and on the assumption that market participants largely extrapolate their past experiences. In some markets, surveys of inflation expectations are available, although these are often biased by the way the questions are asked. A third indicator becomes available when governments issue bonds that adjust in various ways to compensate holders for inflation, such as TIPS. By comparing the interest available on these bonds with other government bonds that do not offer such inflation-linked adjustments, practitioners can gauge the general level of inflation expectations among market participants and factor it into their own inflation forecasts and strategies.

For example, if today's yield on the 10-year nominal bond of a certain country is 3.5 percent and the yield on the 10-year inflation-protected bond of the same country is 1.5 percent, we infer that the market is pricing in a 3.5 − 1.5 = 2 percent average annual inflation over the next 10 years. However, this calculation needs to be treated cautiously because the market for inflation-linked bonds is relatively small and thus yields can be influenced by market other factors. For example, in the last decade TIPS yields appear to have been artificially depressed by very strong demand from pension funds trying to match their liabilities at any cost.

EXAMPLE 16

Velocity of Money (II)

1 Cost-push inflation most likely occurs when:

   A unemployment rates are low.

   B unemployment rates are high.

   C unemployment is either high or low.

2 Unit labor costs measure:

   A hourly wage rates.

   B total labor compensation per hour.

   C a combination of hourly wages and output.

3 Demand-pull inflation:

   A is a discredited concept.

   B depends on the movements in commodity prices.

   C reflects the state of economic activity relative to potential.

4 Monetarists believe inflation reflects:

   A the growth of money.

   B the level of interest rates.

   C that there is no difference between monetarist positions and cost-push inflation.

5   The inflationary potential of a particular inflation rate depends on the economy's NAIRU or NARU, which in turn depends in part on:

   A   the intensity of past cyclical swings.

   B   the bargaining power of trade unions.

   C   the skill set of the workforce relative to the economy's industrial mix.

6   Which of the following is *not* a problem with NARU and NAIRU?

   A   They are not observable directly.

   B   They work only in monetarist models.

   C   They change over time given changes in technology and economic structure.

Solution to 1:

A is correct. When unemployment is below NAIRU, there is a shortage of labor that pushes up labor cost.

Solution to 2:

C is correct. Unit labor costs reflect the labor cost in each unit of output.

Solution to 3:

C is correct. When the economy is operating above its potential capacity allowed by the resources available, inflation will start to rise.

Solution to 4:

A is correct. Monetarists emphasize the role of money growth in determining the inflation rate, especially in the long run. As Milton Friedman famously put it: "Inflation is always and everywhere a monetary phenomenon."

Solution to 5:

C is correct. If the skill set of a large part of the workforce cannot satisfy the hiring need from the employers, the NAIRU of such an economy can be quite high.

Solution to 6:

B is correct. NAIRU or NARU reflects the potential of an economy and thus cannot be directly observed from the economic data. They also change over time depending on technological progress and social factors.

5   ECONOMIC INDICATORS

As used in business cycle contexts, an **economic indicator** is a variable that provides information on the state of the overall economy. Economic indicators are often classified according to whether they lag, lead, or coincide with changes in an economy's growth. **Leading economic indicators** have turning points that usually precede those of the overall economy. They are believed to have value for predicting the economy's future state, usually near-term. **Coincident economic indicators** have turning points that are usually close to those of the overall economy. They are believed to have value for identifying the economy's present state. **Lagging economic indicators** have turning points that take place later than those of the overall economy. They are believed to have value in identifying the economy's past condition.

To get as clear of a picture as possible, practitioners frequently consider several related indicators simultaneously. What follows is a review of these indicators and how practitioners use them.

5.1 Popular Economic Indicators

A very useful approach for practitioners is to take an aggregate perspective on leading, lagging, and coincident indicators. These aggregate measures typically are a composite of economic indicators known respectively to lead the cycle, run coincident with it, or lag it at cyclical turns. For obvious reasons, the leading indicators in particular help with anticipating cyclical turns up or down and allow strategists and others to position themselves and their companies in a secure and timely way to benefit from movements in the economic cycle.

The exact indicators combined into these composites vary from one economy to the other. Even within an economy, they can have a remarkably diverse and eclectic character. In the United States, for instance, the composite leading indicator known as the **Index of Leading Economic Indicators** (LEI) has 10 component parts that run the gamut from orders for capital goods, to changes in the money supply, to swings in stock prices. Such composite indicators in other countries include equally eclectic combinations.

Similar statistics are available for numerous economies. The Conference Board, a US industry research organization, computes leading, lagging, and coincident indicators for the United States and nine other countries plus the Euro area (Eurozone). For about 30 countries and several aggregates, such as the EU and G–7, the Organisation for Economic Co-Operation and Development (OECD) calculates CLI (Composite Leading Indicators) indices, which gauge the state of the business cycle in the economy. One of the interesting features of CLI indices is that they are consistent across countries, and therefore, can be compared more easily to see how each region is faring. The Economic Cycle Research Institute (ECRI), a private company, also computes leading indicator indices for about 20 countries on a weekly basis.

Although specifics for leading, coincident, and lagging indicators vary from one economy to another, they have much in common. In each case, they bring together various economic and financial measures that have displayed a consistently leading, coincident, or lagging relationship to that economy's general cycle. However, as reported by the Conference Board, the timing record of the various composite indices for the United States has varied over the last 50 years. The coincident index closely matches the NBER peak and trough dates, with 8 of the last 13 turning points correspond to the beginning or end of a recession. The leading indicator index displays more variability, leading cyclical contractions by 8 to 20 months and expansions by 1 to 10 months.[13]

Exhibit 7 presents the 10 leading, 4 coincident, and 7 lagging indicators tracked for the United States by the Conference Board. In addition to naming the indicators, it also offers a general description of why each measure fits in each of the three groups.

---

13 The Conference Board, *Business Cycle Indicators Handbook* (2001):pp 14, 15.

Exhibit 7   Leading, Coincident, and Lagging Indicators — USA

Indicator and Description	Reason
Leading	
1 Average weekly hours, manufacturing	Because businesses will cut overtime before laying off workers in a downturn and increase it before rehiring in a cyclical upturn, these measures move up and down before the general economy.
2 Average weekly initial claims for unemployment insurance	This measure offers a very sensitive test of initial layoffs and rehiring.
3 Manufacturers' new orders for consumer goods and materials	Because businesses cannot wait too long to meet demands for consumer goods or materials without ordering, these gauges tend to lead at upturns and downturns. Indirectly, they capture changes in business sentiment as well, which also often leads the cycle.
4 Vendor performance, slower deliveries diffusion index[a]	By measuring the speed at which businesses can complete and deliver an order, this gauge offers a clear signal of unfolding demands on businesses.
5 Manufacturers' new orders for non-defense capital goods	In addition to offering a first signal of movement, up or down, in an important economic sector, movement in this area also indirectly captures business expectations.
6 Building permits for new private housing units	Because most localities require permits before new building can begin, this gauge foretells new construction activity.
7 S&P 500 Stock Index	Because stock prices anticipate economic turning points, both up and down, their movements offer a useful early signal on economic cycles.
8 Money supply, real M^2	Because money supply growth measures the tightness or looseness of monetary policy, increases in money beyond inflation indicate easy monetary conditions and a positive economic response, whereas declines in real M^2 indicate monetary restraint and a negative economic response.
9 Interest rate spread between 10-year treasury yields and overnight borrowing rates (federal funds rate)	Because long-term yields express market expectations about the direction of short-term interest rates, and rates ultimately follow the economic cycle up and down, a wider spread, by anticipating short rate increases, also anticipates an economic upswing. Conversely, a narrower spread, by anticipating short rate decreases, also anticipates an economic downturn.
10 Index of Consumer Expectations, University of Michigan	Because the consumer is about two-thirds of the US economy and will spend more or less freely according to his or her expectations, this gauge offers early insight into future consumer spending and consequently directions in the whole economy.
Coincident	
1 Employees on non-agricultural payrolls	Once recession or recovery is clear, businesses adjust their fulltime payrolls.
2 Aggregate real personal income (less transfer payments)	By measuring the income flow from non-corporate profits and wages, this measure captures the current state of the economy.
3 Industrial Production Index	Measures industrial output, thus capturing the behavior of the most volatile part of the economy. The service sector tends to be more stable.
4 Manufacturing and trade sales	In the same way as aggregate personal income and the industrial production index, this aggregate offers a measure of the current state of business activity.

Exhibit 7	(Continued)	

Indicator and Description		Reason
Lagging		
1	Average Duration of Unemployment	Because businesses wait until downturns look genuine to lay off, and wait until recoveries look secure to rehire, this measure is important because it lags the cycle on both the way down and the way up.
2	Inventory–sales ratio	Because inventories accumulate as sales initially decline and then, once a business adjusts its ordering, become depleted as sales pick up, this ratio tends to lag the cycle.
3	Change in unit labor costs	Because businesses are slow to fire workers, these costs tend to rise into the early stages of recession as the existing workforce is used less intensely. Late in the recovery when the labor market gets tight, upward pressure on wages can also raise such costs. In both cases, there is a clear lag at cyclical turns.
4	Average bank prime lending rate	Because this is a bank administered rate, it tends to lag other rates that move either before cyclical turns or with them.
5	Commercial and industrial loans outstanding	Because these loans frequently support inventory building, they lag the cycle for much the same reason that the inventory–sales ratio does.
6	Ratio of consumer installment debt to income	Because consumers only borrow heavily when confident, this measure lags the cyclical upturn, but debt also overstays cyclical downturns because households have trouble adjusting to income losses, causing it to lag in the downturn.
7	Change in consumer price index for services	Inflation generally adjusts to the cycle late, especially the more stable services area.

[a] A diffusion index usually measures the percentage of components in a series that are rising in the same period. It indicates how widespread a particular movement in the trend is among the individual components.

Let us consider a few examples that show the use of these statistics in identifying a business cycle phase. An increase in the reported ratio of consumer installment debt to income lags (occurs after) cyclical upturns; so the increase, by itself, would be evidence that an upturn has been underway. That could confirm the implication of positive changes in coincident indicators that an expansion is in place. As a leading economic indicator, a positive change in the S&P 500 Index is supposed to lead (come before) an increase in aggregate economic activity. An increase in the S&P 500 would be positive for future economic growth, all else equal. However, if the S&P 500 showed an increase but the aggregate index did not, we would likely not draw a positive conclusion. For a final example, if we observed that the LEI moved up a small amount on two consecutive observations, we might conclude that a modest economic expansion is expected.

The component indicators for other countries, though different in specifics, are similar in most respects. The Eurozone, for instance, composes its leading index from eight components:

1 Economic sentiment index
2 Residential building permits
3 Capital goods orders
4 The Euro Stoxx Equity Index
5 M^2 money supply

6 An interest rate spread

7 Eurozone Manufacturing Purchasing Managers Index

8 Eurozone Service Sector Future Business Activity Expectations Index

The parallels between many of these components and those used in the United States are clear, but Europe has a services component in its business activity measures that the United States lacks, whereas Europe forgoes many of the overtime and employment gauges that the United States includes.

Japan's leading index contains 10 components:

1 New orders for machinery and construction equipment

2 Real operating profits

3 Overtime worked

4 Dwelling units started

5 Six-month growth rate in labor productivity

6 Business failures

7 Business confidence (Tankan Survey)

8 Stock prices

9 Real M^2 money supply

10 Interest rate spread

Again many are similar, but Japan includes labor market indicators more like the United States than Europe and adds a measure of business failures not included in the other two.

Similarities and differences along these lines appear in indicators for the United Kingdom, Australia, South Africa, specific European economies, and other countries. The general tone is, however, similar to the detail provided here for the United States.

EXAMPLE 17

Building Permits as a Leading Economic Indicator

Exhibit 8 shows an example of a leading economic indicator in Germany, the granted building permits along with its relationship to the growth of Germany's GDP. In Exhibit 8, the growth rate of building permits usually peaks one quarter ahead of the GDP growth rate, with the exception for the first half of 2008 and 2010. Before 2006, the growth rate of building permits usually bottomed out earlier than the GDP growth rate by four quarters. But after 2006, the troughs of the two series almost coincide. The uncertainty of the relationships between an indicator and business cycles is very common. Some indicators may be good predictors for economic expansions but poor predictors for recessions. This uncertainty is why economists and statisticians often combine different indicators and try to find common factors among them when building indicator indices.

Exhibit 8   The Growth Rates of Germany GDP and Number of Building Permits

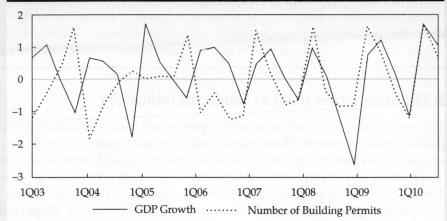

Note: The quarter-to-quarter growth rates are normalized by using the standard deviations of the two series, respectively.
Source: Federal Statistical Office of Germany.

EXAMPLE 18

Diffusion Index of Economic Indicators

In the United States, the Conference Board also compiles a monthly diffusion index of the leading, lagging, and coincident indicators. The **diffusion index** reflects the proportion of the index's components that are moving in a pattern consistent with the overall index. Analysts often rely on these diffusion indices to provide a measure of the breadth of the change in a composite index.

For example, the Conference Board tracks the growth of each of the 10 constituents of its leading indicator measure, assigning a value of 1.0 to each indicator that rises by more than 0.05 percent during the monthly measurement period, a value of 0.5 for each component indicator that changes by less than 0.05 percent, and a value of 0 for each component indicator that falls by more than 0.05 percent. These assigned values, which of course differ in other indices in other countries, are then summed and divided by 10 (the number of components). Then to make the overall measure resemble the more familiar indices, the Board multiplies the result by 100.

A simple numerical example will help explain. Say, for ease of exposition, the indicator has only four component parts: stock prices, money growth, orders, and consumer confidence. In one month, stock prices rise 2.0 percent, money growth rises 1.0 percent, orders are flat, and consumer confidence falls by 0.6 percent. Using the Conference Board's assigned values, these would contribute respectively: 1.0 + 1.0 + 0.5 + 0 to create a numerator of 2.5. When divided by four (the number of components) and multiplied by 100, it generates an indicator of 62.5 for that month.

Assume that the following month stock prices fall 0.8 percent, money grows by 0.5 percent, orders pick up 0.5 percent, and consumer confidence grows 3.5 percent. Applying the appropriate values, the components would add to 0 + 1.0 + 1.0 + 1.0 = 3.0. Divided by the number of components and multiplied by

100, this yields an index value of 75. The 20.0 percent increase in the index value means more components of the composite index are rising. Given this result, an analyst can be more confident that the higher composite index value actually represents broader movements in the economy. In general, a diffusion index does not reflect outliers in any component (like a straight arithmetic mean would do) but instead tries to capture the overall change common to all components.

5.2 Other Variables Used as Economic Indicators

In addition to this array of measures, public agencies and trade associations provide aggregate cyclical measures. These may include surveys of industrialists, bankers, labor associations, and households on the state of their finances, level of activity, and their confidence in the future. In the United States, for instance, the Federal Reserve polls its 12 branches for a qualitative report on business activity and expectations in their respective regions. It summarizes those findings in what it calls the "Beige Book" released every 6 weeks. Also in the United States, the Institute of Supply Management (ISM) polls its members to build indices of manufacturing orders, output, employment, pricing, and comparable gauges for services. Over the last decade, so-called "purchasing managers" indices along the lines of the ISM have been introduced in a wide range of countries, including Europe and China. Japan's industrial organization polls its members in a similar way and releases the findings in what is called the "Tankan Report." These diverse sources multiply within and across economies. Practitioners can use these sources to assess whether they confirm or contradict other more broad-based cyclical indicators, giving pause to, or greater confidence in, those earlier conclusions.

Using a statistical technique called "principal components analysis," the Federal Reserve Bank of Chicago computes the Chicago Fed National Activity Index (CFNAI). The CFNAI is computed using 85 monthly macroeconomic series. These series cover industrial production, personal income, capital utilization, employment by sectors, housing starts, retail sales, and so on. Principal components analysis "extracts" the underlying trend that is common to most of these variables, thus distilling the essence of the US business cycle. Similarly, the Bank of Italy in conjunction with the Centre for Economic Policy Research (CEPR) produces the Euro–Coin statistic, which is also based on principal component analysis. There are more than one hundred macroeconomic series included in Euro–Coin. The Euro–Coin also includes data derived from surveys, interest rates, and other financial variables. Both CFNAI and Euro–Coin are freely available online.

EXAMPLE 19

Economic Indicators

1 Leading, lagging, and coincident indicators are:
  A the same worldwide.
  B based on historical cyclical observations.
  C based on Keynesian and/or Monetarist theory.
2 A diffusion index:
  A measures growth.
  B reflects the consensus change in economic indicators.
  C is roughly analogous to the indices used to measure industrial production.

3 In the morning business news, a financial analyst, Kevin Durbin, learned that average hourly earnings had increased last month. The most appropriate action for Durbin is to:

   A call his clients to inform them of a good trading opportunity today.

   B examine other leading indicators to see any confirmation of a possible turning point for the economy.

   C use the news in his research report as a confirmation for his belief that the economy has recovered from a recession.

4 Which one of the following is *not* thought to be a lagging indicator for the US economy?

   A Real M^2.

   B Unit labor costs.

   C Commercial and industrial loans.

5 The indicator indices created by various organizations or research agencies:

   A include only leading indicators to compute their value.

   B are highly reliable signals on the phase of business cycles.

   C evolve over time in terms of composition and computation formula.

6 Leading indicators are often very useful to investors because:

   A they help investors to predict long-run returns on stocks.

   B their turning points signal possible future change in the trend of economic growth.

   C they may change into coincident indicators to help confirm the current state of the economy.

Solution to 1:

B is correct. The recognition of economic indicators is based on empirical observations for an economy.

Solution to 2:

B is correct. The diffusion indices are constructed to reflect the common trends embedded in the movements of all the indicators included in such an index.

Solution to 3:

B is correct. Financial analysts need to synthesize the information from various indicators in order to gather a reliable reading of the economic trends.

Solution to 4:

A is correct. Real M^2 is a leading indicator.

Solution to 5:

C is correct. The indicator indices are constantly updated for their composition and methodology based on the accumulation of empirical knowledge, and they can certainly include more than just leading indicators.

Solution to 6:

B is correct. Leading indicators can help predict short-term trends but not that much on long-run return on equity. The changing nature of an indicator itself does not help investors that much.

SUMMARY

This reading has summarized business cycle analysis. Among the points made are the following:

- Business cycles are a fundamental feature of market economies but their amplitude and length varies considerably.

- Business cycles have four phases: trough, expansion, peak, and contraction.

- Keynesian theories focus on fluctuations of aggregate demand (AD). If AD shifts left, Keynesians advocate government intervention to restore full employment and avoid a deflationary spiral. Monetarists argue that the timing of government policies is uncertain and it is generally better to let the economy find its new equilibrium unassisted, but ensure that the money supply is kept growing at an even pace.

- New Classical and Real Business Cycle (RBC) theories also consider fluctuations of aggregate supply (AS). If AS shifts left because of an input price increase or right because of a price decrease or technical progress, the economy will gradually converge to its new equilibrium. Government intervention is generally not necessary because it may exacerbate the fluctuation or delay the convergence to equilibrium. New Keynesians argue that frictions in the economy may prevent convergence and government policies may be needed.

- The demand for factors of production may change in the short run as a result of changes in all components of GDP: consumption (e.g., households worry about the future, save more, and thus shift AD left), investment (e.g., companies expect customers to increase demand and buy new equipment, thus shifting AD right; another example is that companies introduce new technologies, thus shifting long-term AS right), government (e.g., fiscal and monetary policies shift AD), and net exports (e.g., faster growth in other countries generates higher demand for the home country's products, thus shifting AD, or higher prices of imported inputs shift AS left). Any shifts in AD and AS will affect the demand for the factors of production (capital and labor) that are used to produce the new level of GDP.

- Unemployment has different subcategories. Frictional (people that are not working because they are in between jobs); structural (people that are unemployed because they do not have the skills required by the openings or reside far away from the jobs); discouraged workers are unemployed people who have given up looking for jobs because they do not believe they can find one (they are considered outside the labor force in unemployment statistics); and voluntarily unemployed are people who do not wish to work, for example because they are in school, retired early, or very rich (they are also considered outside the labor force in unemployment statistics).

- There are different types of inflation. Hyperinflation indicates a high (e.g., 100 percent annual) and increasing rate of inflation; deflation indicates a negative inflation rate (prices decrease); imported inflation is associated with increasing cost of inputs that come from abroad; demand inflation is caused by constraints in production that prevent companies from making as many goods as the market demands (it is sometimes called wartime inflation because in times of war, goods tend to be rationed).

■ Economic indicators are statistics on macroeconomic variables that help in understanding which stage of the business cycle an economy is at. Of particular importance are the leading indicators, which suggest where the economy is likely to be in the near future. No economic indicator is perfect, and many of these statistics are subject to periodic revisions.

■ Price levels are affected by real factors and monetary factors. Real factors include aggregate supply (an increase in supply leads to lower prices) and aggregate demand (an increase in demand leads to higher prices). Monetary factors include the supply of money (more money circulating, if the economy is in equilibrium, will lead to higher prices) and the velocity of money (higher velocity, if the economy is in equilibrium, will lead to higher prices).

■ Inflation is measured by many indices. Consumer price indices reflect the prices of a basket of goods and services that is typically purchased by a normal household. Producer price indices measure the cost of a basket of raw materials, intermediate inputs, and finished products. GDP deflators measure the price of the basket of goods and services produced within an economy in a given year. Core indices exclude volatile items, such as agricultural products and energy, whose prices tend to vary more than other goods.

REFERENCES

Burns, Wesley Clair, and Arthur F. Mitchell. 1946. *Measuring Business Cycles*. National Bureau of Economic Research.

Christiano, Lawrence J., Martin Eichenbaum, and Charles L. Evans. 2005. "Nominal Rigidities and the Dynamic Effects of a Shock to Monetary Policy." *Journal of Political Economy*, vol. 113, no. 1:1–45.

Friedman, Milton. 1968. "The Role of Monetary Policy." *American Economic Review*, vol. 58, no. 1:1–17.

Greenspan, Alan. 2005. "Remarks on Central Banking." Speech given at the annual Kansas City Fed symposium in Jackson Hole, WY. Available online at http://www.federalreserve.gov/boarddocs/speeches/2005/20050826/default.htm.

Mankiw, N. Gregory. 1989. "Real Business Cycles: A New Keynesian Perspective." *Journal of Economic Perspectives*, vol. 3, no. 3:79–90.

McCulley, Paul. 2010. "The Shadow Banking System and Hyman Minsky's Economic Journey." In *Insights into the Global Crisis*. Charlottesville, VA: Research Foundation of CFA Institute.

Plosser, Charles I. 1989. "Understanding Real Business Cycles." *Journal of Economic Perspectives*, vol. 3, no. 3:51–77.

Reinhardt, Carmen, and Kenneth Rogoff. 2009. *This Time Is Different: Eight Centuries of Financial Folly*. Princeton, NJ: Princeton University Press.

Romer, David. 2005. *Advanced Macroeconomics*, 2nd edition. Columbus, OH: McGraw-Hill.

Siegel, Lawrence. 2010. *Insights into the Global Crisis*. Charlottesville, VA: Research Foundation of CFA Institute.

Woodford, Michael. 2009. "Convergence in Macroeconomics: Elements of the New Synthesis." *American Economic Journal: Macroeconomics*, vol. 1, no. 1:267–279.

PRACTICE PROBLEMS

1 Business cycle analysis *most* commonly describes economic activity that is conducted through:

   A state enterprises.

   B agricultural co-ops.

   C private corporations.

2 The characteristic business cycle patterns of trough, expansion, peak, and contraction are:

   A periodic.

   B recurrent.

   C of similar duration.

3 During the contraction phase of a business cycle, it is *most likely* that:

   A inflation indicators are stable.

   B aggregate economic activity is decreasing.

   C investor preference for government securities declines.

4 An economic peak is *most* closely associated with:

   A accelerating inflation.

   B stable unemployment.

   C declining capital spending.

5 Based on typical labor utilization patterns across the business cycle, productivity (output per hours worked) is *most likely* to be highest:

   A at the peak of a boom.

   B into a maturing expansion

   C at the bottom of a recession.

6 In a recession, companies are *most likely* to adjust their stock of physical capital by:

   A selling it at fire sale prices.

   B not maintaining equipment.

   C quickly canceling construction activity.

7 The inventory/sales ratio is *most likely* to be rising:

   A as a contraction unfolds.

   B partially into a recovery.

   C near the top of an economic cycle.

8 The Austrian economic school attributes the primary cause of the business cycle to:

   A misguided government intervention.

   B the creative destruction of technological progress.

   C sticky price and wage expectations that exaggerate trends.

9 Monetarists favor a limited role for the government because they argue:

   A government policies operate with a lag.

   B firms take time to adjust to systemic shocks to the economy.

C   resource use is efficient with marginal revenue and cost equal.

10 The discouraged worker category is defined to include people who:

A   are overqualified for their job.

B   could look for a job but choose not to.

C   currently look for work without finding it.

11 The unemployment rate is considered a lagging indicator because:

A   new job types must be defined to count their workers.

B   multi-worker households change jobs at a slower pace.

C   businesses are slow to hire and fire due to related costs.

12 The factor for which it is *most* difficult to estimate its effect on the unemployment rate is:

A   technological progress.

B   the use of temporary workers.

C   the nature of underemployment.

13 The category of persons who would be *most likely* to be harmed by an increase in the rate of inflation is:

A   homeowners with fixed 30-year mortgages.

B   retirees relying on a fixed annuity payment.

C   workers employed under contracts with escalator clauses.

14 The term that describes when inflation declines but nonetheless remains at a positive level is:

A   deflation.

B   stagflation.

C   disinflation.

15 Deflation is *most likely* to be associated with:

A   a shortage of government revenue.

B   substantial macroeconomic contraction.

C   explicit monetary policy to combat inflation.

16 The *least likely* consequence of a period of hyperinflation is the:

A   reduced velocity of money.

B   increased supply of money.

C   possibility of social unrest.

The following information relates to Questions 17–18

Exhibit 1	Consumption Baskets and Prices Over Two Months			
Date	**November 2010**		**December 2010**	
Goods	**Quantity**	**Price**	**Quantity**	**Price**
Sugar	70 kg	€ 0.90 / kg	120 kg	€ 1.00 / kg
Cotton	60 kg	€ 0.60 / kg	50 kg	€ 0.80 / kg

17 Assuming the base period for 2010 consumption is November and the initial price index is set at 100, then the inflation rate after calculating the December price index as a Laspeyres index is *closest* to:

A 19.2%.

B 36.4%.

C 61.6%.

18 For the December consumption basket in Exhibit 1, the value of the Paasche index is *closest* to:

A 116.

B 148.

C 160.

19 The characteristic of national consumer price indexes which is *most* typically shared across major economies worldwide is:

A the geographic areas covered in their surveys.

B the weights they place on covered goods and services.

C their use in the determination of macroeconomic policy.

20 Of the following statements regarding the Producer Price Index (PPI), which is the *least likely*? The PPI:

A can influence the future CPI.

B category weights can vary more widely than analogous CPI terms.

C is used more frequently than CPI as a benchmark for adjusting labor contract payments.

21 The inflation rate *most likely* relied on to determine public economic policy is:

A core inflation.

B headline inflation.

C index of food and energy prices.

22 What is the *most* important effect of labor productivity in a cost-push inflation scenario?

A Rising productivity indicates a strong economy and a bias towards inflation.

B The productivity level determines the economy's status relative to its "natural rate of unemployment."

    C As productivity growth proportionately exceeds wage increases, product price increases are less likely.

23 Which of the following statements is the *best* description of the characteristics of economic indicators?

    A Leading indicators are important because they track the entire economy.

    B Lagging indicators in measuring past conditions do not require revisions.

    C A combination of leading and coincident indicators can offer effective forecasts.

24 When the spread between 10-year US Treasury yields and the federal funds rate narrows and at the same time the prime rate stays unchanged, this mix of indicators *most likely* forecasts future economic:

    A growth.

    B decline.

    C stability.

25 If relative to prior values of their respective indicators, the inventory–sales ratio has risen, unit labor cost is stable, and real personal income has decreased, it is *most likely* that a peak in the business cycle:

    A has occurred.

    B is just about to occur.

    C will occur sometime into the future.

SOLUTIONS

1 C is correct. Business cycles relate to fluctuations in national economic activity generated mainly through business enterprises.

2 B is correct. The stages of the business cycle occur repeatedly over time.

3 B is correct. The net trend during contraction is negative.

4 A is correct. Inflation is rising at peaks.

5 C is correct. At the end of a recession, firms will run "lean production" to generate maximum output with the fewest number of workers.

6 B is correct. Physical capital adjustments to downturns come through aging of equipment plus lack of maintenance.

7 C is correct. Near the top of a cycle, sales begin to slow before production is cut, leading to an increase in inventories relative to sales.

8 A is correct. Austrian economists see monetary policy mistakes as leading to booms and busts.

9 A is correct. Monetarists caution policy effects can occur long after the need for which they were implemented is no longer an issue.

10 B is correct. Discouraged workers are defined as persons who have stopped looking for work and are outside the labor force.

11 C is correct. This effect makes unemployment rise more slowly as recessions start and fall more slowly as recoveries begin.

12 A is correct. The impact of new technologies can be experienced over a period as long as decades, while unemployment is measured over a much shorter time frame.

13 B is correct. With inflation, a fixed amount of money buys fewer goods and services, thus reducing purchasing power.

14 C is correct. Disinflation is known as a reduction of inflation from a higher to lower, but still above zero, level.

15 B is correct. Deflation is connected to a vicious cycle of reduced spending and higher unemployment.

16 A is correct. In hyperinflation, consumers accelerate their spending to beat prices increases and money circulates more rapidly.

17 A is correct. The Laspeyres index is calculated with these inputs:

- November consumption bundle: $70 \times 0.9 + 60 \times 0.6 = 99$
- December consumption bundle: $70 \times 1 + 60 \times 0.8 = 118$
- December price index: $(118/99) \times 100 = 119.19$
- Inflation rate: $(119.19/100) - 1 = 0.1919 = 19.19\%$

18 A is correct. The Paasche index uses the current product mix of consumption combined with the variation of prices. So for December, its value is

$$(120 \times 1 + 50 \times 0.8)/(120 \times 0.9 + 50 \times 0.6) = (160/138) \times 100 = 115.9$$

19 C is correct. Central banks typically use consumer price indexes to monitor inflation and evaluate their monetary policies.

20 C is correct. The CPI is typically used for this purpose, while the PPI is more closely connected to business contracts.

21 A is correct. Core inflation is less volatile since it excludes food and energy prices and therefore will not be as likely to lead to policy overreactions when serving as a target.

22 C is correct. For productivity, or output per hour, the faster that it can grow, the further that wages can rise without putting pressure on business costs per unit of output.

23 C is correct. While no single indicator is definitive, a mix of them—which can be affected by various economic determinants—can offer the strongest signal of performance.

24 B is correct. The narrowing spread of this leading indicator foretells a drop in short-term rates and a fall in economic activity. The prime rate is a lagging indicator and typically moves after the economy turns.

25 A is correct. Both inventory–sales and unit labor costs are lagging indicators that decline somewhat after a peak. Real personal income is a coincident indicator that by its decline shows a slowdown in business activity.

Monetary and Fiscal Policy

by Andrew Clare, PhD, and Stephen Thomas, PhD

Andrew Clare, PhD, and Stephen Thomas, PhD, are at Cass Business School (United Kingdom).

LEARNING OUTCOMES

Mastery	The candidate should be able to:
☐	a. compare monetary and fiscal policy;
☐	b. describe functions and definitions of money;
☐	c. explain the money creation process;
☐	d. describe theories of the demand for and supply of money;
☐	e. describe the Fisher effect;
☐	f. describe roles and objectives of central banks;
☐	g. contrast the costs of expected and unexpected inflation;
☐	h. describe tools used to implement monetary policy;
☐	i. describe the monetary transmission mechanism;
☐	j. describe qualities of effective central banks;
☐	k. explain the relationships between monetary policy and economic growth, inflation, interest, and exchange rates;
☐	l. contrast the use of inflation, interest rate, and exchange rate targeting by central banks;
☐	m. determine whether a monetary policy is expansionary or contractionary;
☐	n. describe limitations of monetary policy;
☐	o. describe roles and objectives of fiscal policy;
☐	p. describe tools of fiscal policy, including their advantages and disadvantages;
☐	q. describe the arguments about whether the size of a national debt relative to GDP matters;
☐	r. explain the implementation of fiscal policy and difficulties of implementation;

(continued)

1   INTRODUCTION

The economic decisions of households can have a significant impact on an economy. For example, a decision on the part of households to consume more and to save less can lead to an increase in employment, investment, and ultimately profits. Equally, the investment decisions made by corporations can have an important impact on the real economy and on corporate profits. But individual corporations can rarely affect large economies on their own; the decisions of a single household concerning consumption will have a negligible impact on the wider economy.

By contrast, the decisions made by governments can have an enormous impact on even the largest and most developed of economies for two main reasons. First, the public sectors of most developed economies normally employ a significant proportion of the population, and they are usually responsible for a significant proportion of spending in an economy. Second, governments are also the largest borrowers in world debt markets. Exhibit 1 gives some idea of the scale of government borrowing and spending.

Exhibit 1

Panel A. Central Government Debt to GDP, 2009

Total Central Government Debt as % of GDP

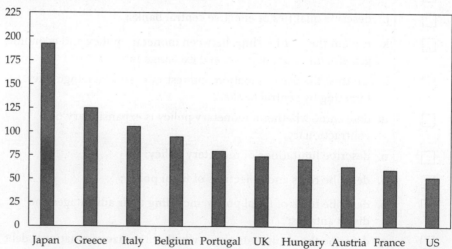

Exhibit 1   (Continued)

Panel B. Public Sector Spending to GDP, 2009

Government Consumption as % of GDP

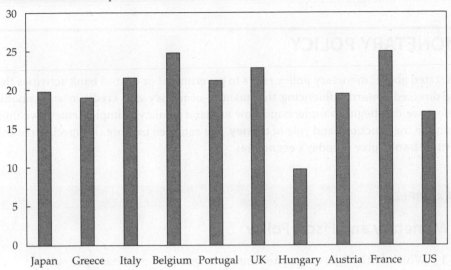

Note: All data are for 2009.
Source: Thomson Financial.

Government policy is ultimately expressed through its borrowing and spending activities. In this reading, we identify and discuss two types of government policy that can affect the macroeconomy and financial markets: monetary policy and fiscal policy.

Monetary policy refers to central bank activities that are directed toward influencing the quantity of money and credit in an economy.[1] By contrast, **fiscal policy** refers to the government's decisions about taxation and spending. Both monetary and fiscal policies are used to regulate economic activity over time. They can be used to accelerate growth when an economy starts to slow or to moderate growth and activity when an economy starts to overheat. In addition, fiscal policy can be used to redistribute income and wealth.

The overarching goal of both monetary and fiscal policy is normally the creation of an economic environment where growth is stable and positive and inflation is stable and low. Crucially, the aim is therefore to steer the underlying economy so that it does not experience economic booms that may be followed by extended periods of low or negative growth and high levels of unemployment. In such a stable economic environment, householders can feel secure in their consumption and saving decisions, while corporations can concentrate on their investment decisions, on making their regular coupon payments to their bond holders and on making profits for their shareholders.

The challenges to achieving this overarching goal are many. Not only are economies frequently buffeted by shocks (such as oil price jumps), but some economists believe that natural cycles in the economy also exist. Moreover, there are plenty of examples from history where government policies—either monetary, fiscal, or both—have exacerbated an economic expansion that eventually led to damaging consequences for the real economy, for financial markets, and for investors.

---

1 Central banks can implement monetary policy almost completely independent of government interference and influence at one end of the scale, or simply as the agent of the government at the other end of the scale.

The balance of the reading is organized as follows. Section 2 provides an introduction to monetary policy and related topics. Section 3 presents fiscal policy. The
interactions between monetary policy and fiscal policy are the subject of Section 4.
A summary and practice problems conclude the reading.

2 MONETARY POLICY

As stated above, monetary policy refers to government or central bank activities that
are directed toward influencing the quantity of money and credit in an economy.
Before we can begin to understand how monetary policy is implemented, we must
examine the functions and role of **money**. We can then explore the special role that
central banks play in today's economies.

EXAMPLE 1

Monetary and Fiscal Policy

1 Which of the following statements *best* describes monetary policy?
   Monetary policy:
   A involves the setting of medium-term targets for broad money
      aggregates.
   B involves the manipulation by a central bank of the government's bud-
      get deficit.
   C seeks to influence the macro economy by influencing the quantity of
      money and credit in the economy.
2 Which of the following statements *best* describes fiscal policy? Fiscal
   policy:
   A is used by governments to redistribute wealth and incomes.
   B is the attempt by governments to balance their budgets from one year
      to the next.
   C involves the use of government spending and taxation to influence
      economy activity.

Solution to 1:

C is correct. Choice A is incorrect because, although the setting of targets for
monetary aggregates is a possible *tool* of monetary policy, monetary policy itself
is concerned with influencing the overall, or macro, economy.

Solution to 2:

C is correct. Note that governments may wish to use fiscal policy to redistribute
incomes and balance their budgets, but the overriding goal of fiscal policy is
usually to influence a broader range of economic activity.

2.1 Money

To understand the nature, role, and development of money in modern economies,
it is useful to think about a world without money—where to purchase any good or
service, an individual would have to "pay" with another good or service. An economy
where such economic agents as households, corporations, and even governments pay

for goods and services in this way is known as a **barter economy**. There are many drawbacks to such an economy. First, the exchange of goods for other goods (or services) would require both economic agents in the transaction to want what the other is selling. This means that there has to be a **double coincidence of wants**. It might also be impossible to undertake transactions where the goods are indivisible—that is, where one agent wishes to buy a certain amount of another's goods, but that agent only has one indivisible unit of another good that is worth more than the good that the agent is trying to buy. Another problem occurs if economic agents do not wish to exchange all of their goods on other goods and services. This may not be a problem, however, when the goods they have to sell can be stored safely so that they retain their value for the future. But if these goods are perishable, they will not be able to store value for their owner. Finally, in a barter economy, there are many measures of value: the price of oranges in terms of pears; of pears in terms of bread; of bread in terms of milk; or of milk in terms of oranges. A barter economy has no common measure of value that would make multiple transactions simple.

2.1.1 *The Functions of Money*

The most generic definition of money is that it is any generally accepted medium of exchange. A **medium of exchange** is any asset that can be used to purchase goods and services or to repay debts. Money can thus eliminate the debilitating double coincidence of the "wants" problem that exists in a barter economy. When this medium of exchange exists, a farmer wishing to sell wheat for wine does not need to identify a wine producer in search of wheat. Instead, he can sell wheat to those who want wheat in exchange for money. The farmer can then exchange this money for wine with a wine producer, who in turn can exchange that money for the goods or services that she wants.

However, for money to act as this liberating medium of exchange, it must possess certain qualities. It must:

 i. be readily acceptable,

 ii. have a known value,

 iii. be easily divisible,

 iv. have a high value relative to its weight, and

 v. be difficult to counterfeit.

Qualities (i) and (ii) are closely related; the medium of exchange will only be acceptable if it has a known value. If the medium of exchange has quality (iii), then it can be used to purchase items of relatively little value and of relatively large value with equal ease. Having a high value relative to its weight is a practical convenience, meaning that people can carry around sufficient wealth for their transaction needs. Finally, if the medium of exchange can be counterfeited easily, then it would soon cease to have a value and would not be readily acceptable as a means of effecting transactions; in other words, it would not satisfy qualities (i) and (ii).

Given the qualities that money needs to have, it is clear why precious metals (particularly gold and silver) often fulfilled the role of medium of exchange in early societies, and as recently as the early part of the twentieth century. Precious metals were acceptable as a medium of exchange because they had a known value, were easily divisible, had a high value relative to their weight, and could not be easily counterfeited.

Thus, precious metals were capable of acting as a medium of exchange. But they also fulfilled two other useful functions that are essential for the characteristics of money. In a barter economy, it is difficult to store wealth from one year to the next when one's produce is perishable, or indeed, if it requires large warehouses in which to store it. Because precious metals like gold had a high value relative to their bulk and were not perishable, they could act as a **store of wealth**. However, their ability to act as a store of wealth not only depended on the fact that they did not perish physically over time, but also on the belief that others would always value precious metals. The value from year to year of precious metals depended on people's continued demand for them in ornaments, jewellery, and so on. For example, people were willing to use gold as a store of wealth because they believed that it would remain highly valued. However, if gold became less valuable to people relative to other goods and services year after year it would not be able to fulfill its role as a **store of value**, and as such might also lose its status as a medium of exchange.

Another important characteristic of money is that it can be used as a universal unit of account. As such, it can create a single unitary **measure of value** for all goods and services. In an economy where gold and silver are the accepted medium of exchange, all prices, debts, and wealth can be recorded in terms of their gold or silver coin exchange value. Money, in its role as a unit of account, drastically reduces the number of prices in an economy compared to barter, which requires that prices be established for a good in terms of all other goods for which it might be exchanged.

In summary, money fulfills three important functions, it:

- acts as a medium of exchange;
- provides individuals with a way of storing wealth; and
- provides society with a convenient measure of value and unit of account.

2.1.2 *Paper Money and the Money Creation Process*

Although precious metals like gold and silver fulfilled the required functions of money relatively well for many years, and although carrying gold coins around was easier than carrying around one's physical produce, it was not necessarily a safe way to conduct business.

A crucial development in the history of money was the **promissory note**. The process began when individuals began leaving their excess gold with goldsmiths, who would look after it for them. In turn the goldsmiths would give the depositors a receipt, stating how much gold they had deposited. Eventually these receipts were traded directly for goods and services, rather than there being a physical transfer of gold from the goods buyer to the goods seller. Of course, both the buyer and seller had to trust the goldsmith because the goldsmith had all the gold and the goldsmith's customers had only pieces of paper. These depository receipts represented a promise to pay a certain amount of gold on demand. This paper money therefore became a proxy for the precious metals on which they were based, that is, they were directly related to a physical commodity. Many of these early goldsmiths evolved into banks, taking in excess wealth and in turn issuing promissory notes that could be used in commerce.

In taking in other people's gold and issuing depository receipts and later promissory notes, it became clear to the goldsmiths and early banks that not all the gold that they held in their vaults would be withdrawn at any one time. Individuals were willing to buy and sell goods and services with the promissory notes, but the majority of the gold that backed the notes just sat in the vaults—although its ownership would change with the flow of commerce over time. A certain proportion of the gold that was not being withdrawn and used directly for commerce could therefore be lent to others at a rate of interest. By doing this, the early banks created money.

The process of **money creation** is a crucial concept for understanding the role that money plays in an economy. Its potency depends on the amount of money that banks keep in reserve to meet the withdrawals of its customers. This practice of lending customers' money to others on the assumption that not all customers will want all of their money back at any one time is known as **fractional reserve banking**.

We can illustrate how it works through a simple example. Suppose that the bankers in an economy come to the view that they need to retain only 10 percent of any money deposited with them. This is known as the **reserve requirement**.[2] Now consider what happens when a customer deposits €100 in the First Bank of Nations. This deposit changes the balance sheet of First Bank of Nations, as shown in Exhibit 2, and it represents a liability to the bank because it is effectively loaned to the bank by the customer. By lending 90 percent of this deposit to another customer the bank has two types of assets: (1) the bank's reserves of €10, and (2) the loan equivalent to €90. Notice that the balance sheet still balances; €100 worth of assets and €100 worth of liabilities are on the balance sheet.

Now suppose that the recipient of the loan of €90 uses this money to purchase some goods of this value and the seller of the goods deposits this €90 in another bank, the Second Bank of Nations. The Second Bank of Nations goes through the same process; it retains €9 in reserve and loans 90 percent of the deposit (€81) to another customer. This customer in turn spends €81 on some goods or services. The recipient of this money deposits it at the Third Bank of Nations, and so on. This example shows how money is created when a bank makes a loan.

Exhibit 2   Money Creation via Fractional Reserve Banking

First Bank of Nations

Assets		Liabilities	
Reserves	€10	Deposits	€100
Loans	€90		

Second Bank of Nations

Assets		Liabilities	
Reserves	€9	Deposits	€90
Loans	€81		

Third Bank of Nations

Assets		Liabilities	
Reserves	€8.1	Deposits	€81
Loans	€72.9		

This process continues until there is no more money left to be deposited and loaned out. The total amount of money 'created' from this one deposit of €100 can be calculated as:

New deposit/Reserve requirement = €100/0.10 = €1,000   (1)

It is the sum of all the deposits now in the banking system. You should also note that the original deposit of €100, via the practice of reserve banking, was the catalyst for €1,000 worth of economic transactions. That is not to say that economic growth would be zero without this process, but instead that it can be an important component in economic activity.

---

2 This is an example of a *voluntary* reserve requirement because it is self-imposed.

The amount of money that the banking system creates through the practice of fractional reserve banking is a function of 1 divided by the reserve requirement, a quantity known as the **money multiplier**.[3] In the case just examined, the money multiplier is 1/0.10 = 10. Equation 1 implies that the smaller the reserve requirement, the greater the money multiplier effect.

In our simplistic example, we assumed that the banks themselves set their own reserve requirements. However, in some economies, the central bank sets the reserve requirement, which is a potential means of affecting money growth. In any case, a prudent bank would be wise to have sufficient reserves such that the withdrawal demands of their depositors can be met in stressful economic and credit market conditions.

Later, when we discuss central banks and central bank policy, we will see how central banks can use the mechanism just described to affect the money supply. Specifically, the central bank could, by purchasing €100 in government securities credited to the bank account of the seller, seek to initiate an increase in the money supply. The central bank may also lend reserves directly to banks, creating excess reserves (relative to any imposed or self-imposed reserve requirement) that can support new loans and money expansion.

EXAMPLE 2

Money and Money Creation

1 To fulfill its role as a medium of exchange, money should:
   A be a conservative investment.
   B have a low value relative to its weight.
   C be easily divisible and a good store of value.

2 If the reserve requirement for banks in an economy is 5 percent, how much money could be created with the deposit of an additional £100 into a deposit account?
   A £500
   B £1,900
   C £2,000

3 Which of the following functions does money normally fulfill for a society? It:
   A acts as a medium of exchange only.
   B provides economic agents with a means of storing wealth only.
   C provides society with a unit of account, acts as a medium of exchange, and acts as a store of wealth.

Solution to 1:

C is correct. Money needs to have a known value and be easily divisible. It should also be readily acceptable, difficult to counterfeit, and have a high value relative to its weight.

---

3 This quantity, known as the simple money multiplier, represents a maximum expansion. To the extent that banks hold excess reserves or that money loaned out is not re-deposited, the money expansion would be less. More complex multipliers incorporating such factors are developed in more advanced texts.

Solution to 2:

C is correct. To calculate the increase in money from an additional deposit in the banking system, use the following expression: new deposit/reserve requirement.

Solution to 3:

C is correct. Money needs to be able to fulfill the functions of acting as a unit of account, a medium of exchange, and a means of storing wealth.

2.1.3 Definitions of Money

The process of money creation raises a fundamental issue: What is money? In an economy with money but without promissory notes and fractional reserve banking, money is relatively easy to define: Money is the total amount of gold and silver coins in circulation, or their equivalent. The money creation process above, however, indicates that a broader definition of money might encompass all the notes and coins in circulation *plus* all bank deposits.

More generally, we might define money as any medium that can be used to purchase goods and services. Notes and coins can be used to fulfill this purpose, and yet such currency is not the only means of purchasing goods and services. Personal cheques can be written based on a bank chequing account, while debit cards can be used for the same purpose. But what about time deposits or savings accounts? Nowadays transfers can be made relatively easily from a savings account to a current account; therefore, these savings accounts might also be considered as part of the stock of money. Credit cards are also used to pay for goods and services; however, there is an important difference between credit card payments and those made by cheques and debit cards. Unlike a cheque or debit card payment, a credit card payment involves a deferred payment. Basically, the greater the complexity of any financial system, the harder it is to define money.

The monetary authorities in most modern economies produce a range of measures of money (see Exhibit 3). But generally speaking, the money stock consists of notes and coins in circulation, plus the deposits in banks and other financial institutions that can be readily used to make purchases of goods and services in the economy. In this regard, economists often speak of the rate of growth of **narrow money** and/or **broad money**. By narrow money, they generally mean the notes and coins in circulation in an economy, plus other very highly liquid deposits. Broad money encompasses narrow money but also includes the entire range of liquid assets that can be used to make purchases.

Because financial systems, practice, and institutions vary from economy to economy, so do definitions of money; thus, it is difficult to make international comparisons. Still, most central banks produce both a narrow and broad measure of money, plus some intermediate ones too. Exhibit 3 shows the money definitions in four economies.

Exhibit 3   Definitions of Money

Money Measures in the United States

The US Federal Reserve produces two measures of money. The first is M1, which comprises notes and coins in circulation, travelers' cheques of non-bank issuers, demand deposits at commercial banks, plus other deposits on which cheques can be written. M2 is the broadest measure of money currently produced by the Federal Reserve and includes M1, plus savings and money market deposits, time deposit accounts of less than $100,000, plus other balances in retail money market and mutual funds.

(continued)

Exhibit 3   (Continued)

Money Measures in the Eurozone

The European Central Bank (ECB) produces three measures of euro area money supply. The narrowest is M1. M1 comprises notes and coins in circulation, plus all overnight deposits. M2 is a broader definition of euro area money that includes M1, plus deposits redeemable with notice up to three months and deposits with maturity up to two years. Finally, the euro area's broadest definition of money is **M3**, which includes M2, plus repurchase agreements, money market fund units, and debt securities with up to two years maturity.

Money Measures in Japan

The Bank of Japan calculates three measures of money. M1 is the narrowest measure and consists of cash currency in circulation. M2 incorporates M1 but also includes certificates of deposit (CDs). The broadest measure, M3, incorporates M2, plus deposits held at post offices, plus other savings and deposits with financial institutions. There is also a "broad measure of liquidity" that encompasses M3 as well as a range of other liquid assets, such as government bonds and commercial paper.

Money Measures in the United Kingdom

The United Kingdom produces a set of four measures of the money stock. **M0** is the narrowest measure and comprises notes and coins held outside the Bank of England, plus Bankers' deposits at the Bank of England. **M2** includes M0, plus (effectively) all retail bank deposits. **M4** includes M2, plus wholesale bank and building society deposits and also certificates of deposit. Finally, the Bank of England produces another measure called **M3H**, which is a measure created to be comparable with money definitions in the EU (see above). M3H includes M4, plus UK residents' and corporations' foreign currency deposits in banks and building societies.

2.1.4 *The Quantity Theory of Money*

The previous section of this reading shows that there are many definitions of money. In this section, we explore the important relationship between money and the price level. This relationship is best expressed in the **quantity theory of money**, which asserts that total spending (in money terms) is proportional to the quantity of money. The theory can be explained in terms of Equation 2, known as the **quantity equation of exchange**:

$$M \times V = P \times Y \tag{2}$$

where M is the quantity of money, V is the velocity of circulation of money (the average number of times in a given period that a unit of currency changes hands), P is the average price level, and Y is real output. The expression is really just an accounting identity. Effectively, it says that over a given period, the amount of money used to purchase all goods and services in an economy, $M \times V$, is equal to monetary value of this output, $P \times Y$. If the velocity of money is approximately constant—which is an assumption of quantity theory—then spending $P \times Y$ is approximately proportional to M. The quantity equation can also be used to explain a consequence of **money neutrality**. If money neutrality holds, then an increase in the money supply, M, will not affect Y, real output, or the speed with which money changed hands, V, because if real output is unaffected, there would be no need for money to change hands more rapidly.[4] However, it will cause the aggregate price level, P, to rise.

The simple quantity theory gave rise to the equally simple idea that the price level, or at least the rate of inflation, could be controlled by manipulating the rate of growth of the money supply. Economists who believe this are referred to as **monetarists**. They argue that there is a causal relationship running from money growth to inflation. In the past, some governments have tried to apply this logic in their efforts to control inflation, most notably and unsuccessfully the United Kingdom's government in 1979 (see Example 5). However, it is possible that causality runs the other way—that is, from real activity to the money supply. This means that the quantity of money in circulation is determined by the level of economic activity, rather than vice versa.

2.1.5 The Demand for Money

The amount of wealth that the citizens of an economy choose to hold in the form of money—as opposed to bonds or equities—is known as the demand for money. There are three basic motives for holding money:

- transactions-related;
- precautionary; and
- speculative.

Money balances that are held to finance transactions are referred to as **transactions money balances**. The size of the transactions balances will tend to increase with the average value of transactions in an economy. Generally speaking, as gross domestic product (GDP) grows over time, transactions balances will also tend to grow; however, the ratio of transactions balances to GDP remains fairly stable over time.

As the name suggests, **precautionary money balances** are held to provide a buffer against unforeseen events that might require money. These balances will tend to be larger for individuals or organizations that enter into a high level of transactions over time. In other words, a precautionary buffer of $100 for a company that regularly enters into transactions worth millions of dollars might be considered rather small. When we extend this logic to the overall economy, we can see that these precautionary balances will also tend to rise with the volume and value of transactions in the economy, and therefore, GDP as well.

Finally, the **speculative demand for money** (sometimes called the **portfolio demand for money**) relates to the demand to hold speculative money balances based on the potential opportunities or risks that are inherent in other financial instruments (e.g., bonds). **Speculative money balances** consist of monies held in anticipation that other assets will decline in value. But in choosing to hold speculative money balances rather than bonds, investors give up the return that could be earned from the bond or other financial assets. Therefore, the speculative demand for money will tend to fall as the returns available on other financial assets rises. However, it will tend to rise as the perceived risk in other financial instruments rises. In equilibrium, individuals will tend to increase their holdings of money relative to riskier assets until the marginal benefit of having a lower risk portfolio of wealth is equal to the marginal cost of giving up a unit of expected return on these riskier assets. In aggregate then, speculative balances will tend to be inversely related to the expected return on other financial assets and directly related to the perceived risk of other financial assets.

---

4 Note that the full version of the quantity theory of money uses the symbol T rather than Y to indicate transactions because money is used not just for buying goods and services but also for financial transactions. We will return to this point in the discussion of quantitative easing.

EXAMPLE 3

Money

1   The transactions demand for money refers to the demand to hold money:

   A   as a buffer against unforeseen events.

   B   to use in the purchase of goods and services.

   C   based on the opportunity or risks available on other financial instruments.

2   The speculative demand for money will tend to:

   A   fall as the perceived risk on other assets rises.

   B   rise as the expected returns on other assets fall.

   C   be inversely related to the transactions demand for money.

3   What is the difference between narrow and broad money? Broad money:

   A   is limited to those liquid assets most commonly used to make purchases.

   B   can be used to purchase a wider range of goods and services than narrow money.

   C   encompasses narrow money and refers to the stock of the entire range of liquid assets that can be used to make purchases.

Solution to 1:

B is correct. The transactions demand for money refers to the amount of money that economic agents wish to hold to pay for goods and services.

Solution to 2:

B is correct. If the expected return on other assets falls, then the opportunity cost of holding money also falls and can, in turn, lead to an increase in the speculative demand for money.

Solution to 3:

C is correct. This is the definition of broad money. Broad money encompasses narrow money.

2.1.6 *The Supply and Demand for Money*

We have now discussed definitions of money, its relationship with the aggregate price level, and the demand for it. We now discuss the interaction between the supply of and demand for money.

   As with most other markets, the supply of money and the demand to hold it will interact to produce an equilibrium price for money. In this market, the price of money is the nominal interest rate that could be earned by lending it to others. Exhibit 4 shows the supply and demand curves for money. The vertical scale represents the rate of interest; the horizontal scale plots the quantity of nominal money in the economy. The supply curve (MS) is vertical because we assume that there is a fixed nominal amount of money circulating at any one time. The demand curve (MD) is downward sloping because as interest rates rise, the speculative demand for money falls. The supply and demand for money are both satisfied at an equilibrium interest rate of I_0. I_0 is the rate of interest at which no excess money balances exist.

Exhibit 4   The Supply and Demand for Money

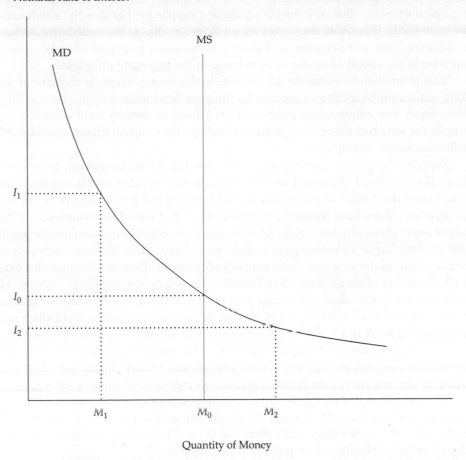

Nominal Rate of Interest

To see why I_0 is the equilibrium rate of interest where there are no excess money balances, consider the following. If the interest rate on bonds were I_1 instead of I_0, there would be excess supply of money ($M_0 - M_1$). Economic agents would seek to buy bonds with their excess money balances, which would force the price of bonds up and the interest rate back down to I_0. Similarly, if bonds offered a rate of interest, I_2, there would be an excess demand for money ($M_2 - M_0$). Corporations and individuals would seek to sell bonds so that individuals could increase their money holdings, but in doing so, the price of bonds would fall and the interest rate offered on them would rise until it reached I_0. Interest rates effectively adjust to bring the market into equilibrium ("clear the market"). In this simple example, we have also assumed that the supply of money and bonds is fixed as economic agents readjust their holdings. In practice, this may not be true, but the dynamics of the adjustment process described here essentially still hold.

Exhibit 4 also reemphasises the relationship between the supply of money and the aggregate price level, which we first encountered when discussing the quantity theory of money. Suppose that the central bank increases the supply of money from M_0 to M_2, so that the vertical supply curve shifts to the right. Because the increase in the supply of money makes it more plentiful and hence less valuable, its price (the interest rate) falls as the price level rises.

This all sounds very simple, but in practice the effects of an increase in the money supply are more complex. The initial increase in the money supply will create excess supply of cash. People and companies could get rid of the excess by loaning the money to others by buying bonds, as implied above, but they might also deposit it in a bank or simply use it to buy goods and services. But an economy's capacity to produce goods and services depends on the availability of real things: notably, natural resources, capital, and labour—that is, factors of production supplied either directly or indirectly by households. Increasing the money supply does not change the availability of these real things. Thus, some economists believe that the long-run impact of an exogenous increase in the supply of money is an increase in the aggregate price level.

This phenomenon—whereby an increase in the money supply is thought in the long run simply to lead to an increase in the price level while leaving real variables like output and employment unaffected—is known as **money neutrality**. To see why in the long run money should have a neutral effect on real things, consider the following simple example.

Suppose the government declared today that 1kg would henceforth be referred to as 2kg and that 1.5kg would be referred to as 3kg. In other words, suppose that they halved the "value" of a kilogram. Would anything real have changed? A 1kg bag of sugar would not have changed physically, although it would be relabelled as a 2kg bag of sugar. However, there might be some short-run effects; confused people might buy too little sugar, and some people might go on crash diets! But ultimately people would adjust. In the long run, the change wouldn't matter. There is a clear parallel here with the theory of money neutrality. Doubling the prices of everything—halving the value of a currency—does not change anything real. This is because, like kilograms, money is a unit of account. However, halving the value of a currency could affect real things in the short run.

There are two points worth making with regard to money neutrality. First, although the simple kilogram analogy above does suggest that money should not affect real things in the long run, as the British economist Keynes said: "*In the long run we are all dead!*" In practice, it is very difficult for economists to be sure that money neutrality holds in the long run. And second, we must assume that monetary authorities do believe that the money supply can affect real things in the short run. If they did not, then there would be almost no point to monetary policy.

2.1.7 The Fisher Effect

The **Fisher effect** is directly related to the concept of money neutrality. Named after the economist Irving Fisher, the Fisher effect states that the real rate of interest in an economy is stable over time so that changes in nominal interest rates are the result of changes in expected inflation. Thus, the nominal interest rate (R_{nom}) in an economy is the sum of the required real rate of interest (R_{real}) and the expected rate of inflation (π^e) over any given time horizon:

$$R_{nom} = R_{real} + \pi^e \qquad\qquad (3)$$

According to money neutrality, over the long term the money supply and/or the growth rate in money should not affect R_{real} but will affect inflation and inflation expectations.

The Fisher effect also demonstrates that embedded in every nominal interest rate is an expectation of future inflation. Suppose that 12-month US government T-bills offered a yield equal to 4 percent over the year. Suppose also that T-bill investors wished to earn a real rate of interest of 2 percent and expected inflation to be 2 percent over the next year. In this case, the return of 4 percent would be sufficient to deliver the investors' desired real return of 2 percent (so long as inflation did not exceed 2 percent). Now suppose that investors changed their view about future inflation and instead expected it to equal 3 percent over the next 12 months. To compensate them for the higher expected inflation, the T-bill rate would have to rise to 5 percent, thereby preserving the required 2 percent real return.

There is one caveat to this example. Investors can never be sure about future values of such economic variables as inflation and real growth. To compensate them for this uncertainty, they require a **risk premium**. The greater the uncertainty, the greater the required risk premium. So all nominal interest rates are actually comprised of three components:

■ a required real return;

■ a component compensating investors for expected inflation; and

■ a risk premium to compensate them for uncertainty.

EXAMPLE 4

Interest Rates and the Supply of Money

1 According to the quantity equation of exchange, an increase in the money supply can lead to an:

   A increase in the aggregate price level, regardless of changes in the velocity of circulation of money.

   B increase in the aggregate price level as long as the velocity of circulation of money rises sufficiently to offset the increase in the money supply.

   C increase in the aggregate price level as long as the velocity of circulation of money does not fall sufficiently to offset the increase in the money supply and real output is unchanged.

2 The nominal interest rate comprises a real rate of interest:

   A plus a risk premium only.

   B plus a premium for expected inflation only.

   C compensation for both expected inflation and risk.

3 An expansion in the money supply would *most likely*:

   A lead to a decline in nominal interest rates.

   B lead to an increase in nominal interest rates.

   C reduce the equilibrium amount of money that economic agents would wish to hold.

Solution to 1:

C is correct. If the velocity of circulation of money does not change with an increase in the money supply and real output is fixed, then the aggregate price level should increase. If the velocity of circulation of money falls sufficiently, or if real output rises sufficiently, then the increase in money may have no impact on prices.

Solution to 2:

C is correct. Investors demand a real rate of interest and compensation for expected inflation and a risk premium to compensate them for uncertainty.

Solution to 3:

A is correct. Increasing the supply of money, all other things being equal, will reduce its "price," that is, the interest rate on money balances.

EXAMPLE 5

Mrs. Thatcher's Monetary Experiment

The Background

Over the 1970s, the United Kingdom had one of the worst inflation records of any developed economy. Retail price inflation averaged 12.6 percent over that decade and peaked at 26.9 percent in August 1975. Over this period, then-Prime Minister Margaret Thatcher and her advisers had become convinced that inflation could not be controlled by the income and price policies used in the United Kingdom in the past. Instead, they believed that inflation could be tamed by controlling the rate of growth of the money supply. Mrs. Thatcher's first administration took power in May 1979 with the intention of pursuing a monetarist agenda—that is, a macroeconomic policy that would be underpinned by targets for money supply growth.

The Medium-Term Financial Strategy

Targets for monetary growth were set for a definition of the money supply known as Sterling M3 (£M3), which was to be kept in the range of 7–11 percent for the period 1980–1981 and then gradually reduced to within 4–8 percent by 1983–1984. This set of targets was known as the Medium Term Financial Strategy (MTFS). The idea was simple: Control the rate of growth of the money supply, and the rate of growth of prices (i.e., inflation) would remain under control too. The instrument of control was the Bank of England's policy interest rate that would be set to achieve the desired rate of growth of the money supply. This was a macroeconomic policy built, however imperfectly, on an interpretation of the quantity theory of money.

The theory was simple, but the practice proved to be less so. Over the first two and a half years of the MTFS, £M3 overshot its target by 100 percent. The inability of the monetary authorities to control the rate of growth of the broad money supply was largely caused by Thatcher's abolition of exchange controls in 1979. By abolishing these controls, there was a significant increase in foreign exchange business that came into the British banking system, which changed the velocity of money and therefore meant that the relationship between broad money and nominal incomes had changed fundamentally.[5]

Despite the inability to control the money supply, in 1983 the Thatcher administration reasserted its confidence in the policy and published a further set of monetary targets for several years ahead. However, the persistent failure to meet these targets, too, eventually led to the abandonment of any type of monetary targeting by the summer of 1985.

The experience of the UK monetary authorities over this period emphasizes how unstable the relationship between money and the policy interest rate could be along with the relationship between money and aggregate demand—particularly in an economy that is experiencing rapid financial innovation, as the UK economy was following the abolition of exchange controls and the introduction of greater competition within the banking industry.

Today the Bank of England is responsible for the operation and implementation of monetary policy in the United Kingdom. The trends in money supply are watched very carefully, but they are not the subject of targets, per se.

---

5 See Goodhart (1989) for a discussion.

2.2 The Roles of Central Banks

Central banks play a number of key roles in modern economies. Generally, a central bank is the monopoly supplier of the currency, the banker to the government and the bankers' bank, the lender of last resort, the regulator and supervisor of the payments system, the conductor of monetary policy, and the supervisor of the banking system. Let us examine these roles in turn.

In its earliest form, money could be exchanged for a pre-specified precious commodity, usually gold, and promissory notes were issued by many private banks. Today, however, state-owned institutions—usually central banks—are designated in law as being the monopoly suppliers of a currency. Initially, these monopolists supplied money that could be converted into a pre-specified amount of gold; they adhered to a **gold standard**. For example, up until 1931, bank notes issued by Britain's central bank, the Bank of England, could be redeemed at the bank for a pre-specified amount of gold. But Britain, like most other major economies, abandoned this convertibility principle in the first half of the twentieth century. Money in all major economics today is not convertible by law into anything else, but it is, in law, **legal tender**. This means that it must be accepted when offered in exchange for goods and services. Money that is not convertible into any other commodity is known as **fiat money**. Fiat money derives its value via government decree and because people accept it for payment of goods and services and for debt repayment.

As long as fiat money is acceptable to everyone as a medium of exchange, and it holds its value over time, then it will also be able to serve as a unit of account. However, once an economy has moved to a system of fiat money, the role of the supplier of that money becomes even more crucial because they could, for example, expand the supply of this money indefinitely should they wish to do so. Central banks therefore play a crucial role in modern economies as the suppliers and guardians of the value of their fiat currencies and as institutions charged with the role of maintaining confidence in their currencies. As the monopoly suppliers of an economy's currency, central banks are at the centre of economic life. As such, they assume other roles in addition to being the suppliers and guardians of the value of their currencies.

Most central banks act as the banker to the government and to other banks. They also act as a **lender of last resort** to banks. Because the central bank effectively has the capacity to print money, it is in the position to be able to supply the funds to banks that are facing a damaging shortage. The facts that economic agents know that the central bank stands ready to provide the liquidity required by any of the banks under its jurisdiction and that they trust government bank deposit insurance help to prevent bank runs in the first place. However, the recent financial crisis has shown that this knowledge is not always sufficient to deter a bank run.

EXAMPLE 6

The Northern Rock Bank Run

In the latter part of the summer of 2007, the fall in US house prices and the related implosion of the US sub-prime mortgage market became the catalyst for a global liquidity crisis. Banks began to hoard cash and refused to lend to other banks at anything other than extremely punitive interest rates through the interbank market. This caused severe difficulties for a UK mortgage bank, Northern Rock. Northern Rock's mortgage book had expanded rapidly in the preceding years as it borrowed aggressively from the money markets. It is now clear that this expansion was at the expense of loan quality. The then UK regulatory authority, the Financial Services Authority (FSA),[6] later reported in 2008 that Northern Rock's lending practices did not pay due regard to either the credit quality of the mortgagees or the values of the properties on which the mortgages were secured. Being at the worst end of banking practice, and relying heavily on international capital markets for its funding, Northern Rock was therefore very susceptible to a global reduction in liquidity. As the liquidity crisis took hold, Northern Rock found that it could not replace its maturing money market borrowings. On 12 September 2007, in desperate need of liquidity, Northern Rock's board approached the UK central bank to ask for the necessary funds.

However, the news of Northern Rock's perilous liquidity position became known by the public and, more pertinently, by Northern Rock's retail depositors. On 14 September, having heard the news, queues began to form outside Northern Rock branches as depositors tried to withdraw their savings. On that day, it was estimated that Northern Rock depositors withdrew around £1bn, representing 5 percent of Northern Rock's deposits. Further panic ensued as investors in "internet only" Northern Rock accounts could not withdraw their money because of the collapse of Northern Rock's website. A further £1bn was withdrawn over the next two days.

Northern Rock's share price dropped rapidly, as did the share prices of other similar UK banks. The crisis therefore threatened to engulf more than one bank. To prevent contagion, the Chancellor of the Exchequer announced on 17 September that the UK government would guarantee all Northern Rock deposits. This announcement was enough to stabilize the situation, and given that lending to Northern Rock was now just like lending to the government, deposits actually started to rise again.

Eventually Northern Rock was nationalized by the UK government, with the hope that at some time in the future it could be privatized once its balance sheet had been repaired.

Central banks are also often charged by the government to supervise the banking system, or at least to supervise those banks that they license to accept deposits. However, in some countries, this role is undertaken by a separate authority. In other countries, the central bank can be jointly responsible with another body for the supervision of its banks.

Exhibit 5 lists the banking supervisors in the G-10 countries; central banks are underlined. As the exhibit shows, most but not all bank systems have a single supervisor, which is not necessarily a central bank. A few countries, such as Germany and the United States, have more than one supervisor.

Exhibit 5	Banking Supervision in the G10
Country	**Institution(s)**
Belgium	Banking and Finance Commission
Canada	Office of the Superintendent of Financial Institutions
France	Commission Bancaire
Germany	Federal Banking Supervisory Office; <u>Deutsche Bundesbank</u>
Italy	<u>Bank of Italy</u>

---

6 In 2013, the Financial Services Authority was replaced by two new regulatory authorities, the Financial Conduct Authority (FCA) and the Prudential Regulation Authority (PRA).

Exhibit 5	(Continued)

Country	Institution(s)
Japan	Financial Services Agency
Netherlands	Bank of Netherlands
Sweden	Swedish Financial Supervisory Authority
Switzerland	Federal Commission
United Kingdom	Bank of England
United States	Office of the Comptroller of the Currency; Federal Reserve; Federal Deposit Insurance Corporation

The United Kingdom is an interesting case study in this regard. Until May 1997, the Bank of England had statutory responsibility for banking supervision in the United Kingdom. In May 1997, banking supervision was removed from the Bank of England and assigned to a new agency, the Financial Services Authority (FSA). However, the removal of responsibility for banking supervision from the central bank was seen by some as being a contributory factor in the run on the mortgage bank Northern Rock, and generally as a contributory factor in the recent banking crisis. Because of this perceived weakness in the separation of the central bank from banking supervision, the Bank of England regained responsibility for banking supervision and regulation in 2013.

Perhaps the least appreciated role of a central bank is its role in the **payments system**. Central banks are usually asked to oversee, regulate, and set standards for a country's payments system. Every day millions of financial transactions take place in a modern economy. For the system to work properly, procedures must be robust and standardized. The central bank will usually oversee the payments system and will also be responsible for the successful introduction of any new processes. Given the international nature of finance, the central bank will also be responsible for coordinating payments systems internationally with other central banks.

Most central banks will also be responsible for managing their country's **foreign currency reserves** and also its gold reserves. With regard to the latter, even though countries abandoned the gold standard in the early part of the twentieth century, the world's central bankers still hold large quantities of gold. As such, if central banks were to decide to sell significant proportions of their gold reserves, it could potentially depress gold prices.

Finally, central banks are usually responsible for the operation of a country's **monetary policy**. This is arguably the highest profile role that these important organizations assume. Recall that monetary policy refers to central bank activities that are directed toward influencing the quantity of money and credit in an economy. As the monopoly supplier of a country's currency, central banks are in the ideal position to implement and/or determine monetary policy.

To summarise, central banks assume a range of roles and responsibilities. They do not all assume responsibility for the supervision of the banks, but all of the other roles listed below are normally assumed by the central bank:

- Monopoly supplier of the currency;
- Banker to the government and the bankers' bank;
- Lender of last resort;
- Regulator and supervisor of the payments system;

- Conductor of monetary policy; and
- Supervisor of the banking system.

2.3 The Objectives of Monetary Policy

Central banks fulfill a variety of important roles, but for what overarching purpose? A brief perusal of the websites of the world's central banks will reveal a wide range of explanations of their objectives. Their objectives are clearly related to their roles, and so there is frequent mention of objectives related to the stability of the financial system and to the payments systems. Some central banks are charged with doing all they can to maintain full employment and output. But some also have related but less tangible roles, like "maintaining confidence in the financial system," or even to "promote understanding of the financial sector." But there is one overarching objective that most seem to acknowledge explicitly, and that is the objective of maintaining **price stability**.

So although central banks usually have to perform many roles, most specify an overarching objective. Exhibit 6 lists what we might call the primary objective(s) of a number of central banks, from both developed and developing economies.

Exhibit 6   The Objectives of Central Banks

The Central Bank of Brazil

Its "institutional mission" is to "ensure the stability of the currency's purchasing power and a solid and efficient financial system."

The European Central Bank

"[T]o maintain price stability is the primary objective of the Euro system and of the single monetary policy for which it is responsible. This is laid down in the Treaty on the Functioning of the European Union, Article 127 (1)."

"Without prejudice to the objective of price stability", the euro system will also "support the general economic policies in the Community with a view to contributing to the achievement of the objectives of the Community." These include a "high level of employment" and "sustainable and non-inflationary growth."

The US Federal Reserve

"The Federal Reserve sets the nation's monetary policy to promote the objectives of maximum employment, stable prices, and moderate long-term interest rates."

The Reserve Bank of Australia

"It is the duty of the Reserve Bank Board, within the limits of its powers, to ensure that the monetary and banking policy of the Bank is directed to the greatest advantage of the people of Australia and that the powers of the Bank ... are exercised in such a manner as, in the opinion of the Reserve Bank Board, will best contribute to:

a   the stability of the currency of Australia;

b   the maintenance of full employment in Australia; and

c   the economic prosperity and welfare of the people of Australia."

The Bank of Korea

"The primary purpose of the Bank, as prescribed by the Bank of Korea Act of 1962, is the pursuit of price stability."

Source: Central bank websites found at http://www.bis.org/cbanks.htm.

EXAMPLE 7

Central Banks

1 A central bank is normally *not* the:

   A lender of last resort.

   B banker to the government and banks.

   C body that sets tax rates on interest on savings.

2 Which of the following *best* describes the overarching, long-run objective of most central banks?

   A Price stability

   B Fast economic growth

   C Current account surplus

Solution to 1:

C is correct. A central bank is normally the lender of last resort and the banker to the banks and government, but the determination of all tax rates is normally the preserve of the government and is a fiscal policy issue.

Solution to 2:

A is correct. Central banks normally have a variety of objectives, but the overriding one is nearly always price stability.

As we have already discussed, one of the essential features of a monetary system is that the medium of exchange should have a relatively stable value from one period to the next. Arguably then, the overarching goal of most central banks in maintaining price stability is the associated goal of controlling inflation. But before we explore the tools central banks use to control inflation, we should first consider the potential costs of inflation. In other words, we should ask why it is that central bankers believe that it is so important to control a nominal variable.

2.3.1 *The Costs of Inflation*

Huge efforts have been put into controlling inflation since the major economies experienced such high levels of inflation in the 1970s. From the early 1970s then, inflation has been seen as a very bad thing. But why? What are the costs of inflation? The debate around the "costs" of inflation really centers on the distinction between **expected inflation** and **unexpected inflation**. Expected inflation is clearly the level of inflation that economic agents expect in the future. Unexpected inflation can be defined as the level of inflation that we experience that is either below or above that which we expected; it is the component of inflation that is a surprise.

At a micro level, high inflation means that businesses constantly have to change the advertised prices of their goods and services. These are known as **menu costs**. There also exists what economists refer to as "shoe leather" costs of inflation. In times of high inflation, people would naturally tend to hold less cash and would therefore wear out their shoe leather (or more likely the engines of their cars) in making frequent trips to the bank to withdraw cash. But these are relatively old arguments, used to demonstrate that inflation is bad. In a modern economy, with the internet and with transactions becoming increasingly cashless, these costs associated with inflation will be lower today than they may have been in the past.

To demonstrate the potentially more significant costs of inflation, consider the following. Imagine a world where inflation is high but where all prices (including asset prices) in an economy are perfectly indexed to inflation, and that technology has eliminated the issues surrounding the menu and shoe leather costs of inflation. In such a world, would economic agents care about inflation? Probably not. If the average price of goods and services rose by 10 percent, people's salaries (and all other prices) would rise by the same amount, which would therefore make economic agents indifferent to the rise in prices.

In practice, however, all prices, wages, salaries, rents, and so forth are not indexed, in which case economic agents would certainly need to think about inflation more carefully. But what if inflation in this world where prices are no longer perfectly indexed is high, but perfectly predictable? In this alternative, imaginary world, economic agents would have to think about inflation, but not too hard as long as they were capable of calculating the impact of the known inflation rate on all future prices. So, if everyone knew that inflation was going to be 10 percent over the next year, then everyone could bargain for a 10 percent increase in their salaries to accommodate this, and companies could plan to put up the prices of their goods and services by 10 percent. Actually, in this world, an expectation of 10 percent inflation would become a self-fulfilling prophecy.

However, economic agents would worry about inflation in a world where all prices were not indexed and, crucially, where inflation was high and unpredictable. In fact this is a crude description the inflationary backdrop in many developed economies over the 1970s and 1980s, including the United States, France, the United Kingdom, Italy, and Canada.

Arguably it is **unexpected inflation** that is most costly. Inflation that is fully anticipated can be factored into wage negotiations and priced into business and financial contracts. But when inflation turns out to be higher than is anticipated, then borrowers benefit at the expense of lenders because the real value of their borrowing declines. Conversely, when inflation is lower than is anticipated, lenders benefit at the expense of borrowers because the real value of the payment on debts rises. Furthermore, if inflation is very uncertain or very volatile, then lenders will ask for a premium to compensate them for this uncertainty. As a result, the costs of borrowing will be higher than would otherwise have been the case. Higher borrowing costs could in turn reduce economic activity, for example, by discouraging investment.

It is also possible that **inflation uncertainty** can exacerbate the economic cycle. Inflation uncertainty is the degree to which economic agents view future rates of inflation as hard to forecast. Take for example the case of an imaginary television manufacturer. Suppose one day that the manufacturer looks out at the market for televisions and sees that the market price of televisions has risen by 10 percent. Armed with this information, the manufacturer assumes that there has been an increase in demand for televisions or maybe a reduction in supply. So to take advantage of the new, higher prices, the manufacturer extends the factory, employs more workers, and begins to produce more televisions.

Having now increased the output of the factory, the manufacturer then attempts to sell the extra televisions that the factory has produced. But to its horror, the manufacturer finds out that there is no extra demand for televisions. Instead, the 10 percent rise in television prices was caused by a generalized 10 percent increase in all consumer prices across the economy. The manufacturer realizes that it has surplus stock, surplus factory capacity, and too many workers. So, it cuts back on production, lays off some of the workforce, and realizes that it won't need to invest in new plant or machinery for a long time.

This example emphasizes the potentially destabilizing impact of unexpected inflation. It demonstrates how unanticipated inflation can reduce the information content of market prices for economic agents. If we scale this example up, it should not be too difficult to imagine how unanticipated increases or decreases in the general price level could help to exacerbate—and in some extreme cases cause—economic booms and busts.

Over the last two to three decades the consensus among economists has been that unanticipated and high levels of inflation can have an impact on real things like employment, investment and profits, and therefore that controlling inflation should be one of the main goals of macroeconomic policy. In summary:

Expected inflation can give rise to:

- menu costs and
- shoe leather costs.

Unanticipated (unexpected) inflation can in addition:

- lead to inequitable transfers of wealth between borrowers and lenders (including losses to savings);
- give rise to risk premia in borrowing rates and the prices of other assets; and
- reduce the information content of market prices.

2.3.2 Monetary Policy Tools[7]

Central banks have three primary tools available to them: open market operations, the refinancing rate, and reserve requirements.

2.3.2.1 Open Market Operations   One of the most direct ways for a central bank to increase or reduce the amount of money in circulation is via **open market operations**. Open market operations involve the purchase and sale of government bonds from and to commercial banks and/or designated market makers. For example, when the central bank buys government bonds from commercial banks, this increases the reserves of private sector banks on the asset side of their balance sheets. If banks then use these surplus reserves by increasing lending to corporations and households, then via the money multiplier process explained in Section 2.1.2, broad money growth expands. Similarly, the central bank can sell government bonds to commercial banks. By doing this, the reserves of commercial banks decline, reducing their capacity to make loans (i.e., create credit) to households and corporations and thus causing broad money growth to decline through the money multiplier mechanism. In using open market operations, the central bank may target a desired level of commercial bank reserves or a desired interest rate for these reserves.

---

7 Monetary policy tools and operations often vary considerably from economy to economy. We have tried to describe the generics of the process here. For a more-detailed review of monetary operations across the world, see Gray and Talbot (2006).

2.3.2.2 The Central Bank's Policy Rate　　The most obvious expression of a central bank's intentions and views comes via the interest rate it sets. The name of the **official interest rate** (or **official policy rate** or just **policy rate**) varies from central bank to central bank, but its purpose is to influence short- and long-term interest rates and ultimately real economic activity.

The interest rate that a central bank sets and that it announces publicly is normally the rate at which it is willing to lend money to the commercial banks (although practices do vary from country to country). This policy rate can be achieved by using short-term collateralized lending rates, known as repo rates. For example, if the central bank wishes to increase the supply of money, it might buy bonds (usually government bonds) from the banks, with an agreement to sell them back at some time in the future. This transaction is known as a **repurchase agreement**. Normally, the maturity of repo agreements ranges from overnight to two weeks. In effect, this represents a secured loan to the banks, and the lender (in this case the central bank) earns the repo rate.

Suppose that a central bank announces an increase in its official interest rate. Commercial banks would normally increase their **base rates** at the same time. A commercial bank's base rate is the reference rate on which it bases lending rates to all other customers. For example, large corporate clients might pay the base rate plus 1 percent on their borrowing from a bank, while the same bank might lend money to a small corporate client at the base rate plus 3 percent. But why would commercial banks immediately increase their base or reference rates just because the central bank's refinancing rate had increased?

The answer is that commercial banks would not want to have lent at a rate of interest that would be lower than they might be charged by the central bank. Effectively, the central bank can force commercial banks to borrow from it at this rate because it can conduct open market operations that create a shortage of money, forcing the banks to sell bonds to it with a pre-agreed repurchase price (i.e., do a repurchase agreement). The repo rate would be such that the central bank earned the official refinancing rate on the transactions.

The name of each central bank's official refinancing rate varies. The Bank of England's refinancing rate is the **two-week repo rate**. In other words, the Bank of England fixes the rate at which it is willing to lend two-week money to the banking sector. The ECB's official policy rate is known as the **refinancing rate** and defines the rate at which it is willing to lend short-term money to the euro area banking sector.

The corresponding rate in the United States is the discount rate, which is the rate for member banks borrowing directly from the Federal Reserve System. But the most important interest rate used in US monetary policy is the **federal funds rate**. The federal funds rate (or **fed funds rate**) is the interbank lending rate on overnight borrowings of reserves. The Federal Open Market Committee (FOMC) seeks to move this rate to a target level by reducing or adding reserves to the banking system by means of open market operations. The level of the rate is reviewed by the FOMC at its meetings held every six weeks (although the target can be changed between meetings, if necessary).

Through the setting of a policy rate, a central bank can manipulate the amount of money in the money markets. Generally speaking, the higher the policy rate, the higher the potential penalty that banks will have to pay to the central bank if they run short of liquidity, the greater will be their willingness to reduce lending, and the more likely that broad money growth will shrink.

2.3.2.3 Reserve Requirements　　The third primary way in which central banks can limit or increase the supply of money in an economy is via their **reserve requirements**. We have already seen that the money creation process is more powerful the lower the percentage reserve requirement of banks. So, a central bank could restrict money creation by raising the reserve requirements of banks. However, this policy tool is not used much nowadays in developed economies. Indeed, some central banks, such as the Bank of England, do not even set minimum reserve requirements for the banks under their jurisdiction anymore. Changing reserve requirements frequently is disruptive for banks. For example, if a central bank increased the reserve requirements, a bank that was short on reserves might have to cease its lending activities until it had built up the necessary reserves, because deposits would be unlikely to rise quickly enough for the bank to build its reserves in this way. However, reserve requirements are still actively used in many developing countries to control lending—for example in China and in India—and they remain a potential policy tool for those central banks that do not currently use it.

To summarize, central banks can manipulate the money supply in one of three ways:

- open market operations;
- its official policy rate and associated actions in the repo market; and
- manipulation of official reserve requirements.

2.3.3 *The Transmission Mechanism*

The overarching goal of a central bank is to maintain price stability. We demonstrated above how a central bank can manipulate the money supply and growth of the money supply. We also indicated how policy rates set and targeted by the central banks are usually very short term in nature; often they target overnight interest rates. However, most businesses and individuals in the real economy borrow and lend over much longer time frames than this. It may not be obvious, then, how changing short-term interest rates can influence the real economy, particularly if money neutrality holds in the long run. The fact that central bankers believe that they can affect real economic variables, in particular economic growth, by influencing broad money growth suggests that they believe that money is not neutral—at least not in the short run.

Exhibit 7 presents a stylized representation of the **monetary transmission mechanism**. This is the process whereby a central bank's interest rate gets transmitted through the economy and ultimately affects the rate of increase of prices—that is, inflation.

Exhibit 7   A Stylized Representation of the Monetary Transmission Mechanism

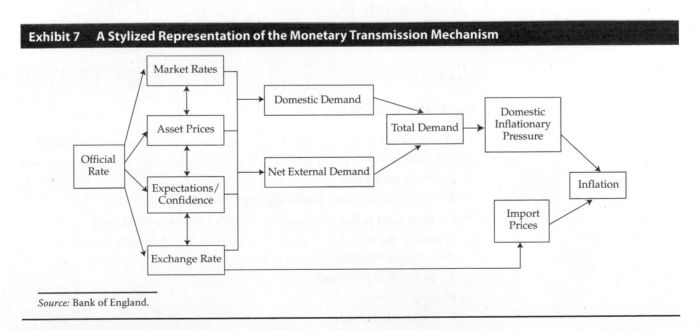

Source: Bank of England.

Suppose that a central bank announces an increase in its official interest rate. The implementation of the policy may begin to work through the economy via four interrelated channels. Those channels include bank lending rates, asset prices, agents' expectations, and exchange rates. First, as described above, the base rates of commercial banks and interbank rates should rise in response to the increase in the official rate. Banks would, in turn, increase the cost of borrowing for individuals and companies over both short- and long-term horizons. Businesses and consumers would then tend to borrow less as interest rates rise. An increase in short-term interest rates could also cause the price of such assets as bonds or the value of capital projects to fall as the discount rate for future cash flows rises.

Market participants would then come to the view that higher interest rates will lead to slower economic growth, reduced profits, and reduced borrowing to finance asset purchases. Exporters' profits might decline if the rise in interest rates causes the country's exchange rate to appreciate, because this would make domestic exports more expensive to overseas buyers and dampen demand to purchase them. The fall in asset prices as well as an increase in prices would reduce household financial wealth and therefore lead to a reduction in consumption growth. Expectations regarding interest rates can play a significant role in the economy. Often companies and individuals will make investment and purchasing decisions based on their interest rate expectations, extrapolated from recent events. If the central bank's interest rate move is widely expected to be followed by other interest rate increases, investors and companies will act accordingly. Consumption, borrowing, and asset prices may all decline as a result of the revision in expectations.

There is a whole range of interconnected ways in which a rise in the central bank's policy rate can reduce real domestic demand and net external demand (that is, the difference between export and import consumption). Weaker total demand would tend to put downward pressure on the rate of domestic inflation—as would a stronger currency, which would reduce the prices of imports. Taken together, these might begin to put downward pressure on the overall measure of inflation.

To summarize, the central bank's policy rate works through the economy via any one, and often all, of the following interconnected channels:

- Short-term interest rates;
- Changes in the values of key asset prices;
- The exchange rate; and
- The expectations of economic agents.

EXAMPLE 8

Central Bank Tools

1. Which of the following variables are *most likely* to be affected by a change in a central bank's policy rate?
   A Asset prices only
   B Expectations about future interest rates only
   C Both asset prices and expectations about future interest rates

2. Which of the following does a central bank seek to influence directly via the setting of its official interest rate?
   A Inflation expectations
   B Import prices
   C Domestic inflation

Solution to 1:

C is correct. The price of equities, for example, might be affected by the expectation of future policy interest rate changes. In other words, a rate change may be taken as a signal of the future stance of monetary policy—contractionary or expansionary.

Solution to 2:

A is correct. By setting its official interest rate, a central bank could expect to have a direct influence on inflation expectations—as well as on other market interest rates, asset prices, and the exchange rate (where this is freely floating). If it can influence these factors, it might ultimately hope to influence import prices (via changes in the exchange rate) and also domestically generated inflation (via its impact on domestic and/or external demand). The problem is that the workings of the transmission mechanism—from the official interest rate to inflation—are complex and can change over time.

2.3.4 Inflation Targeting

Over the 1990s, a consensus began to build among both central bankers and politicians that the best way to control inflation and thereby maintain price stability was to target a certain level of inflation and to ensure that this target was met by monitoring a wide range of monetary, financial, and real economic variables. Nowadays, inflation-targeting frameworks are the cornerstone of monetary policy and macroeconomic policy in many economies. Exhibit 8 shows the growth in the number of inflation-targeting monetary policy regimes over time.

The inflation-targeting framework that is now commonly practiced was pioneered in New Zealand. In 1988, the New Zealand Minister of Finance, Roger Douglas, announced that economic policy would focus on bringing inflation down from the prevailing level of around 6.0 percent to a target range of 0 to 2 percent. This goal was given legal status by the Reserve Bank of New Zealand Act 1989. As part of the Act, the Reserve Bank of New Zealand (RBNZ) was given the role of pursuing this target. The bank was given **operational independence**; it was free to set interest rates in the way that it thought would best meet the inflation target. Although the RBNZ had independent control of monetary policy, it was still accountable to the government and was charged with communicating its decisions in a clear and transparent way. As Exhibit 8 shows, the New Zealand model was widely copied.

Exhibit 8	The Progressive Adoption of Inflation Targeting by Central Banks			
1989	New Zealand				
1990	Chile	Canada			
1991	Israel	United Kingdom			
1992	Sweden	Finland	Australia		
1995	Spain				
1998	Czech Republic	South Korea	Poland		
1999	Mexico	Brazil	Colombia	ECB	
2000	South Africa	Thailand			
2001	Iceland	Norway	Hungary	Peru	Philippines
2005	Guatemala	Indonesia	Romania		
2006	Turkey	Serbia			
2007	Ghana				

Note: Spain and Finland later joined the EMU.
Sources: For 2001 and earlier, Truman (2003). For 2002 to 2007, Roger (2010).

Although these inflation-targeting regimes vary a little from economy to economy, their success is thought to depend on three key concepts: central bank independence, credibility, and transparency.

Central Bank Independence[8]   In most cases, the central bank that is charged with targeting inflation has a degree of independence from its government. This independence is thought to be important. It is conceivable that politicians could announce an inflation target and direct the central bank to set interest rates accordingly. Indeed, this was the process adopted in the United Kingdom between 1994 and 1997. But politicians have a constant eye on re-election and might be tempted, for example, to keep rates "too low" in the lead up to an election in the hope that this might help their re-election prospects. As a consequence, this might lead to higher inflation. Thus, it is now widely believed that monetary policy decisions should rest in the hands of an organization that is remote from the electoral process. The central bank is the natural candidate to be the monopoly supplier of a currency.

However, there are degrees of independence. For example, the head of the central bank is nearly always chosen by government officials. The Chairman of the US Federal Reserve's Board of Governors is appointed by the President of the United States of America; the Head of the ECB is chosen by the committee of Euro area finance ministers; while the Governor of the Bank of England is chosen by the Chancellor of the Exchequer. So, in practice, separating control from political influence completely is probably an impossible (although a desirable) goal.

There are further degrees of independence. Some central banks are both operationally and **target independent**. This means that they not only decide the level of interest rates, but they also determine the definition of inflation that they target, the rate of inflation that they target, and the horizon over which the target is to be achieved. The ECB has independence of this kind. By contrast, other central banks—including those in New Zealand, Sweden, and the United Kingdom—are tasked to hit a definition and level of inflation determined by the government. These central banks are therefore only operationally independent.

Credibility   The independence of the central bank and public confidence in it are key in the design of an inflation-targeting regime.

To illustrate the role of credibility, suppose that instead of the central bank, the government assumes the role of targeting inflation but the government is heavily indebted. Given that higher inflation reduces the real value of debt, the government would have an incentive to avoid reaching the inflation target or to set a high inflation target such that price stability and confidence in the currency could be endangered. As a result, few would believe the government was really intent on controlling inflation; thus, the government would lack credibility. Many governments have very large levels of debt, especially since the 2008–2009 global financial crisis. In such a situation, economic agents might expect a high level of inflation, regardless of the actual, stated target. The target might have little credibility if the organization's likelihood of sticking to it is in doubt.

---

8 For information about the degree of independence of any central bank, the roles that it assumes in an economy, and the framework in which it operates, analysts should go to a central bank's website. A list of central bank websites can be found at http://www.bis.org/cbanks.htm.

If a respected central bank assumes the inflation-targeting role and if economic agents believe that the central bank will hit its target, the belief itself could become self-fulfilling. If everyone believes that the central bank will hit an inflation target of 2 percent next year, this expectation might be built into wage claims and other nominal contracts that would make it hit the 2 percent target. It is for this reason that central bankers pay a great deal of attention to inflation expectations. If these expectations were to rise rapidly, perhaps following a rapid increase in oil prices, unchecked expectations could get embedded into wage claims and eventually cause inflation to rise.

Transparency One way of establishing credibility is for a central bank to be transparent in its decision making. Many, if not all, independent inflation-targeting central banks produce a quarterly assessment of their economies. These **Inflation Reports**, as they are usually known, give central banks' views on the range of indicators that they watch when they come to their (usually) monthly interest rate decision. They will consider and outline their views on the following subjects, usually in this order:

- Broad money aggregates and credit conditions;
- Conditions in financial markets;
- Developments in the real economy (e.g., the labour market); and
- Evolution of prices.

Consideration of all of these important components of an economy is then usually followed by a forecast of growth and inflation over a medium-term horizon, usually two years.

By explaining their views on the economy and by being transparent in decision making, the independent, inflation-targeting central banks seek to gain reputation and credibility, making it easier to influence inflation expectations and hence ultimately easier to meet the inflation target.

The Target
Whether the target is set by the central bank or by the government for the central bank to hit, the level of the target and the horizon over which the target is to be hit is a crucial consideration in all inflation-targeting frameworks.

Exhibit 9	**A Range of Inflation Targets**
Country/Region	
Australia	Australian Federal Reserve's target is inflation between 2.0% and 3.0%.
Canada	Bank of Canada's target is CPI inflation within 1.0% and 3.0%.
Euro-area	ECB's target is CPI inflation below a ceiling of 2%.
South Korea	Bank of Korea's target for 2010–2012 is CPI inflation within ±1.0 percentage of 3.0%.
New Zealand	Reserve Bank of New Zealand's target is inflation between 1.0% and 3.0%.
Sweden	Riksbank's target is CPI inflation within ±1.0 percentage point of 2.0%.
United Kingdom	Bank of England's target is CPI inflation within ±1.0 percentage point of 2.0%.

Source: Central bank websites (http://www.bis.org/cbanks.htm).

Exhibit 9 shows that many central banks in developed economies target an inflation rate of 2 percent based on a consumer price index. Given that the operation of monetary policy is both art and science, the banks are normally allowed a range around the central target of +1 percent or –1 percent. For example, with a 2 percent target, they would be tasked to keep inflation between 1 percent and 3 percent. But why target 2 percent and not 0 percent?

The answer is that aiming to hit 0 percent could result in negative inflation, known as **deflation**. One of the limitations of monetary policy that we discuss below is its ability or inability to deal with periods of deflation. If deflation is something to be avoided, why not target 10 percent? The answer to this question is that levels of inflation that high would not be consistent with price stability; such a high inflation rate would further tend to be associated with high inflation volatility and uncertainty. Central bankers seem to agree that 2 percent is far enough away from the risks of deflation and low enough not to lead to destabilizing inflation shocks.

Finally, we should keep in mind that the headline inflation rate that is announced in most economies every month, and which is the central bank's target, is a measure of how much a basket of goods and services has risen over the previous twelve months. It is history. Furthermore, interest rate changes made today will take some time to have their full effect on the real economy as they make their way through the monetary transmission mechanism. It is for these two reasons that inflation targeters do not target current inflation but instead usually focus on inflation two years ahead.

Although inflation-targeting mandates may vary from country to country, they have common elements: the specification of an explicit inflation target, with permissible bounds, and a requirement that the central bank should be transparent in its objectives and policy actions. This is all usually laid out in legislation that imposes statutory obligations on the central bank. As mentioned earlier, New Zealand pioneered the inflation-targeting approach to monetary policy that has since been copied widely. Below is New Zealand's Policy Targets Agreement, which specifies the inflation-targeting mandate of its central bank, the Reserve Bank of New Zealand.

Exhibit 10   New Zealand's Policy Targets Agreement

"This agreement between the Minister of Finance and the Governor of the Reserve Bank of New Zealand (the Bank) is made under section 9 of the Reserve Bank of New Zealand Act 1989 (the Act). The Minister and the Governor agree as follows:

1   Price stability

   a   Under Section 8 of the Act the Reserve Bank is required to conduct monetary policy with the goal of maintaining a stable general level of prices.

   b   The Government's economic objective is to promote a growing, open and competitive economy as the best means of delivering permanently higher incomes and living standards for New Zealanders. Price stability plays an important part in supporting this objective.

2   Policy target

   a   In pursuing the objective of a stable general level of prices, the Bank shall monitor prices as measured by a range of price indices. The price stability target will be defined in terms of the All Groups Consumers Price Index (CPI), as published by Statistics New Zealand.

   b   For the purpose of this agreement, the policy target shall be to keep future CPI inflation outcomes between 1 per cent and 3 per cent on average over the medium term.

3   Inflation variations around target

Exhibit 10   (Continued)

a For a variety of reasons, the actual annual rate of CPI inflation will vary around the medium-term trend of inflation, which is the focus of the policy target. Amongst these reasons, there is a range of events whose impact would normally be temporary. Such events include, for example, shifts in the aggregate price level as a result of exceptional movements in the prices of commodities traded in world markets, changes in indirect taxes,[9] significant government policy changes that directly affect prices, or a natural disaster affecting a major part of the economy.

b When disturbances of the kind described in clause 3(a) arise, the Bank will respond consistent with meeting its medium-term target.

4   Communication, implementation and accountability

a On occasions when the annual rate of inflation is outside the medium-term target range, or when such occasions are projected, the Bank shall explain in Policy Statements made under section 15 of the Act why such outcomes have occurred, or are projected to occur, and what measures it has taken, or proposes to take, to ensure that inflation outcomes remain consistent with the medium-term target.

b In pursuing its price stability objective, the Bank shall implement monetary policy in a sustainable, consistent and transparent manner and shall seek to avoid unnecessary instability in output, interest rates and the exchange rate.

c The Bank shall be fully accountable for its judgments and actions in implementing monetary policy."

Source: http://www.rbnz.govt.nz/.

To summarize, an inflation-targeting framework normally has the following set of features:

- An independent and credible central bank;
- A commitment to transparency;
- A decision-making framework that considers a wide range of economic and financial market indicators; and
- A clear, symmetric and forward-looking medium-term inflation target, sufficiently above 0 percent to avoid the risk of deflation but low enough to ensure a significant degree of price stability.

Indeed, independence, credibility, and transparency are arguably the crucial ingredients for an effective central bank, whether they target inflation or not.

The Main Exceptions to the Inflation-Targeting Rule

Although the practice of inflation targeting is widespread, there are two prominent central banks that have not adopted a formal inflation target along the lines of the New Zealand model: the Bank of Japan and the US Federal Reserve System.

---

9 "Indirect taxes" refer to such taxes as sales taxes and value-added taxes that are levied on goods and services rather than directly on individuals and companies.

The Bank of Japan

Japan's central bank, the Bank of Japan (BoJ), does not target an explicit measure of inflation. Japan's government and its monetary authorities have been trying to combat deflation for much of the last two decades. However, despite their efforts—including the outright printing of money—inflation has remained very weak. Inflation targeting is seen very much as a way of combating and controlling inflation; as such, it would seem to have no place in an economy that suffers from persistent deflation.

Some economists have argued, however, that an inflation target is exactly what the Japanese economy needs. By announcing that positive inflation of say 3 percent is desired by the central bank, this might become a self-fulfilling prophecy if Japanese consumers and companies factor this target into nominal wage and price contracts. But for economic agents to believe that the target will be achieved, they have to believe that the central bank is capable of achieving it. Given that the BoJ has failed to engineer persistent, positive inflation, it is debatable how much credibility Japanese households and corporations would afford such an inflation-targeting policy.

The US Federal Reserve System

It is perhaps rather ironic that the world's most influential central bank, the US Federal Reserve, which controls the supply of the world's de facto reserve currency, the US dollar, does not have an explicit inflation target. However, it is felt that the single-minded pursuit of inflation might not be compatible with the Fed's statutory goal as laid out in the Federal Reserve Act, which charges the Fed's board to:

> "promote effectively the goals of maximum employment, stable prices, and moderate long-term interest rates."

In other words, it has been argued that inflation targeting might compromise the goal of "maximum employment." In practice, however, the Fed has indicated that it sees core inflation measured by the personal consumption expenditure (PCE) deflator of about, or just below, 2 percent as being compatible with "stable prices." Financial markets therefore watch this US inflation gauge very carefully in order to try and anticipate the rate actions of the Fed.

Monetary Policy in Developing Countries

Developing economies often face significant impediments to the successful operation of any monetary policy—that is, the achievement of price stability. These include:

- the absence of a sufficiently liquid government bond market and developed interbank market through which monetary policy can be conducted;

- a rapidly changing economy, making it difficult to understand what the neutral rate might be and what the equilibrium relationship between monetary aggregates and the real economy might be;

- rapid financial innovation that frequently changes the definition of the money supply;

- a poor track record in controlling inflation in the past, making monetary policy intentions less credible; and

- an unwillingness of governments to grant genuine independence to the central bank.

Taken together, any or all of these impediments might call into question the effectiveness of any developing economy's monetary policy framework, making any related monetary policy goals difficult to achieve.

EXAMPLE 9

Central Bank Effectiveness

1 The reason some inflation-targeting banks may target low inflation and not 0 percent inflation is *best* described by which of the following statements?

A Some inflation is viewed as being good for an economy.

B Targeting zero percent inflation runs a higher risk of a deflationary outcome.

C It is very difficult to eliminate all inflation from a modern economy.

2 The degree of credibility that a central bank is afforded by economic agents is important because:

A they are the lender of last resort.

B their targets can become self-fulfilling prophecies.

C they are the monopolistic suppliers of the currency.

Solution to 1:

B is correct. Inflation targeting is art, not science. Sometimes inflation will be above target and sometimes below. Were central banks to target zero percent, then inflation would almost certainly be negative on some occasions. If a deflationary mindset then sets in among economic agents, it might be difficult for the central bank to respond to this because they cannot cut interest rates below zero.

Solution to 2:

B is correct. If a central bank operates within an inflation-targeting regime and if economic agents believe that it will achieve its target, this expectation will become embedded into wage negotiations, for example, and become a self-fulfilling prophecy. Also, banks need to be confident that the central bank will lend them money when all other sources are closed to them; otherwise, they might curtail their lending drastically, leading to a commensurate reduction in money and economic activity.

2.3.5 *Exchange Rate Targeting*

Many developing economies choose to operate monetary policy by targeting their currency's exchange rate, rather than an explicit level of domestic inflation. Such targeting involves setting a fixed level or band of values for the exchange rate against a major currency, with the central bank supporting the target by buying and selling the national currency in foreign exchange markets. There are recent examples of developed economies using such an approach. In the 1980s, following the failure of its policy of trying to control UK inflation by setting medium-term goals for money supply growth (see Example 5), the UK government decided to operate monetary policy such that the sterling's exchange rate equalled a pre-determined value in terms of German deutschemarks. The basic idea is that by tying a domestic economy's currency to that of an economy with a good track record on inflation, the domestic economy would effectively "import" the inflation experience of the low inflation economy.

Suppose that a developing country wished to maintain the value of its currency against the US dollar. The government and/or central bank would announce the currency exchange rate that they wished to target. To simplify matters, let us assume that the domestic inflation rates are very similar in both countries and that the monetary authorities of the developing economy have set an exchange rate target that is consistent with relative price levels in the two economies. Under these (admittedly unlikely) circumstances, in the absence of shocks, there would be no reason for the exchange rate to deviate significantly from this target level. So as long as domestic inflation closely mirrors US inflation, the exchange rate should remain close to its target (or within a target band). It is in this sense that a successful exchange rate policy imports the inflation of the foreign economy.

Now suppose that economic activity in the developing economy starts to rise rapidly and that domestic inflation in the developing economy rises above the level in the United States. With a freely floating exchange rate regime, the currency of the developing economy would start to fall against the dollar. To arrest this fall, and to protect the exchange rate target, the developing economy's monetary authority sells foreign currency reserves and buys its own currency. This has the effect of reducing the domestic money supply and increasing short-term interest rates. The developing economy experiences a monetary policy tightening which, if expected to bring down inflation, will cause its exchange rate to rise against the dollar.

By contrast, in a scenario in which inflation in the developing country fell relative to the United States, the central bank would need to sell the domestic currency to support the target, tending to increase the domestic money supply and reduce the rate of interest.

In practice, the interventions of the developing economy central bank will simply stabilize the value of its currency, with many frequent adjustments. But this simplistic example should demonstrate one very important fact: *When the central bank or monetary authority chooses to target an exchange rate, interest rates and conditions in the domestic economy must adapt to accommodate this target and domestic interest rates and money supply can become more volatile.*

The monetary authority's commitment to and ability to support the exchange rate target must be credible for exchange rate targeting to be successful. If that is not the case, then speculators may trade against the monetary authority. Speculative attacks forced sterling out of the European Exchange Rate Mechanism in 1992. The fixed exchange rate regime was abandoned and the United Kingdom allowed its currency to float freely. Eventually, the UK government adopted a formal inflation target in 1997. Similarly, in the Asian financial crisis of 1997–1998, Thailand's central bank tried to defend the Thai baht against speculative attacks for much of the first half of 1997 but then revealed at the beginning of July that it had no reserves left. The subsequent devaluation triggered a debt crisis for banks and companies that had borrowed in foreign currency, and contagion spread throughout Asia.

Despite these risks, many economies fix their exchange rate to other currencies, most notably the US dollar. Exhibit 11 shows a list of some of the currencies that were fixed against the US dollar at the end of 2009. Other countries operate a "managed exchange rate policy," where they try to limit the movement of their currency by intervening in the market.

Exhibit 11	Some Markets that Peg Currencies to the US Dollar, as of December 2009
▪ The Netherlands Antilles	▪ Hong Kong SAR
▪ Jordan	▪ Lebanon
▪ Barbados	▪ Saudi Arabia
▪ Maldives	▪ Oman
▪ Belize	▪ Qatar
▪ The Bahamas	

EXAMPLE 10

Exchange Rate Targeting

1 When the central bank chooses to target a specific value for its exchange rate:

    A it must also target domestic inflation.

    B it must also set targets for broad money growth.

    C conditions in the domestic economy must adapt to accommodate this target.

2 With regard to monetary policy, what is the hoped for benefit of adopting an exchange rate target?

    A Freedom to pursue redistributive fiscal policy

    B Freedom to set interest rates according to domestic conditions

    C To "import" the inflation experience of the economy whose currency is being targeted

3 Which of the following is *least* likely to be an impediment to the successful implementation of monetary policy in developing economies?

    A Fiscal deficits

    B Rapid financial innovation

    C Absence of a liquid government bond market

Solution to 1:

C is correct. The adoption of an exchange rate target requires that the central bank set interest rates to achieve this target. If the target comes under pressure, domestic interest rates may have to rise, regardless of domestic conditions. It may have a "target" level of inflation in mind as well as "targets" for broad money growth, but as long as it targets the exchange rate, domestic inflation and broad money trends must simply be allowed to evolve.

Solution to 2:

C is correct. Note that interest rates have to be set to achieve this target and are therefore subordinate to the exchange rate target and partially dependent on economic conditions in the foreign economy.

Solution to 3:

A is correct. Note that the absence of a liquid government bond market through which a central bank can enact open market operations and/or repo transactions will inhibit the implementation of monetary policy—as would rapid financial innovation because such innovation can change the relationship between money and economic activity. Fiscal deficits, on the other hand, are not normally an impediment to the implementation of monetary policy, although they could be if they were perceived to be unsustainable.

2.4 Contractionary and Expansionary Monetary Policies and the Neutral Rate

Most central banks will adjust liquidity conditions by adjusting their official policy rate.[10] When they believe that economic activity is likely to lead to an increase in inflation, they might increase interest rates, thereby reducing liquidity. In these cases, market analysts describe such actions as **contractionary** because the policy is designed to cause the rate of growth of the money supply and the real economy to contract (see Exhibit 7 for the possible transmission mechanism here). Conversely, when the economy is slowing and inflation and monetary trends are weakening, central banks may increase liquidity by cutting their target rate. In these circumstances, monetary policy is said to be **expansionary**.

Thus, when policy rates are high, monetary policy may be described as contractionary; when low, they may be described as expansionary. But what are they "high" and "low" in comparison to?

The **neutral rate of interest** is often taken as the point of comparison. One way of characterizing the neutral rate is to say that it is that rate of interest that neither spurs on nor slows down the underlying economy. As such, when policy rates are above the neutral rate, monetary policy is contractionary; when they are below the neutral rate, monetary policy is expansionary. The neutral rate should correspond to the average policy rate over a business cycle.

However, economists' views of the neutral rate for any given economy might differ, and therefore, their view of whether monetary policy is contractionary, neutral, or expansionary might differ too. What economists do agree on is that the neutral policy rate for any economy comprises two components:

- Real trend rate of growth of the underlying economy, and
- Long-run expected inflation.

The real trend rate of growth of an economy is also difficult to discern, but it corresponds to that rate of economic growth that is achievable in the long run that gives rise to stable inflation. If we are thinking about an economy with a credible inflation-targeting regime, where the inflation target is say 2 percent per year and where an analyst believes that the economy can grow sustainably over the long term at a rate of 2.5 percent per year, then they might also estimate the neutral rate to be:

$$\text{Neutral rate} = \text{Trend growth} + \text{Inflation target} = 2\% + 2.5\% = 4.5\% \qquad (4)$$

The analyst would therefore describe the central bank's monetary policy as being contractionary when its policy rate is above 4.5 percent and expansionary when it is below this level.

In practice, central banks often indicate what they believe to be the neutral rate of interest for their economy too. But determining this "neutral rate" is more art than science. For example, many analysts have recently revised down their estimates of trend growth for many western countries following the collapse of the credit bubble, because in many cases, the governments and private individuals of these economies are now being forced to reduce consumption levels and pay down their debts.

What's the Source of the Shock to the Inflation Rate?

An important aspect of monetary policy for those charged with its conduct is the determination of the source of any shock to the inflation rate. Suppose that the monetary authority sees that inflation is rising beyond its target, or simply in a way that

---

10 Although, if they have reduced their policy rate to 0 percent, to increase liquidity further they have to resort to less-conventional monetary policy measures.

threatens price stability. If this rise was caused by an increase in the confidence of consumers and business leaders, which in turn has led to increases in consumption and investment growth rates, then we could think of it as being a **demand shock**. In this instance, it might be appropriate to tighten monetary policy in order to bring the inflationary pressures generated by these domestic demand pressures under control.

However, suppose instead that the rise in inflation was caused by a rise in the price of oil (for the sake of argument). In this case, the economy is facing a **supply shock**, and raising interest rates might make a bad situation worse. Consumers are already facing an increase in the cost of fuel prices that might cause profits and consumption to fall and eventually unemployment to rise. Putting up interest rates in this instance might simply exacerbate the oil price-induced downturn, which might ultimately cause inflation to fall sharply.

It is important, then, for the monetary authority to try to identify the source of the shock before engineering a contractionary or expansionary monetary policy phase.

2.5 Limitations of Monetary Policy

The limitations of monetary policy include problems in the transmission mechanism and the relative ineffectiveness of interest rate adjustment as a policy tool in deflationary environments.

2.5.1 *Problems in the Monetary Transmission Mechanism*

In Exhibit 7, we presented a stylized representation of the monetary policy transmission mechanism, including the channels of bank lending rates, asset prices, expectations, and exchange rates. The implication of the diagram is that there are channels through which the actions of the central bank or monetary authority are transmitted to both the nominal and real economy. However, there may be some occasions when the will of the monetary authority is not transmitted seamlessly through the economy.

Suppose that a central bank raises interest rates because it is concerned about the strength of underlying inflationary pressures. Long-term interest rates are influenced by the path of expected short-term interest rates, so the outcome of the rate hike will depend on market expectations. Suppose that bond market participants think that short-term rates are already too high, that the monetary authorities are risking a recession, and that the central bank will likely undershoot its inflation target. This fall in inflation expectations could cause long-term interest rates to fall. That would make long-term borrowing cheaper for companies and households, which could in turn stimulate economic activity rather than cause it to contract.

Arguably, the more credible the monetary authority, the more stable the long end of the yield curve; moreover, the monetary authority will be more confident that its "policy message" will be transmitted throughout the economy. A term recently used in the marketplace is **bond market vigilantes**. These "vigilantes" are bond market participants who might reduce their demand for long-term bonds, thus pushing up their yields, if they believe that the monetary authority is losing its grip on inflation. That yield increase could act as a brake on any loose monetary policy stance. Conversely, the vigilantes may push long-term rates down by increasing their demand for long-dated government bonds if they expect that tight monetary policy is likely to cause a sharp slowdown in the economy, thereby loosening monetary conditions for long-term borrowers in the economy.

A credible monetary policy framework and authority will tend not to require the vigilantes to do the work for it.

In very extreme instances, there may be occasions where the demand for money becomes infinitely elastic—that is, where the demand curve is horizontal and individuals are willing to hold additional money balances without any change in the interest rate—so that further injections of money into the economy will not serve to further lower interest rates or affect real activity. This is known as a **liquidity trap**. In this extreme circumstance, monetary policy can become completely ineffective. The economic conditions for a liquidity trap are associated with the phenomenon of **deflation**.

2.5.2 *Interest Rate Adjustment in a Deflationary Environment and Quantitative Easing as a Response*

Deflation is a pervasive and persistent fall in a general price index and is more difficult for conventional monetary policy to deal with than inflation. This is because once the monetary authority has cut nominal interest rates to zero to stimulate the economy, it cannot cut them any further. It is at this point that the economic conditions for a liquidity trap arise.

Deflation raises the real value of debt, while the persistent fall in prices can encourage consumers to put off consumption today, leading to a fall in demand that leads to further deflationary pressure. Thus a deflationary "trap" can develop, which is characterized by weak consumption growth, falling prices, and increases in real debt levels. Japan eventually found itself in such a position following the collapse of its property bubble in the early 1990s.

If conventional monetary policy—the adjustment of short-term interest rates—is no longer capable of stimulating the economy once the zero nominal interest rate bound has been reached, is monetary policy useless?

In the aftermath of the collapse of the high-tech bubble in November 2002, Federal Reserve Governor (now Chairman) Ben Bernanke gave a speech entitled "Deflation: Making Sure 'It' Doesn't Happen Here." In this speech, Bernanke stated that inflation was always and everywhere a monetary phenomenon, and he expressed great confidence that by expanding the money supply by various means (including dropping it out of a helicopter on the population below), the Federal Reserve as the monopoly supplier of money could always engineer positive inflation in the US economy. He said:

> I am confident that the Fed would take whatever means necessary to prevent significant deflation in the United States and, moreover, that the US central bank, in cooperation with other parts of the government as needed, has sufficient policy instruments to ensure that any deflation that might occur would be both mild and brief.

Following the collapse of the credit bubble in 2008, a number of governments along with their central banks cut rates to (near) zero, including those in the United States and the United Kingdom. However, there was concern that the underlying economies might not respond to this drastic monetary medicine, mainly because the related banking crisis had caused banks to reduce their lending drastically. In order to kick start the process, both the Federal Reserve and the Bank of England effectively printed money and pumped it in to their respective economies. This "unconventional" approach to monetary policy, known as **quantitative easing** (QE), is operationally similar to open market purchase operations but conducted on a much larger scale.

The additional reserves created by central banks in a policy of quantitative easing can be used to buy any assets. The Bank of England chose to buy **gilts** (bonds issued by the UK government), where the focus was on gilts with three to five years maturity. The idea was that this additional reserve would kick-start lending, causing broad money growth to expand, which would eventually lead to an increase in real economic activity. But there is no guarantee that banks will respond in this way. In a difficult economic climate, it may be better to hold excess reserves rather than to lend to households and businesses that may default.

In the United States, the formal plan for QE mainly involved the purchase of mortgage bonds issued or guaranteed by Freddie Mac and Fannie Mae. Part of the intention was to push down mortgage rates to support the US housing market, as well as to increase the growth rate of broad money. Before implementing this formal program, the Federal Reserve intervened in several other markets that were failing for lack of liquidity, including interbank markets and the commercial paper market. These interventions had a similar effect on the Federal Reserve's balance sheet and the money supply as the later QE program.

This first round of QE by the Federal Reserve was then followed by a further round of QE, known as QE2. In November 2010, the Federal Reserve judged that the US economy had not responded sufficiently to the first round of QE (QE1). The Fed announced that it would create $600 billion and use this money to purchase long-dated US Treasuries in equal tranches over the following eight months. The purpose of QE2 was to ensure that long bond yields remained low in order to encourage businesses and households to borrow for investment and consumption purposes, respectively.

As long as they have the appropriate authority from the government, central banks can purchase any assets in a quantitative easing program. But the risks involved in purchasing assets with credit risk should be clear. In the end, the central bank is just a special bank. If it accumulates bad assets that then turn out to create losses, it could face a fatal loss of confidence in its main product: fiat money.

2.5.3 Limitations of Monetary Policy: Summary

The ultimate problem for monetary authorities as they try to manipulate the supply of money in order to influence the real economy is that they cannot control the amount of money that households and corporations put in banks on deposit, nor can they easily control the willingness of banks to create money by expanding credit. Taken together, this also means that they cannot always control the money supply. Therefore, there are definite limits to the power of monetary policy.

EXAMPLE 11

The Limits of Monetary Policy: The Case of Japan

The Background

Between the 1950s and 1980s, Japan's economy achieved faster real growth than any other G7 economy. But the terrific success of the economy sowed the seeds of the problems that were to follow. The very high real growth rates achieved by Japan over four decades became built in to asset prices, particularly equity and commercial property prices. Toward the end of the 1980s, asset prices rose to even higher levels when the Bank of Japan followed a very easy monetary policy as it tried to prevent the Japanese yen from appreciating too much against the US dollar. However, when interest rates went up in 1989–1990 and the economy slowed, investors eventually came to believe that the growth assumptions that were built in to asset prices and other aspects of the Japanese economy were unrealistic. This realization caused Japanese asset prices to collapse. For example, the Nikkei 225 stock market index reached 38,915 in 1989; by the end of March 2003, it had fallen by 80 percent to 7,972. The collapse in asset prices caused wealth to decline dramatically. Consumer confidence understandably fell sharply too, and consumption growth slowed. Corporate spending also fell, while bank lending contracted sharply in the weak economic climate. Although many of these phenomena are apparent in all recessions, the situation was made worse when deflation set in. In an environment when prices are falling, consumers may put off discretionary spending today until tomorrow; by doing this, however, they exacerbate the deflationary environment. Deflation also raises the real value of debts; as deflation takes hold, borrowers find the real value of their debts rising and may try to increase their savings accordingly. Once again, such actions exacerbate the recessionary conditions.

The Monetary Policy Response

Faced with such a downturn, the conventional monetary policy response is to cut interest rates to try to stimulate real economic activity. The Japanese central bank, the Bank of Japan, cut rates from 8 percent in 1990 to 1 percent by 1996. By February 2001, the Japanese policy rate was cut to zero. Once this point is reached, a central bank cannot lower rates any further because nominal interest rates cannot be negative. The Bank of Japan has kept rates at zero since February 2001.

Once rates are at zero, there are two broad approaches suggested by theory, though the two are usually complementary. First, the central bank can try to convince markets that interest rates will remain low for a long time, even after the economy and inflation pick up. This will tend to lower interest rates along the yield curve. Second, the central bank can try to increase the money supply by purchasing assets from the private sector, so-called quantitative easing. The Bank of Japan (BoJ) did both in 2001. It embarked on a program of quantitative easing supplemented by an explicit promise not to raise short-term interest rates until deflation had given way to inflation.

Quantitative easing simply involves the printing of money by the central bank. In practice, this involved the BoJ using open market operations to add reserves to the banking system through the direct purchase of government securities in the open market.

The reserve levels became the new target. The BoJ's monetary policy committee determined the level of reserves and the quantity of bond purchases that should be undertaken, rather than voting on the policy rate.

The success of this policy is difficult to judge. As the chart below shows, although deflation turned to inflation for a while, it returned to deflation in 2008–2009 when the Japanese economy suffered a sharp recession along with much of the rest of the world. At that time, having reversed its QE policy during 2004–2008 by reducing its bond holdings, the Bank of Japan began to buy again.

Economists debate the point, but arguably, the Bank of Japan needed to implement a much larger program of QE to eliminate deflation. Japan's program amounted to a cumulative 7–8 percent of GDP spread over three years, whereas the United States and United Kingdom implemented programs totaling 12 percent and 14 percent, respectively, in about one year between 2009 and 2010. The Japanese experience suggests that there may be limits to the power of monetary policy.

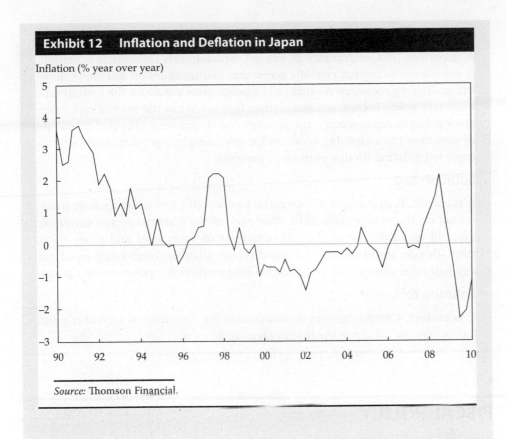

Exhibit 12   Inflation and Deflation in Japan

Inflation (% year over year)

Source: Thomson Financial.

EXAMPLE 12

Evaluating Monetary Policy

1 If an economy's trend GDP growth rate is 3 percent and its central bank has a 2 percent inflation target, which policy rate is *most consistent* with an expansionary monetary policy?

   A   4 percent

   B   5 percent

   C   6 percent

2 An increase in a central bank's policy rate might be expected to reduce inflationary pressures by:

   A   reducing consumer demand.

   B   reducing the foreign exchange value of the currency.

   C   driving up asset prices leading to an increase in personal sector wealth.

3 Which of the following statements *best* describes a fundamental limitation of monetary policy? Monetary policy is limited because central bankers:

   A   cannot control the inflation rate perfectly.

   B   are appointed by politicians and are therefore never truly independent.

   C   cannot control the amount of money that economic agents put in banks, nor the willingness of banks to make loans.

Solution to 1:

A is correct. The neutral rate of interest, which in this example is 5 percent, is considered to be that rate of interest that neither spurs on nor slows down the underlying economy. As such, when policy rates are above the neutral rate, monetary policy is contractionary; when they are below the neutral rate, monetary policy is expansionary. It comprises two components: the real trend rate of growth of the underlying economy (in this example, 3 percent) and long-run expected inflation (in this example, 2 percent).

Solution to 2:

A is correct. If an increase in the central bank's policy rate is successfully transmitted via the money markets to other parts of the financial sector, consumer demand might decline as the rate of interest on mortgages and other credit rises. This decline in consumer demand should, all other things being equal and amongst other affects, lead to a reduction in upward pressure on consumer prices.

Solution to 3:

C is correct. Central bankers do not control the decisions of individuals and banks that can influence the money creation process.

3   FISCAL POLICY

The second set of tools used for influencing economic activity consists of the tools associated with fiscal policy. These involve the use of government spending and changing tax revenue to affect a number of aspects of the economy:

- Overall level of aggregate demand in an economy and hence the level of economic activity.
- Distribution of income and wealth among different segments of the population.
- Allocation of resources between different sectors and economic agents.

Often, a discussion of fiscal policy focuses on the impact of changes in the difference between government spending and revenue on the aggregate economy, rather than on the actual levels of spending and revenue themselves.

3.1 Roles and Objectives of Fiscal Policy

A primary aim for fiscal policy is to help manage the economy through its influence on aggregate national output, that is, real GDP.

3.1.1 Fiscal Policy and Aggregate Demand

Aggregate demand is the amount companies and households plan to spend. We can consider a number of ways that fiscal policy can influence aggregate demand. For example, an **expansionary** policy could take one or more of the following forms:

- Cuts in personal income tax raise disposable income with the objective of boosting aggregate demand.
- Cuts in sales (indirect) taxes to lower prices which raises real incomes with the objective of raising consumer demand.
- Cuts in corporation (company) taxes to boost business profits, which may raise capital spending.

- Cuts in tax rates on personal savings to raise disposable income for those with savings, with the objective of raising consumer demand.

- New public spending on social goods and infrastructure, such as hospitals and schools, boosting personal incomes with the objective of raising aggregate demand.

We must stress, however, that the reliability and magnitude of these relationships will vary over time and from country to country. For example, in a recession with rising unemployment, it is not always the case that cuts in income taxes will raise consumer spending because consumers may wish to raise their precautionary (rainy day) saving in anticipation of further deterioration in the economy. Indeed, in very general terms economists are often divided into two camps regarding the workings of fiscal policy: **Keynesians** believe that fiscal policy can have powerful effects on aggregate demand, output, and employment when there is substantial spare capacity in an economy. **Monetarists** believe that fiscal changes only have a temporary effect on aggregate demand and that monetary policy is a more effective tool for restraining or boosting inflationary pressures. Monetarists tend not to advocate using monetary policy for countercyclical adjustment of aggregate demand. This intellectual division will naturally be reflected in economists' divergent views on the efficacy of the large fiscal expansions observed in many countries following the credit crisis of 2008, along with differing views on the possible impact of quantitative easing.

3.1.2 Government Receipts and Expenditure in Major Economies

In Exhibit 13, we present the total government revenues as a percentage of GDP for some major economies. This is the share of a country's output that is gathered by the government through taxes and such related items as fees, charges, fines, and capital transfers. It is often considered as a summary measure of the extent to which a government is involved both directly and indirectly in the economic activity of a country.

Taxes are formally defined as compulsory, unrequited payments to the general government (they are unrequited in the sense that benefits provided by a government to taxpayers are usually not related to payments). Exhibit 13 contains taxes on incomes and profits, social security contributions, indirect taxes on goods and services, employment taxes, and taxes on the ownership and transfer of property.

Exhibit 13	General Government Revenues as Percent of GDP					
	1995	**2000**	**2005**	**2006**	**2007**	**2008**
Australia	34.5	36.1	36.5	36.4	36.0	35.3
Germany	45.1	46.4	43.6	43.7	43.8	43.8
Japan	31.2	31.4	31.7	34.5	33.5	34.4
United Kingdom	38.2	40.3	40.8	41.4	41.4	42.2
United States	33.8	35.4	33.0	33.8	34.0	32.3
OECD	37.9	39.0	37.7	38.6	38.6	37.9

Source: Organisation for Economic Co-Operation and Development (OECD).

Taxes on income and profits have been fairly constant for the Organisation for Economic Co-Operation and Development (OECD) countries overall at around 12.5–13 percent of GDP since the mid-1990s, while taxes on goods and services have been steady at about 11 percent of GDP for that period. Variations between countries can be substantial; taxes on goods and services are around 5 percent of GDP for the United States and Japan but over 16 percent for Denmark.

Exhibit 14 shows the percentage of GDP represented by government expenditure in a variety of major economies over time. Generally, these have been fairly constant since 1995, though Germany had a particularly high number at the start of the period because of reunification costs.

Exhibit 14	General Government Expenditures as Percent of GDP					
	1995	**2000**	**2005**	**2006**	**2007**	**2008**
Australia	38.2	35.2	34.8	34.5	34.2	34.3
Germany	54.8	45.1	46.9	45.3	43.6	43.8
Japan	36.0	39.0	38.4	36.2	36.0	37.1
United Kingdom	44.1	36.6	44.0	44.1	44.2	47.5
United States	37.1	33.9	36.2	36.0	36.8	38.8
OECD	42.7	38.7	40.5	39.9	39.9	41.4

Source: OECD.

Clearly, the possibility that fiscal policy can influence output means that it may be an important tool for **economic stabilization**. In a recession, governments can raise spending (**expansionary fiscal policy**) in an attempt to raise employment and output. In boom times—when an economy has full employment and wages and prices are rising too fast—then government spending may be reduced and taxes raised (**contractionary fiscal policy**).

Hence, a key concept is the **budget surplus/deficit**, which is the difference between government revenue and expenditure for a fixed period of time, such as a fiscal or calendar year. Government revenue includes tax revenues net of transfer payments; government spending includes interest payments on the government debt. Analysts often focus on changes in the budget surplus or deficit from year to year as indicators of whether the fiscal policy is getting tighter or looser. An increase in a budget surplus would be associated with contractionary fiscal policy, while a rise in a deficit is an expansionary fiscal policy. Of course, over the course of a business cycle the budget surplus will vary automatically in a countercyclical way. For example, as an economy slows and unemployment rises, government spending on social insurance and unemployment benefits will also rise and add to aggregate demand. This is known as an **automatic stabilizer**. Similarly, if boom conditions ensue and employment and incomes are high, then progressive income and profit taxes are rising and also act as automatic stabilizers increasing budget surplus or reducing budget deficit. The great advantage of automatic stabilizers is that they are indeed automatic, not requiring the identification of shocks to which policymakers must consider a response. By reducing the responsiveness of the economy to shocks, these automatic stabilizers reduce output fluctuations. Automatic stabilizers should be distinguished from discretionary fiscal policies, such as changes in government spending or tax rates, which are actively used to stabilize aggregate demand. If government spending and revenues are equal, then the budget is **balanced**.

Exhibit 15	General Government Net Borrowing or Lending as Percent of GDP					
	1995	**2000**	**2005**	**2006**	**2007**	**2008**
Australia	−3.7	0.9	1.7	1.9	1.8	1.0
Germany	−9.7	1.3	−3.3	−1.6	0.2	0.0
Japan	−4.7	−7.6	−6.7	−1.6	−2.5	−2.7
United Kingdom	−5.8	3.7	−3.3	−2.7	−2.7	−5.3
United States	−3.3	1.5	−3.3	−2.2	−2.8	−6.5
OECD	−4.8	0.2	−2.7	−1.3	−1.3	−1.3

Source: OECD.

EXAMPLE 13

Sources and Uses of Government Cash Flows: The Case of the United Kingdom

The precise components of revenue and expenditure will of course vary over time and between countries. But, as an example of the breakdown of expenditure and revenue, in Exhibits 16 and 17 we have presented the budget projections of the United Kingdom for 2010/2011. The budget projected that total spending would come to £697bn, while total revenue would only be £548bn. The government was therefore forecasting a budget shortfall of £149bn for the fiscal year, meaning that it had an associated need to borrow £149bn from the private sector in the United Kingdom or the private and public sectors of other economies.

Exhibit 16   Where Does the Money Go? The United Kingdom, 2010–2011

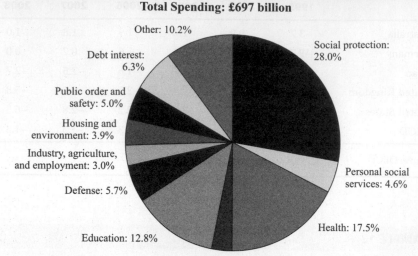

Total Spending: £697 billion

Other: 10.2%

Debt interest: 6.3%

Public order and safety: 5.0%

Housing and environment: 3.9%

Industry, agriculture, and employment: 3.0%

Defense: 5.7%

Education: 12.8%

Transport: 3.0%

Health: 17.5%

Personal social services: 4.6%

Social protection: 28.0%

Note: "Other" includes recreation, culture, religion, public sector pensions, and general public services.
Source: HM Treasury, United Kingdom.

Exhibit 17   Where Does the Money Come From? The United Kingdom, 2010–2011

Total Government Receipts: £548 billion

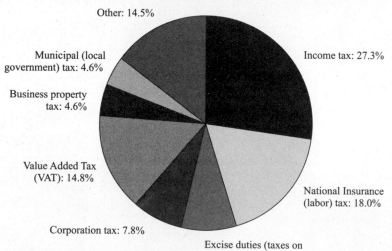

Other: 14.5%

Municipal (local government) tax: 4.6%

Business property tax: 4.6%

Value Added Tax (VAT): 14.8%

Corporation tax: 7.8%

Excise duties (taxes on alcohol, tobacco): 8.4%

National Insurance (labor) tax: 18.0%

Income tax: 27.3%

Note: "Other Receipts" includes capital taxes, stamp duties on share and property transactions, and vehicle excise duties ("road tax").

3.1.3 *Deficits and the National Debt*

Government deficits are the difference between government revenues and expenditures over a period of calendar time, usually a year. Government (or national) debt is the accumulation over time of these deficits. Government deficits are financed by borrowing from the private sector, often via private pension and insurance fund portfolio investments. We saw above that governments are more likely to have deficits than surpluses over long periods of time. As a result, there may exist a large stock of outstanding government debt owned by the private sector. This will vary as the business cycle ebbs and flows. Exhibit 18 shows the time path of the ratio of public debt to GDP for the United Kingdom over several hundred years. It can be clearly seen that the major cause of fluctuations in that ratio through history has been the financing of wars, in particular the Napoleonic Wars of 1799–1815 and the First and Second World Wars of 1914–1918 and 1939–1945.

Exhibit 18   UK National Debt as Percent of GDP (1692–2010)

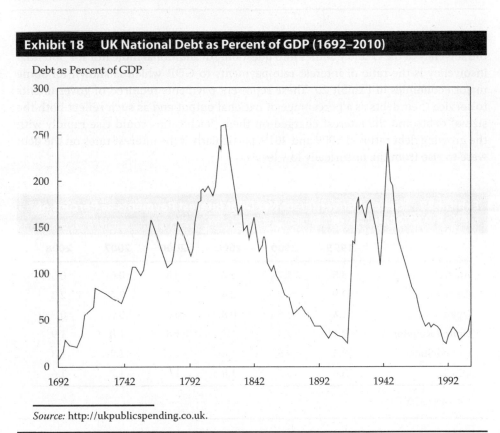

Source: http://ukpublicspending.co.uk.

With the onset of the credit crisis of 2008, governments actively sought to stimulate their economies through increased expenditures without raising taxes and revenues. This led to increased borrowing, shown in Exhibits 15 and 19, which has become a concern in the financial markets in 2010 for such countries as Greece. Indeed, between 2008 and 2009, central government debt rose from $1.2 trillion to $1.6 trillion in the United Kingdom and from $5.8 trillion to $7.5 trillion for the United States.[11]

---

11 www.oecd.org.

Exhibit 19	General Government Gross Financial Liabilities as Percent of GDP					
	1995	2000	2005	2006	2007	2008
Australia	42.5	25.4	16.9	16.2	15.3	14.3
Germany	55.7	60.4	71.1	69.2	65.3	68.8
Japan	86.2	135.4	175.3	172.1	167.1	172.1
United Kingdom	51.6	45.1	46.1	45.9	46.9	56.8
United States	70.6	54.4	61.3	60.8	61.8	70.0
OECD	69.9	68.3	75.9	74.6	73.1	78.4

Source: www.oecd.org.

Ultimately, if the ratio of debt to GDP rises beyond a certain unknown point, then the solvency of the country comes into question. An additional indicator for potential insolvency is the ratio of interest rate payments to GDP, which is shown for some major economies in Exhibit 20. These represent payments required of governments to service their debts as a percentage of national output and as such reflect both the size of debts and the interest charged on them. Such ratios could rise rapidly with the growing debt ratios of 2009 and 2010, particularly if the interest rates on the debt were to rise from the historically low levels.

Exhibit 20	General Government Net Debt Interest Payments as Percent of GDP					
	1995	2000	2005	2006	2007	2008
Australia	3.5	1.7	1.0	0.8	0.6	0.5
Germany	2.9	2.7	2.4	2.4	2.4	2.3
Japan	1.3	1.5	0.8	0.6	0.6	0.9
United Kingdom	3.1	2.4	1.8	1.8	1.8	1.9
United States	3.5	2.5	1.8	1.8	1.9	1.8
OECD	3.6	2.5	1.8	1.7	1.7	1.6

Source: OECD.

Governments' spending was far in excess of revenues following the credit crisis of 2007–2010 as governments tried to stimulate their economies; this level of spending raised concerns in some quarters about the scale of governmental debt accumulation. Exhibit 19 shows that gross government financial liabilities relative to GDP for the OECD countries overall rose from 73.1 percent in 2007 to 78.4 percent in 2008. In Japan, where fiscal spending has been used to stimulate the economy from the early 1990s, the ratio has risen from 86.2 percent in 1995 to 172.1 percent in 2008. If an economy grows in real terms, so do the real tax revenues and hence the ability to service a growing real debt at constant tax rate levels. However, if the real growth in the economy is lower than the real interest rate on the debt, then the debt ratio will worsen even though the economy is growing because the debt burden (i.e., the real interest rate times the debt) grows faster than the economy. Hence, an important issue for governments and their creditors is whether their additional spending leads to sufficiently higher tax revenues to pay the interest on the debt used to finance the extra spending.

However, within a national economy, the real value of the outstanding debt will fall if the overall price level rises (i.e., inflation, and hence a rise in nominal GDP even if real GDP is static) and thus the ratio of debt to GDP may not be rising. But if the general price level falls (i.e., deflation), then the ratio may stay elevated for longer. If net interest payments rise rapidly and investors lose confidence in a government's ability to honour its debts, then financing costs may escalate even more quickly and make the situation unstable.

Should we be concerned about the size of a national debt (relative to GDP)? There are strong arguments both for and against:

The arguments against being concerned about national debt (relative to GDP) are as follows:

- The scale of the problem may be overstated because the debt is owed internally to fellow citizens. This is certainly the case in Japan, where 93 percent is owned by Japanese residents. In the United States and United Kingdom, the figures are 63 percent and 69 percent, respectively. South Korea and Canada have only 7 percent and 5 percent non-resident ownership of government debt, respectively. But Italy has 49 percent.[12]

- A proportion of the money borrowed may have been used for capital investment projects or enhancing human capital (e.g., training, education); these should lead to raised future output and tax revenues.

- Large fiscal deficits require tax changes which may actually reduce distortions caused by existing tax structures.

- Deficits may have no net impact because the private sector may act to offset fiscal deficits by increasing saving in anticipation of future increased taxes. This argument is known as "Ricardian equivalence" and is discussed in more detail later.

- If there is unemployment in an economy, then the debt is not diverting activity away from productive uses (and indeed the debt could be associated with an increase in employment).

The arguments in favour of being concerned are:

- High levels of debt to GDP may lead to higher tax rates in the search for higher tax revenues. This may lead to disincentives to economic activity as the higher marginal tax rates reduce labour effort and entrepreneurial activity, leading to lower growth in the long run.

- If markets lose confidence in a government, then the central bank may have to print money to finance a government deficit. This may lead ultimately to high inflation, as evidenced by the economic history of Germany in the 1920s and more recently in Zimbabwe.

- Government borrowing may divert private sector investment from taking place (an effect known as **crowding out**); if there is a limited amount of savings to be spent on investment, then larger government demands will lead to higher interest rates and lower private sector investing.

An important distinction to make is between long- and short-run effects. Over short periods of time (say, a few years), crowding out may have little effect. If it lasts for a longer time, however, then capital accumulation in an economy may be damaged. Similarly, tax distortions may not be too serious over the short-term but will have a more substantial impact over many years.

---

12 These data come from the Bank for International Settlements (BIS), IMF, and central bank websites. All figures are as of 2008.

EXAMPLE 14

Types of Fiscal Policies

1 Which of the following is *not* associated with an expansionary fiscal policy?

   A A rise in capital gains taxes

   B Cuts in personal income taxes

   C New capital spending by the government on road building

2 Fiscal expansions will *most likely* have the most impact on aggregate output when the economy is in which of the following states?

   A Full employment

   B Near full employment

   C Considerable unemployment

3 Which one of the following is *most likely* a reason to *not* use fiscal deficits as an expansionary tool?

   A They may crowd out private investment.

   B They may facilitate tax changes to reduce distortions in an economy.

   C They may stimulate employment when there is substantial unemployment in an economy.

Solution to 1:

A is correct. A rise in capital gains taxes reduces income available for spending and hence reduces aggregate demand, other things being equal. Cutting income tax raises disposable income, while new road building raises employment and incomes; in both cases, aggregate demand rises and hence policy is expansionary.

Solution to 2:

C is correct. When an economy is close to full employment a fiscal expansion raising aggregate demand can have little impact on output because there are few spare unused resources (e.g., labour or idle factories); instead, there will be upward pressure on prices (i.e., inflation).

Solution to 3:

A is correct. A frequent argument against raises in fiscal deficits is that the additional borrowing to fund the deficit in financial markets will displace private sector borrowing for investment (i.e., "crowd it out").

3.2 Fiscal Policy Tools and the Macroeconomy

We now look at the nature of the fiscal tools available to a government. Government spending can take a variety of forms:

▪ **Transfer payments** are welfare payments made through the social security system and, depending on the country, comprise payments for state pensions, housing benefits, tax credits and income support for poorer families, child benefits, unemployment benefits, and job search allowances. Transfer payments exist to provide a basic minimum level of income for low-income households, and they also provide a means by which a government can change the overall income distribution in a society. Note that these payments are not included in the definition of GDP because they do not reflect a reward to a factor of production for economic activity. Also, they are not considered to be part of general government spending on goods and services.

- **Current government spending** involves spending on goods and services that are provided on a regular, recurring basis—including health, education, and defense. Clearly, such spending will have a big impact on a country's skill level and overall labour productivity.

- **Capital expenditure** includes infrastructure spending on roads, hospitals, prisons, and schools. This investment spending will add to a nation's capital stock and affect productive potential for an economy.

Government spending can be justified on both economic and social grounds:

- To provide such services as defense that benefit all citizens equally.

- For infrastructure capital spending (e.g., roads) to help a country's economic growth.

- To guarantee a minimum level of income for poorer people and hence redistribute income and wealth (e.g., welfare and related benefits).

- To influence a government's economic objectives of low inflation and high employment and growth (e.g., management of aggregate demand).

- To subsidize the development of innovative and high-risk new products or markets (e.g., alternative energy sources).

Government revenues can take several forms:

- **Direct taxes** are levied on income, wealth, and corporate profits and include capital gains taxes, national insurance (or labour) taxes, and corporate taxes. They may also include a local income or property tax for both individuals and businesses. Inheritance tax on a deceased's estate will have both revenue-raising and wealth-redistribution aspects.

- **Indirect taxes** are taxes on spending on a variety of goods and services in an economy—such as the excise duties on fuel, alcohol, and tobacco as well as sales (or value-added tax)—and often exclude health and education products on social grounds. In addition, taxes on gambling may also be considered to have a social aspect in deterring such activity, while fuel duties will have an environmental purpose in making fuel consumption and hence travel more expensive.

Taxes can be justified both in terms of raising revenues to finance expenditures and in terms of income and wealth redistribution policies. Economists typically consider four desirable attributes of a tax policy:

- **Simplicity**: This refers to ease of compliance by the taxpayer and enforcement by the revenue authorities. The final liability should be certain and not easily manipulated.

- **Efficiency**: Taxation should interfere as little as possible in the choices individuals make in the market place. Taxes affect behaviour and should, in general, discourage work and investment as little as possible. A major philosophical issue among economists is whether tax policy should deliberately deviate from efficiency to promote "good" economic activities, such as savings, and discourage harmful ones, such as tobacco consumption. Although most would accept a limited role in guiding consumer choices, some will question how well equipped policymakers are to decide on such objectives and whether there will be unwanted ancillary effects, such as giving tax breaks for saving among people who already save and whose behaviour does not change.

- **Fairness**: This refers to the fact that people in similar situations should pay the same taxes ("horizontal equity") and that richer people should pay more taxes ("vertical equity"). Of course, the concept of fairness is really subjective. Still, most would agree that income tax rates should be progressive—that is, that households and corporations should pay proportionately more as their incomes rise. However, some people advocate "flat" tax rates, whereby all should pay the same proportion of taxable income.

- **Revenue sufficiency**: Although revenue sufficiency may seem obvious as a criterion for tax policy, there may be a conflict with fairness and efficiency. For example, one may believe that increasing income tax rates to reduce fiscal deficits reduces labour effort and that tax rate increases are thus an inefficient policy tool.

EXAMPLE 15

Some Issues with Tax Policy

1 *Incentives*. Some economists believe that income taxes reduce the incentive to work, save, and invest and that the overall tax burden has become excessive. These ideas are often associated with supply-side economics and the US economist Arthur Laffer. A variety of income tax cuts and simplifications have taken place in the United States since 1981, and although there is substantial controversy, some claim that work effort did rise (although tax cuts had little impact on savings). Similarly, some found that business investment did rise, while others claimed it was independent of such cuts.

2 *Fairness*. How do we judge the fairness of the tax system? One way is to calibrate the tax burden falling on different groups of people ranked by their income and to assess how changes in taxes affect these groups. Of course, this imposes huge data demands on investigators and must be considered incomplete. In the United States, it has been found that the federal system is indeed highly progressive. Many countries use such methods to analyze the impact of tax changes on different income groups when they announce their annual fiscal policy plans.

3 *Tax reform*. There is continuous debate on reforming tax policy. Should there be a flat-rate tax on labour income? Should all investment be immediately deducted for corporate taxes? Should more revenue be sourced from consumption taxes? Should taxes be indexed to inflation? Should dividends be taxed when profits have already been subject to tax? Should estates be taxed at all? Many of these issues are raised in the context of their impact on economic growth.

EXAMPLE 16

Fiscal Tools

1 Which of the following is *not* a tool of fiscal policy?

  A A rise in social transfer payments

  B The purchase of new equipment for the armed forces

    C   An increase in deposit requirements for the buying of houses

2 Which of the following is not an indirect tax?

    A   Excise duty

    B   Value-added Tax

    C   Employment taxes

3 Which of the following statements is *most* accurate?

    A   Direct taxes are useful for discouraging alcohol consumption.

    B   Because indirect taxes cannot be changed quickly, they are of no use in fiscal policy.

    C   Government capital spending decisions are slow to plan, implement, and execute and hence are of little use for short-term economic stabilization.

Solution to 1:

C is correct. Rises in deposit requirements for house purchases are intended to reduce the demand for credit for house purchases and hence would be considered a tool of monetary policy. This is a policy used actively in several countries, and is under consideration by regulators in other countries to constrain house price inflation.

Solution to 2:

C is correct. Both excise duty and VAT are applied to prices, whereas taxes on employment apply to labour income and hence are not indirect taxes.

Solution to 3:

C is correct. Capital spending is much slower to implement than changes in indirect taxes; and indirect taxes affect alcohol consumption more directly than direct taxes.

3.2.1 *The Advantages and Disadvantages of Using the Different Tools of Fiscal Policy*

The different tools used to expedite fiscal policy as a means to try to put or keep an economy on a path of positive, stable growth with low inflation have both advantages and disadvantages:

Advantages:

- Indirect taxes can be adjusted almost immediately after they are announced and can influence spending behaviour instantly and generate revenue for the government at little or no cost to the government.

- Social policies, such as discouraging alcohol or tobacco use, can be adjusted almost instantly by raising such taxes.

Disadvantages:

- Direct taxes are more difficult to change without considerable notice, often many months, because payroll computer systems will have to be adjusted (although the announcement itself may well have a powerful effect on spending behaviour more immediately). The same may be said for welfare and other social transfers.

- Capital spending plans take longer to formulate and implement, typically over a period of years. For example, building a road or hospital requires detailed planning, legal permissions, and implementation. This is often a valid criticism of an active fiscal policy and was widely heard during the US fiscal stimulus in 2009–2010. On the other hand, such policies add to the productive potential of an economy, unlike a change in personal or indirect taxes. Of course, the slower the impact of a fiscal change, the more likely other exogenous changes will already be influencing the economy before the fiscal change kicks in.

The above-mentioned tools may also have expectational effects at least as powerful as the direct effects. The announcement of future income tax rises a year ahead could potentially lead to reduced consumption immediately. Such delayed tax rises were a feature of UK fiscal policy of 2009–2010; however, the evidence is anecdotal because spending behaviour changed little until the delayed tax changes actually came into force.

We may also consider the relative potency of the different fiscal tools. Direct government spending has a far bigger impact on aggregate spending and output than income tax cuts or transfer increases; however, if the latter are directed at the poorest in society (basically, those who spend all their income), then this will give a relatively strong boost. Further discussion and examples of these comparisons are given in section 4 below on the interaction between monetary and fiscal policy.

3.2.2 Modeling the Impact of Taxes and Government Spending: The Fiscal Multiplier

The conventional macroeconomic model has government spending, G, adding directly to aggregate demand, AD, and reducing it via taxes, T; these comprise both indirect taxes on expenditures and direct taxes on factor incomes. Further government spending is increased via the payment of transfer benefits, B, such as social security payments. Hence, the net impact of the government sector on aggregate demand is:

$$G - T + B = \text{Budget surplus OR deficit} \qquad (5)$$

Net taxes (NT; taxes less transfers) reduce disposable income (YD) available to individuals relative to national income or output (Y) as follows:

$$YD = Y - NT = (1 - t)\, Y \qquad (6)$$

where t is the **net tax rate**. Net taxes are often assumed to be proportional to national income, Y, and hence total tax revenue from net taxes is tY. If $t = 20\%$ or 0.2, then for every \$1 rise in national income, net tax revenue will rise by 20 cents and household disposable income will rise by 80 cents.

The **fiscal multiplier** is important in macroeconomics because it tells us how much output changes as exogenous changes occur in government spending or taxation. The recipients of the increase in government spending will typically save a proportion $1 - c$ of each additional dollar of disposable income, where c is the **marginal propensity to consume** (MPC) this additional income. Ignoring income taxes, we can see that \$$c$ will, in turn, be spent by these recipients on more goods and services. The recipients of this \$$c$ will themselves spend a proportion c of this additional income (i.e., \$$c \times c$, or c-squared). This process continues with income and spending growing at a constant rate of c as it passes from hand to hand through the economy. This is the familiar geometric progression with constant factor c, where $0 < c < 1$. The sum of this geometric series is $1/(1 - c)$.

We define s as the **marginal propensity to save** (MPS), the amount saved out of an additional dollar of disposable income. Because $c + s = 1$, hence $s = 1 - c$.

Exhibit 21	Disposable Income, Saving, and the MPC			
Income	**Income tax**	**Disposable income**	**Consumption**	**Saving**
$100	$20	$80	$72	$8

In Exhibit 21, the MPC out of disposable income is 90% or 0.9 (72/80).The MPS is therefore $1 - 0.9$ or 0.1

For every dollar of new (additional) spending, total incomes and spending rises by $\$1/(1 - c)$. And because $0 < c < 1$, this must be > 1; this is the multiplier. If $c = 0.9$ (or individuals spend 90 percent of additions to income), then the multiplier $= 1/(1 - 0.9) = 10$.

A formal definition of the multiplier would be the ratio of the change in equilibrium output to the change in autonomous spending that caused the change. This is a monetary measure, but because prices are assumed to be constant in this analysis, real and monetary amounts are identical. Given that fiscal policy is about changes in government spending, G, net taxes, NT, and tax rates, t, we can see that the multiplier is an important tool for calibrating the possible impact of policy changes on output. How can we introduce tax changes into the multiplier concept? We do this by introducing the idea of disposable income, YD, defined as income less income taxes net of transfers, $Y - NT$.

Households spend a proportion c of disposable income, YD, that is, cYD or $c(Y - NT)$ or $c(1 - t)Y$. The **marginal propensity to consume** in the presence of taxes is then $c(1 - t)$. If the government increases spending, say on road building, by an amount, G, then disposable income rises by $(1 - t)G$ and consumer spending by $c(1 - t)G$. Provided there are unused sources of capital and labour in the economy, this leads to a rise in aggregate demand and output; the recipients of this extra consumption spending will have $(1 - t)c(1 - t)G$ extra disposable income available and will spend c of it. This cumulative extra spending and income will continue to spread through the economy at a decreasing rate as $0 < c(1 - t) < 1$. The overall final impact on aggregate demand and output will effectively be the sum of this decreasing geometric series with common ratio $c(1 - t)$, and this sums to $1/[1 - c(1 - t)]$. This is known as the **fiscal multiplier** and is very relevant to studies of fiscal policy as changes in G or tax rates will affect output in an economy through the value of the multiplier.

For example, if the tax rate is 20 percent, or 0.2, and the marginal propensity to spend is 90 percent, or 0.9, then the fiscal multiplier will be: $1/[1 - 0.9(1 - 0.2)]$ or $1/0.28 = 3.57$. In other words, if the government raises G by $1 billion, total incomes and spending rise by $3.57 billion.

Discretionary fiscal policy (see below) will involve changes in these variables with a view to influencing Y.

3.2.3 *The Balanced Budget Multiplier*

If a government increases G by the same amount as it raises taxes, the aggregate output actually rises. Why is this?

It is because the marginal propensity to spend out of disposable income is less than 1, and hence for every dollar less in YD, spending only falls $\$c$. Hence, aggregate spending falls less than the tax rise by a factor of c. A balanced budget leads to a rise in output, which in turn leads to further rises in output and incomes via the multiplier effect.

Suppose an economy has an equilibrium output or income level of $1,000 consisting of $900 of consumption and $100 of investment spending, which is fixed and not related to income. If government spending is set at $200, financed by a tax rate of 20 percent (giving tax revenue of $200), what will happen to output? First, additional government spending of $200 will raise output by that amount; but will taxes of $200 reduce output by a similar amount? Not if the MPC is less than 1; suppose it is 0.9, and hence spending will only fall by 90 percent of $200, or $180. The initial impact of the balanced fiscal package on aggregate demand will be to raise it by $200–$180 = $20. This additional output will, in turn, lead to further increases in income and output through the multiplier effect.

Even though the above policy involved a combination of government spending and tax increases that initially left the government's budget deficit/surplus unchanged, the induced rise in output will lead to further tax revenue increases and a further change in the budget position. Could the government adjust the initial change in spending to offset exactly the eventual total change in tax revenues? The answer is "yes," and we can ask what will be the effect on output of this genuinely balanced budget change? This balanced budget multiplier always takes the value unity.

EXAMPLE 17

Government Debt, Deficits, and Ricardo

The total stock of government debt is the outstanding stock of IOUs issued by a government and not yet repaid. They are issued when the government has insufficient tax revenues to meet expenditures and has to borrow from the public. The size of the outstanding debt equals the cumulative quantity of net borrowing it has done, and the fiscal or budget deficit is added in the current period to the outstanding stock of debt. If the outstanding stock of debt falls, we have a negative deficit or a surplus.

If a government reduces taxation by $10 billion one year and replaces that revenue with borrowing of $10 billion from the public, will it have any real impact on the economy? The important issue here is how people perceive that action: Do they recognize what will happen over time as interest and bond principal have to be repaid out of future taxes? If so, they may think of the bond finance as equivalent to delayed taxation finance; thus, the reduction in current taxation will have no impact on spending because individuals save more in anticipation of higher future taxes to repay the bond. This is called **Ricardian equivalence** after the economist David Ricardo. If people do not correctly anticipate all the future taxes required to repay the additional government debt, then they feel wealthier when the debt is issued and may increase their spending, adding to aggregate demand.

Whether Ricardian equivalence holds in practice is ultimately an empirical issue and is difficult to calibrate conclusively given the number of things that are changing at any time in a modern economy.

3.3 Fiscal Policy Implementation: Active and Discretionary Fiscal Policy

In the following, we discuss major issues in fiscal policy implementation.

3.3.1 *Deficits and the Fiscal Stance*

An important question is the extent to which the budget is a useful measure of the government's fiscal stance. Does the size of the deficit actually indicate whether fiscal policy is **expansionary** or **contractionary**? Clearly, such a question is important for economic policymakers insofar as the deficit can change for reasons unrelated to actual fiscal policy changes. For example, the **automatic stabilizers** mentioned earlier will lead to changes in the budget deficit unrelated to fiscal policy changes; a recession will cause tax revenues to fall and the budget deficit to rise. An observer may conclude that fiscal policy has been loosened and is expansionary and that no further government action is required.

To this end, economists often look at the **structural (or cyclically adjusted) budget deficit** as an indicator of the fiscal stance. This is defined as the deficit that would exist *if the economy was at full employment (or full potential output)*. Hence, if we consider a period of relatively high unemployment, such as 2009–2010 with around 9–10 percent of the workforce out of work in the United States and Europe, then the budget deficits in those countries would be expected to be reduced substantially if the economies returned to full employment. At this level, tax revenues would be higher and social transfers lower. Recent data for major countries are given in Exhibit 22, where negative numbers refer to deficits and positive numbers are surpluses.

Exhibit 22	General Government Net Cyclically Adjusted Borrowing or Lending as Percent of GDP					
	1995	**2000**	**2005**	**2006**	**2007**	**2008**
Australia	−3.1	0.1	1.1	1.4	1.3	0.1
Germany	−9.5	−1.8	−2.3	−1.5	−0.4	−0.5
Japan	−4.6	−7.1	−6.5	−1.8	−3.0	−2.3
United Kingdom	−5.6	0.9	−3.7	−3.3	−3.5	−5.1
United States	−2.9	0.7	−3.6	−2.6	−3.2	−6.1
OECD	−4.6	−1.1	−3.1	−1.9	−2.1	−3.7

Source: OECD.

A further reason why actual government deficits may *not* be a good measure of fiscal stance is the distinction between real and nominal interest rates and the role of inflation adjustment when applied to budget deficits. Although national economic statistics treat the cash interest payments on debt as government expenditure it makes more sense to consider only the inflation-adjusted (or real) interest payments because the real value of the outstanding debt is being eroded by inflation. Automatic stabilizers—such as income tax, VAT, and social benefits—are important because as output and employment fall and reduce tax revenues, so *net* tax revenues also fall as unemployment benefits rise. This acts as a fiscal stimulus and serves to reduce the size of the multiplier, dampening the output response of whatever caused the fall in output in the first place. By their very nature, automatic stabilizers do not require policy changes; no policymaker has to decide that an economic shock has occurred and how to respond. Hence, the responsiveness of the economy to shocks is automatically reduced, as are movements in employment and output.

In addition to these automatic adjustments, governments also use discretionary fiscal adjustments to influence aggregate demand. These will involve tax changes and/or spending cuts or increases usually with the aim of stabilizing the economy. A natural question is why fiscal policy cannot stabilize aggregate demand completely, hence ensuring full employment at all times.

3.3.2 *Difficulties in Executing Fiscal Policy*

Fiscal policy cannot stabilize aggregate demand completely because the difficulties in executing fiscal policy cannot be completely overcome.

First, the policymaker does not have complete information on how the economy functions. It may take several months for policymakers to realize that an economy is slowing, because data appear with a considerable time lag and even then are subject to substantial revision. This is often called the **recognition lag** and has been likened to the problem of driving with the rear view mirror. Then, when policy changes are finally decided on, they may take many months to implement. This is the **action lag**. If a government decides to raise spending on capital projects to increase employment and incomes, for example, these may take many months to plan and put into action. Finally, the result of these actions on the economy will take additional time to become evident; this is the **impact lag**. These types of policy lags also occur in the case of discretionary monetary policy.

A second aspect of time in this process is the uncertainty of where the economy is heading independently of these policy changes. For example, a stimulus may occur simultaneously with a surprise rise in investment spending or in the demand for a country's exports just as discretionary government spending starts to rise. Macroeconomic forecasting models do not generally have a good track record for accuracy and hence cannot be relied on to aid the policy-making process in this context. In addition, when discretionary fiscal adjustments are announced (or are already underway), private sector behaviour may well change leading to rises in consumption or investment, both of which will reinforce the effects of a rise in government expenditure. Again, this will make it difficult to calibrate the required fiscal adjustment to secure full employment.

There are wider macroeconomic issues also involved here.

- If the government is concerned with both unemployment *and* inflation in an economy, then raising aggregate demand toward the full employment level may also lead to a tightening labour market and rising wages and prices. The policymaker may be reluctant to further fine tune fiscal policy in an uncertain world because it might induce inflation.

- If the budget deficit is already large relative to GDP and further fiscal stimulus is required, then the necessary increase in the deficit may be considered unacceptable by the financial markets when government funding is raised, leading to higher interest rates on government debt and political pressure to tackle the deficit.

- Of course, all this presupposes that we know the level of full employment, which is difficult to measure accurately. Fiscal expansion raises demand, but what if we are already at full employment, which will be changing as productive capacity changes and workers' willingness to work at various wage levels changes?

- If unused resources reflect a low supply of labour or other factors rather than a shortage of demand, then discretionary fiscal policy will not add to demand and will be ineffective, raising the risk of inflationary pressures in the economy.

- The issue of crowding out may occur: If the government borrows from a limited pool of savings, the competition for funds with the private sector may crowd out private firms with subsequent less investing and economic growth. In addition, the cost of borrowing may rise, leading to the cancellation of potentially profitable opportunities. This concept is the subject of continuing empirical debate and investigation.

EXAMPLE 18

Evaluating Fiscal Policy

1 Which of the following statements is *least* accurate?

 A The economic data available to policymakers have a considerable time lag.

 B Economic models always offer an unambiguous guide to the future path of the economy.

 C Surprise changes in exogenous economic variables make it difficult to use fiscal policy as a stabilization tool.

2 Which of the following statements is *least* accurate?

 A Discretionary fiscal changes are aimed at stabilizing an economy.

 B In the context of implementing fiscal policy, the recognition lag is often referred to as "driving in the rear view mirror."

 C Automatic fiscal stabilizers include new plans for additional road building by the government.

3 Which of the following statements regarding a fiscal stimulus is *most* accurate?

 A Accommodative monetary policy reduces the impact of a fiscal stimulus

 B Different statistical models will predict different impacts for a fiscal stimulus.

 C It is always possible to predict precisely the impact of a fiscal stimulus on employment.

4 Which of the following statements is *most* accurate?

 A An increase in the budget deficit is always expansionary.

 B An increase in government spending is always expansionary.

 C The structural deficit is always larger than the deficit below full employment.

5 Crowding out refers to a:

 A fall in interest rates that reduces private investment.

 B rise in private investment that reduces private consumption.

 C rise in government borrowing that reduces the ability of the private sector to access investment funds.

6 A contractionary fiscal policy will always involve which of the following?

 A A balanced budget

 B A reduction in government spending

 C A fall in the budget deficit or rise in the surplus

7 Which one of the following statements is *most* accurate?

 A Ricardian equivalence refers to individuals having no idea of future tax liabilities.

> **B** If there is high unemployment in an economy, then easy monetary and fiscal policies should lead to an expansion in aggregate demand.
>
> **C** Governments do not allow political pressures to influence fiscal policies but do allow voters to affect monetary policies.

Solution to 1:

B is correct. Economic forecasts from models will always have an element of uncertainty attached to them and thus are not unambiguous or precise in their prescriptions. Once a fiscal policy decision has been made and implemented, unforeseen changes in other variables may affect the economy in ways that would lead to changes in the fiscal policy if we had perfect foresight. Note that it is true that official economic data may be available with substantial time lags, making fiscal judgements more difficult.

Solution to 2:

C is correct. New plans for road building are discretionary and not automatic.

Solution to 3:

B is correct. Different models embrace differing views on how the economy works, including differing views on the impact of fiscal stimuli.

Solution to 4:

A is correct. Note that increases in government spending may be accompanied by even bigger rises in tax receipts and hence may not be expansionary.

Solution to 5:

C is correct. A fall in interest rates is likely to lead to a rise in investment. Crowding out refers to government borrowing that reduces the ability of the private sector to invest.

Solution to 6:

C is correct. Note that a reduction in government spending could be accompanied by an even bigger fall in taxation, making it be expansionary.

Solution to 7:

B is correct. Note that governments often allow pressure groups to affect fiscal policy and that Ricardian equivalence involves individuals correctly anticipating future taxes, so A and C are not correct choices.

4 THE RELATIONSHIP BETWEEN MONETARY AND FISCAL POLICY

Both monetary and fiscal policies can be used to try and influence the macroeconomy. But the impact of monetary policy on aggregate demand may differ depending on the fiscal policy stance. Conversely, the impact of fiscal policy might vary under various alternative monetary policy conditions. Clearly, policymakers need to understand this interaction. For example, they need to consider the impact of changes to the budget when monetary policy is accommodative as opposed to when it is restrictive: Can we expect the same impact on aggregate demand in both situations?

Although both fiscal and monetary policy can alter aggregate demand, they do so through differing channels with differing impact on the composition of aggregate demand. The two policies are not interchangeable. Consider the following cases in which the assumption is made that *wages and prices are rigid*:

- *Easy fiscal policy/tight monetary policy*: If taxes are cut or government spending rises, the expansionary fiscal policy will lead to a rise in aggregate output. If this is accompanied by a reduction in money supply to offset the fiscal expansion, then interest rates will rise and have a negative effect on private sector demand. We have higher output and higher interest rates, and government spending will be a larger proportion of overall national income.

- *Tight fiscal policy/easy monetary policy*: If a fiscal contraction is accompanied by expansionary monetary policy and low interest rates, then the private sector will be stimulated and will rise as a share of GDP, while the public sector will shrink.

- *Easy monetary policy/easy fiscal policy*: If both fiscal and monetary policy are easy, then the joint impact will be highly expansionary—leading to a rise in aggregate demand, lower interest rates (at least if the monetary impact is larger), and growing private and public sectors.

- *Tight monetary policy/tight fiscal policy*: Interest rates rise (at least if the monetary impact on interest rates is larger) and reduce private demand. At the same time, higher taxes and falling government spending lead to a drop in aggregate demand from both public and private sectors.

4.1 Factors Influencing the Mix of Fiscal and Monetary Policy

Although governments are concerned about stabilizing the level of aggregate demand at close to the full employment level, they are also concerned with the growth of potential output. To this end, encouraging private investment will be important. It may best be achieved by accommodative monetary policy with low interest rates and a tight fiscal policy to ensure free resources for a growing private sector.

At other times, the lack of a good quality, trained workforce—or perhaps a modern capital infrastructure—will be seen as an impediment to growth; thus, an expansion in government spending in these areas may be seen as a high priority. If taxes are not raised to pay for this, then the fiscal stance will be expansionary. If a loose monetary policy is chosen to accompany this expansionary spending, then it is *possible* that inflation may be induced. Of course, it is an open question as to whether policymakers can judge the appropriate levels of interest rates or fiscal spending levels.

Clearly, the mix of policies will be heavily influenced by the political context. A weak government may raise spending to accommodate the demands of competing vested interests (e.g., subsidies to particular sectors, such as agriculture in the EC), and thus a restrictive monetary policy may be needed to hold back the possibly inflationary growth in aggregate demand through raised interest rates and less credit availability.

Both fiscal and monetary policies suffer from lack of precise knowledge of where the economy is today, because data appear initially subject to revision and with a time lag. However, fiscal policy suffers from two further issues with regard to its use in the short run.

As we saw earlier, it is difficult to implement quickly because spending on capital projects takes time to plan, procure, and put into practice. In addition, it is politically easier to loosen fiscal policy than to tighten it; in many cases, automatic stabilizers are the source of fiscal tightening, because tax rates are not changing and political opposition is muted. Similarly, the independence of many central banks means that decisions on raising interest rates are outside the hands of politicians and thus can be taken more easily.

The interaction between monetary and fiscal policies was also implicitly evident in our discussion of Ricardian equivalence because if tax cuts have no impact on private spending as individuals anticipate future higher taxes, then clearly this may lead policymakers to favour monetary tools.

Ultimately, the interaction of monetary and fiscal policies in practice is an empirical question, which we touched on earlier. In their detailed research paper using the IMF'S Global Integrated Monetary and Fiscal Model (IMF 2009), IMF researchers examined four forms of coordinated global fiscal loosening over a two-year period, which will be reversed gradually after the two years are completed. These are:

- an increase in social transfers to all households,
- a decrease in tax on labour income,
- a rise in government investment expenditure, and
- a rise in transfers to the poorest in society.

The two types of monetary policy responses considered are:

- no monetary accommodation, so rising aggregate demand leads to higher interest rates immediately; or
- interest rates are kept unchanged (accommodative policy) for the two years.

The following important policy conclusions from this study emphasize the role of policy interactions:

- *No monetary accommodation*: Government spending increases have a much bigger effect (six times bigger) on GDP than similar size social transfers because the latter are not considered permanent, although real interest rates rise as monetary authorities react to rises in aggregate demand and inflation. Targeted social transfers to the poorest citizens have double the effect of the non-targeted transfers, while labour tax reductions have a slightly bigger impact than the latter.

- *Monetary accommodation:* Except for the case of the cut in labour taxes, fiscal multipliers are now much larger than when there is no monetary accommodation. The cumulative multiplier (i.e., the cumulative effect on real GDP over the two years divided by the percentage of GDP, which is a fiscal stimulus) is now 3.9 for government expenditure compared to 1.6 with no monetary accommodation. The corresponding numbers for targeted social transfer payments are 0.5 without monetary accommodation and 1.7 with it. The larger multiplier effects with monetary accommodation result from rises in aggregate demand and inflation, leading to falls in real interest rates and additional private sector spending (e.g., on investment goods). Labour tax cuts are less positive.

4.2 Quantitative Easing and Policy Interaction

What about the scenario of zero interest rates and deflation? Fiscal stimulus should still raise demand and inflation, lowering real interest rates and stimulating private sector demand. We saw earlier that quantitative easing has been a feature of major economies during 2009–2010. This involves the purchase of government or private securities by the central bank from individuals, institutions, or banks and substituting central bank balances for those securities. The ultimate aim is that recipients will subsequently increase expenditures, lending or borrowing in the face of raised cash balances and lower interest rates.

If the central bank purchases government securities on a large scale, it is effectively funding the budget deficit and the independence of monetary policy is an illusion. This so-called "printing of money" is feared by many economists as the monetization of the government deficit. Note that it is unrelated to the conventional inflation target of central banks, such as the Bank of England. Some economists question whether an independent central bank should engage in such activity.

4.3 The Importance of Credibility and Commitment

The IMF model implies that if governments run persistently high budget deficits, real interest rates rise and crowd out private investment, reducing each country's productive potential. As individuals realize that deficits will persist, inflation expectations and longer-term interest rates rise: This reduces the effect of the stimulus by half.

Further, if there is a real lack of commitment to fiscal discipline over the longer term, (e.g., because of aging populations) and the ratio of government debt to GDP rose by 10 percentage points permanently in the United States alone, then world real interest rates would rise by 0.14 percent—leading to a 0.6 percent permanent fall in world GDP.

EXAMPLE 19

Interactions of Monetary and Fiscal Policy

1 In a world where Ricardian equivalence holds, governments would *most likely* prefer to use monetary rather than fiscal policy because under Ricardian equivalence:

  A real interest rates have a more powerful effect on the real economy.

  B the transmission mechanism of monetary policy is better understood.

  C the future impact of fiscal policy changes are fully discounted by economic agents.

2 If fiscal policy is easy and monetary policy tight, then:

  A interest rates would tend to fall, reinforcing the fiscal policy stance.

  B the government sector would tend to shrink as a proportion of total GDP.

  C the government sector would tend to expand as a proportion of total GDP.

3 Which of the following has the greatest impact on aggregate demand according to an IMF study? A 1 percent of GDP stimulus in:

  A government spending.

  B rise in transfer benefits.

  C cut in labour income tax across all income levels.

Solution to 1:

C is correct. If Ricardian equivalence holds, then economic agents anticipate that the consequence of any current tax cut will be future tax rises, which leads them to increase their saving in anticipation of this so that the tax cut has little effect on consumption and investment decisions. Governments would be forced to use monetary policy to affect the real economy on the assumption that money neutrality did not hold in the short term.

Solution to 2:

C is correct. With a tight monetary policy, real interest rates should rise and reduce private sector activity, which could be at least partially offset by an expansion in government activity via the loosening of fiscal policy. The net effect, however, would be an expansion in the size of the public sector relative to the private sector.

Solution to 3:

A is correct. The study clearly showed that direct spending by the government leads to a larger impact on GDP than changes in taxes or benefits.

SUMMARY

In this reading, we have sought to explain the practices of both monetary and fiscal policy. Both can have a significant impact on economic activity, and it is for this reason that financial analysts need to be aware of the tools of both monetary and fiscal policy, the goals of the monetary and fiscal authorities, and most important the monetary and fiscal policy transmission mechanisms.

- Governments can influence the performance of their economies by using combinations of monetary and fiscal policy. Monetary policy refers to central bank activities that are directed toward influencing the quantity of money and credit in an economy. By contrast, fiscal policy refers to the government's decisions about taxation and spending. The two sets of policies affect the economy via different mechanisms.

- Money fulfills three important functions: It acts as a medium of exchange, provides individuals with a way of storing wealth, and provides society with a convenient unit of account. Via the process of fractional reserve banking, the banking system can create money.

- The amount of wealth that the citizens of an economy choose to hold in the form of money—as opposed to, for example, bonds or equities—is known as the demand for money. There are three basic motives for holding money: transactions-related, precautionary, and speculative.

- The addition of 1 unit of additional reserves to a fractional reserve banking system can support an expansion of the money supply by an amount equal to the money multiplier, defined as 1/reserve requirement (stated as a decimal).

- The nominal rate of interest is comprised of three components: a real required rate of return, a component to compensate lenders for future inflation, and a risk premium to compensate lenders for uncertainty (e.g., about the future rate of inflation).

- Central banks take on multiple roles in modern economies. They are usually the monopoly supplier of their currency, the lender of last resort to the banking sector, the government's bank and bank of the banks, and they often supervise banks. Although they may express their objectives in different ways, the overarching objective of most central banks is price stability.

- For a central bank to be able to implement monetary policy objectively, it should have a degree of independence from government, be credible, and be transparent in its goals and objectives.

- The ultimate challenge for central banks as they try to manipulate the supply of money to influence the economy is that they cannot control the amount of money that households and corporations put in banks on deposit, nor can they easily control the willingness of banks to create money by expanding credit. Taken together, this also means that they cannot always control the money supply. Therefore, there are definite limits to the power of monetary policy.

- The concept of money neutrality is usually interpreted as meaning that money cannot influence the real economy in the long run. However, by the setting of its policy rate, a central bank hopes to influence the real economy via the policy rate's impact on other market interest rates, asset prices, the exchange rate, and the expectations of economic agents.

- Inflation targeting is the most common monetary policy—although exchange rate targeting is also used, particularly in developing economies. Quantitative easing attempts to spur aggregate demand by drastically increasing the money supply.

- Fiscal policy involves the use of government spending and revenue raising (taxation) to impact a number of aspects of the economy: the overall level of aggregate demand in an economy and hence the level of economic activity; the distribution of income and wealth among different segments of the population; and hence ultimately the allocation of resources between different sectors and economic agents.

- The tools that governments use in implementing fiscal policy are related to the way in which they raise revenue and the different forms of expenditure. Governments usually raise money via a combination of direct and indirect taxes. Government expenditure can be current on goods and services or can take the form of capital expenditure, for example, on infrastructure projects.

- As economic growth weakens, or when it is in recession, a government can enact an expansionary fiscal policy—for example, by raising expenditure without an offsetting increase in taxation. Conversely, by reducing expenditure and maintaining tax revenues, a contractionary policy might reduce economic activity. Fiscal policy can therefore play an important role in stabilizing an economy.

- Although both fiscal and monetary policy can alter aggregate demand, they work through different channels, the policies are therefore not interchangeable, and they conceivably can work against one another unless the government and central bank coordinate their objectives.

REFERENCES

Goodhart, Charles A.E. 1989. "The Conduct of Monetary Policy." *Economic Journal*, vol. 99, no. 396:293–346.

Gray, Simon, and Nick Talbot. 2006. *Monetary Operations*. London: Bank of England (http://www.bankofengland.co.uk/education/ccbs/handbooks/ccbshb24.htm).

IMF (International Monetary Fund). 2009. "The Case for Global Fiscal Stimulus" (March): http://www.imf.org/external/pubs/ft/spn/2009/spn0903.pdf.

Roger, Scott. 2010. "Inflation Targeting Turns 20." *Finance and Development*, vol. 47, no. 1:46–49 (March).

Truman, Edwin. 2003. *Inflation Targeting in the World Economy*. Washington, DC: Institute for International Economics.

PRACTICE PROBLEMS

1 As the reserve requirement increases, the money multiplier:

  A increases.

  B decreases.

  C remains the same.

2 Which is the *most* accurate statement regarding the demand for money?

  A Precautionary money demand is directly related to GDP.

  B Transactions money demand is inversely related to returns on bonds.

  C Speculative demand is inversely related to the perceived risk of other assets.

3 The following exhibit shows the supply and demand for money:

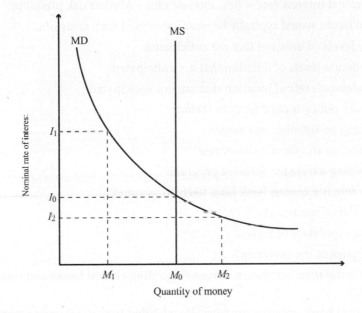

  There is an excess supply of money when the nominal rate of interest is:

  A I_0.

  B I_1.

  C I_2.

4 According to the theory of money neutrality, money supply growth does *not* affect variables such as real output and employment in:

  A the long run.

  B the short run.

  C the long and short run.

5 Which of the following *best* describes a fundamental assumption when monetary policy is used to influence the economy?

  A Financial markets are efficient.

  B Money is not neutral in the short run.

  C Official rates do not affect exchange rates.

6 Monetarists are *most likely* to believe:

   A   there is a causal relationship running from inflation to money.

   B   inflation can be affected by changing the money supply growth rate.

   C   rapid financial innovation in the market increases the effectiveness of monetary policy.

7   The proposition that the real interest rate is relatively stable is *most* closely associated with:

   A   the Fisher effect.

   B   money neutrality.

   C   the quantity theory of money.

8   Which of the following equations is a consequence of the Fisher effect?

   A   Nominal interest rate = Real interest rate + Expected rate of inflation.

   B   Real interest rate = Nominal interest rate + Expected rate of inflation.

   C   Nominal interest rate = Real interest rate + Market risk premium.

9   Central banks would typically be *most* concerned with costs of:

   A   low levels of inflation that are anticipated.

   B   moderate levels of inflation that are anticipated.

   C   moderate levels of inflation that are not anticipated.

10   Monetary policy is *least likely* to include:

   A   setting an inflation rate target.

   B   changing an official interest rate.

   C   enacting a transfer payment program.

11   Which role is a central bank *least likely* to assume?

   A   Lender of last resort.

   B   Sole supervisor of banks.

   C   Supplier of the currency.

12   Which is the *most* accurate statement regarding central banks and monetary policy?

   A   Central bank activities are typically intended to maintain price stability.

   B   Monetary policies work through the economy via four independent channels.

   C   Commercial and interbank interest rates move inversely to official interest rates.

13   When a central bank announces a decrease in its official policy rate, the desired impact is an increase in:

   A   investment.

   B   interbank borrowing rates.

   C   the national currency's value in exchange for other currencies.

14   Which action is a central bank *least likely* to take if it wants to encourage businesses and households to borrow for investment and consumption purposes?

   A   Sell long-dated government securities.

   B   Purchase long-dated government treasuries.

   C   Purchase mortgage bonds or other securities.

15   A central bank that decides the desired levels of interest rates and inflation and the horizon over which the inflation objective is to be achieved is *most* accurately described as being:

   A   target independent and operationally independent.

   B   target independent but not operationally independent.

   C   operationally independent but not target independent.

16 A country that maintains a target exchange rate is *most likely* to have which outcome when its inflation rate rises above the level of the inflation rate in the target country?

   A   An increase in short-term interest rates.

   B   An increase in the domestic money supply.

   C   An increase in its foreign currency reserves.

17 A central bank's repeated open market purchases of government bonds:

   A   decreases the money supply.

   B   is prohibited in most countries.

   C   is consistent with an expansionary monetary policy.

18 In theory, setting the policy rate equal to the neutral interest rate should promote:

   A   stable inflation.

   B   balanced budgets.

   C   greater employment.

19 A prolonged period of an official interest rate of zero without an increase in economic growth *most likely* suggests:

   A   quantitative easing must be limited to be successful.

   B   there may be limits to the effectiveness of monetary policy.

   C   targeting reserve levels is more important than targeting interest rates.

20 Raising the reserve requirement is *most likely* an example of which type of monetary policy?

   A   Neutral.

   B   Expansionary.

   C   Contractionary.

21 Which of the following is a limitation on the ability of central banks to stimulate growth in periods of deflation?

   A   Ricardian equivalence.

   B   The interaction of monetary and fiscal policy.

   C   The fact that interest rates have a minimum value (0%).

22 The *least likely* limitation to the effectiveness of monetary policy is that central banks cannot:

   A   accurately determine the neutral rate of interest.

   B   regulate the willingness of financial institutions to lend.

   C   control amounts that economic agents deposit into banks.

23 Which of the following is the *most likely* example of a tool of fiscal policy?

   A   Public financing of a power plant.

   B   Regulation of the payment system.

   C   Central bank's purchase of government bonds.

24 The *least likely* goal of a government's fiscal policy is to:

   A   redistribute income and wealth.

   B   influence aggregate national output.

C ensure the stability of the purchasing power of its currency.

25 Given an independent central bank, monetary policy actions are *more likely* than fiscal policy actions to be:

A implementable quickly.

B effective when a specific group is targeted.

C effective when combating a deflationary economy.

26 Which statement regarding fiscal policy is *most* accurate?

A To raise business capital spending, personal income taxes should be reduced.

B Cyclically adjusted budget deficits are appropriate indicators of fiscal policy.

C An increase in the budget surplus is associated with expansionary fiscal policy.

27 The *least likely* explanation for why fiscal policy cannot stabilize aggregate demand completely is that:

A private sector behavior changes over time.

B policy changes are implemented very quickly.

C fiscal policy focuses more on inflation than on unemployment.

28 Which of the following *best* represents a contractionary fiscal policy?

A Public spending on a high-speed railway.

B A temporary suspension of payroll taxes.

C A freeze in discretionary government spending.

29 A "pay-as-you-go" rule, which requires that any tax cut or increase in entitlement spending be offset by an increase in other taxes or reduction in other entitlement spending, is an example of which fiscal policy stance?

A Neutral.

B Expansionary.

C Contractionary.

30 Quantitative easing, the purchase of government or private securities by the central banks from individuals and/or institutions, is an example of which monetary policy stance?

A Neutral.

B Expansionary.

C Contractionary.

31 The *most likely* argument against high national debt levels is that:

A the debt is owed internally to fellow citizens.

B they create disincentives for economic activity.

C they may finance investment in physical and human capital.

32 Which statement regarding fiscal deficits is *most* accurate?

A Higher government spending may lead to higher interest rates and lower private sector investing.

B Central bank actions that grow the money supply to address deflationary conditions decrease fiscal deficits.

C According to the Ricardian equivalence, deficits have a multiplicative effect on consumer spending.

33 Which policy alternative is *most likely* to be effective for growing both the public and private sectors?

A Easy fiscal/easy monetary policy.

B Easy fiscal/tight monetary policy.

C Tight fiscal/tight monetary policy.

SOLUTIONS

1   B is correct. There is an inverse relationship between the money multiplier and the reserve requirement. The money multiplier is equal to 1 divided by the reserve requirement.

2   A is correct. Precautionary money demand is directly related to GDP. Precautionary money balances are held to provide a buffer against unforeseen events that might require money. Precautionary balances tend to rise with the volume and value of transactions in the economy, and therefore rise with GDP.

3   B is correct. When the interest rate on bonds is I_1 there is an excess supply of money (equal to $M_0 - M_1 > 0$). Economic agents would seek to buy bonds with their excess money balances, which would force the price of bonds up and the interest rate down to I_0.

4   A is correct. According to the theory of money neutrality, an increase in the money supply ultimately leads to an increase in the price level and leaves real variables unaffected in the long run.

5   B is correct. If money were neutral in the short run, monetary policy would not be effective in influencing the economy.

6   B is correct. By definition, monetarists believe prices may be controlled by manipulating the money supply.

7   A is correct. The Fisher effect is based on the idea that the real interest rate is relatively stable. Changes in the nominal interest rate result from changes in expected inflation.

8   A is correct. The Fisher effect implies that changes in the nominal interest rate reflect changes in expected inflation, which is consistent with Nominal interest rate = Real interest rate + Expected rate of inflation.

9   C is correct. Low levels of inflation has higher economic costs than moderate levels, all else equal; unanticipated inflation has greater costs than anticipated inflation.

10 C is correct. Transfer payment programs represent fiscal, not monetary policy.

11 B is correct. The supervision of banks is not a role that all central banks assume. When it is a central bank's role, responsibility may be shared with one or more entities.

12 A is correct. Central bank activities are typically intended to maintain price stability. Concerning choice B, note that the transmission channels of monetary policy are not independent.

13 A is correct. Investment is expected to move inversely with the official policy rate.

14 A is correct. Such action would tend to constrict the money supply and increase interest rates, all else equal.

15 A is correct. The central bank described is target independent because it set its own targets (e.g., the target inflation rate) and operationally independent because it decides how to achieve its targets (e.g., the time horizon).

16 A is correct. Interest rates are expected to rise to protect the exchange rate target.

17 C is correct. The purchase of government bonds via open market operations increases banking reserves and the money supply; it is consistent with an expansionary monetary policy.

18 A is correct. The neutral rate of interest is that rate of interest that neither stimulates nor slows down the underlying economy. The neutral rate should be consistent with stable long-run inflation.

19 B is correct. A central bank would decrease an official interest rate to stimulate the economy. The setting in which an official interest rate is lowered to zero (the lowest value that could be targeted) without stimulating economic growth suggests that there are limits to monetary policy.

20 C is correct. Raising reserve requirements should slow money supply growth.

21 C is correct. Deflation poses a challenge to conventional monetary policy because once the central bank has cut nominal interest rates to zero to stimulate the economy, they cannot cut them further.

22 A is correct. The inability to determine exactly the neutral rate of interest does not necessarily limit the power of monetary policy.

23 A is correct. Public financing of a power plant could be described as a fiscal policy tool to stimulate investment.

24 C is correct. Ensuring stable purchasing power is a goal of monetary rather than fiscal policy. Fiscal policy involves the use of government spending and tax revenue to affect the overall level of aggregate demand in an economy and hence the level of economic activity.

25 A is correct. Monetary actions may face fewer delays to taking action than fiscal policy, especially when the central bank is independent.

26 B is correct. Cyclically adjusted budget deficits are appropriate indicators of fiscal policy. These are defined as the deficit that would exist if the economy was at full employment (or full potential output).

27 B is correct. Fiscal policy is subject to recognition, action, and impact lags.

28 C is correct. A freeze in discretionary government spending is an example of a contractionary fiscal policy.

29 A is correct. A "pay-as-you-go" rule is a neutral policy because any increases in spending or reductions in revenues would be offset. Accordingly, there would be no net impact on the budget deficit/surplus.

30 B is correct. Quantitative easing is an example of an expansionary monetary policy stance. It attempts to spur aggregate demand by drastically increasing the money supply.

31 B is correct. The belief is that high levels of debt to GDP may lead to higher future tax rates which may lead to disincentives to economic activity.

32 A is correct. Government borrowing may compete with private sector borrowing for investment purposes.

33 A is correct. If both fiscal and monetary policies are "easy," then the joint impact will be highly expansionary, leading to a rise in aggregate demand, low interest rates, and growing private and public sectors.

Economics

Economics in a Global Context

This study session introduces economics in a global context. The first reading explains the flows of goods and services, physical capital, and financial capital across national borders. The reading explains how the different types of flows are linked and how trade may benefit trade partners. The accounting for these flows and the institutions that facilitate and regulate them are also covered. The payment system supporting trade and investment depends on world currency markets. Investment practitioners need to understand how these markets function in detail because of their importance in portfolio management and economic analysis. The second reading provides an overview of currency market fundamentals.

READING ASSIGNMENTS

Reading 20	International Trade and Capital Flows by Usha Nair-Reichert, PhD, and Daniel Robert Witschi, PhD, CFA
Reading 21	Currency Exchange Rates by William A. Barker, CFA, Paul D. McNelis, and Jerry Nickelsburg

READING

20

International Trade and Capital Flows

by Usha Nair-Reichert, PhD, and Daniel Robert Witschi, PhD, CFA

Usha Nair-Reichert, PhD, is at Georgia Institute of Technology (USA). Daniel Robert Witschi, PhD, CFA (Switzerland).

LEARNING OUTCOMES

Mastery	The candidate should be able to:
☐	a. compare gross domestic product and gross national product;
☐	b. describe benefits and costs of international trade;
☐	c. distinguish between comparative advantage and absolute advantage;
☐	d. explain the Ricardian and Heckscher–Ohlin models of trade and the source(s) of comparative advantage in each model;
☐	e. compare types of trade and capital restrictions and their economic implications;
☐	f. explain motivations for and advantages of trading blocs, common markets, and economic unions;
☐	g. describe common objectives of capital restrictions imposed by governments;
☐	h. describe the balance of payments accounts including their components;
☐	i. explain how decisions by consumers, firms, and governments affect the balance of payments;
☐	j. describe functions and objectives of the international organizations that facilitate trade, including the World Bank, the International Monetary Fund, and the World Trade Organization.

INTRODUCTION

1

Global investors must address two fundamentally interrelated questions: where to invest and in what asset classes? Some countries may be attractive from an equity perspective because of their strong economic growth and the profitability of particular domestic sectors or industries. Other countries may be attractive from a fixed income perspective because of their interest rate environment and price stability. To identify markets that are expected to provide attractive investment opportunities, investors must analyze cross-country differences in such factors as expected GDP growth rates, monetary and fiscal policies, trade policies, and competitiveness. From a longer term perspective investors also need to consider such factors as a country's stage of economic and financial market development, demographics, quality and quantity of physical and human capital (accumulated education and training of workers), and its area(s) of comparative advantage.[1]

This reading provides a framework for analyzing a country's trade and capital flows and their economic implications. International trade can facilitate economic growth by increasing the efficiency of resource allocation, providing access to larger capital and product markets, and facilitating specialization based on comparative advantage. The flow of financial capital (funds available for investment) between countries with excess savings and those where financial capital is scarce can increase liquidity, raise output, and lower the cost of capital. From an investment perspective, it is important to understand the complex and dynamic nature of international trade and capital flows because investment opportunities are increasingly exposed to the forces of global competition for markets, capital, and ideas.

This reading is organized as follows. Section 2 defines basic terminology used in the reading and describes patterns and trends in international trade and capital flows. It also discusses the benefits of international trade, distinguishes between absolute and comparative advantage, and explains two traditional models of comparative advantage. Section 3 describes trade restrictions and their implications and discusses the motivation for, and advantages of, trade agreements. Section 4 describes the balance of payments and Section 5 discusses the function and objectives of international organizations that facilitate trade. A summary of key points and practice problems conclude the reading.

2   INTERNATIONAL TRADE

The following sections describe the role, importance, and possible benefits and costs of international trade. Before beginning those discussions, we define some basic terminology used in this area.

2.1 Basic Terminology

The aggregate output of a nation over a specified time period is usually measured as its gross domestic product or its gross national product. Gross domestic product (GDP) measures the market value of all final goods and services produced by factors of production (such as labor and capital) located within a country/economy during a given period of time, generally a year or a quarter. Gross national product (GNP), however, measures the market value of all final goods and services produced by factors of production (such as labor and capital) supplied by residents of a country, regardless of whether such production takes place within the country or outside of the country. The difference between a country's GDP and its GNP is that GDP includes, and GNP excludes, the production of goods and services by foreigners within that country, whereas GNP includes, and GDP excludes, the production of goods and

---

1 Comparative advantage refers to a country's ability to produce a good at a relatively lower cost than other goods it produces, as compared with another country. It will be more precisely defined and illustrated in Section 2.4.

services by its citizens outside of the country. Countries that have large differences between GDP and GNP generally have a large number of citizens who work abroad (for example, Pakistan and Portugal), and/or pay more for the use of foreign-owned capital in domestic production than they earn on the capital they own abroad (for example, Brazil and Canada). Therefore, GDP is more widely used as a measure of economic activity occurring *within* the country, which, in turn, affects employment, growth, and the investment environment.

Imports are goods and services that a domestic economy (i.e., households, firms, and government) purchases from other countries. For example, the US economy imports (purchases) cloth from India and wine from France. **Exports** are goods and services that a domestic economy sells to other countries. For example, South Africa exports (sells) diamonds to the Netherlands, and China exports clothing to the European Union. So how are services imported or exported? If a Greek shipping company transports the wine that the United States imports from France, the United States would classify the cost of shipping as an import of services from Greece and the wine would be classified as an import of goods from France. Similarly, when a British company provides insurance coverage to a South African diamond exporter, Britain would classify the cost of the insurance as an export of services to South Africa. Other examples of services exported/imported include engineering, consulting, and medical services.

The **terms of trade** are defined as the ratio of the price of exports to the price of imports, representing those prices by export and import price indices, respectively. The terms of trade capture the relative cost of imports in terms of exports. If the prices of exports increase relative to the prices of imports, the terms of trade have improved because the country will be able to purchase more imports with the same amount of exports.[2] For example, when oil prices increased during 2007–2008, major oil exporting countries experienced an improvement in their terms of trade because they had to export less oil in order to purchase the same amount of imported goods. In contrast, if the price of exports decreases relative to the price of imports, the terms of trade have deteriorated because the country will be able to purchase fewer imports with the same amount of exports. Because each country exports and imports a large number of goods and services, the terms of trade of a country are usually measured as an index number (normalized to 100 in some base year) that represents a ratio of the average price of exported goods and services to the average price of imported goods and services. Exhibit 1 shows the terms of trade reported in Salvatore (2010). A value over (under) 100 indicates that the country, or group of countries, experienced better (worse) terms of trade relative to the base year of 2000.

Exhibit 1	Data on the Terms of Trade for Industrial and Developing Countries (Unit Export Value/Unit Import Value)				
	1990	**1995**	**2000**	**2005**	**2006**
Industrial countries	99.8	104.8	100	101.3	99
Developing countries	103	101.9	100	99.4	100.5
Africa	100.4	102.8	100	107.9	105.2
Asia	106.8	106.8	100	91.5	89.2

(continued)

---

2 Although the prices of imports and exports are each stated in currency units, the currency units cancel out when we take the ratio, so the terms of trade reflect the relative price of imports and exports in real (i.e., quantity) terms: units of imports per unit of exports. To see this, note that if one unit of imports costs P_M currency units and one unit of exports is priced at P_X currency units, then the country can buy P_X/P_M (= Terms of trade) units of imports for each unit of exports.

Exhibit 1	(Continued)				
	1990	**1995**	**2000**	**2005**	**2006**
Europe	68.7	105.5	100	102.1	99.8
Middle East	109	68.4	100	140.4	155.9
Western hemisphere	129.6	107.1	100	104.3	108.7

Source: Salvatore (2010), case study 3–3. Base year 2000 = 100.

As an example, Exhibit 1 indicates that from 1990 to 2006 both of the broader groups, developing and industrial countries, experienced a slight decline in their terms of trade. Looking at the disaggregated data indicates that developing countries in Asia and the Western hemisphere experienced a considerable decline in terms of trade while those in Europe and the Middle East (which benefited from rising prices of their petroleum exports) experienced a substantial increase. Africa also experienced a small improvement in its terms of trade during this period.

Net exports is the difference between the value of a country's exports and the value of its imports (i.e., value of exports minus imports). If the value of exports equals the value of imports, then trade is balanced. If the value of exports is greater (less) than the value of imports, then there is a **trade surplus (deficit)**. When a country has a trade surplus, it lends to foreigners or buys assets from foreigners reflecting the financing needed by foreigners running trade deficits with that country. Similarly, when a country has a trade deficit, it has to borrow from foreigners or sell some of its assets to foreigners. Section 4 on the balance of payments explains these relationships more fully.

Autarky is a state in which a country does not trade with other countries. This means that all goods and services are produced and consumed domestically. The price of a good or service in such an economy is called its **autarkic price**. An autarkic economy is also known as a **closed economy** because it does not trade with other countries. An **open economy**, in contrast, is an economy that trades with other countries. If there are no restrictions on trade, then members of an open economy can buy and sell goods and services at the price prevailing in the world market, the **world price**. An open economy can provide domestic households with a larger variety of goods and services, give domestic companies access to global markets and customers, and offer goods and services that are more competitively priced. In addition, it can offer domestic investors access to foreign capital markets, foreign assets, and greater investment opportunities. For capital intensive industries, such as automobiles and aircraft, manufacturers can take advantage of economies of scale because they have access to a much larger market. **Free trade** occurs when there are no government restrictions on a country's ability to trade. Under free trade, global aggregate demand and supply determine the equilibrium quantity and price of imports and exports. Government policies that impose restrictions on trade, such as tariffs and quotas (discussed later in the reading), are known as **trade protection** and prevent market forces (demand and supply) from determining the equilibrium price and quantity for imports and exports. According to Deardorff, *globalization* refers to the "increasing worldwide integration of markets for goods, services, and capital that began to attract special attention in the late 1990s."[3] It also references "a variety of other changes that were perceived to occur at about the same time, such as an increased role for large corporations (multinational

---

3 Deardorff, Alan. "Deardorff's Glossary of International Economics" (www-personal.umich.edu/~alandear/ glossary).

corporations) in the world economy and increased intervention into domestic policies and affairs by international institutions," such as the International Monetary Fund, the World Trade Organization, and the World Bank.

The levels of aggregate demand and supply and the quantities of imports and exports in an economy are related to the concepts of *excess demand* and *excess supply*. Exhibit 2 shows supply and demand curves for cars in the United Kingdom. E is the autarkic equilibrium at price P^A and quantity Q^A, with the quantity of cars demanded equaling the quantity supplied. Now, consider a situation in which the country opens up to trade and the world price is P_1. At this price, the quantity demanded domestically is Q^K while the quantity supplied is Q^J. Hence excess demand is $Q^J Q^K$. This quantity is satisfied by imports. For example, at a world price of \$15,000, the quantity of cars demanded in the United Kingdom might be 2 million and UK production of cars only 1.5 million. As a result, the excess demand of 500,000 would be satisfied by imports. Returning to Exhibit 2, now consider a situation in which the world price is P_2. The quantity demanded is Q^C while the quantity supplied is Q^D. Hence, the domestic excess supply at world price P_2 is $Q^C Q^D$, which results in exports of $Q^C Q^D$.

Exhibit 2   Excess Demand, Excess Supply, Imports and Exports

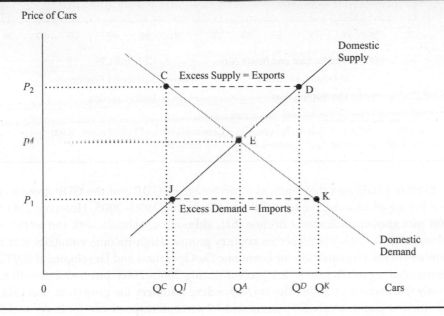

2.2 Patterns and Trends in International Trade and Capital Flows

The importance of trade in absolute and relative terms (trade-to-GDP ratio) is illustrated in Exhibits 3 through 5. Exhibit 3 shows that trade as a percentage of regional GDP increased in all regions of the world during 1970–2006. Developing countries in Asia had the fastest growth in trade, increasing from less than 20 percent of GDP in 1970 to more than 90 percent of GDP in 2006.

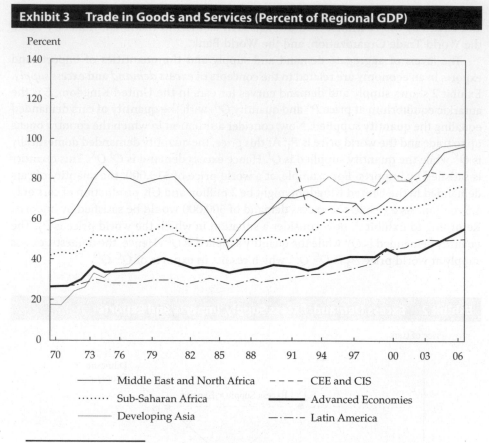

Exhibit 3   Trade in Goods and Services (Percent of Regional GDP)

Middle East and North Africa ——
Sub-Saharan Africa ··········
Developing Asia ——
CEE and CIS – – – –
Advanced Economies ——
Latin America –·–·–

Note: CEE = Central and Eastern Europe; CIS = Commonwealth of Independent States
Source: IMF Issues Brief "Globalization: A Brief Overview," 2008.

Exhibit 4 indicates that trade as a percentage of GDP and the GDP growth rate have increased in most regions of the world during 1990–2006. However, data for 2008 (not shown) indicates a decline that, although consistent with the worldwide economic downturn, varied across country groups. High-income countries that are members of the Organisation for Economic Co-Operation and Development (OECD) experienced a growth rate of 2.4 percent during 2000–2006, but had a growth rate of only 0.3 percent in 2008. The corresponding numbers for growth in non-OECD high-income countries are 5.0 percent and 3.2 percent, respectively; for lower-middle-income countries, they are 7.7 percent and 7.5 percent, respectively. The 2009 World Development Report affirmed the link between trade and growth and noted evidence that all rich and emerging economies are oriented to being open to trade. More specifically, the report indicated:

> …When exports are concentrated in labor-intensive manufacturing, trade increases the wages for unskilled workers, benefiting poor people. It also encourages macroeconomic stability, again benefiting the poor, who are more likely to be hurt by inflation. And through innovation and factor accumulation, it enhances productivity and thus growth. There may be some empirical uncertainty about the strength of trade's relationship with growth. But essentially all rich and emerging economies have a strong trade orientation. (World Bank 2009)

Of course, trade is not the only factor that influences economic growth. Research has also identified such factors as the quality of institutions, infrastructure, and education; economic systems; the degree of development; and global market conditions (World Trade Organization 2008).

Exhibit 4	Trade Openness and GDP Growth					
	Trade as Percent of GDP (averaged over the period)			**Average GDP growth (%)**		
Country Group	**1980–1989**	**1990–1999**	**2000–2006**	**1980–1989**	**1990–1999**	**2000–2006**
World	37.2	41.0	50.7	3.1	2.7	3.2
High income:						
All	38.1	40.3	49.5	3.1	2.6	2.5
OECD	35.3	37.2	44.7	3.1	2.5	2.4
Non-OECD	120.0	128.1	172.5	3.9	4.5	5.0
Low and middle income:						
All	32.4	44.4	56.9	3.4	3.5	5.8
Middle	32.4	44.5	57.1	3.4	3.5	5.8
Upper middle	33.4	44.3	53.5	2.1	1.7	4.1
Lower middle	31.4	44.8	61.4	6.0	6.1	7.7
Low	32.5	39.9	51.7	2.6	2.7	4.8

Note: Averages indicate the average of the annual data for the period covered.
Source: World Bank.

Exhibit 5 presents trade and foreign direct investment as a percentage of GDP for select countries for 1980–2007. **Foreign direct investment** (FDI) refers to direct investment by a firm in one country (the *source country*) in productive assets in a foreign country (the *host country*). When a firm engages in FDI, it becomes a **multinational corporation** (MNC) operating in more than one country or having subsidiary firms in more than one country. It is important to distinguish FDI from **foreign portfolio investment** (FPI), which refers to shorter-term investment by individuals, firms, and institutional investors (e.g., pension funds) in such foreign financial instruments as foreign stocks and foreign government bonds. Exhibit 5 shows that trade as a percentage of GDP for the world as a whole increased from 38 percent in 1980 to 57 percent in 2007. In Argentina, trade as a percentage of GDP increased from 12 percent in 1980 to 45 percent in 2007, while in India during this same period it increased from 15.5 percent to 45 percent. Among the more advanced economies, trade expanded sharply in Germany (from 45 percent to 87 percent), but in the United States trade expanded more modestly (from 21 percent to 29 percent).

Exhibit 5	Increasing Global Interdependence FDI and Trade as a percentage of GDP				
Country	**Type of Flow**	**1980**	**1990**	**2000**	**2007**
World	Trade	38.4	38.0	48.8	57.3
	FDI: Net Inflows	0.6	1.0	5.1	4.3
	FDI: Net Outflows	0.6	1.1	3.6	4.5

(continued)

Exhibit 5   (Continued)

Country	Type of Flow	1980	1990	2000	2007
Argentina	Trade	11.5	15.0	22.4	45.0
	FDI: Net Inflows	−0.1	0.0	0.3	0.6
	FDI: Net Outflows	0.9	1.3	3.7	2.5
Germany	Trade	45.3	49.7	66.4	86.7
	FDI: Net Inflows	0.5	1.4	3.1	4.9
	FDI: Net Outflows	0.0	0.2	11.1	2.3
India	Trade	15.6	15.7	27.4	45.2
	FDI: Net Inflows	0.0	0.0	0.1	1.4
	FDI: Net Outflows	0.0	0.1	0.8	2.0
United States	Trade	20.8	20.5	25.9	28.7
	FDI: Net Inflows	0.7	0.6	1.6	2.9
	FDI: Net Outflows	0.6	0.8	3.2	1.9

Source: World Development Indicators, World Bank.

The increasing importance of multinational corporations is also apparent in Exhibit 5. Net FDI inflows and outflows increased as a percentage of GDP between 1980 and 2000 for each of the countries shown. Trade between multinational firms and their subsidiaries (i.e., intra-firm trade) has become an important part of world trade. For example, 46 percent of US imports occur between related parties (Bernard, Jensen, Redding, and Schott 2010). Globalization of production has increased the productive efficiency of manufacturing firms because they are able to decompose their value chain into individual components or parts, and then outsource their production to different countries where these components can be produced most efficiently.[4] For example, Nintendo's Wii remote is manufactured with components sourced from several countries in the world: the accelerometer is manufactured in the United States; the base memory chip in Italy; the data converter in the United States, Thailand, and India; the plastic casing is assembled in China and designed in Japan; the Bluetooth chip is manufactured in Taiwan and designed in California (US); and the rumble pack is manufactured in various countries in Asia.[5] Foreign direct investment and outsourcing have increased business investment in these countries and provided smaller and less developed countries the opportunity to participate in international trade. For example, the World Investment Report (2002) indicates that in January 2002 Intel had 13 fabrication plants and 11 assembly and testing sites in 7 countries. It was the leading national exporter from Ireland, Philippines, and Costa Rica, and 17th among foreign exporters from China. These trends indicate the increasing global interdependence of economies, although the degree of interdependence varies among regions and countries. Greater interdependence also means that countries are now more exposed to global competition. As a result they must be more flexible in their production structure in order to respond effectively to changes in global demand and supply.

4 Hill (2007, pp. 412) explains the idea of the firm as a value chain: "The operations of the firms can be thought of as a value chain composed of a series of distinct value creation activities including production, marketing and sales, materials management, R&D, human resources, information systems, and firm infrastructure." Production itself can be broken down into distinct components and each component outsourced separately.

5 http://money.cnn.com/magazines/fortune/storysupplement/wiiremote/index.htm.

The complexity of trading relationships has also increased with the development of sophisticated global supply chains that include not only final goods but also intermediate goods and services. Increased global interdependence has changed the risk and return profiles of many countries. Countries that have greater international links are more exposed to, and affected by, economic downturns and crises occurring in other parts of the world. The contagion effect of the Asian financial crisis, which began in Thailand in July 1997, spread to many other markets, such as Indonesia, Malaysia, South Korea, Philippines, Hong Kong, Singapore, and Taiwan. It even affected Brazil and Russia to some degree, although there is less clarity about the mechanisms by which the crisis spread beyond Asia. Among the outward symptoms of the crisis were exchange rate problems, such as currency speculation and large depreciation of currencies, capital flight, and financial and industrial sector bankruptcies. However, recovery was surprisingly swift and all these countries exhibited positive growth by the second quarter of 1999 (Gerber 2010).

2.3 Benefits and Costs of International Trade

The preceding sections have described the growth of world trade and the increasing interdependence of national economies. Has trade been beneficial? The benefits and costs of international trade have been widely debated. The most compelling arguments supporting international trade are: countries gain from exchange and specialization, industries experience greater economies of scale, households and firms have greater product variety, competition is increased, and resources are allocated more efficiently.

Gains from exchange occur when trade enables each country to receive a higher price for its exports (and greater profit) and/or pay a lower price for imported goods instead of producing these goods domestically at a higher cost (i.e., less efficiently). This exchange, in turn, leads to a more efficient allocation of resources by increasing production of the export good and reducing production of the import good in each country (trading partner). This efficiency allows consumption of a larger bundle of goods, thus increasing overall welfare. The fact that trade increases overall welfare does not, of course, mean that every individual consumer and producer is better off. What it does mean is that the winners could, in theory, compensate the losers and still be better off.

Trade also leads to greater efficiency by fostering specialization based on comparative advantage. Traditional trade models, such as the Ricardian model and the Heckscher–Ohlin model, focus on specialization and trade according to comparative advantage arising from differences in technology and factor endowments, respectively. These models will be discussed in the next section.

Newer models of trade focus on the gains from trade that result from economies of scale, greater product variety, and increased competition. In an open economy, increased competition from foreign firms reduces the monopoly power of domestic firms and forces them to become more efficient, as compared to a closed economy. Industries that exhibit increasing returns to scale (for example, the automobile and steel industries) benefit from increased market size as a country starts trading because the average cost of production declines as output increases in these industries. Monopolistically competitive models of trade have been used to explain why there is significant two-way trade (known as *intra-industry trade*) between countries within the same industry. Intra-industry trade occurs when a country exports and imports goods in the same product category or classification.

In a monopolistically competitive industry, there are many firms; each firm produces a unique or differentiated product, there are no exit or entry barriers, and long-run economic profits are zero. In such a model, even though countries may be similar, they gain from trade because each country focuses on the production and export of one or more varieties of the good and imports other varieties of the good. For example, the

European Union exports and imports different types of cars. Consumers gain from having access to a greater variety of final goods. Firms benefit from greater economies of scale because firms both within and outside the EU are able to sell their goods in both markets. Hence, scale economies allow firms to benefit from the larger market size and experience lower average cost of production as a result of trade.

Research suggests that trade liberalization can lead to increased real (that is, inflation-adjusted) GDP although the strength of this relationship is still debated. The positive influence of trade on GDP can arise from more efficient allocation of resources, learning by doing, higher productivity, knowledge spillovers, and trade-induced changes in policies and institutions that affect the incentives for innovation.[6] In industries where there is "learning by doing," such as the semiconductor industry, the cost of production per unit declines as output increases because of expertise and experience acquired in the process of production. Trade can lead to increased exchange of ideas, freer flow of technical expertise, and greater awareness of changing consumer tastes and preferences in global markets. It can also contribute to the development of higher quality and more effective institutions and policies that encourage domestic innovation. For example, Coe and Helpman (1995) show that foreign research and development (R&D) has beneficial effects on domestic productivity. These effects become stronger the more open a country is to foreign trade. They estimate that about a quarter of the benefits of R&D investment in a G–7 country accrues to their trading partners.[7] Hill (2007) discusses the case of Logitech, a Swiss company that manufactures computer mice. In order to win original equipment manufacturer (OEM) contracts from IBM and Apple, Logitech needed to develop innovative designs and provide high-volume production at a low cost. So in the late 1980s they moved to Taiwan, which had a highly qualified labor force, competent parts suppliers, a rapidly expanding local computer industry, and offered Logitech space in a science park at a very competitive rate. Soon thereafter, Logitech was able to secure the Apple contract.

Opponents of free trade point to the potential for greater income inequality and the loss of jobs in developed countries as a result of import competition. As a country moves toward free trade, there will be adjustments in domestic industries that are exporters as well as those that face import competition. Resources (investments) may need to be reallocated into or out of an industry depending on whether that industry is expanding (exporters) or contracting (i.e., facing import competition). As a result of this adjustment process, less-efficient firms may be forced to exit the industry, which may, in turn, lead to higher unemployment and the need for displaced workers to be retrained for jobs in expanding industries. The counter argument is that although there may be short-term and even some medium-term costs, these resources are likely to be more effectively (re-)employed in other industries in the long run. Nonetheless, the adjustment process is virtually certain to impose costs on some groups of stakeholders. For example, the US textile industry has undergone significant changes over the past 30 years as a result of competition from lower-priced imports produced in developing countries, including increased outsourcing of production by US firms. Example 1 discusses recent developments and projections for future employment in the industry.

---

6 "Knowledge spillovers" occur when investments in knowledge creation generate benefits that extend beyond the investing entity and facilitate learning and innovation by other firms or entities.
7 G–7 countries include Canada, France, Germany, Italy, Japan, the United Kingdom, and the United States.

EXAMPLE 1

The US Textile Industry

According to the US Bureau of Labor Statistics (BLS) the textile, textile product, and apparel manufacturing industry is very labor intensive and faces strong import competition. Changing trade regulations have a big impact on employment in this industry. In 2005, members of the World Trade Organization terminated the Multi Fiber Agreement that imposed quotas for apparel and textile products. This agreement included most US trading partners and, in particular, China. The expiration of quotas in 2005 has allowed more apparel and textile products to be imported into the United States. Although some bilateral quotas have been re-imposed between the United States and China, imports have increased substantially. The low-skilled, labor intensive parts of the industry, such as fabric for apparel, have lost many jobs as firms shift their operations to countries with very cheap labor costs. The more skill-intensive jobs, such as design jobs and custom or high-end items that are produced domestically, have not been as adversely affected by trade. Firms in the highly automated and innovative sectors of the industry, such as industrial fabrics, carpets, and specialty yarns, are competitive on a global scale, and it is expected that they will increase their exports as a result of the liberalization of trade in textiles.

The BLS estimates in Exhibit 6 indicate that in 2008 there were 497,100 wage and salary workers in the textile, textile product, and apparel manufacturing industries. California, Georgia, and North Carolina together accounted for about 44 percent of these workers. The BLS also estimates that there will be a 47.9 percent decline in employment in this sector between 2008 and 2018. Increased labor productivity and foreign competition will both continue to contribute to this trend.

Exhibit 6	Employment in Textile, Textile Product, and Apparel Manufacturing by Industry Segment	
2008 and Projected Change 2008–2018 (Employment in Thousands)		
Industry Segment	**2008 Employment**	**2008–2018 Percent Change**
Textile, textile product, and apparel manufacturing	497.1	–47.9
Textile mills	151.1	–47.6
Textile product mills	147.6	–38.1
Apparel manufacturing	198.4	–55.4

Source: BLS National Employment Matrix, 2008–2018.

The segment of the industry that remains in the United States has responded to competitive pressures by adopting new and more advanced technologies and becoming very labor efficient. Advanced technology includes computers and computer-controlled equipment that aid in many functions, such as design, pattern making and cutting, wider looms, and the use of robotics to move material within the plant. All these initiatives are boosting productivity, providing workers with increased training and new skills, and changing the nature of work in the industry. Among the domestic industry's advantages are its proximity to the domestic market and its ability to respond to fashion trends more rapidly than foreign competitors. The domestic industry is also better positioned to participate in retailers' move to just-in-time inventory management systems and electronic data exchange systems.

1 What are the key changes in trade policy that affected the US textile, textile product, and apparel manufacturing industry?

2 How did increased import competition affect the US industry?

Solution to 1:

The Multi Fiber Agreement that imposed quotas for apparel and textile products came to an end in 2005. This affected trade with most US trading partners and, in particular, China. The expiration of quotas in 2005 has allowed more apparel and textile products to be imported into the United States. Although some bilateral quotas have been re-imposed between the United States and China, imports have increased substantially.

Solution to 2:

One of the main impacts was that many low-skilled workers lost their jobs as firms moved production out of the United States to lower-wage countries. The effect on more skill-intensive jobs, such as those involved with design and domestically produced custom and high-end items, has been less severe. The highly automated and innovative sectors of the industry, such as industrial fabrics, carpets, and specialty yarns, are competitive on a global scale. The industry has responded to competitive pressures by adopting new and advanced technologies and becoming very labor efficient.

EXAMPLE 2

Benefits of Trade

Consider two countries that each produce two goods. Suppose the cost of producing cotton relative to lumber is lower in Cottonland than in Lumberland.

1 How would trade between the two countries affect the lumber industry in Lumberland?

2 How would trade between the two countries affect the lumber industry in Cottonland?

3 What would happen to the lumber industry workers in Cottonland in the long run?

4 What is the meaning of the expression "gains from trade"?

5 What are some of the benefits from trade?

Solution to 1:

The lumber industry in Lumberland would benefit from trade. Because the cost of producing lumber relative to producing cotton is lower in Lumberland than in Cottonland (i.e., lumber is relatively cheap in Lumberland), Lumberland will export lumber and the industry will expand.

Solution to 2:

The lumber industry in Cottonland would not benefit from trade, at least in the short run. Because lumber is relatively expensive to produce in Cottonland, the domestic lumber industry will shrink as lumber is imported from Lumberland.

Solution to 3:

The overall welfare effect in both countries is positive. However, in the short run, many lumber producers in Cottonland (and cotton producers in Lumberland) are likely to find themselves without jobs as the lumber industry in Cottonland and the cotton industry in Lumberland contract. Those with skills that are also needed in the other industry may find jobs fairly quickly. Others are likely to do so after some re-training. In the long run, displaced workers should be able to find jobs in the expanding export industry. However, those who remain in the import-competing industry may be permanently worse off because their industry-specific skills are now less valuable. Thus, even in the long run, trade does not necessarily make every stakeholder better off. But the winners could compensate the losers and still be better off, so the overall welfare effect of opening trade is positive.

Solution to 4:

Gains from trade imply that the overall benefits of trade outweigh the losses from trade. It does not mean that all stakeholders (producers, consumers, government) benefit (or benefit equally) from trade.

Solution to 5:

Some of the benefits from trade include: gains from exchange and specialization based on relative cost advantage; gains from economies of scale as the companies add new markets for their products; greater variety of products available to households and firms; greater efficiency from increased competition; and more efficient allocation of resources.

2.4 Comparative Advantage and the Gains from Trade

Up to this point, we have not been precise about what it means for a country to have a comparative advantage in the production of specific goods and services. In this section, we define comparative advantage, distinguish it from the notion of absolute advantage, and demonstrate the gains from trading in accordance with comparative advantage. We then explain two traditional models of trade—the Ricardian and Heckscher–Ohlin models—and the source of comparative advantage in each model.

2.4.1 *Gains from Trade: Absolute and Comparative Advantage*

A country has an **absolute advantage** in producing a good (or service) if it is able to produce that good at a lower cost or use fewer resources in its production than its trading partner. For example, suppose a worker in Brazil can produce either 20 pens or 40 pencils in a day. A worker in China can produce either 10 pens or 60 pencils. A Chinese worker produces 60 pencils a day while a Brazilian worker produces only 40 pencils a day. Hence, China produces pencils at a lower cost than Brazil, and has an absolute advantage in the production of pencils. Similarly, Brazil produces pens at a lower cost than China, and hence has an absolute advantage in the production of pens. A country has a **comparative advantage** in producing a good if its opportunity cost of producing that good is less than that of its trading partner. In our example, the opportunity cost of producing an extra pen in China is 6 pencils. It is the opportunity foregone; namely, the number of pencils China would have to give up to produce an extra pen. If Brazil does not trade and has to produce both pens and pencils, it will have to give up 2 pencils in order to produce a pen. Similarly, in China each pen will cost 6 pencils. Hence, the opportunity cost of a pen in Brazil is 2 pencils, whereas in China it is 6 pencils. Brazil has the lower opportunity cost and thus a comparative advantage in the production of pens. China has a lower opportunity cost (1 pencil costs ⅙th of a pen) than Brazil (1 pencil costs ½ a pen) in the production of pencils and thus has a comparative advantage in the production of pencils. Example 3 further illustrates these concepts.

EXAMPLE 3

Absolute and Comparative Advantages

Suppose there are only two countries, India and the United Kingdom. India exports cloth to the United Kingdom and imports machinery. The output per worker per day in each country is shown in Exhibit 7:

Exhibit 7	Output per Worker per Day	
	Machinery	**Cloth (yards)**
United Kingdom	4	8
India	2	16

Based only on the information given, address the following:

1 Which country has an absolute advantage in the production of:

   A machinery?

   B cloth?

2 Do the countries identified in Question 1 as having an absolute advantage in the production of A) machinery and B) cloth, also have a comparative advantage in those areas?

Solution to 1A:

The United Kingdom has an absolute advantage in the production of machinery because it produces more machinery per worker per day than India.

Solution to 1B:

India has an absolute advantage in the production of cloth because it produces more cloth per worker per day than the United Kingdom.

Solution to 2A and 2B:

In both cases, the answer is "yes." In the case of machinery, the opportunity cost of a machine in the United Kingdom is 2 yards of cloth (8 ÷ 4 or 1 machine = 2 yards cloth). This amount is the autarkic price of machines in terms of cloth in the United Kingdom. In India, the opportunity cost of a machine is 8 yards of cloth (16 ÷ 2 or 1 machine = 8 yards cloth). Thus, the United Kingdom has a comparative advantage in producing machines. In contrast, the opportunity cost of a yard of cloth in the United Kingdom and in India is ½ and ⅛ of a machine, respectively. India has a lower opportunity cost (⅛ of a machine) and, therefore, a comparative advantage in the production of cloth.

It is important to note that even if a country does not have an absolute advantage in producing any of the goods, it can still gain from trade by exporting the goods in which it has a comparative advantage. In Example 3, if India could produce only 6 yards of cloth per day instead of 16 yards of cloth, the United Kingdom would have an *absolute* advantage in both machines and cloth. However, India would still have a *comparative* advantage in the production of cloth because the opportunity cost of a yard of cloth in India, ⅓ of a machine in this case, would still be less than the opportunity cost of a yard of cloth in the United Kingdom (½ of a machine as before).

Let us now illustrate the gains from trading according to comparative advantage. In Example 3, if the United Kingdom could sell a machine for more than 2 yards of cloth and if India could purchase a machine for less than 8 yards of cloth, both countries would gain from trade. Although it is not possible to determine the exact world price without additional details regarding demand and supply conditions, both countries would gain from trade as long as the world price for machinery in terms of cloth is between the autarkic prices of the trading partners. In our example, this price corresponds to a price of between 2 and 8 yards of cloth for a machine. *The further away the world price of a good or service is from its autarkic price in a given country, the more that country gains from trade.* For example, if the United Kingdom was able to sell a machine to India for 7 yards of cloth (i.e., closer to India's autarkic price), it would gain 5 yards of cloth per machine sold to India compared with its own autarkic price (with no trade) of 1 machine for 2 yards of cloth. However, if the United Kingdom was able to sell a machine to India for only 3 yards of cloth (closer to the UK autarkic price), it would gain only 1 yard of cloth per machine sold to India compared with its own autarkic price.

Exhibits 8 and 9 provide the production and consumption schedules of both countries at autarky and after trade has commenced. In autarky (Exhibit 8), the United Kingdom produces and consumes 200 machines and 400 yards of cloth (without trade, consumption of each product must equal domestic production). Similarly, India produces 100 machines and 800 yards of cloth in autarky. In a world economy consisting of only these two countries, total output for each commodity is the sum of production in both countries. Therefore, total world output is 300 machines and 1,200 yards of cloth.

Exhibit 8   Production and Consumption in Autarky

	Autarkic Production	Autarkic Consumption
United Kingdom		
Machinery (m)	200	200
Cloth (yards) (c)	400	400
India		
Machinery	100	100
Cloth (yards)	800	800
Total World:		
Machinery	300	300
Cloth (yards)	1200	1200

Now, assume that the United Kingdom and India start trading and that the world price of 1 machine is 4 yards of cloth (1m = 4c). This price is within the range of acceptable world trading prices discussed earlier because this price lies between the autarkic prices of the United Kingdom (1m = 2c) and India (1m = 8c). Exhibit 9 shows that in an open economy, the United Kingdom would specialize in machines and India would specialize in cloth. As a result, the United Kingdom produces 400 machines and no cloth, while India produces 1,600 yards of cloth and no machines. The United Kingdom exports 160 machines to India in exchange for 640 yards of cloth. After trade begins with India, the United Kingdom consumes 240 machines and 640 yards of cloth. Consumption in the United Kingdom increases by 40 machines and 240 yards of cloth. Similarly, India consumes 160 machines and 960 yards of cloth, an increase of 60 machines and 160 yards of cloth. World production and consumption is now 400 machines and 1,600 yards of cloth. Post-trade production and consumption exceeds the autarkic situation by 100 machines and 400 yards of cloth.

Exhibit 9	Gains from Trade		
	Post-trade Production	Post-trade Consumption	Change in Consumption (compared with autarky)
UK			
Machinery	400	240	+40
Cloth (yards)	0	640	+240
India			
Machinery	0	160	+60
Cloth (yards)	1600	960	+160
Total World:			
Machinery	400	400	+100
Cloth (yards)	1600	1600	+400

Exhibit 10 shows a more general case of gains from trade under increasing costs. In Panel A, the curve connecting the X and Y axes is the UK production possibilities frontier (PPF).[8] That is, it represents the combinations of cloth and machinery that the United Kingdom can produce given its technology and resources (capital and labor). The slope of the PPF at any point is the opportunity cost of one good in terms of the other. The shape of the PPF indicates increasing opportunity cost in terms of machines as more cloth is produced and vice versa. To maximize the value of output, production occurs where the slope of the PPF equals the relative price of the goods. P_A represents the autarkic price line, which is tangent to the PPF at A, the autarkic equilibrium. The slope of the autarkic price line represents the opportunity cost before trade. In autarky, the United Kingdom produces and consumes 60 machines and 60 thousand yards cloth, and is on indifference curve I.[9] When the United Kingdom starts trading with India, it faces the world price line P^*. This new price line is tangent to the PPF at B. The change in relative prices of the goods encourages the United Kingdom to increase the production of the good in which it has comparative advantage (machines) and produce at B instead of A. We note that at B the United Kingdom has increased the production of machines to 120 units and reduced the production of cloth to 30 thousand yards. We also note that trade has expanded the UK consumption possibilities. The United Kingdom consumes at point E after trade, exports 80 machines to India and imports 80 thousand yards of cloth from India. Note that E is outside the PPF, but on the world price line that is tangent to the PPF at B.

---

8 Modified from Salvatore (2010).
9 An indifference curve represents the various combinations of goods (machines and cloth) that provide the same level of utility or welfare. Higher indifference curves represent higher levels of utility or welfare.

This line is also the trading possibilities line because trade occurs along this line. The slope of this line is the opportunity cost of a machine in terms of cloth in the world market. The United Kingdom has clearly increased its welfare through trade because it is able to consume at point E, which is on a higher indifference curve (III) and thus represents a higher level of welfare compared with the autarkic consumption point A on indifference curve I.

Panel B shows the corresponding situation for India. When trade opens with the United Kingdom, India shifts production from A' to B', producing more cloth, the good in which it has a comparative advantage, and fewer machines. It now exports 80 thousand yards of cloth to the United Kingdom and imports 80 machines from the United Kingdom. India now consumes at E' which is on the world price line and also on a higher indifference curve, III', than the autarkic consumption point (A') on indifference curve I'. Thus, by specializing (incompletely, as is typically the case with increasing production costs) in the good in which it has a comparative advantage, each country increases its welfare. We should also note that P^* is the price at which trade is balanced. At this relative world price, the export of cloth from India equals the import of cloth into the United Kingdom (80 thousand yards) and the export of machines from the United Kingdom equals the imports of machines into India (80 machines).

| **Exhibit 10** | **Graphical Depiction of Gains from Trade with Increasing Costs** |

Panel A. United Kingdom

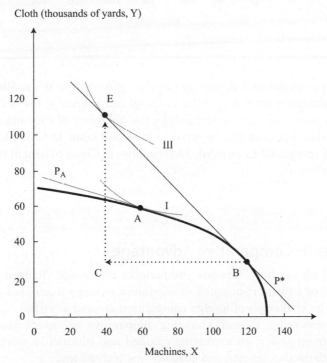

(continued)

Exhibit 10   (Continued)

Panel B. India

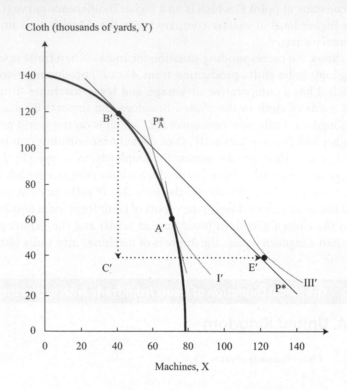

Cloth (thousands of yards, Y)

A country's comparative advantage can change over time as a result of structural shifts in its domestic economy, shifts in the global economy, the accumulation of physical or human capital, new technology, the discovery of such natural resources as oil, and so on. For example, an increase in skilled labor in China has led several multinational companies to establish R&D facilities in China to benefit from its highly educated workforce.

EXAMPLE 4

Changes in Comparative Advantage

Exhibit 11 shows how Taiwan's comparative advantage changed over time as a result of an export-oriented development strategy it adopted during the 1960s.[10] The challenges of foreign competition created a "virtuous circle" that was self-reinforcing. Taiwan's changing comparative advantage was the result of government policy, an increasingly skilled and productive workforce, and proactive firms that learned and adapted new technology.

---

10 Prior to the 1960s, Taiwan had an import-substitution policy—that is, a development policy aimed at replacing imports with domestic production that was supported by US aid. However, US aid ended in the 1960s, forcing Taiwan toward export promotion policies.

Exhibit 11	Changes in Structure of Taiwan's Merchandise Exports, 1963–2003 (Percentage Shares)				
Products	1963	1973	1983	1993	2003
Agricultural products	59.3	15.4	8.0	5.1	2.5
Mining products	2.7	0.9	2.4	1.7	3.5
Manufactures	38	83.3	89.1	93	93.7
Iron and steel	3.0	1.3	2.5	1.6	3.9
Chemicals	5.1	1.5	2.4	5.1	8.1
Other semi-manufactures	11.7	12.1	11.6	9.6	6.8
Machinery and transport equipment	1.5	23.5	26.2	44.4	55.7
Office and telecom equipment	0.3	16.3	13.9	23.8	35.8
Electrical machinery and apparatus	0.3	2.7	3.6	6.5	8.1
Textiles	11.7	12.8	7.2	9.6	6.2
Clothing	3.0	16.1	11.9	4.4	1.4
Other consumer goods	1.8	16.3	27.4	18.4	11.6

Source: World Trade Report (2008).

1 How has Taiwan's structure of exports changed over time?
2 How did increased foreign competition impact the economy?
3 What were the factors that helped to change Taiwan's comparative advantage?

Solution to 1:

The economy moved from exporting agricultural products and textiles during the 1960s to exporting clothes and other consumer goods during the 1970s and 1980s to exporting office and telecommunications equipment in the 1990s. In 1960, agriculture and manufacturing accounted for 59.3 percent and 38 percent of Taiwan's exports, respectively. By 2003, the corresponding figures were 2.5 percent and 93.7 percent. The share of machinery and transport equipment (a subcategory of manufacturing) had increased from 1.5 percent in 1960 to 55.7 percent in 2003.

Solution to 2:

The challenges of foreign competition created a "virtuous circle" that was self-reinforcing. Success in export markets increased the confidence of Taiwanese firms and led to greater success in exports through increased productivity, higher-quality products, acquisition of new skills, and adoption of technologies.

Solution to 3:

The factors that helped change Taiwan's comparative advantage included government policy, an increasingly skilled and productive workforce, and proactive firms that learned and adapted new technology.

From an investment perspective, it is critical for analysts to be able to examine a country's comparative and absolute advantages and to analyze changes in them. It is also important to understand changes in government policy and regulations, demographics, human capital, demand conditions, and other factors that may influence comparative advantage and production and trade patterns. This information can then be used to identify sectors, industries within those sectors, and companies within those industries that will benefit.

2.4.2 *Ricardian and Heckscher–Ohlin Models of Comparative Advantage*

A discussion of absolute and comparative advantage and the gains from specialization would be incomplete without a discussion of two important theories of trade, the Ricardian Model and the Heckscher–Ohlin Model. These models are based on cross-country differences in technology and in factor endowments, respectively. These theoretical models are based on several assumptions, some of which may not be fully satisfied in the real world; nonetheless they provide extremely useful insights into the determinants and patterns of trade.

Adam Smith argued that a country could gain from trade if it had an absolute advantage in the production of a good. David Ricardo extended Smith's idea of the gains from trade by arguing that even if a country did not have an absolute advantage in the production of any good, it could still gain from trade if it had a comparative advantage in the production of a good. In the Ricardian model, labor is the only (variable) factor of production. Differences in labor productivity, reflecting underlying differences in technology, are the source of comparative advantage and hence the key driver of trade in this model. A country with a lower opportunity cost in the production of a good has a comparative advantage in that good and will specialize in its production. In our two-country model, if countries vary in size, the smaller country may specialize completely, but may not be able to meet the total demand for the product. Hence, the larger country may be incompletely specialized, producing and exporting the good in which it has a comparative advantage but still producing (and consuming) some of the good in which it has a comparative disadvantage. It is important to recognize that although differences in technology may be a major source of comparative advantage at a given point in time, other countries can close the technology gap or even gain a technological advantage. The shift of information technology services from developed countries to India is an example of comparative advantage shifting over time.[11] This shift was facilitated by India's growing pool of highly skilled and relatively low-wage labor, the development and growth of its telecommunication infrastructure, and government policies that liberalized trade in the 1990s.

In the Heckscher–Ohlin Model (also known as the factor-proportions theory), both capital and labor are variable factors of production. That is, each good can be produced with varying combinations of labor and capital. According to this model, differences in the relative endowment of these factors are the source of a country's comparative advantage. This model assumes that technology in each industry is the same among countries, but it varies between industries. According to the theory, a country has a comparative advantage in goods whose production is intensive in the factor with which it is relatively abundantly endowed, and would tend to specialize in and export that good. Capital is relatively more (less) abundant in a country if the ratio of its endowment of capital to labor is greater (less) than that of its trading partner.[12] This scenario means a country in which labor is relatively abundant would export relatively labor-intensive goods and import relatively capital-intensive goods. For example, because the manufacture of textiles and clothing is relatively labor intensive, they are exported by such countries as China and India where labor is relatively abundant.

---

11 According to NASSCOM (India's prominent IT-BPO trade association), Indian firms offer a wide range of information technology services that include consulting, systems integration, IT outsourcing/managed services/hosting services, training, and support/maintenance. See www.nasscom.in.

12 Alternatively, factor abundance can be defined in terms of the relative factor prices that prevail in autarky. Under this definition, labor is more (less) abundant in a country if the cost of labor relative to the cost of capital is lower (higher) in that country.

Relative factor intensities in production can be illustrated with the following example. In 2002, capital per worker in the Canadian paper industry was C$118,777, whereas in the clothing manufacturing sector it was C$8,954.[13] These amounts indicate that manufacturing paper is more capital intensive than clothing production. Canada trades with Thailand and, being relatively capital abundant compared with Thailand, it exports relatively capital intensive paper to Thailand and imports relatively labor intensive clothing from Thailand.

Because the Heckscher–Ohlin model has two factors of production, labor and capital, (unlike the Ricardian model that has only labor), it allows for the possibility of income redistribution through trade. The demand for an input is referred to as a *derived demand* because it is derived from the demand for the product it is used to produce. As a country opens up to trade, it has a favorable impact on the abundant factor, and a negative impact on the scarce factor. This result is because trade causes output prices to change; more specifically, the price of the export good increases and the price of the import good declines. These price changes affect the demand for factors used to produce the import and export goods, and hence affect the incomes received by each factor of production.

To illustrate this point, consider again the opening of trade between the United Kingdom and India in Exhibit 10. When trade opened, the United Kingdom expanded production of machines—which are assumed to be the capital-intensive industry—and reduced production of clothing. India did the opposite. Machines became more expensive relative to clothing in the United Kingdom (line P^* is steeper than line P^A). The relative price change, along with the shift in output it induces, leads to a redistribution of income from labor to capital in the United Kingdom. The opposite occurs in India—machines become cheaper relative to clothing (line P^* is flatter than $P^{A'}$), production shifts toward clothing, and income is redistributed from capital to labor.

Note that in each country, the relatively cheap good and the relatively cheap factor of production both get more expensive when trade is opened. That raises an interesting question: If free trade equalizes the prices of goods among countries, does it also equalize the prices of the factors of production? In the simple Heckscher–Ohlin world of homogeneous products, homogeneous inputs, and identical technologies among countries, the answer is yes: The absolute and relative factor prices are equalized in both countries if there is free trade. In the real world, we see that factor prices do not converge completely even if there is free trade because several assumptions of the models are not fully satisfied in the real world. Nonetheless, it is important to note that *with international trade factor prices display a tendency to move closer together in the long run.*

Changes in factor endowments can cause changes in the patterns of trade and can create profitable investment opportunities. For example, in 1967 Japan had a comparative advantage in unskilled-labor-intensive goods, such as textiles, apparel, and leather. Meier (1998) notes that by 1980, Japan had greatly increased its skilled labor and consequently had a comparative advantage in skill-intensive products, especially non-electrical machinery.

It is important to note that technological differences, as emphasized in the Ricardian trade model, and differences in factor abundance, as emphasized in the Heckscher–Ohlin model, are both important drivers of trade. They are complementary, not mutually exclusive. Tastes and preferences can also vary among countries and can change over time, leading to changes in trade patterns and trade flows.

---

13 Appleyard, Field, and Cobb (2010), p. 131.

3   TRADE AND CAPITAL FLOWS: RESTRICTIONS AND AGREEMENTS

Trade restrictions (or trade protection) are government policies that limit the ability of domestic households and firms to trade freely with other countries. Examples of trade restrictions include tariffs, import quotas, voluntary export restraints (VER), subsidies, embargoes, and domestic content requirements. **Tariffs** are taxes that a government levies on imported goods. **Quotas** restrict the quantity of a good that can be imported into a country, generally for a specified period of time. A voluntary export restraint is similar to a quota but is imposed by the exporting country. An **export subsidy** is paid by the government to the firm when it exports a unit of a good that is being subsidized. The goal here is to promote exports, but it reduces welfare by encouraging production and trade that is inconsistent with comparative advantage. **Domestic content provisions** stipulate that some percentage of the value added or components used in production should be of domestic origin. Trade restrictions are imposed by countries for several reasons including protecting established domestic industries from foreign competition, protecting new industries from foreign competition until they mature (infant industry argument), protecting and increasing domestic employment, protecting strategic industries for national security reasons, generating revenues from tariffs (especially for developing countries), and retaliation against trade restrictions imposed by other countries.

    Capital restrictions are defined as controls placed on foreigners' ability to own domestic assets and/or domestic residents' ability to own foreign assets. Thus, in contrast with trade restrictions, which limit the openness of goods markets, capital restrictions limit the openness of financial markets. Sections 3.1 through 3.4 discuss trade restrictions. Section 3.5 briefly addresses capital restrictions.

3.1   Tariffs

Tariffs are taxes that a government levies on imported goods.[14] The primary objective of tariffs is to protect domestic industries that produce the same or similar goods. They may also aim to reduce a trade deficit. Tariffs reduce the demand for imported goods by increasing their price above the free trade price. The economic impact of a tariff on imports in a small country is illustrated in Exhibit 12. In this context, a small country is not necessarily small in size, population, or GDP. Instead, a **small country** is one that is a price taker in the world market for a product and cannot influence the world market price. For example, by many measures Brazil is a large country, but it is a price taker in the world market for cars. A large country, however, is a large importer of the product and can exercise some influence on price in the world market. When a large country imposes a tariff, the exporter reduces the price of the good to retain some of the market share it could lose if it did not lower its price. This reduction in price alters the terms of trade and represents a redistribution of income from the exporting country to the importing country. So, in theory it is possible for a large country to increase its welfare by imposing a tariff if 1) its trading partner does not retaliate and 2) the deadweight loss as a result of the tariff (see below) is smaller than the benefit of improving its terms of trade. However, there would still be a net reduction in global welfare—the large country cannot gain by imposing a tariff unless it imposes an even larger loss on its trading partner.

---

14 Governments may also impose taxes on exports, although they are less common.

In Exhibit 12, the world price (free trade price) is P^*. Under free trade, domestic supply is Q^1, domestic consumption is Q^4, and imports are Q^1Q^4. After the imposition of a per-unit tariff t, the domestic price increases to P_t, which is the sum of the world price and the per-unit tariff t. At the new domestic price, domestic production increases to Q^2 and domestic consumption declines to Q^3, resulting in a reduction in imports to Q^2Q^3.

The welfare effects can be summarized as follows:

- Consumers suffer a loss of consumer surplus because of the increase in price.[15] This effect is represented by areas A + B + C + D in Exhibit 12.

- Local producers gain producer surplus from a higher price for their output. This effect is represented by area A.

- The government gains tariff revenue on imports Q^2Q^3. This effect is represented by area C.

The net welfare effect is the sum of these three effects. The loss in consumer surplus is greater than the sum of the gain in producer surplus and government revenue and results in a deadweight loss to the country's welfare of B + D.

Welfare Effects of an Import Tariff or Quota

	Importing Country
Consumer surplus	$-(A + B + C + D)$
Producer surplus	$+A$
Tariff revenue or Quota rents	$+C$
National welfare	$-B - D$

Tariffs create deadweight loss because they give rise to inefficiencies on both the consumption and production side. D represents inefficiencies in production. Instead of being able to import goods at the world price P^*, tariffs encourage inefficient producers whose cost of production is greater than P^* to enter (or remain in) the market, leading to an inefficient allocation of resources. On the consumption side, tariffs prevent mutually beneficial exchanges from occurring because consumers who were willing to pay more than P^* but less than P_t are now unable to consume the good.

---

15 Consumer surplus, producer surplus, and deadweight loss are defined and discussed in the Level I curriculum reading "Demand and Supply Analysis: Introduction."

Exhibit 12   Welfare Effects of Tariff and Import Quota

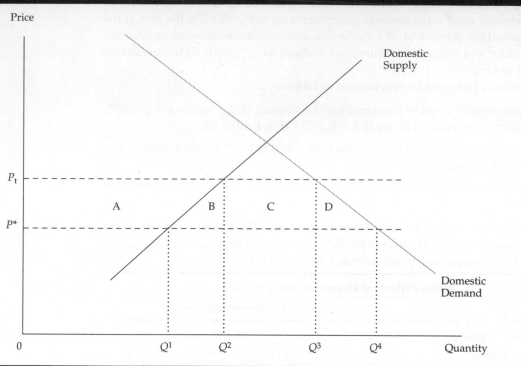

EXAMPLE 5

Analysis of a Tariff

South Africa manufactures 110,000 tons of paper. However, domestic demand for paper is 200,000 tons. The world price for paper is $5 per ton. South Africa will import 90,000 tons of paper from the world market at free trade prices. If the South African government (a small country) decides to impose a tariff of 20 percent on paper imports, the price of imported paper will increase to $6. Domestic production after the imposition of the tariff increases to 130,000 tons, while the quantity demanded declines to 170,000 tons.

1 Calculate the loss in consumer surplus arising from the imposition of the tariff.

2 Calculate the gain in producer surplus arising from the imposition of the tariff.

3 Calculate the gain in government revenue arising from the imposition of the tariff.

4 Calculate the deadweight loss arising from the imposition of the tariff.

Solution to 1:

The loss in consumer surplus = $1 × 170,000 + 1/2 × $1 × 30,000 = $185,000. This calculation is represented by areas A + B + C + D in Exhibit 12.

Solution to 2:

Gain in producer surplus = $1 × 110,000 + 1/2 × ($1 × 20,000) = $120,000; Area A in Exhibit 12.

> **Solution to 3:**
>
> Change in government revenue = $1 \times 40{,}000 = \$40{,}000$; Area C in Exhibit 12.
>
> **Solution to 4:**
>
> Deadweight loss because of the tariff = $1/2 \times \$1 \times 20{,}000 + 1/2 \times \$1 \times 30{,}000 = \$25{,}000$; Areas B + D in Exhibit 12.

3.2 Quotas

A **quota** restricts the quantity of a good that can be imported into a country, generally for a specified period of time. An **import license** specifies the quantity that can be imported. For example, the European Union operates a system of annual import quotas for steel producers who are not members of the World Trade Organization. The 2010 quota was 0.2 million tons a year for Kazakhstan. In the case of Russia, the 2010 quota of 3.2 million tons per year was a part of an EU–Russia agreement.[16] A key difference between tariffs and quotas is that the government is able to collect the revenue generated from a tariff. This effect is uncertain under a quota. With quotas, foreign producers can often raise the price of their goods and earn greater profits than they would without the quota. These profits are called **quota rents**. In Exhibit 12, if the quota is Q^2Q^3, the equivalent tariff that will restrict imports to Q^2Q^3 is t and the domestic price after the quota is P_t. This is the same as the domestic price after the tariff t was imposed. Area C, however, is now the quota rent or profits that are likely to be captured by the foreign producer rather than tariff revenue that is captured by the domestic government. If the foreign producer or foreign government captures the quota rent, C, then the welfare loss to the importing country, represented by areas B + D + C in Exhibit 12, under a quota is greater than under the equivalent tariff. If the government of the country that imposes the quota can capture the quota rents by auctioning the import licenses for a fee, then the welfare loss under the quota is similar to that of a tariff, represented by areas B + D.

A **voluntary export restraint** (VER) is a trade barrier under which the exporting country agrees to limit its exports of the good to its trading partners to a specific number of units. The main difference between an import quota and a VER is that the former is imposed by the importer, whereas the latter is imposed by the exporter. The VER allows the quota rent resulting from the decrease in trade to be captured by the exporter (or exporting country), whereas in the case of an import quota there is ambiguity regarding who captures the quota rents. Hence, a VER results in welfare loss in the importing country. For example, in 1981 the Japanese government imposed VERs on automobile exports to the United States.

3.3 Export Subsidies

An export subsidy is a payment by the government to a firm for each unit of a good that is exported. Its goal is to stimulate exports. But it interferes with the functioning of the free market and may distort trade away from comparative advantage. Hence, it reduces welfare. *Countervailing duties* are duties that are levied by the importing country against subsidized exports entering the country. As an example, agricultural subsidies in developed countries, notably the EU, have been a contentious issue in trade negotiations with less-developed countries and developed countries that are agricultural exporters, such as New Zealand and Australia.

---

16 For more information, see http://ec.europa.eu/trade/creating-opportunities/economic-sectors/industrial-goods/steel/.

In the case of an export subsidy, the exporter has the incentive to shift sales from the domestic to the export market because it receives the international price plus the per-unit subsidy for each unit of the good exported. This scenario raises the price in the domestic market by the amount of the subsidy in the small country case (price before subsidy plus subsidy). In the large country case, the world price declines as the large country increases exports. The net welfare effect is negative in both the large and small country cases, with a larger decline in the large country case. This result is because in the large country case, the decline in world prices implies that a part of the subsidy is transferred to the foreign country, unlike in the small country case.

Exhibit 13 summarizes some of these effects.

Exhibit 13

Panel A. Effects of Alternative Trade Policies

	Tariff	Import Quota	Export Subsidy	VER
Impact on	Importing country	Importing country	Exporting country	Importing country
Producer surplus	Increases	Increases	Increases	Increases
Consumer surplus	Decreases	Decreases	Decreases	Decreases
Government revenue	Increases	Mixed (depends on whether the quota rents are captured by the importing country through sale of licenses or by the exporters)	Falls (government spending rises)	No change (rent to foreigners)
National welfare	Decreases in small country. Could increase in large country	Decreases in small country. Could increase in large country	Decreases	Decreases

Panel B. Effects of Alternative Trade Policies on Price, Production, Consumption, and Trade

	Tariff	Import Quota	Export Subsidy	VER
Impact on	Importing country	Importing country	Exporting country	Importing country
Price	Increases	Increases	Increases	Increases
Domestic consumption	Decreases	Decreases	Decreases	Decreases
Domestic production	Increases	Increases	Increases	Increases
Trade	Imports decrease	Imports decrease	Exports increase	Imports decrease

EXAMPLE 6

Tariffs, Quotas, and VERs

Thailand, a small country, has to decide whether to impose a tariff or a quota on the import of computers. You are considering investing in a local firm that is a major importer of computers.

1   What will be the impact of a tariff on prices, quantity produced, and quantity imported in Thailand (the importing country)?

2   If Thailand imposes a tariff, what will the impact be on prices in the exporting country?

3 How would a tariff affect consumer surplus, producer surplus, and government revenue in Thailand?

4 Explain whether the net welfare effect of a tariff is the same as that of a quota.

5 Which policy, a tariff or a quota, would be most beneficial to the local importer in which you may invest and why?

6 If Thailand were to negotiate a VER with the countries from which it imports computers, would this be better or worse than an import quota for the local importing firm in which you may invest? Why?

Solution to 1:

A tariff imposed by a small country, such as Thailand, raises the price of computers in the importing country, reduces the quantity imported, and increases domestic production.

Solution to 2:

A tariff imposed by a small country would not change the price of computers in the exporting country.

Solution to 3:

When a small country imposes a tariff, it reduces consumer surplus, increases producer surplus, and increases government revenue in that country.

Solution to 4:

The quota can lead to a greater welfare loss than a tariff if the quota rents are captured by the foreign government or foreign firms.

Solution to 5:

A tariff will hurt importers because it will reduce their share of the computer market in Thailand. The impact of a quota depends on whether the importers can capture a share of the quota rents. Assuming importers can capture at least part of the rents, they will be better off with a quota.

Solution to 6:

The VER would not be better for the local importer than the import quota and would most likely be worse. Under the VER, all of the quota rents will be captured by the exporting countries whereas with an import quota at least part of the quota rents may be captured by local importers.

It is important to understand existing trade policies and the potential for policy changes that may impact return on investment. Changes in the government's trade policy can affect the pattern and value of trade and may result in changes in industry structure. These changes may have important implications for firm profitability and growth because they can affect the goods a firm can import/export, change demand for its products, impact its pricing policies, and create delays through increased paperwork, procurement of licenses, approvals, and so on. For example, changes in import policies that affect the ability of a firm to import vital inputs for production may increase the cost of production and reduce firm profitability.

3.4 Trading Blocs, Common Markets, and Economic Unions

There has been a proliferation of trading blocs or regional trading agreements (RTA) in recent years. Important examples of regional integration include the North American Free Trade Agreement (NAFTA) and the European Union (EU). A regional trading bloc is a group of countries that have signed an agreement to reduce and progressively eliminate barriers to trade and movement of factors of production among the members of the bloc. It may or may not have common trade barriers against countries that are not members of the bloc.

There are many different types of regional trading blocs, depending on the level of integration that takes place. **Free trade areas** (FTA) are one of the most prevalent forms of regional integration in which all barriers to the flow of goods and services among members have been eliminated. However, each country maintains its own polices against non-members. The North American Free Trade Agreement (NAFTA) among the United States, Canada, and Mexico is an example of a FTA. A **customs union** extends the FTA by not only allowing free movement of goods and services among members but also creating a common trade policy against non-members. In 1947, Belgium, the Netherlands, and Luxemburg ("Benelux") formed a customs union that became a part of the European Community in 1958. The **common market** is the next level of economic integration that incorporates all aspects of the customs union and extends it by allowing free movement of factors of production among members. The Southern Cone Common Market (MERCOSUR) of Argentina, Brazil, Paraguay, and Uruguay is an example of a common market.[17] An **economic union** requires an even greater degree of integration. It incorporates all aspects of a common market and in addition requires common economic institutions and coordination of economic policies among members. The European Community became the European Union in 1993. If the members of the economic union decide to adopt a common currency, then it is also a **monetary union**. For example, with the adoption of the euro, 11 EU member countries also formed a monetary union.[18]

EXAMPLE 7

Trading Blocs

1 Chile and Australia have a free trade with each other but have separate trade barriers on imports from other countries. Chile and Australia are a part of a(n)

   A FTA.

   B Economic union.

   C Customs union.

   D Common market.

2 An RTA that removes all tariffs on imports from member countries, has common external tariffs against all non-members, but does not advance further in deepening economic integration is called a(n)

---

17 For more information, visit the OECD website, http://stats.oecd.org/glossary/.
18 On 1 January 1999, Austria, Belgium, Finland, France, Germany, Ireland, Italy, Luxembourg, the Netherlands, Portugal, and Spain adopted the euro. This adoption meant that these countries had to surrender control over their domestic monetary policy to the European Central Bank. Greece joined in 2001. Euro coins and notes went into circulation on 1 January 2002, and these countries gave up the last vestiges of their national currencies. Other members now include Slovenia (2007), Cyprus (2008), Malta (2008), Slovakia (2009), and Estonia (2011). The eurozone (i.e., the monetary union) is only a subset of the EU membership because some EU members, notably the United Kingdom, have not adopted the euro.

A   FTA.

B   Economic union.

C   Customs union.

D   Common market.

Solution to 1:

A is correct. Chile and Australia do not a have customs union because they do not have a common trade policy with respect to other trade partners (C is incorrect). A common market or a economic union entail even more integration (B and D are incorrect).

Solution to 2:

C is correct. A basic FTA does not entail common external tariffs (A is incorrect), whereas a common market and an economic union entail integration beyond common external tariffs (B and D are incorrect).

Regional integration is popular because eliminating trade and investment barriers among a small group of countries is easier, politically less contentious, and quicker than multilateral trade negotiations under the World Trade Organization (WTO). The WTO is a negotiating forum that deals with the rules of global trade between nations and where member countries can go to sort out trade disputes. The latest rounds of trade negotiations launched by the WTO in 2001 at Doha, Qatar, included several contentious issues of specific concern to developing countries, such as the cost of implementing trade policy reform in developing countries, market access in developed countries for developing countries' agricultural products, and access to affordable pharmaceuticals in developing countries. After nearly a decade of negotiations, very limited progress has been made on the major issues. Hence, it is not surprising to see a renewed interest in bilateral and multilateral trade liberalization on a smaller scale. Policy coordination and harmonization are also easier among a smaller group of countries. Regional integration can be viewed as a movement toward freer trade.

Regional integration results in preferential treatment for members compared with non-members and can lead to changes in the patterns of trade. Member countries move toward freer trade by eliminating or reducing trade barriers against each other, leading to a more efficient allocation of resources. But regional integration may also result in trade and production being shifted from a lower-cost non-member who still faces trade barriers to a higher-cost member who faces no trade barriers. This shift leads to a less-efficient allocation of resources and could reduce welfare. Hence, there are two static effects that are direct results of the formation of the customs union: trade creation and trade diversion.

Trade creation occurs when regional integration results in the replacement of higher-cost domestic production by lower-cost imports from other members. For example, consider two hypothetical countries, Qualor and Vulcan. Qualor produces 10 million shirts annually and imports 2 million shirts from Vulcan, which has a lower cost of production. Qualor has 10 percent tariffs on imports from Vulcan. Qualor and Vulcan then agree to form a customs union. Qualor reduces its production of shirts to 7 million and now imports 11 million shirts from Vulcan. The decline in Qualor's domestic production (from 10 million to 7 million shirts) is replaced by importing 3 million additional shirts from the low-cost producer, Vulcan. This scenario represents trade creation. The rest of the additional imports (6 million shirts) represent increased consumption by Qualor's consumers because the price of shirts declines after formation of the custom union.

Trade diversion occurs when lower-cost imports from nonmember countries are replaced with higher-cost imports from members. In the example in the preceding paragraph, suppose Qualor initially imposes a 10 percent tariff on imports from both Vulcan and Aurelia. Aurelia is the lowest-cost producer of shirts, so Qualor initially imports 2 million shirts from Aurelia instead of from Vulcan. Qualor and Vulcan then form a customs union, which eliminates tariffs on imports from Vulcan but maintains a 10 percent tariff on imports from Aurelia. Now trade diversion could occur if the free trade price on imports from Vulcan is lower than the price on imports from Aurelia. Even though Aurelia is the lowest-cost producer, it may be a higher-priced source of imports because of the tariff. If this is the case, then Qualor will stop importing from Aurelia, a non-member, and divert its imports to Vulcan, a member of the RTA. Both trade creation and trade diversion are possible in an RTA. If trade creation is larger than trade diversion, then the net welfare effect is positive. However, there are concerns that this may not always be the case.

The benefits ascribed to free trade—greater specialization according to comparative advantage, reduction in monopoly power because of foreign competition, economies of scale from larger market size, learning by doing, technology transfer, knowledge spillovers, greater foreign investment, and better quality intermediate inputs at world prices—also apply to regional trading blocs. In addition, fostering greater interdependence among members of the regional trading bloc reduces the potential for conflict. Members of the bloc also have greater bargaining power and political clout in the global economy by acting together instead of as individual countries.

The 2009 World Development Report points to spillover of growth across borders as one of the main benefits of regional integration (Collier and O'Connell 2007). There is evidence of considerable spillovers among OECD countries, which are highly integrated both as a group and within their own geographic regions. The long-run growth of integrated countries is interconnected because members have greater access to each other's markets. Strong growth in any RTA country could have a positive impact on growth in other RTA member countries. RTAs also enhance the benefits of good policy and lead to convergence in living standards. For example, growth spillovers are likely to be much smaller among Sub-Saharan African countries because of a lack of integration arising from deficiencies in RTAs and inadequate levels of transportation and telecommunications infrastructure. Roberts and Deichmann (2008) estimated what the cumulative loss in real GDP between 1970 and 2000 would have been if Switzerland, which is landlocked and fully integrated with both its immediate neighbors and the world economy, had been subject to the same level of spillovers as the Central African Republic. Under such a scenario, Switzerland's GDP per capita in 2000 would have been 9.3 percent lower. The cumulative GDP loss would have been $334 billion (constant US dollars, 2000), which was the equivalent of 162 percent of Switzerland's real GDP in 2000.

Although regional integration has many advantages, it may impose costs on some groups. For example, there was significant concern in the United States that NAFTA and especially low-skilled-labor intensive imports from Mexico could hurt low-skilled workers. Adjustment costs arose as import competition caused inefficient firms to exit the market, and the workers in those firms were at least temporarily unemployed as they sought new jobs. However, the surviving firms experienced an increase in productivity, and US consumers benefited from the increase in product varieties imported from Mexico. Feenstra and Taylor (2008) estimated that the product varieties exported from Mexico to the United States had grown by an average of 2.2 percent a year across all industries. They estimated that NAFTA imposed private costs of nearly $5.4 billion a year in the United States during 1994–2002, but that these costs were offset by an average welfare gain of $5.5 billion a year accruing from increased varieties imported from Mexico. Consumer gains from more varieties of products continued over time as long as the imports continued, while adjustment costs arising from job losses declined over time. In 2003, the gain from increased product varieties from Mexico was $11 billion, far exceeding the adjustment costs of $5.4 billion.[19] Their analysis concluded:

> ...Thus the consumer gains from increased product variety, when summed over the years, considerably exceed the private loss from displacement. This outcome is guaranteed to occur because the gains from expanded import varieties occur every year that the imports are available, whereas labor displacement is a temporary phenomenon. (Feenstra and Taylor 2008, p. 208)

It is important to recognize, however, that workers displaced by regional integration may have to bear long-term losses if they are unable to find jobs with wages comparable with the jobs they lost or they remain unemployed for a long period. For example, although import competition was certainly not the only factor that led to a dramatic contraction of the US automobile industry, the impact on employment in that industry is likely to be permanent and many former autoworkers, especially older workers, may never find comparable jobs.

Concerns regarding national sovereignty, especially where big and small nations may be part of the same bloc, have also been an impediment to the formation of FTAs. The proposal for a South Asian regional bloc has faced challenges regarding India's role because it is one of the biggest economies in the region.

Regional integration is important from an investment perspective because it offers new opportunities for trade and investment. The cost of doing business in a large, single, regional market is lower and firms can benefit from economies of scale. However, it is important to note that differences in tastes, culture, and competitive conditions still exist among members of a trading bloc. These differences may limit the potential benefits from investments within the bloc. In addition, depending on the level of integration and the safeguards in place, problems faced by individual member countries in an RTA may quickly spread to other countries in the bloc.

There are at least two challenges in the formation of an RTA and in its potential progression from a free trade area to deeper integration in the form of a customs union, common market, or economic union. First, cultural differences and historical considerations—for example, wars and conflicts—may complicate the social/political process of integration. Second, maintaining a high degree of economic integration limits the extent to which member countries can pursue independent economic and social policies. Free trade and mobility of labor and capital tend to thwart policies aimed at controlling relative prices and/or quantities within a country, while balance of payments and fiscal credibility considerations limit the viability of divergent macroeconomic policies. This situation is especially true in the case of a monetary union because monetary policy is not under the control of individual countries and currency devaluation/revaluation is not available as a tool to correct persistent imbalances.[20] When persistent imbalances do arise, they may lead to a crisis that spills over to other countries facing similar problems. A recent example is the fear of contagion caused by the Greek fiscal crisis in 2010. In May 2010, Standard & Poor's reduced the credit ratings on Greece's government from investment grade to junk status. It also downgraded the government debt of Spain and Portugal. These countries were suffering from a combination of high government deficits and slow GDP growth. The credit downgrades increased fears that Greece, in particular, would default on its debt and cause economic turmoil not only among the healthier countries in the EU but also

---

19 Feenstra and Taylor (2008) discuss in their book on pages 207–208 the data limitations and various assumptions they made in their analysis.

20 These limitations are inherent in any system with fixed exchange rates and a high degree of capital mobility. They are not unique to a monetary union (i.e., a common currency). For a discussion of currency regimes, see the Level I curriculum reading on "Currency Exchange Rates," (CFA Institute).

in the United States and Asia. The EU and the International Monetary Fund (IMF) agreed on a USD145 billion (EUR110 billion) bailout for Greece in May 2010, and provided Ireland with a financing package of about USD113 billion (EUR85 billion) in November 2010. As of late 2010, there were continuing concerns about the financial health of Greece, Ireland, Portugal, and Spain. The EU, which created the European Financial Stability Facility (EFSF) in 2010 to help EU countries in need, has been debating the need for an expansion in the scope and financing capacity of the EFSF.

EXAMPLE 8

Trade Agreements

Bagopia, Cropland, and Technopia decide to enter into an RTA. In the first stage, they decide to sign a free trade agreement (FTA). After several successful years, they decide that it is time to form a common market.

1　Does an FTA make exporting firms in member countries more attractive as investment options?

2　How does the common market affect firms doing business in these countries compared with an FTA?

Solution to 1:

The first stage, where there is free movement of goods and services among RTA members, is called a free trade area. It makes exporting firms a more attractive investment proposition because they are able to serve markets in member countries without the additional costs imposed by trade barriers.

Solution to 2:

Unlike an FTA, a common market allows for free movement of factors of production, such as labor and capital, among the member economies. Like an FTA, it provides access to a much larger market and free movement of goods and services. But the common market can create more profitable opportunities for firms than an FTA by allowing them to locate production in and purchase components from anywhere in the common market according to comparative advantage.

3.5 Capital Restrictions

There are many reasons for governments to restrict inward and outward flow of capital. For example, the government may want to meet some objective regarding employment or regional development, or it may have a strategic or defense-related objective. Many countries require approval for foreigners to invest in their country and for citizens to invest abroad. Control over inward investment by foreigners results in restrictions on how much can be invested, and on the type of industries in which capital can be invested. For example, such strategic industries as defense and telecommunications are often subject to ownership restrictions. Outflow restrictions can include restrictions on repatriation of capital, interest, profits, royalty payments, and license fees. Citizens are often limited in their ability to invest abroad, especially in foreign exchange–scarce economies, and there can be deadlines for repatriation of income earned from any investments abroad.

Economists consider free movement of financial capital to be beneficial because it allows capital to be invested where it will earn the highest return. Inflows of capital also allow countries to invest in productive capacity at a rate that is higher than could be achieved with domestic savings alone, and it can enable countries to achieve a higher rate of growth. Longer-term investments by foreign firms that establish a presence in the local economy can bring in not only much needed capital but also new technology, skills, and advanced production and management practices as well as create spillover benefits for local firms. Investment by foreign firms can also create a network of local suppliers if they source some of their components locally. Such suppliers may receive advanced training and spillover benefits from a close working relationship with the foreign firms. On the one hand, increased competition from foreign firms in the market may force domestic firms to become more efficient. On the other hand, it is possible that the domestic industry may be hurt because domestic firms that are unable to compete are forced to exit the market.

In times of macroeconomic crisis, capital mobility can result in capital flight out of the country, especially if most of the inflow reflects short-term portfolio flows into stocks, bonds, and other liquid assets rather than foreign direct investment (FDI) in productive assets. In such circumstances, capital restrictions are often used in conjunction with other policy instruments, such as fixed exchange rate targets. Capital restrictions and fixed exchange rate targets are complementary instruments because in a regime of perfect capital mobility, governments cannot achieve domestic and external policy objectives simultaneously using only standard monetary and fiscal policy tools.[21] By limiting the free flow of capital, capital controls provide a way to exercise control over a country's external balance whereas more traditional macro-policy tools are used to address other objectives. As an example, China has pegged its currency to the US dollar in a narrow range. At the same time, it limits the free flow of capital into and out of the country. The capital controls serve two purposes. First, they make it easier to maintain the tight exchange rate peg that is crucial in fostering the nation's export sector. Second, the capital controls shield domestic interest rates from external market forces. Control over domestic interest rates is crucial for managing the domestic banking and real estate sectors. In essence, the capital controls allow China to exercise a degree of monetary policy independence that would not be achievable under a fixed exchange rate regime with free capital flows.

Modern capital controls were developed by the belligerents in World War I as a method to finance the war effort. At the start of the war, all major powers restricted capital outflows (i.e., the purchase of foreign assets or loans abroad). These restrictions raised revenues by keeping capital in the domestic economy, facilitating the taxation of wealth, and producing interest income. Moreover, capital controls helped to maintain a low level of interest rates, reducing the government's borrowing costs on its liabilities. Since WWI, controls on capital outflows have been used similarly in other countries, mostly developing nations, to generate revenue for governments or to permit them to allocate credit in the domestic economy without risking capital flight. In broad terms, a capital restriction is any policy designed to limit or redirect capital flows. Such restrictions may take the form of taxes, price or quantity controls, or outright prohibitions on international trade in assets. Price controls may take the form of special taxes on returns to international investment, taxes on certain types of transactions, or mandatory reserve requirements—that is, a requirement forcing foreign parties wishing to deposit money in a domestic bank account to deposit some percentage of the inflow with the central bank for a minimum period at zero interest. Quantity restrictions on capital flows may include rules imposing ceilings or requiring special authorization for new or existing borrowing from foreign creditors. Or there may be administrative controls on cross-border capital movements in which a government agency must approve transactions for certain types of assets.

---

21 Section 4.1 of the Level I curriculum reading on "Currency Exchange Rates" (CFA Institute), provides a concise discussion of the policy implications of capital mobility with fixed versus floating exchange rates.

Effective implementation of capital restrictions may entail non-trivial administration costs, particularly if the measures have to be broadened to close potential loopholes. There is also the risk that protecting the domestic financial markets by capital restrictions may postpone necessary policy adjustments or impede private-sector adaptation to changing international circumstances. Most importantly, controls may give rise to negative market perceptions, which may, in turn, make it more costly and difficult for the country to access foreign funds.

In a study on the effectiveness of capital controls, the International Monetary Fund considered restrictions on capital outflows and inflows separately.[22] The authors concluded that for restrictions on capital inflows to be effective (i.e., not circumvented), the coverage needs to be comprehensive and the controls need to be implemented forcefully. Considerable administrative costs are incurred in continuously extending, amending, and monitoring compliance with the regulations. Although controls on inflows appeared to be effective in some countries, it was difficult to distinguish the impact of the controls from the impact of other policies, such as strengthening of prudential regulations, increased exchange rate flexibility, and adjustment of monetary policy. In the case of capital outflows, the imposition of controls during episodes of financial crisis seems to have produced mixed results, providing only temporary relief of varying duration to some countries, while successfully shielding others (e.g., Malaysia) and providing them with sufficient time to restructure their economies.

EXAMPLE 9

Capital Restrictions: Malaysia's Capital Controls in 1998–2001

After the devaluation of the Thai baht in July 1997, Southeast Asia suffered from significant capital outflows that led to falling local equity and real estate prices and declining exchange rates. To counter the outflows of capital, the IMF urged many of the countries in the region to increase interest rates, thus making their assets more attractive to foreign investors. Higher interest rates, however, weighed heavily on the domestic economies. In response to this dilemma, Malaysia imposed capital controls on 1 September 1998. These controls prohibited transfers between domestic and foreign accounts, eliminated credit facilities to offshore parties, prevented repatriation of investment until 1 September 1999, and fixed the exchange rate of the Malaysian ringgit at 3.8 per US dollar. In February 1999, a system of taxes on capital flows replaced the prohibition on repatriation of capital. Although the details were complex, the net effect was to discourage short-term capital flows while permitting long-term transactions. By imposing capital controls, Malaysia hoped to regain monetary independence, and to be able to cut interest rates without provoking a fall in the value of its currency as investors avoided Malaysian assets. The imposition of outflow controls indeed curtailed speculative capital outflows and allowed interest rates to be reduced substantially. At the same time, under the umbrella of the capital controls, the authorities pursued bank and corporate restructuring and achieved a strong economic recovery in 1999 and 2000. With the restoration of economic and financial stability, administrative controls on portfolio outflows were replaced by a two-tier, price-based exit system in February 1999, which was finally eliminated in May 2001. Although Malaysia's capital controls did contribute to a stabilization of its economy, they came with long-term costs associated with the country's removal from the MSCI developed equity market

---

22 Ariyoshi, et al. (2000).

index, an important benchmark in the institutional asset management industry, and its relegation to the emerging market universe. The Malaysian market was no longer seen as on par with developed equity markets whose institutional and regulatory frameworks provide a higher standard of safety for investors. As a consequence, it became more difficult for Malaysia to attract net long-term capital inflows (Kawai and Takagi 2003).

1   Under what economic circumstances were Malaysia's capital restrictions imposed?

2   What was the ultimate objective of Malaysia's capital restrictions?

3   How successful were the country's capital restrictions?

Solution to 1:

As a result of the Southeast Asian crisis, Malaysia suffered substantial net capital outflows pushing up the domestic interest rate level.

Solution to 2:

The restrictions were designed to limit and redirect capital flows to allow the government to reduce interest rates and pursue bank and corporate restructurings.

Solution to 3:

Although the capital controls helped stabilize Malaysia's economy, they contributed to a change in investors' perception of Malaysian financial markets and removal of the Malaysian equity market from the MSCI benchmark universe of developed equity markets. This situation undermined international demand for Malaysian equities and made it more difficult to attract net long-term capital inflows.

THE BALANCE OF PAYMENTS   **4**

The **balance of payments** (BOP) is a double-entry bookkeeping system that summarizes a country's economic transactions with the rest of the world for a particular period of time, typically a calendar quarter or year. In this context, a transaction is defined as "an economic flow that reflects the creation, transformation, exchange, or extinction of economic value and involves changes in ownership of goods and/or financial assets, the provision of services, or the provision of labour and capital."[23] In other words, the BOP reflects payments for exports and imports as well as financial transactions and financial transfers. Analyzing the BOP is an important element in assessing a country's macroeconomic environment, its monetary and fiscal policies, and its long-term growth potential. Investors use data on trade and capital flows to evaluate a country's overall level of capital investment, profitability, and risk. The following section describes the balance of payments, the factors that influence it, and its impact on exchange rates, interest rates, and capital market transactions.

---

23 IMF Balance of Payments Handbook, chapter II, page 6.

4.1 Balance of Payments Accounts

The BOP is a double-entry system in which every transaction involves both a debit and credit. In principle, the sum of all debit entries should equal the sum of all credit entries, and the net balance of all entries on the BOP statement should equal zero. In practice, however, this is rarely the case because the data used to record balance of payments transactions are often derived from different sources.

Debit entries reflect purchases of imported goods and services, purchases of foreign financial assets, payments received for exports, and payments (interest and principal) received from debtors. Credit entries reflect payments for imported goods and services, payments for purchased foreign financial assets, and payments to creditors (see Exhibit 14, Panel A). Put differently, a debit represents an increase in a country's assets (the purchase of foreign assets or the receipt of cash from foreigners) or a decrease in its liabilities (the amount owed to foreigners); a credit represents a decrease in assets (the sale of goods and services to foreigners or the payment of cash to foreigners) or an increase in liabilities (an amount owed to foreigners).

For example, as shown in Panel B of Exhibit 14, on 1 September Country A purchases $1 million of goods from Country B and agrees to pay for these goods on 1 December. On 1 September, Country A would record in its BOP a $1 million debit to reflect the value of the goods purchased (i.e., increase in assets) and $1 million credit to reflect the amount owed to Country B. On 1 December, Country A would record in its BOP a $1 million debit to reflect a decrease in the amount owed (liability) to Country B and $1 million a credit to reflect the actual payment to Country B (decrease in assets).

From Country B's perspective, on 1 September it would record in its BOP a $1 million debit to reflect the amount owed by Country A and a $1 million credit to reflect the sale of goods (exports). On 1 December, Country B would record a $1 million debit to reflect the cash received from Country A, and $1 million credit to reflect the fact that it is no longer owed $1 million by Country A.

Exhibit 14　Basic Entries in a BOP Context

Panel A

DEBITS Increase in Assets, Decrease in Liabilities	CREDITS Decrease in Assets, Increase in Liabilities
■ Value of imported goods and services	■ Payments for imports of goods and services
■ Purchases of foreign financial assets	■ Payments for foreign financial assets
■ Receipt of payments from foreigners	■ Value of exported goods and services
■ Increase in debt owed by foreigners	■ Payment of debt by foreigners
■ Payment of debt owed to foreigners	■ Increase in debt owed to foreigners

Panel B

Country A	Debits	Credits
1 September	$1 million Goods purchased from Country B *(increase in real assets)*	$1 million Short-term liability for goods purchased from Country B *(increase in financial liabilities)*
1 December	$1 million Elimination of short-term liability for goods purchased from Country B *(decrease in financial liabilities)*	$1 million Payment for goods purchased from Country B *(decrease in financial assets)*

Country B	Debits	Credits
1 September	$1 million Short-term claim for goods delivered to Country A *(increase in financial assets)*	$1 million Goods delivered to Country A *(decrease in real assets)*
1 December	$1 million Receipt of payment for goods delivered to Country A *(increase in financial assets)*	$1 million Elimination of claim for goods delivered to Country A *(decrease in financial assets)*

Exhibit 14   (Continued)

4.2 Balance of Payment Components

The BOP is composed of the **current account** that measures the flow of goods and services, the **capital account** that measures transfers of capital, and the **financial account** that records investment flows. These accounts are further disaggregated into sub-accounts:

Current Account

The current account can be decomposed into four sub-accounts:

1 **Merchandise trade** consists of all commodities and manufactured goods bought, sold, or given away.

2 **Services** include tourism, transportation, engineering, and business services, such as legal services, management consulting, and accounting. Fees from patents and copyrights on new technology, software, books, and movies are also recorded in the services category.

3 **Income receipts** include income derived from ownership of assets, such as dividends and interest payments; income on foreign investments is included in the current account because that income is compensation for services provided by foreign investments. When a German company builds a plant in China, for instance, the services the plant generates are viewed as a service export from Germany to China equal in value to the profits the plant yields for its German owner.

4 **Unilateral transfers** represent one-way transfers of assets, such as worker remittances from abroad to their home country and foreign direct aid or gifts.

Capital Account

The capital account consists of two sub-accounts:

1 **Capital transfers** include debt forgiveness and migrants' transfers (goods and financial assets belonging to migrants as they leave or enter the country).[24] Capital transfers also include the transfer of title to fixed assets and the transfer of funds linked to the sale or acquisition of fixed assets, gift and inheritance taxes, death duties, uninsured damage to fixed assets, and legacies.

2 **Sales and purchases of non-produced, non-financial assets**, such as the rights to natural resources, and the sale and purchase of intangible assets, such as patents, copyrights, trademarks, franchises, and leases.

Financial Account

The financial account can be broken down in two sub-accounts: financial assets abroad and foreign-owned financial assets within the reporting country.

1 A country's assets abroad are further divided into official reserve assets, government assets, and private assets. These assets include gold, foreign currencies, foreign securities, the government's reserve position in the International Monetary Fund,[25] direct foreign investment, and claims reported by resident banks.

2 Foreign-owned assets in the reporting country are further divided into official assets and other foreign assets. These assets include securities issued by the reporting country's government and private sectors (e.g., bonds, equities, mortgage-backed securities), direct investment, and foreign liabilities reported by the reporting country's banking sector.

EXAMPLE 10

US Current Account Balance

Exhibit 15 shows a simplified version of the US balance of payments for 1970–2009.

Exhibit 15   US International Transactions Accounts Data

	(USD millions)					
(Credits+, Debits–)	**1970**	**1980**	**1985**	**1990**	**2000**	**2009**
Current Account						
Exports of goods and services and income receipts	68,387	344,440	387,612	706,975	1,421,515	2,159,000
Exports of goods and services	56,640	271,834	289,070	535,233	1,070,597	1,570,797
Income receipts	11,748	72,606	98,542	171,742	350,918	588,203
Imports of goods and services and income payments	−59,901	−333,774	−483,769	−759,290	−1,779,241	−2,412,489

---

24 Immigrants bring with them goods and financial assets already in their possession. Hence, these goods are imported on grounds other than commercial transactions.
25 These are in effect official currency reserves held with the International Monetary Fund.

Exhibit 15 (Continued)

(Credits+, Debits–)	(USD millions)					
	1970	1980	1985	1990	2000	2009
Imports of goods and services	−54,386	−291,241	−410,950	−616,097	−1,449,377	−1,945,705
Income payments	−5,515	−42,532	−72,819	−143,192	−329,864	−466,783
Unilateral current transfers, net	−6,156	−8,349	−21,998	−26,654	−58,645	−124,943
Capital Account						
Capital account transactions, net	....	....	....	−7,220	−1	−140
Financial Account						
US-owned assets abroad, ex derivatives (increase/ financial outflow (−))	−9,337	−86,967	−44,752	−81,234	−560,523	−140,465
Foreign-owned assets in the United States, ex derivatives (increase/ financial inflow (+))	7,226	62,037	144,231	139,357	1,038,224	305,736
Financial derivatives, net	NA	NA	NA	NA	NA	50,804
Statistical discrepancy (sum of above items with sign reversed)	−219	22,613	18,677	28,066	−61,329	162,497

Based only on the information given, address the following:

1 Calculate the current account balance for each year.
2 Calculate the financial account balance for each year.
3 Describe the long-term change in the current account balance.
4 Describe the long-term change in the financial account balance.

Solutions to 1 and 2:

(Credits+, Debits–)	1970	1980	1985	1990	2000	2009
Current Account	2,330	2,317	−118,155	−78,969	−416,371	−378,432
Financial Account	−2,111	−24,930	99,479	58,123	477,701	216,075

Solution to 3:

The United States had a current account surplus until 1980. After 1985, the US current account had an increasing deficit as a result of strong import growth.

Solution to 4:

Mirroring the growing US current account deficit, the US financial account, after 1985, registered increasing net capital inflows in similar proportions to the deficit in the current account.

4.3 Paired Transactions in the BOP Bookkeeping System

The following examples illustrate how some typical cross-border transactions are recorded in the BOP framework outlined previously. They include commercial exports and imports, the receipt of income from foreign investments, loans made to borrowers abroad, and purchases of home-country currency by foreign central banks. Exhibit 16 illustrates the various individual bookkeeping entries from the perspective of an individual country, in this case Germany.

Commercial Exports: Transactions (ia) and (ib)

A company in Germany sells technology equipment to a South Korean auto manufacturer for a total price of EUR50 million, including freight charges of EUR1 million to be paid within 90 days. The merchandise will be shipped via a German cargo ship. In this case, Germany is exporting two assets: equipment and transportation services. The cargo shipped is viewed as being created in Germany and used by South Korean customers. In return for relinquishing these two assets, Germany acquires a financial asset—the promise by the South Korean manufacturer to pay for the equipment in 90 days.

Germany would record a EUR50 million debit to an account called "private short-term claims" to show an increase in this asset. It would also record a credit of EUR49 million to "goods" and another credit of EUR1 million to "services." Both credit entries are listed in the export category and show the decrease in assets available to German residents. These figures are entered as credits on lines 2 and 3 and as a debit on 19 in Exhibit 16 and are marked with (ia) to identify a typical commercial export transaction. To pay for the technology equipment purchased from Germany, the South Korean auto manufacturer may purchase euros from its local bank (i.e., a EUR demand deposit held by the Korean bank in a German bank) and then transfer them to the German exporter. As a result, German liabilities to South Korean residents (i.e., South Korean private short-term claims) would be debited. The respective entries, marked with (ib) are on lines 19 and 23 in Exhibit 16.

Commercial Imports: Transaction (ii)

A German utility company imports gas from Russia valued at EUR 45 million (ii), and agrees to pay the Russian company within three months. The imported gas generates a debit on line 6. The obligation pay is recorded as a credit to foreign private short-term claims on line 23.

Loans to Borrowers Abroad: Transaction (iii)

A German commercial bank purchases EUR 100 million in intermediate-term bonds issued by a Ukrainian steel company. The bonds are denominated in euros, so payment is made in euros (i.e., by transferring EUR demand deposits). A debit entry on line 18 records the increase in German holdings of Ukrainian bonds, and a credit entry on line 23 records the increase in demand deposits held by Ukrainians in German banks.

Exhibit 16	Hypothetical Transactions between German Residents and Foreigners			
Item no	Account	Debit	Credit	Balance
		−	+	+/−
1	**Exports of goods and services, income received**			55
2	Goods		49 (ia)	49
3	Services		1 (ia)	1

Exhibit 16   (Continued)

Item no	Account	Debit −	Credit +	Balance +/−
4	Income on residents' investments abroad		5 (v)	5
5	**Imports of goods and services, income paid**			−45
6	Goods	45 (ii)		−45
7	Services			
8	Income on foreign investments in home country			
9	**Unilateral transfers**			
10	**Changes in residents' claims on foreigners**			−105
11	Official reserve assets			
12	Gold			
13	Foreign currency balances			
14	Other			
15	Government claims			
16	Private claims			
17	Direct investments			
18	Other private long-term claims	100 (iii)		−100
19	Private short-term claims	50 (ia), 5 (v)	50 (ib)	−5
20	**Changes in foreign claims on residents**			195
21	Foreign official claims		20 (iv)	20
22	Foreign private long-term claims			
23	Foreign private short-term claims	20 (iv), 50 (ib)	45 (ii), 100 (iii), 100 (vi)	175
24	**Other**	100 (vi)		−100
	Total	~~270~~ 370	~~270~~ 370	0
	Current Account: (1) + (5) + (9)			**10**
	Capital Account: (24)			**−100**
	Financial Account: (10) + (20)			**90**

Purchases of Home-Country Currency by Foreign Central Banks: Transaction (iv)

Private foreigners may not wish to retain euro balances acquired in earlier transactions. Those who are holding foreign currency, in our example euro claims, typically do so for purposes of financing purchases from Germany (or other euro area member countries). Assume for instance, that Swiss residents attempt to sell EUR20 million in exchange for their native currency, the Swiss franc (CHF), but there is a lack of demand for EUR funds in Switzerland. In such circumstances, the CHF would appreciate against the EUR. To prevent an undesired CHF appreciation, the Swiss National Bank (SNB) might sell CHF in exchange for EUR balances.

Suppose that the Swiss National Bank purchased EUR20 million, typically in the form of a EUR demand deposit held with a German bank, from local commercial banks in Switzerland. The German BOP would register an increase of EUR20 million in German liabilities held by foreign monetary authorities, the Swiss National Bank (line 21), and an equivalent decline in short-term liabilities held by private foreigners (i.e.,

Swiss private investors, line 23). It may be noteworthy that when the SNB purchases EUR funds from Swiss commercial banks, it also credits them the CHF equivalent of EUR20 million. The SNB's liabilities to Swiss commercial banks arising from this transaction are in fact reserve deposits that Swiss banks can use when they expand their lending business and create new deposits. Currency interventions by central banks, therefore, can contribute to an increase in a country's overall money supply, all else remaining unchanged.

Receipts of Income from Foreign Investments: Transaction (v)

Each year, residents of Germany receive billions of EUR in interest and dividends from capital invested in foreign securities and other financial claims. German residents receive these payments in return for allowing foreigners to use German capital that otherwise could be put to work in Germany. Foreign residents, in turn, receive similar returns for their investments in Germany. Assume that a German firm has a long-term capital investment in a profitable subsidiary abroad, and that the subsidiary transfers to its German parent EUR5 million in dividends in the form of funds held in a foreign bank. The German firm then has a new (or increased) demand deposit in a foreign bank as compensation for allowing its capital to be used by its subsidiary. A debit entry on line 19 shows German private short-term claims on foreigners have increased by EUR5 million, and a credit entry on line 4 reflects the fact that German residents have given up an asset (the services of capital covered over the period) valued at EUR5 million.

Purchase of Non-financial Assets: Transaction (vi)

In a move to safeguard its long-term supply of uranium, a German utility company purchases the rights to exploit a uranium mine from the government of Kazakhstan. It agrees to pay within three months. The respective entries are on lines 23 and 24. Because a non-financial, non-produced asset is involved in this transaction, it is recorded in Germany's capital account.

Note that the sum of all BOP entries in Exhibit 16 is 0. Transactions (i)–(iv) produce a current account surplus of EUR10 million, a capital account deficit of EUR100 million, and a financial account surplus of EUR90 million.

Although it is important to understand the detailed structure of official balance of payments accounts as described in the preceding paragraphs, this example is not necessarily how investment professionals think about the balance of payments day-to-day. Practitioners often think of the current account as roughly synonymous with the trade balance (merchandise trade + services) and lump all the financing flows (financial account + capital account) into one category that is usually referred to simply as the "capital account." They then think of the capital account as consisting of two types of flows—portfolio investment flows and foreign direct investment (FDI). The former are shorter-term investments in foreign assets (stocks, bonds, etc.), whereas the latter are long-term investments in production capacity abroad. Although not completely accurate, this way of thinking about the balance of payments focuses attention on the components—trade, portfolio flows, and FDI—that are most sensitive to, and most likely to affect, market conditions, prices of goods and services, asset prices, and exchange rates. In addition, this perspective fits well with the role that the balance of payments plays in the macroeconomy.

4.4 National Economic Accounts and the Balance of Payments

In a closed economy, all output Y is consumed or invested by the private sector—domestic households and businesses—or purchased by the government. Letting Y denote GDP, C private consumption, I investment, and G government purchases of goods and services, the national income identity for a closed economy is given by:

$$Y = C + I + G \tag{1}$$

Once foreign trade is introduced, however, some output is purchased by foreigners (exports) whereas some domestic spending is used for purchases of foreign goods and services (imports). The national income identity for an open economy is thus

$$Y = C + I + G + X - M \tag{2}$$

where X denotes exports and M denotes imports.

For most countries, exports rarely equal imports. Net exports or the difference between exports and imports $(X - M)$ is the equivalent of the current account balance from a BOP perspective.[26] When a country's imports exceed its exports, the current account is in deficit. When a country's exports exceed its imports, the current account is in surplus. As the right side of Equation 2 shows, a current account surplus or deficit can affect GDP (and also employment). The balance of the current account is also important because it measures the size and direction of international borrowing.

In order for the balance of payments to balance, a deficit or surplus in the current account must be offset by an opposite balance in the sum of the capital and financial accounts. This requirement means that a country with a current account deficit has to increase its net foreign debts by the amount of the current account deficit. For example, the United States has run current account deficits for many years while accumulating net foreign liabilities: The current account deficit was financed by net capital imports (i.e., direct investments by foreigners), loans by foreign banks, and the sale of US equities and fixed-income securities to foreign investors. By the same token, an economy with a current account surplus is earning more for its exports than it spends for its imports. Japan, Germany, and China are traditional current account surplus countries accumulating substantial net foreign claims, especially against the United States. An economy with a current account surplus finances the current account deficit of its trading partners by lending to them—that is, granting bank loans and investing in financial and real assets. As a result, the foreign wealth of a surplus country rises because foreigners pay for imports by issuing liabilities that they will eventually have to redeem.

By rearranging Equation 2, we can define the current account balance from the perspective of the national income accounts as:

$$CA = X - M = Y - (C + I + G) \tag{3}$$

Only by borrowing money from foreigners can a country have a current account deficit and consume more output than it produces. If it consumes less output than it produces, it has a current account surplus and can (indeed must) lend the surplus to foreigners. International capital flows essentially reflect an *inter-temporal trade*. An economy with a current account deficit is effectively importing present consumption and exporting future consumption.

---

26 Strictly speaking, net exports as defined here is the trade balance rather than the current account balance because it excludes income receipts and unilateral transfers. This distinction arises because we have defined income Y as GDP rather than GNP (see section 2.1). Because the trade balance is usually the dominant component of the current account, the terms "trade balance" and "current account" are often used interchangeably. We will do so here unless the distinction is important to the discussion.

Let us now turn to the relationship between output Y and disposable income Y^d. We have to recognize that part of income is spent on taxes T, and that the private sector receives net transfers R in addition to (national) income. Disposable income Y^d is thus equal to income plus transfers minus taxes:

$$Y^d = Y + R - T \tag{4}$$

Disposable income, in turn, is allocated to consumption and saving so that we can write

$$Y^d = C + S_p \tag{5}$$

where S_p denotes private sector saving. Combining Equations 4 and 5 allows us to write consumption as income plus transfers minus taxes and saving.

$$C = Y^d - S_p = Y + R - T - S_p \tag{6}$$

We can now use the right side of Equation 6 to substitute for C in Equation 3. With some rearrangement we obtain

$$CA = S_p - I + (T - G - R) \tag{7}$$

Because $(T - G - R)$ is taxes minus government spending and transfers, it is the government surplus, or put differently, government savings S_g. Equation 7 can therefore be restated as

$$S_p + S_g = I + CA \tag{8}$$

Equation 8 highlights an essential difference between open and closed economies: An open economy can use its saving for domestic investment or for foreign investment (i.e., by exporting its savings and acquiring foreign assets), while in a closed economy savings can only be used for domestic investment. Put another way, an open economy with promising investment opportunities is not constrained by its domestic savings rate in order to exploit these opportunities. As Equation 8 shows, it can raise investment by increasing foreign borrowing (a reduction in CA) without increasing domestic savings. For example, if India decides to build a network of high-speed trains, it can import all the required materials it needs from France and then borrow the funds, perhaps also from France, to pay for the materials. This transaction increases India's domestic investment because the imported materials contribute to the expansion in the country's capital stock. All else being equal, this transaction will also produce a current account deficit for India by an amount equal to the increase in investment. India's savings does not have to increase, even though investment increases. This example can be interpreted as an inter-temporal trade, in which India imports present consumption (when it borrows to fund current expenditure) and exports future consumption (when it repays the loan).

Rearranging Equation 8, we can write

$$S_p = I + CA - S_g \tag{9}$$

Equation 9 states that an economy's private savings can be used in three ways: (1) investment in domestic capital (I), (2) purchases of assets from foreigners (CA), and (3) net purchases (or redemptions) of government debt ($-S_g$).

Finally, we can rearrange Equation 8 again to illustrate the macroeconomic sources of a current account imbalance:

$$CA = S_p + S_g - I \tag{10}$$

A current account deficit tends to result from low private savings, high private investment, a government deficit ($S_g < 0$), or a combination of the three. Alternatively, a current account surplus reflects high private savings, low private investment, or a government surplus.

As outlined above, trade deficits can result from a lack of private or government savings or booming investments. If trade deficits primarily reflect high private or government consumption (i.e., scarce savings = $S_p + S_g$), the deficit country's capacity to repay its liabilities from future production remains unchanged. If a trade deficit primarily reflects strong investments (*I*), however, the deficit country can increase its productive resources and its ability to repay its liabilities.

We can also see from Equation 3 that a current account deficit tends to reflect a strong domestic economy (elevated consumer, government, and investment spending), which is usually accompanied by elevated domestic credit demand and high interest rates. In such an environment, widening interest rate differentials vis-à-vis other countries can lead to growing net capital imports and produce an appreciating currency. In the long run, however, a persistent current account deficit leads to a permanent increase in the claims held by other countries against the deficit country. As a result, foreign investors may require rising risk premiums for such claims, a process that appears to lead to a depreciating currency.

EXAMPLE 11

The United Kingdom Budget

A financial newspaper had the following item:

> The UK's budget deficit is the highest in the G-20, in Europe, only Ireland borrows more. These are the stark facts facing Chancellor of the Exchequer George Osborne as he plans his first Budget tomorrow. He intends to tackle the problem even if that involves severe spending cuts and large tax increases.

> *Source: Financial Times*, 21 June 2010.

1 What are the likely consequences for the UK current account balance from the planned fiscal policy moves mentioned in the above article?

2 Describe the impact spending cuts and tax increases are likely to have on UK imports.

Solution to 1:

The combination of spending cuts and tax increases will, all else the same, lead to an improvement in the UK current account position.

Solution to 2:

UK imports are likely to be reduced by tax increases and spending cuts because government demand for foreign goods will fall and growth in private household income, which finances private imports, will be restricted as more household income goes to taxes.

EXAMPLE 12

Global Current Account Imbalances since 1996

As a result of growing financial integration and trade liberalization, the world economy has entered a period of rapid growth in cross-border trade since the late 1980s. In synch with surging international trade, current account imbalances widened substantially in the 1990s and the first decade of the new millennium. Exhibit 17 shows current account balances for 1996–2009 for four specific country groups—the United States, oil exporters, Germany and Japan (DEU + JPN), China and emerging Asia (CHN + EMA)—and two broad categories: the rest of the world (ROW) and other current account deficit countries (OCADC), which includes Central and Eastern European countries, Australia, New Zealand, and a wide range of smaller developed and emerging countries. The United States ran a current account deficit in every year, and in every year its deficit represented most of the aggregate value of such deficits worldwide. Only recently, in the wake of the 2007–2009 recession, has the US deficit declined both in absolute terms and relative to the global aggregate of current account deficits. In the first half of the 1990s, Germany and Japan were the traditional current account surplus countries, providing net exports of goods and services to and accumulating net claims against the United States. In the late 1990s, China and other emerging Asian nations and oil exporting nations became new and even more important surplus countries.

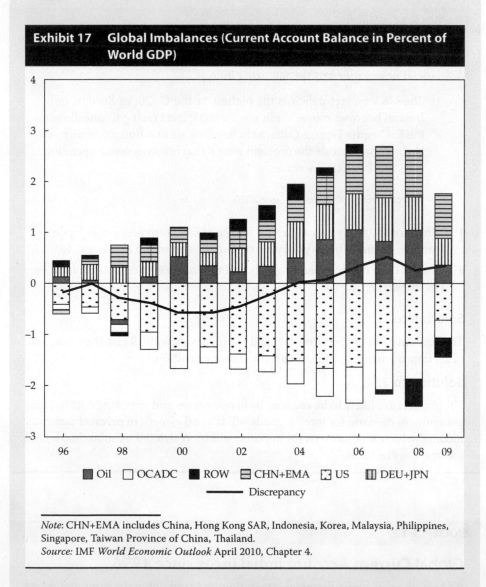

Exhibit 17   Global Imbalances (Current Account Balance in Percent of World GDP)

Note: CHN+EMA includes China, Hong Kong SAR, Indonesia, Korea, Malaysia, Philippines, Singapore, Taiwan Province of China, Thailand.
Source: IMF *World Economic Outlook* April 2010, Chapter 4.

As illustrated in Equation 10, current account deficits or surpluses reflect imbalances between national savings (including government savings) and investments. Current account deficits are often related to expansionary fiscal policy and government deficits. In the 1980s, for instance, the growing deficit in the US current account was widely seen as the consequence of tax cuts and rising defence spending adopted by the Reagan administration. Since the mid-1990s, however, the current account imbalances depicted in Exhibit 17 appear to reflect other, more complex factors. Exhibit 18 illustrates US net savings ($S-I$) for private domestic businesses, households, and the government (i.e., federal, state, and local) from 1996 to the second quarter of 2010. The exhibit indicates that business sector net savings and government net savings as a percentage of GDP have been near mirror-images since 1996. During the technology bubble businesses invested heavily and ran progressively larger savings deficits while the government moved to a surplus. After the bubble burst the pattern reversed with businesses moving to net positive savings and the government fiscal balance deteriorating sharply. Meanwhile, the household sector gradually reduced its savings rate. By 2006, each of the three sectors was dis-saving roughly 2 percent of US GDP. From that point, the public and private sectors diverged sharply. In the wake of the global financial crisis, households and businesses cut spending and increased savings sharply while the government deficit exploded to more than 12 percent of GDP.

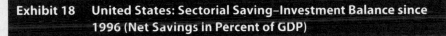

Exhibit 18   United States: Sectorial Saving–Investment Balance since 1996 (Net Savings in Percent of GDP)

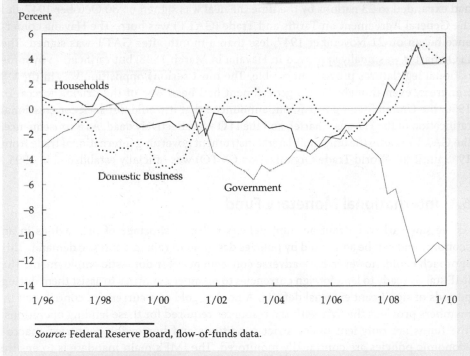

Source: Federal Reserve Board, flow-of-funds data.

TRADE ORGANIZATIONS

5

During the Great Depression in the 1930s, countries attempted to support their failing economies by sharply raising barriers to foreign trade, devaluing their currencies to compete against each other for export markets, and restricting their citizens' freedom to hold foreign exchange. These attempts proved to be self-defeating. World trade declined dramatically and employment and living standards fell sharply in many countries. By the 1940s, it had become a wide-spread conviction that the world economy was in need of organizations that would help promote international economic cooperation. In July 1944, during the United Nations Monetary and Financial Conference in Bretton Woods, New Hampshire, representatives of 45 governments agreed on a framework for international economic cooperation. Two crucial, multinational organizations emanated from this conference—the World Bank, which was founded during the conference, and the International Monetary Fund (IMF), which came into formal existence in December 1945. Although the IMF was founded with the goal to stabilize exchange rates and assist the reconstruction of the world's international payment system, the World Bank was created to facilitate post-war reconstruction and development.

A third institution, the International Trade Organization (ITO), was to be created to handle the trade side of international economic cooperation, joining the other two "Bretton Woods" institutions. The draft ITO charter was ambitious, extending beyond world trade regulations to include rules on employment, commodity agreements, restrictive business practices, international investment, and services. The objective was to create the ITO at a United Nations Conference on Trade and Employment in Havana, Cuba in 1947. Meanwhile, 15 countries had begun negotiations in December 1945 to reduce and regulate customs tariffs. With World War II only barely ended, they wanted to give an early boost to trade liberalization and begin to correct the legacy of protectionist measures that had remained in place since the early 1930s. The group had expanded to 23 nations by the time the deal was signed on 30 October 1947 and the General Agreement on Tariffs and Trade (GATT) was born. The Havana conference began on 21 November 1947, less than a month after GATT was signed. The ITO charter was finally approved in Havana in March 1948, but ratification in some national legislatures proved impossible. The most serious opposition was in the US Congress, even though the US government had been one of the driving forces. In 1950, the United States government announced that it would not seek congressional ratification of the Havana Charter, and the ITO was effectively dead. As a consequence, the GATT became the only multilateral instrument governing international trade from 1948 until the World Trade Organization (WTO) was officially established in 1995.

5.1 International Monetary Fund

As we saw earlier, current account deficits reflect a shortage of net savings in an economy and can be addressed by policies designed to rein in domestic demand. This approach could, however, have adverse consequences for domestic employment. The IMF stands ready to lend foreign currencies to member countries to assist them during periods of significant external deficits. A pool of gold and currencies contributed by members provides the IMF with the resources required for these lending operations. The funds are only lent under strict conditions and borrowing countries' macroeconomic policies are continually monitored. The IMF's main mandate is to ensure the stability of the international monetary system, the system of exchange rates and international payments that enables countries to buy goods and services from each other. More specifically, the IMF:

▪ provides a forum for cooperation on international monetary problems;

▪ facilitates the growth of international trade and promotes employment, economic growth, and poverty reduction;

- supports exchange rate stability and an open system of international payments; and

- lends foreign exchange to members when needed, on a temporary basis and under adequate safeguards, to help them address balance of payments problems.

The global financial crisis of 2007–2009 demonstrated that domestic and international financial stability cannot be taken for granted, even in the world's most developed countries. In light of these events, the IMF has redefined and deepened its operations by:[27]

- *enhancing its lending facilities*: The IMF has upgraded its lending facilities to better serve its members. As part of a wide-ranging reform of its lending practices, it has also redefined the way it engages with countries on issues related to structural reform of their economies. In this context, it has doubled member countries' access to fund resources and streamlined its lending approach to reduce the stigma of borrowing for countries in need of financial help.

- *improving the monitoring of global, regional, and country economies*: The IMF has taken several steps to improve economic and financial surveillance, which is its framework for providing advice to member countries on macroeconomic policies and warning member countries of risks and vulnerabilities in their economies.

- *helping resolve global economic imbalances*: The IMF's analysis of global economic developments provides finance ministers and central bank governors with a common framework for discussing the global economy.

- *analyzing capital market developments*: The IMF is devoting more resources to the analysis of global financial markets and their links with macroeconomic policy. It also offers training to country officials on how to manage their financial systems, monetary and exchange regimes, and capital markets.

- *assessing financial sector vulnerabilities*: Resilient, well-regulated financial systems are essential for macroeconomic stability in a world of ever-growing capital flows. The IMF and the World Bank jointly run an assessment program aimed at alerting countries to vulnerabilities and risks in their financial sectors.

From an investment perspective, the IMF helps to keep country-specific market risk and global systemic risk under control. The Greek sovereign debt crisis, which threatened to destabilize the entire European banking system, is a recent example. In early 2010, the Greek sovereign debt rating was downgraded to non-investment grade by leading rating agencies as a result of serious concerns about the sustainability of Greece's public sector debt load. Yields on Greek government bonds rose substantially following the downgrading and the country's ability to refinance its national debt was seriously questioned in international capital markets. Bonds issued by some other European governments fell and equity markets worldwide declined in response to spreading concerns of a Greek debt default. The downgrading of Greek sovereign debt was the ultimate consequence of persistent and growing budget deficits the Greek government had run before and after the country had joined the European Monetary Union (EMU) in 2001. Most of the budget shortfalls reflected elevated outlays for public-sector jobs, pensions, and other social benefits as well as persistent tax evasion. Reports that the Greek government had consistently and deliberately misreported the country's official economic and budget statistics contributed to further erosion of confidence in Greek government bonds in international financial markets. Facing default, the Greek government requested that a joint European Union/IMF bailout package be

---

27 Visit www.imf.org/ for more information.

activated, and a loan agreement was reached between Greece, the other EMU member countries, and the IMF. The deal consisted of an immediate EUR45 billion in loans to be provided in 2010, with more funds available later. A total of EUR110 billion was agreed depending on strict economic policy conditions that included cuts in wages and benefits, an increase in the retirement age for public-sector employees, limits on public pensions, increases in direct and indirect taxes, and a substantial reduction in state-owned companies. By providing conditional emergency lending facilities to the Greek government and designing a joint program with the European Union on how to achieve fiscal consolidation, the IMF prevented a contagious wave of sovereign debt crises in global capital markets.

Another example of IMF activities is the East Asian Financial Crisis in the late 1990s. It began in July 1997, when Thailand was forced to abandon its currency's peg with the US dollar. Currency devaluation subsequently hit other East Asian countries that had similar balance of payment problems, such as South Korea, Malaysia, the Philippines, and Indonesia. They had run persistent and increasing current account deficits, financed mainly with short-term capital imports, in particular, domestic banks borrowing in international financial markets. External financing was popular because of the combination of lower foreign, especially US, interest rates and fixed exchange rates. Easy money obtained from abroad led to imprudent investment, which contributed to overcapacities in several industries and inflated prices on real estate and stock markets. The IMF came to the rescue of the affected countries with considerable loans, accompanied by policies designed to control domestic demand, which included fiscal austerity and tightened monetary reins.

5.2 World Bank Group

The World Bank's main objective is to help developing countries fight poverty and enhance environmentally sound economic growth. For developing countries to grow and attract business, they have to

▪ strengthen their governments and educate their government officials;

▪ implement legal and judicial systems that encourage business;

▪ protect individual and property rights and honour contracts;

▪ develop financial systems robust enough to support endeavours ranging from micro credit to financing larger corporate ventures; and

▪ combat corruption.

Given these targets, the World Bank provides funds for a wide range of projects in developing countries worldwide and financial and technical expertise aimed at helping those countries reduce poverty.

The World Bank's two closely affiliated entities—the International Bank for Reconstruction and Development (IBRD) and the International Development Association (IDA)—provide low or no-interest loans and grants to countries that have unfavourable or no access to international credit markets. Unlike private financial institutions, neither the IBRD nor the IDA operates for profit. The IBRD is market-based, and uses its high credit rating to pass the low interest it pays for funds on to its borrowers—developing countries. It pays for its own operating costs because it does not look to outside sources to furnish funds for overhead.

IBRD lending to developing countries is primarily financed by selling AAA-rated bonds in the world's financial markets. Although the IBRD earns a small margin on this lending, the greater proportion of its income comes from lending out its own capital. This capital consists of reserves built up over the years and money paid in from the Bank's 185 member country shareholders. IBRD's income also pays for World Bank operating expenses and has contributed to IDA and debt relief. IDA is the world's largest source of interest-free loans and grant assistance to the poorest countries. IDA's funds are replenished every three years by 40 donor countries. Additional funds are regenerated through repayments of loan principal on 35-to-40-year, no-interest loans, which are then available for re-lending. At the end of September 2010, the IBRD had net loans outstanding of USD125.5 billion, while its borrowings amounted to USD132 billion.

Besides acting as a financier, the World Bank also provides analysis, advice, and information to its member countries to enable them to achieve the lasting economic and social improvements their people need. Another of the Bank's core functions is to increase the capabilities of its partners, people in developing countries, and its own staff. Links to a wide range of knowledge-sharing networks have been set up by the Bank to address the vast need for information and dialogue about development.

From an investment perspective, the World Bank helps to create the basic economic infrastructure that is essential for the creation of domestic financial markets and a well-functioning financial industry in developing countries. Moreover, the IBRD is one of the most important supranational borrowers in the international capital markets. Because of its strong capital position and its very conservative financial, liquidity, and lending policies, it enjoys the top investment-grade rating from the leading agencies and investors have confidence in its ability to withstand adverse events. As a result, IBRD bonds denominated in various major currencies are widely held by institutional and private investors.

5.3 World Trade Organization

The WTO provides the legal and institutional foundation of the multinational trading system. It is the only international organization that regulates cross-border trade relationships among nations on a global scale. It was founded on 1 January 1995, replacing the General Agreement on Tariffs and Trade (GATT) that had come into existence in 1947. The GATT was the only multilateral body governing international trade from 1947 to 1995. It operated for almost half a century as a quasi-institutionalized, provisional system of multilateral treaties. Several rounds of negotiations took place under the GATT, of which the Tokyo round and the Uruguay round may have been the most far reaching. The Tokyo round was the first major effort to address a wide range of non-tariff trade barriers, whereas the Uruguay round focused on the extension of the world trading system into several new areas, particularly trade in services and intellectual property, but also to reform trade in agricultural products and textiles. The GATT still exists in an updated 1994 version and is the WTO's principal treaty for trade in goods. The GATT and the General Agreement on Trade in Services (GATS) are the major agreements within the WTO's body of treaties that encompasses a total of about 60 agreements, annexes, decisions, and understandings.

In November 2001, the most recent and still ongoing round of negotiations was launched by the WTO in Doha, Qatar. The Doha round was an ambitious effort to enhance globalization by slashing barriers and subsidies in agriculture and addressing a wide range of cross-border services. So far, under GATS, which came into force in January 1995, banks, insurance companies, telecommunication firms, tour operators, hotel chains, and transport companies that want to do business abroad can enjoy the same principles of free and fair trade that had previously applied only to international trade in goods. No agreement has been reached in Doha so far, however, despite intense negotiations at several ministerial conferences and at other sessions. The start of the Doha round nevertheless marks one of the most crucial events in global trade over the past decade: China's accession to the WTO in December 2001.

The WTO's most important functions are the implementation, administration, and operation of individual agreements; acting as a platform for negotiations; and settling disputes. Moreover, the WTO has the mandate to review and propagate its members' trade policies and ensure the coherence and transparency of trade policies through surveillance in a global policy setting. The WTO also provides technical cooperation and training to developing, least-developed, and low-income countries to assist with their adjustment to WTO rules. In addition, the WTO is a major source of economic research and analysis, producing ongoing assessments of global trade in its publications and research reports on special topics. Finally, the WTO is in close cooperation with the other two Bretton Woods institutions, the IMF and the World Bank.

From an investment perspective, the WTO's framework of global trade rules provides the major institutional and regulatory base without which today's global multinational corporations would be hard to conceive. Modern financial markets would look different without the large, multinational companies whose stocks and bonds have become key elements in investment portfolios. In the equity universe, for instance, investment considerations focusing on global sectors rather than national markets would make little sense without a critical mass of multinational firms competing with each other in a globally defined business environment.

EXAMPLE 13

Function and Objective of International Organizations

On 10 May 2010, the Greek government officially applied for emergency lending facilities extended by the International Monetary Fund. It sent the following letter to Dominique Strauss-Kahn, the IMF's Managing Director:

Request for Stand-By Arrangement

This paper was prepared based on the information available at the time it was completed on Monday, May 10, 2010. The views expressed in this document are those of the staff team and do not necessarily reflect the views of the government of Greece or the Executive Board of the IMF. The policy of publication of staff reports and other documents by the IMF allows for the deletion of market-sensitive information.

Mr. Dominique Strauss-Kahn Athens, May 3, 2010
Managing Director
International Monetary Fund
Washington DC

Dear Mr. Strauss-Kahn:

The attached Memorandum of Economic and Financial Policies (MEFP)[28] outlines the economic and financial policies that the Greek government and the Bank of Greece, respectively, will implement during the remainder of 2010 and in the period 2011–2013 to strengthen market confidence and Greece's fiscal and financial position during a difficult transition period toward a more open and competitive economy. The government is fully committed to the policies stipulated in this document and its attachments, to frame tight budgets in the coming years with the aim to reduce the fiscal deficit to below 3 percent in 2014 and achieve a downward trajectory in the public debt-GDP ratio beginning in 2013, to safeguard the stability of the Greek financial system, and to implement structural reforms to boost competitiveness and the economy's capacity to

---

28 The detailed memorandum is available from www.imf.org/external/pubs/ft/scr/2010/cr10111.pdf.

produce, save, and export. (...) The government is strongly determined to lower the fiscal deficit, (...) by achieving higher and more equitable tax collections, and constraining spending in the government wage bill and entitlement outlays, among other items. In view of these efforts and to signal the commitment to effective macroeconomic policies, the Greek government requests that the Fund supports this multi-year program under a Stand-By Arrangement (SBA) for a period of 36 months in an amount equivalent to SDR26.4 billion.[29] (...) A parallel request for financial assistance to euro area countries for a total amount of €80 billion has been sent. The implementation of the program will be monitored through quantitative performance criteria and structural benchmarks as described in the attached MEFP and Technical Memorandum of Understanding (TMU). There will be twelve quarterly reviews of the program supported under the SBA by the Fund, (....) to begin with the first review that is expected to be completed in the course of the third calendar quarter of 2010, and then every quarter thereafter until the last quarterly review envisaged to be completed during the second calendar quarter of 2013, to assess progress in implementing the program and reach understandings on any additional measures that may be needed to achieve its objectives. (....) The Greek authorities believe that the policies set forth in the attached memorandum are adequate to achieve the objectives of the economic program, and stand ready to take any further measures that may become appropriate for this purpose. The authorities will consult with the Fund in accordance with its policies on such consultations, (....) and in advance of revisions to the policies contained in the MEFP. All information requested by the Fund (....) to assess implementation of the program will be provided. (....)

Sincerely,

George Papaconstantinou	George Provopoulos
Minister of Finance	Governor of the Bank of Greece

---

1. What is the objective of the IMF's emergency lending facilities?

2. What are the macroeconomic policy conditions under which the IMF provides emergency lending to Greece?

3. What is the amount Greece requests from the IMF as emergency funds?

Solution to 1:

The program seeks to safeguard the stability of the Greek financial system and to implement structural reforms to boost competitiveness and the economy's capacity to produce, save and export.

Solution to 2:

The Greek government has to reduce the country's fiscal deficit by achieving higher and more equitable tax collections as well as constrain spending in the government wage bill and entitlement outlays.

---

29 A SDR (special drawing right) is a basket of four leading currencies: Japanese yen (JPY), US dollar (USD), British pound (GBP), and euro (EUR). It consists of 18.4 yen, 0.6320 USD, 0.0903 GBP, and 0.41 EUR. One SDR was worth 1.4975 USD or 1.1547 EUR on 10 May 2010.

Solution to 3:

Greece applied for a standby arrangement in an amount equivalent to SDR26.4 billion (approximately USD39.5 billion, based on the 10 May 2010 exchange rate).

SUMMARY

This reading provides a framework for analyzing a country's trade and capital flows and their economic implications. It examines basic models that explain trade based on comparative advantage and provides a basis for understanding how international trade can affect the rate and composition of economic growth as well as the attractiveness of investment in various sectors.

- The benefits of trade include
  - gains from exchange and specialization;
  - gains from economies of scale as companies add new markets for their products;
  - greater variety of products available to households and firms; and
  - increased competition and more efficient allocation of resources.

- A country has an absolute advantage in producing a good (or service) if it is able to produce that good at a lower absolute cost or use fewer resources in its production than its trading partner. A country has a comparative advantage in producing a good if its *opportunity cost* of producing that good is less than that of its trading partner.

- Even if a country does not have an absolute advantage in the production of any good, it can gain from trade by producing and exporting the good(s) in which it has a comparative advantage and importing good(s) in which it has a comparative disadvantage.

- In the Ricardian model of trade, comparative advantage and the pattern of trade are determined by differences in technology between countries. In the Heckscher–Ohlin model of trade, comparative advantage and the pattern of trade are determined by differences in factor endowments between countries. In reality, technology and factor endowments are complementary, not mutually exclusive, determinants of trade patterns.

- Trade barriers prevent the free flow of goods and services among countries. Governments impose trade barriers for various reasons including: to promote specific developmental objectives, to counteract certain imperfections in the functioning of markets, or to respond to problems facing their economies.

- For purposes of international trade policy and analysis, a small country is defined as one that cannot affect the world price of traded goods. A large country's production and/or consumption decisions do alter the relative prices of trade goods.

- In a small country, trade barriers generate a net welfare loss arising from distortion of production and consumption decisions and the associated inefficient allocation of resources.

- Trade barriers can generate a net welfare gain in a large country if the gain from improving its terms of trade (higher export prices and lower import prices) more than offsets the loss from the distortion of resource allocations. However, the large country can only gain if it imposes an even larger welfare loss on its trading partner(s).

- An import tariff and an import quota have the same effect on price, production, and trade. With a quota, however, some or all of the revenue that would be raised by the equivalent tariff is instead captured by foreign producers (or the foreign government) as quota rents. Thus, the welfare loss suffered by the importing country is generally greater with a quota.

- A voluntary export restraint is imposed by the exporting country. It has the same impact on the importing country as an import quota from which foreigners capture all of the quota rents.

- An export subsidy encourages firms to export their product rather than sell it in the domestic market. The distortion of production, consumption, and trade decisions generates a welfare loss. The welfare loss is greater for a large country because increased production and export of the subsidized product reduces its global price—that is, worsens the country's terms of trade.

- Capital restrictions are defined as controls placed on foreigners' ability to own domestic assets and/or domestic residents' ability to own foreign assets. In contrast to trade restrictions, which limit the openness of goods markets, capital restrictions limit the openness of financial markets.

- A regional trading bloc is a group of countries who have signed an agreement to reduce and progressively eliminate barriers to trade and movement of factors of production among the members of the bloc.

  - They may or may not have common trade barriers against those countries that are not members of the bloc. In a free trade area all barriers to the flow of goods and services among members are eliminated, but each country maintains its own polices against non-members.

  - A customs union extends the FTA by not only allowing free movement of goods and services among members but also creating a common trade policy against non-members.

  - A common market incorporates all aspects of a customs union and extends it by allowing free movement of factors of production among members.

  - An economic union incorporates all aspects of a common market and requires common economic institutions and coordination of economic policies among members.

  - Members of a monetary union adopt a common currency.

- From an investment perspective, it is important to understand the complex and dynamic nature of trading relationships because they can help identify potential profitable investment opportunities as well as provide some advance warning signals regarding when to disinvest in a market or industry.

- The major components of the balance of payments are the
  - current account balance, which largely reflects trade in goods and services.
  - capital account balance, which mainly consists of capital transfers and net sales of non-produced, non-financial assets.
  - financial account, which measures net capital flows based on sales and purchases of domestic and foreign financial assets.

- Decisions by consumers, firms, and governments influence the balance of payments.

- Low private savings and/or high investment tend to produce a current account deficit that must be financed by net capital imports; high private savings and/or low investment, however, produce a current account surplus, balanced by net capital exports.

- All else the same, a government deficit produces a current account deficit and a government surplus leads to a current account surplus.

- All else the same, a sustained current account deficit contributes to a rise in the risk premium for financial assets of the deficit country. Current account surplus countries tend to enjoy lower risk premiums than current account deficit countries.

■ Created after WWII, the International Monetary Fund, the World Bank, and the World Trade Organization are the three major international organizations that provide necessary stability to the international monetary system and facilitate international trade and development.

- The IMF's mission is to ensure the stability of the international monetary system, the system of exchange rates and international payments that enables countries to buy goods and services from each other. The IMF helps to keep country-specific market risk and global systemic risk under control.

- The World Bank helps to create the basic economic infrastructure essential for creation and maintenance of domestic financial markets and a well-functioning financial industry in developing countries.

- The World Trade Organization's mission is to foster free trade by providing a major institutional and regulatory framework of global trade rules without which today's global multinational corporations would be hard to conceive.

REFERENCES

Appleyard, Dennis, Alfred Field, and Steven Cobb. 2010. *International Economics*. 7th ed. Boston: McGraw-Hill/Irwin.

Ariyoshi, Akira, Karl Habermeier, Bernard Laurens, Inci Otker-Robe, Jorge Iván Canales-Kriljenko, and Andrei Kirilenko. 2000. "Capital Controls: Country Experiences with Their Use and Liberalization." IMF Occasional Paper 190, Washington, DC (May 17).

Bernard, Andrew B., J. Bradford Jensen, Stephen J. Redding, and Peter K. Schott. 2010. "Intrafirm Trade and Product Contractibility." *American Economic Review*, vol. 100, no. 2 (May):444–448.

Bureau of Labor Statistics.Textile, Textile Product, and Apparel Manufacturing." In *Career Guide to Industries*: 2010–11 Edition.

Coe, David T., and Elhanan Helpman. 1995. "International R&D Spillovers." *European Economic Review*, vol. 39, no. 5 (May):859–887.

Collier, Paul, and Stephen A. O'Connell. 2007. "Opportunities and Choices." In *The Political Economy of Economic Growth in Africa, 1960–2000*, vol. 1. Edited by Benno J. Ndulu, Stephen A. O'Connell, Robert H. Bates, Paul Collier, and Charles C. Soludo. Cambridge, U.K.: Cambridge University Press.

Feenstra, Robert C., and Alan M. Taylor. 2008. *International Economics*. New York: Worth Publishers.

Gerber, James. 2010. *International Economics*. 5th ed. New York: Prentice Hall.

Hill, Charles W.L. 2007. *International Business: Competing in the Global Marketplace*. 6th ed. Boston: Irwin/McGraw-Hill.

IMF. 2008. *Globalization: A Brief Overview*. Issues Brief, International Monetary Fund (May).

IMF. 2010a. *Balance of Payments and International Investment Position Manual*. 6th ed. Washington, DC: International Monetary Fund.

IMF. 2010b. *World Economic Outlook*: April 2010. Washington, DC: International Monetary Fund.

IMF. 2011. "The IMF at a Glance." International Monetary Fund (February): www.imf.org/external/np/exr/facts/glance.htm.

Kawai, Masahiro, and Shinji Takagi. 2003. "Rethinking Capital Controls: The Malaysian Experience." PRI Discussion Paper Series No. 03A-05, Policy Research Institute, Ministry of Finance Japan, Tokyo (May).

Meier, Gerald M. 1998. *The International Environment of Business: Competition and Governance in the Global Economy*. New York: Oxford University Press.

Roberts, Mark, and Uwe Deichmann. 2008. "Regional Spillover Estimation." Background paper for the *World Development Report 2009: Reshaping Economic Geography*, World Bank.

Salvatore, Dominick. 2010. *Introduction to International Economics*. 2nd ed. Hoboken, NJ: John Wiley & Sons.

United Nations. 2002. *World Investment Report 2002: Transnational Corporations and Export Competitiveness*. New York: United Nations Conference on Trade and Development (UNCTAD).

World Bank. 2009. *World Development Report 2009: Reshaping Economic Geography*. Washington, DC: World Bank.

World Trade Organization. 2008. *World Trade Report 2008: Trade in a Globalizing World*. Geneva: World Trade Organization.

PRACTICE PROBLEMS

1   Which of the following statements *best* describes the benefits of international trade?

   A   Countries gain from exchange and specialization.

   B   Countries receive lower prices for their exports and pay higher prices for imports.

   C   Absolute advantage is required for a country to benefit from trade in the long term.

2   Which of the following statements *best* describes the costs of international trade?

   A   Countries without an absolute advantage in producing a good cannot benefit significantly from international trade.

   B   Resources may need to be allocated into or out of an industry and less-efficient companies may be forced to exit an industry, which in turn may lead to higher unemployment.

   C   Loss of manufacturing jobs in developed countries as a result of import competition means that developed countries benefit far less than developing countries from trade.

3   Suppose the cost of producing tea relative to copper is lower in Tealand than in Copperland. With trade, the copper industry in Copperland would *most likely*:

   A   expand.

   B   contract.

   C   remain stable.

4   A country has a comparative advantage in producing a good if:

   A   it is able to produce the good at a lower cost than its trading partner.

   B   its opportunity cost of producing the good is less than that of its trading partner.

   C   its opportunity cost of producing the good is more than that of its trading partner.

5   Suppose Mexico exports vegetables to Brazil and imports flashlights used for mining from Brazil. The output per worker per day in each country is as follows:

	Flashlights	Vegetables
Mexico	20	60
Brazil	40	80

   Which country has a comparative advantage in the production of vegetables and what is the *most* relevant opportunity cost?

   A   Brazil: 2 vegetables per flashlight.

   B   Mexico: 1.5 vegetables per flashlight.

   C   Mexico: ⅓ flashlight per vegetable.

6   Suppose three countries produce rulers and pencils with output per worker per day in each country as follows:

	Rulers	Pencils
Mexico	20	40
Brazil	30	90
China	40	160

Which country has the greatest comparative advantage in the production of rulers?

A China.

B Brazil.

C Mexico.

7 In the Ricardian trade model, comparative advantage is determined by:

A technology.

B the capital-to-labor ratio.

C the level of labor productivity.

8 In the Ricardian trade model, a country captures more of the gains from trade if:

A it produces all products while its trade partner specializes in one good.

B the terms of trade are closer to its autarkic prices than to its partner's autarkic prices.

C the terms of trade are closer to its partner's autarkic prices than to its autarkic prices.

9 Germany has much more capital per worker than Portugal. In autarky each country produces and consumes both machine tools and wine. Production of machine tools is relatively capital intensive whereas winemaking is labor intensive. According to the Heckscher–Ohlin model, when trade opens:

A Germany should export machine tools and Portugal should export wine.

B Germany should export wine and Portugal should export machine tools.

C Germany should produce only machine tools and Portugal should produce only wine.

10 According to the Heckscher–Ohlin model, when trade opens:

A the scarce factor gains relative to the abundant factor in each country.

B the abundant factor gains relative to the scarce factor in each country.

C income is redistributed between countries but not within each country.

11 Which type of trade restriction would *most likely* increase domestic government revenue?

A Tariff.

B Import quota.

C Export subsidy.

12 Which of the following trade restrictions is likely to result in the greatest welfare loss for the importing country?

A A tariff.

B An import quota.

C A voluntary export restraint.

13 A large country can:

A benefit by imposing a tariff.

B benefit with an export subsidy.

C not benefit from any trade restriction.

14 If Brazil and South Africa have free trade with each other, a common trade policy against all other countries, but no free movement of factors of production between them, then Brazil and South Africa are part of a:

A customs union.

B common market.

C free trade area (FTA).

15 Which of the following factors *best* explains why regional trading agreements are more popular than larger multilateral trade agreements?

A Minimal displacement costs.

B Trade diversions benefit members.

C Quicker and easier policy coordination.

16 The sale of mineral rights would be captured in which of the following balance of payments components?

A Capital account.

B Current account.

C Financial account.

17 Patent fees and legal services are recorded in which of the following balance of payments components?

A Capital account.

B Current account.

C Financial account.

18 During the most recent quarter, a steel company in South Korea had the following transactions

- Bought iron ore from Australia for AUD50 million.
- Sold finished steel to the United States for USD65 million.
- Borrowed AUD50 million from a bank in Sydney.
- Received a USD10 million dividend from US subsidiary.
- Paid KRW550 million to a Korean shipping company.

Which of the following would be reflected in South Korea's current account balance for the quarter?

A The loan.

B The shipping.

C The dividend.

19 Which of the following *most likely* contributes to a current account deficit?

A High taxes.

B Low private savings.

C Low private investment.

20 Which of the following chronic deficit conditions is *least* alarming to the deficit country's creditors?

A High consumption.

B High private investment.

C High government spending.

21 Which of the following international trade organizations regulates cross-border exchange among nations on a global scale?

A World Bank Group (World Bank).

B World Trade Organization (WTO).

C International Monetary Fund (IMF).

22 Which of the following international trade organizations has a mission to help developing countries fight poverty and enhance environmentally sound economic growth?

A World Bank Group (World Bank).

B World Trade Organization (WTO).

C International Monetary Fund (IMF).

23 Which of the following organizations helps to keep global systemic risk under control by preventing contagion in scenarios such as the 2010 Greek sovereign debt crisis?

A World Bank Group (World Bank).

B World Trade Organization (WTO).

C International Monetary Fund (IMF).

24 Which of the following international trade bodies was the only multilateral body governing international trade from 1948 to 1995?

A World Trade Organization (WTO).

B International Trade Organization (ITO).

C General Agreement on Tariffs and Trade (GATT).

SOLUTIONS

1   A is correct. Countries gain from exchange when trade enables each country to receive a higher price for exported goods and/or pay a lower price for imported goods. This leads to more efficient resource allocation and allows consumption of a larger variety of goods.

2   B is correct. Resources may need to be reallocated into or out of an industry, depending on whether that industry is an exporting sector or an import-competing sector of that economy. As a result of this adjustment process, less-efficient companies may be forced to exit the industry, which in turn may lead to higher unemployment and the need for retraining in order for displaced workers to find jobs in expanding industries.

3   A is correct. The copper industry in Copperland would benefit from trade. Because the cost of producing copper relative to producing tea is lower in Copperland than in Tealand, Copperland will export copper and the industry will expand.

4   B is correct. Comparative advantage is present when the opportunity cost of producing a good is less than that of a trading partner.

5   C is correct. While Brazil has an absolute advantage in the production of both flashlights and vegetables, Mexico has a comparative advantage in the production of vegetables. The opportunity cost of vegetables in Mexico is ⅓ per flashlight, while the opportunity cost of vegetables in Brazil is ½ per flashlight.

6   C is correct. Mexico has the lowest opportunity cost to produce an extra ruler. The opportunity cost is 2 pencils per ruler in Mexico, 3 pencils per ruler in Brazil, and 4 pencils per ruler in China.

7   A is correct. In the Ricardian model, comparative advantage is determined by technology differences between countries. Technology determines output per worker in each industry in each country. Differences in technology between countries cause output per worker in each industry to differ between countries. These ratios determine the pattern of comparative advantage.

8   C is correct. A country gains if trade increases the price of its exports relative to its imports as compared to its autarkic prices, i.e. the final terms of trade are more favorable than its autarkic prices. If the relative price of exports and imports remains the same after trade opens, then the country will consume the same basket of goods before and after trade opens, and it gains nothing from the ability to trade. In that case, its trade partner will capture all of the gains. Of course, the opposite is true if the roles are reversed. More generally, a country captures more of the gains from trade the more the final terms of trade differ from its autarkic prices.

9   A is correct. In the Heckscher–Ohlin model a country has a comparative advantage in goods whose production is intensive in the factor with which it is relatively abundantly endowed. In this case, capital is relatively abundant in Germany so Germany has a comparative advantage in producing the capital-intensive product: machine tools. Portugal is relatively labor abundant, hence should produce and export the labor-intensive product: wine.

10 B is correct. As a country opens up to trade, it has a favorable impact on the abundant factor, and a negative impact on the scarce factor. This is because trade causes the output mix to change and therefore changes the relative demand for the factors of production. Increased output of the export product increases demand for the factor that is used intensively in its production, while

reduced output of the import product decreases demand for the factor used intensively in its production. Because the export (import) product uses the abundant (scarce) factor intensively, the abundant factor gains relative to the scarce factor in each country.

11 A is correct. The imposition of a tariff will most likely increase domestic government revenue. A tariff is a tax on imports collected by the importing country's government.

12 C is correct. With a voluntary export restraint, the price increase induced by restricting the quantity of imports (= quota rent for equivalent quota = tariff revenue for equivalent tariff) accrues to foreign exporters and/or the foreign government.

13 A is correct. By definition, a large country is big enough to affect the world price of its imports and exports. A large country can benefit by imposing a tariff if its terms of trade improve by enough to outweigh the welfare loss arising from inefficient allocation of resources.

14 A is correct. A customs union extends a free trade area (FTA) by not only allowing free movement of goods and services among members, but also creating common trade policy against non-members. Unlike a more integrated common market, a customs union does not allow free movement of factors of production among members.

15 C is correct. Regional trading agreements are politically less contentious and quicker to establish than multilateral trade negotiations (for example, under the World Trade Organization). Policy coordination and harmonization is easier among a smaller group of countries.

16 A is correct. The capital account measures capital transfers and sale and purchase of non-produced, non-financial assets such as mineral rights and intangible assets.

17 B is correct. The current account measures the flows of goods and services (including income from foreign investments). Patent fees and legal services are both captured in the services sub-account of the current account.

18 C is correct. The current account includes income received on foreign investments. The Korean company effectively "exported" the use of its capital during the quarter to its US subsidiary, and the dividend represents payment for those services.

19 B is correct. A current account deficit tends to result from low private saving, high private investment, a government deficit, or a combination of the three. Of the choices, only low private savings contributes toward a current account deficit.

20 B is correct. A current account deficit tends to result from low private saving, high private investment, low government savings, or a combination of the three. Of these choices, only high investments can increase productive resources and improve future ability to repay creditors.

21 B is correct. The WTO provides the legal and institutional foundation of the multinational trading system and is the only international organization that regulates cross-border trade relations among nations on a global scale. The WTO's mission is to foster free trade by providing a major institutional and regulatory framework of global trade rules. Without such global trading rules, today's global transnational corporations would be hard to conceive.

22 A is correct. The World Bank's mission is to help developing countries fight poverty and enhance environmentally sound economic growth. The World Bank helps to create the basic economic infrastructure essential for creation and maintenance of domestic financial markets and a well-functioning financial industry in developing countries.

23 C is correct. From an investment perspective, the IMF helps to keep country-specific market risk and global systemic risk under control. The Greek sovereign debt crisis on 2010, which threatened to destabilize the entire European banking system, is a recent example. The IMF's mission is to ensure the stability of the international monetary system, the system of exchange rates and international payments which enables countries to buy goods and services from each other.

24 C is correct. The GATT was the only multilateral body governing international trade from 1948 to 1995. It operated for almost half a century as a quasi-institutionalized, provisional system of multilateral treaties and included several rounds of negotiations.

READING

21

Currency Exchange Rates

by William A. Barker, CFA, Paul D. McNelis, and Jerry Nickelsburg

William A. Barker, CFA (USA). Paul D. McNelis is at Fordham University (USA). Jerry Nickelsburg (USA).

LEARNING OUTCOMES

Mastery	The candidate should be able to:
☐	a. define an exchange rate and distinguish between nominal and real exchange rates and spot and forward exchange rates;
☐	b. describe functions of and participants in the foreign exchange market;
☐	c. calculate and interpret the percentage change in a currency relative to another currency;
☐	d. calculate and interpret currency cross-rates;
☐	e. convert forward quotations expressed on a points basis or in percentage terms into an outright forward quotation;
☐	f. explain the arbitrage relationship between spot rates, forward rates, and interest rates;
☐	g. calculate and interpret a forward discount or premium;
☐	h. calculate and interpret the forward rate consistent with the spot rate and the interest rate in each currency;
☐	i. describe exchange rate regimes;
☐	j. explain the effects of exchange rates on countries' international trade and capital flows.

INTRODUCTION

1

Measured by daily turnover, the foreign exchange (FX) market—the market in which currencies are traded against each other—is by far the world's largest market. Current estimates put daily turnover at approximately USD4 trillion for 2010. This is about 10 to 15 times larger than daily turnover in global fixed-income markets and about

50 times larger than global turnover in equities. Moreover, volumes in FX turnover continue to grow: Some predict that daily FX turnover will reach USD10 trillion by 2020 as market participation spreads and deepens.

The FX market is also a truly global market that operates 24 hours a day, each business day. It involves market participants from every time zone connected through electronic communications networks that link players as large as multibillion-dollar investment funds and as small as individuals trading for their own account—all brought together in real time. International trade would be impossible without the trade in currencies that facilitates it, and so too would cross-border capital flows that connect all financial markets globally through the FX market.

These factors make foreign exchange a key market for investors and market participants to understand. The world economy is increasingly transnational in nature, with both production processes and trade flows often determined more by global factors than by domestic considerations. Likewise, investment portfolio performance increasingly reflects global determinants because pricing in financial markets responds to the array of investment opportunities available worldwide, not just locally. All of these factors funnel through, and are reflected in, the foreign exchange market. As investors shed their "home bias" and invest in foreign markets, the exchange rate—the price at which foreign-currency-denominated investments are valued in terms of the domestic currency—becomes an increasingly important determinant of portfolio performance.

Even investors adhering to a purely "domestic" portfolio mandate are increasingly affected by what happens in the foreign exchange market. Given the globalization of the world economy, most large companies depend heavily on their foreign operations (for example, by some estimates about 40 percent of S&P 500 Index earnings are from outside the United States). Almost all companies are exposed to some degree of foreign competition, and the pricing for domestic assets—equities, bonds, real estate, and others—will also depend on demand from foreign investors. All of these various influences on investment performance reflect developments in the foreign exchange market.

This reading introduces the foreign exchange market, providing the basic concepts and terminology necessary to understand exchange rates as well as some of the basics of exchange rate economics.

The reading is divided up as follows. Section 2 describes the organization of the foreign exchange market and discusses the major players—who they are, how they conduct their business, and how they respond to exchange rate changes. Section 3 takes up the mechanics of exchange rates: definitions, quotes, and calculations. This section shows that the reader has to pay close attention to conventions used in various foreign exchange markets around the world because they can vary widely. Sometimes exchange rates are quoted in the number of domestic currency units per unit of foreign currency, and sometimes they are quoted in the opposite way. The exact notation used to represent exchange rates can vary widely as well, and occasionally the same exchange rate notation will be used by different sources to mean completely different things. The notation used here may not be the same as that encountered elsewhere. Therefore, the focus should be on understanding the underlying concepts rather than relying on rote memorization of formulas. We also show how to calculate cross-exchange rates and how to compute the forward exchange rate given either the forward points or the percentage forward premium or discount. In Section 4, we discuss alternative exchange rate regimes operating throughout the world. Finally, in Section 5, we discuss how exchange rates affect a country's international trade (exports and imports) and capital flows. A summary and practice problems conclude the reading.

THE FOREIGN EXCHANGE MARKET

To understand the FX market, it is necessary to become familiar with some of its basic conventions. Individual currencies are often referred to by standardized three-letter codes that the market has agreed upon through the International Organization for Standardization (ISO). Exhibit 1 lists some of the major global currencies and their identification codes.

Exhibit 1   Standard Currency Codes

Three-Letter Currency Code	Currency
USD	US dollar
EUR	Euro
JPY	Japanese yen
GBP	British pound
CHF	Swiss franc
CAD	Canadian dollar
AUD	Australian dollar
NZD	New Zealand dollar
ZAR	South African rand
SEK	Swedish krona
NOK	Norwegian krone
BRL	Brazilian real
SGD	Singapore dollar
MXN	Mexican peso
CNY	Chinese yuan
HKD	Hong Kong dollar
INR	Indian rupee
KRW	South Korean won
RUB	Russian ruble

It is important to understand that there is a difference between referring to an *individual currency* and an *exchange rate*. One can hold an individual currency (for example, in a EUR100 million deposit), but an exchange rate refers to the price of one currency in terms of another (for example, the exchange rate between the EUR and USD). An individual currency can be singular, but there are always two currencies involved in an exchange rate: the price of one currency relative to another. The exchange rate is the number of units of one currency (called the *price currency*) that one unit of another currency (called the *base currency*) will buy. An equivalent way of describing the exchange rate is as the cost of one unit of the base currency in terms of the price currency.

This distinction between individual currencies and exchange rates is important because, as we will see in a later section, these three-letter currency codes can be used both ways. (For example, when used as an exchange rate in the professional FX market, EUR is understood to be the exchange rate between the euro and US dollar). But be aware of the context (either as a currency or as an exchange rate) in which these three-letter currency codes are being used. To avoid confusion, this reading will identify exchange rates using the convention of "A/B," referring to the number of units of currency A that one unit of currency B will buy. For example, a USD/EUR exchange rate of 1.2875 means that 1 euro will buy 1.2875 US dollars (i.e., 1 euro costs 1.2875 US dollars).[1] In this case, the euro is the base currency and the US dollar is the price currency. A decrease in this exchange rate would mean that the euro costs less or that fewer US dollars are needed to buy one euro. In other words, a decline in this exchange rate indicates that the USD is *appreciating* against the EUR or, equivalently, the EUR is *depreciating* against the USD.

The exchange rates described above are referred to as *nominal* exchange rates. This is to distinguish them from *real* exchange rates, which are indices often constructed by economists and other market analysts to assess changes in the relative purchasing power of one currency compared with another. Creating these indices requires adjusting the nominal exchange rate by using the price levels in each country of the currency pair (hence the name "real exchange rates") in order to compare the relative purchasing power between countries.

In a world of homogenous goods and services and with no market frictions or trade barriers, the relative purchasing power across countries would tend to equalize: Why would you pay more, in real terms, domestically for a "widget" if you could import an identical "widget" from overseas at a cheaper price? This basic concept is the intuition behind a theory known as "purchasing power parity" (PPP), which describes the long-term equilibrium of nominal exchange rates. PPP asserts that nominal exchange rates adjust so that identical goods (or baskets of goods) will have the same price in different markets. Or, put differently, the purchasing power of different currencies is equalized for a standardized basket of goods.

In practice, the conditions required to enforce PPP are not satisfied: Goods and services are not identical across countries; countries typically have different baskets of goods and services produced and consumed; many goods and services are not traded internationally; there are trade barriers and transaction costs (e.g., shipping costs and import taxes); and capital flows are at least as important as trade flows in determining nominal exchange rates. As a result, nominal exchange rates exhibit persistent deviations from PPP. Moreover, relative purchasing power among countries displays a weak, if any, tendency toward long-term equalization. A simple example of a cross-country comparison of the purchasing power of a standardized good is the "Big Mac" index produced by the *Economist*, which shows the relative price of this standardized hamburger in different countries. The Big Mac index shows that fast-food hamburger prices can vary widely internationally and that this difference in purchasing power is typical of most goods and services. Hence, movements in real exchange rates provide meaningful information about changes in relative purchasing power among countries.

Consider the case of an individual who wants to purchase goods from a foreign country. The individual would be able to buy fewer of these goods if the nominal spot exchange rate for the foreign currency appreciated or if the foreign price level increased. Conversely, the individual could buy more foreign goods if the individual's domestic income increased. (For this example, we will assume that changes in the individual's income are proportional to changes in the domestic price level.) Hence, in *real* purchasing power terms, the real exchange rate that an individual faces is an increasing function of the nominal exchange rate (quoted in terms of the number of units of domestic currency per one unit of foreign currency) and the foreign price level and a decreasing function of the domestic price level. The *higher* the real exchange

---

1 This convention is consistent with the meaning of "/" in mathematics and the straightforward interpretation of "A/B" as "A per B" is helpful in understanding exchange rates as the price of one currency in terms of another. Nevertheless, other notation conventions exist. "B/A" and "B:A" are sometimes used to denote what this reading denotes as "A/B." Careful attention to the context will usually make the convention clear.

rate that this individual faces, the *fewer* foreign goods, in real terms, the individual can purchase and the *lower* that individual's relative purchasing power compared with the other country.

An equivalent way of viewing the real exchange rate is that it represents the relative price levels in the domestic and foreign countries. Mathematically, we can represent the foreign price level in terms of the domestic currency as:

Foreign price level in domestic currency = $S_{d/f} \times P_f$

where $S_{d/f}$ is the spot exchange rate (quoted in terms of the number of units of domestic currency per one unit of foreign currency) and P_f is foreign price level quoted in terms of the foreign currency. We can define the domestic price level, in terms of the domestic currency, as P_d. Hence, the ratio between the foreign and domestic price levels is:

Real exchange rate$_{(d/f)}$ = $(S_{d/f} \times P_f)/P_d = S_{d/f} \times (P_f/P_d)$

For example, for a British consumer wanting to buy goods made in the Eurozone, the real exchange rate (defined in GBP/EUR terms; note that the domestic currency for the United Kingdom is the price currency, not the base currency) will be an increasing function of the nominal spot exchange rate (GBP/EUR) and the Eurozone price level and a decreasing function of the UK price level. This is written as:

$$\text{Real exchange rate}_{\frac{GBP}{EUR}} = S_{\frac{GBP}{EUR}} \times \left(\frac{CPI_{eur}}{CPI_{UK}} \right)$$

Let's examine the effect of movements in the domestic and foreign price levels, and the nominal spot exchange rate, on the real purchasing power of an individual in the United Kingdom wanting to purchase Eurozone goods. Assume that the nominal spot exchange rate (GBP/EUR) increases by 10 percent, the Eurozone price level by 5 percent, and the UK price level by 2 percent. The change in the real exchange rate is then:

$$\left(1 + \frac{\Delta S_{\frac{d}{f}}}{S_{\frac{d}{f}}} \right) \times \frac{\left(1 + \frac{\Delta P_f}{P_f} \right)}{\left(1 + \frac{\Delta P_d}{P_d} \right)} - 1 = (1 + 10\%) \times \frac{1 + 5\%}{1 + 2\%} - 1 \approx 10\% + 5\% - 2\% \approx 13\%$$

In this case, the real exchange rate for the UK-based individual has *increased* about 13 percent, meaning that it now costs *more*, in real terms, to buy Eurozone goods. Or put differently, the UK individual's real purchasing power relative to Eurozone goods has *declined* by about 13 percent. An easy way to remember this relationship is to consider the real exchange rate (stated with the domestic currency as the price currency) as representing the real price you face in order to purchase foreign goods and services: The *higher* the price (real exchange rate), the *lower* your relative purchasing power.

The real exchange rate for a currency can be constructed for the domestic currency relative to a single foreign currency or relative to a basket of foreign currencies. In either case, these real exchange rate indices depend on the assumptions made by the analyst creating them. Several investment banks and central banks create proprietary measures of real exchange rates. It is important to note that real exchange rates are *not* quoted or traded in global FX markets: They are only indices created by analysts to understand the international competitiveness of an economy and the real purchasing power of a currency.

In this context, real exchange rates can be useful for understanding trends in international trade and capital flows and hence can be seen as one of the influences on nominal spot exchange rates. As an example, consider the exchange rate between the Chinese yuan and the US dollar. During 2010, the nominal yuan exchange rate against the US dollar (CNY/USD) declined by approximately 3 percent—meaning that the US dollar depreciated against the yuan. However, the annual inflation rates in the United States and China were different during 2010—approximately 1.5 percent for the United States and 4.5 percent for China. This means that the real exchange rate (in CNY/USD terms) was depreciating more rapidly than the nominal CNY/USD exchange rate:

$$\left(1 + \%\Delta S_{\frac{CNY}{USD}}\right) \times \frac{\left(1 + \%\Delta P_{US}\right)}{\left(1 + \%\Delta P_{China}\right)} - 1 \approx -3\% + 1.5\% - 4.5\% \approx -6\%$$

This combination of a stronger yuan and a higher Chinese inflation rate meant that the real exchange rate faced by China was declining, thus increasing Chinese purchasing power in USD terms.

Movements in real exchange rates can have a similar effect as movements in nominal exchange rates in terms of affecting relative prices and hence trade flows. Even if the nominal spot exchange rate does not move, differences in inflation rates between countries affect their relative competitiveness.

Although real exchange rates can exert some influence on nominal exchange rate movements, they are only one of many factors; it can be difficult to disentangle all of these inter-relationships in a complex and dynamic FX market. As discussed earlier, PPP is a poor guide to predicting future movements in nominal exchange rates because these rates can deviate from PPP equilibrium—and even continue to trend away from their PPP level—for years at a time. Hence, it should not be surprising that real exchange rates, which reflect changes in relative purchasing power, have a poor track record as a predictor of future nominal exchange rate movements.

EXAMPLE 1

Nominal and Real Exchange Rates

An investment adviser located in Sydney, Australia, is meeting with a local client who is looking to diversify her domestic bond portfolio by adding investments in fixed-rate, long-term bonds denominated in HKD. The client frequently visits Hong Kong, and many of her annual expenses are denominated in HKD. The client, however, is concerned about the foreign currency risks of offshore investments and whether the investment return on her HKD-denominated investments will maintain her purchasing power—both domestically (i.e., for her AUD-denominated expenses) and in terms of her foreign trips (i.e., denominated in HKD, for her visits to Hong Kong). The investment adviser explains the effect of changes in nominal and real exchange rates to the client and illustrates this explanation by making the following statements:

Statement 1   All else equal, an increase in the nominal AUD/HKD exchange rate will lead to an increase in the AUD-denominated value of your foreign investment.

Statement 2   All else equal, an increase in the nominal AUD/HKD exchange rate means that your relative purchasing power for your Hong Kong trips will increase (based on paying for your trip with the income from your HKD-denominated bonds).

Statement 3   All else equal, an increase in the Australian inflation rate will lead to an increase in the real exchange rate (AUD/HKD). A higher real exchange rate means that the relative purchasing power of your AUD-denominated income is higher.

> Statement 4   All else equal, a decrease in the nominal exchange rate (AUD/HKD) will decrease the real exchange rate (AUD/HKD) and increase the relative purchasing power of your AUD-denominated income.

To demonstrate the effects of the changes in inflation and nominal exchange rates on relative purchasing power, the adviser uses the following scenario: "Suppose that the AUD/HKD exchange rate increases by 5 percent, the price of goods and services in Hong Kong goes up by 5 percent, and the price of Australian goods and services goes up by 2 percent."

1   Statement 1 is:

A   correct.

B   incorrect, because based on the quote convention the investment's value would be decreasing in AUD terms.

C   incorrect, because the nominal AUD value of the foreign investments will depend on movements in the Australian inflation rate.

2   Statement 2 is:

A   correct.

B   incorrect, because purchasing power is not affected in this case.

C   incorrect, because based on the quote convention, the client's relative purchasing power would be decreasing.

3   Statement 3 is:

A   correct.

B   incorrect with respect to the real exchange rate only.

C   incorrect with respect to both the real exchange rate and the purchasing power of AUD-denominated income.

4   Statement 4 is:

A   correct.

B   incorrect with respect to the real exchange rate.

C   incorrect with respect to the purchasing power of AUD-denominated income.

5   Based on the adviser's scenario and assuming that the HKD value of the HKD bonds remained unchanged, the nominal AUD value of the client's HKD investments would:

A   decrease by about 5 percent.

B   increase by about 5 percent.

C   remain approximately the same.

6   Based on the adviser's scenario, the change in the relative purchasing power of the client's AUD-denominated income is *closest* to:

A   −8 percent.

B   +8 percent.

C   +12 percent.

Solution to 1:

A is correct. Given the quoting convention, an increase in the AUD/HKD rate means that the base currency (HKD) is appreciating (one HKD will buy more AUD). This is increasing the nominal value of the HKD-denominated investments when measured in AUD terms.

Solution to 2:

B is correct. When paying for HKD-denominated expenses with HKD-denominated income, the value of the AUD/HKD spot exchange rate (or any other spot exchange rate) would not be relevant. In fact, this is a basic principle of currency risk management: reducing FX risk exposures by denominating assets and liabilities (or income and expenses) in the same currency.

Solution to 3:

C is correct. An increase in the Australian (i.e., domestic) inflation rate means that the real exchange rate (measured in domestic/foreign, or AUD/HKD, terms) would be decreasing, not increasing. Moreover, an increase in the real exchange rate ($R_{AUD/HKD}$) would be equivalent to a reduction of the purchasing power of the Australian client: Goods and services denominated in HKD would cost more.

Solution to 4:

A is correct. As the spot AUD/HKD exchange rate decreases, the HKD is depreciating against the AUD; or equivalently, the AUD is appreciating against the HKD. This is reducing the real exchange rate ($R_{AUD/HKD}$) and increasing the Australian client's purchasing power.

Solution to 5:

B is correct. As the AUD/HKD spot exchange rate increases by 5 percent, the HKD is appreciating against the AUD by 5 percent and, all else equal, the value of the HKD-denominated investment is increasing by 5 percent in AUD terms.

Solution to 6:

A is correct. The real exchange rate ($R_{AUD/HKD}$) is expressed as:

$$R_{\frac{AUD}{HKD}} = S_{\frac{AUD}{HKD}} \times \frac{P_{HKD}}{P_{AUD}}$$

The information in the adviser's scenario can be expressed as:

$$\%\Delta R_{\frac{AUD}{HKD}} \approx \%\Delta S_{\frac{AUD}{HKD}} + \%\Delta P_{HKD} - \%\Delta P_{AUD} \approx +5\% + 5\% - 2\% \approx +8\%$$

Because the real exchange rate (expressed in AUD/HKD terms) has gone up by about 8 percent, the real purchasing power of the investor based in Australia has declined by about 8 percent. This can be seen from the fact that HKD has appreciated against the AUD in nominal terms, and the Hong Kong price level has also increased. This increase in the cost of Hong Kong goods and services (measured in AUD) is only partially offset by the small (2 percent) increase in the investor's income (assumed equal to the change in the Australian price level).

2.1 Market Functions

FX markets facilitate international trade in goods and services, where companies and individuals need to make transactions in foreign currencies. This would cover everything from companies and governments buying and selling products in other countries, to tourists engaged in cross-border travel (for example, a German tourist selling euros and buying sterling for a visit to London). Although this is an important dimension of FX markets, and despite the growth of global trade in recent years, an even larger proportion of the daily turnover in FX markets is accounted for by capital market transactions, where investors convert between currencies for the purpose of moving funds into (or out of) foreign assets. These types of transactions cover the range from direct investments (for example, companies buying such fixed assets as factories) in other countries to portfolio investments (the purchase of stocks, bonds, and other financial assets denominated in foreign currencies). Because capital is extremely mobile in modern financial markets, this ebb and flow of money across international borders and currencies generates a huge and growing volume of FX transactions.

Regardless of the underlying motivation for the FX transaction, it will eventually require that one currency be exchanged for another in the FX market. In advance of that required transaction, market participants are exposed to the risk that the exchange rate will move against them. Often they will try to reduce (hedge) this risk through a variety of FX instruments (described in more detail later). Conversely, market participants may form opinions about future FX movements and undertake speculative FX risk exposures through a variety of FX instruments in order to profit from their views.

The distinction between hedging and speculative positions is not always clear cut. For example, consider the case of a corporation selling its products overseas. This creates an FX risk exposure because the revenue from foreign sales will ultimately need to be converted into the corporation's home currency. This risk exposure is typically hedged, and corporate hedging often accounts for large FX flows passing through the market. The amount and timing of foreign revenue, however, are generally hard to predict with precision: They will depend on the pace of foreign sales, the sales prices realized, the pace at which foreign clients pay for their purchases, and so forth. In the face of this uncertainty, the corporate treasury will estimate the timing and amount of foreign revenue and will then hedge a portion of this estimated amount. Many corporate treasuries have hedging targets based on this estimate, but they also have the flexibility to under-hedge or over-hedge based on their opinions about future FX rate movements. In order to judge the effectiveness of these discretionary trades, the performance of the corporate treasury is compared with a benchmark, usually stated in terms of a fixed amount hedged relative to total sales. (For example, the benchmark may be a 100 percent fully hedged position. The profitability of the hedge actually implemented—which, based on the treasury's discretion, can vary above or below 100 percent—is then compared with what would have been achieved with a passive, 100 percent fully hedged position.) Treasury managers' performance is judged based on gains or losses relative to the benchmark, just as an investment fund manager's performance is benchmarked against performance targets.

At the other end of the spectrum between hedging and speculation, consider the archetypical speculative account: a hedge fund. Although it is true that hedge funds will seek out, accept, and manage risk for profit, a hedge fund is, after all, a hedge fund: Strict risk control procedures are critical to the fund's success, especially when leverage is involved. This mixture of speculative and hedging motives is common throughout the FX space as market participants shape their FX exposures to suit their market forecasts, operational mandates, and appetites for risk.

The FX market provides a variety of products that provide the flexibility to meet this varied and complex set of financial goals. *Spot* transactions involve the exchange of currencies for immediate delivery. For most currencies, this corresponds to "T + 2" delivery, meaning that the exchange of currencies is settled two business days after the trade is agreed to by the two sides of the deal. (One exception is the Canadian dollar, for which spot settlement against the US dollar is on a T + 1 basis.) The exchange rate used for these spot transactions is referred to as the spot exchange rate, and it is the exchange rate that most people refer to in their daily lives (for example, this is the exchange rate usually quoted by the financial press, on the evening news, and so forth).

It is important to realize, however, that spot transactions make up only a minority of total daily turnover in the global FX market: The rest is accounted for by trade in outright forward contracts, FX swaps, and FX options. Although these products will be covered in more depth in a subsequent section, and at Level II of the CFA curriculum, we will provide a brief introduction to these products here.

Outright *forward contracts* (often referred to simply as forwards) are agreements to deliver foreign exchange at a future date at an exchange rate agreed upon today. For example, suppose that a UK-based company expects to receive a payment of 100 million euros in 85 days. Although it could convert these euros to British pounds with a spot transaction (the spot rate would be the GBP/EUR rate in 83 days, because of T + 2 settlement), this future spot rate is currently unknown and represents a foreign exchange risk to the company. The company can avoid this risk by entering into a transaction with a foreign exchange dealer to sell 100 million euros against the British pound for settlement 85 days from today at a rate—the forward exchange rate—agreed upon today.

As such, forward contracts are any exchange rate transactions that occur with currency settlement longer than the usual T + 2 settlement for spot delivery. Each of these contracts requires two specifications: the date at which the currencies are to be exchanged and the exchange rate to be applied on the settlement date. Accordingly, exchange rates for these transactions are called *forward exchange rates* to distinguish them from spot rates.

Dealers will typically quote forward rates for a variety of standard forward settlement dates (for example, one week, one month, or 90 days) on their dealing screens. In an over-the-counter (OTC) market, however, traders can arrange forward settlement at *any* future date they agree upon, with the forward exchange rate scaled appropriately for the specific term to settlement. Standard forward settlement dates (such as three months) are defined in terms of the spot settlement date, which is generally T + 2. For example, if today is 18 October and spot settlement is for 20 October, then a three-month forward settlement would be defined as 20 January of the following year. Note as well that these standard forward settlement dates may not always be good business days: 20 January could be a weekend or a holiday. In that case, the forward settlement date is set to the closest good business day. Traders always confirm the exact forward settlement date when making these types of trades, and the forward rate is scaled by the exact number of days to settlement.

In an OTC market, the size of the forward contracts can also be any size that the two counterparties agree upon. In general, however, liquidity in forward markets declines the longer the term to maturity and the larger the trade size. The concept of the forward exchange rate and exchange hedging is developed further in Section 3.

Although the OTC market accounts for the majority of foreign exchange trades with future (i.e., greater than T + 2) settlement dates, there is also a deep, liquid market in exchange-traded *futures* contracts for currencies. Although there are technical differences between futures and forward contracts, the basic concept is the same: The price is set today for settlement on a specified future date. Futures contracts on currencies trade on several exchanges globally, but the majority of volume in exchange-traded currency futures contracts is found on the International Monetary Market (IMM) division of the Chicago Mercantile Exchange (CME). Futures contracts differ from OTC forward contracts in several important ways: They trade on exchanges (such as the CME) rather than OTC; they are only available for fixed contract amounts and fixed settlement dates; the exchanges demand that a fixed amount of collateral be posted against the futures contract trade; and this collateral is marked-to-market daily, with counterparties asked to post further collateral if their positions generate losses. On balance, futures contracts are somewhat less flexible than forward contracts. Nonetheless, they provide deep, liquid markets for deferred delivery with a minimum of counterparty (i.e., default) risk—a proposition that many FX traders find attractive. Accordingly, daily turnover in FX futures contracts is huge. As of 2010, the average daily trading volume of FX futures on the CME alone was estimated to be about USD140 billion, which is almost comparable in size to the interbank volume of spot transactions.

Because forward contracts eventually expire, existing speculative positions or FX hedges that need to be extended must be rolled prior to their settlement dates. This typically involves a spot transaction to offset (settle) the expiring forward contract and a new forward contract to be set at a new, more distant settlement date. The combination of an offsetting spot transaction and a new forward contract is referred to as an **FX swap**.[2]

An FX swap is best illustrated by an example. Suppose that a trader sells 100 million euros with settlement 95 days from today at a forward exchange rate (USD/EUR) of 1.2500. In 93 days, the forward contract is two days from settlement, specifically the T + 2 days to spot settlement. To roll the forward contract, the trader will engage in the following FX swap. First, the trader will need to buy 100 million euros spot, for which T + 2 settlement will fall on day 95, the same day as the settlement of the expiring forward contract. The purchase of the 100 million euros spot will be used to satisfy the delivery of the 100 million euros sold in the expiring forward contract. Because 100 million euros are being both bought and sold on day 95, there is no exchange of euros between counterparties on that day: The amounts net to zero. However, there will be an exchange of US dollars, reflecting the movement in exchange rates between the date the forward contract was agreed to (day 0) and day 93. Suppose that on day 93 the spot exchange rate for USD/EUR is 1.2400. This means that the trader will see a cash flow on day 95 of USD1,000,000. This is calculated as follows:

$$EUR100,000,000 \times (1.2500 - 1.2400) = USD1,000,000$$

The trader receives USD1,000,000 from the counterparty because the euro was *sold* forward to day 95 at a price of 1.2500; it was *bought* (on day 93) for spot settlement on day 95 at a price of 1.2400. This *price* movement in the euro indicates a profit to the trader, but because the euro *quantities* exchanged on day 95 net to zero (100,000,000 euros both bought and sold), this cash flow is realized in US dollars. The second leg of the FX swap is then to initiate a new forward sale of 100 million euros at the USD/EUR forward exchange rate being quoted on day 93. This renews the forward position (a forward sale of the euro) to a new date.

FX swaps will be dealt with in more detail at Level II in the curriculum. For the purposes of this reading, it is only necessary to understand that (1) an FX swap consists of a simultaneous spot and forward transaction; (2) these swap transactions can extend (roll) an existing forward position to a new future date; and (3) rolling the position forward leads to a cash flow on settlement day. This cash flow can be thought of as a mark-to-market on the forward position. FX swaps are a large component of daily FX market turnover because market participants have to roll over existing speculative or hedging positions as the underlying forward contracts mature in order to extend the hedge or speculative position (otherwise, the position is closed out on the forward settlement date).

One other area where FX swaps are used in FX markets also bears mentioning: They are often used by market participants as a funding source (called swap funding). Consider the case of a UK-based firm that needs to borrow GBP100 million for 90 days, starting 2 days from today. One way to do this is simply to borrow 90-day money in GBP-denominated funds starting at T + 2. An alternative is to borrow in US dollars and exchange these for British pounds in the spot FX market (both with T + 2 settlement) and then sell British pounds 90 days forward against the US dollar. (Recall that the maturity of a forward rate contract is defined in terms of the spot settlement date, so the 90-day forward rate would be for settlement in 92 days from today.) The company has the use of GBP100 million for 90 days, starting on T + 2, and at the end of this

---

2 Note that an "FX swap" is not the same as a "currency swap." An FX swap is simply the combination of a spot and a forward FX transaction (i.e., only two settlement dates—spot and forward—are involved). A currency swap is generally used for multiple periods and payments.

period can pay off the US dollar loan at a known, pre-determined exchange rate (the 90-day forward rate). By engaging in simultaneous spot and forward transactions (i.e., an FX swap), the company has eliminated any FX risk from the foreign borrowing. The all-in financing rate using an FX swap will typically be close to that of domestic borrowing, usually within a few basis points. This near equivalence is enforced by an arbitrage relationship that will be described in Section 3.3. On large borrowing amounts, however, even a small differential can add up to substantial cost savings.

Another way to hedge FX exposures, or implement speculative FX positions, is to use options on currencies. FX options are contracts that, for an upfront premium or fee, give the purchaser the right, but not the obligation, to make an FX transaction at some future date at an exchange rate agreed upon today (when the contract is agreed to). The holder of an FX option will exercise the option only if it is advantageous to do so—that is, if the agreed upon exchange rate for the FX option contract is better than the FX rate available in the market at option expiry. As such, options are extremely flexible tools for managing FX exposures and account for a large percentage of daily turnover in the FX market.

Another concept to bear in mind is that spot, forward, swap, and option products are typically not used in isolation. Most major market participants manage their FX transactions and FX risk exposures through concurrent spot, forward, swap, and option positions. Taken together, these instruments (the building blocks of the FX market) provide an extremely flexible way for market participants to shape their FX risk exposures to match their operational mandate, risk tolerance, and market opinion. Moreover, FX transactions are often made in conjunction with transactions in other financial markets—such as equities, fixed income, and commodities. These markets have a variety of instruments as well, and market participants jointly tailor their *overall* position simultaneously using the building blocks of the FX market and these other markets.

EXAMPLE 2

Spot and Forward Exchange Rates

The investment adviser based in Sydney, Australia, continues her meeting with the local client who has diversified her domestic bond portfolio by adding investments in fixed-rate, long-term bonds denominated in HKD. Given that the client spends most of the year in Australia, she remains concerned about the foreign exchange risk of her foreign investments and asks the adviser how these might be managed. The investment adviser explains the difference between spot and forward exchange rates and their role in determining foreign exchange risk exposures. The investment adviser suggests the following investment strategy to the client: "You can exchange AUD for HKD in the spot exchange market, invest in a risk-free, one-year HKD-denominated zero coupon bond, and use a one-year forward contract for converting the proceeds back into AUD."

Spot exchange rate (AUD/HKD)	0.1429
One-year HKD interest rate	7.00%
One-year forward exchange rate (AUD/HKD)	0.1402

1 Which of the following statements is *most* correct? Over a one-year horizon, the exchange rate risk of the client's investment in HKD-denominated bonds is determined by uncertainty over:

   A today's AUD/HKD forward rate.

   B the AUD/HKD spot rate one year from now.

C   the AUD/HKD forward rate one year from now.

2   To reduce the exchange rate risk of the Hong Kong investment, the client should:

   A   sell AUD spot.

   B   sell AUD forward.

   C   sell HKD forward.

3   Over a one-year horizon, the investment proposed by the investment adviser is *most* likely:

   A   risk free.

   B   exposed to interest rate risk.

   C   exposed to exchange rate risk.

4   To set up the investment proposed by the adviser, the client would need to:

   A   sell AUD spot; sell a one-year, HKD-denominated bond; and buy AUD forward.

   B   buy AUD spot; buy a one-year, HKD-denominated bond; and sell AUD forward.

   C   sell AUD spot; buy a one-year, HKD-denominated bond; and buy AUD forward.

5   The return (in AUD) on the investment proposed by the investment adviser is *closest* to:

   A   5.00 percent.

   B   6.00 percent.

   C   7.00 percent.

Solution to 1:

B is correct. The exchange rate risk (for an unhedged investment) is defined by the uncertainty over future spot rates. In this case, the relevant spot rate is that which would prevail one year from now. Forward rates that would be in effect one year from now would be irrelevant, and the current forward rate is known with certainty.

Solution to 2:

C is correct. The Australian-based investor owns HKD-denominated bonds, meaning that she is long HKD exposure. To hedge this exposure, she could enter into a forward contract to sell the HKD against the AUD for future delivery (that is, match a long HKD exposure in the cash market with a short HKD exposure in the derivatives market). The forward rate is established at the time the forward contract is entered into, eliminating any uncertainty about what exchange rate would be used to convert HKD-denominated cash flows back into AUD.

Solution to 3:

A is correct. The investment is risk free because the investment is based on a risk-free, one-year, zero coupon, HKD-denominated bond—meaning there is no default or reinvestment risk. The investment will mature in one-year at par; there is no interest rate risk. The use of a forward contract to convert the HKD-denominated proceeds back to AUD eliminates any exchange rate risk.

> ### Solution to 4:
>
> C is correct. To create the investment, the client needs to convert AUD to HKD in the spot exchange market, invest in (buy) the one-year HKD bond, and sell the HKD forward/buy the AUD forward. Note that this process is directly comparable to the swap financing approach described in this section of the reading.
>
> ### Solution to 5:
>
> A is correct. Converting one AUD to HKD in the spot market gives the client (1/0.1429) = HKD7.00. Investing this for one year leads to 7.00 × (1.07) = HKD7.49. Selling this amount of HKD at the forward rate gives 7.49 × 0.1402 = AUD1.05 (rounding to two decimal places). This implies an AUD-denominated return of 5 percent.

2.2 Market Participants

We now turn to the counterparties that participate in FX markets. As mentioned previously, there is an extremely diverse range of market participants, ranging in size from multi-billion-dollar investment funds down to individuals trading for their own account (including foreign tourists exchanging currencies at airport kiosks).

To understand the various market participants, it is useful to separate them into broad categories. One broad distinction is between what the market refers to as the *buy side* and the *sell side*. The sell side generally consists of large FX trading banks (such as Citigroup, UBS, and Deutsche Bank); the buy side consists of clients who use these banks to undertake FX transactions (i.e., buy FX products) from the sell-side banks.

The buy side can be further broken down into several categories:

- *Corporate accounts*: Corporations of all sizes undertake FX transactions during cross-border purchases and sales of goods and services. Many of their FX flows can also be related to cross-border investment flows—such as international mergers and acquisitions (M&A) transactions, investment of corporate funds in foreign assets, and foreign currency borrowing.

- *Real money accounts*: These are investment funds managed by insurance companies, mutual funds, pension funds, endowments, exchange-traded funds (ETFs), and other institutional investors. These accounts are referred to as real money because they are usually restricted in their use of leverage or financial derivatives. This distinguishes them from leveraged accounts (discussed next); although, many institutional investors often engage in some form of leverage, either directly through some use of borrowed funds or indirectly using financial derivatives.

- *Leveraged accounts*: This category, often referred to as the professional trading community, consists of hedge funds, proprietary trading shops, commodity trading advisers (CTAs), high-frequency algorithmic traders, and the proprietary trading desks at banks—and indeed, almost any active trading account that accepts and manages FX risk for profit. The professional trading community accounts for a large and growing proportion of daily FX market turnover. These active trading accounts also have a wide diversity of trading styles. Some are macro-hedge funds that take longer term FX positions based on their views of the underlying economic fundamentals of a currency. Others are high-frequency algorithmic traders that use technical trading strategies (such as those based on moving averages or Fibonacci levels) and whose trading cycles and investment horizons are sometimes measured in milliseconds.

- *Retail accounts*: The simplest example of a retail account is the archetypical foreign tourist exchanging currency at an airport kiosk. However, it is important to realize that as electronic trading technology has reduced the barriers to entry into FX markets and the costs of FX trading, there has been a huge surge in speculative trading activity by retail accounts—consisting of individuals trading for their own accounts as well as smaller hedge funds and other active traders. This also includes households using electronic trading technology to move their savings into foreign currencies (this is relatively widespread among households in Japan, for example). It is estimated that retail trading accounts for as much as 10 percent of all spot transactions in some currency pairs and that this proportion is growing.

- *Governments*: Public entities of all types often have FX needs, ranging from relatively small (e.g., maintaining consulates in foreign countries) to large (e.g., military equipment purchases or maintaining overseas military bases). Sometimes these flows are purely transactional—the business simply needs to be done—and sometimes government FX flows reflect, at least in part, the public policy goals of the government. Some government FX business resembles that of investment funds, although sometimes with a public policy mandate as well. In some countries, public sector pension plans and public insurance schemes are run by a branch of the government. One example is the Caisse de dépôt et placement du Québec, which was created by the Québec provincial government in Canada to manage that province's public sector pension plans. The Caisse, as it is called, is a relatively large player in financial markets, with about CAD200 billion of assets under management as of 2010. Although it has a mandate to invest these assets for optimal return, it is also called upon to help promote the economic development of Québec. It should be noted that many governments—both at the federal and provincial/state levels—issue debt in foreign currencies; this, too, creates FX flows. Such supranational agencies as the World Bank and the African Development Bank issue debt in a variety of currencies as well.

- *Central banks*: These entities sometimes intervene in FX markets in order to influence either the level or trend in the domestic exchange rate. This often occurs when the central banks judge their domestic currency to be too weak and when the exchange rate has overshot any concept of equilibrium level (e.g., because of a speculative attack) to the degree that the exchange rate no longer reflects underlying economic fundamentals. Alternatively, central banks also intervene when the FX market has become so erratic and dysfunctional that end-users such as corporations can no longer transact necessary FX business. Conversely, sometimes central banks intervene when they believe that their domestic currency has become too strong, to the point that it undercuts that country's export competitiveness. The Bank of Japan intervened against yen strength versus the US dollar in 2004 and again in September 2010. Similarly, in 2010 the Swiss National Bank intervened against strength in the Swiss franc versus the euro by selling the Swiss franc on the euro–Swiss (CHF/EUR) cross-rate. Central bank reserve managers are also frequent participants in FX markets in order to manage their country's FX reserves. In this context, they act much like real money investment funds—although generally with a cautious, conservative mandate to safeguard the value of their country's foreign exchange reserves. The foreign exchange reserves of some countries are enormous (e.g., China has about USD2.5 trillion in reserves as of 2010), and central bank participation in FX markets can sometimes have a material impact on exchange rates even when these reserve managers are not intervening for public policy purposes. Exhibit 2 provides information on central bank reserve holdings as of the second quarter of 2010.[3]

Exhibit 2	Currency Composition of Official Foreign Exchange Reserves, as of 2nd Quarter 2010 (USD billion)
Total foreign exchange holdings globally	8,422
Held by advanced economies	2,927
Held by emerging and developing economies	5,495
Percent of global holdings held in the US dollar[a]	62%

[a] This percentage is calculated using that amount of global currency reserves for which the currency composition can be identified.

Note that the amount of foreign exchange reserves now held by emerging economies comfortably exceeds those held by developed economies. This largely reflects the rapid growth in foreign reserves held by Asian central banks, because these countries typically run large current account surpluses with the United States and other developed economies. Reserve accumulation by energy exporting countries in the Middle East and elsewhere is also a factor. Most of the global currency reserves are held in US dollars; the percentage held in USD is more than twice the portion held in the euro, the second most widely held currency in central bank foreign exchange reserves.

▪ *Sovereign wealth funds (SWFs)*: Many countries with large current account surpluses have diverted some of the resultant international capital flows into SWFs rather than into foreign exchange reserves managed by central banks. Although SWFs are government entities, their mandate is usually more oriented to purely investment purposes rather than public policy purposes. As such, SWFs can be thought of as akin to real money accounts, although some SWFs can employ derivatives or engage in aggressive trading strategies. It is generally understood that SWFs use their resources to help fulfill the public policy mandate of their government owners. The SWFs of many current account surplus countries (such as exporting countries in East Asia or oil-exporting countries) are enormous, and their FX flows can be an important determinant of exchange rate movements in almost all of the major currency pairs.

As mentioned, the sell side generally consists of the FX dealing banks that sell FX products to the buy side. Even here, however, distinctions can be made.

▪ A large and growing proportion of the daily FX turnover is accounted for by the very largest dealing banks, such as Deutsche Bank, Citigroup, UBS, HSBC, and a few other multinational banking behemoths. Maintaining a competitive advantage in FX requires huge fixed-cost investments in the electronic technology that connects the FX market, and it also requires a broad, global client base. As a result, only the largest banks are able to compete successfully in providing competitive price quotes to clients across the broad range of FX products. In fact, among the largest FX dealing banks, a large proportion of their business

---

3 See International Monetary Fund (2010).

is crossed internally, meaning that these banks are able to connect buyers and sellers within their own extremely diverse client base and have no need to show these FX flows outside of the bank.

- All other banks fall into the second and third tier of the FX market sell side. Many of these financial institutions are regional or local banks with well-developed business relationships, but they lack the economies of scale, broad global client base, or information technology (IT) expertise required to offer competitive pricing across a wide range of currencies and FX products. In many cases, these are banks in emerging markets that don't have the business connections or credit lines required to access the FX market on a cost-effective basis on their own. As a result, these banks often outsource FX services by forming business relationships with the larger tier-one banks; otherwise, they depend on the deep, competitive liquidity provided by the largest FX market participants.

All of the categories and sub-categories listed above, on both the buy side and sell side, are relatively loose, and there is substantial blurring among these groups. For example, in the past, FX price quotes were provided exclusively by sell-side banks; more recently, however, hedge funds and other large players are accessing the professional FX market on equal terms with the dealing banks. Often it is these more aggressive players that act as market makers rather than the banks themselves: Banks sometimes depend on liquidity supplied by accounts that might otherwise be described as buy side.

One of the most important ideas to draw from this categorization of market participants is that there is an extremely wide variety of FX market participants, reflecting a complex mix of trading motives and strategies that can vary with time. Most market participants reflect a combination of hedging and speculative motives in tailoring their FX risk exposures. Among public sector market participants, public policy motives may also be a factor. The dynamic, complex interaction of FX market participants and their trading objectives makes it difficult to analyze or predict movements in FX rates with any precision, or to describe the FX market adequately with simple characterizations.

2.3 Market Size and Composition

In this section, we present a descriptive overview of the global FX market drawn from the 2010 Triennial Survey undertaken by the Bank for International Settlements (2010). The BIS is an umbrella organization for the world's central banks. Every three years, participating central banks undertake a survey of the FX market in their jurisdictions, the results of which are aggregated and compiled at the BIS. The most recent survey, taken in April 2010, gives a broad indication of the current size and distribution of global FX market flows.

As of April 2010, the BIS estimates that average daily turnover in the traditional FX market (comprised of spot, outright forward, and FX swap transactions) totaled approximately USD3.9 trillion. Exhibit 3 shows the approximate percentage allocation among FX product types, including both traditional FX products and exchange-traded FX derivatives. Note that this table of percentage allocations adds exchange-traded derivatives to the BIS estimate of average daily turnover of USD3.9 trillion; the "Spot" and "OTC forwards" categories include only transactions that are not executed as part of a swap transaction.

Exhibit 3	FX Turnover by Instrument
Spot	36%
OTC forwards	12

(continued)

Exhibit 3 (Continued)	
Exchange-traded derivatives	4
Swaps[a]	44
OTC options[b]	4
Total	**100%**

[a] Includes both FX and currency swaps.
[b] Includes what the BIS categorizes as "other FX products."

The survey also provides a percentage breakdown of the average daily flows between sell-side banks (called the interbank market), between banks and financial customers (all non-bank financial entities, such as real money and leveraged accounts, SWFs, and central banks), and between banks and non-financial customers (such as corporations, retail accounts, and governments). The breakdown is provided in Exhibit 4. It bears noting that the proportion of average daily FX flow accounted for by financial clients is much larger than that for non-financial clients. The BIS also reports that the proportion of financial client flows has been growing rapidly, and as of 2010, it exceeded interbank trading volume for the first time. This underscores the fact that only a minority of the daily FX flow is accounted for by corporations and individuals buying and selling foreign goods and services. Huge investment pools and professional traders are accounting for a large and growing proportion of the FX business.

Exhibit 4 FX Flows by Counterparty	
Interbank	39%
Financial clients	48
Non-financial clients	13

The 2010 BIS survey also identifies the top five currency pairs in terms of their percentage share of average daily global FX turnover. These are shown in Exhibit 5. Note that each of these most active pairs includes the US dollar (USD).

Exhibit 5 FX Turnover by Currency Pair	
USD/EUR	28%
JPY/USD	14
USD/GBP	9
USD/AUD	6
CAD/USD	5

The largest proportion of global FX trading occurs in London, followed by New York. This means that FX markets are most active between approximately 8:00 A.M. and 11:30 A.M. New York time, when banks in both cities are open. (The official London close is at 11:00 A.M. New York time, but London markets remain relatively active for a period after that.) Tokyo is the third-largest FX trading hub.

EXAMPLE 3

Market Participants and Composition of Trades

The investment adviser based in Sydney, Australia, makes the following statements to her client when describing some of the basic characteristics of the foreign exchange market:

Statement 1 "Foreign exchange transactions for spot settlement see the most trade volume in terms of average daily turnover because the FX market is primarily focused on settling international trade flows."

Statement 2 "The most important foreign exchange market participants on the buy side are corporations engaged in international trade; on the sell side they are the local banks that service their FX needs."

1 Statement 1 is:

A correct.

B incorrect with respect to the importance of spot settlements.

C incorrect both with respect to the importance of spot settlements and international trade flows.

2 Statement 2 is:

A correct.

B incorrect with respect to corporations engaged in international trade.

C incorrect with respect to both corporations and the local banks that service their trade needs.

Solution to 1:

C is correct. Although the media generally focus on the spot market when discussing foreign exchange, the majority of average daily trade volume involves the FX swap market as market participants either roll over or modify their existing hedging and speculative positions (or engage in FX swap financing). Although it is true that all international trade transactions eventually result in some form of spot settlement, this typically generates a great deal of hedging (and speculative) activity in advance of spot settlement. Moreover, an important group of FX market participants engages in purely speculative positioning with no intention of ever delivering/receiving the principal amount of the trades. Most FX trading volume is not related to international trade: Portfolio flows (cross-border capital movements) and speculative activities dominate.

Solution to 2:

C is correct. As of 2010, the most important foreign exchange market participants in terms of average daily turnover are found not among corporations engaged in international trade but among huge investment managers, both private (e.g., pension funds) and public (e.g., central bank reserve managers or sovereign wealth funds). A large and growing amount of daily turnover is also being generated by high-frequency traders who use computer algorithms to automatically execute extremely high numbers of speculative trades (although their individual ticket sizes are generally small, they add up to large aggregate flows). On the sell side, the largest money center banks (e.g., Deutsche Bank, Citigroup, HSBC, UBS) are increasingly dominating the amount of trading activity routed through dealers. Regional and local banks are increasingly being marginalized in terms of their share of average daily turnover in FX markets.

3 CURRENCY EXCHANGE RATE CALCULATIONS

3.1 Exchange Rate Quotations

Exchange rates represent the relative price of one currency in terms of another. This price can be represented in two ways: 1) currency A buys how many units of currency B; or 2) currency B buys how many units of currency A. Of course, these two prices are simply the inverse of each other.

To distinguish between these two prices, market participants sometimes distinguish between *direct* and *indirect* exchange rates. In the quoting convention A/B (where there is a certain number of units of currency A per one unit of currency B), we refer to currency A as the *price currency* (or quote currency); currency B is referred to as the *base currency*. (The reason for this choice of names will become clearer below.) The base currency is always set at a quantity of one. A *direct* currency quote takes the domestic country as the price currency and the foreign country as the base currency. For example, for a Paris-based trader, the domestic currency would be the euro (EUR) and a foreign currency would be the UK pound (GBP). For this Paris-based trader, a *direct* quote would be EUR/GBP. An exchange rate quote of EUR/GBP = 1.2225 means that 1 GBP costs 1.2225 EUR. For this Paris-based trader, an *indirect* quote has the domestic currency—the euro—as the base currency. An indirect quote of GBP/EUR = 0.8180 means that 1 EUR costs 0.8180 GBP. *Direct and indirect quotes are just the inverse (reciprocal) of each other.*

It can be confusing to describe exchange rates as either being direct or indirect because determining the domestic currency and the foreign currency depends on where one is located. For a London-based market participant, the UK pound (GBP) is the domestic currency and the euro (EUR) is a foreign currency. For a Paris-based market participant, it would be the other way around.

To avoid confusion, the professional FX market has developed a set of market conventions that all market participants typically adhere to when making and asking for FX quotes. Exhibit 6 displays some of these for the major currencies: the currency code used for obtaining exchange rate quotes, how the market lingo refers to this currency pair, and the actual ratio—price currency per unit of base currency—represented by the quote.

Exhibit 6	Exchange Rate Quote Conventions	
FX Rate Quote Convention	**Name Convention**	**Actual Ratio (Price currency/Base currency)**
EUR	Euro	USD/EUR
JPY	Dollar–yen	JPY/USD
GBP	Sterling	USD/GBP
CAD	Dollar–Canada	CAD/USD
AUD	Aussie	USD/AUD
NZD	Kiwi	USD/NZD
CHF	Swiss franc	CHF/USD

Exhibit 6   (Continued)

FX Rate Quote Convention	Name Convention	Actual Ratio (Price currency/Base currency)
EURJPY	Euro–yen	JPY/EUR
EURGBP	Euro–sterling	GBP/EUR
EURCHF	Euro–Swiss	CHF/EUR
GBPJPY	Sterling–yen	JPY/GBP
EURCAD	Euro–Canada	CAD/EUR
CADJPY	Canada–yen	JPY/CAD

Several things should be noted in this exhibit. First, the three-letter currency codes in the first column (for FX rate quotes) refer to what are considered the major exchange rates. Remember that an exchange rate is the price of one currency in terms of another: There are always two currencies involved in the price. This is different from referring to a single currency in its own right. For example, one can refer to the euro (EUR) as a *currency*; but if we refer to a euro *exchange rate* (EUR), it is always the price of the euro in terms of another currency, in this case the US dollar. This is because in the professional FX market, the three-letter code EUR is always taken to refer to the euro–US dollar exchange rate, which is quoted in terms of the number of US dollars per euro (USD/EUR). Second, where there are six-letter currency codes in the first column, these refer to some of the major *cross-rates*. This topic will be covered in the next section, but generally these are secondary exchange rates and they are not as common as the main exchange rates. (It can be noted that three-letter codes are always in terms of an exchange rate involving the US dollar, while the six-letter codes are not.) Third, when both currencies are mentioned in the code or the name convention, *the base currency is always mentioned first, the opposite order of the actual ratio (price currency/base currency)*. Thus, the code for "Sterling–yen" is "GBPJPY," but the actual number quoted is the number of yen per sterling (JPY/GBP). It should also be noted that *the codes may appear in a variety of formats that all mean the same thing*. For example, GBPJPY might instead appear as GBP:JPY or GBP–JPY. Fourth, regardless of where a market participant is located, there is always a mix of direct and indirect quotes in common market usage. For example, a trader based in Toronto will typically refer to the euro–Canada and Canada–yen exchange rates—a mixture of direct (CAD/EUR) and indirect (JPY/CAD) quotes for a Canadian-based trader. There is no overall consistency in this mixture of direct and indirect quoting conventions in the professional FX market; a market participant just has to get familiar with how the conventions are used.[4]

Another concept involving exchange rate quotes in professional FX markets is that of a *two-sided price*. When a client asks a bank for an exchange rate quote, the bank will provide a "*bid*" (the price at which the bank is willing to buy the currency) and an "*offer*" (the price at which the bank is willing to sell the currency). But there are *two* currencies involved in an exchange rate quote, which is always the price of one currency relative to the other. So, which one is being bought and sold in this two-sided price quote? This is where the lingo involving the price currency (or quote currency)

---

4 In general, however, there is a hierarchy for quoting conventions. For quotes involving the EUR, it serves as the base currency (e.g., GBP/EUR). Next in the priority sequence, for quotes involving the GBP (but not the EUR) it serves as the base currency (e.g., USD/GBP). Finally, for quotes involving the USD (but not the GBP or EUR) it serves as the base currency (e.g., CAD/USD). Exceptions among the major currencies are the AUD and NZD: they serve as the base currency when quoted against the USD (i.e., USD/AUD, USD/NZD).

and the base currency, explained above, becomes useful. *The two-sided price quoted by the dealer is in terms of buying/selling the base currency.* It shows the number of units of the *price* currency that the client will receive from the dealer for one unit of the base currency (the bid) and the number of units of the price currency that the client must sell to the dealer to obtain one unit of the base currency (the offer). Consider the case of a client that is interested in a transaction involving the Swiss franc (CHF) and the euro (EUR). As we have seen above, the market convention is to quote this as euro–Swiss (CHF/EUR). The EUR is the base currency, and the two-sided quote (price) shows the number of units of the price currency (CHF) that must be paid or will be received for 1 euro. For example, a two-sided price in euro–Swiss (CHF/EUR) might look like: 1.3405–1.3407. The client will receive CHF1.3405 for selling EUR1 to the dealer and must pay CHF1.3407 to the dealer to buy EUR1. Note that *the price is shown in terms of the price currency* and that *the bid is always less than the offer*: The bank buys the base currency (EUR, in this case) at the low price and sells the base currency at the high price. Buying low and selling high is profitable for banks, and spreading clients—trying to widen the bid/offer spread—is how dealers try to increase their profit margins. However, it should be noted that the electronic dealing systems currently used in professional FX markets are extremely efficient in connecting buyers and sellers globally. Moreover, this worldwide competition for business has compressed most bid/offer spreads to very tight levels. For simplicity, in the remainder of this reading we will focus on exchange rates as a single number (with no bid/offer spread).

One last thing that can be pointed out in exchange rate quoting conventions is that most major spot exchange rates are typically quoted to four decimal places. One exception among the major currencies involves the yen, for which spot exchange rates are usually quoted to two decimal places. (For example, using spot exchange rates from the middle of 2010, a USD/EUR quote would be expressed as 1.2875, while a JPY/EUR quote would be expressed as 110.25.) This difference involving the yen comes from the fact that the units of yen per unit of other currencies is typically relatively large already, and hence extending the exchange rate quote to four decimal places is viewed as unnecessary.

Regardless of what quoting convention is used, changes in an exchange rate can be expressed as a percentage appreciation of one currency against the other: One simply has to be careful in identifying which currency is the price currency and which is the base currency. For example, let's suppose the exchange rate for the euro (USD/EUR) increases from 1.2500 to 1.3000. This represents an (un-annualized) percentage change of:

$$\frac{1.3000}{1.2500} - 1 = 4.00\%$$

This represents a 4 percent appreciation in the euro against the US dollar (and not an appreciation of the US dollar against the euro) because the USD/EUR exchange rate is expressed with the dollar as the price currency.

Note that this appreciation of the euro against the US dollar can also be expressed as a depreciation of the US dollar against the euro; but in this case, the depreciation is not equal to 4.0 percent. Inverting the exchange rate quote from USD/EUR to EUR/USD, so that the euro is now the price currency, leads to:

$$\frac{\left(\dfrac{1}{1.3000}\right)}{\left(\dfrac{1}{1.2500}\right)} - 1 = \frac{1.2500}{1.3000} - 1 = -3.85\%$$

Note that the US dollar depreciation is not the same, in percentage terms, as the euro appreciation. This will always be true; it is simply a matter of arithmetic.

EXAMPLE 4

Exchange Rate Conventions

A dealer based in New York City provides a spot exchange rate quote of 12.4035 MXN/USD to a client in Mexico City. The inverse of 12.4035 is 0.0806.

1 From the perspective of the Mexican client, the *most* accurate statement is that the:

   A direct exchange rate quotation is equal to 0.0806.

   B direct exchange rate quotation is equal to 12.4035.

   C indirect exchange rate quotation is equal to 12.4035.

2 If the bid/offer quote from the dealer was 12.4020 ~ 12.4060 MXN/USD, then the bid/offer quote in USD/MXN terms would be *closest* to:

   A 0.08061 ~ 0.08063.

   B 0.08063 ~ 0.08061.

   C 0.08062 ~ 0.08062.

Solution to 1:

B is correct. A direct exchange rate uses the domestic currency as the price currency and the foreign currency as the base currency. For an MXN/USD quote, the MXN is the price currency; therefore, the direct quote for the Mexican client is 12.4035 (it costs 12.4035 pesos to purchase 1 US dollar). Another way of understanding a *direct* exchange rate quote is that it is the price of one unit of foreign currency in terms of your own currency. This purchase of a unit of foreign currency can be thought of as a purchase much like any other you might make; think of the unit of foreign currency as just another item that you might be purchasing with your domestic currency. For example, for someone based in Canada, a liter of milk currently costs about CAD1.25 and USD1 costs about CAD1.03. This *direct* currency quote uses the *domestic* currency (the Canadian dollar, in this case) as the *price* currency and simply gives the price of a unit of foreign currency that is being purchased.

Solution to 2:

A is correct. An MXN/USD quote means the amount of MXN the dealer is bidding (offering) to buy (sell) USD1. The dealer's bid to buy USD1 at MXN12.4020 is equivalent to the dealer paying MXN12.4020 to buy USD1. Dividing both terms by 12.4020 means the dealer is paying (i.e., selling) MXN1 to buy USD0.08063. This is the offer in USD/MXN terms: The dealer offers to sell MXN1 at a price of USD0.08063. In USD/MXN terms, the dealer's bid for MXN1 is 0.08061, calculated by inverting the offer of 12.4060 in MXN/USD terms (1/12.4060 = 0.08061). Note that in any bid/offer quote, no matter what the base or price currencies, the bid is always lower than the offer.

3.2 Cross-Rate Calculations

Given two exchange rates involving three currencies, it is possible to back out what the cross-rate must be. For example, as we have seen, the FX market convention is to quote the exchange rate between the US dollar and the euro as euro–dollar (USD/ EUR). The FX market also quotes the exchange rate between the Canadian dollar and US dollar as dollar–Canada (CAD/USD). Given these two exchange rates, it is possible to back out the cross-rate between the euro and the Canadian dollar, which according to market convention is quoted as euro–Canada (CAD/EUR). This calculation is shown as:

$$\frac{CAD}{USD} \times \frac{USD}{EUR} = \frac{CAD}{\cancel{USD}} \times \frac{\cancel{USD}}{EUR} = \frac{CAD}{EUR}$$

Hence, to get a euro–Canada (CAD/EUR) quote, we must multiply the dollar–Canada (CAD/USD) quote by the euro–dollar (USD/EUR) quote. For example, assume the exchange rate for dollar–Canada is 1.0460 and the exchange rate for euro–dollar is 1.2880. Using these sample spot exchange rates, calculating the euro–Canada cross-rate equals:

1.0460 × 1.2880 = 1.3472 CAD per EUR

It is best to avoid talking in terms of direct or indirect quotes because, as noted above, these conventions depend on where one is located and hence what the domestic and foreign currencies are. Instead, focus on how the math works: Sometimes it is necessary to invert one of the quotes in order to get the intermediary currency to cancel out in the equation to get the cross-rate. For example, to get a Canada–yen (JPY/CAD) quote, one is typically using the dollar–Canada (CAD/USD) rate and dollar–yen (JPY/USD) rate, which are the market conventions. This Canada–yen calculation requires that the dollar–Canada rate (CAD/USD) be inverted to a USD/CAD quote for the calculations to work, as shown below:

$$\left(\frac{CAD}{USD}\right)^{-1} \times \frac{JPY}{USD} = \frac{USD}{CAD} \times \frac{JPY}{USD} = \frac{\cancel{USD}}{CAD} \times \frac{JPY}{\cancel{USD}} = \frac{JPY}{CAD}$$

Hence, to get a Canada–yen (JPY/CAD) quote, we must first invert the dollar–Canada (CAD/USD) quote before multiplying by the dollar–yen (JPY/USD) quote. As an example, let's assume that we have spot exchange rates of 1.0460 for dollar–Canada (CAD/USD) and 85.50 for dollar–yen (JPY/USD). The dollar–Canada rate of 1.0460 inverts to 0.9560; multiplying this value by the dollar–yen quote of 85.50 gives a Canada–yen quote of:

0.9560 × 85.50 = 81.74 JPY per CAD

Market participants asking for a quote in a cross-rate currency pair typically will not have to do this calculation themselves: Either the dealer or the electronic trading platform will provide a quote in the specified currency pair. (For example, a client asking for a quote in Canada–yen will receive that quote from the dealer; he will not be given separate dollar–Canada and dollar–yen quotes in order to do the math.) But be aware that dealers providing the quotes often have to do this calculation themselves if only because the dollar–Canada and dollar–yen currency pairs often trade on different trading desks and involve different traders. Electronic dealing machines used in both the interbank market and bank-to-client markets often provide this mathematical operation to calculate cross-rates automatically.

Because market participants can receive both a cross-rate quote (for example, Canada–yen) as well as the component underlying exchange rate quotes (for example, dollar–Canada and dollar–yen), these cross-rate quotes must be consistent with the above equation; otherwise, the market will arbitrage the mispricing. Extending our example above, we calculate a Canada–yen (JPY/CAD) rate of 81.74 based on underlying dollar–Canada (CAD/USD) and dollar–yen (JPY/USD) rates of 1.0460 and 85.50, respectively. Now suppose that at the same time a misguided dealer quotes a Canada–yen rate of 82.00. This is a different price in JPY/CAD for an identical service: converting yen into Canadian dollars. Hence, any trader could buy CAD1 at the lower price of JPY81.74 and then turn around and sell CAD1 at JPY82.00 (recall our earlier discussion of how price and base currencies are defined). The riskless arbitrage profit is JPY0.26 per CAD1. The arbitrage—called *triangular arbitrage*, "tri-," because it involves three currencies—would continue until the price discrepancy was removed.

In reality, however, these discrepancies in cross-rates almost never occur because both human traders and automatic trading algorithms are constantly on alert for any pricing inefficiencies. In practice, and for the purposes of this reading, we can consider cross-rates as being consistent with their underlying exchange rate quotes and that given any two exchange rates involving three currencies, we can back out the third cross-rate.

EXAMPLE 5

Cross Exchange Rates and Percentage Changes

A research report produced by a dealer includes the following exhibit:

	Spot Rate	Expected Spot Rate in One Year
USD/EUR	1.3960	1.3863
CHF/USD	0.9585	0.9551
USD/GBP	1.5850	1.5794

1 The spot CHF/EUR cross-rate is *closest* to:

   A 0.6866.

   B 0.7473.

   C 1.3381.

2 The spot GBP/EUR cross-rate is *closest* to:

   A 0.8808.

   B 1.1354.

   C 2.2127.

3 Based on the exhibit, the euro is expected to appreciate by how much against the US dollar over the next year?

   A −0.7 percent

   B +0.7 percent

   C +1.0 percent

4 Based on the exhibit, the US dollar is expected to appreciate by how much against the British pound over the next year?

   A +0.6 percent

   B −0.4 percent

   C +0.4 percent

5 Over the next year, the Swiss franc is expected to:

   A depreciate against the GBP.

   B depreciate against the EUR.

   C appreciate against the GBP, EUR, and USD.

6 Based on the exhibit, which of the following lists the three currencies from strongest to weakest over the next year?

   A USD, GBP, EUR

   B USD, EUR, GBP

C   EUR, USD, GBP

7   Based on the exhibit, which of the following lists the three currencies in order of appreciating the most to appreciating the least (in percentage terms) against the USD over the next year?

A   GBP, CHF, EUR

B   CHF, GBP, EUR

C   EUR, CHF, GBP

Solution to 1:

C is correct:

$$\frac{CHF}{EUR} = \frac{USD}{EUR} \times \frac{CHF}{USD} = 1.3960 \times 0.9585 = 1.3381$$

Solution to 2:

A is correct:

$$\frac{GBP}{EUR} = \frac{USD}{EUR} \times \left(\frac{USD}{GBP}\right)^{-1} = \frac{USD}{EUR} \times \frac{GBP}{USD} = \frac{1.3960}{1.5850} = 0.8808$$

Solution to 3:

A is correct. The euro is the base currency in the USD/EUR quote, and the expected decrease in the USD/EUR rate indicates that the EUR is depreciating (in one year it will cost less USD to buy one EUR). Mathematically:

$$\frac{1.3863}{1.3960} - 1 = -0.7\%$$

Solution to 4:

C is correct. The GBP is the base currency in the USD/GBP quote, and the expected decrease in the USD/GBP rate means that the GBP is expected to depreciate against the USD. Or equivalently, the USD is expected to appreciate against the GBP. Mathematically:

$$\left(\frac{1.5794}{1.5850}\right)^{-1} - 1 = \frac{1.5850}{1.5794} - 1 = +0.4\%$$

Solution to 5:

C is correct: Because the question does not require calculating the magnitude of the appreciation or depreciation, we can work with CHF as either the price currency or the base currency. In this case, it is easiest to use it as the price currency. According to the table, CHF/USD is expected to decline from 0.9585 to 0.9551, so CHF is expected to be stronger (i.e., it should appreciate against the USD). CHF/EUR is currently 1.3381 (see the solution to problem 1) and is expected to be 1.3241 (= 0.9551 × 1.3863), so CHF is expected to appreciate against the EUR. CHF/GBP is currently 1.5192 (= 0.9585 × 1.5850) and is expected to be 1.5085 (= 0.9551 × 1.5794), so CHF is also expected to appreciate against the GBP.

Alternatively, we can derive this answer intuitively. The table shows that the CHF/USD rate is expected to decline: That is, the USD is expected to depreciate against the CHF, or alternatively, the CHF is expected to appreciate against the USD. The table also shows that the USD/EUR and USD/GBP rates are also decreasing, meaning that the EUR and GBP are expected to depreciate against the USD, or alternatively, the USD is expected to appreciate against the EUR and GBP. If the CHF is expected to appreciate against the USD and the USD is expected to appreciate against both the EUR and GBP, it follows that the CHF is expected to appreciate against both the EUR and GBP.

Solution to 6:

A is correct. According to the table, USD/EUR is expected to decline from 1.3960 to 1.3863, while USD/GBP is expected to decline from 1.5850 to 1.5794. So, the USD is expected to be stronger than both the EUR and GBP. GBP/EUR is currently 0.8808 [= $(1.5850)^{-1} \times 1.3960$] and is expected to be 0.8777 [= $(1.5794)^{-1} \times 1.3863$], so the GBP is expected to be stronger than the EUR.

Solution to 7:

B is correct. The USD/EUR rate depreciates by −0.7 percent (= [1.3863/1.3960] − 1), which is the depreciation of the base currency EUR against the USD. The USD/GBP rate declines −0.4 percent (= [1.5794/1.5850] − 1), which is the depreciation of the GBP against the USD. Inverting the CHF/USD rate to a USD/CHF convention shows that the base currency CHF appreciates by +0.4 percent against the USD (= [1.0470/1.0433] − 1).

3.3 Forward Calculations

In professional FX markets, forward exchange rates are typically quoted in terms of points (also sometimes referred to as "pips"). The points on a forward rate quote are simply the difference between the forward exchange rate quote and the spot exchange rate quote, with the points scaled so that they can be related to the last decimal in the spot quote. When the forward rate is higher than the spot rate, the points are positive and the base currency is said to be trading at a *forward premium*. Conversely, if the forward rate is less than the spot rate, the points (forward rate minus spot rate) are negative and the base currency is said to be trading at a *forward discount*. Of course, if the base currency is trading at a forward premium, then the price currency is trading at a forward discount, and vice versa.

This can best be explained by means of an example. At one point during 2010, the spot euro–dollar exchange rate (USD/EUR) was 1.2875 and the one-year forward rate was 1.28485. Hence, the forward rate was trading at a discount to the spot rate (the forward rate was smaller than the spot rate) and the one-year forward points were quoted as −26.5. This −26.5 comes from:

1.28485 − 1.2875 = −0.00265

Recall that most non-yen exchange rates are quoted to four decimal places, so in this case we would scale up by four decimal places (multiply by 10,000) so that this −0.00265 would be represented as −26.5 points. Notice that the points are scaled to the size of the last digit in the spot exchange rate quote—usually the fourth decimal place. Notice as well that points are typically quoted to one (or more) decimal places, meaning that the forward rate will typically be quoted to five or more decimal places. The exception among the major currencies is the yen, which is typically quoted to two decimal places for spot rates. Here, forward points are scaled up by two decimal places—the last digit in the spot rate quote—by multiplying the difference between forward and spot rates by 100.

Typically, quotes for forward rates are shown as the number of forward points at each maturity.[5] These forward points are also called *swap points* because an FX swap consists of simultaneous spot and forward transactions. In the middle of 2010, a trader would have faced a spot rate and forward points in the euro–dollar (USD/EUR) currency pair similar to those in Exhibit 7:

Exhibit 7	Sample Spot and Forward Quotes
Maturity	**Spot Rate or Forward Points**
Spot	1.2875
One week	−0.3
One month	−1.1
Three months	−5.5
Six months	−13.3
Twelve months	−26.5

Notice that the absolute number of points generally increases with maturity. This is because the number of points is proportional to the yield differential between the two countries (the Eurozone and the United States, in this case) scaled by the term to maturity. Given the interest rate differential, the longer the term to maturity, the greater the absolute number of forward points. Similarly, given the term to maturity, a wider interest rate differential implies a greater absolute number of forward points. (This will be explained and demonstrated in more detail later in this section.)

To convert any of these quoted forward points into a forward rate, one would divide the number of points by 10,000 (to scale down to the fourth decimal place, the last decimal place in the spot quote) and then add the result to the spot exchange rate quote.[6] For example, using the data in Exhibit 7, the three-month forward rate in this case would be:

$$1.2875 + \left(\frac{-5.5}{10,000} \right) = 1.2875 - 0.00055 = 1.28695$$

Occasionally, one will see the forward rate or forward points represented as a percentage of the spot rate rather than as an absolute number of points. Continuing our example from above, the three-month forward rate for USD/EUR can be represented as:

$$\frac{1.28750 - 0.00055}{1.28750} - 1 = \left(\frac{1.28695}{1.28750} \right) - 1 = -0.043\%$$

This shows that either the forward rate or the forward points can be used to calculate the percentage discount (or premium) in the forward market—in this case, −0.043 percent rounding to three decimal places. To convert a spot quote into a forward quote when the points are shown as a percentage, one simply multiples the spot rate by one plus the percentage premium or discount:

$$1.28750 \times (1 - 0.043\%) = 1.28750 \times (1.0000 - 0.00043) \approx 1.28695$$

---

5 As mentioned earlier, "maturity" is defined in terms of the time between spot settlement (usually T + 2) and the settlement of the forward contract.
6 Because the JPY/USD exchange rate is only quoted to two decimal places, forward points for the dollar–yen currency pair are divided by 100.

Note that, rounded to the fifth decimal place, this is equal to our previous calculation. However, it is typically the case in professional FX markets that forward rates will be quoted in terms of pips rather than percentages.

We now turn to the relationship between spot rates, forward rates, and interest rates and how their relationship is derived. Forward exchange rates are based on an arbitrage relationship that equates the investment return on two alternative but equivalent investments. Consider the case of an investor with funds to invest. For simplicity, we will assume that there is one unit of the investor's domestic currency to be invested for one period. One alternative is to invest for one period at the domestic risk-free rate (i_d); at the end of the period, the amount of funds held is equal to $(1 + i_d)$. An alternative investment is to convert this one unit of domestic currency to foreign currency using the spot rate of $S_{f/d}$ (number of units of foreign currency per one unit of domestic currency). This can be invested for one period at the foreign risk-free rate; at the end of the period, the investor would have $S_{f/d}(1 + i_f)$ units of foreign currency. These funds must then be converted back to the investor's domestic currency. If the exchange rate to be used for this end-of-period conversion was pre-contracted at the start of the period (i.e., a forward rate was used), it would eliminate any foreign exchange risk from converting at a future, unknown spot rate. Given the assumed exchange rate convention here (foreign/domestic), the investor would obtain $(1/F_{f/d})$ units of the domestic currency for each unit of foreign currency sold forward. Note that this process of converting domestic funds in the spot FX market, investing at the foreign risk-free rate, and then converting back to the domestic currency with a forward rate is identical to the concept of swap financing described in an earlier section of this reading.

Hence, we have two alternative investments—both risk-free because both are invested at risk-free interest rates and because any foreign exchange risk was eliminated (hedged) by using a forward rate. Because these two investments are equal in risk characteristics, they must have the same return. Bearing in mind that the currency quoting convention is the number of foreign currency units per single domestic unit (f/d), this relationship can be stated as:

$$(1 + i_d) = S_{f/d}(1 + i_f)\left(\frac{1}{F_{f/d}}\right)$$

This is an arbitrage relationship because it describes two alternative investments (one on either side of the equal sign) that should have equal returns. If they do not, a riskless arbitrage opportunity exists because an investor can sell short the investment with the lower return and invest the funds in the investment with the higher return; the difference between the two returns is pure profit.[7]

This formula is perhaps the easiest and most intuitive way to remember the formula for the forward rate because it is based directly on the underlying intuition (the arbitrage relationship of two alternative but equivalent investments, one on either side of the equal sign). Also, the right-hand side of the equation, for the hedged foreign investment alternative, is arranged in proper time sequence: a) convert domestic to foreign currency; then b) invest the foreign currency at the foreign interest rate; and finally c) convert the foreign currency back to the domestic currency.[8]

---

7 It is because of this arbitrage relationship that the all-in financing rate using swap financing is close to the domestic interest rate.

8 Recall that this equation is based on an f/d exchange rate quoting convention. If the exchange rate data were presented in d/f form, one could either invert these quotes back to f/d form and use the above equation or use the following equivalent equation: $(1 + i_d) = (1/S_{d/f})(1 + i_f)F_{d/f}$. If this latter equation were used, remember that forward and spot exchange rates are now being quoted on a d/f convention.

This arbitrage equation can be re-arranged as needs require. For example, to get the formula for the forward rate, the above equation can be restated as:

$$F_{f/d} = S_{f/d}\left(\frac{1+i_f}{1+i_d}\right)$$

Another way of looking at this is, given the spot exchange rate and the domestic and foreign risk-free interest rates, the forward rate is whatever value completes this equation and eliminates any arbitrage opportunity. For example, let's assume that the spot exchange rate ($S_{f/d}$) is 1.6535, the domestic 12-month risk-free rate is 3.50 percent, and the foreign 12-month risk-free rate is 5.00 percent. The 12-month forward rate ($F_{f/d}$) must then be equal to:

$$1.6535\left(\frac{1.0500}{1.0350}\right) = 1.6775$$

Suppose instead that, with the spot exchange rate and interest rates unchanged, you were given a quote on the 12-month forward rate ($F_{f/d}$) of 1.6900. Because this misquoted forward rate does not agree with the arbitrage equation, it would present a riskless arbitrage opportunity. This can be seen by using the arbitrage equation to compute the return on the two alternative investment strategies. The return on the domestic-only investment approach is the domestic risk-free rate (3.50 percent). In contrast, the return on the hedged foreign investment when this misquoted forward rate is put into the arbitrage equation equals:

$$S_{f/d}\left(1+i_f\right)\left(\frac{1}{F_{f/d}}\right) = 1.6535\left(1.05\right)\left(\frac{1}{1.6900}\right) = 1.0273$$

This defines a return of 2.73 percent. Hence, the investor could make riskless arbitrage profits by borrowing at the higher foreign risk-free rate, selling the foreign currency at the spot exchange rate, hedging the currency exposure (buying the foreign currency back) at the misquoted forward rate, investing the funds at the lower domestic risk-free rate, and thereby getting a profit of 77 basis points (3.50% − 2.73%) for each unit of domestic currency involved—all with no upfront commitment of the investor's own capital. Any such opportunity in real-world financial markets would be quickly "arbed" away. It is interesting to note that in this example, the investor actually borrows at the higher of the two interest rates but makes a profit because the foreign currency is underpriced in the forward market.

The underlying arbitrage equation can also be re-arranged to show the forward rate as a percentage of the spot rate:

$$\frac{F_{f/d}}{S_{f/d}} = \left(\frac{1+i_f}{1+i_d}\right)$$

This shows that, given an f/d quoting convention, the forward rate will be higher than (be at a premium to) the spot rate if foreign interest rates are higher than domestic interest rates. More generally, and regardless of the quoting convention, *the currency with the higher (lower) interest rate will always trade at a discount (premium) in the forward market.*

One context in which forward rates are quoted as a percentage of spot rates occurs when forward rates are interpreted as expected future spot rates, or:

$$F_t = \hat{S}_{t+1}$$

Substituting this expression into the previous equation and doing some re-arranging leads to:

$$\frac{\hat{S}_{t+1}}{S_t} - 1 = \%\Delta\hat{S}_{t+1} = \left(\frac{i_f - i_d}{1 + i_d}\right)$$

This shows that if forward rates are interpreted as expected future spot rates, the expected percentage change in the spot rate is proportional to the interest rate differential $(i_f - i_d)$.

It is intuitively appealing to see forward rates as expected future spot rates. However, this interpretation of forward rates should be used cautiously. First, the direction of the expected change in spot rates is somewhat counter-intuitive. All else being equal, an increase in domestic interest rates (for example, the central bank tightens monetary policy) would typically be expected to lead to an increase in the value of the domestic currency. In contrast, the equation above indicates that, all else equal, a higher domestic interest rate implies slower expected appreciation (or greater expected depreciation) of the domestic currency (recall that this equation is based on an f/d quoting convention).

More important, historical data show that forward rates are poor predictors of future spot rates. Although various econometric studies suggest that forward rates may be unbiased predictors of future spot rates (i.e., they do not systematically over- or under-estimate future spot rates), this is not particularly useful information because the margin of error for these forecasts is so large. As we have seen in our introductory section, the FX market is far too complex and dynamic to be captured by a single variable, such as the level of the yield differential between countries. Moreover, as can be seen in the formula above for the forward rate, forward rates are based on domestic and foreign interest rates. This means that anything that affects the level and shape of the yield curve in either the domestic or foreign market will also affect the relationship between spot and forward exchange rates. In other words, FX markets do not operate in isolation but will reflect almost all factors affecting other markets globally; anything that affects expectations or risk premia in these other markets will reverberate in forward exchange rates as well. Although the level of the yield differential is one factor that the market may look at in forming spot exchange rate expectations, it is only one of many factors. (Many traders look to the trend in the yield differential rather than the level of the differential.) Moreover, there is a lot of noise in FX markets that makes almost any model—no matter how complex—a relatively poor predictor of spot rates at any given point in the future. In practice, FX traders and market strategists do *not* base either their currency expectations or trading strategies solely on forward rates.

For the purposes of this reading, *it is best to understand forward exchange rates simply as a product of the arbitrage equation outlined earlier and forward points as being related to the (time-scaled) interest rate differential between the two countries.* Reading any more than that into forward rates or interpreting them as the "market forecast" can be potentially misleading.

To understand the relationship between maturity and forward points, we need to generalize our arbitrage formula slightly. Suppose the investment horizon is a fraction, τ, of the period for which the interest rates are quoted. Then the interest earned in the domestic and foreign markets would be $(i_d\tau)$ and $(i_f\tau)$, respectively. Substituting this into our arbitrage relationship and solving for the difference between the forward and spot exchange rates gives:

$$F_{f/d} - S_{f/d} = S_{f/d}\left(\frac{i_f - i_d}{1 + i_d\tau}\right)\tau$$

This equation shows that forward points (appropriately scaled) are proportional to the spot exchange rate and to the interest rate differential and approximately (but not exactly) proportional to the horizon of the forward contract.

Let's demonstrate this using an example. Suppose that we wanted to determine the 30-day forward exchange rate given a 30-day domestic risk-free interest rate of 2.00 percent per year, a 30-day foreign risk-free interest rate of 3.00 percent per year, and a spot exchange rate ($S_{f/d}$) of 1.6555. The risk-free assets used in this arbitrage relationship are typically bank deposits quoted using the London Interbank Offered Rate (Libor) for the currencies involved. The day count convention for Libor deposits is Actual/360.[9] Incorporating the fractional period (τ) as above and inserting the data into the forward rate equation leads to a 30-day forward rate of:

$$F_{f/d} = S_{f/d}\left(\frac{1+i_f\tau}{1+i_d\tau}\right) = 1.6555\left(\frac{1+0.0300\left[\frac{30}{360}\right]}{1+0.0200\left[\frac{30}{360}\right]}\right) = 1.6569$$

This means that, for a 30-day term, forward rates are trading at a premium of 14 pips (1.6569 – 1.6555). This can also be calculated using the above formula for swap points:

$$F_{f/d} - S_{f/d} = S_{f/d}\left(\frac{i_f-i_d}{1+i_d\tau}\right)\tau = 1.6555\left(\frac{0.0300-0.0200}{1+0.0200\left[\frac{30}{360}\right]}\right)\left[\frac{30}{360}\right] = 0.0014$$

As should be clear from this expression, the absolute number of swap points will be closely related to the term of the forward contract (i.e., approximately proportional to τ = Actual/360). For example, leaving the spot exchange rate and interest rates unchanged, let's set the term of the forward contract to 180 days:

$$F_{f/d} - S_{f/d} = 1.6555\left(\frac{0.0300-0.0200}{1+0.0200\left[\frac{180}{360}\right]}\right)\left[\frac{180}{360}\right] = 0.0082$$

This leads to the forward rate trading at a premium of 82 pips. The increase in the number of forward points is approximately proportional to the increase in the term of the contract (from 30 days to 180 days). Note that although the term of the 180-day forward contract is six times longer than that of a 30-day contract, the number of forward points is not exactly six times larger: 6 × 14 = 84.

Similarly, the number of forward points is proportional to the spread between foreign and domestic interest rates ($i_f - i_d$). For example, with reference to the original 30-day forward contract, let's set the foreign interest rate to 4.00 percent leaving the domestic interest rate and spot exchange rate unchanged. This doubles the interest rate differential ($i_f - i_d$) from 1.00 percent to 2.00 percent; it also doubles the forward points (rounding to four decimal places):

$$F_{f/d} - S_{f/d} = 1.6555\left(\frac{0.0400-0.0200}{1+0.0200\left[\frac{30}{360}\right]}\right)\left[\frac{30}{360}\right] = 0.0028$$

---

9 This means that for interest calculation purposes, it is assumed that there are 360 days in the year. However, the actual number of days the funds are on deposit is used to calculate the interest payable.

EXAMPLE 6

Forward Rates

A French company has recently finalized a sale of goods to a UK-based client and expects to receive a payment of GBP50 million in 32 days. The corporate treasurer at the French company wants to hedge the foreign exchange risk of this transaction and receives the following exchange rate information from a dealer:

GBP/EUR spot rate	0.8752
One-month forward points	−1.4

1   Given the above data, the treasurer could hedge the foreign exchange risk by:

   A   buying EUR (selling GBP) at a forward rate of 0.87380.

   B   buying EUR (selling GBP) at a forward rate of 0.87506.

   C   selling EUR (buying GBP) at a forward rate of 0.87506.

2   The *best* interpretation of the forward discount shown is that:

   A   the euro is expected to depreciate over the next 30 days.

   B   one-month UK interest rates are higher than those in the Eurozone.

   C   one-month Eurozone interest rates are higher than those in the United Kingdom.

3   If the 12-month forward rate is 0.87295 GBP/EUR, then based on the data the 12-month forward points are *closest* to:

   A   −22.5.

   B   −2.25.

   C   −0.00225.

4   If a second dealer quotes GBP/EUR at a 12-month forward discount of 0.30 percent on the same spot rate, the French company could:

   A   trade with either dealer because the 12-month forward quotes are equivalent.

   B   lock in a profit in 12 months by buying EUR from the second dealer and selling it to the original dealer.

   C   lock in a profit in 12 months by buying EUR from the original dealer and selling it to the second dealer.

5   If the 270-day Libor rates (annualized) for the EUR and GBP are 1.370% and 1.325%, respectively, and the spot GBP/EUR exchange rate is 0.8489, then the number of forward points for a 270-day forward rate ($F_{GBP/EUR}$) is *closest* to:

   A   −22.8.

   B   −3.8.

   C   −2.8.

Solution to 1:

B is correct. The French company would want to convert the GBP to its domestic currency, the EUR (it wants to sell GBP, buy EUR). The forward rate would be equal to: 0.8752 + (−1.4/10,000) = 0.87506.

Solution to 2:

C is correct. A forward discount indicates that interest rates in the base currency country (France in this case, which uses the euro) are higher than those in the price currency country (the United Kingdom).

Solution to 3:

A is correct. The number of forward points is equal to the scaled difference between the forward rate and the spot rate. In this case: 0.87295 − 0.87520 = −0.00225. This is then multiplied by 10,000 to convert to the number of forward points.

Solution to 4:

B is correct. A 0.30 percent discount means that the second dealer will sell euros 12 months forward at 0.8752 × (1 − 0.0030) = 0.87257, a lower price per euro than the original dealer's quote of 0.87295. Buying euros at the cheaper 12-month forward rate (0.87257) and selling the same amount of euros 12 months forward at the higher 12-month forward rate (0.87295) means a profit of (0.87295 − 0.87257 = GBP 0.00038) per euro transacted, receivable when both forward contracts settle in 12 months.

Solution to 5:

C is correct, because the forward rate is calculated as:

$$F_{\frac{GBP}{EUR}} = S_{\frac{GBP}{EUR}}\left(\frac{1 + i_{GBP}\left[\frac{Actual}{360}\right]}{1 + i_{EUR}\left[\frac{Actual}{360}\right]}\right) = 0.8489\left(\frac{1 + 0.01325\left[\frac{270}{360}\right]}{1 + 0.01370\left[\frac{270}{360}\right]}\right) = 0.84862$$

This shows that the forward points are at a discount of: 0.84862 − 0.84890 = −0.00028, or −2.8 points. This can also be seen using the swap points formula:

$$F_{\frac{GBP}{EUR}} - S_{\frac{GBP}{EUR}} = 0.8489\left(\frac{0.01325 - 0.01370}{1 + 0.01370\left[\frac{270}{360}\right]}\right)\left[\frac{270}{360}\right] = -0.00028$$

The calculation of −3.8 points omits the day count (270/360), and −22.8 points gets the scaling wrong.

4   EXCHANGE RATE REGIMES

Highly volatile exchange rates create uncertainty that undermines the efficiency of real economic activity and the financial transactions required to facilitate that activity. Exchange rate volatility also has a direct impact on investment decisions because it is a key component of the risk inherent in foreign (i.e., foreign-currency-denominated) assets. Exchange rate volatility is also a critical factor in selecting hedging strategies for foreign currency exposures.

The amount of foreign exchange rate volatility will depend, at least in part, on the institutional and policy arrangements associated with trade in any given currency. Virtually every exchange rate is managed to some degree by central banks. The policy framework that each central bank adopts is called an *exchange rate regime*. Although there are many potential variations, these regimes fall into a few general categories. Before describing each of these types, we consider the possibility of an ideal regime and provide some historical perspective on the evolution of currency arrangements.

4.1 The Ideal Currency Regime

The ideal currency regime would have three properties. First, the exchange rate between any two currencies would be credibly fixed. This would eliminate currency-related uncertainty with respect to the prices of goods and services as well as real and financial assets. Second, all currencies would be fully convertible (i.e., currencies could be freely exchanged for any purpose and in any amount). This condition ensures unrestricted flow of capital. Third, each country would be able to undertake fully independent monetary policy in pursuit of domestic objectives, such as growth and inflation targets.

Unfortunately, these three conditions are not consistent. If the first two conditions were satisfied—credibly fixed exchange rates and full convertibility—then there would really be only one currency in the world. Converting from one national currency to another would have no more significance (indeed less) than deciding whether to carry coins or paper currency in your wallet. Any attempt to influence interest rates, asset prices, or inflation by adjusting the supply of one currency versus another would be futile. Thus, it should be clear that independent monetary policy is not possible if exchange rates are credibly fixed and currencies are fully convertible. *There can be no ideal currency regime.*

The impact of the currency regime on a country's ability to exercise independent monetary policy is a recurring theme in open-economy macroeconomics. It will be covered in more detail in other readings; however, it is worthwhile to emphasize the basic point by considering what would happen in an idealized world of perfect capital mobility. If the exchange rate were credibly fixed, then any attempt to decrease default-free interest rates in one country below those in another—that is, to undertake independent, expansionary monetary policy—would result in a potentially unlimited outflow of capital because funds would seek the higher return. The central bank would be forced to sell foreign currency and buy domestic currency to maintain the fixed exchange rate. The loss of reserves and reduction in the domestic money supply would put upward pressure on domestic interest rates until rates were forced back to equality, negating the initial expansionary policy. Similarly, contractionary monetary policy (higher interest rates) would be thwarted by an inflow of capital.

The situation is quite different, however, with a floating exchange rate. A decrease in the domestic interest rate would make the domestic currency less attractive. The resulting depreciation of the domestic currency would shift demand toward domestically produced goods (i.e., exports rise and imports fall), reinforcing the expansionary impact of the initial decline in the interest rate. Similarly, a contractionary increase in the interest rate would be reinforced by appreciation of the domestic currency.

In practice, of course, capital is not perfectly mobile and the impact on monetary policy is not so stark. The fact remains, however, that fixed exchange rates limit the scope for independent monetary policy and that national monetary policy regains potency and independence, at least to some degree, if the exchange rate is allowed to fluctuate and/or restrictions are placed on convertibility. In general, the more freely the exchange rate is allowed to float and the more tightly convertibility is controlled, the more effective the central bank can be in addressing domestic macroeconomic objectives. The downside, of course, is the potential distortion of economic activity caused by exchange rate risk and inefficient allocation of financial capital.

4.2 Historical Perspective on Currency Regimes

How currencies exchange for one another has evolved over the centuries. At any point in time, different exchange rate systems may coexist; still, there tends to be one dominant system in the world economy. Throughout most of the 19th century and the early 20th century until the start of World War I, the US dollar and the UK pound sterling operated on the "classical gold standard." The price of each currency was fixed in terms of gold. Gold was the numeraire[10] for each currency; therefore, it was indirectly the numeraire for all other prices in the economy. Many countries (e.g., the colonies of the United Kingdom) fixed their currencies relative to sterling and were therefore implicitly also operating on the classical gold standard.

The classical gold standard operated by what is called the *price-specie-flow mechanism*. This mechanism operated through the impact of trade imbalances on capital flows, namely gold. As countries experienced a trade surplus, they accumulated gold as payment, their domestic money supply expanded by the amount dictated by the fixed parity, prices rose, and exports fell. Similarly, when a country ran a trade deficit, there was an automatic outflow of gold, a contraction of the domestic money supply, and a fall in prices leading to increased exports.

In this system, national currencies were backed by gold. A country could only print as much money as its gold reserve warranted. The system was limited by the amount of gold, but it was self-adjusting and inspired confidence. With a fixed stock of gold, the price-specie-flow mechanism would work well. Still, new gold discoveries as well as more efficient methods of refining gold would enable a country to increase its gold reserves and increase its money supply apart from the effect of trade flows. In general, however, trade flows drove changes in national money supplies.[11]

There is much disagreement among economic historians about the effect of the classical gold standard on overall macroeconomic stability. Was it destabilizing? On the one hand, monetary policy was tied to trade flows, so a country could not engage in expansionary policies when there was a downturn in the non-traded sector. On the other hand, it has been argued that tying monetary policy to trade flows kept inflation in check.

During the 1930s, the use of gold as a clearing device for settlement of trade imbalances, combined with increasing protectionism on the part of economies struggling with depression as well as episodes of deflation and hyperinflation, created a chaotic environment for world trade. As a consequence of these factors, world trade dropped by over 50 percent and the gold standard was abandoned.

In the later stages of World War II, a new system of fixed exchange rates with periodic realignments was devised by John Maynard Keynes and Harry Dexter White, representing the UK and US Treasuries, respectively. The Bretton Woods system, named after the town where it was negotiated, was adopted by 44 countries in 1944. From the end of the war until the collapse of the system in the early 1970s, the United States, Japan, and most of the industrialized countries of Europe maintained a system of fixed parities for exchange rates between currencies. When the parities were significantly and persistently out of line with the balancing of supply and demand, there would be a realignment of currencies with some appreciating in value and others depreciating in value. These periodic realignments were viewed as a part of standard monetary policy.

---

10 Economists refer to the unit of account in terms of which other goods, services, and assets are priced as the *numeraire*. Under the classical gold standard, the official value of each currency was expressed in ounces of gold.

11 The European inflation of the 17th century was an important exception. Discoveries of gold in South America led to an increase in the world gold stock and in prices throughout Europe. The impact was especially pronounced in Imperial Spain, the primary importing country. Historians have attributed the decline of the Spanish Empire, in part, to the loss of control of domestic prices.

By 1973, with chronic inflation taking hold throughout the world, most nations abandoned the Bretton Woods system in favor of a flexible exchange rate system under what are known as the Smithsonian Agreements. Milton Friedman had called for such a system as far back as the 1950s.[12] His argument was that the fixed parity system with periodic realignments would become unsustainable. When the inevitable realignments were imminent, large speculative profit opportunities would appear. Speculators would force the hand of monetary policy authorities, and their actions would distort the data needed to ascertain appropriate trade-related parities. It is better, he argued, to let the market, rather than central bank governors and treasury ministers, determine the exchange rate.

After 1973, most of the industrialized world changed to a system of flexible exchange rates. The original thinking was that the forces that caused exchange rate chaos in the 1930s—poor domestic monetary policy and trade barriers—would not be present in a flexible exchange rate regime, and therefore exchange rates would move in response to the exchange of goods and services among countries. As it turned out, however, exchange rates moved around much more than anyone expected. Academic economists and financial analysts alike soon realized that the high degree of exchange rate volatility was the manifestation of a highly liquid, forward-looking asset market.[13] Investment-driven FX transactions—for both long-term investment and short-term speculation—mattered much more in setting the spot exchange rate than anyone had previously imagined.

There are costs, of course, to a high degree of exchange rate volatility. These include difficulty planning without hedging exchange rate risks—a form of insurance cost, domestic price fluctuations, uncertain costs of raw materials, and short-term interruptions in financing transactions. For these reasons, in 1979 the European Union opted for a system of limited flexibility, the European Exchange Rate Mechanism (ERM).

Initially, the system called for European currency values to fluctuate within a narrow band called "the snake." This did not last long. The end of the Cold War and the re-unification of Germany created conditions ripe for speculative attack. In the early 1990s, the United Kingdom was in a recession and the Bank of England's monetary policy leaned toward low interest rates to stimulate economic recovery. Germany was issuing large amounts of debt to pay for re-unification, and the German central bank (the Deutsche Bundesbank) opted for high interest rates to ensure price stability. Capital began to flow from sterling to Deutsche marks to obtain the higher interest rate. The Bank of England tried to lean against these flows and maintain the exchange rate within the Exchange Rate Mechanism, but eventually it began to run out of marks to sell. Because it was almost certain that devaluation would be required, holders of sterling rushed to purchase marks at the old rate and the speculative attack forced the United Kingdom out of the ERM in September 1992, only two years after it finally joined the system.

Despite these difficulties, 1999 saw the creation of a common currency for most Western European countries, without Switzerland or the United Kingdom, called the euro.[14] The hope was that the common currency would increase transparency of prices across borders in Europe, enhance market competition, and facilitate more

---

12 Friedman (1953).

13 Whether or not FX markets satisfy recognized definitions of market efficiency—correctly reflecting all available information—is debatable (e.g., some point to evidence of trending as a clear violation of efficiency). However, there is no doubt that FX market participants attempt to incorporate new information, which is often lumpy and difficult to decipher, into their expectations about the future. Changing expectations—accurate or otherwise—affect the value that investors place on holding different currencies and, in a highly liquid market, lead to rapid and sometimes violent exchange rate movements.

14 The number of European countries adopting the euro has continued to expand since its inception; the most recent country to join the euro (as of this writing) was Estonia, on 1 January 2011.

efficient allocation of resources. The drawback, of course, is that each member country lost the ability to manage its exchange rate and therefore to engage in independent monetary policy.

4.3 A Taxonomy of Currency Regimes

Although the pros and cons of fixed and flexible exchange rate regimes continue to be debated, many countries adopt regimes that lie somewhere between these polar cases. Countries adopt specific regimes for a variety of reasons. In some cases, the driving force is the lack of credibility with respect to sound monetary policy. A country with a history of hyperinflation may be forced to adopt a form of fixed-rate regime because its promise to maintain a sound currency with a floating rate regime would not be credible. This has been a persistent issue in Latin America. In other cases, the driving force is as much political as economic. The decision to create the euro was strongly influenced by the desire to enhance political union within the European Community, whose members had been at war with each other twice in the 20th century.

As of April 2008, the International Monetary Fund (IMF) classified the actual (as opposed to officially stated) exchange rate regimes of its members into the eight categories shown in Exhibit 8.

Exhibit 8   Exchange Rate Regimes for Selected Markets[15] As of 30 April 2008

Type of Regime	Currency Anchor		
	USD	EUR	Basket/None
No separate legal tender			
Dollarized	Ecuador, El Salvador, Panama	Montenegro, San Marino	
Monetary union		EMU: Austria, Belgium, Cyprus, Finland, France, Germany, Greece, Ireland, Italy, Luxembourg, Malta, Netherlands, Portugal, Slovenia, Spain	
Currency board	Antigua, Hong Kong	Bosnia and Herzegovina, Bulgaria	
Fixed parity	Argentina, Belarus, Lebanon, Saudi Arabia, Venezuela, Vietnam	Croatia, Denmark	Kuwait, Libya, Russia
Target zone		Slovak Republic	Syria
Crawling peg	Bolivia, China, Iraq		Iran
Crawling band	Costa Rica		Azerbaijan

---

15 The classifications are described in International Monetary Fund (2006). In some cases, the labels used by the IMF do not clearly distinguish among the regimes. Hence, the names applied here to the regimes differ somewhat from the IMF's original taxonomy.

Exhibit 8   (Continued)

	Currency Anchor		
Type of Regime	USD	EUR	Basket/None
Managed float	Cambodia, Liberia, Ukraine		Algeria, Colombia, Egypt, India, Indonesia, Malaysia, Peru, Singapore, Thailand
Independent float			Australia, Canada, Chile, Hungary, Iceland, Israel, South Korea, Mexico, New Zealand, Norway, Philippines, Poland, South Africa, Sweden, Turkey, United Kingdom, Japan, Switzerland, United States

It should be noted that global financial markets are too complex and diverse to be fully captured by this (or any other) classification system. A government's control over the domestic currency's exchange rate will depend on many factors; for example, the degree of capital controls used to prevent the free flow of funds in and out of the country. Also, even those countries classified as using an "independent float" regime will occasionally intervene in foreign exchange markets in order to influence the value of their domestic currency. Additionally, the specifics of exchange rate policy implementation are subject to change. (For example, the Chinese yuan was officially pegged against a basket of currencies prior to the 2008 crisis in the global financial market, but the Chinese government switched back toward focusing on the rate against the US dollar after market volatility rose.)

This means that the classifications in Exhibit 8 are somewhat arbitrary and subject to interpretation, as well as change, over time. The important point to be drawn from this discussion is that the prices and flows in foreign exchange markets will, to varying degrees, reflect the legal and regulatory framework imposed by governments, not just "pure" market forces. Governments have a variety of motives and tools for attempting to manage exchange rates. The taxonomy in Exhibit 8 can be used to help understand the main distinctions among currency regimes and the rationales for adopting them, but the specific definitions should not be interpreted too rigidly. Instead, the focus should be on the diversity of foreign exchange markets globally as well as the implications of these various currency regimes for market pricing.

4.3.1 Arrangements with No Separate Legal Tender

The IMF identifies two types of arrangements in which a country does not have its own legal tender. In the first, known as *dollarization*, the country uses the currency of another nation as its medium of exchange and unit of account. In the second, the country participates in a monetary union whose members share the same legal tender. In either case, the country gives up the ability to conduct its own monetary policy.

In principle, a country could adopt any currency as its medium of exchange and unit of account, but the main reserve currency, the US dollar, is an obvious choice—hence the name dollarization. Many countries are dollarized: East Timor, El Salvador, Ecuador, and Panama, for example. By adopting another country's currency as legal tender, a dollarized country inherits that country's currency credibility, but not its credit-worthiness. For example, although local banks may borrow, lend, and accept deposits in US dollars, they are not members of the US Federal Reserve System nor are they backed by deposit insurance from the Federal Deposit Insurance Corporation. Thus, interest rates on US dollars in a dollarized economy need not be, and generally are not, the same as on dollar deposits in the United States.

Dollarization imposes fiscal discipline by eliminating the possibility that the central bank will be induced to monetize government debt (i.e., to persistently purchase government debt with newly created local currency). For countries with a history of fiscal excess or lack of monetary discipline, dollarizing the economy can facilitate growth of international trade and capital flows if it creates an expectation of economic and financial stability. In the process, however, it removes another potential source of stabilization—domestic monetary policy.

The European Economic and Monetary Union (EMU) is the most prominent example of the second type of arrangement lacking separate legal tender. Each EMU member uses the euro as its currency. Although member countries cannot have their own monetary policies, they jointly determine monetary policy through their representation at the European Central Bank (ECB). As with dollarization, a monetary union confers currency credibility on members with a history of fiscal excess and/or a lack of monetary discipline. However, as shown by the 2010 EMU sovereign debt crisis, monetary union alone cannot confer credit-worthiness.

4.3.2 Currency Board System

The IMF defines a *currency board system* (CBS) as:

> A monetary regime based on an explicit legislative commitment to exchange domestic currency for a specified foreign currency at a fixed exchange rate, combined with restrictions on the issuing authority to ensure fulfillment of its legal obligation. This implies that domestic currency will be issued only against foreign exchange and it remains fully backed by foreign assets....[16]

Hong Kong is the leading example of a long-standing (since 1983) currency board. US dollar reserves are held to cover, at the fixed parity, the entire *monetary base*— essentially bank reserves plus all HKD notes and coins in circulation.[17] Note that HKD-denominated bank deposits are not fully collateralized by US dollar reserves; to do so would mean that banks could not lend against their deposits. The Hong Kong Monetary Authority (HKMA) does not function as a traditional central bank under this system because the obligation to maintain 100 percent foreign currency reserves against the monetary base prevents it from acting as a lender-of-last-resort for troubled financial institutions. However, it can provide short-term liquidity by lending against foreign currency collateral.

A CBS works much like the classical gold standard in that expansion and contraction of the monetary base are directly linked to trade and capital flows. As with the gold standard, a CBS works best if domestic prices and wages are very flexible, non-traded sectors of the domestic economy are relatively small, and the global supply of the reserve asset grows at a slow, steady rate consistent with long-run real growth with stable prices. The first two of these conditions are satisfied in Hong Kong. Until and unless Hong Kong selects a new reserve asset, however, the third condition depends on US monetary policy.

In practice, the HKD exhibits modest fluctuations around the official parity of HKD/USD = 7.80 because the HKMA buys (sells) USD at a pre-announced level slightly below (above) the parity. Persistent flows on one side of this convertibility zone or the other result in interest rate adjustments rather than exchange rate adjustments. Inside

---

16 International Monetary Fund (2006).
17 For a description of Hong Kong's currency board system, see Hong Kong Monetary Authority (2005).

the zone, however, the exchange rate is determined by the market and the HKMA is free to conduct limited monetary operations aimed at dampening transitory interest rate movements.

One of the advantages of a CBS as opposed to dollarization is that the monetary authority can earn a profit by paying little or no interest on its liability—the monetary base—and can earn a market rate on its asset—the foreign currency reserves. This profit is called *seigniorage*.[18] Under dollarization, the seigniorage goes to the country whose currency is used.

4.3.3 *Fixed Parity*

A simple fixed-rate system differs from a CBS in two important respects. First, there is no legislative commitment to maintaining the specified parity. Thus, market participants know that the country may choose to adjust or abandon the parity rather than endure other, potentially more painful, adjustments. Second, the target level of foreign exchange reserves is discretionary; it bears no particular relationship to domestic monetary aggregates. Thus, although monetary independence is ultimately limited as long as the exchange peg is maintained, the central bank can carry out traditional functions, such as serving as lender of last resort.

In the conventional fixed-rate system, the exchange rate may be pegged to a single currency—for example, the US dollar—or to a basket index of the currencies of major trading partners. There is a band of up to ±1 percent around the parity level within which private flows are allowed to determine the exchange rate. The monetary authority stands ready to spend its foreign currency reserves, or buy foreign currency, in order to maintain the rate within these bands.

The credibility of the fixed parity depends on the country's willingness and ability to offset imbalances in private sector demand for its currency. Both excess and deficient private demand for the currency can exert pressure to adjust or abandon the parity. Excess private demand for the domestic currency implies a rapidly growing stock of foreign exchange reserves, expansion of the domestic money supply, and potentially accelerating inflation. Deficient demand for the currency depletes foreign exchange reserves and exerts deflationary pressure on the economy. If market participants believe the foreign exchange reserves are insufficient to sustain the parity, then that belief may be self-fulfilling because the resulting speculative attack will drain reserves and may force an immediate devaluation. Thus, the level of reserves required to maintain credibility is a key issue for a simple fixed exchange rate regime.

4.3.4 *Target Zone*

A target zone regime has a fixed parity with fixed horizontal intervention bands that are somewhat wider—up to ±2 percent around the parity—than in the simple fixed parity regime. The wider bands provide the monetary authority with greater scope for discretionary policy.

4.3.5 *Active and Passive Crawling Pegs*

Crawling pegs for the exchange rate—usually against a single currency, such as the US dollar—were common in the 1980s in Latin America, particularly Brazil, during the high inflation periods. To prevent a run on the US dollar reserves, the exchange rate was adjusted frequently (weekly or daily) to keep pace with the inflation rate. Such a system was called a passive crawl. An adaptation used in Argentina, Chile, and Uruguay was the active crawl: The exchange rate was pre-announced for the coming

---

18 More generally, seigniorage is the profit earned when the value of money issued exceeds the cost of producing it. For physical currency, seigniorage arises when a coin is minted for a fraction of its face value and then issued (sold) at its face value.

weeks with changes taking place in small steps. The aim of the active crawl was to manipulate expectations of inflation. Because the domestic prices of many goods were directly tied to import prices, announced changes in the exchange rate would effectively signal future changes in the inflation rate of these goods.

4.3.6 *Fixed Parity with Crawling Bands*

A country can also have a fixed central parity with crawling bands. Initially, a country may fix its rates to a foreign currency to anchor expectations about future inflation but then gradually permit more and more flexibility in the form of a pre-announced widening band around the central parity. Such a system has the desirable property of allowing a gradual exit strategy from the fixed parity. A country might want to introduce greater flexibility and greater scope for monetary policy, but it may not yet have the credibility or financial infrastructure for full flexibility. So it maintains a fixed parity with slowly widening bands.

4.3.7 *Managed Float*

A country may simply follow an exchange rate policy based on either internal or external policy targets—intervening or not to achieve trade balance, price stability, or employment objectives. Such a policy, often called *dirty floating*, invites trading partners to respond likewise with their exchange rate policy and potentially decreases stability in foreign exchange markets as a whole. The exchange rate target, in terms of either a level or a rate of change, is typically not explicit.

4.3.8 *Independently Floating Rates*

In this case, the exchange rate is left to market determination and the monetary authority is able to exercise independent monetary policy aimed at achieving such objectives as price stability and full employment. The central bank also has latitude to act as a lender of last resort to troubled financial institutions, if necessary.

It should be clear from recent experience that the concepts of float, managed float, crawl, and target zone are not hard and fast rules. Central banks do occasionally engage, implicitly or explicitly, in regime switches—even in countries nominally following an independently floating exchange rate regime. For example, when the US dollar appreciated in the mid-1980s with record US trade deficits, then-US Treasury Secretary James Baker engineered the Plaza Accord, in which Japan and Germany engineered an appreciation of their currencies against the US dollar. (The "Plaza Accord" is so named because it was negotiated at the Plaza Hotel in New York City.) This 1985 policy agreement involved a combination of fiscal and monetary policy measures by the countries involved as well as direct intervention in foreign exchange markets. The Plaza Accord was a clear departure from a pure independently floating exchange rate system.

There are more recent examples of government intervention in foreign exchange markets. In September 2000, the European Central Bank, the Federal Reserve Board, the Bank of Japan, the Bank of England, and the Bank of Canada engaged in "concerted" intervention in order to support the value of the euro, a "freely floating" currency which was then under pressure within foreign exchange markets. (This intervention was described as "concerted" because it was pre-arranged and coordinated among the central banks involved.) During 2010, many countries engaged in unilateral intervention to prevent the rapid appreciation of their currencies against the US dollar. Several of these countries also employed various fiscal and regulatory measures (for example, taxes on capital inflows) in order to further affect exchange rate movements.

The important point to draw from this discussion is that exchange rates do not only reflect private sector market forces but will also, to varying degrees, be influenced by the legal and regulatory framework (currency regimes) within which foreign exchange markets operate. Moreover, they will occasionally be influenced by government polices (fiscal, monetary, and intervention) intended to manage exchange rates. All of these can vary widely among countries and are subject to change with time.

Nonetheless, the most widely traded currencies in foreign exchange markets (the US dollar, yen, euro, UK pound, Swiss franc, and the Canadian and Australian dollars) are typically considered to be free floating, although subject to relatively infrequent intervention.

EXAMPLE 7

Currency Regimes

An investment adviser in Los Angeles, USA, is meeting with a client who wishes to diversify her portfolio by including more international investments. In order to evaluate the suitability of international diversification for the client, the adviser attempts to explain some of the characteristics of foreign exchange markets. The adviser points out that countries often follow different exchange rate regimes, and the choice of regime will affect the performance of their domestic economies as well as the amount of foreign exchange risk posed by international investments.

The client and her adviser discuss potential investments in Hong Kong, Panama, and Canada. The adviser notes that the currency regimes of these countries are a currency board, dollarization, and a free float, respectively. The adviser tells his client that these regimes imply different degrees of foreign exchange risk for her portfolio.

The discussion between the investment adviser and his client then turns to potential investments in other countries with different currency regimes. The adviser notes that some countries follow fixed parity regimes against the US dollar. The client asks whether a fixed parity regime would imply less foreign currency risk for her portfolio than would a currency board. The adviser replies: "Yes, a fixed parity regime means a constant exchange rate and is more credible than a currency board."

The adviser goes on to explain that some countries allow their exchange rates to vary, although with different degrees of foreign exchange market intervention to limit exchange rate volatility. Citing examples, he notes that China has a crawling peg regime with reference to the US dollar, but the average daily percentage changes in the China/US exchange rate are very small compared with the average daily volatility for a freely floating currency. The adviser also indicates that Denmark has a target zone regime with reference to the euro, and South Korea usually follows a freely floating currency regime but sometimes switches to a managed float regime. The currencies of China, Denmark, and South Korea are the yuan renminbi (CNY), krone (DKK), and won (KRW), respectively.

1 Based solely on the exchange rate risk the client would face, what is the correct ranking (from most to least risky) of the following investment locations?

    A Panama, Canada, Hong Kong.

    B Canada, Hong Kong, Panama.

    C Hong Kong, Panama, Canada.

2 Based solely on their foreign exchange regimes, which country is least likely to import inflation or deflation from the United States?

    A Canada.

    B Panama.

    C Hong Kong.

3 The adviser's statement about fixed parity regimes is incorrect with regard to:

   A credibility.

   B a constant exchange rate.

   C both a constant exchange rate and credibility.

4 Based on the adviser's categorization of China's currency regime, if the USD is depreciating against the KRW, then it is *most* likely correct that the CNY is:

   A fixed against the KRW.

   B appreciating against the KRW.

   C depreciating against the KRW.

5 Based on the adviser's categorization of Denmark's currency regime, it would be *most* correct to infer that the:

   A krone is allowed to float against the euro within fixed bands.

   B Danish central bank will intervene if the exchange rate strays from its target level.

   C target zone will be adjusted periodically in order to manage inflation expectations.

6 Based on the adviser's categorization of South Korea's currency policy, it would be *most* correct to infer that the:

   A Korean central bank is engineering a gradual exit from a fixed-rate regime.

   B government is attempting to peg the exchange rate within a predefined zone.

   C won is allowed to float, but with occasional intervention by the Korean central bank.

Solution to 1:

B is correct. The CAD/USD exchange rate is a floating exchange rate, and Canadian investments would therefore carry exchange rate risk for a US-based investor. Although Hong Kong follows a currency board system, the HKD/USD exchange rate nonetheless does display some variation, albeit much less than in a floating exchange rate regime. In contrast, Panama has a dollarized economy (i.e., it uses the US dollar as the domestic currency); therefore, there is no foreign exchange risk for a US investor.

Solution to 2:

A is correct. The Canadian dollar floats independently against the US dollar leaving the Bank of Canada able to adjust monetary policy to maintain price stability. Neither Hong Kong (currency board) nor Panama (dollarized) can exercise independent monetary policy to buffer its economy from the inflationary/deflationary consequences of US monetary policy.

Solution to 3:

C is correct. A fixed exchange rate regime does not mean that the exchange rate is rigidly fixed at a constant level. In practice, both a fixed-rate regime and a currency board allow the exchange rate to vary within a band around the country's stated parity level. Thus, both regimes involve at least a modest amount of exchange rate risk. The fixed parity regime exposes the investor to the additional risk that the country may be unable or unwilling to maintain the parity. In a fixed parity regime, the level of foreign currency reserves is discretionary and typically only a small fraction of the domestic money supply. With no legal obligation to maintain the parity, the country may adjust the parity (devalue or revalue its currency) or allow its currency to float if doing so is deemed to be less painful than other adjustment mechanisms (e.g., fiscal restraint). In contrast, a currency board entails a legal commitment to maintain the parity and to fully back the domestic currency with reserve currency assets. Hence, there is little risk that the parity will be abandoned.

Solution to 4:

C is correct. If the CNY is subject to a crawling peg with very small daily adjustments versus the USD and the USD is depreciating against the KRW, then the CNY would *most* likely be depreciating against the KRW as well. In fact, this was an important issue in foreign exchange markets through the latter part of 2010: As the USD depreciated against most Asian currencies (and less so against the CNY), many Asian countries felt that they were losing their competitive export advantage because the CNY was so closely tied to the USD. This led many Asian countries to intervene in FX markets against the strength of their domestic currencies in order not to lose an export pricing advantage against China.

Solution to 5:

A is correct. A target zone means that the exchange rate between the euro and Danish krone (DKK) will be allowed to vary within a fixed band (as of 2010, the target zone for the DKK/EUR is a ± 2.5 percent band). This does not mean that the DKK/EUR rate is fixed at a certain level (B is incorrect) or that the target zone will vary in order to manage inflation expectations (this is a description of a crawling peg, which makes C incorrect).

Solution to 6:

C is correct. Similar to the monetary authorities responsible for many of the world's major currencies, the South Korean policy typically involves letting market forces determine the exchange rate (an independent floating rate regime). But this approach does not mean that market forces are the sole determinant of the won exchange rate. As with most governments, the South Korean policy is to intervene in foreign exchange markets when movements in the exchange rate are viewed as undesirable (a managed float). For example, during the later part of 2010, South Korea and many other countries intervened in foreign exchange markets to moderate the appreciation of their currencies against the US dollar. Answer A describes a fixed parity with a crawling bands regime, and B describes a target zone regime: Both answers are incorrect.

EXCHANGE RATES, INTERNATIONAL TRADE, AND CAPITAL FLOWS

5

Just as a family that spends more than it earns must borrow or sell assets to finance the excess, a country that imports more goods and services than it exports must borrow from foreigners or sell assets to foreigners to finance the trade deficit. Conversely, a country that exports more goods and services than it imports must invest the excess either by lending to foreigners or by buying assets from foreigners. Thus, a trade deficit (surplus) must be exactly matched by an offsetting *capital account* surplus (deficit).[19] This implies that any factor that affects the trade balance must have an equal and opposite impact on the capital account, and vice versa. To put this somewhat differently, the *impact of exchange rates and other factors on the trade balance must be mirrored by their impact on capital flows*: They cannot affect one without affecting the other.

Using a fundamental identity from macroeconomics, the relationship between the trade balance and expenditure/saving decisions can be expressed as:[20]

$$X - M = (S - I) + (T - G)$$

where X represents exports, M is imports, S is private savings, I is investment in plant and equipment, T is taxes net of transfers, and G is government expenditure. From this relationship, we can see that a trade surplus ($X > M$) must be reflected in a fiscal surplus ($T > G$), an excess of private saving over investment ($S > I$), or both. Because a fiscal surplus can be viewed as government saving, we can summarize this relationship more simply by saying that a trade surplus means the country saves more than enough to fund its investment (I) in plant and equipment. The excess saving is used to accumulate financial claims on the rest of the world. Conversely, a trade deficit means the country does not save enough to fund its investment spending (I) and must reduce its net financial claims on the rest of the world.

Although this identity provides a key link between real expenditure/saving decisions and the aggregate flow of financial assets into or out of a country, it does not tell us what type of financial assets will be exchanged or in what currency they will be denominated. All that can be said is that asset prices and exchange rates at home and abroad must adjust so that all financial assets are willingly held by investors.

If investors anticipate a significant change in an exchange rate, they will try to sell the currency that is expected to depreciate and buy the currency that is expected to appreciate. This implies an incipient (i.e., potential) flow of capital from one country to the other, which must either be accompanied by a simultaneous shift in the trade balance or be discouraged by changes in asset prices and exchange rates. Because expenditure/saving decisions and prices of goods change much more slowly than financial investment decisions and asset prices, most of the adjustment usually occurs within the financial markets. That is, *asset prices and exchange rates adjust so that the potential flow of financial capital is mitigated and actual capital flows remain consistent with trade flows*. In a fixed exchange rate regime, the central bank offsets the private capital flows in the process of maintaining the exchange rate peg and the adjustment occurs in other asset prices, typically interest rates, until and unless the central bank is forced to allow the exchange rate to adjust.[21] In a floating exchange rate regime, the main adjustment is often a rapid change in the exchange rate that dampens an investor's conviction that further movement will be forthcoming. Thus, *capital flows—potential and actual—are the primary determinant of exchange rate movements in the short-to-intermediate term*. Trade flows become increasingly important in the longer term as expenditure/saving decisions and the prices of goods and services adjust.

---

19 In official balance of payments accounts, investment/financing flows are separated into two categories: the capital account and the financial account. Because the technical distinction is immaterial for present purposes, we will simply refer to the balance of investment/financing flows as the capital account. Similarly, we ignore the technical distinction between the trade balance and the *current account* balance. The details of balance of payments accounting are presented in the Level I curriculum reading on "International Trade and Capital Flows" (CFA Institute).

20 This relationship is developed in the Level I curriculum reading on "Aggregate Output, Prices, and Economic Growth," (CFA Institute).

21 A classic example of this occurred in September 1992, when the United Kingdom was forced to withdraw from the European Exchange Rate Mechanism, the forerunner of the current European Economic and Monetary Union (EMU).

With the correspondence between the trade balance and capital flows firmly established, we can now examine the impact of exchange rate changes on the trade balance from two perspectives. The first approach focuses on the effect of changing the relative price of domestic and foreign goods. This approach, which is called the *elasticities approach*, highlights changes in the composition of spending. The second approach, called the *absorption approach*, focuses on the impact of exchange rates on aggregate expenditure/saving decisions.

5.1 Exchange Rates and the Trade Balance: The Elasticities Approach

The effectiveness of devaluation (in a fixed system) or depreciation (in a flexible system) of the currency for reducing a trade deficit depends on well-behaved demand and supply curves for goods and services. The condition that guarantees that devaluations improve the trade balance is called the Marshall–Lerner condition. The usual statement of this condition assumes that trade is initially balanced. We will present a generalization of the condition that allows for an initial trade imbalance and hence is more useful in addressing whether exchange rate movements will correct such imbalances.

Recall from microeconomics that the price elasticity of demand is given by:[22]

$$\varepsilon = -\frac{\%\ change\ in\ quantity}{\%\ change\ in\ price} = -\frac{\%\Delta Q}{\%\Delta P}$$

For example, a demand elasticity of 0.6 means that quantity demanded increases by 6 percent if price declines by 10 percent. Note that the elasticity of demand is defined so that it is a positive number. Because expenditure (R) equals price multiplied by quantity ($P \times Q$), by re-arranging the above expression to solve and substitute for $\%\Delta Q$, we can see that:

$$\%\ change\ in\ expenditure = \%\Delta R = \%\Delta P + \%\Delta Q = (1 - \varepsilon)\%\Delta P$$

From this we can see that an increase in price decreases expenditure if $\varepsilon > 1$, but it increases expenditure if $\varepsilon < 1$. By convention, if $\varepsilon > 1$ demand is described as being "elastic," while if $\varepsilon < 1$ demand is described as "inelastic."

The basic idea behind the Marshall–Lerner condition is that demand for imports and exports must be sufficiently price-sensitive so that increasing the relative price of imports increases the difference between export receipts and import expenditures. The generalized Marshall–Lerner condition is:

$$\omega_X \varepsilon_X + \omega_M(\varepsilon_M - 1) > 0$$

where ω_X and ω_M are the shares of exports and imports, respectively, in total trade (i.e., imports + exports) and ε_X and ε_M are the price elasticities of foreign demand for domestic country exports and domestic country demand for imports, respectively. Note that ($\omega_X + \omega_M$) = 1 and that an initial trade deficit implies $\omega_M > \omega_X$. If this condition is satisfied, a devaluation/depreciation of the domestic currency will move the trade balance toward surplus.

The first term in the generalized Marshall–Lerner condition reflects the change in export receipts assuming the domestic currency price of exports is unchanged (i.e., foreigners are billed in the domestic currency). It will be positive as long as export demand is not totally insensitive to price. Depreciation of the domestic currency makes exports cheaper in foreign currency and induces an increase in the quantity demanded by foreigners. This is reflected by the elasticity ε_x. There is no direct price impact on domestic currency export revenue because the domestic currency price is assumed

---

22 See the Level I curriculum reading on "Demand and Supply Analysis: An Introduction," (CFA Institute).

to be unchanged. Hence, the percentage change in export revenue corresponding to a 1 percent depreciation of the currency is simply ε_X. The second term in the generalized Marshall–Lerner condition reflects the impact on import expenditures. Assuming that imports are billed in a foreign currency, the domestic currency price of imports rises as the domestic currency depreciates. The direct price effect increases import expenditures, while the induced reduction in the quantity of imports decreases import expenditures. The net effect depends on the elasticity of import demand, ε_M. Import expenditure declines only if import demand is elastic (i.e., $\varepsilon_M > 1$).

Examination of the generalized Marshall–Lerner condition indicates that more elastic demand—for either imports or exports—makes it more likely that the trade balance will improve. Indeed, if the demand for imports is elastic, $\varepsilon_M > 1$, then the trade balance will definitely improve. It should also be clear that the elasticity of import demand becomes increasingly important, and the export elasticity less important, as the initial trade deficit gets larger—that is, as ω_M increases. In the special case of initially balanced trade, $\omega_X = \omega_M$, the condition reduces to ($\varepsilon_X + \varepsilon_M > 1$), which is the classic Marshall–Lerner condition.

Exhibit 9 illustrates the impact of depreciation on the trade balance. For ease of reference, we assume the domestic currency is the euro. A 10 percent depreciation of the euro makes imports 10 percent more expensive in euro terms. With an import elasticity of 0.65, this induces a 6.5 percent reduction in the quantity of imports. But import expenditures increase by 3.5 percent [10% × (1 − 0.65)] or €21,000,000 because the drop in quantity is not sufficient to offset the increase in price. On the export side, the euro price of exports does not change but the foreign currency price of exports declines by 10 percent. This induces a 7.5 percent increase in the quantity of exports given an elasticity of 0.75. The euro value of exports therefore increases by 7.5 percent or €30,000,000. The net effect is a €9,000,000 improvement in the trade balance and a €51,000,000 increase in total trade.

Exhibit 9	Marshall–Lerner Condition with a 10 Percent Depreciation of Domestic Currency (€)	
Assumptions	**Exports**	**Imports**
Demand elasticity	0.75	0.65
Percent price change		
In domestic currency (€)	0	10%
In foreign currency	−10%	0
Results	**Initial value(€)**	**Change(€)**
Exports	400,000,000	30,000,000
Imports	600,000,000	21,000,000
Trade balance	−200,000,000	9,000,000
Total trade	1,000,000,000	51,000,000

The balance of trade improves after the depreciation of the euro because the Marshall–Lerner condition is satisfied: The increase in the euro-value of exports exceeds the increase in the value of imports. Based on the data in Exhibit 9, $\omega_M = 0.6$ (i.e., 600,000,000/1,000,000,000) and $\omega_X = 0.4$ (i.e., 1 − 0.6). Thus, the Marshall–Lerner equation is greater than zero:

$$\omega_X \varepsilon_X + \omega_M (\varepsilon_M - 1) = 0.4 \times 0.75 + 0.6(0.65 - 1) = 0.09$$

The elasticity of demand for any good or service depends on at least four factors: 1) the existence or absence of close substitutes, 2) the structure of the market for that product (e.g., a monopoly or perfect competition), 3) its share in people's budgets, and 4) the nature of the product and its role in the economy. Demand for a product with close substitutes is highly price-sensitive, whereas demand for a unique product tends to be much less elastic. The demand curve faced by any producer also depends on the nature and level of competition among producers of that product. If there are many sellers of identical products, then each producer faces highly elastic demand for its output even if global demand for that product is insensitive to price. Producers who are able to differentiate their product, perhaps through branding, face somewhat less elastic demand. In markets with only a few sellers, each producer faces demand that is highly dependent upon strategic maneuvers by its competitors. If competitors match price decreases but not increases, then the producer loses market share by raising his price but fails to gain market share by reducing his price.

Price changes have two effects on demand. The *substitution effect* refers to changes in the composition of spending across different products. As a product gets more expensive (cheaper) relative to other products, customers demand less (more) of it. This is what people usually think of first when they consider the effect of a price change. The *income effect* refers to the fact that price changes affect real purchasing power. When the price of a good rises (falls), people's purchasing power is reduced (increased). The strength of this effect depends on the product's share in people's budgets—the more important the product, the stronger the income effect. The income effect also depends on the nature of the product. The demand for luxuries is highly sensitive to income, whereas the demand for necessities is fairly insensitive to income.

To illustrate the differential impact of the two drivers of the income effect—share of expenditure and nature of the product—consider the demand for food. Clearly, food is a necessity. Based on this fact, we would expect demand to be inelastic. However, the share of expenditures that go to food varies across countries. In poor countries, food represents a much larger share of expenditure than in rich countries. Hence, all else being equal, we would expect the demand for food to be more price elastic in poorer countries. Of course, even in rich countries, the composition of spending on food may change considerably even if overall demand for food does not.

A significant portion of international trade occurs in intermediate products—products that are used as inputs into the production of other goods. Demand for these products derives from supply and demand decisions for the final products. However, the same basic considerations apply for intermediate products as for final products. Are there close substitutes for it in the production process? If not, its demand will tend to be less elastic than would be the case if there were readily available substitutes. How important is it to the overall economy? All else equal, the larger its share in overall production costs for the economy, the bigger its impact on production decisions and therefore the more price-elastic its derived demand. Oil is a classic example of a widely used input with few readily adoptable substitutes, at least in the short run. Lack of substitutes tends to make oil demand price-inelastic. However, it is so important in modern industrial economies that changes in its price can induce expansion or contraction of aggregate output. This makes short-run oil demand somewhat more elastic—at least for significant price changes. In the longer run, the feasibility of substitution among energy sources enhances the price sensitivity of oil demand.

Exhibit 10 shows estimates of demand elasticity for various products. The estimates range from essentially zero for pediatric doctor visits—a necessity for which there is virtually no substitute—to 3.8 for Coca-Cola, a specific brand for which there are many substitutes. Note that the elasticity of demand for soft drinks in general is much lower than for Coca-Cola, roughly 0.9. The elasticity of demand for rice in Japan versus in Bangladesh clearly illustrates the impact of expenditure share on price sensitivity. Similarly, although air travel for pleasure (a luxury) is quite price elastic, demand for first-class air travel is fairly insensitive to price. This is most likely because many first-class passengers are either traveling on business (presumably deemed to have high value added) or wealthy enough that the cost of first-class airfare is inconsequential.

Exhibit 10	Estimates of Demand Elasticities	
Product Description	**Elasticity**	**Rationale/Comment**
Travel and transport		
Airline travel (US)		
For pleasure	1.5	Luxury
1st class	0.3	Business and wealthy travelers
Car fuel (US, long term)	0.6	
Bus travel (US)	0.2	
Ford compact car	2.8	Large purchase; specific brand
Food and beverages		
Rice		Necessity; staple food
Bangladesh	0.8	Poor country
Japan	0.3	Wealthy country
Soft drinks		
All	0.8–1.0	
Coca-Cola	3.8	Specific brand; competitive market
Medical care (US)		
Health insurance	0.3	
Pediatric doctor visit	0.0–0.1	No good substitute
Materials and energy		Necessary inputs
Steel	0.2–0.3	
Oil	0.4	

Sources: Various studies cited in Wikipedia, "Price Elasticity of Demand," as of December 2010 (http://en.wikipedia.org/wiki/Price_elasticity_of_demand).

In practice, most countries import and export a variety of products. Hence, the overall price elasticities of their imports and exports reflect a composite of the products they trade. In conjunction with the Marshall–Lerner condition, our review of the factors that determine price elasticities suggests that exchange rate changes will be a more-effective mechanism for trade balance adjustment if a country imports and exports the following:

- Goods for which there are good substitutes

- Goods that trade in competitive markets

- Luxury goods, rather than necessities

- Goods that represent a large portion of consumer expenditures or a large portion of input costs for final producers

Note that each of these conditions is associated with higher demand elasticities (ε_X and ε_M).

Even when the Marshall–Lerner condition is satisfied, it is still possible that devaluation (in a fixed parity regime) or depreciation (in a floating regime) of the currency will initially make the trade balance worse before making it better. This effect, called the *J*-curve effect, is illustrated in Exhibit 11.

Exhibit 11   Trade Balance Dynamics: The *J*-Curve

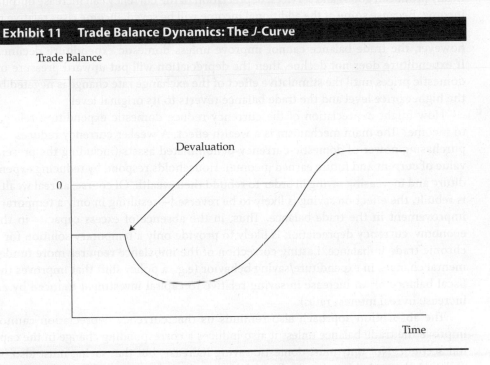

In the very short run, the *J* curve reflects the order delivery lags that take place in import and export transactions. Imagine a clothing importer in Washington. Orders are placed in January for French spring fashions. Market forces cause the dollar to depreciate in February, but contracts were already signed for payment in euros. When the fashions arrive in March, more dollars have to go out to pay for the order signed in euros. Thus, the trade balance gets worse. However, after the depreciation, the clothing importer has to put in new orders for summer fashions. As a result of the currency depreciation, the French summer fashions are now more expensive, so the clothing store cuts the demand for imported clothes from France. The depreciation eventually improves the trade balance, even though it initially made it worse.

A *J*-curve pattern may also arise if short-term price elasticities do not satisfy the Marshall–Lerner condition but long-term elasticities do satisfy it. As noted above in the case of oil, significant changes in spending patterns often take time. Thus, the trade balance may worsen initially and then gradually improve following a depreciation of the currency as firms and consumers adapt.

5.2 Exchange Rates and the Trade Balance: The Absorption Approach

The elasticities approach focuses on the expenditure-switching effect of changing the relative prices of imports and exports. It is essentially a microeconomic view of the relationship between exchange rates and the trade balance. The absorption approach adopts an explicitly macroeconomic view of this relationship.

Recall from above that the trade balance is equal to the country's saving, including the government fiscal balance, minus its investment in new plants and equipment. Equivalently, it is equal to the difference between income (GDP) and domestic expenditure, or absorption. Thus, in order to move the trade balance toward surplus, a devaluation/depreciation of the domestic currency must increase income relative to expenditure or, equivalently, increase national saving relative to investment in physical capital.

If there is excess capacity in the economy, then by switching demand toward domestically produced goods and services, depreciation of the currency can increase output/income. Because some of the additional income will be saved, income rises relative to expenditure and the trade balance improves. If the economy is at full employment, however, the trade balance cannot improve unless domestic expenditure declines. If expenditure does not decline, then the depreciation will put upward pressure on domestic prices until the stimulative effect of the exchange rate change is negated by the higher price level and the trade balance reverts to its original level.

How might depreciation of the currency reduce domestic expenditure relative to income? The main mechanism is a wealth effect. A weaker currency reduces the purchasing power of domestic-currency-denominated assets (including the present value of current and future earned income). Households respond by reducing expenditure and increasing saving in order to rebuild their wealth. Of course, as real wealth is rebuilt, the effect on saving is likely to be reversed—resulting in only a temporary improvement in the trade balance. Thus, in the absence of excess capacity in the economy, currency depreciation is likely to provide only a temporary solution for a chronic trade imbalance. Lasting correction of the imbalance requires more fundamental changes in expenditure/saving behavior (e.g., a policy shift that improves the fiscal balance or an increase in saving relative to capital investment induced by an increase in real interest rates).

The absorption approach also reminds us that currency depreciation cannot improve the trade balance unless it also induces a corresponding change in the capital account. Not only must domestic saving increase, but that saving must also be willingly channeled into buying financial assets from foreigners. All else equal, this implies that foreign and domestic asset prices must change such that foreign assets become relatively more attractive and domestic assets relatively less attractive to both foreign and domestic investors.

EXAMPLE 8

Exchange Rates and the Trade Balance

An analyst at a foreign exchange dealing bank is examining the exchange rate for the Australian dollar (AUD), which is a freely floating currency. Currently, Australia is running a trade surplus with the rest of the world, primarily reflecting strong demand for Australian resource exports generated by rapid growth in emerging market economies in the Western Pacific region. In turn, Australia imports food and energy from a variety of foreign countries that compete with each other as well as with Australian producers of these products. The analyst uses data in the following table to estimate the effect of changes in the AUD exchange rate on Australia's balance of trade.

	Volume (AUD billions)	Demand Elasticity
Exports	200	0.3
Imports	180	0.6

The analyst's research report on this topic notes that the mix of products that Australia imports and exports seems to be changing and that this will affect the relation between the exchange rates and the trade surplus. The proportion of Australian exports accounted for by fine wines is increasing. These are considered a luxury good and must compete with increased wine exports from comparable-producing regions (such as Chile and New Zealand). At the same time, rising income levels in Australia are allowing the country to increase the proportion of its imports accounted for by luxury goods, and these represent a rising proportion of consumer expenditures. The analyst's report states: "Given the changing export mix, an appreciation of the currency will be more likely to reduce Australia's trade surplus. In contrast, the changing import mix will have the opposite effect."

1   Given the data in the table, an appreciation in the AUD will:

   A   cause the trade balance to increase.

   B   cause the trade balance to decrease.

   C   have no effect on the trade balance.

2   All else equal, an appreciation in the AUD will be *more* likely to reduce the trade surplus if the demand:

   A   elasticities for imports and exports increase.

   B   elasticity for exports and the export share in total trade decrease.

   C   elasticity for imports decreases and the import share in total trade increases.

3   All else equal, an appreciation in the AUD will be *more* likely to reduce the trade surplus if it leads to an increase in Australian:

   A   tax receipts.

   B   private sector investment.

   C   government budget surpluses.

4   The report's statement about the effect of changing import and export mixes is *most* likely:

   A   correct.

   B   incorrect with respect to the import effect.

   C   incorrect with respect to the export effect.

5   Suppose the Australian government imposed capital controls that prohibited the flow of financial capital into or out of the country. What impact would this have on the Australian trade balance?

   A   The trade surplus would increase.

   B   The trade balance would go to zero.

   C   The trade balance would not necessarily be affected.

6   Suppose the Australian government imposed capital controls that prohibited the flow of financial capital into or out of the country. The impact on the trade balance, if any, would most likely take the form of:

   A   a decrease in private saving.

   B   a decrease in private investment.

   C   an increase in the government fiscal balance.

Solution to 1:

A is correct. As the AUD appreciates, the price of exports to *offshore buyers* goes up and they demand fewer of them; hence, the AUD-denominated revenue from exports decreases. (Although export demand is inelastic, or $\varepsilon_X < 1$, recall that the *Australian* price of these exports is assumed not to have changed, so the amount of export revenue received by Australia, in AUD-terms, unambiguously declines as the quantity of exports declines.) Australian expenditure for imports also declines. Although the price of imports declines as the AUD appreciates, the Australians do not increase their import purchases enough to lead to higher expenditures. This is because import demand is also inelastic ($\varepsilon_M < 1$). This effect on import expenditure can be seen from: $\%\Delta R_M = (1 - \varepsilon_M)\%\Delta P_M$, where $\%\Delta P_M$ is negative (import prices are declining) and import demand is inelastic (so $(1 - \varepsilon_M) > 0$). With both import expenditures and export revenues declining, the net effect on the trade balance comes down to the relative size of the import and export weights (ω_M and ω_X, respectively). In this case, $\omega_X = 0.53$ (i.e., 200/380) and $\omega_M = 0.47$ (i.e., 180/380). Putting this into the Marshall–Lerner equation leads to:

$$\omega_X\varepsilon_X + \omega_M(\varepsilon_M - 1) = 0.53 \times 0.3 + 0.47(0.6 - 1) = -0.03$$

Because the Marshall–Lerner condition is not satisfied, exchange rate movements do not move the trade balance in the expected direction [i.e., appreciation (depreciation) of the currency does not decrease (increase) the trade balance]. However, note that with different import/export weights and the same elasticities, the Marshall–Lerner condition would be met. In particular, the condition would be met for any value of ω_X greater than 4/7 (≈ 0.571).

Solution to 2:

A is correct. The basic intuition of the Marshall–Lerner condition is that in order for an exchange rate movement to rebalance trade, the demands for imports and exports must be sufficiently price-sensitive (i.e., they must have sufficiently high elasticities). However, the relative share of imports and exports in total trade must also be considered. The generalized Marshall–Lerner condition requires:

$$\omega_X\varepsilon_X + \omega_M(\varepsilon_M - 1) > 0$$

An increase in both ε_X and ε_M will clearly make this expression increase (A is correct). In contrast, a decrease in both ω_X and ε_X tends to make the expression smaller (B is incorrect).[23] If ε_M decreases and ω_M increases, import demand will respond less to an exchange rate movement and will have a larger role in determining the trade balance (C is incorrect).

Solution to 3:

B is correct. An Australian trade surplus means that Australia is spending less than it earns and is accumulating claims on foreigners. Equivalently, Australian saving, inclusive of both private saving and the government fiscal balance, is more than sufficient to fund Australian private sector investment. The relationship between the trade balance and expenditure/saving decisions is given by:

$$X - M = (S - I) + (T - G) > 0$$

For Australia's trade balance to decline, it must save less (S down), invest more (I up), decrease its fiscal balance ($T - G$ down), or some combination of these. Increasing tax receipts (T up) increases rather than decreases the fiscal balance, so answer A is incorrect. Similarly, answer C, increasing the government budget surplus, is incorrect. Increasing private investment (I up) does decrease the trade balance, so answer B is correct.

Solution to 4:

B is correct. As Australian exports become more dominated by luxury goods that face highly competitive market conditions, the elasticity of export demand (ε_X) is likely to be increasing. Increasing export elasticity makes the trade

---

23 Because $\omega_M = 1 - \omega_X$ and $\varepsilon_M < 1$ in this example, a decrease in ω_X also decreases the second terms, $\omega_M(\varepsilon_M - 1)$, in the Marshall–Lerner condition.

surplus more responsive to an AUD appreciation (the increase in ε_X will tend to increase the computed value for the Marshall–Lerner equation). Similarly, as Australian imports become more dominated by luxury goods that are an increasing proportion of household expenditure, import elasticity (ε_M) will most likely increase. This will also tend to increase the computed value for the Marshall–Lerner equation.

Solution to 5:

B is correct. A trade deficit (surplus) must be exactly matched by an offsetting capital account surplus (deficit). Anything that impacts the trade balance must impact the capital account, and vice versa. If capital flows are prohibited, then both the capital account and the trade balance must be zero.

Solution to 6:

A is correct. The trade balance must go to zero. An increase in the fiscal balance implies an increase in the existing trade surplus, so answer C is incorrect. A decrease in private investment will also cause an increase in the trade surplus, so answer B is incorrect. A decrease in private saving will decrease the trade surplus as required, so answer A is correct: A decrease in saving will most likely reflect a decline in national income, especially the profit component, as export demand is choked off by the inability to extend credit to foreigners.

SUMMARY

Foreign exchange markets are crucial for understanding both the functioning of the global economy as well as the performance of investment portfolios. In this reading, we have described the diverse array of FX market participants and have introduced some of the basic concepts necessary to understand the structure and functions of these markets. The reader should be able to understand how exchange rates—both spot and forward—are quoted and be able to calculate cross exchange rates and forward rates. We also have described the array of exchange rate regimes that characterize foreign exchange markets globally and how these regimes determine the flexibility of exchange rates, and hence, the degree of foreign exchange rate risk that international investments are exposed to. Finally, we have discussed how movements in exchange rates affect international trade flows (imports and exports) and capital flows.

The following points, among others, are made in this reading:

- Measured by average daily turnover, the foreign exchange market is by far the largest financial market in the world. It has important effects, either directly or indirectly, on the pricing and flows in all other financial markets.

- There is a wide diversity of global FX market participants that have a wide variety of motives for entering into foreign exchange transactions.

- Individual currencies are usually referred to by standardized three-character codes. These currency codes can also be used to define exchange rates (the price of one currency in terms of another). There are a variety of exchange rate quoting conventions commonly used.

- A direct currency quote takes the domestic currency as the price currency and the foreign currency as the base currency (i.e., $S_{d/f}$). An indirect quote uses the domestic currency as the base currency (i.e., $S_{f/d}$). To convert between direct and indirect quotes, the inverse (reciprocal) is used. Professional FX markets use standardized conventions for how the exchange rate for specific currency pairs will be quoted.

■ Currencies trade in foreign exchange markets based on nominal exchange rates. An increase (decrease) in the exchange rate, quoted in indirect terms, means that the domestic currency is appreciating (depreciating) versus the foreign currency.

■ The real exchange rate, defined as the nominal exchange rate multiplied by the ratio of price levels, measures the relative purchasing power of the currencies. An increase in the real exchange rate ($R_{d/f}$) implies a reduction in the relative purchasing power of the domestic currency.

■ Given exchange rates for two currency pairs—A/B and A/C—we can compute the cross-rate (B/C) between currencies B and C. Depending on how the rates are quoted, this may require inversion of one of the quoted rates.

■ Spot exchange rates are for immediate settlement (typically, T + 2), while forward exchange rates are for settlement at agreed-upon future dates. Forward rates can be used to manage foreign exchange risk exposures or can be combined with spot transactions to create FX swaps.

■ The spot exchange rate, the forward exchange rate, and the domestic and foreign interest rates must jointly satisfy an arbitrage relationship that equates the investment return on two alternative but equivalent investments. Given the spot exchange rate and the foreign and domestic interest rates, the forward exchange rate must take the value that prevents riskless arbitrage.

■ Forward rates are typically quoted in terms of forward (or swap) points. The swap points are added to the spot exchange rate in order to calculate the forward rate. Occasionally, forward rates are presented in terms of percentages relative to the spot rate.

■ The base currency is said to be trading at a forward premium if the forward rate is above the spot rate (forward points are positive). Conversely, the base currency is said to be trading at a forward discount if the forward rate is below the spot rate (forward points are negative).

■ The currency with the higher (lower) interest rate will trade at a forward discount (premium).

■ Swap points are proportional to the spot exchange rate and to the interest rate differential and approximately proportional to the term of the forward contract.

■ Empirical studies suggest that forward exchange rates may be unbiased predictors of future spot rates, but the margin of error on such forecasts is too large for them to be used in practice as a guide to managing exchange rate exposures. FX markets are too complex and too intertwined with other global financial markets to be adequately characterized by a single variable, such as the interest rate differential.

■ Virtually every exchange rate is managed to some degree by central banks. The policy framework that each central bank adopts is called an exchange rate regime. These regimes range from using another country's currency (dollarization), to letting the market determine the exchange rate (independent float). In practice, most regimes fall in between these extremes. The type of exchange rate regime used varies widely among countries and over time.

■ An ideal currency regime would have three properties: (1) the exchange rate between any two currencies would be credibly fixed; (2) all currencies would be fully convertible; and (3) each country would be able to undertake fully independent monetary policy in pursuit of domestic objectives, such as growth and inflation targets. However, these conditions are inconsistent. In particular, a fixed exchange rate and unfettered capital flows severely limit a country's ability to undertake independent monetary policy. Hence, there cannot be an ideal currency regime.

- The IMF identifies the following types of regimes: arrangements with no separate legal tender (dollarization, monetary union), currency board, fixed parity, target zone, crawling peg, crawling band, managed float, and independent float. Most major currencies traded in FX markets are freely floating, albeit subject to occasional central bank intervention.

- A trade surplus (deficit) must be matched by a corresponding deficit (surplus) in the capital account. Any factor that affects the trade balance must have an equal and opposite impact on the capital account, and vice versa.

- A trade surplus reflects an excess of domestic saving (including the government fiscal balance) over investment spending. A trade deficit indicates that the country invests more than it saves and must finance the excess by borrowing from foreigners or selling assets to foreigners.

- The impact of the exchange rate on trade and capital flows can be analyzed from two perspectives. The elasticities approach focuses on the effect of changing the relative price of domestic and foreign goods. This approach highlights changes in the composition of spending. The absorption approach focuses on the impact of exchange rates on aggregate expenditure/saving decisions.

- The elasticities approach leads to the Marshall–Lerner condition, which describes combinations of export and import demand elasticities such that depreciation (appreciation) of the domestic currency will move the trade balance toward surplus (deficit).

- The idea underlying the Marshall–Lerner condition is that demand for imports and exports must be sufficiently price-sensitive so that an increase in the relative price of imports increases the difference between export receipts and import expenditures.

- In order to move the trade balance toward surplus (deficit), a change in the exchange rate must decrease (increase) domestic expenditure (also called absorption) relative to income. Equivalently, it must increase (decrease) domestic saving relative to domestic investment.

- If there is excess capacity in the economy, then currency depreciation can increase output/income by switching demand toward domestically produced goods and services. Because some of the additional income will be saved, income rises relative to expenditure and the trade balance improves.

- If the economy is at full employment, then currency depreciation must reduce domestic expenditure in order to improve the trade balance. The main mechanism is a wealth effect: A weaker currency reduces the purchasing power of domestic-currency-denominated assets (including the present value of current and future earned income), and households respond by reducing expenditure and increasing saving.

REFERENCES

Bank for International Settlements (BIS). 2010. "Triennial Central Bank Survey of Foreign Exchange and Derivatives Market Activity in 2010" (www.bis.org).

Friedman, Milton. 1953. "The Monetarist Theory of Flexible Exchange Rate Systems." In *Essays in Positive Economics.* Chicago: University of Chicago Press.

Hong Kong Monetary Authority (HKMA). 2005. *HKMA Background Brief No. 1: Hong Kong's Linked Exchange Rate System.* 2nd ed. (November): www.info.gov.hk.

International Monetary Fund (IMF). 2006. "De Facto Classification of Exchange Rate Regimes and Monetary Policy Framework" (www.imf.org).

International Monetary Fund (IMF). 2010. "Currency Composition of Official Foreign Exchange Reserves (COFER)" report (www.imf.org).

PRACTICE PROBLEMS

1 An exchange rate:

   A is most commonly quoted in real terms.

   B is the price of one currency in terms of another.

   C between two currencies ensures they are fully convertible.

2 A decrease in the real exchange rate (quoted in terms of domestic currency per unit of foreign currency) is *most likely* to be associated with an increase in which of the following?

   A Foreign price level.

   B Domestic price level.

   C Nominal exchange rate.

3 In order to minimize the foreign exchange exposure on a euro-denominated receivable due from a German company in 100 days, a British company would *most likely* initiate a:

   A spot transaction.

   B forward contract.

   C real exchange rate contract.

4 Which of the following counterparties is *most likely* to be considered a sell-side foreign-exchange market participant?

   A A large corporation that borrows in foreign currencies.

   B A sovereign wealth fund that influences cross-border capital flows

   C A multinational bank that trades foreign exchange with its diverse client base.

5 What will be the effect on a direct exchange rate quote if the domestic currency appreciates?

   A Increase

   B Decrease

   C No change

6 An executive from Switzerland checked into a hotel room in Spain and was told by the hotel manager that 1 EUR will buy 1.2983 CHF. From the executive's perspective, an indirect exchange rate quote would be:

   A 0.7702 EUR per CHF.

   B 0.7702 CHF per EUR.

   C 1.2983 EUR per CHF.

7 Over the past month, the Swiss Franc (CHF) has depreciated 12 percent against pound sterling (GBP). How much has the pound sterling appreciated against the Swiss Franc?

   A 12%

   B Less than 12%

   C More than 12%

8 An exchange rate between two currencies has increased to 1.4500. If the base currency has appreciated by 8% against the price currency, the initial exchange rate between the two currencies was *closest* to:

   A   1.3340.

   B   1.3426.

   C   1.5660.

The following information relates to Questions 9–10

A dealer provides the following quotes:

Ratio	Spot rate
CNY/HKD	0.8422
CNY/ZAR	0.9149
CNY/SEK	1.0218

9   The spot ZAR/HKD cross-rate is *closest* to:

   A   0.9205.

   B   1.0864.

   C   1.2978.

10   Another dealer is quoting the ZAR/SEK cross-rate at 1.1210. The arbitrage profit that can be earned is *closest* to:

   A   ZAR 3671 per million SEK traded.

   B   SEK 4200 per million ZAR traded.

   C   ZAR 4200 per million SEK traded.

---

11   A BRL/MXN spot rate is listed by a dealer at 0.1378. The 6-month forward rate is 0.14193. The 6-month forward points are *closest* to:

   A   −41.3.

   B   +41.3.

   C   +299.7.

12   A three-month forward exchange rate in CAD/USD is listed by a dealer at 1.0123. The dealer also quotes 3-month forward points as a percentage at 6.8%. The CAD/USD spot rate is *closest* to:

   A   0.9478.

   B   1.0550.

   C   1.0862.

13   If the base currency in a forward exchange rate quote is trading at a forward discount, which of the following statements is *most* accurate?

   A   The forward points will be positive.

   B   The forward percentage will be negative.

   C   The base currency is expected to appreciate versus the price currency.

14   A forward premium indicates:

   A   an expected increase in demand for the base currency.

   B   the interest rate is higher in the base currency than in the price currency.

C the interest rate is higher in the price currency than in the base currency.

15 The JPY/AUD spot exchange rate is 82.42, the JPY interest rate is 0.15%, and the AUD interest rate is 4.95%. If the interest rates are quoted on the basis of a 360-day year, the 90-day forward points in JPY/AUD would be *closest* to:

    A −377.0.

    B −97.7.

    C 98.9.

16 Which of the following is *not* a condition of an ideal currency regime?

    A Fully convertible currencies.

    B Fully independent monetary policy.

    C Independently floating exchange rates.

17 In practice, both a fixed parity regime and a target zone regime allow the exchange rate to float within a band around the parity level. The *most likely* rationale for the band is that the band allows the monetary authority to:

    A be less active in the currency market.

    B earn a spread on its currency transactions.

    C exercise more discretion in monetary policy.

18 A fixed exchange rate regime in which the monetary authority is legally required to hold foreign exchange reserves backing 100% of its domestic currency issuance is best described as:

    A dollarization.

    B a currency board.

    C a monetary union.

19 A country with a trade deficit will *most likely*:

    A have an offsetting capital account surplus.

    B save enough to fund its investment spending.

    C buy assets from foreigners to fund the imbalance.

20 A large industrialized country has recently devalued its currency in an attempt to correct a persistent trade deficit. Which of the following domestic industries is *most likely* to benefit from the devaluation?

    A Luxury cars.

    B Branded prescription drugs.

    C Restaurants and live entertainment venues.

21 A country with a persistent trade surplus is being pressured to let its currency appreciate. Which of the following *best* describes the adjustment that must occur if currency appreciation is to be effective in reducing the trade surplus?

    A Domestic investment must decline relative to saving.

    B Foreigners must increase investment relative to saving.

    C Global capital flows must shift toward the domestic market.

SOLUTIONS

1 B is correct. The exchange rate is the number of units of the price currency that 1 unit of the base currency will buy. Equivalently, it is the number of units of the price currency required to buy 1 unit of the base currency.

2 B is correct. The real exchange rate (quoted in terms of domestic currency per unit of foreign currency) is given by:

$$\text{Real exchange rate}_{(d/f)} = S_{d/f} \times (P_f/P_d)$$

An increase in the domestic price level (P_d) *decreases* the real exchange rate because it implies an *increase* in the relative purchasing power of the domestic currency.

3 B is correct. The receivable is due in 100 days. To reduce the risk of currency exposure, the British company would initiate a forward contract to sell euros/ buy pounds at an exchange rate agreed to today. The agreed-upon rate is called the forward exchange rate.

4 C is correct. The sell side generally consists of large banks that sell foreign exchange and related instruments to buy-side clients. These banks act as market makers, quoting exchange rates at which they will buy (the bid price) or sell (the offer price) the base currency.

5 B is correct. In the case of a direct exchange rate, the domestic currency is the price currency (the numerator) and the foreign currency is the base currency (the denominator). If the domestic currency appreciates, then fewer units of the domestic currency are required to buy 1 unit of the foreign currency and the exchange rate (domestic per foreign) declines. For example, if sterling (GBP) appreciates against the euro (EUR), then euro–sterling (GBP/EUR) might decline from 0.8650 to 0.8590.

6 A is correct. An indirect quote takes the foreign country as the price currency and the domestic country as the base currency. To get CHF—which is the executive's domestic currency—as the base currency, the quote must be stated as EUR/CHF. Using the hotel manager's information, the indirect exchange rate is (1/1.2983) = 0.7702.

7 C is correct. The appreciation of sterling against the Swiss franc is simply the inverse of the 12% depreciation of the Swiss franc against Sterling: [1/(1 − 0.12)] − 1 = (1/0.88) − 1 = 0.1364, or 13.64%.

8 B is correct. The percentage appreciation of the base currency can be calculated by dividing the appreciated exchange rate by the initial exchange rate. In this case, the unknown is the initial exchange rate. The initial exchange is the value of X that satisfies the formula:

$$1.4500/X = 1.08$$

Solving for X leads to 1.45/1.08 = 1.3426.

9 A is correct. To get to the ZAR/HKD cross-rate, it is necessary to take the inverse of the CNY/ZAR spot rate and then multiply by the CNY/HKD exchange rate:

ZAR/HKD = (CNY/ZAR)$^{-1}$ × (CNY/HKD)

= (1/0.9149) × 0.8422 = 0.9205

10 C is correct. The ZAR/SEK cross-rate from the original dealer is (1.0218/0.9149) = 1.1168, which is lower than the quote from the second dealer. To earn an arbitrage profit, a currency trader would buy SEK (sell ZAR) from the original dealer and sell SEK (buy ZAR) to the second dealer. On 1 million SEK the profit would be

SEK 1,000,000 × (1.1210 − 1.1168) = ZAR 4200

11 B is correct. The number of forward points equals the forward rate minus the spot rate, or 0.14193 − 0.1378 = 0.00413, multiplied by 10,000: 10,000 × 0.00413= 41.3 points. By convention, forward points are scaled so that ±1 forward point corresponds to a change of ±1 in the last decimal place of the spot exchange rate.

12 A is correct. Given the forward rate and forward points as a percentage, the unknown in the calculation is the spot rate. The calculation is as follows:

Spot rate × (1 + Forward points as a percentage) = Forward rate

Spot rate × (1 + 0.068) = 1.0123

Spot = 1.0123/1.068 =0.9478

13 B is correct. The base currency trading at a forward discount means that 1 unit of the base currency costs less for forward delivery than for spot delivery; i.e., the forward exchange rate is less than the spot exchange rate. The forward points, expressed either as an absolute number of points or as a percentage, are negative.

14 C is correct. To eliminate arbitrage opportunities, the spot exchange rate (S), the forward exchange rate (F), the interest rate in the base currency (i_b), and the interest rate in the price currency (i_p) must satisfy:

$$\frac{F}{S} = \left(\frac{1 + i_p}{1 + i_b}\right)$$

According to this formula, the base currency will trade at forward premium ($F > S$) if, and only if, the interest rate in the price currency is higher than the interest rate in the base currency ($i_p > i_b$).

15 B is correct. The forward exchange rate is given by

$$F_{JPY/AUD} = S_{JPY/AUD}\left(\frac{1 + i_{JPY}\tau}{1 + i_{AUD}\tau}\right) = 82.42\left[\frac{1 + .0015\left(\frac{90}{360}\right)}{1 + .0495\left(\frac{90}{360}\right)}\right]$$

= 82.42 × .98815 = 81.443

The forward points are 100 × ($F − S$) = 100 × (81.443 − 82.42) = 100 × (−0.977) = −97.7. Note that because the spot exchange rate is quoted with two decimal places, the forward points are scaled by 100.

16 C is correct. An ideal currency regime would have credibly fixed exchange rates among all currencies. This would eliminate currency-related uncertainty with respect to the prices of goods and services as well as real and financial assets.

17 C is correct. Fixed exchange rates impose severe limitations on the exercise of independent monetary policy. With a rigidly fixed exchange rate, domestic interest rates, monetary aggregates (e.g., money supply), and credit conditions are dictated by the requirement to buy/sell the currency at the rigid parity. Even a narrow band around the parity level allows the monetary authority to exercise some discretionary control over these conditions. In general, the wider the band, the more independent control the monetary authority can exercise.

18 B is correct. With a currency board, the monetary authority is legally required to exchange domestic currency for a specified foreign currency at a fixed exchange rate. It cannot issue domestic currency without receiving foreign currency in exchange, and it must hold that foreign currency as a 100% reserve against the domestic currency issued. Thus, the country's monetary base (bank reserves plus notes and coins in circulation) is fully backed by foreign exchange reserves.

19 A is correct. A trade deficit must be exactly matched by an offsetting capital account surplus to fund the deficit. A capital account surplus reflects borrowing from foreigners (an increase in domestic liabilities) and/or selling assets to foreigners (a decrease in domestic assets). A capital account surplus is often referred to as a "capital inflow" because the net effect is foreign investment in the domestic economy.

20 A is correct. A devaluation of the domestic currency means domestic producers are cutting the price faced by their foreign customers. The impact on their unit sales and their revenue depends on the elasticity of demand. Expensive luxury goods exhibit high price elasticity. Hence, luxury car producers are likely to experience a sharp increase in sales and revenue due to the devaluation.

21 C is correct. The trade surplus cannot decline unless the capital account deficit also declines. Regardless of the mix of assets bought and sold, foreigners must buy more assets from (or sell fewer assets to) domestic issuers/investors.

Glossary

A priori probability   A probability based on logical analysis rather than on observation or personal judgment.

Abnormal profit   Equal to accounting profit less the implicit opportunity costs not included in total accounting costs; the difference between total revenue (TR) and total cost (TC).

Abnormal return   The amount by which a security's actual return differs from its expected return, given the security's risk and the market's return.

Absolute advantage   A country's ability to produce a good or service at a lower absolute cost than its trading partner.

Absolute dispersion   The amount of variability present without comparison to any reference point or benchmark.

Absolute frequency   The number of observations in a given interval (for grouped data).

Accelerated book build   An offering of securities by an investment bank acting as principal that is accomplished in only one or two days.

Accelerated methods   Depreciation methods that allocate a relatively large proportion of the cost of an asset to the early years of the asset's useful life.

Account   With the accounting systems, a formal record of increases and decreases in a specific asset, liability, component of owners' equity, revenue, or expense.

Accounting (or explicit) costs   Payments to non-owner parties for services or resources they supply to the firm.

Accounting loss   When accounting profit is negative.

Accounting profit   Income as reported on the income statement, in accordance with prevailing accounting standards, before the provisions for income tax expense. Also called *income before taxes* or *pretax income*.

Accounts payable   Amounts that a business owes to its vendors for goods and services that were purchased from them but which have not yet been paid.

Accounts receivable   Amounts customers owe the company for products that have been sold as well as amounts that may be due from suppliers (such as for returns of merchandise). Also called *commercial receivables* or *trade receivables*.

Accounts receivable turnover   Ratio of sales on credit to the average balance in accounts receivable.

Accrued expenses   Liabilities related to expenses that have been incurred but not yet paid as of the end of an accounting period—an example of an accrued expense is rent that has been incurred but not yet paid, resulting in a liability "rent payable." Also called *accrued liabilities*.

Accrued interest   Interest earned but not yet paid.

Accrued revenue   Revenue that has been earned but not yet billed to customers as of the end of an accounting period.

Accumulated depreciation   An offset to property, plant, and equipment (PPE) reflecting the amount of the cost of PPE that has been allocated to current and previous accounting periods.

Acid-test ratio   A stringent measure of liquidity that indicates a company's ability to satisfy current liabilities with its most liquid assets, calculated as (cash + short-term marketable investments + receivables) divided by current liabilities.

Acquisition method   A method of accounting for a business combination where the acquirer is required to measure each identifiable asset and liability at fair value. This method was the result of a joint project of the IASB and FASB aiming at convergence in standards for the accounting of business combinations.

Action lag   Delay from policy decisions to implementation.

Active investment   An approach to investing in which the investor seeks to outperform a given benchmark.

Active return   The return on a portfolio minus the return on the portfolio's benchmark.

Active strategy   In reference to short-term cash management, an investment strategy characterized by monitoring and attempting to capitalize on market conditions to optimize the risk and return relationship of short-term investments.

Activity ratio   The ratio of the labor force to total population of working age. Also called *participation ratio*.

Activity ratios   Ratios that measure how efficiently a company performs day-to-day tasks, such as the collection of receivables and management of inventory. Also called *asset utilization ratios* or *operating efficiency ratios*.

Add-on rates   Bank certificates of deposit, repos, and indices such as Libor and Euribor are quoted on an add-on rate basis (bond equivalent yield basis).

Addition rule for probabilities   A principle stating that the probability that A or B occurs (both occur) equals the probability that A occurs, plus the probability that B occurs, minus the probability that both A and B occur.

Agency bonds   See *quasi-government bond*.

Agency RMBS   In the United States, securities backed by residential mortgage loans and guaranteed by a federal agency or guaranteed by either of the two GSEs (Fannie Mae and Freddie Mac).

Aggregate demand   The quantity of goods and services that households, businesses, government, and foreign customers want to buy at any given level of prices.

Aggregate demand curve   Inverse relationship between the price level and real output.

Aggregate income   The value of all the payments earned by the suppliers of factors used in the production of goods and services.

Aggregate output   The value of all the goods and services produced in a specified period of time.

Aggregate supply   The quantity of goods and services producers are willing to supply at any given level of price.

Aggregate supply curve   The level of domestic output that companies will produce at each price level.

Aging schedule   A breakdown of accounts into categories of days outstanding.

All-or-nothing (AON) orders   An order that includes the instruction to trade only if the trade fills the entire quantity (size) specified.

Allocationally efficient   Said of a market, a financial system, or an economy that promotes the allocation of resources to their highest value uses.

Allowance for bad debts   An offset to accounts receivable for the amount of accounts receivable that are estimated to be uncollectible.

Alternative investment markets   Market for investments other than traditional securities investments (i.e., traditional common and preferred shares and traditional fixed income instruments). The term usually encompasses direct and indirect investment in real estate (including timberland and farmland) and commodities (including precious metals); hedge funds, private equity, and other investments requiring specialized due diligence.

Alternative trading systems   Trading venues that function like exchanges but that do not exercise regulatory authority over their subscribers except with respect to the conduct of the subscribers' trading in their trading systems. Also called *electronic communications networks* or *multilateral trading facilities*.

American depository receipt   A US dollar-denominated security that trades like a common share on US exchanges.

American depository share   The underlying shares on which American depository receipts are based. They trade in the issuing company's domestic market.

American-style   Said of an option contract that can be exercised at any time up to the option's expiration date.

Amortisation   The process of allocating the cost of intangible long-term assets having a finite useful life to accounting periods; the allocation of the amount of a bond premium or discount to the periods remaining until bond maturity.

Amortised cost   The historical cost (initially recognised cost) of an asset, adjusted for amortisation and impairment.

Amortizing bond   Bond with a payment schedule that calls for periodic payments of interest and repayments of principal.

Amortizing loan   Loan with a payment schedule that calls for periodic payments of interest and repayments of principal.

Annual percentage rate   The cost of borrowing expressed as a yearly rate.

Annuity   A finite set of level sequential cash flows.

Annuity due   An annuity having a first cash flow that is paid immediately.

Anticipation stock   Excess inventory that is held in anticipation of increased demand, often because of seasonal patterns of demand.

Antidilutive   With reference to a transaction or a security, one that would increase earnings per share (EPS) or result in EPS higher than the company's basic EPS—antidilutive securities are not included in the calculation of diluted EPS.

Arbitrage   1) The simultaneous purchase of an undervalued asset or portfolio and sale of an overvalued but equivalent asset or portfolio, in order to obtain a riskless profit on the price differential. Taking advantage of a market inefficiency in a risk-free manner. 2) The condition in a financial market in which equivalent assets or combinations of assets sell for two different prices, creating an opportunity to profit at no risk with no commitment of money. In a well-functioning financial market, few arbitrage opportunities are possible. 3) A risk-free operation that earns an expected positive net profit but requires no net investment of money.

Arbitrage-free pricing   The overall process of pricing derivatives by arbitrage and risk neutrality. Also called the *principle of no arbitrage*.

Arbitrageurs   Traders who engage in arbitrage. See *arbitrage*.

Arc elasticity   An elasticity based on two points, in contrast with (point) elasticity. With reference to price elasticity, the percentage change in quantity demanded divided by the percentage change in price between two points for price.

Arithmetic mean   The sum of the observations divided by the number of observations.

Arms index   A flow of funds indicator applied to a broad stock market index to measure the relative extent to which money is moving into or out of rising and declining stocks.

Ascending price auction   An auction in which an auctioneer calls out prices for a single item and potential buyers bid directly against each other, with each subsequent bid being higher than the previous one.

Asian call option   A European-style option with a value at maturity equal to the difference between the stock price at maturity and the average stock price during the life of the option, or $0, whichever is greater.

Ask   The price at which a dealer or trader is willing to sell an asset, typically qualified by a maximum quantity (ask size). See *offer*.

Ask size   The maximum quantity of an asset that pertains to a specific ask price from a trader. For example, if the ask for a share issue is $30 for a size of 1,000 shares, the trader is offering to sell at $30 up to 1,000 shares.

Asset allocation   The process of determining how investment funds should be distributed among asset classes.

Asset-backed securities   A type of bond issued by a legal entity called a *special purpose entity* (SPE) on a collection of assets that the SPE owns. Also, securities backed by receivables and loans other than mortgages.

Asset-based loan   A loan that is secured with company assets.

Asset-based valuation models   Valuation based on estimates of the market value of a company's assets.

Asset beta   The unlevered beta; reflects the business risk of the assets; the asset's systematic risk.

Asset class   A group of assets that have similar characteristics, attributes, and risk/return relationships.

Asset swap   Converts the periodic fixed coupon of a specific bond to a Libor plus or minus a spread.

Asset utilization ratios   Ratios that measure how efficiently a company performs day-to-day tasks, such as the collection of receivables and management of inventory.

Assets   Resources controlled by an enterprise as a result of past events and from which future economic benefits to the enterprise are expected to flow.

Assignment of accounts receivable   The use of accounts receivable as collateral for a loan.

At the money   An option in which the underlying's price equals the exercise price.

At-the-money   Said of an option in which the underlying's price equals the exercise price.

Auction   A type of bond issuing mechanism often used for sovereign bonds that involves bidding.

Autarkic price   The price of a good or service in an autarkic economy.

Autarky   A state in which a country does not trade with other countries.

Automated Clearing House (ACH)   An electronic payment network available to businesses, individuals, and financial institutions in the United States, US Territories, and Canada.

Automatic stabilizer   A countercyclical factor that automatically comes into play as an economy slows and unemployment rises.

Available-for-sale Debt and equity securities not classified as either held-to-maturity or held-for-trading securities. The investor is willing to sell but not actively planning to sell. In general, available-for-sale securities are reported at fair value on the balance sheet.

Average fixed cost Total fixed cost divided by quantity.

Average life See *weighted average life*.

Average product Measures the productivity of inputs on average and is calculated by dividing total product by the total number of units for a given input that is used to generate that output.

Average revenue Quantity sold divided into total revenue.

Average total cost Total costs divided by quantity.

Average variable cost Total variable cost divided by quantity.

Back simulation Another term for the historical method of estimating VAR. This term is somewhat misleading in that the method involves not a *simulation* of the past but rather what *actually happened* in the past, sometimes adjusted to reflect the fact that a different portfolio may have existed in the past than is planned for the future.

Back-testing With reference to portfolio strategies, the application of a strategy's portfolio selection rules to historical data to assess what would have been the strategy's historical performance.

Backup lines of credit A type of credit enhancement provided by a bank to an issuer of commercial paper to ensure that the issuer will have access to sufficient liquidity to repay maturing commercial paper if issuing new paper is not a viable option.

Balance of payments A double-entry bookkeeping system that summarizes a country's economic transactions with the rest of the world for a particular period of time, typically a calendar quarter or year.

Balance of trade deficit When the domestic economy is spending more on foreign goods and services than foreign economies are spending on domestic goods and services.

Balance sheet The financial statement that presents an entity's current financial position by disclosing resources the entity controls (its assets) and the claims on those resources (its liabilities and equity claims), as of a particular point in time (the date of the balance sheet). Also called *statement of financial position* or *statement of financial condition*.

Balance sheet ratios Financial ratios involving balance sheet items only.

Balanced With respect to a government budget, one in which spending and revenues (taxes) are equal.

Balloon payment Large payment required at maturity to retire a bond's outstanding principal amount.

Bank discount basis A quoting convention that annualizes, on a 360-day year, the discount as a percentage of face value.

Bar chart A price chart with four bits of data for each time interval—the high, low, opening, and closing prices. A vertical line connects the high and low. A cross-hatch left indicates the opening price and a cross-hatch right indicates the close.

Barter economy An economy where economic agents as house-holds, corporations, and governments "pay" for goods and services with another good or service.

Base rates The reference rate on which a bank bases lending rates to all other customers.

Basic EPS Net earnings available to common shareholders (i.e., net income minus preferred dividends) divided by the weighted average number of common shares outstanding.

Basis point Used in stating yield spreads, one basis point equals one-hundredth of a percentage point, or 0.01%.

Basket of listed depository receipts An exchange-traded fund (ETF) that represents a portfolio of depository receipts.

Bearer bonds Bonds for which ownership is not recorded; only the clearing system knows who the bond owner is.

Behavioral equations With respect to demand and supply, equations that model the behavior of buyers and sellers.

Behavioral finance A field of finance that examines the psychological variables that affect and often distort the investment decision making of investors, analysts, and portfolio managers.

Behind the market Said of prices specified in orders that are worse than the best current price; e.g., for a limit buy order, a limit price below the best bid.

Benchmark A comparison portfolio; a point of reference or comparison.

Benchmark issue The latest sovereign bond issue for a given maturity. It serves as a benchmark against which to compare bonds that have the same features but that are issued by another type of issuer.

Benchmark rate Typically the yield-to-maturity on a government bond having the same, or close to the same, time-to-maturity.

Benchmark spread The yield spread over a specific benchmark, usually measured in basis points.

Bermuda-style Said of an option contract that can be exercised on specified dates up to the option's expiration date.

Bernoulli random variable A random variable having the outcomes 0 and 1.

Bernoulli trial An experiment that can produce one of two outcomes.

Best bid The highest bid in the market.

Best effort offering An offering of a security using an investment bank in which the investment bank, as agent for the issuer, promises to use its best efforts to sell the offering but does not guarantee that a specific amount will be sold.

Best offer The lowest offer (ask price) in the market.

Beta A measure of the sensitivity of a given investment or portfolio to movements in the overall market.

Bid The price at which a dealer or trader is willing to buy an asset, typically qualified by a maximum quantity.

Bid–ask spread The difference between the prices at which dealers will buy from a customer (bid) and sell to a customer (offer or ask). It is often used as an indicator of liquidity.

Bid–offer spread The difference between the prices at which dealers will buy from a customer (bid) and sell to a customer (offer or ask). It is often used as an indicator of liquidity.

Bid size The maximum quantity of an asset that pertains to a specific bid price from a trader.

Bilateral loan A loan from a single lender to a single borrower.

Binomial model A model for pricing options in which the underlying price can move to only one of two possible new prices.

Binomial random variable The number of successes in n Bernoulli trials for which the probability of success is constant for all trials and the trials are independent.

Binomial tree The graphical representation of a model of asset price dynamics in which, at each period, the asset moves up with probability p or down with probability $(1 - p)$.

Block brokers A broker (agent) that provides brokerage services for large-size trades.

Blue chip   Widely held large market capitalization companies that are considered financially sound and are leaders in their respective industry or local stock market.

Bollinger Bands   A price-based technical analysis indicator consisting of a moving average plus a higher line representing the moving average plus a set number of standard deviations from average price (for the same number of periods as used to calculate the moving average) and a lower line that is a moving average minus the same number of standard deviations.

Bond   Contractual agreement between the issuer and the bondholders.

Bond equivalent yield   A calculation of yield that is annualized using the ratio of 365 to the number of days to maturity. Bond equivalent yield allows for the restatement and comparison of securities with different compounding periods.

Bond indenture   The governing legal credit agreement, typically incorporated by reference in the prospectus. Also called *trust deed*.

Bond market vigilantes   Bond market participants who might reduce their demand for long-term bonds, thus pushing up their yields.

Bond yield plus risk premium approach   An estimate of the cost of common equity that is produced by summing the before-tax cost of debt and a risk premium that captures the additional yield on a company's stock relative to its bonds. The additional yield is often estimated using historical spreads between bond yields and stock yields.

Bonus issue of shares   A type of dividend in which a company distributes additional shares of its common stock to shareholders instead of cash.

Book building   Investment bankers' process of compiling a "book" or list of indications of interest to buy part of an offering.

Book value   The net amount shown for an asset or liability on the balance sheet; book value may also refer to the company's excess of total assets over total liabilities. Also called *carrying value*.

Boom   An expansionary phase characterized by economic growth "testing the limits" of the economy.

Bottom-up analysis   With reference to investment selection processes, an approach that involves selection from all securities within a specified investment universe, i.e., without prior narrowing of the universe on the basis of macroeconomic or overall market considerations.

Break point   In the context of the weighted average cost of capital (WACC), a break point is the amount of capital at which the cost of one or more of the sources of capital changes, leading to a change in the WACC.

Breakeven point   The number of units produced and sold at which the company's net income is zero (revenues = total costs); in the case of perfect competition, the quantity where price, average revenue, and marginal revenue equal average total cost.

Bridge financing   Interim financing that provides funds until permanent financing can be arranged.

Broad money   Encompasses narrow money plus the entire range of liquid assets that can be used to make purchases.

Broker   1) An agent who executes orders to buy or sell securities on behalf of a client in exchange for a commission. 2) See *futures commission merchants*.

Broker–dealer   A financial intermediary (often a company) that may function as a principal (dealer) or as an agent (broker) depending on the type of trade.

Brokered market   A market in which brokers arrange trades among their clients.

Budget constraint   A constraint on spending or investment imposed by wealth or income.

Budget surplus/deficit   The difference between government revenue and expenditure for a stated fixed period of time.

Business risk   The risk associated with operating earnings. Operating earnings are uncertain because total revenues and many of the expenditures contributed to produce those revenues are uncertain.

Buy-side firm   An investment management company or other investor that uses the services of brokers or dealers (i.e., the client of the sell side firms).

Buyback   A transaction in which a company buys back its own shares. Unlike stock dividends and stock splits, share repurchases use corporate cash.

Buyout fund   A fund that buys all the shares of a public company so that, in effect, the company becomes private.

Call   An option that gives the holder the right to buy an underlying asset from another party at a fixed price over a specific period of time.

Call market   A market in which trades occur only at a particular time and place (i.e., when the market is called).

Call money rate   The interest rate that buyers pay for their margin loan.

Call option   An option that gives the holder the right to buy an underlying asset from another party at a fixed price over a specific period of time.

Call protection   The time during which the issuer of the bond is not allowed to exercise the call option.

Callable bond   A bond containing an embedded call option that gives the issuer the right to buy the bond back from the investor at specified prices on pre-determined dates.

Callable common shares   Shares that give the issuing company the option (or right), but not the obligation, to buy back the shares from investors at a call price that is specified when the shares are originally issued.

Candlestick chart   A price chart with four bits of data for each time interval. A candle indicates the opening and closing price for the interval. The body of the candle is shaded if the opening price was higher than the closing price, and the body is clear if the opening price was lower than the closing price. Vertical lines known as wicks or shadows extend from the top and bottom of the candle to indicate the high and the low prices for the interval.

Cannibalization   Cannibalization occurs when an investment takes customers and sales away from another part of the company.

Capacity   The ability of the borrower to make its debt payments on time.

Capital account   A component of the balance of payments account that measures transfers of capital.

Capital allocation line   (CAL) A graph line that describes the combinations of expected return and standard deviation of return available to an investor from combining the optimal portfolio of risky assets with the risk-free asset.

Capital asset pricing model   (CAPM) An equation describing the expected return on any asset (or portfolio) as a linear function of its beta relative to the market portfolio.

Capital budgeting   The allocation of funds to relatively long-range projects or investments.

Capital consumption allowance   A measure of the wear and tear (depreciation) of the capital stock that occurs in the production of goods and services.

Capital deepening investment   Increases the stock of capital relative to labor.

Capital expenditure   Expenditure on physical capital (fixed assets).

Capital-indexed bonds   Type of index-linked bond. The coupon rate is fixed but is applied to a principal amount that increases in line with increases in the index during the bond's life.

Capital lease   See *finance lease*.

Capital market expectations   An investor's expectations concerning the risk and return prospects of asset classes.

Capital market line   (CML) The line with an intercept point equal to the risk-free rate that is tangent to the efficient frontier of risky assets; represents the efficient frontier when a risk-free asset is available for investment.

Capital market securities   Securities with maturities at issuance longer than one year.

Capital markets   Financial markets that trade securities of longer duration, such as bonds and equities.

Capital rationing   A capital rationing environment assumes that the company has a fixed amount of funds to invest.

Capital restrictions   Controls placed on foreigners' ability to own domestic assets and/or domestic residents' ability to own foreign assets.

Capital stock   The accumulated amount of buildings, machinery, and equipment used to produce goods and services.

Capital structure   The mix of debt and equity that a company uses to finance its business; a company's specific mixture of long-term financing.

Captive finance subsidiary   A wholly-owned subsidiary of a company that is established to provide financing of the sales of the parent company.

Carry   The net of the costs and benefits of holding, storing, or "carrying" an asset.

Carrying amount   The amount at which an asset or liability is valued according to accounting principles.

Carrying value   The net amount shown for an asset or liability on the balance sheet; book value may also refer to the company's excess of total assets over total liabilities. For a bond, the purchase price plus (or minus) the amortized amount of the discount (or premium).

Cartel   Participants in collusive agreements that are made openly and formally.

Cash   In accounting contexts, cash on hand (e.g., petty cash and cash not yet deposited to the bank) and demand deposits held in banks and similar accounts that can be used in payment of obligations.

Cash collateral account   Form of external credit enhancement whereby the issuer immediately borrows the credit-enhancement amount and then invests that amount, usually in highly rated short-term commercial paper.

Cash conversion cycle   A financial metric that measures the length of time required for a company to convert cash invested in its operations to cash received as a result of its operations; equal to days of inventory on hand + days of sales outstanding − number of days of payables. Also called *net operating cycle*.

Cash equivalents   Very liquid short-term investments, usually maturing in 90 days or less.

Cash flow additivity principle   The principle that dollar amounts indexed at the same point in time are additive.

Cash flow from operating activities   The net amount of cash provided from operating activities.

Cash flow from operations   The net amount of cash provided from operating activities.

Cash flow yield   The internal rate of return on a series of cash flows.

Cash market securities   Money market securities settled on a "same day" or "cash settlement" basis.

Cash markets   See *spot markets*.

Cash prices   See *spot prices*.

Cash-settled forwards   See *non-deliverable forwards*.

CBOE Volatility Index   A measure of near-term market volatility as conveyed by S&P 500 stock index option prices.

CD equivalent yield   A yield on a basis comparable to the quoted yield on an interest-bearing money market instrument that pays interest on a 360-day basis; the annualized holding period yield, assuming a 360-day year.

Central bank funds market   The market in which deposit-taking banks that have an excess reserve with their national central bank can loan money to banks that need funds for maturities ranging from overnight to one year. Called the Federal or Fed funds market in the United States.

Central bank funds rates   Interest rates at which central bank funds are bought (borrowed) and sold (lent) for maturities ranging from overnight to one year. Called Federal or Fed funds rates in the United States.

Central banks   The dominant bank in a country, usually with official or semi-official governmental status.

Certificate of deposit   An instrument that represents a specified amount of funds on deposit with a bank for a specified maturity and interest rate. It is issued in small or large denominations, and can be negotiable or non-negotiable.

Change in polarity principle   A tenet of technical analysis that once a support level is breached, it becomes a resistance level. The same holds true for resistance levels; once breached, they become support levels.

Change in quantity supplied   A movement along a given supply curve.

Change in supply   A shift in the supply curve.

Change of control put   A covenant giving bondholders the right to require the issuer to buy back their debt, often at par or at some small premium to par value, in the event that the borrower is acquired.

Character   The quality of a debt issuer's management.

Chart of accounts   A list of accounts used in an entity's accounting system.

Classified balance sheet   A balance sheet organized so as to group together the various assets and liabilities into subcategories (e.g., current and noncurrent).

Clawback   A requirement that the GP return any funds distributed as incentive fees until the LPs have received back their initial investment and a percentage of the total profit.

Clearing   The process by which the exchange verifies the execution of a transaction and records the participants' identities.

Clearing instructions   Instructions that indicate how to arrange the final settlement ("clearing") of a trade.

Clearinghouse   An entity associated with a futures market that acts as middleman between the contracting parties and guarantees to each party the performance of the other.

Closed economy   An economy that does not trade with other countries; an *autarkic economy*.

Closed-end fund   A mutual fund in which no new investment money is accepted. New investors invest by buying existing shares, and investors in the fund liquidate by selling their shares to other investors.

Coefficient of variation (CV) The ratio of a set of observations' standard deviation to the observations' mean value.

Coincident economic indicators Turning points that are usually close to those of the overall economy; they are believed to have value for identifying the economy's present state.

Collateral The quality and value of the assets supporting an issuer's indebtedness.

Collateral manager Buys and sells debt obligations for and from the CDO's portfolio of assets (i.e., the collateral) to generate sufficient cash flows to meet the obligations to the CDO bondholders.

Collateral trust bonds Bonds secured by securities such as common shares, other bonds, or other financial assets.

Collateralized bond obligations A structured asset-backed security that is collateralized by a pool of bonds.

Collateralized debt obligation Generic term used to describe a security backed by a diversified pool of one or more debt obligations.

Collateralized loan obligations A structured asset-backed security that is collateralized by a pool of loans.

Collateralized mortgage obligation A security created through the securitization of a pool of mortgage-related products (mortgage pass-through securities or pools of loans).

Collaterals Assets or financial guarantees underlying a debt obligation above and beyond the issuer's promise to pay.

Combination A listing in which the order of the listed items does not matter.

Commercial paper A short-term, negotiable, unsecured promissory note that represents a debt obligation of the issuer.

Commercial receivables Amounts customers owe the company for products that have been sold as well as amounts that may be due from suppliers (such as for returns of merchandise). Also called *trade receivables* or *accounts receivable*.

Committed capital The amount that the limited partners have agreed to provide to the private equity fund.

Committed lines of credit A bank commitment to extend credit up to a pre-specified amount; the commitment is considered a short-term liability and is usually in effect for 364 days (one day short of a full year).

Commodity swap A swap in which the underlying is a commodity such as oil, gold, or an agricultural product.

Common market Level of economic integration that incorporates all aspects of the customs union and extends it by allowing free movement of factors of production among members.

Common shares A type of security that represent an ownership interest in a company.

Common-size analysis The restatement of financial statement items using a common denominator or reference item that allows one to identify trends and major differences; an example is an income statement in which all items are expressed as a percent of revenue.

Common stock See *common shares*.

Common value auction An auction in which the item being auctioned has the same value to each auction participant, although participants may be uncertain as to what that value is.

Company analysis Analysis of an individual company.

Comparable company A company that has similar business risk; usually in the same industry and preferably with a single line of business.

Comparative advantage A country's ability to produce a good or service at a lower relative cost, or opportunity cost, than its trading partner.

Competitive strategy A company's plans for responding to the threats and opportunities presented by the external environment.

Complements Said of goods which tend to be used together; technically, two goods whose cross-price elasticity of demand is negative.

Complete markets Informally, markets in which the variety of distinct securities traded is so broad that any desired payoff in a future state-of-the-world is achievable.

Complete preferences The assumption that a consumer is able to make a comparison between any two possible bundles of goods.

Completed contract A method of revenue recognition in which the company does not recognize any revenue until the contract is completed; used particularly in long-term construction contracts.

Component cost of capital The rate of return required by suppliers of capital for an individual source of a company's funding, such as debt or equity.

Compounding The process of accumulating interest on interest.

Comprehensive income The change in equity of a business enterprise during a period from nonowner sources; includes all changes in equity during a period except those resulting from investments by owners and distributions to owners; comprehensive income equals net income plus other comprehensive income.

Conditional expected value The expected value of a stated event given that another event has occurred.

Conditional probability The probability of an event given (conditioned on) another event.

Conditional variances The variance of one variable, given the outcome of another.

Consistent With reference to estimators, describes an estimator for which the probability of estimates close to the value of the population parameter increases as sample size increases.

Conspicuous consumption Consumption of high status goods, such as a luxury automobile or a very expensive piece of jewelry.

Constant-cost industry When firms in the industry experience no change in resource costs and output prices over the long run.

Constant returns to scale The characteristic of constant per-unit costs in the presence of increased production.

Constant-yield price trajectory A graph that illustrates the change in the price of a fixed-income bond over time assuming no change in yield-to-maturity. The trajectory shows the "pull to par" effect on the price of a bond trading at a premium or a discount to par value.

Constituent securities With respect to an index, the individual securities within an index.

Consumer choice theory The theory relating consumer demand curves to consumer preferences.

Consumer surplus The difference between the value that a consumer places on units purchased and the amount of money that was required to pay for them.

Consumption The purchase of final goods and services by individuals.

Consumption basket A specific combination of the goods and services that a consumer wants to consume.

Consumption bundle   A specific combination of the goods and services that a consumer wants to consume.

Contingency provision   Clause in a legal document that allows for some action if a specific event or circumstance occurs.

Contingent claims   Derivatives in which the payoffs occur if a specific event occurs; generally referred to as options.

Contingent convertible bonds   Bonds that automatically convert into equity if a specific event or circumstance occurs, such as the issuer's equity capital falling below the minimum requirement set by the regulators. Also called *CoCos*.

Continuation patterns   A type of pattern used in technical analysis to predict the resumption of a market trend that was in place prior to the formation of a pattern.

Continuous random variable   A random variable for which the range of possible outcomes is the real line (all real numbers between $-\infty$ and $+\infty$ or some subset of the real line).

Continuous time   Time thought of as advancing in extremely small increments.

Continuous trading market   A market in which trades can be arranged and executed any time the market is open.

Continuously compounded return   The natural logarithm of 1 plus the holding period return, or equivalently, the natural logarithm of the ending price over the beginning price.

Contra account   An account that offsets another account.

Contract rate   See *mortgage rate*.

Contraction   The period of a business cycle after the peak and before the trough; often called a *recession* or, if exceptionally severe, called a *depression*.

Contraction risk   The risk that when interest rates decline, the security will have a shorter maturity than was anticipated at the time of purchase because borrowers refinance at the new, lower interest rates.

Contractionary   Tending to cause the real economy to contract.

Contractionary fiscal policy   A fiscal policy that has the objective to make the real economy contract.

Contracts for differences   See *non-deliverable forwards*.

Contribution margin   The amount available for fixed costs and profit after paying variable costs; revenue minus variable costs.

Convenience yield   A non-monetary advantage of holding an asset.

Conventional bond   See *plain vanilla bond*.

Conventional cash flow   A conventional cash flow pattern is one with an initial outflow followed by a series of inflows.

Convergence   The tendency for differences in output per capita across countries to diminish over time; in technical analysis, a term that describes the case when an indicator moves in the same manner as the security being analyzed.

Conversion price   For a convertible bond, the price per share at which the bond can be converted into shares.

Conversion ratio   For a convertible bond, the number of common shares that each bond can be converted into.

Conversion value   For a convertible bond, the current share price multiplied by the conversion ratio.

Convertible bond   Bond that gives the bondholder the right to exchange the bond for a specified number of common shares in the issuing company.

Convertible preference shares   A type of equity security that entitles shareholders to convert their shares into a specified number of common shares.

Convexity adjustment   For a bond, one half of the annual or approximate convexity statistic multiplied by the change in the yield-to-maturity squared.

Core inflation   The inflation rate calculated based on a price index of goods and services except food and energy.

Correlation   A number between -1 and $+1$ that measures the comovement (linear association) between two random variables.

Correlation coefficient   A number between -1 and $+1$ that measures the consistency or tendency for two investments to act in a similar way. It is used to determine the effect on portfolio risk when two assets are combined.

Cost averaging   The periodic investment of a fixed amount of money.

Cost of capital   The rate of return that suppliers of capital require as compensation for their contribution of capital.

Cost of carry   See *carry*.

Cost of debt   The cost of debt financing to a company, such as when it issues a bond or takes out a bank loan.

Cost of goods sold   For a given period, equal to beginning inventory minus ending inventory plus the cost of goods acquired or produced during the period.

Cost of preferred stock   The cost to a company of issuing preferred stock; the dividend yield that a company must commit to pay preferred stockholders.

Cost-push   Type of inflation in which rising costs, usually wages, compel businesses to raise prices generally.

Cost recovery method   A method of revenue recognition in which the seller does not report any profit until the cash amounts paid by the buyer—including principal and interest on any financing from the seller—are greater than all the seller's costs for the merchandise sold.

Cost structure   The mix of a company's variable costs and fixed costs.

Counterparty risk   The risk that the other party to a contract will fail to honor the terms of the contract.

Coupon rate   The interest rate promised in a contract; this is the rate used to calculate the periodic interest payments.

Cournot assumption   Assumption in which each firm determines its profit-maximizing production level assuming that the other firms' output will not change.

Covariance   A measure of the co-movement (linear association) between two random variables.

Covariance matrix   A matrix or square array whose entries are covariances; also known as a variance–covariance matrix.

Covenants   The terms and conditions of lending agreements that the issuer must comply with; they specify the actions that an issuer is obligated to perform (affirmative covenant) or prohibited from performing (negative covenant).

Covered bond   Debt obligation secured by a segregated pool of assets called the cover pool. The issuer must maintain the value of the cover pool. In the event of default, bondholders have recourse against both the issuer and the cover pool.

Covered call   An option strategy involving the holding of an asset and sale of a call on the asset.

Credit   With respect to double-entry accounting, a credit records increases in liability, owners' equity, and revenue accounts or decreases in asset accounts; with respect to borrowing, the willingness and ability of the borrower to make promised payments on the borrowing.

Credit analysis   The evaluation of credit risk; the evaluation of the creditworthiness of a borrower or counterparty.

Credit curve   A curve showing the relationship between time to maturity and yield spread for an issuer with comparable bonds of various maturities outstanding, usually upward sloping.

Credit default swap (CDS)   A type of credit derivative in which one party, the credit protection buyer who is seeking credit protection against a third party, makes a series of regularly scheduled payments to the other party, the credit protection seller. The seller makes no payments until a credit event occurs.

Credit derivatives   A contract in which one party has the right to claim a payment from another party in the event that a specific credit event occurs over the life of the contract.

Credit enhancements   Provisions that may be used to reduce the credit risk of a bond issue.

Credit-linked coupon bond   Bond for which the coupon changes when the bond's credit rating changes.

Credit-linked note   Fixed-income security in which the holder of the security has the right to withhold payment of the full amount due at maturity if a credit event occurs.

Credit-linked note (CLN)   A type of structured financial instrument that provides investors yield enhancement. It is a bond that pays regular coupons but whose redemption value depends on the occurrence of a well-defined credit event, such as a rating downgrade or the default of an underlying asset.

Credit migration risk   The risk that a bond issuer's creditworthiness deteriorates, or migrates lower, leading investors to believe the risk of default is higher. Also called *downgrade risk*.

Credit risk   The risk of loss caused by a counterparty's or debtor's failure to make a promised payment. Also called *default risk*.

Credit scoring model   A statistical model used to classify borrowers according to creditworthiness.

Credit spread option   An option on the yield spread on a bond.

Credit tranching   A structure used to redistribute the credit risk associated with the collateral; a set of bond classes created to allow investors a choice in the amount of credit risk that they prefer to bear.

Credit-worthiness   The perceived ability of the borrower to pay what is owed on the borrowing in a timely manner; it represents the ability of a company to withstand adverse impacts on its cash flows.

Cross-default provisions   Provisions whereby events of default such as non-payment of interest on one bond trigger default on all outstanding debt; implies the same default probability for all issues.

Cross-price elasticity of demand   The percent change in quantity demanded for a given small change in the price of another good; the responsiveness of the demand for Product A that is associated with the change in price of Product B.

Cross-sectional analysis   Analysis that involves comparisons across individuals in a group over a given time period or at a given point in time.

Cross-sectional data   Observations over individual units at a point in time, as opposed to time-series data.

Crossing networks   Trading systems that match buyers and sellers who are willing to trade at prices obtained from other markets.

Crowding out   The thesis that government borrowing may divert private sector investment from taking place.

Cumulative distribution function   A function giving the probability that a random variable is less than or equal to a specified value.

Cumulative preference shares   Preference shares for which any dividends that are not paid accrue and must be paid in full before dividends on common shares can be paid.

Cumulative relative frequency   For data grouped into intervals, the fraction of total observations that are less than the value of the upper limit of a stated interval.

Cumulative voting   Voting that allows shareholders to direct their total voting rights to specific candidates, as opposed to having to allocate their voting rights evenly among all candidates.

Currencies   Monies issued by national monetary authorities.

Currency option bonds   Bonds that give the bondholder the right to choose the currency in which he or she wants to receive interest payments and principal repayments.

Currency swap   A swap in which each party makes interest payments to the other in different currencies.

Current account   A component of the balance of payments account that measures the flow of goods and services.

Current assets   Assets that are expected to be consumed or converted into cash in the near future, typically one year or less. Also called *liquid assets*.

Current cost   With reference to assets, the amount of cash or cash equivalents that would have to be paid to buy the same or an equivalent asset today; with reference to liabilities, the undiscounted amount of cash or cash equivalents that would be required to settle the obligation today.

Current government spending   With respect to government expenditures, spending on goods and services that are provided on a regular, recurring basis including health, education, and defense.

Current liabilities   Short-term obligations, such as accounts payable, wages payable, or accrued liabilities, that are expected to be settled in the near future, typically one year or less.

Current ratio   A liquidity ratio calculated as current assets divided by current liabilities.

Current yield   The sum of the coupon payments received over the year divided by the flat price; also called the *income* or *interest yield* or *running yield*.

Curve duration   The sensitivity of the bond price (or the market value of a financial asset or liability) with respect to a benchmark yield curve.

Customs union   Extends the free trade area (FTA) by not only allowing free movement of goods and services among members, but also creating a common trade policy against nonmembers.

CVaR   Conditional VaR, a tail loss measure. The weighted average of all loss outcomes in the statistical distribution that exceed the VaR loss.

Cyclical   See *cyclical companies*.

Cyclical companies   Companies with sales and profits that regularly expand and contract with the business cycle or state of economy.

Daily settlement   See *mark to market* and *marking to market*.

Dark pools   Alternative trading systems that do not display the orders that their clients send to them.

Data mining   The practice of determining a model by extensive searching through a dataset for statistically significant patterns. Also called *data snooping*.

Data snooping   See *data mining*.

Date of book closure   The date that a shareholder listed on the corporation's books will be deemed to have ownership of the shares for purposes of receiving an upcoming dividend; two business days after the ex-dividend date.

Date of record   The date that a shareholder listed on the corporation's books will be deemed to have ownership of the shares for purposes of receiving an upcoming dividend; two business days after the ex-dividend date.

Day order   An order that is good for the day on which it is submitted. If it has not been filled by the close of business, the order expires unfilled.

Day's sales outstanding   Estimate of the average number of days it takes to collect on credit accounts.

Days in receivables   Estimate of the average number of days it takes to collect on credit accounts.

Days of inventory on hand   An activity ratio equal to the number of days in the period divided by inventory turnover over the period.

Dead cross   A technical analysis term that describes a situation where a short-term moving average crosses from above a longer-term moving average to below it; this movement is considered bearish.

Deadweight loss   A net loss of total (consumer and producer) surplus.

Dealers   A financial intermediary that acts as a principal in trades.

Dealing securities   Securities held by banks or other financial intermediaries for trading purposes.

Debentures   Type of bond that can be secured or unsecured.

Debit   With respect to double-entry accounting, a debit records increases of asset and expense accounts or decreases in liability and owners' equity accounts.

Debt incurrence test   A financial covenant made in conjunction with existing debt that restricts a company's ability to incur additional debt at the same seniority based on one or more financial tests or conditions.

Debt-rating approach   A method for estimating a company's before-tax cost of debt based upon the yield on comparably rated bonds for maturities that closely match that of the company's existing debt.

Debt-to-assets ratio   A solvency ratio calculated as total debt divided by total assets.

Debt-to-capital ratio   A solvency ratio calculated as total debt divided by total debt plus total shareholders' equity.

Debt-to-equity ratio   A solvency ratio calculated as total debt divided by total shareholders' equity.

Declaration date   The day that the corporation issues a statement declaring a specific dividend.

Decreasing-cost industry   An industry in which per-unit costs and output prices are lower when industry output is increased in the long run.

Decreasing returns to scale   Increase in cost per unit resulting from increased production.

Deductible temporary differences   Temporary differences that result in a reduction of or deduction from taxable income in a future period when the balance sheet item is recovered or settled.

Default probability   The probability that a borrower defaults or fails to meet its obligation to make full and timely payments of principal and interest, according to the terms of the debt security. Also called *default risk*.

Default risk   The probability that a borrower defaults or fails to meet its obligation to make full and timely payments of principal and interest, according to the terms of the debt security. Also called *default probability*.

Default risk premium   An extra return that compensates investors for the possibility that the borrower will fail to make a promised payment at the contracted time and in the contracted amount.

Defensive companies   Companies with sales and profits that have little sensitivity to the business cycle or state of the economy.

Defensive interval ratio   A liquidity ratio that estimates the number of days that an entity could meet cash needs from liquid assets; calculated as (cash + short-term marketable investments + receivables) divided by daily cash expenditures.

Deferred coupon bond   Bond that pays no coupons for its first few years but then pays a higher coupon than it otherwise normally would for the remainder of its life. Also called *split coupon bond*.

Deferred income   A liability account for money that has been collected for goods or services that have not yet been delivered; payment received in advance of providing a good or service.

Deferred revenue   A liability account for money that has been collected for goods or services that have not yet been delivered; payment received in advance of providing a good or service.

Deferred tax assets   A balance sheet asset that arises when an excess amount is paid for income taxes relative to accounting profit. The taxable income is higher than accounting profit and income tax payable exceeds tax expense. The company expects to recover the difference during the course of future operations when tax expense exceeds income tax payable.

Deferred tax liabilities   A balance sheet liability that arises when a deficit amount is paid for income taxes relative to accounting profit. The taxable income is less than the accounting profit and income tax payable is less than tax expense. The company expects to eliminate the liability over the course of future operations when income tax payable exceeds tax expense.

Defined benefit pension plans   Plan in which the company promises to pay a certain annual amount (defined benefit) to the employee after retirement. The company bears the investment risk of the plan assets.

Defined-benefit plan   A pension plan that specifies the plan sponsor's obligations in terms of the benefit to plan participants.

Defined contribution pension plans   Individual accounts to which an employee and typically the employer makes contributions, generally on a tax-advantaged basis. The amounts of contributions are defined at the outset, but the future value of the benefit is unknown. The employee bears the investment risk of the plan assets.

Defined-contribution plan   A pension plan that specifies the sponsor's obligations in terms of contributions to the pension fund rather than benefits to plan participants.

Deflation   Negative inflation.

Degree of confidence   The probability that a confidence interval includes the unknown population parameter.

Degree of financial leverage   (DFL) The ratio of the percentage change in net income to the percentage change in operating income; the sensitivity of the cash flows available to owners when operating income changes.

Degree of operating leverage (DOL) The ratio of the percentage change in operating income to the percentage change in units sold; the sensitivity of operating income to changes in units sold.

Degree of total leverage The ratio of the percentage change in net income to the percentage change in units sold; the sensitivity of the cash flows to owners to changes in the number of units produced and sold.

Degrees of freedom (df) The number of independent observations used.

Delta The sensitivity of the derivative price to a small change in the value of the underlying asset.

Demand The willingness and ability of consumers to purchase a given amount of a good or service at a given price.

Demand and supply analysis The study of how buyers and sellers interact to determine transaction prices and quantities.

Demand curve Graph of the inverse demand function.

Demand function A relationship that expresses the quantity demanded of a good or service as a function of own-price and possibly other variables.

Demand-pull Type of inflation in which increasing demand raises prices generally, which then are reflected in a business's costs as workers demand wage hikes to catch up with the rising cost of living.

Demand shock A typically unexpected disturbance to demand, such as an unexpected interruption in trade or transportation.

Dependent With reference to events, the property that the probability of one event occurring depends on (is related to) the occurrence of another event.

Depository bank A bank that raises funds from depositors and other investors and lends it to borrowers.

Depository institutions Commercial banks, savings and loan banks, credit unions, and similar institutions that raise funds from depositors and other investors and lend it to borrowers.

Depository receipt A security that trades like an ordinary share on a local exchange and represents an economic interest in a foreign company.

Depreciation The process of systematically allocating the cost of long-lived (tangible) assets to the periods during which the assets are expected to provide economic benefits.

Depression See *contraction*.

Derivative pricing rule A pricing rule used by crossing networks in which a price is taken (derived) from the price that is current in the asset's primary market.

Derivatives A financial instrument whose value depends on the value of some underlying asset or factor (e.g., a stock price, an interest rate, or exchange rate).

Descending price auction An auction in which the auctioneer begins at a high price, then lowers the called price in increments until there is a willing buyer for the item being auctioned.

Descriptive statistics The study of how data can be summarized effectively.

Development capital Minority equity investments in more mature companies that are looking for capital to expand or restructure operations, enter new markets, or finance major acquisitions.

Diffuse prior The assumption of equal prior probabilities.

Diffusion index Reflects the proportion of the index's components that are moving in a pattern consistent with the overall index.

Diluted EPS The EPS that would result if all dilutive securities were converted into common shares.

Diluted shares The number of shares that would be outstanding if all potentially dilutive claims on common shares (e.g., convertible debt, convertible preferred stock, and employee stock options) were exercised.

Diminishing balance method An accelerated depreciation method, i.e., one that allocates a relatively large proportion of the cost of an asset to the early years of the asset's useful life.

Diminishing marginal productivity Describes a state in which each additional unit of input produces less output than previously.

Direct debit program An arrangement whereby a customer authorizes a debit to a demand account; typically used by companies to collect routine payments for services.

Direct financing leases A type of finance lease, from a lessor perspective, where the present value of the lease payments (lease receivable) equals the carrying value of the leased asset. The revenues earned by the lessor are financing in nature.

Direct format With reference to the cash flow statement, a format for the presentation of the statement in which cash flow from operating activities is shown as operating cash receipts less operating cash disbursements. Also called *direct method*.

Direct method See *direct format*.

Direct taxes Taxes levied directly on income, wealth, and corporate profits.

Direct write-off method An approach to recognizing credit losses on customer receivables in which the company waits until such time as a customer has defaulted and only then recognizes the loss.

Disbursement float The amount of time between check issuance and a check's clearing back against the company's account.

Discount To reduce the value of a future payment in allowance for how far away it is in time; to calculate the present value of some future amount. Also, the amount by which an instrument is priced below its face (par) value.

Discount interest A procedure for determining the interest on a loan or bond in which the interest is deducted from the face value in advance.

Discount margin See *required margin*.

Discount rates In general, the interest rate used to calculate a present value. In the money market, however, discount rate is a specific type of quoted rate.

Discounted cash flow models Valuation models that estimate the intrinsic value of a security as the present value of the future benefits expected to be received from the security.

Discouraged worker A person who has stopped looking for a job or has given up seeking employment.

Discrete random variable A random variable that can take on at most a countable number of possible values.

Discriminatory pricing rule A pricing rule used in continuous markets in which the limit price of the order or quote that first arrived determines the trade price.

Diseconomies of scale Increase in cost per unit resulting from increased production.

Dispersion The variability around the central tendency.

Display size The size of an order displayed to public view.

Distressed investing Investing in securities of companies in financial difficulties. Private equity funds typically buy the debt of mature companies in financial difficulties.

Divergence In technical analysis, a term that describes the case when an indicator moves differently from the security being analyzed.

Diversification ratio The ratio of the standard deviation of an equally weighted portfolio to the standard deviation of a randomly selected security.

Dividend A distribution paid to shareholders based on the number of shares owned.

Dividend discount model (DDM) A present value model that estimates the intrinsic value of an equity share based on the present value of its expected future dividends.

Dividend discount model based approach An approach for estimating a country's equity risk premium. The market rate of return is estimated as the sum of the dividend yield and the growth rate in dividends for a market index. Subtracting the risk-free rate of return from the estimated market return produces an estimate for the equity risk premium.

Dividend payout ratio The ratio of cash dividends paid to earnings for a period.

Dividend yield Annual dividends per share divided by share price.

Divisor A number (denominator) used to determine the value of a price return index. It is initially chosen at the inception of an index and subsequently adjusted by the index provider, as necessary, to avoid changes in the index value that are unrelated to changes in the prices of its constituent securities.

Domestic content provisions Stipulate that some percentage of the value added or components used in production should be of domestic origin.

Double bottoms In technical analysis, a reversal pattern that is formed when the price reaches a low, rebounds, and then sells off back to the first low level; used to predict a change from a downtrend to an uptrend.

Double coincidence of wants A prerequisite to barter trades, in particular that both economic agents in the transaction want what the other is selling.

Double declining balance depreciation An accelerated depreciation method that involves depreciating the asset at double the straight-line rate. This rate is multiplied by the book value of the asset at the beginning of the period (a declining balance) to calculate depreciation expense.

Double-entry accounting The accounting system of recording transactions in which every recorded transaction affects at least two accounts so as to keep the basic accounting equation (assets = liabilities + owners' equity) in balance.

Double top In technical analysis, a reversal pattern that is formed when an uptrend reverses twice at roughly the same high price level; used to predict a change from an uptrend to a downtrend.

Down transition probability The probability that an asset's value moves down in a model of asset price dynamics.

Downgrade risk The risk that a bond issuer's creditworthiness deteriorates, or migrates lower, leading investors to believe the risk of default is higher. Also called *credit migration risk*.

Drag on liquidity When receipts lag, creating pressure from the decreased available funds.

Drawdown A reduction in net asset value (NAV).

Dual-currency bonds Bonds that make coupon payments in one currency and pay the par value at maturity in another currency.

DuPont analysis An approach to decomposing return on investment, e.g., return on equity, as the product of other financial ratios.

Duration A measure of the approximate sensitivity of a security to a change in interest rates (i.e., a measure of interest rate risk).

Duration gap A bond's Macaulay duration minus the investment horizon.

Dutch auction An auction in which the auctioneer begins at a high price, then lowers the called price in increments until there is a willing buyer for the item being auctioned.

Dutch Book theorem A result in probability theory stating that inconsistent probabilities create profit opportunities.

Early repayment option See *prepayment option*.

Earnings per share The amount of income earned during a period per share of common stock.

Earnings surprise The portion of a company's earnings that is unanticipated by investors and, according to the efficient market hypothesis, merits a price adjustment.

Economic costs All the remuneration needed to keep a productive resource in its current employment or to acquire the resource for productive use; the sum of total accounting costs and implicit opportunity costs.

Economic indicator A variable that provides information on the state of the overall economy.

Economic loss The amount by which accounting profit is less than normal profit.

Economic order quantity–reorder point (EOQ–ROP) An approach to managing inventory based on expected demand and the predictability of demand; the ordering point for new inventory is determined based on the costs of ordering and carrying inventory, such that the total cost associated with inventory is minimized.

Economic profit Equal to accounting profit less the implicit opportunity costs not included in total accounting costs; the difference between total revenue (TR) and total cost (TC). Also called *abnormal profit* or *supernormal profit*.

Economic rent The surplus value that results when a particular resource or good is fixed in supply and market price is higher than what is required to bring the resource or good onto the market and sustain its use.

Economic stabilization Reduction of the magnitude of economic fluctuations.

Economic union Incorporates all aspects of a common market and in addition requires common economic institutions and coordination of economic policies among members.

Economics The study of the production, distribution, and consumption of goods and services; the principles of the allocation of scarce resources among competing uses. Economics is divided into two broad areas of study: macroeconomics and microeconomics.

Economies of scale Reduction in cost per unit resulting from increased production.

Effective annual rate The amount by which a unit of currency will grow in a year with interest on interest included.

Effective annual yield (EAY) An annualized return that accounts for the effect of interest on interest; EAY is computed by compounding 1 plus the holding period yield forward to one year, then subtracting 1.

Effective convexity A *curve convexity* statistic that measures the secondary effect of a change in a benchmark yield curve on a bond's price.

Effective duration The sensitivity of a bond's price to a change in a benchmark yield curve.

Effective interest rate The borrowing rate or market rate that a company incurs at the time of issuance of a bond.

Efficient market   A market in which asset prices reflect new information quickly and rationally.

Elastic   Said of a good or service when the magnitude of elasticity is greater than one.

Elasticity   The percentage change in one variable for a percentage change in another variable; a measure of how sensitive one variable is to a change in the value of another variable.

Elasticity of supply   A measure of the sensitivity of quantity supplied to a change in price.

Electronic communications networks   See *alternative trading systems*.

Electronic funds transfer (EFT)   The use of computer networks to conduct financial transactions electronically.

Elliott wave theory   A technical analysis theory that claims that the market follows regular, repeated waves or cycles.

Embedded option   Contingency provisions that provide the issuer or the bondholders the right, but not the obligation, to take action. These options are not part of the security and cannot be traded separately.

Empirical probability   The probability of an event estimated as a relative frequency of occurrence.

Employed   The number of people with a job.

Endogenous variables   Variables whose equilibrium values are determined within the model being considered.

Enterprise risk management   An overall assessment of a company's risk position. A centralized approach to risk management sometimes called firmwide risk management.

Enterprise value   A measure of a company's total market value from which the value of cash and short-term investments have been subtracted.

Equal weighting   An index weighting method in which an equal weight is assigned to each constituent security at inception.

Equilibrium condition   A condition necessary for the forces within a system to be in balance.

Equipment trust certificates   Bonds secured by specific types of equipment or physical assets.

Equity   Assets less liabilities; the residual interest in the assets after subtracting the liabilities.

Equity risk premium   The expected return on equities minus the risk-free rate; the premium that investors demand for investing in equities.

Equity swap   A swap transaction in which at least one cash flow is tied to the return to an equity portfolio position, often an equity index.

Estimate   The particular value calculated from sample observations using an estimator.

Estimation   With reference to statistical inference, the subdivision dealing with estimating the value of a population parameter.

Estimator   An estimation formula; the formula used to compute the sample mean and other sample statistics are examples of estimators.

Eurobonds   Type of bond issued internationally, outside the jurisdiction of the country in whose currency the bond is denominated.

European-style   Said of an option contract that can only be exercised on the option's expiration date.

Event   Any outcome or specified set of outcomes of a random variable.

Ex-date   The first date that a share trades without (i.e. "ex") the dividend.

Ex-dividend date   The first date that a share trades without (i.e. "ex") the dividend.

Excess kurtosis   Degree of peakedness (fatness of tails) in excess of the peakedness of the normal distribution.

Excess supply   A condition in which the quantity ready to be supplied is greater than the quantity demanded.

Exchanges   Places where traders can meet to arrange their trades.

Execution instructions   Instructions that indicate how to fill an order.

Exercise   The process of using an option to buy or sell the underlying.

Exercise price   The fixed price at which an option holder can buy or sell the underlying. Also called *strike price*, *striking price*, or *strike*.

Exercise value   The value obtained if an option is exercised based on current conditions. Also known as *intrinsic value*.

Exhaustive   Covering or containing all possible outcomes.

Exogenous variables   Variables whose equilibrium values are determined outside of the model being considered.

Expansion   The period of a business cycle after its lowest point and before its highest point.

Expansionary   Tending to cause the real economy to grow.

Expansionary fiscal policy   Fiscal policy aimed at achieving real economic growth.

Expected inflation   The level of inflation that economic agents expect in the future.

Expected loss   Default probability times Loss severity given default.

Expected value   The probability-weighted average of the possible outcomes of a random variable.

Expenses   Outflows of economic resources or increases in liabilities that result in decreases in equity (other than decreases because of distributions to owners); reductions in net assets associated with the creation of revenues.

Experience curve   A curve that shows the direct cost per unit of good or service produced or delivered as a typically declining function of cumulative output.

Export subsidy   Paid by the government to the firm when it exports a unit of a good that is being subsidized.

Exports   Goods and services that an economy sells to other countries.

Extension risk   The risk that when interest rates rise, fewer prepayments will occur because homeowners are reluctant to give up the benefits of a contractual interest rate that now looks low. As a result, the security becomes longer in maturity than anticipated at the time of purchase.

Externality   An effect of a market transaction that is borne by parties other than those who transacted.

Extra dividend   A dividend paid by a company that does not pay dividends on a regular schedule, or a dividend that supplements regular cash dividends with an extra payment.

Extreme value theory   A branch of statistics that focuses primarily on extreme outcomes.

Face value   The amount of cash payable by a company to the bondholders when the bonds mature; the promised payment at maturity separate from any coupon payment.

Factor   A common or underlying element with which several variables are correlated.

Factor markets   Markets for the purchase and sale of factors of production.

Fair value   The amount at which an asset could be exchanged, or a liability settled, between knowledgeable, willing parties in an arm's-length transaction; the price that would be received to sell an asset or paid to transfer a liability in an orderly transaction between market participants.

Fed funds rate   The US interbank lending rate on overnight borrowings of reserves.

Federal funds rate   The US interbank lending rate on overnight borrowings of reserves.

Fiat money   Money that is not convertible into any other commodity.

Fibonacci sequence   A sequence of numbers starting with 0 and 1, and then each subsequent number in the sequence is the sum of the two preceding numbers. In Elliott Wave Theory, it is believed that market waves follow patterns that are the ratios of the numbers in the Fibonacci sequence.

Fiduciary call   A combination of a European call and a risk-free bond that matures on the option expiration day and has a face value equal to the exercise price of the call.

FIFO method   The first in, first out, method of accounting for inventory, which matches sales against the costs of items of inventory in the order in which they were placed in inventory.

Fill or kill   See *immediate or cancel order*.

Finance lease   Essentially, the purchase of some asset by the buyer (lessee) that is directly financed by the seller (lessor). Also called *capital lease*.

Financial account   A component of the balance of payments account that records investment flows.

Financial flexibility   The ability to react and adapt to financial adversities and opportunities.

Financial leverage   The extent to which a company can effect, through the use of debt, a proportional change in the return on common equity that is greater than a given proportional change in operating income; also, short for the financial leverage ratio.

Financial leverage ratio   A measure of financial leverage calculated as average total assets divided by average total equity.

Financial risk   The risk that environmental, social, or governance risk factors will result in significant costs or other losses to a company and its shareholders; the risk arising from a company's obligation to meet required payments under its financing agreements.

Financing activities   Activities related to obtaining or repaying capital to be used in the business (e.g., equity and long-term debt).

Firm commitment offering   See *underwritten offering*.

First-degree price discrimination   Where a monopolist is able to charge each customer the highest price the customer is willing to pay.

First lien debt   Debt secured by a pledge of certain assets that could include buildings, but may also include property and equipment, licenses, patents, brands, etc.

First mortgage debt   Debt secured by a pledge of a specific property.

First price sealed bid auction   An auction in which envelopes containing bids are opened simultaneously and the item is sold to the highest bidder.

Fiscal multiplier   The ratio of a change in national income to a change in government spending.

Fiscal policy   The use of taxes and government spending to affect the level of aggregate expenditures.

Fisher effect   The thesis that the real rate of interest in an economy is stable over time so that changes in nominal interest rates are the result of changes in expected inflation.

Fisher index   The geometric mean of the Laspeyres index.

Fixed charge coverage   A solvency ratio measuring the number of times interest and lease payments are covered by operating income, calculated as (EBIT + lease payments) divided by (interest payments + lease payments).

Fixed costs   Costs that remain at the same level regardless of a company's level of production and sales.

Fixed-for-floating interest rate swap   An interest rate swap in which one party pays a fixed rate and the other pays a floating rate, with both sets of payments in the same currency. Also called *plain vanilla swap* or *vanilla swap*.

Fixed price tender offer   Offer made by a company to repurchase a specific number of shares at a fixed price that is typically at a premium to the current market price.

Fixed rate perpetual preferred stock   Nonconvertible, noncallable preferred stock that has a fixed dividend rate and no maturity date.

Flags   A technical analysis continuation pattern formed by parallel trendlines, typically over a short period.

Flat price   The full price of a bond minus the accrued interest; also called the *quoted* or *clean* price.

Float   In the context of customer receipts, the amount of money that is in transit between payments made by customers and the funds that are usable by the company.

Float-adjusted market-capitalization weighting   An index weighting method in which the weight assigned to each constituent security is determined by adjusting its market capitalization for its market float.

Float factor   An estimate of the average number of days it takes deposited checks to clear; average daily float divided by average daily deposit.

Floaters   See *floating-rate notes*.

Floating-rate notes   A note on which interest payments are not fixed, but instead vary from period to period depending on the current level of a reference interest rate.

Flotation cost   Fees charged to companies by investment bankers and other costs associated with raising new capital.

Foreclosure   Allows the lender to take possession of a mortgaged property if the borrower defaults and then sell it to recover funds.

Foreign currency reserves   Holding by the central bank of non-domestic currency deposits and non-domestic bonds.

Foreign direct investment   Direct investment by a firm in one country (the source country) in productive assets in a foreign country (the host country).

Foreign exchange gains (or losses)   Gains (or losses) that occur when the exchange rate changes between the investor's currency and the currency that foreign securities are denominated in.

Foreign portfolio investment   Shorter-term investment by individuals, firms, and institutional investors (e.g., pension funds) in foreign financial instruments such as foreign stocks and foreign government bonds.

Forward commitments   Class of derivatives that provides the ability to lock in a price to transact in the future at a previously agreed-upon price.

Forward contract   An agreement between two parties in which one party, the buyer, agrees to buy from the other party, the seller, an underlying asset at a later date for a price established at the start of the contract.

Forward curve   A series of forward rates, each having the same timeframe.

Forward market   For future delivery, beyond the usual settlement time period in the cash market.

Forward price   The fixed price or rate at which the transaction scheduled to occur at the expiration of a forward contract will take place. This price is agreed on at the initiation date of the contract.

Forward rate   The interest rate on a bond or money market instrument traded in a forward market. A forward rate can be interpreted as an incremental, or marginal, return for extending the time-to-maturity for an additional time period.

Forward rate agreements   A forward contract calling for one party to make a fixed interest payment and the other to make an interest payment at a rate to be determined at the contract expiration.

Fractile   A value at or below which a stated fraction of the data lies.

Fractional reserve banking   Banking in which reserves constitute a fraction of deposits.

Free cash flow   The actual cash that would be available to the company's investors after making all investments necessary to maintain the company as an ongoing enterprise (also referred to as free cash flow to the firm); the internally generated funds that can be distributed to the company's investors (e.g., shareholders and bondholders) without impairing the value of the company.

Free cash flow to equity (FCFE)   The cash flow available to a company's common shareholders after all operating expenses, interest, and principal payments have been made, and necessary investments in working and fixed capital have been made.

Free-cash-flow-to-equity models   Valuation models based on discounting expected future free cash flow to equity.

Free cash flow to the firm (FCFF)   The cash flow available to the company's suppliers of capital after all operating expenses have been paid and necessary investments in working capital and fixed capital have been made.

Free float   The number of shares that are readily and freely tradable in the secondary market.

Free trade   When there are no government restrictions on a country's ability to trade.

Free trade areas   One of the most prevalent forms of regional integration, in which all barriers to the flow of goods and services among members have been eliminated.

Frequency distribution   A tabular display of data summarized into a relatively small number of intervals.

Frequency polygon   A graph of a frequency distribution obtained by drawing straight lines joining successive points representing the class frequencies.

Full price   The price of a security with accrued interest; also called the *invoice* or *dirty* price.

Fundamental analysis   The examination of publicly available information and the formulation of forecasts to estimate the intrinsic value of assets.

Fundamental value   The underlying or true value of an asset based on an analysis of its qualitative and quantitative characteristics. Also called *intrinsic value*.

Fundamental weighting   An index weighting method in which the weight assigned to each constituent security is based on its underlying company's size. It attempts to address the disadvantages of market-capitalization weighting by using measures that are independent of the constituent security's price.

Funds of hedge funds   Funds that hold a portfolio of hedge funds.

Future value (FV)   The amount to which a payment or series of payments will grow by a stated future date.

Futures contract   A variation of a forward contract that has essentially the same basic definition but with some additional features, such as a clearinghouse guarantee against credit losses, a daily settlement of gains and losses, and an organized electronic or floor trading facility.

Futures price   The agreed-upon price of a futures contract.

FX swap   The combination of a spot and a forward FX transaction.

G-spread   The yield spread in basis points over an actual or interpolated government bond.

Gains   Asset inflows not directly related to the ordinary activities of the business.

Game theory   The set of tools decision makers use to incorporate responses by rival decision makers into their strategies.

Gamma   A numerical measure of how sensitive an option's delta (the sensitivity of the derivative's price) is to a change in the value of the underlying.

GDP deflator   A gauge of prices and inflation that measures the aggregate changes in prices across the overall economy.

General equilibrium analysis   An analysis that provides for equilibria in multiple markets simultaneously.

General partner   The partner that runs the business and theoretically bears unlimited liability.

Geometric mean   A measure of central tendency computed by taking the nth root of the product of n non-negative values.

Giffen good   A good that is consumed more as the price of the good rises.

Gilts   Bonds issued by the UK government.

Giro system   An electronic payment system used widely in Europe and Japan.

Global depository receipt   A depository receipt that is issued outside of the company's home country and outside of the United States.

Global minimum-variance portfolio   The portfolio on the minimum-variance frontier with the smallest variance of return.

Global registered share   A common share that is traded on different stock exchanges around the world in different currencies.

Gold standard   With respect to a currency, if a currency is on the gold standard a given amount can be converted into a prespecified amount of gold.

Golden cross   A technical analysis term that describes a situation where a short-term moving average crosses from below a longer-term moving average to above it; this movement is considered bullish.

Good-on-close   An execution instruction specifying that an order can only be filled at the close of trading. Also called *market on close*.

Good-on-open   An execution instruction specifying that an order can only be filled at the opening of trading.

Good-till-cancelled order   An order specifying that it is valid until the entity placing the order has cancelled it (or, commonly, until some specified amount of time such as 60 days has elapsed, whichever comes sooner).

Goods markets   Markets for the output of production.

Goodwill   An intangible asset that represents the excess of the purchase price of an acquired company over the value of the net assets acquired.

Government equivalent yield   A yield that restates a yield-to-maturity based on 30/360 day-count to one based on actual/actual.

Greenmail   The purchase of the accumulated shares of a hostile investor by a company that is targeted for takeover by that investor, usually at a substantial premium over market price.

Grey market   The forward market for bonds about to be issued. Also called "when issued" market.

Gross domestic product   The market value of all final goods and services produced within the economy in a given period of time (output definition) or, equivalently, the aggregate income earned by all households, all companies, and the government within the economy in a given period of time (income definition).

Gross margin   Sales minus the cost of sales (i.e., the cost of goods sold for a manufacturing company).

Gross profit   Sales minus the cost of sales (i.e., the cost of goods sold for a manufacturing company).

Gross profit margin   The ratio of gross profit to revenues.

Grouping by function   With reference to the presentation of expenses in an income statement, the grouping together of expenses serving the same function, e.g. all items that are costs of goods sold.

Grouping by nature   With reference to the presentation of expenses in an income statement, the grouping together of expenses by similar nature, e.g., all depreciation expenses.

Growth cyclical   A term sometimes used to describe companies that are growing rapidly on a long-term basis but that still experience above-average fluctuation in their revenues and profits over the course of a business cycle.

Growth investors   With reference to equity investors, investors who seek to invest in high-earnings-growth companies.

Guarantee certificate   A type of structured financial instrument that provides investors capital protection. It combines a zero-coupon bond and a call option on some underlying asset.

Haircut   See repo margin.

Harmonic mean   A type of weighted mean computed by averaging the reciprocals of the observations, then taking the reciprocal of that average.

Head and shoulders pattern   In technical analysis, a reversal pattern that is formed in three parts: a left shoulder, head, and right shoulder; used to predict a change from an uptrend to a downtrend.

Headline inflation   The inflation rate calculated based on the price index that includes all goods and services in an economy.

Hedge funds   Private investment vehicles that typically use leverage, derivatives, and long and short investment strategies.

Hedge portfolio   A hypothetical combination of the derivative and its underlying that eliminates risk.

Held for trading   Debt or equity financial assets bought with the intention to sell them in the near term, usually less than three months; securities that a company intends to trade. Also called *trading securities*.

Held-to-maturity   Debt (fixed-income) securities that a company intends to hold to maturity; these are presented at their original cost, updated for any amortization of discounts or premiums.

Herding   Clustered trading that may or may not be based on information.

Hidden order   An order that is exposed not to the public but only to the brokers or exchanges that receive it.

High water marks   The highest value, net of fees, which a fund has reached. It reflects the highest cumulative return used to calculate an incentive fee.

Histogram   A bar chart of data that have been grouped into a frequency distribution.

Historical cost   In reference to assets, the amount paid to purchase an asset, including any costs of acquisition and/or preparation; with reference to liabilities, the amount of proceeds received in exchange in issuing the liability.

Historical equity risk premium approach   An estimate of a country's equity risk premium that is based upon the historical averages of the risk-free rate and the rate of return on the market portfolio.

Historical simulation   Another term for the historical method of estimating VAR. This term is somewhat misleading in that the method involves not a *simulation* of the past but rather what *actually happened* in the past, sometimes adjusted to reflect the fact that a different portfolio may have existed in the past than is planned for the future.

Holder-of-record date   The date that a shareholder listed on the corporation's books will be deemed to have ownership of the shares for purposes of receiving an upcoming dividend; two business days after the ex-dividend date.

Holding period return   The return that an investor earns during a specified holding period; a synonym for total return.

Holding period yield (HPY)   The return that an investor earns during a specified holding period; holding period return with reference to a fixed-income instrument.

Homogeneity of expectations   The assumption that all investors have the same economic expectations and thus have the same expectations of prices, cash flows, and other investment characteristics.

Horizon yield   The internal rate of return between the total return (the sum of reinvested coupon payments and the sale price or redemption amount) and the purchase price of the bond.

Horizontal analysis   Common-size analysis that involves comparing a specific financial statement with that statement in prior or future time periods; also, cross-sectional analysis of one company with another.

Horizontal demand schedule   Implies that at a given price, the response in the quantity demanded is infinite.

Household   A person or a group of people living in the same residence, taken as a basic unit in economic analysis.

Human capital   The accumulated knowledge and skill that workers acquire from education, training, or life experience and the corresponding present value of future earnings to be generated by said skilled individual.

Hurdle rate   The rate of return that must be met for a project to be accepted.

Hypothesis   With reference to statistical inference, a statement about one or more populations.

Hypothesis testing   With reference to statistical inference, the subdivision dealing with the testing of hypotheses about one or more populations.

I-spread   The yield spread of a specific bond over the standard swap rate in that currency of the same tenor.

Iceberg order   An order in which the display size is less than the order's full size.

If-converted method   A method for accounting for the effect of convertible securities on earnings per share (EPS) that specifies what EPS would have been if the convertible securities had been converted at the beginning of the period, taking account of the effects of conversion on net income and the weighted average number of shares outstanding.

Immediate or cancel order An order that is valid only upon receipt by the broker or exchange. If such an order cannot be filled in part or in whole upon receipt, it cancels immediately. Also called *fill or kill*.

Impact lag The lag associated with the result of actions affecting the economy with delay.

Imperfect competition A market structure in which an individual firm has enough share of the market (or can control a certain segment of the market) such that it is able to exert some influence over price.

Implicit price deflator for GDP A gauge of prices and inflation that measures the aggregate changes in prices across the overall economy.

Implied forward rates Calculated from spot rates, an implied forward rate is a break-even reinvestment rate that links the return on an investment in a shorter-term zero-coupon bond to the return on an investment in a longer-term zero-coupon bond.

Implied volatility The volatility that option traders use to price an option, implied by the price of the option and a particular option-pricing model.

Import license Specifies the quantity of a good that can be imported into a country.

Imports Goods and services that a domestic economy (i.e., house-holds, firms, and government) purchases from other countries.

In the money Options that, if exercised, would result in the value received being worth more than the payment required to exercise.

In-the-money Options that, if exercised, would result in the value received being worth more than the payment required to exercise.

Incentive fee (or performance fee) Funds distributed by the general partner to the limited partner(s) based on realized profits.

Income Increases in economic benefits in the form of inflows or enhancements of assets, or decreases of liabilities that result in an increase in equity (other than increases resulting from contributions by owners).

Income constraint The constraint on a consumer to spend, in total, no more than his income.

Income elasticity of demand A measure of the responsiveness of demand to changes in income, defined as the percentage change in quantity demanded divided by the percentage change in income.

Income statement A financial statement that provides information about a company's profitability over a stated period of time. Also called *statement of operations* or *profit and loss statement*.

Income tax paid The actual amount paid for income taxes in the period; not a provision, but the actual cash outflow.

Income tax payable The income tax owed by the company on the basis of taxable income.

Income trust A type of equity ownership vehicle established as a trust issuing ownership shares known as units.

Increasing-cost industry An industry in which per-unit costs and output prices are higher when industry output is increased in the long run.

Increasing marginal returns Where the marginal product of a resource increases as additional units of that input are employed.

Increasing returns to scale Reduction in cost per unit resulting from increased production.

Incremental cash flow The cash flow that is realized because of a decision; the changes or increments to cash flows resulting from a decision or action.

Indenture Legal contract that describes the form of a bond, the obligations of the issuer, and the rights of the bondholders. Also called the *trust deed*.

Independent With reference to events, the property that the occurrence of one event does not affect the probability of another event occurring.

Independent projects Independent projects are projects whose cash flows are independent of each other.

Independently and identically distributed (IID) With respect to random variables, the property of random variables that are independent of each other but follow the identical probability distribution.

Index-linked bond Bond for which coupon payments and/or principal repayment are linked to a specified index.

Index of Leading Economic Indicators A composite of economic variables used by analysts to predict future economic conditions.

Indexing An investment strategy in which an investor constructs a portfolio to mirror the performance of a specified index.

Indifference curve A curve representing all the combinations of two goods or attributes such that the consumer is entirely indifferent among them.

Indifference curve map A group or family of indifference curves, representing a consumer's entire utility function.

Indirect format With reference to cash flow statements, a format for the presentation of the statement which, in the operating cash flow section, begins with net income then shows additions and subtractions to arrive at operating cash flow. Also called *indirect method*.

Indirect method See *indirect format*.

Indirect taxes Taxes such as taxes on spending, as opposed to direct taxes.

Industry A group of companies offering similar products and/or services.

Industry analysis The analysis of a specific branch of manufacturing, service, or trade.

Inelastic Insensitive to price changes.

Inelastic supply Said of supply that is insensitive to the price of goods sold.

Inferior goods A good whose consumption decreases as income increases.

Inflation The percentage increase in the general price level from one period to the next; a sustained rise in the overall level of prices in an economy.

Inflation-linked bond Type of index-linked bond that offers investors protection against inflation by linking the bond's coupon payments and/or the principal repayment to an index of consumer prices. Also called *linkers*.

Inflation premium An extra return that compensates investors for expected inflation.

Inflation rate The percentage change in a price index—that is, the speed of overall price level movements.

Inflation Reports A type of economic publication put out by many central banks.

Inflation uncertainty   The degree to which economic agents view future rates of inflation as difficult to forecast.

Information cascade   The transmission of information from those participants who act first and whose decisions influence the decisions of others.

Information-motivated traders   Traders that trade to profit from information that they believe allows them to predict future prices.

Informationally efficient market   A market in which asset prices reflect new information quickly and rationally.

Initial margin   The amount that must be deposited in a clearinghouse account when entering into a futures contract.

Initial margin requirement   The margin requirement on the first day of a transaction as well as on any day in which additional margin funds must be deposited.

Initial public offering   (IPO) The first issuance of common shares to the public by a formerly private corporation.

Installment method   With respect to revenue recognition, a method that specifies that the portion of the total profit of the sale that is recognized in each period is determined by the percentage of the total sales price for which the seller has received cash.

Installment sales   With respect to revenue recognition, a method that specifies that the portion of the total profit of the sale that is recognized in each period is determined by the percentage of the total sales price for which the seller has received cash.

Intangible assets   Assets lacking physical substance, such as patents and trademarks.

Interbank market   The market of loans and deposits between banks for maturities ranging from overnight to one year.

Interbank money market   The market of loans and deposits between banks for maturities ranging from overnight to one year.

Interest   Payment for lending funds.

Interest coverage   A solvency ratio calculated as EBIT divided by interest payments.

Interest-only mortgage   A loan in which no scheduled principal repayment is specified for a certain number of years.

Interest rate   A rate of return that reflects the relationship between differently dated cash flows; a discount rate.

Interest rate swap   A swap in which the underlying is an interest rate. Can be viewed as a currency swap in which both currencies are the same and can be created as a combination of currency swaps.

Intergenerational data mining   A form of data mining that applies information developed by previous researchers using a dataset to guide current research using the same or a related dataset.

Intermarket analysis   A field within technical analysis that combines analysis of major categories of securities— namely, equities, bonds, currencies, and commodities—to identify market trends and possible inflections in a trend.

Intermediate goods and services   Goods and services purchased for use as inputs to produce other goods and services.

Internal rate of return   (IRR) The discount rate that makes net present value equal 0; the discount rate that makes the present value of an investment's costs (outflows) equal to the present value of the investment's benefits (inflows).

Interpolated spread   The yield spread of a specific bond over the standard swap rate in that currency of the same tenor.

Interquartile range   The difference between the third and first quartiles of a dataset.

Interval   With reference to grouped data, a set of values within which an observation falls.

Interval scale   A measurement scale that not only ranks data but also gives assurance that the differences between scale values are equal.

Intrinsic value   See *exercise value.*

Inventory   The unsold units of product on hand.

Inventory blanket lien   The use of inventory as collateral for a loan. Though the lender has claim to some or all of the company's inventory, the company may still sell or use the inventory in the ordinary course of business.

Inventory investment   Net change in business inventory.

Inventory turnover   An activity ratio calculated as cost of goods sold divided by average inventory.

Inverse demand function   A restatement of the demand function in which price is stated as a function of quantity.

Inverse floater   A type of leveraged structured financial instrument. The cash flows are adjusted periodically and move in the opposite direction of changes in the reference rate.

Investing activities   Activities which are associated with the acquisition and disposal of property, plant, and equipment; intangible assets; other long-term assets; and both long-term and short-term investments in the equity and debt (bonds and loans) issued by other companies.

Investment banks   Financial intermediaries that provide advice to their mostly corporate clients and help them arrange transactions such as initial and seasoned securities offerings.

Investment opportunity schedule   A graphical depiction of a company's investment opportunities ordered from highest to lowest expected return. A company's optimal capital budget is found where the investment opportunity schedule intersects with the company's marginal cost of capital.

Investment policy statement   (IPS) A written planning document that describes a client's investment objectives and risk tolerance over a relevant time horizon, along with constraints that apply to the client's portfolio.

Investment property   Property used to earn rental income or capital appreciation (or both).

IRR rule   An investment decision rule that accepts projects or investments for which the IRR is greater than the opportunity cost of capital.

January effect   Calendar anomaly that stock market returns in January are significantly higher compared to the rest of the months of the year, with most of the abnormal returns reported during the first five trading days in January. Also called *turn-of-the-year effect.*

Joint probability   The probability of the joint occurrence of stated events.

Joint probability function   A function giving the probability of joint occurrences of values of stated random variables.

Just-in-time (JIT) method   Method of managing inventory that minimizes in-process inventory stocks.

Key rate duration   A method of measuring the interest rate sensitivities of a fixed-income instrument or portfolio to shifts in key points along the yield curve.

Keynesians   Economists who believe that fiscal policy can have powerful effects on aggregate demand, output, and employment when there is substantial spare capacity in an economy.

Kondratieff wave   A 54-year long economic cycle postulated by Nikolai Kondratieff.

Kurtosis   The statistical measure that indicates the peakedness of a distribution.

Labor force   The portion of the working age population (over the age of 16) that is employed or is available for work but not working (unemployed).

Labor markets   Markets for labor services.

Labor productivity   The quantity of goods and services (real GDP) that a worker can produce in one hour of work.

Laddering strategy   A form of active strategy which entails scheduling maturities on a systematic basis within the investment portfolio such that investments are spread out equally over the term of the ladder.

Lagging economic indicators   Turning points that take place later than those of the overall economy; they are believed to have value in identifying the economy's past condition.

Laspeyres index   A price index created by holding the composition of the consumption basket constant.

Law of demand   The principle that as the price of a good rises, buyers will choose to buy less of it, and as its price falls, they will buy more.

Law of diminishing returns   The smallest output that a firm can produce such that its long run average costs are minimized.

Law of one price   The condition in a financial market in which two equivalent financial instruments or combinations of financial instruments can sell for only one price. Equivalent to the principle that no arbitrage opportunities are possible.

Law of supply   The principle that a rise in price usually results in an increase in the quantity supplied.

Lead underwriter   The lead investment bank in a syndicate of investment banks and broker–dealers involved in a securities underwriting.

Leading economic indicators   Turning points that usually precede those of the overall economy; they are believed to have value for predicting the economy's future state, usually near-term.

Legal tender   Something that must be accepted when offered in exchange for goods and services.

Lender of last resort   An entity willing to lend money when no other entity is ready to do so.

Leptokurtic   Describes a distribution that is more peaked than a normal distribution.

Lessee   The party obtaining the use of an asset through a lease.

Lessor   The owner of an asset that grants the right to use the asset to another party.

Letter of credit   Form of external credit enhancement whereby a financial institution provides the issuer with a credit line to reimburse any cash flow shortfalls from the assets backing the issue.

Level of significance   The probability of a Type I error in testing a hypothesis.

Leverage   In the context of corporate finance, leverage refers to the use of fixed costs within a company's cost structure. Fixed costs that are operating costs (such as depreciation or rent) create operating leverage. Fixed costs that are financial costs (such as interest expense) create financial leverage.

Leveraged buyout   (LBO) A transaction whereby the target company management team converts the target to a privately held company by using heavy borrowing to finance the purchase of the target company's outstanding shares.

Liabilities   Present obligations of an enterprise arising from past events, the settlement of which is expected to result in an outflow of resources embodying economic benefits; creditors' claims on the resources of a company.

Life-cycle stage   The stage of the life cycle: embryonic, growth, shakeout, mature, declining.

LIFO layer liquidation   With respect to the application of the LIFO inventory method, the liquidation of old, relatively low-priced inventory; happens when the volume of sales rises above the volume of recent purchases so that some sales are made from relatively old, low-priced inventory. Also called *LIFO liquidation*.

LIFO method   The last in, first out, method of accounting for inventory, which matches sales against the costs of items of inventory in the reverse order the items were placed in inventory (i.e., inventory produced or acquired last are assumed to be sold first).

LIFO reserve   The difference between the reported LIFO inventory carrying amount and the inventory amount that would have been reported if the FIFO method had been used (in other words, the FIFO inventory value less the LIFO inventory value).

Likelihood   The probability of an observation, given a particular set of conditions.

Limit down   A limit move in the futures market in which the price at which a transaction would be made is at or below the lower limit.

Limit order   Instructions to a broker or exchange to obtain the best price immediately available when filling an order, but in no event accept a price higher than a specified (limit) price when buying or accept a price lower than a specified (limit) price when selling.

Limit order book   The book or list of limit orders to buy and sell that pertains to a security.

Limit up   A limit move in the futures market in which the price at which a transaction would be made is at or above the upper limit.

Limitations on liens   Meant to put limits on how much secured debt an issuer can have.

Limited partners   Partners with limited liability. Limited partnerships in hedge and private equity funds are typically restricted to investors who are expected to understand and to be able to assume the risks associated with the investments.

Line chart   In technical analysis, a plot of price data, typically closing prices, with a line connecting the points.

Linear interpolation   The estimation of an unknown value on the basis of two known values that bracket it, using a straight line between the two known values.

Linear scale   A scale in which equal distances correspond to equal absolute amounts. Also called *arithmetic scale*.

Linker   See *inflation-linked bond*.

Liquid market   Said of a market in which traders can buy or sell with low total transaction costs when they want to trade.

Liquidating dividend   A dividend that is a return of capital rather than a distribution from earnings or retained earnings.

Liquidation   To sell the assets of a company, division, or subsidiary piecemeal, typically because of bankruptcy; the form of bankruptcy that allows for the orderly satisfaction of creditors' claims after which the company ceases to exist.

Liquidity   The ability to purchase or sell an asset quickly and easily at a price close to fair market value. The ability to meet short-term obligations using assets that are the most readily converted into cash.

Liquidity premium   An extra return that compensates investors for the risk of loss relative to an investment's fair value if the investment needs to be converted to cash quickly.

Liquidity ratios   Financial ratios measuring the company's ability to meet its short-term obligations.

Liquidity risk   The risk that a financial instrument cannot be purchased or sold without a significant concession in price due to the size of the market.

Liquidity trap   A condition in which the demand for money becomes infinitely elastic (horizontal demand curve) so that injections of money into the economy will not lower interest rates or affect real activity.

Load fund   A mutual fund in which, in addition to the annual fee, a percentage fee is charged to invest in the fund and/or for redemptions from the fund.

Loan-to-value ratio   The ratio of a property's purchase price to the amount of its mortgage.

Lockbox system   A payment system in which customer payments are mailed to a post office box and the banking institution retrieves and deposits these payments several times a day, enabling the company to have use of the fund sooner than in a centralized system in which customer payments are sent to the company.

Locked limit   A condition in the futures markets in which a transaction cannot take place because the price would be beyond the limits.

Lockup period   The minimum period before investors are allowed to make withdrawals or redeem shares from a fund.

Logarithmic scale   A scale in which equal distances represent equal proportional changes in the underlying quantity.

London Interbank offered rate (Libor)   Collective name for multiple rates at which a select set of banks believe they could borrow unsecured funds from other banks in the London interbank market for different currencies and different borrowing periods ranging from overnight to one year.

Long   The buyer of a derivative contract. Also refers to the position of owning a derivative.

Long-lived assets   Assets that are expected to provide economic benefits over a future period of time, typically greater than one year. Also called *long-term assets*.

Long position   A position in an asset or contract in which one owns the asset or has an exercisable right under the contract.

Long-run average total cost curve   The curve describing average total costs when no costs are considered fixed.

Long-run industry supply curve   A curve describing the relationship between quantity supplied and output prices when no costs are considered fixed.

Long-term contract   A contract that spans a number of accounting periods.

Longitudinal data   Observations on characteristic(s) of the same observational unit through time.

Look-ahead bias   A bias caused by using information that was unavailable on the test date.

Loss aversion   The tendency of people to dislike losses more than they like comparable gains.

Loss severity   Portion of a bond's value (including unpaid interest) an investor loses in the event of default.

Losses   Asset outflows not directly related to the ordinary activities of the business.

Lower bound   The lowest possible value of an option.

M^2   A measure of what a portfolio would have returned if it had taken on the same total risk as the market index.

Macaulay duration   The approximate amount of time a bond would have to be held for the market discount rate at purchase to be realized if there is a single change in interest

rate. It indicates the point in time when the coupon reinvestment and price effects of a change in yield-to-maturity offset each other.

Macroeconomics   The branch of economics that deals with aggregate economic quantities, such as national output and national income.

Maintenance covenants   Covenants in bank loan agreements that require the borrower to satisfy certain financial ratio tests while the loan is outstanding.

Maintenance margin   The minimum amount that is required by a futures clearinghouse to maintain a margin account and to protect against default. Participants whose margin balances drop below the required maintenance margin must replenish their accounts.

Maintenance margin requirement   The margin requirement on any day other than the first day of a transaction.

Management buy-ins   Leveraged buyout in which the current management team is being replaced and the acquiring team will be involved in managing the company.

Management buyout   (MBO) An event in which a group of investors consisting primarily of the company's existing management purchase all of its outstanding shares and take the company private.

Management fee   A fee based on assets under management or committed capital, as applicable. Also called *base fee*.

Manufacturing resource planning (MRP)   The incorporation of production planning into inventory management. A MRP analysis provides both a materials acquisition schedule and a production schedule.

Margin   The amount of money that a trader deposits in a margin account. The term is derived from the stock market practice in which an investor borrows a portion of the money required to purchase a certain amount of stock. In futures markets, there is no borrowing so the margin is more of a down payment or performance bond.

Margin bond   A cash deposit required by the clearinghouse from the participants to a contract to provide a credit guarantee. Also called a *performance bond*.

Margin call   A request for the short to deposit additional funds to bring their balance up to the initial margin.

Margin loan   Money borrowed from a broker to purchase securities.

Marginal cost   The cost of producing an additional unit of a good.

Marginal probability   The probability of an event *not* conditioned on another event.

Marginal product   Measures the productivity of each unit of input and is calculated by taking the difference in total product from adding another unit of input (assuming other resource quantities are held constant).

Marginal propensity to consume   The proportion of an additional unit of disposable income that is consumed or spent; the change in consumption for a small change in income.

Marginal propensity to save   The proportion of an additional unit of disposable income that is saved (not spent).

Marginal rate of substitution   The rate at which one is willing to give up one good to obtain more of another.

Marginal revenue   The change in total revenue divided by the change in quantity sold; simply, the additional revenue from selling one more unit.

Marginal revenue product   The amount of additional revenue received from employing an additional unit of an input.

Marginal value   The added value from an additional unit of a good.

Marginal value curve   A curve describing the highest price consumers are willing to pay for each additional unit of a good.

Mark to market   The revaluation of a financial asset or liability to its current market value or fair value.

Market   A means of bringing buyers and sellers together to exchange goods and services.

Market anomaly   Change in the price or return of a security that cannot directly be linked to current relevant information known in the market or to the release of new information into the market.

Market bid–ask spread   The difference between the best bid and the best offer.

Market-capitalization weighting   An index weighting method in which the weight assigned to each constituent security is determined by dividing its market capitalization by the total market capitalization (sum of the market capitalization) of all securities in the index. Also called *value weighting*.

Market discount rate   The rate of return required by investors given the risk of the investment in a bond; also called the *required yield* or the *required rate of return*.

Market equilibrium   The condition in which the quantity willingly offered for sale by sellers at a given price is just equal to the quantity willingly demanded by buyers at that same price.

Market float   The number of shares that are available to the investing public.

Market liquidity risk   The risk that the price at which investors can actually transact—buying or selling—may differ from the price indicated in the market.

Market mechanism   The process by which price adjusts until there is neither excess supply nor excess demand.

Market model   A regression equation that specifies a linear relationship between the return on a security (or portfolio) and the return on a broad market index.

Market multiple models   Valuation models based on share price multiples or enterprise value multiples.

Market-on-close   An execution instruction specifying that an order can only be filled at the close of trading.

Market order   Instructions to a broker or exchange to obtain the best price immediately available when filling an order.

Market-oriented investors   With reference to equity investors, investors whose investment disciplines cannot be clearly categorized as value or growth.

Market rate of interest   The rate demanded by purchases of bonds, given the risks associated with future cash payment obligations of the particular bond issue.

Market risk   The risk that arises from movements in interest rates, stock prices, exchange rates, and commodity prices.

Market structure   The competitive environment (perfect competition, monopolistic competition, oligopoly, and monopoly).

Market value   The price at which an asset or security can currently be bought or sold in an open market.

Marketable limit order   A buy limit order in which the limit price is placed above the best offer, or a sell limit order in which the limit price is placed below the best bid. Such orders generally will partially or completely fill right away.

Markowitz efficient frontier   The graph of the set of portfolios offering the maximum expected return for their level of risk (standard deviation of return).

Matching principle   The accounting principle that expenses should be recognized when the associated revenue is recognized.

Matching strategy   An active investment strategy that includes intentional matching of the timing of cash outflows with investment maturities.

Matrix pricing   Process of estimating the market discount rate and price of a bond based on the quoted or flat prices of more frequently traded comparable bonds.

Maturity premium   An extra return that compensates investors for the increased sensitivity of the market value of debt to a change in market interest rates as maturity is extended.

Maturity structure   A factor explaining the differences in yields on similar bonds; also called *term structure*.

Mean absolute deviation   With reference to a sample, the mean of the absolute values of deviations from the sample mean.

Mean excess return   The average rate of return in excess of the risk-free rate.

Mean–variance analysis   An approach to portfolio analysis using expected means, variances, and covariances of asset returns.

Measure of central tendency   A quantitative measure that specifies where data are centered.

Measure of value   A standard for measuring value; a function of money.

Measurement scales   A scheme of measuring differences. The four types of measurement scales are nominal, ordinal, interval, and ratio.

Measures of location   A quantitative measure that describes the location or distribution of data; includes not only measures of central tendency but also other measures such as percentiles.

Median   The value of the middle item of a set of items that has been sorted into ascending or descending order; the 50th percentile.

Medium of exchange   Any asset that can be used to purchase goods and services or to repay debts; a function of money.

Medium-term note   A corporate bond offered continuously to investors by an agent of the issuer, designed to fill the funding gap between commercial paper and long-term bonds.

Menu costs   A cost of inflation in which businesses constantly have to incur the costs of changing the advertised prices of their goods and services.

Mesokurtic   Describes a distribution with kurtosis identical to that of the normal distribution.

Mezzanine financing   Debt or preferred shares with a relationship to common equity due to a feature such as attached warrants or conversion options and that is subordinate to both senior and high yield debt. It is referred to as mezzanine because of its location on the balance sheet.

Microeconomics   The branch of economics that deals with markets and decision making of individual economic units, including consumers and businesses.

Minimum efficient scale   The smallest output that a firm can produce such that its long run average cost is minimized.

Minimum-variance portfolio   The portfolio with the minimum variance for each given level of expected return.

Minsky moment   Named for Hyman Minksy: A point in a business cycle when, after individuals become overextended in borrowing to finance speculative investments, people start realizing that something is likely to go wrong and a panic ensues leading to asset sell-offs.

Mismatching strategy   An active investment strategy whereby the timing of cash outflows is not matched with investment maturities.

Modal interval With reference to grouped data, the most frequently occurring interval.

Mode The most frequently occurring value in a set of observations.

Modern portfolio theory (MPT) The analysis of rational portfolio choices based on the efficient use of risk.

Modified duration A measure of the percentage price change of a bond given a change in its yield-to-maturity.

Momentum oscillators A graphical representation of market sentiment that is constructed from price data and calculated so that it oscillates either between a high and a low or around some number.

Monetarists Economists who believe that the rate of growth of the money supply is the primary determinant of the rate of inflation.

Monetary policy Actions taken by a nation's central bank to affect aggregate output and prices through changes in bank reserves, reserve requirements, or its target interest rate.

Monetary transmission mechanism The process whereby a central bank's interest rate gets transmitted through the economy and ultimately affects the rate of increase of prices.

Monetary union An economic union in which the members adopt a common currency.

Money A generally accepted medium of exchange and unit of account.

Money convexity For a bond, the annual or approximate convexity multiplied by the full price.

Money creation The process by which changes in bank reserves translate into changes in the money supply.

Money duration A measure of the price change in units of the currency in which the bond is denominated given a change in its yield-to-maturity.

Money market The market for short-term debt instruments (one-year maturity or less).

Money market securities Fixed-income securities with maturities at issuance of one year or less.

Money market yield A yield on a basis comparable to the quoted yield on an interest-bearing money market instrument that pays interest on a 360-day basis; the annualized holding period yield, assuming a 360-day year.

Money multiplier Describes how a change in reserves is expected to affect the money supply; in its simplest form, 1 divided by the reserve requirement.

Money neutrality The thesis that an increase in the money supply leads in the long-run to an increase in the price level, while leaving real variables like output and employment unaffected.

Money-weighted return The internal rate of return on a portfolio, taking account of all cash flows.

Moneyness The relationship between the price of the underlying and an option's exercise price.

Monopolist Said of an entity that is the only seller in its market.

Monopolistic competition Highly competitive form of imperfect competition; the competitive characteristic is a notably large number of firms, while the monopoly aspect is the result of product differentiation.

Monopoly In pure monopoly markets, there are no substitutes for the given product or service. There is a single seller, which exercises considerable power over pricing and output decisions.

Monte Carlo simulation An approach to estimating a probability distribution of outcomes to examine what might happen if particular risks are faced. This method is widely used in the sciences as well as in business to study a variety of problems.

Mortgage-backed securities Debt obligations that represent claims to the cash flows from pools of mortgage loans, most commonly on residential property.

Mortgage loan A loan secured by the collateral of some specified real estate property that obliges the borrower to make a predetermined series of payments to the lender.

Mortgage pass-through security A security created when one or more holders of mortgages form a pool of mortgages and sell shares or participation certificates in the pool.

Mortgage rate The interest rate on a mortgage loan; also called *contract rate* or *note rate*.

Moving average The average of the closing price of a security over a specified number of periods. With each new period, the average is recalculated.

Moving-average convergence/divergence oscillator (MACD) A momentum oscillator that is constructed based on the difference between short-term and long-term moving averages of a security's price.

Multi-factor model A model that explains a variable in terms of the values of a set of factors.

Multi-market indices Comprised of indices from different countries, designed to represent multiple security markets.

Multi-step format With respect to the format of the income statement, a format that presents a subtotal for gross profit (revenue minus cost of goods sold).

Multilateral trading facilities See *alternative trading systems*.

Multinational corporation A company operating in more than one country or having subsidiary firms in more than one country.

Multiplication rule for probabilities The rule that the joint probability of events A and B equals the probability of A given B times the probability of B.

Multiplier models Valuation models based on share price multiples or enterprise value multiples.

Multivariate distribution A probability distribution that specifies the probabilities for a group of related random variables.

Multivariate normal distribution A probability distribution for a group of random variables that is completely defined by the means and variances of the variables plus all the correlations between pairs of the variables.

Muni A type of non-sovereign bond issued by a state or local government in the United States. It very often (but not always) offers income tax exemptions.

Municipal bonds A type of non-sovereign bond issued by a state or local government in the United States. It very often (but not always) offers income tax exemptions.

Mutual fund A professionally managed investment pool in which investors in the fund typically each have a pro-rata claim on the income and value of the fund.

Mutually exclusive projects Mutually exclusive projects compete directly with each other. For example, if Projects A and B are mutually exclusive, you can choose A or B, but you cannot choose both.

***n* Factorial** For a positive integer *n*, the product of the first *n* positive integers; 0 factorial equals 1 by definition. *n* factorial is written as *n*!.

Narrow money The notes and coins in circulation in an economy, plus other very highly liquid deposits.

Nash equilibrium   When two or more participants in a non-coop-erative game have no incentive to deviate from their respective equilibrium strategies given their opponent's strategies.

National income   The income received by all factors of production used in the generation of final output. National income equals gross domestic product (or, in some countries, gross national product) minus the capital consumption allowance and a statistical discrepancy.

Natural rate of unemployment   Effective unemployment rate, below which pressure emerges in labor markets.

Negative externality   A negative effect (e.g., pollution) of a market transaction that is borne by parties other than those who transacted; a spillover cost.

Neo-Keynesians   A group of dynamic general equilibrium models that assume slow-to-adjust prices and wages.

Net book value   The remaining (undepreciated) balance of an asset's purchase cost. For liabilities, the face value of a bond minus any unamortized discount, or plus any unamortized premium.

Net exports   The difference between the value of a country's exports and the value of its imports (i.e., value of exports minus imports).

Net income   The difference between revenue and expenses; what remains after subtracting all expenses (including depreciation, interest, and taxes) from revenue.

Net operating cycle   An estimate of the average time that elapses between paying suppliers for materials and collecting cash from the subsequent sale of goods produced.

Net present value   (NPV) The present value of an investment's cash inflows (benefits) minus the present value of its cash outflows (costs).

Net profit margin   An indicator of profitability, calculated as net income divided by revenue; indicates how much of each dollar of revenues is left after all costs and expenses. Also called *profit margin* or *return on sales*.

Net realisable value   Estimated selling price in the ordinary course of business less the estimated costs necessary to make the sale.

Net revenue   Revenue after adjustments (e.g., for estimated returns or for amounts unlikely to be collected).

Net tax rate   The tax rate net of transfer payments.

Neutral rate of interest   The rate of interest that neither spurs on nor slows down the underlying economy.

New classical macroeconomics   An approach to macroeconomics that seeks the macroeconomic conclusions of individuals maximizing utility on the basis of rational expectations and companies maximizing profits.

New-issue DRP   Dividend reinvestment plan in which the company meets the need for additional shares by issuing them instead of purchasing them.

New Keynesians   A group of dynamic general equilibrium models that assume slow-to-adjust prices and wages.

No-load fund   A mutual fund in which there is no fee for investing in the fund or for redeeming fund shares, although there is an annual fee based on a percentage of the fund's net asset value.

Node   Each value on a binomial tree from which successive moves or outcomes branch.

Nominal GDP   The value of goods and services measured at current prices.

Nominal rate   A rate of interest based on the security's face value.

Nominal risk-free interest rate   The sum of the real risk-free interest rate and the inflation premium.

Nominal scale   A measurement scale that categorizes data but does not rank them.

Non-accelerating inflation rate of unemployment   Effective unemployment rate, below which pressure emerges in labor markets.

Non-agency RMBS   In the United States, securities issued by private entities that are not guaranteed by a federal agency or a GSE.

Non-cumulative preference shares   Preference shares for which dividends that are not paid in the current or subsequent periods are forfeited permanently (instead of being accrued and paid at a later date).

Non-current assets   Assets that are expected to benefit the company over an extended period of time (usually more than one year).

Non-current liabilities   Obligations that broadly represent a probable sacrifice of economic benefits in periods generally greater than one year in the future.

Non-cyclical   A company whose performance is largely independent of the business cycle.

Non-deliverable forwards   Cash-settled forward contracts, used predominately with respect to foreign exchange forwards. Also called *contracts for differences*.

Non-financial risks   Risks that arise from sources other than changes in the external financial markets, such as changes in accounting rules, legal environment, or tax rates.

Non-participating preference shares   Preference shares that do not entitle shareholders to share in the profits of the company. Instead, shareholders are only entitled to receive a fixed dividend payment and the par value of the shares in the event of liquidation.

Non-recourse loan   Loan in which the lender does not have a shortfall claim against the borrower, so the lender can look only to the property to recover the outstanding mortgage balance.

Non-renewable resources   Finite resources that are depleted once they are consumed, such as oil and coal.

Non-satiation   The assumption that the consumer could never have so much of a preferred good that she would refuse any more, even if it were free; sometimes referred to as the "more is better" assumption.

Non-sovereign bonds   A bond issued by a government below the national level, such as a province, region, state, or city.

Non-sovereign government bonds   A bond issued by a government below the national level, such as a province, region, state, or city.

Nonconventional cash flow   In a nonconventional cash flow pattern, the initial outflow is not followed by inflows only, but the cash flows can flip from positive (inflows) to negative (outflows) again (or even change signs several times).

Nonparametric test   A test that is not concerned with a parameter, or that makes minimal assumptions about the population from which a sample comes.

Nonsystematic risk   Unique risk that is local or limited to a particular asset or industry that need not affect assets outside of that asset class.

Normal distribution   A continuous, symmetric probability distribution that is completely described by its mean and its variance.

Normal good   A good that is consumed in greater quantities as income increases.

Normal profit   The level of accounting profit needed to just cover the implicit opportunity costs ignored in accounting costs.

Notching   Ratings adjustment methodology where specific issues from the same borrower may be assigned different credit ratings.

Note rate   See *mortgage rate*.

Notes payable   Amounts owed by a business to creditors as a result of borrowings that are evidenced by (short-term) loan agreements.

Notice period   The length of time (typically 30 to 90 days) in advance that investors may be required to notify a fund of their intent to redeem.

Notional principal   An imputed principal amount.

NPV rule   An investment decision rule that states that an investment should be undertaken if its NPV is positive but not undertaken if its NPV is negative.

Number of days of inventory   An activity ratio equal to the number of days in a period divided by the inventory ratio for the period; an indication of the number of days a company ties up funds in inventory.

Number of days of payables   An activity ratio equal to the number of days in a period divided by the payables turnover ratio for the period; an estimate of the average number of days it takes a company to pay its suppliers.

Number of days of receivables   Estimate of the average number of days it takes to collect on credit accounts.

Objective probabilities   Probabilities that generally do not vary from person to person; includes a priori and objective probabilities.

Off-the-run   Seasoned government bonds are off-the-run securities; they are not the most recently issued or the most actively traded.

Offer   The price at which a dealer or trader is willing to sell an asset, typically qualified by a maximum quantity (ask size).

Official interest rate   An interest rate that a central bank sets and announces publicly; normally the rate at which it is willing to lend money to the commercial banks. Also called *official policy rate* or *policy rate*.

Official policy rate   An interest rate that a central bank sets and announces publicly; normally the rate at which it is willing to lend money to the commercial banks.

Oligopoly   Market structure with a relatively small number of firms supplying the market.

On-the-run   The most recently issued and most actively traded sovereign securities.

One-sided hypothesis test   A test in which the null hypothesis is rejected only if the evidence indicates that the population parameter is greater than (smaller than) θ_0. The alternative hypothesis also has one side.

One-tailed hypothesis test   A test in which the null hypothesis is rejected only if the evidence indicates that the population parameter is greater than (smaller than) θ_0. The alternative hypothesis also has one side.

Open economy   An economy that trades with other countries.

Open-end fund   A mutual fund that accepts new investment money and issues additional shares at a value equal to the net asset value of the fund at the time of investment.

Open interest   The number of outstanding contracts in a clearinghouse at any given time. The open interest figure changes daily as some parties open up new positions, while other parties offset their old positions.

Open-market DRP   Dividend reinvestment plan in which the company purchases shares in the open market to acquire the additional shares credited to plan participants.

Open market operations   The purchase or sale of bonds by the national central bank to implement monetary policy. The bonds traded are usually sovereign bonds issued by the national government.

Operating activities   Activities that are part of the day-to-day business functioning of an entity, such as selling inventory and providing services.

Operating breakeven   The number of units produced and sold at which the company's operating profit is zero (revenues = operating costs).

Operating cash flow   The net amount of cash provided from operating activities.

Operating cycle   A measure of the time needed to convert raw materials into cash from a sale; it consists of the number of days of inventory and the number of days of receivables.

Operating efficiency ratios   Ratios that measure how efficiently a company performs day-to-day tasks, such as the collection of receivables and management of inventory.

Operating lease   An agreement allowing the lessee to use some asset for a period of time; essentially a rental.

Operating leverage   The use of fixed costs in operations.

Operating profit   A company's profits on its usual business activities before deducting taxes. Also called *operating income*.

Operating profit margin   A profitability ratio calculated as operating income (i.e., income before interest and taxes) divided by revenue. Also called *operating margin*.

Operating risk   The risk attributed to the operating cost structure, in particular the use of fixed costs in operations; the risk arising from the mix of fixed and variable costs; the risk that a company's operations may be severely affected by environmental, social, and governance risk factors.

Operational independence   A bank's ability to execute monetary policy and set interest rates in the way it thought would best meet the inflation target.

Operational risk   The risk of loss from failures in a company's systems and procedures.

Operationally efficient   Said of a market, a financial system, or an economy that has relatively low transaction costs.

Opportunity cost   The value that investors forgo by choosing a particular course of action; the value of something in its best alternative use.

Option   A financial instrument that gives one party the right, but not the obligation, to buy or sell an underlying asset from or to another party at a fixed price over a specific period of time. Also referred to as *contingent claim* or *option contract*.

Option-adjusted price   The value of the embedded option plus the flat price of the bond.

Option-adjusted spread   OAS = Z-spread − Option value (in basis points per year).

Option-adjusted yield   The required market discount rate whereby the price is adjusted for the value of the embedded option.

Option contract   See *option*.

Option premium   The amount of money a buyer pays and seller receives to engage in an option transaction.

Order   A specification of what instrument to trade, how much to trade, and whether to buy or sell.

Order-driven markets   A market (generally an auction market) that uses rules to arrange trades based on the orders that traders submit; in their pure form, such markets do not make use of dealers.

Order precedence hierarchy   With respect to the execution of orders to trade, a set of rules that determines which orders execute before other orders.

Ordinal scale   A measurement scale that sorts data into categories that are ordered (ranked) with respect to some characteristic.

Ordinary annuity   An annuity with a first cash flow that is paid one period from the present.

Ordinary shares   Equity shares that are subordinate to all other types of equity (e.g., preferred equity). Also called *common stock* or *common shares*.

Organized exchange   A securities marketplace where buyers and seller can meet to arrange their trades.

Other comprehensive income   Items of comprehensive income that are not reported on the income statement; comprehensive income minus net income.

Other receivables   Amounts owed to the company from parties other than customers.

Out-of-sample test   A test of a strategy or model using a sample outside the time period on which the strategy or model was developed.

Out of the money   Options that, if exercised, would require the payment of more money than the value received and therefore would not be currently exercised.

Out-of-the-money   Options that, if exercised, would require the payment of more money than the value received and therefore would not be currently exercised.

Outcome   A possible value of a random variable.

Over-the-counter (OTC) markets   A decentralized market where buy and sell orders initiated from various locations are matched through a communications network.

Overbought   A market condition in which market sentiment is thought to be unsustainably bullish.

Overcollateralization   Form of internal credit enhancement that refers to the process of posting more collateral than needed to obtain or secure financing.

Oversold   A market condition in which market sentiment is thought to be unsustainably bearish.

Own-price   The price of a good or service itself (as opposed to the price of something else).

Own-price elasticity of demand   The percentage change in quantity demanded for a percentage change in own price, holding all other things constant.

Owner-of-record date   The date that a shareholder listed on the corporation's books will be deemed to have ownership of the shares for purposes of receiving an upcoming dividend; two business days after the ex-dividend date.

Owners' equity   The excess of assets over liabilities; the residual interest of shareholders in the assets of an entity after deducting the entity's liabilities. Also called *shareholders' equity*.

Paasche index   An index formula using the current composition of a basket of products.

Paired comparisons test   A statistical test for differences based on paired observations drawn from samples that are dependent on each other.

Paired observations   Observations that are dependent on each other.

Pairs arbitrage trade   A trade in two closely related stocks involving the short sale of one and the purchase of the other.

Panel data   Observations through time on a single characteristic of multiple observational units.

Par curve   A sequence of yields-to-maturity such that each bond is priced at par value. The bonds are assumed to have the same currency, credit risk, liquidity, tax status, and annual yields stated for the same periodicity.

Par value   The amount of principal on a bond.

Parallel shift   A parallel yield curve shift implies that all rates change by the same amount in the same direction.

Parameter   A descriptive measure computed from or used to describe a population of data, conventionally represented by Greek letters.

Parametric test   Any test (or procedure) concerned with parameters or whose validity depends on assumptions concerning the population generating the sample.

Pari passu   On an equal footing.

Partial duration   See *key rate duration*.

Partial equilibrium analysis   An equilibrium analysis focused on one market, taking the values of exogenous variables as given.

Participating preference shares   Preference shares that entitle shareholders to receive the standard preferred dividend plus the opportunity to receive an additional dividend if the company's profits exceed a pre-specified level.

Pass-through rate   The coupon rate of a mortgage pass-through security.

Passive investment   A buy and hold approach in which an investor does not make portfolio changes based on short-term expectations of changing market or security performance.

Passive strategy   In reference to short-term cash management, it is an investment strategy characterized by simple decision rules for making daily investments.

Payable date   The day that the company actually mails out (or electronically transfers) a dividend payment.

Payment date   The day that the company actually mails out (or electronically transfers) a dividend payment.

Payments system   The system for the transfer of money.

Payout   Cash dividends and the value of shares repurchased in any given year.

Payout policy   A company's set of principles guiding payouts.

Peak   The highest point of a business cycle.

Peer group   A group of companies engaged in similar business activities whose economics and valuation are influenced by closely related factors.

Pennants   A technical analysis continuation pattern formed by trendlines that converge to form a triangle, typically over a short period.

Per capita real GDP   Real GDP divided by the size of the population, often used as a measure of the average standard of living in a country.

Per unit contribution margin   The amount that each unit sold contributes to covering fixed costs—that is, the difference between the price per unit and the variable cost per unit.

Percentage-of-completion   A method of revenue recognition in which, in each accounting period, the company estimates what percentage of the contract is complete and then reports that percentage of the total contract revenue in its income statement.

Percentiles   Quantiles that divide a distribution into 100 equal parts.

Perfect competition   A market structure in which the individual firm has virtually no impact on market price, because it is assumed to be a very small seller among a very large number of firms selling essentially identical products.

Perfectly elastic   Said of a good or service that is infinitely sensitive to a change in the value of a specified variable (e.g., price).

Perfectly inelastic   Said of a good or service that is completely insensitive to a change in the value of a specified variable (e.g., price).

Performance appraisal   The evaluation of risk-adjusted performance; the evaluation of investment skill.

Performance bond   See *margin bond*.

Performance evaluation   The measurement and assessment of the outcomes of investment management decisions.

Performance measurement   The calculation of returns in a logical and consistent manner.

Period costs   Costs (e.g., executives' salaries) that cannot be directly matched with the timing of revenues and which are thus expensed immediately.

Periodicity   The assumed number of periods in the year, typically matches the frequency of coupon payments.

Permanent differences   Differences between tax and financial reporting of revenue (expenses) that will not be reversed at some future date. These result in a difference between the company's effective tax rate and statutory tax rate and do not result in a deferred tax item.

Permutation   An ordered listing.

Perpetual bonds   Bonds with no stated maturity date.

Perpetuity   A perpetual annuity, or a set of never-ending level sequential cash flows, with the first cash flow occurring one period from now. A bond that does not mature.

Personal consumption expenditures   All domestic personal consumption; the basis for a price index for such consumption called the PCE price index.

Personal disposable income   Equal to personal income less personal taxes.

Personal income   A broad measure of household income that includes all income received by households, whether earned or unearned; measures the ability of consumers to make purchases.

Plain vanilla bond   Bond that makes periodic, fixed coupon payments during the bond's life and a lump-sum payment of principal at maturity. Also called *conventional bond*.

Planning horizon   A time period in which all factors of production are variable, including technology, physical capital, and plant size.

Platykurtic   Describes a distribution that is less peaked than the normal distribution.

Point and figure chart   A technical analysis chart that is constructed with columns of X's alternating with columns of O's such that the horizontal axis represents only the number of changes in price without reference to time or volume.

Point estimate   A single numerical estimate of an unknown quantity, such as a population parameter.

Point of sale (POS)   Systems that capture transaction data at the physical location in which the sale is made.

Policy rate   An interest rate that a central bank sets and announces publicly; normally the rate at which it is willing to lend money to the commercial banks.

Population   All members of a specified group.

Population mean   The arithmetic mean value of a population; the arithmetic mean of all the observations or values in the population.

Population standard deviation   A measure of dispersion relating to a population in the same unit of measurement as the observations, calculated as the positive square root of the population variance.

Population variance   A measure of dispersion relating to a population, calculated as the mean of the squared deviations around the population mean.

Portfolio company   In private equity, the company that is being invested in.

Portfolio demand for money   The demand to hold speculative money balances based on the potential opportunities or risks that are inherent in other financial instruments.

Portfolio planning   The process of creating a plan for building a portfolio that is expected to satisfy a client's investment objectives.

Position   The quantity of an asset that an entity owns or owes.

Positive externality   A positive effect (e.g., improved literacy) of a market transaction that is borne by parties other than those who transacted; a spillover benefit.

Posterior probability   An updated probability that reflects or comes after new information.

Potential GDP   The level of real GDP that can be produced at full employment; measures the productive capacity of the economy.

Power of a test   The probability of correctly rejecting the null—that is, rejecting the null hypothesis when it is false.

Precautionary money balances   Money held to provide a buffer against unforeseen events that might require money.

Precautionary stocks   A level of inventory beyond anticipated needs that provides a cushion in the event that it takes longer to replenish inventory than expected or in the case of greater than expected demand.

Preference shares   A type of equity interest which ranks above common shares with respect to the payment of dividends and the distribution of the company's net assets upon liquidation. They have characteristics of both debt and equity securities. Also called *preferred stock*.

Preferred stock   See *preference shares*.

Premium   In the case of bonds, premium refers to the amount by which a bond is priced above its face (par) value. In the case of an option, the amount paid for the option contract.

Prepaid expense   A normal operating expense that has been paid in advance of when it is due.

Prepayment option   Contractual provision that entitles the borrower to prepay all or part of the outstanding mortgage principal prior to the scheduled due date when the principal must be repaid. Also called *early repayment option*.

Prepayment penalty mortgages   Mortgages that stipulate a monetary penalty if a borrower prepays within a certain time period after the mortgage is originated.

Prepayment risk   The uncertainty that the timing of the actual cash flows will be different from the scheduled cash flows as set forth in the loan agreement due to the borrowers' ability to alter payments, usually to take advantage of interest rate movements.

Present value (PV)   The present discounted value of future cash flows: For assets, the present discounted value of the future net cash inflows that the asset is expected to generate; for liabilities, the present discounted value of the future net cash outflows that are expected to be required to settle the liabilities.

Present value models   Valuation models that estimate the intrinsic value of a security as the present value of the future benefits expected to be received from the security. Also called *discounted cash flow models.*

Pretax margin   A profitability ratio calculated as earnings before taxes divided by revenue.

Price   The market price as established by the interactions of the market demand and supply factors.

Price elasticity of demand   Measures the percentage change in the quantity demanded, given a percentage change in the price of a given product.

Price floor   A minimum price for a good or service, typically imposed by government action and typically above the equilibrium price.

Price index   Represents the average prices of a basket of goods and services.

Price limits   Limits imposed by a futures exchange on the price change that can occur from one day to the next.

Price multiple   A ratio that compares the share price with some sort of monetary flow or value to allow evaluation of the relative worth of a company's stock.

Price priority   The principle that the highest priced buy orders and the lowest priced sell orders execute first.

Price relative   A ratio of an ending price over a beginning price; it is equal to 1 plus the holding period return on the asset.

Price return   Measures *only* the price appreciation or percentage change in price of the securities in an index or portfolio.

Price return index   An index that reflects *only* the price appreciation or percentage change in price of the constituent securities. Also called *price index.*

Price stability   In economics, refers to an inflation rate that is low on average and not subject to wide fluctuation.

Price takers   Producers that must accept whatever price the market dictates.

Price to book value   A valuation ratio calculated as price per share divided by book value per share.

Price to cash flow   A valuation ratio calculated as price per share divided by cash flow per share.

Price to earnings ratio   (P/E ratio or P/E) The ratio of share price to earnings per share.

Price to sales   A valuation ratio calculated as price per share divided by sales per share.

Price value of a basis point   A version of money duration, it is an estimate of the change in the full price of a bond given a 1 basis point change in the yield-to-maturity.

Price weighting   An index weighting method in which the weight assigned to each constituent security is determined by dividing its price by the sum of all the prices of the constituent securities.

Priced risk   Risk for which investors demand compensation for bearing (e.g. equity risk, company-specific factors, macroeconomic factors).

Primary bond markets   Markets in which issuers first sell bonds to investors to raise capital.

Primary capital markets (primary markets)   The market where securities are first sold and the issuers receive the proceeds.

Primary dealers   Financial institutions that are authorized to deal in new issues of sovereign bonds and that serve primarily as trading counterparties of the office responsible for issuing sovereign bonds.

Primary market   The market where securities are first sold and the issuers receive the proceeds.

Prime brokers   Brokers that provide services including custody, administration, lending, short borrowing, and trading.

Principal   The amount of funds originally invested in a project or instrument; the face value to be paid at maturity.

Principal amount   Amount that an issuer agrees to repay the debt holders on the maturity date.

Principal business activity   The business activity from which a company derives a majority of its revenues and/or earnings.

Principal value   Amount that an issuer agrees to repay the debt holders on the maturity date.

Principle of no arbitrage   See *arbitrage-free pricing.*

Prior probabilities   Probabilities reflecting beliefs prior to the arrival of new information.

Priority of claims   Priority of payment, with the most senior or highest ranking debt having the first claim on the cash flows and assets of the issuer.

Private equity securities   Securities that are not listed on public exchanges and have no active secondary market. They are issued primarily to institutional investors via non-public offerings, such as private placements.

Private investment in public equity   An investment in the equity of a publicly traded firm that is made at a discount to the market value of the firm's shares.

Private placement   Typically a non-underwritten, unregistered offering of securities that are sold only to an investor or a small group of investors. It can be accomplished directly between the issuer and the investor(s) or through an investment bank.

Private value auction   An auction in which the value of the item being auctioned is unique to each bidder.

Probability   A number between 0 and 1 describing the chance that a stated event will occur.

Probability density function   A function with non-negative values such that probability can be described by areas under the curve graphing the function.

Probability distribution   A distribution that specifies the probabilities of a random variable's possible outcomes.

Probability function   A function that specifies the probability that the random variable takes on a specific value.

Producer price index   Reflects the price changes experienced by domestic producers in a country.

Producer surplus   The difference between the total revenue sellers receive from selling a given amount of a good and the total variable cost of producing that amount.

Production function   Provides the quantitative link between the level of output that the economy can produce and the inputs used in the production process.

Production opportunity frontier   Curve describing the maximum number of units of one good a company can produce, for any given number of the other good that it chooses to manufacture.

Productivity   The amount of output produced by workers in a given period of time—for example, output per hour worked; measures the efficiency of labor.

Profit   The return that owners of a company receive for the use of their capital and the assumption of financial risk when making their investments.

Profit and loss (P&L) statement   A financial statement that provides information about a company's profitability over a stated period of time.

Profit margin   An indicator of profitability, calculated as net income divided by revenue; indicates how much of each dollar of revenues is left after all costs and expenses.

Profitability ratios   Ratios that measure a company's ability to generate profitable sales from its resources (assets).

Project sequencing   To defer the decision to invest in a future project until the outcome of some or all of a current project is known. Projects are sequenced through time, so that investing in a project creates the option to invest in future projects.

Promissory note   A written promise to pay a certain amount of money on demand.

Property, plant, and equipment   Tangible assets that are expected to be used for more than one period in either the production or supply of goods or services, or for administrative purposes.

Prospectus   The document that describes the terms of a new bond issue and helps investors perform their analysis on the issue.

Protective put   An option strategy in which a long position in an asset is combined with a long position in a put.

Pseudo-random numbers   Numbers produced by random number generators.

Public offer   See *public offering*.

Public offering   An offering of securities in which any member of the public may buy the securities. Also called *public offer*.

Pull on liquidity   When disbursements are paid too quickly or trade credit availability is limited, requiring companies to expend funds before they receive funds from sales that could cover the liability.

Pure discount bonds   See *zero-coupon bonds*.

Pure discount instruments   Instruments that pay interest as the difference between the amount borrowed and the amount paid back.

Pure-play method   A method for estimating the beta for a company or project; it requires using a comparable company's beta and adjusting it for financial leverage differences.

Put   An option that gives the holder the right to sell an underlying asset to another party at a fixed price over a specific period of time.

Put–call–forward parity   The relationship among puts, calls, and forward contracts.

Put–call parity   An equation expressing the equivalence (parity) of a portfolio of a call and a bond with a portfolio of a put and the underlying, which leads to the relationship between put and call prices.

Put/call ratio   A technical analysis indicator that evaluates market sentiment based upon the volume of put options traded divided by the volume of call options traded for a particular financial instrument.

Put option   An option that gives the holder the right to sell an underlying asset to another party at a fixed price over a specific period of time.

Putable bonds   Bonds that give the bondholder the right to sell the bond back to the issuer at a predetermined price on specified dates.

Putable common shares   Common shares that give investors the option (or right) to sell their shares (i.e., "put" them) back to the issuing company at a price that is specified when the shares are originally issued.

Quantile   A value at or below which a stated fraction of the data lies. Also called *fractile*.

Quantitative easing   An expansionary monetary policy based on aggressive open market purchase operations.

Quantity   The amount of a product that consumers are willing and able to buy at each price level.

Quantity demanded   The amount of a product that consumers are willing and able to buy at each price level.

Quantity equation of exchange   An expression that over a given period, the amount of money used to purchase all goods and services in an economy, $M \times V$, is equal to monetary value of this output, $P \times Y$.

Quantity theory of money   Asserts that total spending (in money terms) is proportional to the quantity of money.

Quartiles   Quantiles that divide a distribution into four equal parts.

Quasi-fixed cost   A cost that stays the same over a range of production but can change to another constant level when production moves outside of that range.

Quasi-government bonds   A bond issued by an entity that is either owned or sponsored by a national government. Also called *agency bond*.

Quick assets   Assets that can be most readily converted to cash (e.g., cash, short-term marketable investments, receivables).

Quick ratio   A stringent measure of liquidity that indicates a company's ability to satisfy current liabilities with its most liquid assets, calculated as (cash + short-term marketable investments + receivables) divided by current liabilities.

Quintiles   Quantiles that divide a distribution into five equal parts.

Quota rents   Profits that foreign producers can earn by raising the price of their goods higher than they would without a quota.

Quotas   Government policies that restrict the quantity of a good that can be imported into a country, generally for a specified period of time.

Quote-driven market   A market in which dealers acting as principals facilitate trading.

Quoted interest rate   A quoted interest rate that does not account for compounding within the year. Also called *stated annual interest rate*.

Quoted margin   The specified yield spread over the reference rate, used to compensate an investor for the difference in the credit risk of the issuer and that implied by the reference rate.

Random number   An observation drawn from a uniform distribution.

Random number generator   An algorithm that produces uniformly distributed random numbers between 0 and 1.

Random variable   A quantity whose future outcomes are uncertain.

Range   The difference between the maximum and minimum values in a dataset.

Ratio scales   A measurement scale that has all the characteristics of interval measurement scales as well as a true zero point as the origin.

Real GDP   The value of goods and services produced, measured at base year prices.

Real income   Income adjusted for the effect of inflation on the purchasing power of money.

Real interest rate   Nominal interest rate minus the expected rate of inflation.

Real risk-free interest rate   The single-period interest rate for a completely risk-free security if no inflation were expected.

Realizable (settlement) value   With reference to assets, the amount of cash or cash equivalents that could currently be obtained by selling the asset in an orderly disposal; with reference to liabilities, the undiscounted amount of cash or cash equivalents expected to be paid to satisfy the liabilities in the normal course of business.

Rebalancing Adjusting the weights of the constituent securities in an index.

Rebalancing policy The set of rules that guide the process of restoring a portfolio's asset class weights to those specified in the strategic asset allocation.

Recession A period during which real GDP decreases (i.e., negative growth) for at least two successive quarters, or a period of significant decline in total output, income, employment, and sales usually lasting from six months to a year.

Recognition lag The lag in government response to an economic problem resulting from the delay in confirming a change in the state of the economy.

Record date The date that a shareholder listed on the corporation's books will be deemed to have ownership of the shares for purposes of receiving an upcoming dividend; two business days after the ex-dividend date.

Recourse loan Loan in which the lender has a claim against the borrower for any shortfall between the outstanding mortgage balance and the proceeds received from the sale of the property.

Redemption yield See *yield to maturity*.

Redemptions Withdrawals of funds by investors.

Refinancing rate A type of central bank policy rate.

Registered bonds Bonds for which ownership is recorded by either name or serial number.

Relative dispersion The amount of dispersion relative to a reference value or benchmark.

Relative frequency With reference to an interval of grouped data, the number of observations in the interval divided by the total number of observations in the sample.

Relative price The price of a specific good or service in comparison with those of other goods and services.

Relative strength analysis A comparison of the performance of one asset with the performance of another asset or a benchmark based on changes in the ratio of the securities' respective prices over time.

Relative strength index A technical analysis momentum oscillator that compares a security's gains with its losses over a set period.

Renewable resources Resources that can be replenished, such as a forest.

Rent Payment for the use of property.

Reorganization Agreements made by a company in bankruptcy under which a company's capital structure is altered and/or alternative arrangements are made for debt repayment; US Chapter 11 bankruptcy. The company emerges from bankruptcy as a going concern.

Replication The creation of an asset or portfolio from another asset, portfolio, and/or derivative.

Repo A form of collateralized loan involving the sale of a security with a simultaneous agreement by the seller to buy the same security back from the purchaser at an agreed-on price and future date. The party who sells the security at the inception of the repurchase agreement and buys it back at maturity is borrowing money from the other party, and the security sold and subsequently repurchased represents the collateral.

Repo margin The difference between the market value of the security used as collateral and the value of the loan. Also called *haircut*.

Repo rate The interest rate on a repurchase agreement.

Repurchase agreement A form of collateralized loan involving the sale of a security with a simultaneous agreement by the seller to buy the same security back from the purchaser at an agreed-on price and future date. The party who sells the security at the inception of the repurchase agreement and buys it back at maturity is borrowing money from the other party, and the security sold and subsequently repurchased represents the collateral.

Repurchase date The date when the party who sold the security at the inception of a repurchase agreement buys the security back from the cash lending counterparty.

Repurchase price The price at which the party who sold the security at the inception of the repurchase agreement buys the security back from the cash lending counterparty.

Required margin The yield spread over, or under, the reference rate such that an FRN is priced at par value on a rate reset date.

Required rate of return See *market discount rate*.

Required yield See *market discount rate*.

Required yield spread The difference between the yield-to-maturity on a new bond and the benchmark rate; additional compensation required by investors for the difference in risk and tax status of a bond relative to a government bond. Sometimes called the *spread over the benchmark*.

Reservation prices The highest price a buyer is willing to pay for an item or the lowest price at which a seller is willing to sell it.

Reserve accounts Form of internal credit enhancement that relies on creating accounts and depositing in these accounts cash that can be used to absorb losses. Also called *reserve funds*.

Reserve funds See *reserve accounts*.

Reserve requirement The requirement for banks to hold reserves in proportion to the size of deposits.

Residual claim The owners' remaining claim on the company's assets after the liabilities are deducted.

Resistance In technical analysis, a price range in which selling activity is sufficient to stop the rise in the price of a security.

Restricted payments A bond covenant meant to protect creditors by limiting how much cash can be paid out to shareholders over time.

Retail method An inventory accounting method in which the sales value of an item is reduced by the gross margin to calculate the item's cost.

Retracement In technical analysis, a reversal in the movement of a security's price such that it is counter to the prevailing longterm price trend.

Return-generating model A model that can provide an estimate of the expected return of a security given certain parameters and estimates of the values of the independent variables in the model.

Return on assets (ROA) A profitability ratio calculated as net income divided by average total assets; indicates a company's net profit generated per dollar invested in total assets.

Return on equity (ROE) A profitability ratio calculated as net income divided by average shareholders' equity.

Return on sales An indicator of profitability, calculated as net income divided by revenue; indicates how much of each dollar of revenues is left after all costs and expenses.

Return on total capital A profitability ratio calculated as EBIT divided by the sum of short- and long-term debt and equity.

Revaluation model The process of valuing long-lived assets at fair value, rather than at cost less accumulated depreciation. Any resulting profit or loss is either reported on the income statement and/or through equity under revaluation surplus.

Revenue The amount charged for the delivery of goods or services in the ordinary activities of a business over a stated period; the inflows of economic resources to a company over a stated period.

Reversal patterns A type of pattern used in technical analysis to predict the end of a trend and a change in direction of the security's price.

Reverse repo A repurchase agreement viewed from the perspective of the cash lending counterparty.

Reverse repurchase agreement A repurchase agreement viewed from the perspective of the cash lending counterparty.

Reverse stock split A reduction in the number of shares outstanding with a corresponding increase in share price, but no change to the company's underlying fundamentals.

Revolving credit agreements The strongest form of short-term bank borrowing facilities; they are in effect for multiple years (e.g., 3–5 years) and may have optional medium-term loan features.

Rho The sensitivity of the option price to the risk-free rate.

Ricardian equivalence An economic theory that implies that it makes no difference whether a government finances a deficit by increasing taxes or issuing debt.

Risk Exposure to uncertainty. The chance of a loss or adverse outcome as a result of an action, inaction, or external event.

Risk averse The assumption that an investor will choose the least risky alternative.

Risk aversion The degree of an investor's inability and unwillingness to take risk.

Risk budgeting The establishment of objectives for individuals, groups, or divisions of an organization that takes into account the allocation of an acceptable level of risk.

Risk exposure The state of being exposed or vulnerable to a risk. The extent to which an entity is sensitive to underlying risks.

Risk governance The top-down process and guidance that directs risk management activities to align with and support the overall enterprise.

Risk management The process of identifying the level of risk an entity wants, measuring the level of risk the entity currently has, taking actions that bring the actual level of risk to the desired level of risk, and monitoring the new actual level of risk so that it continues to be aligned with the desired level of risk.

Risk management framework The infrastructure, process, and analytics needed to support effective risk management in an organization.

Risk-neutral pricing Sometimes said of derivatives pricing, uses the fact that arbitrage opportunities guarantee that a risk-free portfolio consisting of the underlying and the derivative must earn the risk-free rate.

Risk-neutral probabilities Weights that are used to compute a binomial option price. They are the probabilities that would apply if a risk-neutral investor valued an option.

Risk premium An extra return expected by investors for bearing some specified risk.

Risk shifting Actions to change the distribution of risk outcomes.

Risk tolerance The amount of risk an investor is willing and able to bear to achieve an investment goal.

Risk transfer Actions to pass on a risk to another party, often, but not always, in the form of an insurance policy.

Robust The quality of being relatively unaffected by a violation of assumptions.

Rule of 72 The principle that the approximate number of years necessary for an investment to double is 72 divided by the stated interest rate.

Running yield See *current yield.*

Safety-first rules Rules for portfolio selection that focus on the risk that portfolio value will fall below some minimum acceptable level over some time horizon.

Safety stock A level of inventory beyond anticipated needs that provides a cushion in the event that it takes longer to replenish inventory than expected or in the case of greater than expected demand.

Sales Generally, a synonym for revenue; "sales" is generally understood to refer to the sale of goods, whereas "revenue" is understood to include the sale of goods or services.

Sales returns and allowances An offset to revenue reflecting any cash refunds, credits on account, and discounts from sales prices given to customers who purchased defective or unsatisfactory items.

Sales risk Uncertainty with respect to the quantity of goods and services that a company is able to sell and the price it is able to achieve; the risk related to the uncertainty of revenues.

Sales-type leases A type of finance lease, from a lessor perspective, where the present value of the lease payments (lease receivable) exceeds the carrying value of the leased asset. The revenues earned by the lessor are operating (the profit on the sale) and financing (interest) in nature.

Salvage value The amount the company estimates that it can sell the asset for at the end of its useful life. Also called *residual value.*

Sample A subset of a population.

Sample excess kurtosis A sample measure of the degree of a distribution's peakedness in excess of the normal distribution's peakedness.

Sample kurtosis A sample measure of the degree of a distribution's peakedness.

Sample mean The sum of the sample observations, divided by the sample size.

Sample selection bias Bias introduced by systematically excluding some members of the population according to a particular attribute—for example, the bias introduced when data availability leads to certain observations being excluded from the analysis.

Sample skewness A sample measure of degree of asymmetry of a distribution.

Sample standard deviation The positive square root of the sample variance.

Sample statistic A quantity computed from or used to describe a sample.

Sample variance A sample measure of the degree of dispersion of a distribution, calculated by dividing the sum of the squared deviations from the sample mean by the sample size minus 1.

Sampling The process of obtaining a sample.

Sampling distribution The distribution of all distinct possible values that a statistic can assume when computed from samples of the same size randomly drawn from the same population.

Sampling error The difference between the observed value of a statistic and the quantity it is intended to estimate.

Sampling plan   The set of rules used to select a sample.

Saving   In economics, income not spent.

Say's law   Named for French economist J.B. Say: All that is produced will be sold because supply creates its own demand.

Scenario analysis   Analysis that shows the changes in key financial quantities that result from given (economic) events, such as the loss of customers, the loss of a supply source, or a catastrophic event; a risk management technique involving examination of the performance of a portfolio under specified situations. Closely related to stress testing.

Screening   The application of a set of criteria to reduce a set of potential investments to a smaller set having certain desired characteristics.

Scrip dividend schemes   Dividend reinvestment plan in which the company meets the need for additional shares by issuing them instead of purchasing them.

Sealed bid auction   An auction in which bids are elicited from potential buyers, but there is no ability to observe bids by other buyers until the auction has ended.

Search costs   Costs incurred in searching; the costs of matching buyers with sellers.

Seasoned offering   An offering in which an issuer sells additional units of a previously issued security.

Second-degree price discrimination   When the monopolist charges different per-unit prices using the quantity purchased as an indicator of how highly the customer values the product.

Second lien   A secured interest in the pledged assets that ranks below first lien debt in both collateral protection and priority of payment.

Second price sealed bid   An auction (also known as a Vickery auction) in which bids are submitted in sealed envelopes and opened simultaneously. The winning buyer is the one who submitted the highest bid, but the price paid is equal to the second highest bid.

Secondary bond markets   Markets in which existing bonds are traded among investors.

Secondary market   The market where securities are traded among investors.

Secondary precedence rules   Rules that determine how to rank orders placed at the same time.

Sector   A group of related industries.

Sector indices   Indices that represent and track different economic sectors—such as consumer goods, energy, finance, health care, and technology—on either a national, regional, or global basis.

Secured bonds   Bonds secured by assets or financial guarantees pledged to ensure debt repayment in case of default.

Secured debt   Debt in which the debtholder has a direct claim—a pledge from the issuer—on certain assets and their associated cash flows.

Securitization   A process that involves moving assets into a special legal entity, which then uses the assets as guarantees to secure a bond issue.

Securitized assets   Assets that are typically used to create asset-backed bonds; for example, when a bank securitizes a pool of loans, the loans are said to be securitized.

Security characteristic line   A plot of the excess return of a security on the excess return of the market.

Security market index   A portfolio of securities representing a given security market, market segment, or asset class.

Security market line   (SML) The graph of the capital asset pricing model.

Security selection   The process of selecting individual securities; typically, security selection has the objective of generating superior risk-adjusted returns relative to a portfolio's benchmark.

Self-investment limits   With respect to investment limitations applying to pension plans, restrictions on the percentage of assets that can be invested in securities issued by the pension plan sponsor.

Sell-side firm   A broker or dealer that sells securities to and provides independent investment research and recommendations to investment management companies.

Semi-strong-form efficient market   A market in which security prices reflect all publicly known and available information.

Semiannual bond basis yield   An annual rate having a periodicity of two; also known as a *semiannual bond equivalent yield*.

Semiannual bond equivalent yield   See *semiannual bond basis yield*.

Semideviation   The positive square root of semivariance (sometimes called *semistandard deviation*).

Semilogarithmic   Describes a scale constructed so that equal intervals on the vertical scale represent equal rates of change, and equal intervals on the horizontal scale represent equal amounts of change.

Semivariance   The average squared deviation below the mean.

Seniority ranking   Priority of payment of various debt obligations.

Sensitivity analysis   Analysis that shows the range of possible outcomes as specific assumptions are changed.

Separately managed account   (SMA) An investment portfolio managed exclusively for the benefit of an individual or institution.

Serial maturity structure   Structure for a bond issue in which the maturity dates are spread out during the bond's life; a stated number of bonds mature and are paid off each year before final maturity.

Settlement   The process that occurs after a trade is completed, the securities are passed to the buyer, and payment is received by the seller.

Settlement date   Date when the buyer makes cash payment and the seller delivers the security.

Settlement price   The official price, designated by the clearinghouse, from which daily gains and losses will be determined and marked to market.

Share repurchase   A transaction in which a company buys back its own shares. Unlike stock dividends and stock splits, share repurchases use corporate cash.

Shareholder-of-record date   The date that a shareholder listed on the corporation's books will be deemed to have ownership of the shares for purposes of receiving an upcoming dividend; two business days after the ex-dividend date.

Shareholder wealth maximization   To maximize the market value of shareholders' equity.

Shareholders' equity   Assets less liabilities; the residual interest in the assets after subtracting the liabilities.

Sharpe ratio   The average return in excess of the risk-free rate divided by the standard deviation of return; a measure of the average excess return earned per unit of standard deviation of return.

Shelf registration   Type of public offering that allows the issuer to file a single, all-encompassing offering circular that covers a series of bond issues.

Short   The seller of an asset or derivative contract. Also refers to the position of being short an asset or derivative contract.

Short position   A position in an asset or contract in which one has sold an asset one does not own, or in which a right under a contract can be exercised against oneself.

Short-run average total cost curve   The curve describing average total costs when some costs are considered fixed.

Short-run supply curve   The section of the marginal cost curve that lies above the minimum point on the average variable cost curve.

Short selling   A transaction in which borrowed securities are sold with the intention to repurchase them at a lower price at a later date and return them to the lender.

Shortfall risk   The risk that portfolio value will fall below some minimum acceptable level over some time horizon.

Shutdown point   The point at which average revenue is less than average variable cost.

Simple interest   The interest earned each period on the original investment; interest calculated on the principal only.

Simple random sample   A subset of a larger population created in such a way that each element of the population has an equal probability of being selected to the subset.

Simple random sampling   The procedure of drawing a sample to satisfy the definition of a simple random sample.

Simple yield   The sum of the coupon payments plus the straight-line amortized share of the gain or loss, divided by the flat price.

Simulation   Computer-generated sensitivity or scenario analysis that is based on probability models for the factors that drive outcomes.

Simulation trial   A complete pass through the steps of a simulation.

Single price auction   A Dutch auction variation, also involving a single price, is used in selling US Treasury securities.

Single-step format   With respect to the format of the income statement, a format that does not subtotal for gross profit (revenue minus cost of goods sold).

Sinking fund arrangement   Provision that reduces the credit risk of a bond issue by requiring the issuer to retire a portion of the bond's principal outstanding each year.

Skewed   Not symmetrical.

Skewness   A quantitative measure of skew (lack of symmetry); a synonym of skew.

Small country   A country that is a price taker in the world market for a product and cannot influence the world market price.

Solvency   With respect to financial statement analysis, the ability of a company to fulfill its long-term obligations.

Solvency ratios   Ratios that measure a company's ability to meet its long-term obligations.

Solvency risk   The risk that an entity does not survive or succeed because it runs out of cash, even though it might otherwise be solvent.

Sovereign bonds   A bond issued by a national government.

Sovereign yield spread   An estimate of the country spread (country equity premium) for a developing nation that is based on a comparison of bonds yields in country being analyzed and a developed country. The sovereign yield spread is the difference between a government bond yield in the country being analyzed, denominated in the currency of the developed country, and the Treasury bond yield on a similar maturity bond in the developed country.

Sovereigns   A bond issued by a national government.

Spearman rank correlation coefficient   A measure of correlation applied to ranked data.

Special dividend   A dividend paid by a company that does not pay dividends on a regular schedule, or a dividend that supplements regular cash dividends with an extra payment.

Special purpose entity   A non-operating entity created to carry out a specified purpose, such as leasing assets or securitizing receivables; can be a corporation, partnership, trust, limited liability, or partnership formed to facilitate a specific type of business activity. Also called *special purpose vehicle* or *variable interest entity*.

Special purpose vehicle   See *special purpose entity*.

Specific identification method   An inventory accounting method that identifies which specific inventory items were sold and which remained in inventory to be carried over to later periods.

Speculative demand for money   The demand to hold speculative money balances based on the potential opportunities or risks that are inherent in other financial instruments. Also called *portfolio demand for money*.

Speculative money balances   Monies held in anticipation that other assets will decline in value.

Split coupon bond   See *deferred coupon bond*.

Sponsored   A type of depository receipt in which the foreign company whose shares are held by the depository has a direct involvement in the issuance of the receipts.

Spot curve   A sequence of yields-to-maturity on zero-coupon bonds. Sometimes called *zero* or *strip curve* because coupon payments are "stripped" off of the bonds.

Spot markets   Markets in which assets are traded for immediate delivery.

Spot prices   The price of an asset for immediate delivery.

Spot rates   A sequence of market discount rates that correspond to the cash flow dates; yields-to-maturity on zero-coupon bonds maturing at the date of each cash flow.

Spread   In general, the difference in yield between different fixed income securities. Often used to refer to the difference between the yield-to-maturity and the benchmark.

Spread over the benchmark   See *required yield spread*.

Spread risk   Bond price risk arising from changes in the yield spread on credit-risky bonds; reflects changes in the market's assessment and/or pricing of credit migration (or downgrade) risk and market liquidity risk.

Stable   With reference to an equilibrium, one in which price, when disturbed away from the equilibrium, tends to converge back to it.

Stackelberg model   A prominent model of strategic decisionmaking in which firms are assumed to make their decisions sequentially.

Stagflation   When a high inflation rate is combined with a high level of unemployment and a slowdown of the economy.

Standard cost   With respect to inventory accounting, the planned or target unit cost of inventory items or services.

Standard deviation   The positive square root of the variance; a measure of dispersion in the same units as the original data.

Standard normal distribution   The normal density with mean (μ) equal to 0 and standard deviation (σ) equal to 1.

Standardizing   A transformation that involves subtracting the mean and dividing the result by the standard deviation.

Standing limit orders   A limit order at a price below market and which therefore is waiting to trade.

Stated annual interest rate   A quoted interest rate that does not account for compounding within the year. Also called *quoted interest rate*.

Statement of cash flows A financial statement that reconciles beginning-of-period and end-of-period balance sheet values of cash; provides information about an entity's cash inflows and cash outflows as they pertain to operating, investing, and financing activities. Also called *cash flow statement*.

Statement of changes in equity (statement of owners' equity) A financial statement that reconciles the beginning-of-period and end-of-period balance sheet values of shareholders' equity; provides information about all factors affecting shareholders' equity. Also called *statement of owners' equity*.

Statement of financial condition The financial statement that presents an entity's current financial position by disclosing resources the entity controls (its assets) and the claims on those resources (its liabilities and equity claims), as of a particular point in time (the date of the balance sheet).

Statement of financial position The financial statement that presents an entity's current financial position by disclosing resources the entity controls (its assets) and the claims on those resources (its liabilities and equity claims), as of a particular point in time (the date of the balance sheet).

Statement of operations A financial statement that provides information about a company's profitability over a stated period of time.

Statement of owners' equity A financial statement that reconciles the beginning of-period and end-of-period balance sheet values of shareholders' equity; provides information about all factors affecting shareholders' equity. Also called *statement of changes in shareholders' equity*.

Statement of retained earnings A financial statement that reconciles beginning-of-period and end-of-period balance sheet values of retained income; shows the linkage between the balance sheet and income statement.

Statistic A quantity computed from or used to describe a sample of data.

Statistical inference Making forecasts, estimates, or judgments about a larger group from a smaller group actually observed; using a sample statistic to infer the value of an unknown population parameter.

Statistically significant A result indicating that the null hypothesis can be rejected; with reference to an estimated regression coefficient, frequently understood to mean a result indicating that the corresponding population regression coefficient is different from 0.

Statutory voting A common method of voting where each share represents one vote.

Step-up coupon bond Bond for which the coupon, which may be fixed or floating, increases by specified margins at specified dates.

Stock dividend A type of dividend in which a company distributes additional shares of its common stock to shareholders instead of cash.

Stock-out losses Profits lost from not having sufficient inventory on hand to satisfy demand.

Stop-loss order See *stop order*.

Stop order An order in which a trader has specified a stop price condition. Also called *stop-loss order*.

Store of value The quality of tending to preserve value.

Store of wealth Goods that depend on the fact that they do not perish physically over time, and on the belief that others would always value the good.

Straight-line method A depreciation method that allocates evenly the cost of a long-lived asset less its estimated residual value over the estimated useful life of the asset.

Strategic analysis Analysis of the competitive environment with an emphasis on the implications of the environment for corporate strategy.

Strategic asset allocation The set of exposures to IPS-permissible asset classes that is expected to achieve the client's long-term objectives given the client's investment constraints.

Strategic groups Groups sharing distinct business models or catering to specific market segments in an industry.

Street convention Yield measure that neglects weekends and holidays; the internal rate of return on cash flows assuming payments are made on the scheduled dates, even when the scheduled date falls on a weekend or holiday.

Stress testing A specific type of scenario analysis that estimates losses in rare and extremely unfavorable combinations of events or scenarios.

Strong-form efficient market A market in which security prices reflect all public and private information.

Structural (or cyclically adjusted) budget deficit The deficit that would exist if the economy was at full employment (or full potential output).

Structural subordination Arises in a holding company structure when the debt of operating subsidiaries is serviced by the cash flow and assets of the subsidiaries before funds can be passed to the holding company to service debt at the parent level.

Structured financial instruments Financial instruments that share the common attribute of repackaging risks. Structured financial instruments include asset-backed securities, collateralized debt obligations, and other structured financial instruments such as capital protected, yield enhancement, participation and leveraged instruments.

Subjective probability A probability drawing on personal or subjective judgment.

Subordinated debt A class of unsecured debt that ranks below a firm's senior unsecured obligations.

Subordination Form of internal credit enhancement that relies on creating more than one bond tranche and ordering the claim priorities for ownership or interest in an asset between the tranches. The ordering of the claim priorities is called a senior/subordinated structure, where the tranches of highest seniority are called senior followed by subordinated or junior tranches. Also called *credit tranching*.

Substitutes Said of two goods or services such that if the price of one increases the demand for the other tends to increase, holding all other things equal (e.g., butter and margarine).

Sunk cost A cost that has already been incurred.

Supernormal profit Equal to accounting profit less the implicit opportunity costs not included in total accounting costs; the difference between total revenue (TR) and total cost (TC).

Supply The willingness of sellers to offer a given quantity of a good or service for a given price.

Supply curve The graph of the inverse supply function.

Supply function The quantity supplied as a function of price and possibly other variables.

Supply shock A typically unexpected disturbance to supply.

Support In technical analysis, a price range in which buying activity is sufficient to stop the decline in the price of a security.

Support tranche   A class or tranche in a CMO that protects the PAC tranche from prepayment risk.

Supranational bonds   A bond issued by a supranational agency such as the World Bank.

Surety bond   Form of external credit enhancement whereby a rated and regulated insurance company guarantees to reimburse bondholders for any losses incurred up to a maximum amount if the issuer defaults.

Survey approach   An estimate of the equity risk premium that is based upon estimates provided by a panel of finance experts.

Survivorship bias   The bias resulting from a test design that fails to account for companies that have gone bankrupt, merged, or are otherwise no longer reported in a database.

Sustainable growth rate   The rate of dividend (and earnings) growth that can be sustained over time for a given level of return on equity, keeping the capital structure constant and without issuing additional common stock.

Sustainable rate of economic growth   The rate of increase in the economy's productive capacity or potential GDP.

Swap contract   An agreement between two parties to exchange a series of future cash flows.

Syndicated loans   Loans from a group of lenders to a single borrower.

Syndicated offering   A bond issue that is underwritten by a group of investment banks.

Synthetic lease   A lease that is structured to provide a company with the tax benefits of ownership while not requiring the asset to be reflected on the company's financial statements.

Systematic risk   Risk that affects the entire market or economy; it cannot be avoided and is inherent in the overall market. Systematic risk is also known as non-diversifiable or market risk.

Systematic sampling   A procedure of selecting every kth member until reaching a sample of the desired size. The sample that results from this procedure should be approximately random.

t-Test   A hypothesis test using a statistic (t-statistic) that follows a t-distribution.

Tactical asset allocation   The decision to deliberately deviate from the strategic asset allocation in an attempt to add value based on forecasts of the near-term relative performance of asset classes.

Target balance   A minimum level of cash to be held available—estimated in advance and adjusted for known funds transfers, seasonality, or other factors.

Target capital structure   A company's chosen proportions of debt and equity.

Target independent   A bank's ability to determine the definition of inflation that they target, the rate of inflation that they target, and the horizon over which the target is to be achieved.

Target semideviation   The positive square root of target semivariance.

Target semivariance   The average squared deviation below a target value.

Tariffs   Taxes that a government levies on imported goods.

Tax base   The amount at which an asset or liability is valued for tax purposes.

Tax expense   An aggregate of an entity's income tax payable (or recoverable in the case of a tax benefit) and any changes in deferred tax assets and liabilities. It is essentially the income tax payable or recoverable if these had been determined based on accounting profit rather than taxable income.

Tax loss carry forward   A taxable loss in the current period that may be used to reduce future taxable income.

Taxable income   The portion of an entity's income that is subject to income taxes under the tax laws of its jurisdiction.

Taxable temporary differences   Temporary differences that result in a taxable amount in a future period when determining the taxable profit as the balance sheet item is recovered or settled.

Technical analysis   A form of security analysis that uses price and volume data, which is often displayed graphically, in decision making.

Technology   The process a company uses to transform inputs into outputs.

Technology of production   The "rules" that govern the transformation of inputs into finished goods and services.

Tenor   The time-to-maturity for a bond or derivative contract. Also called *term to maturity*.

Term maturity structure   Structure for a bond issue in which the bond's notional principal is paid off in a lump sum at maturity.

Term structure   See *maturity structure*.

Term structure of credit spreads   The relationship between the spreads over the "risk-free" (or benchmark) rates and times-to-maturity.

Term structure of yield volatility   The relationship between the volatility of bond yields-to-maturity and times-to-maturity.

Terminal stock value   The expected value of a share at the end of the investment horizon—in effect, the expected selling price. Also called *terminal value*.

Terminal value   The expected value of a share at the end of the investment horizon—in effect, the expected selling price.

Terms of trade   The ratio of the price of exports to the price of imports, representing those prices by export and import price indices, respectively.

Theory of the consumer   The branch of microeconomics that deals with consumption—the demand for goods and services—by utility-maximizing individuals.

Theory of the firm   The branch of microeconomics that deals with the supply of goods and services by profit-maximizing firms.

Third-degree price discrimination   When the monopolist segregates customers into groups based on demographic or other characteristics and offers different pricing to each group.

Time-period bias   The possibility that when we use a time-series sample, our statistical conclusion may be sensitive to the starting and ending dates of the sample.

Time-series data   Observations of a variable over time.

Time tranching   The creation of classes or tranches in an ABS/MBS that possess different (expected) maturities.

Time value   The difference between the market price of the option and its intrinsic value, determined by the uncertainty of the underlying over the remaining life of the option.

Time value decay   Said of an option when, at expiration, no time value remains and the option is worth only its exercise value.

Time value of money   The principles governing equivalence relationships between cash flows with different dates.

Time-weighted rate of return   The compound rate of growth of one unit of currency invested in a portfolio during a stated measurement period; a measure of investment performance that is not sensitive to the timing and amount of withdrawals or additions to the portfolio.

Top-down analysis   With reference to investment selection processes, an approach that starts with macro selection (i.e., identifying attractive geographic segments and/or industry segments) and then addresses selection of the most attractive investments within those segments.

Total comprehensive income   The change in equity during a period resulting from transaction and other events, other than those changes resulting from transactions with owners in their capacity as owners.

Total costs   The summation of all costs, where costs are classified according to fixed or variable.

Total expenditure   The total amount spent over a time period.

Total factor productivity   A scale factor that reflects the portion of growth that is not accounted for by explicit factor inputs (e.g. capital and labor).

Total fixed cost   The summation of all expenses that do not change when production varies.

Total invested capital   The sum of market value of common equity, book value of preferred equity, and face value of debt.

Total probability rule   A rule explaining the unconditional probability of an event in terms of probabilities of the event conditional on mutually exclusive and exhaustive scenarios.

Total probability rule for expected value   A rule explaining the expected value of a random variable in terms of expected values of the random variable conditional on mutually exclusive and exhaustive scenarios.

Total product   The aggregate sum of production for the firm during a time period.

Total return   Measures the price appreciation, or percentage change in price of the securities in an index or portfolio, plus any income received over the period.

Total return index   An index that reflects the price appreciation or percentage change in price of the constituent securities plus any income received since inception.

Total return swap   A swap in which one party agrees to pay the total return on a security. Often used as a credit derivative, in which the underlying is a bond.

Total revenue   Price times the quantity of units sold.

Total surplus   The difference between total value to buyers and the total variable cost to sellers; made up of the sum of consumer surplus and producer surplus.

Total variable cost   The summation of all variable expenses.

Tracking error   The standard deviation of the differences between a portfolio's returns and its benchmark's returns; a synonym of active risk.

Tracking risk   The standard deviation of the differences between a portfolio's returns and its benchmark's returns; a synonym of active risk. Also called *tracking error*.

Trade creation   When regional integration results in the replacement of higher cost domestic production by lower cost imports from other members.

Trade credit   A spontaneous form of credit in which a purchaser of the goods or service is financing its purchase by delaying the date on which payment is made.

Trade diversion   When regional integration results in lower-cost imports from non-member countries being replaced with higher-cost imports from members.

Trade payables   Amounts that a business owes to its vendors for goods and services that were purchased from them but which have not yet been paid.

Trade protection   Government policies that impose restrictions on trade, such as tariffs and quotas.

Trade receivables   Amounts customers owe the company for products that have been sold as well as amounts that may be due from suppliers (such as for returns of merchandise) Also called *commercial receivables* or *accounts receivable*.

Trade surplus (deficit)   When the value of exports is greater (less) than the value of imports.

Trading securities   Securities held by a company with the intent to trade them. Also called *held-for-trading securities*.

Traditional investment markets   Markets for traditional investments, which include all publicly traded debts and equities and shares in pooled investment vehicles that hold publicly traded debts and/or equities.

Transactions money balances   Money balances that are held to finance transactions.

Transactions motive   In the context of inventory management, the need for inventory as part of the routine production–sales cycle.

Transfer payments   Welfare payments made through the social security system that exist to provide a basic minimum level of income for low-income households.

Transitive preferences   The assumption that when comparing any three distinct bundles, A, B, and C, if A is preferred to B and simultaneously B is preferred to C, then it must be true that A is preferred to C.

Transparency   Said of something (e.g., a market) in which information is fully disclosed to the public and/or regulators.

Treasury Inflation-Protected Securities   A bond issued by the United States Treasury Department that is designed to protect the investor from inflation by adjusting the principal of the bond for changes in inflation.

Treasury shares   Shares that were issued and subsequently repurchased by the company.

Treasury stock   Shares that were issued and subsequently repurchased by the company.

Treasury stock method   A method for accounting for the effect of options (and warrants) on earnings per share (EPS) that specifies what EPS would have been if the options and warrants had been exercised and the company had used the proceeds to repurchase common stock.

Tree diagram   A diagram with branches emanating from nodes representing either mutually exclusive chance events or mutually exclusive decisions.

Trend   A long-term pattern of movement in a particular direction.

Treynor ratio   A measure of risk-adjusted performance that relates a portfolio's excess returns to the portfolio's beta.

Triangle patterns   In technical analysis, a continuation chart pattern that forms as the range between high and low prices narrows, visually forming a triangle.

Trimmed mean   A mean computed after excluding a stated small percentage of the lowest and highest observations.

TRIN   A flow of funds indicator applied to a broad stock market index to measure the relative extent to which money is moving into or out of rising and declining stocks.

Triple bottoms   In technical analysis, a reversal pattern that is formed when the price forms three troughs at roughly the same price level; used to predict a change from a downtrend to an uptrend.

Triple tops In technical analysis, a reversal pattern that is formed when the price forms three peaks at roughly the same price level; used to predict a change from an uptrend to a downtrend.

Trough The lowest point of a business cycle.

True yield The internal rate of return on cash flows using the actual calendar including weekends and bank holidays.

Trust deed The governing legal credit agreement, typically incorporated by reference in the prospectus. Also called *bond indenture*.

Trust receipt arrangement The use of inventory as collateral for a loan. The inventory is segregated and held in trust, and the proceeds of any sale must be remitted to the lender immediately.

Turn-of-the-year effect Calendar anomaly that stock market returns in January are significantly higher compared to the rest of the months of the year, with most of the abnormal returns reported during the first five trading days in January.

Two-fund separation theorem The theory that all investors regardless of taste, risk preferences, and initial wealth will hold a combination of two portfolios or funds: a risk-free asset and an optimal portfolio of risky assets.

Two-sided hypothesis test A test in which the null hypothesis is rejected in favor of the alternative hypothesis if the evidence indicates that the population parameter is either smaller or larger than a hypothesized value.

Two-tailed hypothesis test A test in which the null hypothesis is rejected in favor of the alternative hypothesis if the evidence indicates that the population parameter is either smaller or larger than a hypothesized value.

Two-week repo rate The interest rate on a two-week repurchase agreement; may be used as a policy rate by a central bank.

Type I error The error of rejecting a true null hypothesis.

Type II error The error of not rejecting a false null hypothesis.

Unanticipated (unexpected) inflation The component of inflation that is a surprise.

Unbilled revenue Revenue that has been earned but not yet billed to customers as of the end of an accounting period. Also called *accrued revenue*.

Unclassified balance sheet A balance sheet that does not show subtotals for current assets and current liabilities.

Unconditional probability The probability of an event *not* conditioned on another event.

Underemployed A person who has a job but has the qualifications to work a significantly higher-paying job.

Underlying An asset that trades in a market in which buyers and sellers meet, decide on a price, and the seller then delivers the asset to the buyer and receives payment. The underlying is the asset or other derivative on which a particular derivative is based. The market for the underlying is also referred to as the *spot market*.

Underwriter A firm, usually an investment bank, that takes the risk of buying the newly issued securities from the issuer, and then reselling them to investors or to dealers, thus guaranteeing the sale of the securities at the offering price negotiated with the issuer.

Underwritten offering A type of securities issue mechanism in which the investment bank guarantees the sale of the securities at an offering price that is negotiated with the issuer. Also known as *firm commitment offering*.

Unearned fees Unearned fees are recognized when a company receives cash payment for fees prior to earning them.

Unearned revenue A liability account for money that has been collected for goods or services that have not yet been delivered; payment received in advance of providing a good or service. Also called *deferred revenue* or *deferred income*.

Unemployed People who are actively seeking employment but are currently without a job.

Unemployment rate The ratio of unemployed to the labor force.

Unexpected inflation The component of inflation that is a surprise.

Unit elastic An elasticity with a magnitude of 1.

Unit labor cost The average labor cost to produce one unit of output.

Unit normal distribution The normal density with mean (μ) equal to 0 and standard deviation (σ) equal to 1.

Unitary elastic An elasticity with a magnitude of 1.

Units-of-production method A depreciation method that allocates the cost of a long-lived asset based on actual usage during the period.

Univariate distribution A distribution that specifies the probabilities for a single random variable.

Unlimited funds An unlimited funds environment assumes that the company can raise the funds it wants for all profitable projects simply by paying the required rate of return.

Unsecured debt Debt which gives the debtholder only a general claim on an issuer's assets and cash flow.

Unsponsored A type of depository receipt in which the foreign company whose shares are held by the depository has no involvement in the issuance of the receipts.

Unstable With reference to an equilibrium, one in which price, when disturbed away from the equilibrium, tends not to return to it.

Up transition probability The probability that an asset's value moves up.

Utility function A mathematical representation of the satisfaction derived from a consumption basket.

Utils A unit of utility.

Validity instructions Instructions which indicate when the order may be filled.

Valuation allowance A reserve created against deferred tax assets, based on the likelihood of realizing the deferred tax assets in future accounting periods.

Valuation ratios Ratios that measure the quantity of an asset or flow (e.g., earnings) in relation to the price associated with a specified claim (e.g., a share or ownership of the enterprise).

Value at risk (VaR) A money measure of the minimum value of losses expected during a specified time period at a given level of probability.

Value investors With reference to equity investors, investors who are focused on paying a relatively low share price in relation to earnings or assets per share.

VaR See *value at risk*.

Variable costs Costs that fluctuate with the level of production and sales.

Variable-rate note Similar to a floating-rate note, except that the spread is variable rather than constant.

Variance The expected value (the probability-weighted average) of squared deviations from a random variable's expected value.

Variation margin Additional margin that must be deposited in an amount sufficient to bring the balance up to the initial margin requirement.

Veblen good A good that increases in desirability with price.

Vega   A measure of the sensitivity of an option's price to changes in the underlying's volatility.

Venture capital   Investments that provide "seed" or start-up capital, early-stage financing, or mezzanine financing to companies that are in the early stages of development and require additional capital for expansion.

Venture capital fund   A fund for private equity investors that provides financing for development-stage companies.

Vertical analysis   Common-size analysis using only one reporting period or one base financial statement; for example, an income statement in which all items are stated as percentages of sales.

Vertical demand schedule   Implies that some fixed quantity is demanded, regardless of price.

Volatility   As used in option pricing, the standard deviation of the continuously compounded returns on the underlying asset.

Voluntarily unemployed   A person voluntarily outside the labor force, such as a jobless worker refusing an available vacancy.

Voluntary export restraint   A trade barrier under which the exporting country agrees to limit its exports of the good to its trading partners to a specific number of units.

Vote by proxy   A mechanism that allows a designated party—such as another shareholder, a shareholder representative, or management—to vote on the shareholder's behalf.

Warehouse receipt arrangement   The use of inventory as collateral for a loan; similar to a trust receipt arrangement except there is a third party (i.e., a warehouse company) that supervises the inventory.

Warrant   Attached option that gives its holder the right to buy the underlying stock of the issuing company at a fixed exercise price until the expiration date.

Weak-form efficient market hypothesis   The belief that security prices fully reflect all past market data, which refers to all historical price and volume trading information.

Wealth effect   An increase (decrease) in household wealth increases (decreases) consumer spending out of a given level of current income.

Weighted average cost method   An inventory accounting method that averages the total cost of available inventory items over the total units available for sale.

Weighted average cost of capital   A weighted average of the aftertax required rates of return on a company's common stock, preferred stock, and long-term debt, where the weights are the fraction of each source of financing in the company's target capital structure.

Weighted average coupon rate   Weighting the mortgage rate of each mortgage loan in the pool by the percentage of the mortgage outstanding relative to the outstanding amount of all the mortgages in the pool.

Weighted average life   A measure that gives investors an indication of how long they can expect to hold the MBS before it is paid off; the convention-based average time to receipt of all principal repayments. Also called *average life*.

Weighted average maturity   Weighting the remaining number of months to maturity for each mortgage loan in the pool by the amount of the outstanding mortgage balance.

Weighted mean   An average in which each observation is weighted by an index of its relative importance.

Wholesale price index   Reflects the price changes experienced by domestic producers in a country.

Winner's curse   The tendency for the winner in certain competitive bidding situations to overpay, whether because of overestimation of intrinsic value, emotion, or information asymmetries.

Winsorized mean   A mean computed after assigning a stated percent of the lowest values equal to one specified low value, and a stated percent of the highest values equal to one specified high value.

Working capital   The difference between current assets and current liabilities.

Working capital management   The management of a company's short-term assets (such as inventory) and short-term liabilities (such as money owed to suppliers).

World price   The price prevailing in the world market.

Yield   The actual return on a debt security if it is held to maturity.

Yield duration   The sensitivity of the bond price with respect to the bond's own yield-to-maturity.

Yield to maturity   Annual return that an investor earns on a bond if the investor purchases the bond today and holds it until maturity. It is the discount rate that equates the present value of the bond's expected cash flows until maturity with the bond's price. Also called *yield-to-redemption* or *redemption yield*.

Yield to redemption   See *yield to maturity*.

Yield-to-worst   The lowest of the sequence of yields-to-call and the yield-to-maturity.

Zero-coupon bonds   Bonds that do not pay interest during the bond's life. It is issued at a discount to par value and redeemed at par. Also called *pure discount bonds*.

Zero volatility spread (Z-spread)   Calculates a constant yield spread over a government (or interest rate swap) spot curve.